The Urbanism of Exception

This book challenges the conventional (modernist-inspired) understanding of urbanization as a universal process tied to the ideal-typical
model of the modern metropolis with its origins in the grand Western experience of city-building. At the start of the twenty-first century, the familiar idea of the 'city' – or 'urbanism' as we know it –
has experienced such profound mutations in both structure and form
that the customary epistemological categories and prevailing conceptual frameworks that predominate in conventional urban theory are
no longer capable of explaining the evolving patterns of city-making.
Global urbanism has increasingly taken shape as vast, distended city-
regions, where urbanizing landscapes are increasingly fragmented into
discontinuous assemblages of enclosed enclaves characterized by global
connectivity and concentrated wealth, on the one side, and distressed
zones of neglect and impoverishment, on the other. These emergent patterns of what might be called enclave urbanism have gone hand-in-hand
with the new modes of urban governance, where the crystallization of
privatized regulatory regimes has effectively shielded wealthy enclaves
from public oversight and interference.

Martin J. Murray is a professor of Urban Planning at Taubman College
urban planning faculty. He is also Adjunct Professor in the Department
of Afroamerican and African Studies at the University of Michigan, Ann
Arbor. His current research engages the fields of urban studies and planning, global urbanism, cultural geography, distressed urbanism, development, historical sociology, and African studies. In addition to six
books and three co-edited volumes, he has produced close to eighty
journal articles and book chapters that focus on diverse geographical
areas of the world at different historical periods (ranging from colonial
Indochina to contemporary southern Africa).

The Urbanism of Exception

The Dynamics of Global City Building in the Twenty-First Century

MARTIN J. MURRAY

University of Michigan

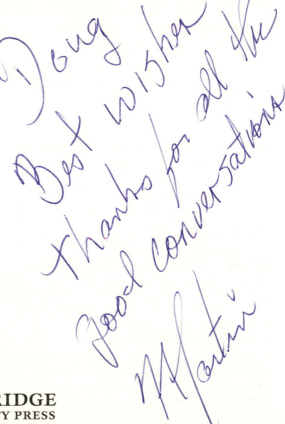

Doug
Best wishes
Thanks for all the
good conversations.
Martin

CAMBRIDGE
UNIVERSITY PRESS

CAMBRIDGE
UNIVERSITY PRESS

University Printing House, Cambridge CB2 8BS, United Kingdom

One Liberty Plaza, 20th Floor, New York, NY 10006, USA

477 Williamstown Road, Port Melbourne, VIC 3207, Australia

4843/24, 2nd Floor, Ansari Road, Daryaganj, Delhi - 110002, India

79 Anson Road, #06-04/06, Singapore 079906

Cambridge University Press is part of the University of Cambridge.

It furthers the University's mission by disseminating knowledge in the pursuit of education, learning, and research at the highest international levels of excellence.

www.cambridge.org
Information on this title: www.cambridge.org/9781107169241
DOI: 10.1017/9781316718438

First published 2017

Printed in the United States of America by Sheridan Books, Inc.

A catalog record for this publication is available from the British Library.

Library of Congress Cataloging-in-Publication Data
Names: Murray, Martin J., author.
Title: The urbanism of exception : the dynamics of global city building in the twenty-first century / Martin J. Murray.
Description: New York, NY : Cambridge University Press, 2017. |
Includes bibliographical references.
Identifiers: LCCN 2016052793 | ISBN 9781107169241
Subjects: LCSH: Urbanization. | Cities and towns–Growth.
Classification: LCC HT361 .M88 2017 | DDC 307.76–dc23
LC record available at https://lccn.loc.gov/2016052793

ISBN 978-1-107-16924-1 Hardback
ISBN 978-1-316-62052-6 Paperback

Contents

List of Illustrations

Preface

Over the past decade or so, increasing numbers of scholars operating within the broad field of critical urban studies have struggled with how to break away from the reigning paradigms and axiomatic regulative principles that have dominated theories of urbanization since at least the 1960s, if not before. This book originated as a response to this intellectual challenge that called upon scholars to make sense of the changing contours of urbanism and urbanization on a global scale at the start of the twenty-first century. Precisely what long-standing ideas like "the city," "urbanism," and "urbanization" refer to, and what they mean, have become increasingly blurred.

As a general rule, conventional understandings of the processes of urbanization in the modern age of industrial capitalism operated on the deeply held belief that leading cities in the core areas of the capitalist world economy created the basic template for city building everywhere throughout the nineteenth and twentieth centuries, and even earlier. This imitative impulse bordering on outright plagiarism was particularly acute in the cities built under the yoke of European colonial rule.[1] Yet at the start of the twenty-first century, the term *urban* no longer suggests, as Ilka Ruby and Andreas Ruby have so eloquently put it, "a normative cultural concept – such as expressed, for instance, in the 'European City.'" Instead the idea of "the urban" opens up a Pandora's box of "extremely varied" ideas and conceptualizations shaped by the intersection of all sorts of geographical, socioeconomic, cultural, and political pressures. If we want to truly understand what it means to talk of urbanism at the start of

---

[1] For an excellent treatment of the export of European building practices to colonial cities, see Mia Fuller, *Modernists Abroad: Architecture, Cities and Italian Imperialism* (New York: Routledge, 2007).

the new millennium, "we have to capture it in all its disguises, gradations, and transformations occurring simultaneously on a global scale."[2]

The point of departure for this book is what Ilka Ruby and Andreas Ruby have referred to as "a double failure": on one side, the inability of the master narrative of modernism (and its kindred spirit named "modernization theory") to subject our understanding of urban realities to the singular, reductive model of the ideal-typical *modern metropolis* with its origins in the grand Western experience of city building; and, on the other side, the inadequacy of the largely romanticized postmodernist call for a return to a kind of idyllic, small-scale, and manageable urbanism that is nostalgically imagined from a "past that never [really] existed." In other words, when the all-too-familiar idea of the "city" – or "urbanism" as we know it – experiences profound and exaggerated mutations in structure and form, then the object itself becomes invisible to our customary epistemological categories and prevailing conceptual frameworks. The profound shifts in the evolving patterns of global urbanism have taken place in not so self-evident ways that make it nearly impossible to detect or grasp when we depend exclusively on conventional ways of knowing. As the prevailing paradigmatic approaches to understanding urbanization as a process and a condition have proven to be largely incapable of registering "differences" in ways that do not involve (almost by definition) ranked hierarchies of superiority/inferiority and normative judgements about "leading" and "lagging" cities, we need to adopt a new language of global urbanism that enables us "to embrace the city" in all its diversity and complexity in ways that do not correspond with a single perspective or "conform to one universal model."[3]

One underlying aim of this book is to problematize and unsettle the very idea of "the city" itself, what constitutes its essential structure and form, and where to locate the boundaries between the urban and nonurban. To make sense of global urbanism at the start of the twenty-first century requires us to cast our gaze upon vast, distended global city-regions without a recognizable, singular, and dynamic urban core, where metropolitan landscapes are increasingly fragmented into distinct zones characterized by concentrated wealth, global connectivity, excess, and fantasy, on the one side, and neglect, impoverishment, and deprivation, on the other. These polar extremes exert a counterbalancing gravitational force, pulling at cities and fragmenting urban landscapes into terrains of difference that are largely unequal and disconnected. The steady accretion of deterritorialized enclaves of concentrated wealth linked with global flows of capital and finance have come into existence as relatively isolated nodes connected with the world-at-large through up-to-date telecommunications, luxury accommodation, and world-class transportation linkages. These

---

[2] Ilka Ruby and Andreas Ruby, "Forward," in Ilka and Andreas Ruby (eds.), *Urban Transformations* (Berlin: Ruby Press, 2008), pp. 10–13 (quotation from p. 12).

[3] Ruby and Ruby, "Forward," p. 12. See also Jennifer Robinson, *Ordinary Cities: Between Modernity and Development* (New York: Routledge, 2003).

sequestered enclaves are surrounded by myriad sites of abandonment and deprivation where ordinary residents are partially, if not completely, excluded from incorporation into the mainstream of urban life.

Building a relational urban theory that approaches the "urban question" through the lens of "organized complexity" challenges the core principles of modernist thinking, a mode of thought that conceives of urban space as a deliberately engineered configuration of discrete zones arranged around their specialized functions. From the start, the goal of modernist planning was to create predictability, permanence, and order out of the instability of everyday urban living. Looking at cities as ever-changing "works-in-progress" that assume an actual existence through connections between a complex multiplicity of urban assemblages (building typologies, associations, interpersonal networks, districts, neighborhoods) offers an alternative to modernist-inspired approaches to urban theory and planning practice.[4]

Despite the postmodernist praise for the seemingly random heterogeneity of urban environments and the celebration of the serendipitous, playful qualities of urban life, the unfolding patterns of urbanization in the contemporary age of neoliberal globalization largely correspond with a spatial ordering of urban landscapes that is far from the self-reflexive eclecticism and carefree "anything goes" ethos of postmodernity.[5] While it is true that "the clearly defined spatial hierarchies of pre-industrial and industrial cities" of the past have declined in significance, city-building efforts at the start of the twenty-first century largely conform to distinctive spatialized logics that have put into motion new patterns of urban fragmentation and dispersal. These logics are clearly distinguished from modernist normative fixation on land-use zoning – a regulatory framework that "prescribed a form of urban spatial order [rooted] in the idea of a structured arrangement of the different basic functions which supposedly constitute[d]" the ideal modern metropolis.[6] Compared to this modernist logic, which actually managed to partially shape the spatial form of cities during the twentieth century, the "anti-planning" gestures of postmodern urbanism at the start of the twenty-first century seem to suggest the paradigmatic opposite to the orderly structured form of the modern metropolis. However, behind this contrived image of layered pastiche, nonconformity, and "pure contingency," there exists a different organizing principle that has produced a distinct kind of geographical order: the discontinuous and uneven spatiality of an "urban

---

4 See Todd May, *Gilles Deleuze: An Introduction* (Cambridge: Cambridge University Press, 2005).
5 Nan Ellin, *Postmodern Urbanism* [Revised Edition] (New York: Princeton Architectural Press, 1999), pp. 1–4, 13–20; and David Harvey, *The Condition of Postmodernity: An Enquiry into the Origins of Cultural Change* (Malden, MA: Basil Blackwell, 1989), pp. 66–99.
6 Stavros Stavrides, "Occupied Squares and the Urban "State of Exception: In, Against and Beyond the City of Enclaves," in Estela Schindel and Pamela Columbo (eds.), *Space and the Memories of Violence: Landscapes of Erasure, Disappearance and Exception* (New York: Palgrave Macmillan, 2014), pp. 231–243 (esp. pp. 232, source of quotation).

archipelago." The makeshift assemblage of disconnected enclaves that comprise this patchwork city consists of a jumbled montage of island-like spaces only loosely connected one to the other. Cobbled together in ways that seem to defy the familiar patterns of the formal legibility which characterized the modernist impulse, the "city of enclaves" resembles a random assortment of "spatial enclosures," which themselves constitute "self-contained worlds with recognizable boundaries," and which are dispersed haphazardly across spatially uneven landscapes.[7] This emergent "post-urban" moment brings together new patterns of urbanization that have broken free from the rigid formality and rational orderliness of modernist city building.[8]

Another aim of this book is to unpack and expose these centrifugal forces that have brought about new kinds of "disaggregated urbanism" on a world scale. While these emergent patterns of spatial fragmentation and splintered urban form signal what might be considered only provisional and tentative steps into an-as-yet unknown urban future, the impulses toward disaggregation are sufficiently powerful to warrant serious attention. As "stand-alone" entities roughly inserted into urban landscapes without much forethought into the overall consequences, the "city-as-zone" and its mirror image – the "zone-as-city" – are geographically demarcated territories that establish differential forms of governance along with largely private regulatory regimes that shield them from unwanted public oversight. While self-governing enclaves and planned utopian experiments with city building are certainly not new, what distinguishes the bewildering patchwork of such disconnected spaces at the start of the twenty-first century is not only the sheer scale and scope of their impact on urban landscapes around the world, but also their association with the enterprise culture of market-driven hypercapitalism.

The contradictory dynamics of what might be called enclave urbanism, or the "urbanism of exception," represent the tentative beginnings of a new era of urbanization on a global scale at the start of the twenty-first century. For the past two to three decades, scholars, journalists, and policy advocates have drawn our collective attention to the shifting contours of urban transformation on a global scale. In countless numbers of ways and in various venues, they have launched penetrating critiques of the worst excesses of global urbanism through exposure, illustration, and example. Bits and pieces of this unfolding story, which combines the geographical spread of planetary urbanism, the eclipse of modernist planning, city building as the aggregation of enclaves, the unbundling of territorial sovereignty, the proliferation of autonomous zones, and the implantation of what might be called concessionary urbanism have

---

[7] Stavrides, "Occupied Squares and the Urban State of Exception," pp. 232–233 (source of quotation).

[8] Edward Soja, *Postmetropolis: Critical Studies of Cities and Regions* (Malden, MA: Blackwell, 2000), p. 299. See also Douglas Kelbaugh, *Repairing The American Metropolis* (Seattle: University of Washington Press, 2002).

appeared in scholarly research, visual imagery, photographic montages, journalistic accounts, and popular essays. What this book offers is an integrated synthesis that brings together these disparate microstories in a more overarching and comprehensive treatment of the opening stages of a new phase of global urbanism. The tentative emergence of this new kind of city building – the makeshift patchwork city of discontinuous enclaves – cuts unevenly across the familiar categorical distinctions between Global North and Global South, First-World City versus Third-World City, and West versus the Rest. Taken at face value, these customary dividing lines still help us to grasp the variety of "urbanisms" and the diverse experiences that characterize the historical unevenness of unfolding urbanization on a global scale. However, these conventional classificatory schemes can actually obscure deeper, subterranean structural dynamics that work to connect global urbanism at the start of the twenty-first century.[9]

The arguments that I offer are supported by stitching together a *mélange* of illustrative examples, vignettes, and singular anecdotes about particular cities and places. This mixture of micro-stories functions as a lens through which to grasp the dynamics of urban transformation at work at the start of the new millennium. Rather than seeing these seemingly odd places as discrete objects or disconnected and unrelated monadic particularisms, I treat them as visible manifestations – and interdependent instances – of imbricated processes bound inextricably together in ways that are often not immediately evident. As a kind of deliberate tactic, I have selected extreme (seemingly "outlier") cases because, as Saskia Sassen has argued, "They make sharply visible what might otherwise remain confusingly vague."[10] These extreme cases serve as exemplary expressions of largely invisible structural processes at work in building cities for the future. The steady multiplication of these exceptions and exemptions that give rise to more and more "extreme cases" has exposed the limitations of our familiar analytic frameworks, and thus has rendered our long-standing fixation with finding the singular logic, the universal rule, or the essential driving force behind the processes of urbanization a global scale no longer useful and increasingly out-of-date.

---

[9] These ideas are derived from a reading of Saskia Sassen, *Expulsions: Brutality and Complexity in the World Economy* (Cambridge, MA: Harvard University Press, 2014), pp. 5–6.

[10] Sassen, *Expulsions*, p. 1.

Acknowledgments

Scholarly research and writing never take place in a vacuum. We all owe a tremendous debt to scholars whose ideas influenced our own thinking, and to friends, family, and colleagues who were often drawn inadvertently into dialogue and conversation. This book originated out of a long and drawn-out critical engagement with the spatial configuration of Johannesburg in the post-apartheid era. I gradually came to realize that Johannesburg is not one city, but many cities occupying and competing for the same geographical space. In so many ways, the fractured urban landscape of Johannesburg consists of a hybrid collection of disconnected enclaves that create almost hermetically sealed social worlds. Those who use and inhabit these cocooned spheres typically do not engage in meaningful and intimate social interaction with those on the "outside." This observation led me to cast my gaze more broadly onto the global terrain, and to critically explore how city building at the start of the twenty-first century has largely moved along pathways quite different than the trajectories that characterized the modernist urbanism of the nineteenth and twentieth centuries.

The Urbanism of Exception is a work of synthesis. I have tried to weave together the research and writing of others in order to create a rather grand story that captures what is happening with global urbanism in the age of late modernity. Hopefully, the whole is greater than the sum of its parts. Over many years, I have engaged in countless conversations about the ideas in this book with numerous colleagues, but Anne Pitcher, Garth Myers, Idalina Baptista, Gavin Shatkin, and David Bieri stand out as key persons with whom I drew into dialogue about the themes that I explore in this book.

I am grateful for the assistance that I received from the School of Architecture and Urban Planning (Taubman College), and the Department of Afroamerican and African Studies at the University of Michigan. Colleagues, including but not restricted to Derek Peterson, Becky Peterson, Danny Herwitz, Lucia Saks, Sean

Jacobs, Jessica Blat, Marieke Krijnen, Howard Stein, Kelly Askew, Omolade Adunbi, Damola Osinulu, Adam Ashforth, Ana Paula Pimentel-Walker, Harley Etienne, Robert Goodspeed, Lesli Hoey, and Scott Campbell provided a great deal of encouragement and intellectual support.

I would also like to acknowledge the support that I have received from Robert Dreesen, my editor at Cambridge University Press. From the start, he certainly expressed a great deal of faith in this project, and cleared away potential impediments blocking a smooth passage forward. In addition, I would like to acknowledge the logistical and financial support of the University of Michigan. Most importantly, and as always, my wife Anne Pitcher is my greatest inspiration. She has always challenged me to refine my ideas and get to the point. I owe a great deal to her encouragement and her support. I would also like to acknowledge Jeremy, Andrew, and Alida. Their presence is always there, sometimes obscured by time and distance. I dedicate this book to them with the hope that the cities they may inhabit in the coming decades will be more inclusive and more welcoming than they are at present.

Introduction

The Modern Metropolis and the Eclipse of Modernist City Building

Cast in bold strokes, the birth of the modern metropolis can trace its origins to the dawn of the industrial capitalist age in the mid- to late-nineteenth century. Animated by the modernist ethos that shaped thinking at the time, a new generation of city builders embarked on a far-reaching strategy to reshape urban landscapes in conformity with the machine-age principles of rational ordering of urban space, functional specialization of land use, spatial differentiation of the built environment, and efficient circulation of people and commodities. In seeking to break free from the strictures of jumbled (and allegedly chaotic) urban form that characterized the preindustrial city, sometimes tight and sometimes loose alliances of real-estate developers and city officials joined forces to adopt the *tabula rasa* approach of erasure and reinscription, clearing away old buildings, streetscapes, and entire neighborhoods that stood in the way of anticipated progress.[1] In a kind of proleptic projection, modernist city builders imagined a future in conformity with their planned interventions to create it.[2] Like industrial production itself in the "machine-age," city building was subjected to the modernist principles of standardization of building typologies, the speed of movement, and top-down organization of municipal administration.[3] This modernizing impulse involving the creative destruction of existing urban

[1] James Holston, *The Modernist City: An Anthropological Critique of Brasília* (Chicago: University of Chicago Press, 1989), pp. 7–11; and David Pinder, *Visions of the City: Utopianism, Power and Politics in Twentieth-Century Urbanism* (New York: Routledge, 2013), pp. 89–126. See also Dietrich Neumann, "The Unbuilt City of Modernity," in Thorsten Scheer, Josef-Paul Kleihues, and Paul Kahlfeldt (eds.), *City of Architecture/Architecture of the City/Berlin 1900–2000* (Berlin: Nicolaische Verlagsbuchhandlung, 2000), pp. 161–173.
[2] See Anthony Vidler, *The Architectural Uncanny: Essays in the Modern Unhomely* (Cambridge, MA: The MIT Press, 1992), pp. 182, 199.
[3] See Shawn Natrasony and Don Alexander, "The Rise of Modernism and the Decline of Place: The Case of Surrey City Centre, Canada," *Planning Perspectives* 20, 4 (2005), pp. 413–433.

fabrics to clear the way for rebuilding spilled out of the core areas at the center of the world economy, as a new kind of dependent urbanism emerged in
the European colonial territories and elsewhere at "the margins of modernity."
Despite the persistence of enduring socioeconomic inequalities and the distortion of urban form brought about by the implantation of rules governing
racial segregation, these new cities in the peripheral zones of the world economy looked strikingly similar to modernist prototypes from which they were
so blatantly copied.[4]

Classical understandings of the modern metropolis have long rested on theories, fears, and hopes associated with the conjoined processes of historical
transformation and progress ("modernization") and the sociocultural practices
of innovation and novelty ("modernity"). As a general rule, early scholarly
contributions to the field of urban studies traced the origins of the modern
metropolis as a distinctive and evolving spatial form to the historical specificity
of particular urban experiences, particularly mid-nineteenth century London,
late nineteenth-century Berlin, Vienna, and Paris, or early twentieth-century
New York and Chicago. In other words, these core theoretical currents in urban
studies "drew on a specific (western) version of urban modernity" to identify
those universalizing (and homogenizing) impulses that were seen to define the
pathways of urbanism everywhere. The singular urban experiences of leading
"western" cities of North America and Europe became the universal standard
through which to evaluate progress toward "development" in cities around the
world as they moved along evolutionary, linear pathways already forged by
those which came before.[5]

---

4 This phrase is borrowed from Daniel Herwitz, "Modernism at the Margins," in Hilton Judin and
   Ivan Vladislavić (eds.), *Blank___: Architecture, Apartheid and After* (Rotterdam: NAi, 1999),
   pp. 405–421. See also Anthony King, *Colonial Urban Development: Culture, Social Power and
   Environment* (London and Boston: Routledge & Kegan Paul, 1976); Anthony King, *Urbanism,
   Colonialism, and the World-Economy: Cultural and Spatial Foundations of the World Urban
   System* (London and Boston: Routledge Kegan & Paul, 1990); and Robert Home, *Of Planting
   and Planning: The Making of British Colonial Cities* [Second Edition] (New York: Routledge,
   2013). See also David Simon, "Colonial Cities, Postcolonial Africa and the World Economy:
   A Reinterpretation," *International Journal of Urban and Regional Research* 13, 1 (1989), pp.
   68–91; Anthony King, "The Times and Spaces of Modernity (or who needs Postmodernism?),"
   in Mike Featherstone, Scott Lash, and Roland Robertson (eds.), *Global Modernities* (Thousand
   Oaks, CA: Sage, 1995), pp. 108–123; Mauro Guillén, "Modernism without Modernity: The
   Rise of Modernist Architecture in Mexico, Brazil, and Argentina, 1890–1940," *Latin American
   Research Review* 39, 2 (2004), pp. 6–34; Uğur Ümit Üngör, "Creative Destruction: Shaping a
   High-Modernist City in Interwar Turkey," *Journal of Urban History* 39, 2 (2012), pp. 297–314;
   Manish Chalana and Tyler Sprague, "Beyond Le Corbusier and the Modernist City: Reframing
   Chandigarh's 'World Heritage' Legacy," *Planning Perspectives* 28, 2 (2013), pp. 199–222; and
   Mia Fuller, *Moderns Abroad: Architecture, Cities, and Italian Imperialism* (New York: Rout-
   ledge, 2007).
5 These ideas are derived from Jennifer Robinson, "The Urban Now: Theorising Cities beyond the
   New," *European Journal of Cultural Studies* 16, 6 (2013), pp. 659–677 (esp. p. 659; quotation
   p. 660).

Thinking about the modern metropolis has always careened back and forth between imaginings of urban futures that are either romantically utopian or catastrophically dystopian.[6] This new kind of city – at once vibrant and ever-changing, and sinister and unforgiving – triggered an outpouring of social commentary captured in the much celebrated writings of Charles Baudelaire (the aimless anonymity of the peripatetic *flaneur*), Georg Simmel (overstimulation, the money economy, and the *blasé* attitude), Louis Wirth ("urbanism as a way of life"), and Walter Benjamin (the phantasmagoria of the arcades as the central organizing metaphor for the meteoric rise of commodity capitalism).[7] This scholarly work focused a great deal of attention on the emergence of new modes of urban living, particularly the dynamics of social mingling with strangers and heterogeneous crowds in urban public space and the *anomie* brought about by the superficial, anonymous, and fleeting interactions characteristic of the transitory nature of urban relationships. Originating out of the anxiety provoked by the encounter with strangeness, the urban uncanny operated alongside (and sometimes in contradiction with) the modernist ethos that praised the virtues of an open and distinctive civic public culture and the positive values fostered by a vibrant public realm.[8]

Starting in the 1920s, a group of urban scholars associated with the so-called "Chicago School" of urban sociology codified what they regarded as the defining characteristics of the modern metropolis into an elaborate theorization of urban evolution and transformation. The Chicago School developed a set of standard assumptions and cohesive themes guiding their work. For the Chicago School, the modern metropolis was the archetypical prototype for understanding urbanization on a world scale. In the view of scholars affiliated with this school of thought, what they found in studying Chicago amounted to virtually universal principles that could be applied to cities everywhere.[9]

[6] See Gyan Prakash, "Introduction: Imagining the Modern City, Darkly," in Gyan Prakash (ed.), *Noir Urbanism: Dystopic Images of the Modern City* (Princeton, NJ: Princeton University Press, 2010), pp. 1–14.

[7] Walter Benjamin [edited by Michael Jennings], *The Writer of Modern Life: Essays on Charles Baudelaire* (Cambridge, MA: Harvard University Press, 2006). See David Frisby, *Cityscapes of Modernity: Critical Explorations* (Malden, MA: Polity Press, 2001); and Steve Baker, "The Sign of the Self in the Metropolis," *Journal of Design History* 3, 4 (1990), pp. 227–234.

[8] For a broad treatment of some of these issues, see Marshall Berman, *All That is Solid Melts into Air: The Experience of Modernity* (New York: Penguin, 1998). For the uncanny, see Vidler, *The Architectural Uncanny*, pp. 4–8. For the idea of publics, see Sophie Watson, *City Publics* (London: Routledge, 2006); Nancy Fraser, "Rethinking the Public Sphere: A Contribution to the Critique of Actually Existing Democracy," in Craig Calhoun (ed.), *Habermas and the Public Sphere* (Cambridge, MA: The MIT Press, 1991), pp. 109–142; and Jürgen Habermas, *The Structural Transformation of the Public Sphere: An Inquiry into a Category of Bourgeois Society* (Cambridge, MA: The MIT Press, 1989).

[9] See Dennis Judd, Dick Simpson, and Janet Abu-Lughod (eds.), *The City Revisited: Urban Theory from Chicago, Los Angeles, and New York* (Minneapolis: University of Minnesota Press, 2011); and Michael Dear (ed.), *From Chicago to LA: Making Sense of Urban Theory* (Thousand Oaks, CA: Sage, 2001).

As a general rule, the Chicago School looked at cities as complex yet predictable social worlds operated in ways analogous to natural processes, where urban growth and development conformed to expected and orderly patterns that could be observed and measured with the application of objective scientific principles.[10] In seeking to understand why redevelopment and land use varied over the urban landscape, the Chicago School relied upon organic metaphors and ecological models as appropriate and useful framing devices for the investigation of urban social relations. The use of such concepts as "ecological niche" ("or natural areas") crystallized into a theory of ever-expanding, or maturing, concentric circles of land use extending outward from the high-density core to the surrounding low-density periphery. For the most part, urban theorists associated with the Chicago School viewed urban social structures as complex webs of dynamic processes, somewhat akin to components of an eco-system, progressing through various stages of growth toward maturity. The resulting ecological models, thus, emerged from the examination of the parallels between natural and social systems. A preoccupation that permeated the investigations of the Chicago School was the search for the rules – or law-like regularities – that governed the growth of the city-system. As the dominant paradigm in urban studies for close to half a century, the Chicago School left its mark on mainstream approaches to urban studies: the uncritical use of naturalistic and organic metaphors, and the widespread deployment of such key framing ideas as stages of urban growth, linear pathways of urbanization, functional specialization, the invasion-succession ecological model, and concentric rings became embedded in the accepted canon of mainstream urban studies.[11]

In the waning decades of the twentieth century, theoretical challenges put forward by such alternative perspectives as the Los Angeles (LA) School exposed the limitations in the foundational principles that guided the researching and writing of the Chicago School.[12] More generally, scholarly inquiry over the past several decades has amounted to a sustained critique of the mainstream canon of conventional urban studies. These critiques have focused the uncritical dependence upon (so-called) Western models of urban development as the basic template for understanding the trajectories of global urbanism.[13] A

---

[10] Andrew Abbott, "Of Time and Space: The Contemporary Relevance of the Chicago School," *Social Forces* 75, 4 (1997), pp. 1149–1182; and James Short, *The Social Fabric of the Metropolis: Contributions of the Chicago School of Urban Sociology* (Chicago: University of Chicago Press, 1971).

[11] Simon Parker, *Urban Theory and the Urban Experience: Encountering the City* [2nd edition] (New York: Routledge, 2015). See also David Wachsmuth, "City as Ideology: Reconciling the Explosion of the City Form with the Tenacity of the City Concept," *Environment and Planning D* 32, 1 (2014), pp. 75–90.

[12] See Judd, Simpson, and Abu-Lughod, The City Revisited; and Dear, *From Chicago to LA: Making Sense of Urban Theory.*

[13] Jennifer Robinson, *Ordinary Cities: Between Modernity and Development* (New York: Routledge, 2003); Ananya Roy, "Slumdog Cities: Rethinking Subaltern Urbanism," *International Journal of Urban and Regional Research* 35, 2 (2011), pp. 223–238; Ryan Bishop, John Phillips,

variety of alternative framing devices – most notably postmodernist, poststructuralist, and postcolonialist perspectives – have provided spirited critiques of modernist orthodoxies.[14] Yet none of these theoretical orientations have offered sufficiently coherent road maps for understanding the evolving trajectories of global urbanism at the start of the twenty-first century.[15]

Starting in the latter half of the nineteenth century, the dominant mode of urbanization that characterized the era of the modern metropolis produced a dual structure consisting of a dense central core surrounded by expansive rings of suburban dependencies tied umbilically to the center via various networks of circulation. At the risk of oversimplification, this crude structure of high-density "urban core" versus low-density "suburban periphery" has long dominated the public imagination as well as the scholarly literature on cities. With some variation, the prevailing view of the urbanization process – what stands as the ideal typical model – looks at urban growth and development as a process fueled by migration to the dense inner city, where the clustering of employment opportunities and the agglomeration of services produced a particular kind of concentrated urban realm. In this formulation, expansion has generally taken place through roughly concentric waves of sprawling suburbanization, thereby "pushing the outer edge of the metropolis into a rural or nonurban countryside."[16]

For close to a century, this core-centric, centripetal model of hierarchical urban growth and development has dominated analytical thinking about cities.[17] Yet the processes of urbanization that began to take shape in the late twentieth century were significantly different from what came before. At this time, a distinctive mode of worldwide urbanization put into motion the geographical concentration of "the world's population, primarily through rural to urban migration, not just in cities *per se*, but in larger and often sprawling metropolitan regions."[18] The sheer scale and scope of the growing population size of cities on a world scale has led to claims that we have entered a new Urban Age, where for the first time in history, more than half the world's

Wei Yeo (eds.), *Postcolonial Urbanism: Southeast Asian Cities and Global Processes* (New York: Routledge, 2003); and Ananya Roy and Aihwa Ong (eds.), *Worlding Cities: Asian Experiments and the Art of Being Global* (Malden, MA: Wiley-Blackwell, 2011).

[14] See, for example, Colin Rowe and Fred Koetter, *Collage City* (Cambridge, MA: The MIT Press, 1975).

[15] Matthew Gandy, *Concrete and Clay: Reworking Nature in New York City* (Cambridge, MA: The MIT Press, 2003), pp. 15–17; and Robert Beauregard, "Without a Net: Modernist Planning and the Postmodern Abyss," *Journal of Planning Education and Research* 10, 3 (1991), pp. 189–194.

[16] Edward Soja, "Regional Urbanization and the Future of Megacities," in Steef Bujijs, Wendy Tan, and Devisari Tunas (eds.), *Megacities: Exploring a Sustainable Future* (Rotterdam: 010 Publishers, 2010), pp. 56–75 (esp. p. 58).

[17] See, for example, Sebastian Dembski, "Structure and Imagination of Changing Cities: Manchester, Liverpool and the Spatial In-between," *Urban Studies* 52, 9 (2015), pp. 1647–1664.

[18] Soja, "Regional Urbanization and the Future of Megacities," pp. 57–58 (quotation from p. 57).

population lives within cities.[19] The trope of this new Urban Age has spawned its own vocabulary: megacities, hypergrowth, planetary urbanism, posturbanism, exopolis, and the postmetropolis. Yet to view urbanization simply through the narrow lens of expanding population size – which has resulted in ever-larger numbers of megacities of hypergrowth on a world scale – tends to ignore how contemporary modes of urbanization have not only eroded "inherited morphologies of urbanism at all spatial scales" but also produced "new, rescaled formulations of urbanized territorial organization."[20]

The modes of urbanization that have unfolded at the start of the twenty-first century have produced highly uneven urban fabrics that have assumed "extremely complex polycentric forms that no longer remotely approximate the concentric rings and linear density gradients associated with the relatively bounded industrial city of the nineteenth century," nor "the metropolitan forms of urban development that were consolidated during the opening decades of the twentieth century."[21] The steady accretion of differences and discontinuities with past waves of urban growth and development have marked a qualitative shift in the dominant modes of urbanization, thereby resulting in what some scholars have called "extended regional urbanization" or "a polycentric and networked city region."[22]

Challenging Foundational Principles: the Modern Metropolis and the Modernist Imagination

Scholarly challenges to the iconic status of the classic modern metropolis as the prototype for understanding global urbanism have emerged in fits and starts, and have yet to gain a fully developed and coherent footing in mainstream urban studies. Old ideas (and paradigms) die slowly. It is often the case that they live on – in the form of a ghostly afterlife – well beyond the time of their analytic and epistemological usefulness. Paradigmatic scaffolding inherited from earlier efforts to understand cities and urbanization has continued to maintain a tight grip over conceptual frameworks, classification schemes, and modes of analysis that are no longer fully capable of making sense of urbanism on a global scale.

As a general rule, mainstream thinking about urbanization as a global process has tried in vain to rationalize the steadily rising numbers of cities on a world scale that do not conform to the classical conception of the modern

---

[19] Neil Brenner and Christian Schmid, "The 'Urban Age' in Question," in Neil Brenner (ed.), *Implosions/Explosions: Towards a Study of Planetary Urbanism* (Berlin: Jovis, 2014), pp. 310–337 (esp. p. 310).

[20] Brenner and Schmid, "The 'Urban Age' in Question," p. 324.

[21] Brenner and Schmid, "The 'Urban Age' in Question," pp. 310–337.

[22] See Edward Soja and Miguel Kanai, "The Urbanization of the World," in Ricky Burdett and Deyan Sudjic (eds.), *The Endless City: The Urban Age Project by the London School of Economics and the Deutsche Bank's Alfred Herrhausen Society* (London: Phaidon, 2007), pp. 54–69.

metropolis. By treating seemingly extreme cases as extraordinary (that is, outside the expected mainstream), conventional theorizing about cities typically classifies the exceptions as inexplicable outliers or curious anomalies, or else dismisses them as unfortunate expressions of failed urbanism, either subjected to the abnormal pressures of super-fast, hypergrowth or suffering from asphyxiating shrinkage and decline. These exceptional cities that do not correspond with expected patterns of urbanization, those that take unexpected detours by expanding too quickly or by seemingly reversing direction through decline and abandonment, either become inconsistent aberrations that require further refinement and elaboration, or they are pushed "off the map" of significance, because they are not forcefully present at the heart of theoretical and paradigmatic expectations.[23]

But the extreme is no longer the exception, but the norm. The failure of existing conceptual frameworks to capture extreme versions of those familiar conditions associated with expected patterns of urbanization on a world scale requires a rethinking of mainstream paradigms that dominate research and writing in urban studies. Beginning with the exception – or what Saskia Sassen has called the "systemic edge" – enables us to question what conventional theorizing about cities and city-making has long regarded as the norm, the expected, and the exemplary.[24]

Rethinking conventional paradigms in contemporary urban studies requires us to challenge, and at least partially dismantle (if not completely discard), the foundational pillars that have guided theory-making for quite some time. While they proved quite useful in assisting us in theorizing about cities and urbanization in earlier times, they seem to have suffered from diminishing capacity to illuminate contemporary processes of urbanization on a global scale. To be sure, this exercise of rethinking does not necessarily mean rejecting every idea inherited from earlier rounds of theorizing about cities and urbanism, and simply starting *de novo*. Yet it does demand that we critically engage with and interrogate the borderlands, or "fuzzy edges," of existing paradigmatic knowledge frameworks, and that we expose largely unquestioned assumptions and examine their continued usefulness.[25]

As a general rule, four key *regulative principles* – that is, taken-for-granted ways of thinking – accompanied the growth and development of the modern metropolis. These ideas have not only animated theories of the "good city" for at least the past half century, but also empowered the practice of city building

---

[23] See Jennifer Robinson, "Global and World Cities: A View from Off the Map," *International Journal of Urban and Regional Research* 26, 3 (2002), pp. 531–554.

[24] These ideas here and earlier are taken and adapted from Saskia Sassen, "At the Systemic Edge," *Cultural Dynamics* 27, 1 (2015), pp. 173–181.

[25] A good place to start is Saskia Sassen, *Expulsions: Brutality and Complexity in the World Economy* (Cambridge, MA: Harvard University Press, 2014). See also Saskia Sassen, *Territory Authority Rights: From Medieval to Global Assemblages* [Updated Edition] (Princeton, NJ: Princeton University Press, 2008), pp. 1–23.

over the same period.[26] But they may not be as readily self-evident, singularly objective, and blandly unproblematic as they may appear at first glance. The structural dynamics, urban form, and social characteristics of cities have "no pregiven or fixed ontological status, but are socially produced and continually transformed" in accordance with changing pressures and entanglements brought about by the encounter with the contradictory dynamics of globalization.[27]

The breakdown and gradual disappearance of the key elements that characterized the modern metropolis from the mid-nineteenth until the late twentieth century marks the eclipse of a particular historically demarcated phase of urbanization and the start of a new mode of urban transformation on a global scale. Tracing the partial disappearance if not complete disintegration of these four foundational pillars enables us to more fully comprehend the contours and trajectories of global urbanism at the start of the twenty-first century. Looking at the fading dominance of the classic "modern metropolis" as the ideal-typical model for urban life in general and the main paradigmatic template for theorizing about global urbanism allows us to rethink conventional theories, conceptual frameworks, and categorical distinctions that have often assumed the elevated status of universal applicability with general relevance for urbanization on a world scale.[28]

The unraveling of these four key regulative principles provides a platform for a rethinking of conventional urban theories and opens up the possibilities for paradigmatic shifts in theorizing about global urbanism. First, the continued reliance in mainstream urban studies on somewhat static conceptualizations of the city as a bounded territory, or recognizable spatial unit, with recognizable borders and edges (producing a distinctive urban form) has hindered our capacity to understand global urbanism at the start of the twenty-first century.[29] Second, the modernist (and high-modernist) principles that shaped thinking about city building beginning at the end of the nineteenth century and continuing to the end of the twentieth century have largely fallen out of favor.[30] Third, the steady encroachment of new kinds of largely privatized regulatory regimes have undermined, and often replaced, the public administration of urban space.

---

[26] See, for example, Malcolm Miles and Tim Hall (eds.), *Urban Futures: Critical Commentaries on Shaping the City* (New York: Routledge, 2003); and Robert Fishman, *Urban Utopias in the Twentieth Century* [Revised Edition] (Cambridge, MA: The MIT Press, 1982).

[27] See Ash Amin, "Spatialities of Globalization," *Environment and Planning A* 34, 3 (2002), pp. 385–399 (quotation from p. 386).

[28] For a classic statement, see Hans Blumenfeld, *The Modern Metropolis: Its Origins, Growth, Characteristics, and Planning: Selected Essays* [edited by Paul Spreiregen] (Cambridge, MA: The MIT Press, 1967).

[29] See Ryan Bishop and John Phillips, "The Urban Problematic," *Theory, Culture & Society* 30, 7–8 (2013), pp. 221–241.

[30] Nigel Taylor, "Anglo-American Town Planning Theory since 1945: Three Significant Developments but no Paradigm Shifts," *Planning Perspectives* 14, 4 (1999), pp. 327–345.

Fourth, and finally, the emergence of new kinds of socially accessible yet privately owned and managed space has become the dominant mode of social congregation, casual mixing, and chance encounter in cities today. While city builders in older cities have clung tenaciously to conventional approaches to organizing urban life around classical understandings of accessible public space, dominant stakeholders in newer cities have gradually jettisoned these commitments in favor of new ways of partitioning urban landscapes.[31]

The shifting patterns of extended urbanization on a global scale have destabilized inherited epistemological assumptions, analytic frameworks, and paradigmatic models that have guided urban theorizing and research for quite some time. Conventional ways of thinking about urbanization have become ingrained habits of thought, expressions of "common sense," that are still widely in use. Received ideas about global urbanism have an enduring afterlife long after their universalizing and essentializing impulses have disappeared. To call into question conventional approaches to urban studies is not to suggest that existing interpretive frameworks are completely outmoded and irrelevant. On the contrary, scholars calling for conceptual renewal and realignment are not in agreement regarding the precise limitations of inherited analytic frameworks and models, and, as a consequence, they have not reached consensus about what "updated or reinvented interpretive frameworks that can more effectively orient and animate" urban theory and research.[32]

The Instability of "the City" as Coherent Object of Inquiry

At first glance, "the city" appears as an obvious fact of contemporary life. Yet the closer one inquires into its inner workings, the more difficult it is to comprehend it as a coherent object.[33] In so many ways, cities are somewhat akin to a "disassembled jigsaw puzzle," which from a distance resemble "a confused mass to which it is difficult to apply models constructed from theories of urban order." Without an organizing focus, it is almost as if, as the anthropologist Nestor Garcia Canclini has suggested about Mexico City, cities are "everywhere without really being anywhere,"[34] just like Jorge Luis Borges's *Aleph*.

The hybrid patterns of global urbanism at the start of the twenty-first century contradict the historicist meta-narrative according to which urban

[31] Anastasia Loukaitou-Sideris, "Privatisation of Public Open Space: The Los Angeles Experience," *Town Planning Review* 64, 2 (1993), pp. 139–168.

[32] Neil Brenner and Christian Schmid, "Combat, Caricature and Critique in the Study of Planetary Urbanization" [Urban Theory Lab, Graduate School of Design, Harvard University, April 2015], pp. 1–11 (quotation from p. 3).

[33] See Hilary Angelo and David Wachmuth, "Urbanizing Urban Political Ecology: A Critique of Methodological Cityism," *International Journal of Urban and Regional Research* 39, 1 (2015), pp. 16–27.

[34] Nestor Garcia Canclini, "Mexico City: Cultural Globalization in a Disintegrating City," *American Ethnologist* 22, 4 (1995), pp. 743–755 (quotations from 748).

transformation takes place in coherent and distinct stages *en route* to a common end point of mature development. The search for internal coherence in the city distorts its most fundamental features and obscures social practices characteristic of the everyday life of the metropolis. The vast extension of urban agglomerations and the actual realities of global connections have together made the boundaries of cities difficult to define. Clarifying the coordinates of object of inquiry is no easy task. When we refer to a city, we generally designate a material object and identify an imagined place. Assuming a unified social whole implies bounded coherence. Yet the force of globalization has undermined both the implied unity of the metropolis and ideal-typical designations of a clear demarcation between "inside" and "outside." If buildings and infrastructure define the city as a place, then multiscaled processes, complex and conflicting relations, and dense interconnections mark the metropolis as a historically specific site. As Henri Lefebvre cautioned a long time ago, neither modernity nor the metropolis have an ontological essence: each is a historically contingent condition located in time as well as in a place.[35]

One of the ironies of modern urban planning – itself the product of circulating ideas originating more than a century ago – is that its practitioners generally assume that cities form unified social wholes with an implied bounded coherence. By operating under the illusory belief in the comprehensiveness, internal logic, and boundedness of urban space, planning practice typically presumes that it is possible to capture the essential characteristics of cities through cartographic representation.[36] The imaginary wholeness of the city acts as a kind of "metaphorical glue," presuming that assembled elements come together as an autochthonous condition and bounded and coherent social system. As Thomas Bender has warned, reification is a real danger, "for it masks as it unifies, thus misleading our understanding of urban processes and [the] lived experience" of urban life.[37]

Conventional urban theories have long been premised on the assumption that cities are more or less self-enclosed, distinctive, discrete, and territorially bounded types of human settlement-space that can be contrasted to putatively "nonurban" zones that lie outside or beyond them (such as suburbs, the countryside, rural hinterlands, and, ultimately, the realm of nature).[38] Yet the accelerated pace of extensive urbanization on a global scale has undermined the once meaningful distinctions between city and country, metropolis and

[35] Henri Lefebvre, *Writings on Cities* [edited and translated by Eleonore Kotman and Elizabeth Lebas] (Oxford: Blackwell, 1996), p. 12.
[36] Thomas Bender, "History, Theory and the Metropolis" (CMS Working Paper Series, No. 005–2206. Center for Metropolitan Studies, Technical University Berlin D-10587, 2006), pp. 1–15 (esp. pp. 6–7).
[37] Bender, "History, Theory and the Metropolis," p. 7.
[38] See, for example, Neil Brenner and Christian Schmid, "Towards a New Epistemology of the Urban?" *City* 19, 2–3 (2015), pp. 151–182; Matthew Gandy, "When Does the City End?" in Neil Brenner (ed.), *Implosions/Explosions: Towards a Study of Planetary Urbanization* (Berlin: Jovis, 2014), pp. 86–89; and Wachsmuth, "City as Ideology," pp. 75–90.

hinterlands, and urban core and periurban periphery. While mainstream urban theories have continued to conceptualize cities as discrete territorial entities and relatively self-enclosed sociogeographical units with a spatial integrity all their own, the "ever-thickening commodity chains, infrastructural circuits, migration streams and circulatory-logistical networks that today crisscross the planet" have triggered processes of extensive urbanization at the start of the twenty-first century that seem almost boundless, with an almost limitless territorial reach.[39]

New geographies of uneven spatial development have unfolded "through a contradictory interplay between rapid, explosive processes of urbanization and various forms of stagnation, shrinkage, and marginalization, often in close proximity to one another." In contrast to the evolving geographies of territorial inequality associated with previous cycles of capitalist industrialization (and deindustrialization), this new mosaic of spatial unevenness cannot be captured adequately through conventional models of urbanization, with their typological differentiation of space between urban/rural, metropole/colony, First/Second/Third World, North/South, East/West, and so forth. At the start of the twenty-first century, divergent processes of extended urbanization have produced the polarities of wealth and poverty, growth and decline, inclusion and exclusion, and centrality and marginality. These processes mutually reinforce one another at all spatial scales, from the microsetting of the neighborhood to the macrouniverse of the planetary.[40] These new patterns of extended urbanization that have unfolded around the world over the past quarter century challenge inherited conceptions of the city (or the urban) as "a fixed, bounded, and universally generalizable settlement type."[41]

The Collapse of Modernist (and High Modernist) Comprehensive Master-Planned City Building

In projecting an image of the functionally specialized city, modernist city builders stressed the rational and efficient use of space through holistic,

---

[39] Neil Brenner, "Theses on Urbanization," *Public Culture* 25, 1 [69] (2013), pp. 85–114; and Neil Brenner, "Urban Theory without an Outside," in Neil Brenner (ed.), *Implosions/Explosions: Towards a Study of Planetary Urbanization* (Berlin: Jovis, 2013), pp. 14–35 (quotation from p. 16). See also Christian Schmid, "Patterns and Pathways of Global Urbanization: Towards Comparative Analysis," in *Implosions/Explosions*, pp. 203–217.

[40] Neil Brenner and Christian Schmid, "Towards a New Epistemology of the Urban?" *City* 19, 2–3 (2015), pp. 151–182 (esp. pp. 151–152; quotation from p. 151; the following two sentences taken almost verbatim from p. 152). For a critique of the planetary urbanism thesis, see, for example, Richard Walker, "Building a Better Theory of the Urban: A Response to 'Towards a New Epistemology of the Urban?'" *City* 19, 5 (2015), pp. 183–191; and Mark Davidson and Kurt Iveson, "Beyond City Limits: A Conceptual and Political Defense of 'the City' as an Anchoring Concept for Critical Urban Theory," *City* 19, 5 (2015), pp. 646–664.

[41] Brenner and Schmid, "Towards a New Epistemology of the Urban?" p. 151 (source of quotation). See also Neil Brenner and Christian Schmid, "The 'Urban Age' in Question," *International Journal of Urban and Regional Research* 38, 3 (2014), pp. 731–755.

comprehensive master planning. As a distinctive technology of power in the service of one particular vision of modernity, modernist master-planning (embedded in a techno-positivist rationality) connoted the officially sanctioned reshaping of urban space that blended functionalist spatial ideologies with particular design morphologies.[42] As a historically specific ideology associated with the idea of progress, modernist planning offered an authoritative promise of the better city yet-to-come.[43]

The core ideas of modernist city building (and linked with conventional planning theory and practice) have long revolved around the firm conviction that social processes can be controlled and improved through the proper and efficient engineering of space. Calls for the wholesale eradication of such dystopic spaces as blighted streetscapes, underutilized buildings, and insalubrious slums required radical intervention to surgically remove what stood in the way of anticipated progress. Erasure and reinscription – the elimination of the unwanted built environment to pave the way for "blank-slate" renewal – dominated modernist thinking about urban landscapes. The principles of modernist-inspired urban planning effectively reduced the "urban question" to little more than the imposition of a standardized ("one-size-fits-all") set of efficient land use zoning regulations and transportation decisions. This conviction has remained so resilient that, despite significant criticism and countermovements challenging the deleterious effects of wholesale demolition and transportation corridor development, the field of contemporary urban planning continues to be largely dominated by heroic "big plans" and the reliance on technical expertise (or what Timothy Mitchell has called "the rule of experts").[44]

Modernist planning has always relied upon a tacit faith in the unmediated link between representation and a future reality yet-to-come. In critiquing modernist-inspired urban planning for its unapologetic functionalism and for mistaking cities as "problems of simplicity," Jane Jacobs once posed the question: "Why have cities not been identified, understood and treated as problems of organized complexity?"[45] For Jacobs, coming to grips with urban complexity meant focusing on social processes – networks, relationships, connections – rather than on fixed places and stable identities. Physical objects located in cities – whether they are buildings, streets, parks, districts, landmarks, or anything else – can have radically differing effects on their surroundings, depending upon the circumstances and contexts in which they exist. Thus, for instance,

[42] See, for example, M. Christine Boyer, *Dreaming the Rational City: The Myth of American City Planning* (Cambridge, MA: The MIT Press, 1983); and Edward Relph, *The Modern Urban Landscape* (London: Croon Helm, 1986).

[43] See Austin Zeiderman, Sobia Ahmad Kaker, Jonathan Silver, and Astrid Wood, "Uncertainty and Urban Life," Public Culture 27, 2 [76] (2015), pp. 281–304 (esp. p. 282).

[44] Kenneth Kolson, *Big Plans: The Allure and Folly of Urban Design* (Baltimore, MD: The Johns Hopkins University Press, 2001), pp. 1–14. See Timothy Mitchell, *Rule of Experts: Egypt, Techno-Politics, Modernity* (Berkeley: University of California Press, 2002).

[45] Jane Jacobs, *The Death and Life of America's Great Cities* (New York: Vintage, 1961), p. 434.

as Jacobs suggested, "almost nothing useful can be understood or can be done about improving city dwellings if those are considered in the abstract as "housing." Residential dwellings – whether they exist or are planned – "are specific and particularized buildings," *always* subject to differing and historically specific processes, such as neglect and abandonment, blight, gentrification, and, as Jacobs put it, "the generation of diversity, [and] self-destruction of diversity."[46]

Despite its confident vision of creating the Radiant City of Tomorrow, modernist (and high-modernist) city building sowed the seeds of its own eventual destruction. Urban landscapes proved to be much too complicated, illegible, and indeterminate to easily conform to the disciplinary logic of rational order and the efficient ("highest and best") use of space.[47] The hallucinogenic "delirium of power" inscribed in the totalizing vision of comprehensive master planning rested on the flawed promise that it was possible to shape the urban landscape to the desired ends of an integrated whole.[48] By the last decades of the twentieth century, as Matthew Gandy has argued, "The omniscient perspective of comprehensive "total planning" had become both a technical and philosophical anachronism." The dynamics of urban decline fatally damaged the utopian ideals of modernist thinkers and urban futurists who had put their faith in state-driven comprehensive master planning. The rejection of modernist urbanism signaled a resistance to technical rationality as the principal solution to urban disorder and dysfunctionalities.[49] The utopian ambitions (and professional arrogance) of modernist (and high-modernist) city builders failed to achieve their goal of molding urban landscapes in conformity with their principles of spatial differentiation and functional specialization, disciplinary order, and the rational and efficient use of space.[50]

The abandonment of the holistic utopianism of modernist city building has given way to largely piecemeal, incremental approaches to urban redevelopment.[51] The end of "top-down," state-sponsored, comprehensive

[46] Jacobs, *The Death and Life of America's Great Cities*, p. 440.

[47] Beatriz Jaguaribe, "Modernist Ruins: National Narratives and Architectural Forms," *Public Culture* 11, 1 (1999), pp. 295–312.

[48] See Holston, *The Modernist City*, pp. 8–9. See also Robert Beauregard, "Between Modernity and Postmodernity: The Ambiguous Position of U.S. Planning," *Environment and Planning D* 7 (1989), pp. 381–395; and Ray Gindroz, "City Life and New Urbanism," *Fordham Urban Law Journal* 29, 4 (2001), pp. 1419–1437.

[49] See Gandy, *Concrete and Clay*, p. 15.

[50] Boyer, *Dreaming the Rational City*, pp. 285–287. See also Georg Leidenberger, "Review Essay: The Search for a Useable Past: Modernist Urban Planning in a Postmodern Age," *Journal of Urban History* 32, 3 (2006), pp. 451–465.

[51] M. Christine Boyer, *The City of Collective Memory: Its Historical Imagery and Architectural Entertainments* (Cambridge, MA: The MIT Press, 1998), pp. 46–70. See also Mariana Valverde, "Seeing like a City: The Dialectic of Modern and Premodern Ways of Seeing in Urban Governance," *Law & Society Review* 45, 2 (2011), pp. 277–312; and Graeme Evans, "Branding the City of Culture: The Death of City Planning?" in Javier Monclús and Manuel Guardia (eds.), *Culture, Urbanism and Planning* (Aldershot: Ashgate, 2006), pp. 197–214.

master planning (with its holistic vision of spatial integration and functional specialization) has not meant the end of deliberately planned environments. At a time when state-sponsored comprehensive master planning has declined in significance around the world, large-scale, private, real-estate developers have often filled the void, promising to use the power of the capitalist marketplace in landed property as a way of rejuvenating urban fortunes through strategic interventions in large-scale mega-projects.[52]

Yet there are also large-scale, city-building projects where state enterprises have played a significant role in orchestrating land acquisition, arranging public financing, and attracting private real-estate developers with a range of incentives (including long-term leases on landed property, tax rebates, and more). Correlatively, state-owned enterprises and state agencies (sometimes acting alone and sometimes joining into public–private partnerships with real-estate developers) have also demonstrated an uncanny ability to capitalize on opportunities for profit-making ventures in city-building projects. In aspiring world-class cities as different as Astana (Kazakhstan) and Luanda, and Macao and Beijing, the fusion of powerful state agencies and private (profit-seeking) enterprise has often gone hand-in-hand with the construction of large-scale urban redevelopment projects. Through their ability to control or manipulate market forces to their distinct advantage, state enterprises have in numerous instances engaged in the production of new satellite towns and huge mega-projects that operate as profit-making businesses.[53]

Hollowing Out the Public Administration of Urban Space

As a core principle of modernist planning, single-use (or Euclidean) zoning established rigid land-use tenets that not only segregated everyday uses such as commercial, residential, and leisure-time activities into their own precincts, but also placed arbitrary limitations on real-estate development (such as height restrictions). At the start of the twenty-first century, the declining significance of comprehensive master planning under the direction of a hierarchically organized public administration has meant that single-use zoning

---

[52] Susan Fainstein, "Mega-Projects in New York, London and Amsterdam," *International Journal of Urban and Regional Research* 32, 4 (2008), pp. 768–785; and Paul Gellert and Barbara Lynch, "Mega-Projects as Displacements," *International Social Science Journal* 55, 175 (2003), pp. 15–25.

[53] Laura Adams and Asel Rustemova, "Mass Spectacle and Styles of Governmentality in Kazakhstan and Uzbekistan," *Europe-Asia Studies* 61, 7 (2009), pp. 1249–1276; Natalie Koch, "The Monumental and the Miniature: Imagining 'Modernity' in Astana," *Social and Cultural Geography* 11, 8 (2010), pp. 769–787; Edward Schatz, "What Capital Cities Say About State and Nation Building," *Nationalism and Ethnic Politics* 9, 4 (2004), pp. 111–140; Tim Simpson, "Macao, Capital of the 21st Century?" *Environment and Planning D* 26 (2008), pp. 1053–1079; and You Tien Hsing, *The Great Urban Transformation: Politics of Land and Property in China* (Oxford: Oxford University Press, 2010).

has become – especially in the eyes of real-estate developers – inflexible and outdated. Wanting free rein to build what they want, property developers (along with their assembled coterie of architects and design specialists) have to a certain extent reclaimed urban planning from civil engineers and technocratic "experts," applying flexible principles of spatial land use (the floating zone or spot zoning) to create mixed-use environments that operate under the jurisdiction of various public–private partnerships and other hybrid regulatory regimes.[54]

The spread of extraterritorial zones with their autonomous regulatory regimes have undermined the modernist ideal of territorial sovereignty that enabled public authorities to establish a comprehensive and uniform set of institutionally enforced rules governing the authorized use of urban space. New modes of extraterritoriality have created regulatory regimes that are exempt from the juridical oversight of legally sanctioned local authorities. The replacement of the public administration of urban space with new "privatized planning" initiatives has shifted the power to shape the built environment in the hands of property owners and real-estate developers. The emergence of new modes of urban governance has brought about the reconfiguration of conventional idea of the one-to-one correspondence between sovereignty and territoriality, and its replacement with a host of new privatized regulatory regimes that are able to erode and undermine public authority and oversight. The disjuncture between sovereignty and territoriality has resulted in the blurring of juridical boundaries separating various regimes of authority.[55]

At the start of the twenty-first century, urban governance has shifted away from conventional, old-style "managerialist" approaches to the public management of urban space and toward new hybrid models that depend upon the mobilization of a variety of engaged participants, including institutionalized (formal) public–private partnerships, informal (that is, unregulated) "stakeholder" coalitions, and other nominally public but quasi-private entities that promote private initiative and entrepreneurial solutions to urban management questions.[56] These new regimes of urban governance constitute a kind of "governance-beyond-the-state," whereby urban management is conducted

---

54 The term comes from a legal case in 1926 regarding the town of Euclid, Ohio. See Russell Reno, "Non-Euclidean Zoning: The Use of the Floating Zone," *Maryland Law Review* 23, 2 (1963), pp. 105–120.

55 Aihwa Ong, *Neoliberalism as Exception: Mutations in Citizenship and Sovereignty* (Durham, NC: Duke University Press, 2006); John Agnew, "Sovereignty Regimes: Territoriality and State Authority in Contemporary World Politics," *Annals of the Association of American Geographers* 95, 2 (2005), pp. 437–461; and Gavin Shatkin, "The City and the Bottom Line: Urban Megaprojects and the Privatization of Planning in Southeast Asia," *Environment and Planning A* 40, 2 (2008), pp. 383–401.

56 David Harvey, "From Managerialism to Entrepreneurialism: The Transformation in Urban Governance in Late Capitalism," *Geografiska Annaler Series B, Human Geography* 71, 1 (1989), pp. 3–17.

under the aegis of new institutional arrangements that involve a significant realignment and "redistribution of policymaking powers, competencies, and responsibilities."[57] These mechanisms of governance-beyond-the-state entail new constellations of representation, participation, and power that are articulated via a "proliferating maze of opaque networks, fuzzy institutional arrangements," and informal organizational connections with ill-defined responsibilities, ambiguous objectives, and hidden priorities.[58] These new regimes of urban governance depend upon the subordination of formal (top-down) mechanisms of urban public management to fragmented, horizontally organized, and polycentric ensembles where power is dispersed across a range of public officials, civil society organizations, and private entrepreneurs.[59] These new institutional arrangements create fertile settings for rule-making and rule-implementation outside conventional governance structures. This changing set of circumstances have increasingly eroded the capacity of public authorities to set urban management agendas by allowing the encroachment of market competition (and the rigid adherence to "cost-recovery") to set the "rules of the game."[60] These diffuse and unregulated mechanisms of representation give participating stakeholder coalitions a great deal of room for maneuver to operate outside of public scrutiny and oversight.[61] The lack of formalized mechanisms of representation has meant that "it is often difficult, if not impossible, to identify who represents what, who, and how." As Erik Swygnedouw has put it, "Participation is rarely a statutory and regulated right, but operates through co-optation and invitation."[62]

A defining feature of new city-building efforts at the start of the twenty-first century is the proliferation of a broad range of highly specialized assemblages that bring together hybrid mixtures of territory, authority, and rights in ways that have begun to escape the grip of conventional institutionalized modes of

---

[57] Erik Swyngedouw, "City or Polis? Profitable Politics ... or the End of the Political," in Steef Buijs, Wendy Tan, and Devisari Tunis (eds.), *Megacities: Exploring a Sustainable Future* (Rotterdam: 010 Publishers, 2010), pp. 214–234 (quotation from p. 215).

[58] Swyngedouw, "City or Polis? Profitable Politics ... or the End of the Political," in *Megacities*, p. 221 (source of quotation).

[59] See Maarten Hajer, "Policy without Polity? Policy Analysis and the Institutional Void," *Policy Sciences* 36, 2 (2003), pp. 175–195 (esp. p. 175).

[60] Erik Swyngedouw, "Governance Innovation and the Citizen: The Janus Face of Governance-beyond-the-State," *Urban Studies* 42, 11 (2005), pp. 1991–2006 (esp. p. 1991).

[61] Nikolas Rose and Peter Miller, "Political Power Beyond the State: Problematics of Government," *British Journal of Sociology* 43, 2 (1992), pp. 173–205; Katheryne Mitchell, "Transnationalism, Neoliberalism, and the Rise of the Shadow State," *Economy and Society* 30, 2 (2001), pp. 165–189; Bob Jessop, "Liberalism, Neoliberalism and Urban Governance: a State-Theoretical Perspective," *Antipode* 34, 2 (2002), pp. 452–472; and Gerald Stoker, "Public–Private Partnerships in Urban Governance," in Jon Pierre (ed.), *Partnerships in Urban Governance: European and American Experience* (Basingstoke: Macmillan, 1998), pp. 34–51.

[62] Swyngedouw, "City or Polis? Profitable Politics ... or the End of the Political," p. 217. (source of quotations)

regulation. By introducing new modalities for ordering urban space, these specialized assemblages have produced new typologies of territoriality.[63]

The proliferation of urban enclaves has fundamentally reconfigured the recipes and protocols for city building in the twenty-first century. Outfitted with a whole infrastructural matrix of unconventional rule-sets, these urban enclaves have mutated into spatial operating systems that assume the characteristics of autonomous zones. Functioning as self-contained islands, quarantined and set apart, the zone format has become arguably the most important experimental prototype for the anticipatory urbanism of the future. Mutating outside and beyond the spatial terrain of singularly crafted spatial enclosures and iconic building typologies, the spread of autonomous zones amounts to serial replication of generic spatial products that reproduce familiar logistical formulas for city building. Operating as a rationalized instrument of economic liberalism freed from restrictive regulation, the zone format has materialized as the preferred platform for new kinds of incentivized urbanism. As sites for multiple, intersecting, and nested forms of sovereignty, autonomous zones have become the organizational vessel or the opaque medium for what Keller Easterling has called *extrastatecraft*, a portmanteau concept that can be described as those "often undisclosed activities outside of, in addition to, and sometimes even in partnership with statecraft."[64] The administration of autonomous zones often takes place through undeclared modes of regulation that operate outside of any recognized laws and beyond the reach of public jurisdiction and oversight. These sites of transgressive practice operate as a kind of "secret weapon" of socioeconomic engineering, taking shape in new and unexpected ways. These relaxed regimes of governance are so stealthy, amorphous, and slippery that they are able to evade and outmaneuver even the most vigilant state authority intent on legislating them.[65]

The zone format has become the key building block for city-making, a *modus operandi* that conspires to build entirely new cities not through the incremental accumulation of masterpiece buildings and retrofitting the existing built environment, but through the serial replication of generic blueprints and formulaic prescriptive codes. Autonomous zones function in ways that are analogous to what Daniel Heller-Roazen has called the "paradigm of piracy." As a telling metaphor, this figural construction of piracy offers a useful way of thinking about extraterritoriality and the contravention, if not outright abrogation, of the conventional rule of law.[66] The "paradigm of piracy" refers to a sociospatial condition that consists, among other things, of locations beyond

---

[63] See Saskia Sassen, "Toward a Multiplication of Specialized Assemblages of Territory, Authority and Rights," *Parallax* 13, 1 (2007), pp. 87–94.

[64] Keller Easterling, *Extrastatecraft: The Power of Infrastructure Space* (New York: Verso, 2014), pp. 15, 68.

[65] Easterling, *Extrastatecraft*, pp. 16, 67.

[66] On "seas" and "piracy," see Keller Easterling, *Enduring Innocence: Global Architecture and Its Political Masquerades* (Cambridge, MA: The MIT Press, 2005).

territorial jurisdiction where the collapse of the distinction between legally bound practices and extralegality "translate[s] into open, boundless areas of indiscriminate negotiation."[67] The multiplication of autonomous zones over previously unaffected spatial terrains constitutes what Lauren Benton termed "imperfect geographies," that is, the discontinuous distribution of fragmented enclave-outposts scattered across disjointed space.[68]

The zone format is the perfect incubator for transgressive practices that break the rules and make them up at the spur of the moment. Operating as a kind of *de facto* polity, autonomous zones can readily become testing grounds for unadulterated neoliberal experiments in entrepreneurialism. As an active form with seemingly endless ambition, the zone format is a stealthy carrier of repeatable formulas that contain a seemingly covert desire to "swallow the city," that is, to become the city itself.[69]

The Erosion of Public Space as Principal Site for Social Congregation

Put broadly, this movement toward the privatization of public space, and the accompanying commercialization of the public realm, has produced new types of administered space in cities.[70] Neither "public" nor "private" in the conventional use of these terms, these hybrid spaces are subjected to new kinds of private regulation and domination.[71] Variously referred to as privatized public space,[72]

---

[67] Daniel Heller-Roazen, *The Enemy of All: Piracy and the Law of Nations* (Cambridge, MA: The MIT Press, 2009).

[68] Lauren Benton, *A Search for Sovereignty: Law and Geography in European Empires, 1400–1900* (Cambridge: Cambridge University Press, 2010), pp. 2–3.

[69] Keller Easterling, "Shadow States," in Jack Shelf and Shumi Bose (eds.), *Fulcrum: Real Estates: Life without Debt* (Germany: Bedford Press, 2014), pp. 27–33 (p. 31, source of quotation).

[70] See Setha Low, "The Erosion of Public Space and the Public Realm: Paranoia, Surveillance and Privatization in New York City," *City & Society* 18, 1 (2006), pp. 43–49; Matthew Carmona, "Contemporary Public Space: Critique and Classification, Part One: Critique," *Journal of Urban Design* 15, 1 (2010), pp. 123–148; and Matthew Carmona, "Contemporary Public Space, Part Two: Classification," *Journal of Urban Design* 15, 2 (2010), pp. 157–173. See also Elizabeth Wilson, "The Rhetoric of Urban Space," *New Left Review* 1/209 (1995), pp. 146–160.

[71] For a thoughtful survey of the evolving mixture of public and private, see Jeff Weintraub, "The Theory and Politics of the Public/Private Distinction," in Jeff Weintraub and Krishan Kumar (eds.), *Public and Private in Thought and Practice: Perspectives on a Grand Dichotomy* (Chicago: University of Chicago Press, 1997), pp. 1–40. See also Peter Goheen, "Public Space and the Geography of the Modern City," *Progress in Human Geography* 24, 4 (1998), pp. 479–496.

[72] Neil Smith and Setha Low, "Introduction: The Imperative of Public Space," in Setha Low and Neil Smith (eds.), *The Politics of Public Space* (New York: Routledge, 2006), pp. 1–16; Setha Low, "How Private Interests Take Over Public Space: Zoning, Taxes, and Incorporation of Gated Communities," in *The Politics of Public Space*, pp. 81–104; Ali Madanipour, *Public and Private Spaces of the City* (London: Routledge, 2003), pp. 215–216; Anastasia Loukaitou-Sideris and Tridib Banerjee, *Urban Design Downtown: Poetics and Politics of Form* (Berkeley: University of California Press, 1998), p. 288; and Tridib Banerjee, "The Future of Public Space:

privately owned public space,[73] quasi-public space,[74] private-public space,[75] pseudo-public space,[76] postliberal space,[77] third space,[78] or postpublic space,[79] these administered spaces signal the wholesale restructuring of urban landscapes to reflect the interests of corporate power and private enterprise.[80] The increasingly privatized management of urban space has irrevocably problematized the conventional understanding of the "public interest," the urban commons, and the public sphere.[81] The production of various typologies of

Beyond Invented Streets and Reinvented Places," *Journal of the American Planning Association* 67, 1 (2001), pp. 9–24 (esp. p. 12).

[73] Jeremy Németh, "Defining a Public: The Management of Privately Owned Public Space," *Urban Studies* 46, 11 (2009), pp. 2463–2490; and Stephan Schmidt, Jeremy Németh and Erik Botsford, "The Evolution of Privately Owned Public Spaces in New York City," *Urban Design International* 16, 4 (2011), pp. 270–284.

[74] Mark Button, "Private Security and the Policing of Quasi-Public Space," *International Journal of the Sociology of Law* 31, 3 (2003), pp. 227–237; Jack Byers, "The Privatization of Downtown Public Space: The Emerging Grade-Separated City in North America," *Journal of Planning Education and Research* 17, 3 (1998), pp. 189–205; Margaret Kohn, "The Mauling of Public Space," *Dissent* (Spring, 2001), pp. 71–77; Margaret Kohn, "Privatization and Protest: Occupy Wall Street, Occupy Toronto, and the Occupation of Public Space in a Democracy," *Perspectives on Politics* 11, 1 (2013), pp. 99–110; and John Michael Roberts, "Public Spaces of Dissent," *Sociology Compass* 2, 2 (2008), pp. 654–674.

[75] Anna Minton, *What Kind of World Are We Building? The Privatisation of Public Space* (London: RICS, 2006), pp. 3, 10; Andrew Kirby, "The Production of Private Space and its Implications for Urban Social Relations," *Political Geography* 27, 1 (2008), pp. 74–95; and Stephen Graham and Alessandro Aurigi, "Virtual Cities, Social Polarization, and the Crisis in Urban Public Space," *The Journal of Urban Technology* 4, 1 (1997), pp. 19–52.

[76] Darrell Crilley, "Megastructures and Urban Change: Aesthetics, Ideology, and Design," in Paul Knox (ed.), *The Restless Urban Landscape* (Englewood Cliffs, NJ: Prentice-Hall, 1993), pp. 126–164.

[77] Mike Davis, *City of Quartz: Excavating the Future of Los Angeles* (New York: Vintage, 1992), pp. 223–224.

[78] Banerjee, "The Future of Public Space," pp. 19–20; and Ray Oldenburg, *The Great Good Place: Cafes, Coffee Shops, Bookstores, Bars, Hair Salons and the Other Hangouts at the Heart of a Community* [2nd edition] (New York: Marlowe, 1999).

[79] Matthew Carmona and Claudio De Magalhães, "Public Space Management – Present and Potential," *Journal of Environmental Planning and Management* 49, 1 (2006), pp. 75–99; Matthew Carmona, Claudio De Magalhães, and Leo Hammond, *Public Space: The Management Dimension* (London: Routledge, 2008); and Matthew Carmona, Tim Heath, Taner Oc, and Steve Tiesdell, *Public Places Urban Spaces, The Dimensions of Urban Design* (Oxford: Architectural Press, 2003); Claudio De Magalhães and Matthew Carmona, "Innovations in the Management of Public Space, Reshaping and Refocusing Governance," *Planning Theory and Practice* 17, 3 (2006), pp. 289–303; Ted Kilian, "Public and Private, Power and Space," in Andrew Light and Jonathan Smith (eds.), *Philosophy and Geography II: The Production of Public Space* (Lanham, MD: Rowman & Littlefield, 1998), pp. 115–134; Stephan Schmidt and Jeremy Németh, "Space, Place and the City: Emerging Research on Public Space Design and Planning," *Journal of Urban Design* 15, 4 (2010), pp. 453–457.

[80] Don Mitchell, "The End of Public Space? People's Park, Definitions of the Public, and Democracy," *Annals of the Association of American Geographers* 85 (1995), pp. 108–133.

[81] Gandy, *Concrete and Clay*, p. 15.

postpublic space has replaced the ideal-typical vision of open public space as the normative goal of what a "good city" should aspire to attain. The breakdown of the idea of the exclusive role of public administration of shared spaces of social congregation – streetscapes, parklands, open plazas, public buildings – has given way to overlapping and sometimes conflicting modes of regulation where private propertied interests have assumed greater responsibility for administering social spaces in the city.[82]

While much has been written on the spatial fragmentation of the contemporary city, very little is understood about the influence of these patterns on what it means to inhabit urban space. Such exclusionary spaces as gated residential estates, enclosed shopping malls, themed entertainment redoubts, luxurious holiday resorts, and securitized office parks represent increasingly prevalent building typologies for the urban future. Because these postpublic places (in their various ways) operate outside the framework of public oversight, they constitute extralegal territories, or spaces of exception. The new social logic of postpublic space is one of indifference and indistinction, that is, not necessarily one of deliberate exclusion, but a kind of selective inclusion that welcomes some but discourages others.[83]

[82] Paul Goldberger, "The Rise of the Private City," in Julia Vitullo-Martin (ed.), *Breaking Away: The Future of Cities* (New York: Century Fund Press, 1996), pp. 135–147.

[83] Bülent Diken and Carsten Bagge Laustsen, *The Culture of Exception: Sociology Facing the Camp* (New York: Routledge, 2005), p. 7.

PART I

SETTING THE STAGE

Global Urbanism at the Start of the Twenty-First Century

Cities are the principal spatial landscapes of modernity, the privileged sites where the great social forces that have shaped humanity for well over a century (if not more) – industrial capitalism, state-making, and globalization – have been played out in dramatic fashion. The experience of living in the key metropolitan centers of global capitalism served as the wellspring for novel experiments in urban design, for path-breaking innovations in building typologies, for enduring achievements in art and architecture, for bold advances in infrastructure, and for critical engagements with civic life and public culture. Writers and scholars have looked upon cities as their source of inspiration for ideas, theories, and utopian imaginings about the social world around them.[1]

The origins of the modern metropolis can be traced to the mid- to late nineteenth century at a time when the explosive growth of industrial capitalism fundamentally reshaped the core areas of the capitalist world economy. For more than a century, the growth and development of the leading industrial cities of North America and Europe served as the basic template – and the source of ideas – for understanding the evolving contours of urbanization on a global scale. In all its variations, modernization theory offered perhaps the clearest and most unblinkered vision of the desired future and a sign-posted road map on how to get there. As a self-fulfilling and self-justifying approach to understanding the human condition, modernization theory belongs to that small family of theoretical interventions that – to borrow from Arjun

---

[1] The ideas in this and the following paragraphs are derived from a reading of Gyan Prakash, "Introduction," in Gyan Prakash and Kevin Kruse (eds.), *The Spaces of the Modern City: Imaginaries, Politics and Everyday Life* (Princeton, NJ: Princeton University Press, 2008), pp. 1–18 (esp. p. 1).

Appardurai – "both declares and desires universal applicability for itself."[2] The point of departure for modernization theory was the historically specific experience of so-called Western cities located in the industrialized heartlands of the capitalist world economy. As both theory and practice, modernization attached itself to the grand meta-narrative of anticipated progress along a well-marked pathway. These modern-industrial cities served as the benchmark for measuring and promoting "development" as the singular, linear route toward the ultimate achievement of the coveted end point of modernity.[3]

At the dawn of the new millennium, the conjoined processes of deindustrialization, decentralization, and unfettered suburban sprawl have called into question the idea of the modern-industrial metropolis as the paradigmatic exemplar of late-twentieth–century urbanism. As the twentieth century came to a close, the emergence of wealthy metropolitan centers of global finance (like London, New York, and Tokyo, along with a host of second-tier rivals) at the commanding heights of the capitalist world economy signaled a decisive shift in thinking about cities on a world scale. These leading financial hubs were able to commandeer the lion's share of global wealth through their management and control over the global flows of capital, commodities, and ideas, and to simultaneously oversee the dispersal of manufacturing and industrial production to faraway sites scattered around the world. What came to be called "global cities" quickly became the new standard for making sense of urbanism on a scale, where so-called "globalizing cities" with world-class aspirations were ranked in hierarchies of importance marking their connections to global flows of finance and corporate enterprise.[4]

At the start of the twenty-first century, the accelerating pace of urbanization on a global scale has brought into sharp relief the shifting balance of city-making as a global process. The explosive growth of urbanization has been concentrated in the peripheral zones of the world economy, as the geographical footprint and population size of such megacities of hypergrowth as Kinshasa, Lagos, Karachi, Cairo, Jakarta, Mexico City, Manila, Mumbai, Delhi, Beijing, Tianjin, and Shanghai has dwarfed even the "big cities" of Europe and North America. These shifting patterns of global urbanization have called into question the idea of holding onto the leading "world-class" cities of Europe and North America – defined as a bounded and largely unitary entities in

[2] Arjun Appardurai, "Here and Now," in Arjun Appadurai (ed.), *Modernity at Large: Cultural Dimensions of Globalization* (Minneapolis: University of Minnesota Press, 1996), pp. 1–11 (quotation from p. 1).

[3] For a thoughtful intervention into this discussion, see Marshall Berman, *All That is Solid Melts into Air: The Experience of Modernity* (New York: Penguin, 1982).

[4] Peter Hall, "Global City-Regions in the Twenty-first Century," in Alan Scott (ed.), *Global City-Regions: Trends, Theory, Policy* (Oxford: Oxford University Press, 2001), pp. 59–77; Saskia Sassen, *The Global City: New York, London, Tokyo* [second edition] (Princeton, NJ: Princeton University Press, 2001); and Saskia Sassen, (ed.), *Global Networks, Linked Cities* (London: Routledge, 2002).

conventional urban theories – as both the paradigmatic modern metropolises, and the starting point for theorizing about transnational urbanism.[5] The conjoined forces of globalization have increasingly penetrated urban life around the world. The transnational flows of finance, commodities, labor, images, communication, and ideas have integrated existing cities into vast urbanized systems of production and consumption. As such, the once reigning idea of the city as a kind of bounded living organism, characterized by an internally coherent civic life and by clearly demarcated boundaries between center and periphery, and structured by clear relationships to the region, nation, and wider world, appears anachronistic and obsolete.[6]

Understanding the Modern Metropolis

At the start of the twenty-first century, cities around the world are being made and remade at a faster pace and at a greater scale than at any other time in history. Yet the current discussions about the future of urbanism are mired in an intellectual impasse that is, at best, several decades out of date and rooted in largely Western-centric (e.g., North American and European) preoccupations about urbanization. As a general rule, debates over urban futures have remained trapped in a conceptual paradigm that has stressed the allegedly powerful and instrumental role of large-scale property developers, policymakers, and urban planners in implanting order and coherence in largely unruly and disorderly urban environments. Yet at the present moment, the everyday realities of urban life are largely shaped by a very different set of unregulated, quotidian practices that operate outside the sanctioned authority of official policymaking and planning initiatives. Despite the complexity and novelty of the contemporary urban condition on a global scale, old models rooted in an abstract idealization of the modern metropolis and the attendant rational and efficient ("highest and best") use of space continue to largely frame debates about how cities should be planned, managed, and governed.[7]

The intensity of fast-paced urban transformation in such rapidly growing cities as Mumbai and Lagos, and São Paulo and Mexico City, has outpaced the capacities of urban planners and policymakers to anticipate those spatial frictions associated with unplanned and haphazard growth, let alone manage and regulate existing built environments. Entirely new patterns of urban growth on a global scale have given rise to novel challenges concerned with sustainability, livability, and social inclusion into the mainstream of urban life that

---

[5] See Jennifer Robinson, *Ordinary Cities: Between Modernity and Development* (New York: Routledge, 2006).

[6] Prakash, "Introduction," p. 1.

[7] Ricky Burdett, "Accretion and Rupture in the Global City," in Pedro Gadanho (ed.), *Uneven Growth: Tactical Urbanisms for Expanding Megacities* (New York: Museum of Modern Art, 2014), pp. 32–39 (esp. 33).

have never been seen before. Planning and design professionals have not been able to adequately conceptualize and implement spatial strategies that are capable of effectively adapting to unpredictable change at a time when everyday urban dynamics are both volatile and uncertain. Instead, they often choose to fall back upon unidimensional, rigid, and anachronistic canons of conventional urban policy and planning discourse that have largely failed to respond to "the social and environmental exigencies of twenty-first century urbanism."[8] These once-regnant models, instruments, and paradigms appear antiquated when set against the backdrop of unregulated urban environments and informal practices. The unruly disorder that characterizes those megacities of hypergrowth has in so many instances proved impossible to subject to the protocols of the paradigmatic "planned city" of formal regulations and orderly space.[9]

In his essay "Whatever Happened to Urbanism?" the celebrated architect Rem Koolhaas has criticized architecture and urban planning for focusing too much on an idealized model of the classical modern city, for failing to understand the rapidly changing patterns of global urbanism, and for a lack of ideas about how to deal with the contemporary challenges of the accelerated pace of urbanization on a world scale.[10] Taken together, these observations provide a useful point of departure for rethinking the principal tenets of mainstream urban studies scholarship. Dispensing with the conventional fixation on ideal-types and paradigmatic exemplars of leading (and lagging), or developed (and developing), cities as yardsticks through which to evaluate and judge urban "progress" on a global scale enables us to see more clearly the kinds of ruptures, breaks, and discontinuities that characterize global urbanism at the start of the twenty-first century.

At present, the global mega-urban condition encompasses a variety of discordant realities, from the glittering generic city-state of Singapore to the *favelas* climbing up the hillsides around São Paulo, and from fortress-like luxury enclaves of northern Johannesburg to the sprawling slums of Mexico City. As a general rule, globalizing cities with world-class aspirations have experienced relentless pressures that either incrementally corrode, or spectacularly destroy, the existing built environment – and, correlatively, undermine the social fabric of urban life. These inexorable processes of disintegration and transformation have produced highly uneven, hybrid urban landscapes where new luxury enclaves are juxtaposed against impoverished zones of broken-down infrastructure, overcrowded streetscapes, and self-built housing. In cities as diverse as Mumbai and Rio de Janeiro, concentrations of extreme wealth (often enclosed and fortified) coexist in close proximity to vast informal markets, neglected

---

[8] Burdett, "Accretion and Rupture in the Global City," p. 34 (source of quotation).
[9] Matthew Gandy, "Planning, Anti-Planning and the Infrastructure Crisis Facing Metropolitan Lagos," *Urban Geography* 43, 2 (2006), pp. 371–396; and Marcello Balbo, "Urban Planning and the Fragmented City of Developing Countries," *Third World Planning Review* 15, 1 (1993), pp. 23–35.
[10] Rem Koolhaas, "Whatever Happened to Urbanism?" in Rem Koolhaas and Bruce Mau (eds.), *S, M, L, XL* (New York: Monacelli Press, 1995), pp. 958–971 (esp. p. 969).

buildings, and sprawling squatter settlements. New business districts or upscale residential neighborhoods on the fringes of Shanghai, Istanbul, Buenos Aires, or Beirut, or "new towns" and satellite cities on the edges of Lagos, Phenom Penh, Ho Chi Minh City, Cairo, or Mumbai, consist of similar building typologies: large-scale, distinctive, monochromatic assemblages of look-alike buildings – with the occasional iconic landmark structure –surrounded by a *cordon sanitaire* of "barrier landscaping" and designed to be set apart.[11]

This kind of city building conforms to a form of deliberate intervention that relies on a drastic intrusion into the metropolitan landscape that has little to do with the existing scale and texture of the built environment of established neighborhoods, streetscapes, and residential communities, and has displayed scant regard for cultural heritage. Mega-projects, superblocks, and spatially separate enclaves disconnected from their local contexts are the hallmarks of this new brand of hybrid, aggregate, and disjointed urbanism. This kind of city building has produced discontinuous ruptures in the urban social fabric, or what some have called the "Archipelago City."[12] To be sure, this concept "archipelago city" conjures up a spatial image of globalizing urbanism as an assemblage or odd assortment of fragments, each with their own distinctive and pronounced identities and mutually exclusive rules of engagement.[13] The production of "new towns," satellite cities, and special development zones at the edge of existing built environments resemble fragmented islands of social activity, separated by indeterminate and marginal spaces that are inhabited by the urban underclasses. In this sense, the "archipelago city" is the prototype of global urbanism at the start of the twenty-first century: polycentric urban landscapes consisting of a patchwork of enclaves, autonomous zones, and sequestered "microcities" scattered across vast and expansive metropolitan regions.[14] These dispersed spatial patterns represent the antithesis of modernist design and planning principles that yearned for spatial coherence, connectivity, and rational order.[15]

The "archipelago city" masks the deeper realities of a kind of supply-side, speculative urbanism, directed at creating new property markets rather than responding to existing demand. City building under the dominance of real-estate capitalism represents one side of the urban future. In aspiring world-class cities, the social and political demands of propertied middle-class residents have revolved around a defense of up-to-date and reliable infrastructure, "protected" spaces of social congregation, good governance, and social order. It is in the

---

[11] The ideas expressed here are taken from Burdett, "Accretion and Rupture in the Global City," p. 36.
[12] See Rem Koolhaas, "Imagining Nothingness," in *S, M, L, XL*, pp. 198–203.
[13] See Klaus Kunzmann, "The Future of the City Region in Europe," in Koos Bosma and Helma Hellinga (eds.), *Mastering the City: North European City Planning 1900–2000* (Rotterdam: NAi Publishers, 1997), pp. 16–29.
[14] See Pier Vittorio Aureli, *The Possibility of an Absolute Architecture* (Cambridge, MA: The MIT Press, 2011), pp. 1–47.
[15] See Robert Beauregard, "Between Modernity and Postmodernity: The Ambiguous Position of U.S. Planning," *Environment and Planning D* 7, 4 (1989), pp. 381–395.

name of these values (grounded in an alleged attachment to 'propriety' and 'civility') that new experiments with privatized modes of urban governance are put into motion. It is also in the name of these values that calls arise to banish the underemployed urban poor – and their messy brand of disorderly "informal" urbanism – from city streets and from public gathering places.[16]

Aggregate Urbanism: Enclaves and Modularity

The hallmark of modernist city building has been its engagement with state-driven, comprehensive, and holistic master planning. Modernist planners sought homogeneity and predictability by imposing a material and spatial order that was intended to "rationalize" all aspects of urban social life. As an exemplary expression of physical determinism (or the idea that the design of the built environment could adequately address and resolve social problems), modernist planning confidently projected an imagined future "without contradictions, without conflict." In short, it uncritically assumed a "rational domination" of this imagined future "in which its total and totalizing plan dissolves any conflict between the imagined and existing [state of affairs] in the imposed coherence of its order." Its failure to include – "as *constituent* elements" of its master plans – the ambiguities, indeterminacies, and conflicts of actual social life undermined this imagined future.[17]

The collapse of the modernist fixation on comprehensive, holistic master planning – that is, integrating the constituent parts into a rationally ordered and coherent whole – has given way to alternative, piecemeal approaches to city building that primarily rely upon market-led redevelopment and entrepreneurial interventions as the primary mechanisms for reshaping the built environment. Spurred by the latest wave of capitalist globalization and neoliberal urban policies, city building at the start of the twenty-first century has increasingly come to resemble a distinct kind of "modular urbanism" (or "aggregate urbanism") where the proliferation of stand-alone, cocooned enclaves spread haphazardly across metropolitan landscapes and deliberately set apart from the surrounding urban environment have produced mosaic-like patterns of urban growth and development. While the fracturing of urban landscapes into distinct enclaves is not new in cities around the world, what distinguish the global patterns of fragmentation at the start of the twenty-first century is the entrenchment of spatial exclusivity and the durability of social inequalities.[18]

---

[16] Ananya Roy, "Postcolonial Urbanism: Speed, Hysteria, Mass Dreams," in Ananya Roy and Aihwa Ong (eds.), *Worlding Cities: Asian Experiments and the Art of Being Global* (Oxford: Blackwell, 2011), pp. 307–335 (esp. p. 326).

[17] James Holston, "Spaces of Insurgent Citizenship," in Leonie Sandercock (ed.), *Making the Invisible Visible: A Multicultural Planning History* (Berkeley and Los Angeles: University of California, 1998), pp. 37–56 (quotations from p. 46).

[18] Tom Angotti, *The New Century of the Metropolis: Urban Enclaves and Orientalism* (New York: Routledge, 2013), pp. 113–114, 133–134.

With its grid-like pattern, rigid hierarchical differentiation, and spatial demarcation of distinct functional specializations, the structured "city of form" constituted the dominant mode of urban production for at least the past century. Because of its important functional role, this "city of form" still commands our urban imagination, despite its gradual disappearance as the *primum mobile* behind city building. The continued association of urbanism with structured form accounts for some of the "blind spots" in mainstream urban theories. As Albert Pope has suggested, "Our understanding or imagination of the [contemporary] city runs counter to the urbanism that is currently being produced." In other words, the ways that mainstream urban theories have thought about the growth and development of cities does not coincide with the actual social production of urban space and the contemporary logic of city-building practices. Despite its increasing obsolescence, the city of structured form has continued to dominate conventional thinking about urbanism. The inability of conventional mainstream thinking about cities to keep abreast of what is happening on the ground has limited our understanding about the actual patterns of urban transformation and the emergence of unstructured urban morphologies. The continued use of such pejorative terms – backward (or failed) urbanism, slums, sprawl, decline, informality, and the like – provide ample testimony to the failure of mainstream urban studies to think about urbanism in ways other than the presumption that incremental growth is the *sine qua non* of progress and that the pathways of urban transformation are linear and lead in the same direction.[19]

At the start of the twenty-first century, the "gridiron metropolis" (to borrow a term from Albert Pope) – or "an urbanism of mechanically structured form" – has given way to the unstructured space of the contemporary megalopolis. The replacement of the structured "city of form" with the unstructured "city of space" has effaced what was for at least a century the wellspring of urban modernity – the centerpiece of the modern urban experience – into something as "outmoded as the medieval hill town." Unlike the structured "city of form," the unstructured "city of space" has "no intrinsic subdivisions, no topographical ruptures of fissures, and no obvious breaking points."[20] As the dominant mode of spatial organization, "aggregation" (whether layered vertically or attached horizontally) has become the underlying structuring logic of global urbanism at the start of the twenty-first century. What distinguishes "aggregation" from comprehensive master planning is that the object of spatial design is not the urban landscape as a connected, relational whole, but the single aggregate unit. Put in another way, the unstructured space of the contemporary megalopolis consists of the repetitive aggregation of various spatial typologies that construct

---

[19] Albert Pope, "From Form to Space," in Roger Sherman and Dana Cuff (eds.), *Fast-Forward Urbanism: Rethinking Architecture's Engagement with the City* (New York: Princeton Architectural Press, 2011), pp. 143–175 (quotations from pp. 143, 144).

[20] Pope, "From Form to Space," pp. 143, 154–155 (sources of quotation). See also Albert Pope, "The Unified Project," *Architectural Design* 82, 5 (2012), 80–87.

a tentative (and ever-evolving) whole that is constantly in flux and never finished. This kind of urban production is not random or arbitrary, but rather conforms to underlying patterns of agglomeration and/or accretion.[21]

If the modern metropolis of the industrial capitalist age represents the quintessential structured "city of form" (with its ordered legibility and recognizable patterns), then the contemporary megalopolis resembles the unstructured "city of space." As a term coined by the Scottish geographer Patrick Geddes in the 1920s (and later popularized by Lewis Mumford and Jean Gottman), the idea of *megalopolis* has come to signify an entirely new form of urban development that originated in the second half of the twentieth century. As the ties that bound ex-urban peripheries to dominant centers were loosened, the centrifugal force of urbanization pushed outward, producing new kinds of dispersed, polycentric networks, or sprawling conurbations no longer tethered to the gravitational pull of a historic downtown core.[22] The resulting "urbanization of suburbia" – or peripheral urbanization – cemented these dispersed patterns of discontinuous urban growth, thereby putting into motion new kinds of formless urbanism.[23]

With the coming of the megalopolis, the structured logic of the "city of form" gave way to the explosive growth of unstructured urban space. Unlike the structured "city of form," the unstructured "city of space" has no innate coherence and no clearly demarcated distinctions between "inside" and "outside."[24] New patterns of urban production that once would have engendered a cityscape dominated by structured form instead gave way to one dominated by unfamiliar and unexpected kinds of unstructured urban space. In turn, these new haphazard patterns of unstructured urban space have unfolded upon a continuous, seemingly infinitely expandable field – where the logical outcome resembles a seemingly never-ending city without obvious boundaries.[25]

The expansion of the contemporary megalopolis has created "'exterior' spaces tethered to loose aggregations of polycentric forms." In short, these new cities of tomorrow consist of an ever-expanding succession of asymmetric urban forms occupying a vast field of amorphous and indifferent space. As

---

[21] Pope, "From Form to Space," pp. 143–144 (source of quotation, p. 143).

[22] Elizabeth Baigent, "Patrick Geddes, Lewis Mumford and Jean Gottmann: Divisions over 'Megalopolis'," *Progress in Human Geography* 28,6 (2008), pp. 687–700. See also Eric Pawson, "Gottmann, J. 1961: Megalopolis. The Urbanized Northeastern Seaboard of the United States. New York: The Twentieth Century Fund," *Progress in Human Geography* 32,3 (2008), pp. 441–444.

[23] Edward Soja, "Los Angeles: 1965–1992: From Crisis-led Restructuring to Restructuring-Generated Crisis," in Allen Scott and Edward Soja (eds.), *The City: Los Angeles and Urban Theory at the End of the Twentieth Century* (Berkeley: University of California Press, 1996), pp. 426–446 (esp. pp. 434–436); and Edward Soja, *My Los Angeles: From Urban Restructuring to Regional Urbanization* (Berkeley: University of California Press, 2014), p. 185–186.

[24] Pope, "From Form to Space," pp. 154–155 (source of quotation).

[25] Pope, "From Form to Space," p. 147. See Ricky Burdett and Deyan Sudjic (eds.), *The Endless City* (London: Phaidon, 2011).

a kind of embryonic urbanism only in its formative stages, the contemporary megalopolis expands to no appreciable cumulative effect – it is no more than the sum of its parts. In a nutshell, this kind of aggregate urbanism "refuses to add up to anything coherent or legible." The contemporary megalopolis is unable to sustain a cumulative urban whole, remaining instead a seemingly random aggregation and spatially discontinuous collection of fragments always in motion.[26]

The expansion of aggregate urbanism on a global scale has triggered new hybrid forms of modernity that arise in the tension between the global flows of capital, commodities, and information on the one hand, and overcrowded streetscapes, broken-down or nonexistent infrastructure, and inadequate regulatory regimes on the other.[27] In distressed megacities of hypergrowth, the steady accretion of upscale urban enclaves that have seemingly appeared out of nowhere, like alien spaceships, has produced highly uneven spatial landscapes increasingly divided between upscale sites of luxury and vast zones of deprivation. Unencumbered by the visible signs of distressed urbanism within which they are incongruously set, these sequestered islands of privilege are at once functional and efficient, that is, they both serve the purpose of concentrating the key elements of a comfortable and safe-and-secure urban life in a single space, and they operate without the frictions, inconveniences, and unpredictability of the everyday modes of life which surround them.[28]

These patterns of enclave urbanism have called into question the classical portrait of the so-called Third World City – mired in 'underdevelopment' and backwardness, and defined by what it lacks. The caricatured image of deadening homogeneity – characterized by slums and informality – is far too flattened out and simplified to capture the emergent realities on the ground. As the signifier of monochromatic urban distress and deprivation, the prototypical Third World City has literally ceased to exist as an actual place, replaced by a hybrid assemblage of sequestered luxury enclaves (or privileged sites for the wealthy) surrounded by vast territories of deprivation and neglect.[29] It is here where the utopian dreams of escape into cocooned laagers of privilege and convenience come face-to-face in uneasy tension with the everyday, "do-it-yourself" (DIY) urbanism of the struggling urban poor.[30]

---

[26] Pope, "From Form to Space," pp. 147, 152, 154 (source of quotations).

[27] Ananya Roy, "The 21st-Century Metropolis: New Geographies of Theory," *Regional Studies* 43, 6 (2009), pp. 819–830.

[28] Rafael Pizarro, Liang Wei, and Tridip Banerjee, "Agencies of Globalization and Third World Urban Form: A Review," *Journal of Planning Literature* 18, 2 (2003), pp. 111–130; and David Drakakis-Smith, *Third World Cities* [2nd Edition] (New York: Routledge, 2000).

[29] Howard Dick and Peter Rimmer, "Beyond the Third World City: The New Urban Geography," *Urban Studies* 35, 12 (1998), pp. 2303–2021.

[30] See Eduardo Mendieta, "Invisible Cities: A Phenomenology of Globalization from Below," *City* 5, 1 (2001), pp. 7–26; and Ananya Roy, "Slumdog Cities: Rethinking Subaltern Urbanism," *International Journal of Urban and Regional Research* 35, 2 (2011), pp. 223–238.

The New Transnational Urban Imaginary: The "Business Consultancy City"

In what Ash Amin has termed the "business consultancy city," mainstream policymakers have worked energetically for the past several decades to propose emerging "globalizing cities" as potential engines of the new knowledge economy, as catalysts driving innovation and creativity for corporate enterprise, and as powerhouses for productivity growth and consumer demand.[31] In the contemporary Urban Age, global city-regions have returned to the economic calculus, fueled by a rising tide of celebratory accounts theorizing cities as the emergent centers of competitive advantage and as the wellsprings of future prosperity.[32] Just as rapidly industrializing cities of the late nineteenth century (with their sprawling factories and manufacturing sites, expanding middle class with consumerist aspirations, and the largely unregulated spirit of entrepreneurialism) became the driving force behind the development of industrial capitalism, mainstream policymakers have once again at the start of the twenty-first century turned their attention to so-called "cities of the third wave" (and the attendant "creative economy," "cognitive-cultural economy," and "cognitive capitalism") as the source of future global economic growth and the expansion of opportunities for upward mobility in the postindustrial world economy.[33]

This story of the renewed economic centrality of cities is a familiar one.[34] In mainstream urban thinking, the vitality of cities has long depended upon a mixture of ingredients, including an "abundance of supply-side readiness," entrepreneurial dynamism, advantageous locational agglomeration, and knowledge (creativity and innovation) clustering, which, taken together, are

---

[31] Ideas expressed here are derived from Ash Amin, "Telescopic Urbanism and the Urban Poor," *City* 17, 4 (2013), pp. 476–492 (esp. p. 478).

[32] Edward Glaeser, *Triumph of the City* (New York: Penguin, 2011); Doug Saunders, *Arrival City: How the Largest Migration in History is Reshaping Our World* (New York: Pantheon Books, 2011), and Jeb Brugmann, *Welcome to the Urban Revolution: How Cities are Changing the World* (St Lucia: University of Queensland Press, 2009). See also Ricky Burdett and Philipp Rode, "Living in the Urban Age," in Ricky Burdett and Deyan Sudjic (eds.), *Living in the Endless City* (London: Phaidon, 2011), pp. 8–43.

[33] See Allen Scott, "Beyond the Creative City: Cognitive-Cultural Capitalism and the New Urbanism," *Regional Studies* 48, 4 (2014), pp. 565–578; Allen Scott, "Emerging Cities of the Third Wave," *City* 15, 3/4 (2011), pp. 289–381; Allen Scott, "Capitalism and Urbanization in a New Key? The Cognitive-Cultural Dimension," *Social Forces* 85, 4 (2007), pp. 1465–1482; Allen Scott, "Cultural Economy and the Creative Field of the City," *Geografiska Annaler: Series B, Human Geography* 92, 2 (2010), pp. 115–130; and Yann Moulier-Boutang, *Cognitive Capitalism* (Cambridge, UK: Polity Press, 2011).

[34] Ash Amin, "The Urban Condition: A Challenge to Social Science," *Public Culture* 25, 2 (2013), pp. 201–208. See Saskia Sassen, "The Economies of Cities," in *Living in the Endless City*, pp. 56–65; and Saskia Sassen, "New Frontiers Facing Urban Sociology at the Millennium," *British Journal of Sociology* 51, 1 (2000), pp. 143–159.

the keys to creating opportunities for jump-starting market-led growth.[35] As a general rule, the new urbanology has positioned itself as offering a progressive agenda for betterment, when in fact this approach is actually very much entrenched within neoliberal ideology, with a vision firmly aligned to cities as launching pads for private initiative, individual self-betterment, and entrepreneurialism.[36]

Yet the Panglossian glow of this new celebratory urbanology seems strangely out of touch with the seamy side of global urbanism as it actually exists.[37] Despite widespread evidence that impoverished living conditions (with limited opportunities for regular work) have become durable features of urban life around the globe, urban optimists like Edward Glaeser, Jeb Brugmann, and Doug Saunders have tended to look upon deprived zones of cities as wellsprings of creative innovation and entrepreneurial zeal – that is, places "rich with possibility and insight."[38] This blinkered gaze yields strange pronouncements. As Glaeser has argued, "There's a lot to like about urban poverty." With distressed cities like Detroit in mind, he makes the surprising (and unsubstantiated) claim that "cities don't make people poor; they attract poor people."[39] This claim certainly does not hold true for Detroit. In seeking to advance the claim that urbanization by itself is a largely self-optimizing process, Glaeser has argued that "cities are expanding enormously because urban density provides the clearest path from poverty to prosperity."[40] Framed within such a totalizing, universalizing, and law-bound view of urbanization, it is not hard to sense the

---

35 Quoted phrase is taken from Amin, "Telescopic Urbanism," p. 478. For mainstream approach, see also Edward Glaeser and Joshua Gottlieb, "The Wealth of Cities: Agglomeration Economies and Spatial Equilibrium in the United States," National Bureau Economic Research Working Paper, No. 14806 (March 2009), 76 pp.; William Strange, Walid Hejazi, and Jianmin Tang, "The Uncertain City: Competitive Instability, Skills, Innovation and the Strategy of Agglomeration," *Journal of Urban Economics* 59, 3 (2006), pp. 331–351; and Edward Glaeser, Stuart Rosenthal, and William Strange, "Urban Economics and Entrepreneurship," *Journal of Urban Economics* 67, 1 (2010), pp. 1–14. See also Allen Scott, "Creative Cities: Conceptual Issues and Policy Questions," *Journal of Urban Affairs* 28, 1 (2006), pp. 1–17; Allen Scott and Michael Storper, "Regions, Globalization, and Development," *Regional Studies* 37, 6&7 (2003), pp. 579–593; and Allen Scott and Michael Storper, "The Nature of Cities: The Scope and Limits of Urban Theory," *International Journal of Urban and Regional Research* 39, 1 (2015), pp. 1–15.

36 For a discussion of this theme, see Brendan Gleeson, "Critical Commentary: The Urban Age: Paradox and Prospect," *Urban Studies* 49, 5 (2012), pp. 931–943; and Kathryn Davidson and Brendan Gleeson, "The Sustainability of an Entrepreneurial City?" *International Planning Studies* 19, 2 (2014), pp. 173–191.

37 Lisa Weinstein, *The Durable Slum: Dharavi and the Right to Stay Put in Globalizing Mumbai* (Minneapolis: University of Minnesota Press, 2014); and Marie Huchzermeyer, *Cities with 'Slums': From Informal Settlement Eradication to a Right to the City in Africa* (Cape Town: University of Cape Town Press, 2011).

38 For evidence of urban impoverishment, see Mike Davis, *Planet of Slums* (New York: Verso, 2006), pp. 174–198. See also Gleeson, "The Urban Age: Paradox and Prospect," pp. 931–943 (p. 934 for source of quotation).

39 Glaeser, *Triumph of the City*, p. 9.   40 Glaeser, *Triumph of the City*, p. 1.

rigid specter of (deterministic) naturalism in this recent wave of triumphalist urbanology.[41]

The Evolving Terrain of Global Urbanism

What has changed over the past three decades is that this robust evocation of urban competitiveness and vitality is no longer confined exclusively to the so-called "emblematic North," but also includes globalizing cities from the "aspiring South."[42] Besides the familiar litany of first- or second-tier global cities (like London, New York, Tokyo, Frankfurt, Paris, Toronto, Chicago, Los Angeles, Hong Kong, Singapore, Sydney, and Stockholm), scholars and policymakers have identified such globalizing cities that fall outside the conventional core areas of the world economy as Shanghai, Mumbai, São Paulo, Johannesburg, Cape Town, and Istanbul as new engines of growth. Urban theorists attached to the Global Cities and World Cities paradigms have traced the cutting edge of growth – industrial and nonindustrial – to a specific set of characteristics of urban composition and global connectivity rather than "to the national economic and political environment." It should not be surprising, then, as Ash Amin has put it, that "these cities have also begun to act like a Hanseatic League," forming cooperative alliances and collaborative partnerships, sharing ideas about "best practices," and, on the whole, "generalizing a new ontology of future prosperity from their collective experiences."[43] As a general rule, cities around the world – ranging from globalizing ones with world-class aspirations to those "loser cities" in need of a large dose of remedial intervention – have increasingly undertaken strategic visioning exercises designed, *inter alia*, to improve the quality of life for their residents, to promote economic growth, and to ensure long-term sustainability. A host of policy experts, international development organizations, and independent consultants have actively promoted these comprehensive plans for city futures as tools for urban redevelopment and competitive advantage. These strategic initiatives "share remarkably similar analyses, conclusions, and policy ambitions."[44]

In the new mantra of success, key watchwords like creativity, innovation, and entrepreneurialism have become rhetorical platforms for measuring upward mobility in the ranked hierarchies of aspiring world-class cities.[45]

---

[41] Gleeson, "The Urban Age: Paradox and Prospect," p. 933. For a critique of the new urbanology, see Nicholaus Lemann, "Get Out of Town," *The New Yorker* (June 27, 2011), pp. 76–80.

[42] These expressive terms are borrowed from Amin, "Telescopic Urbanism," p. 478.

[43] Amin, "Telescopic Urbanism," p. 478.

[44] Jennifer Robinson, "The Spaces of Circulating Knowledge: City Strategies and Global Urban Governmentality," in Eugene McCann and Kevin Ward (eds.), *Mobile Urbanism: Cities and Policymaking in the Global Age* (Minneapolis: University of Minnesota Press, 2011), pp. 15–40 (quotation from p. 15).

[45] See Allen Scott, "Creative Cities: Conceptual Issues and Policy Questions," *Journal of Urban Affairs* 28, 1 (2006), pp. 1–17.

Competitive cities are those that have become entrepreneurial because they have jettisoned the old managerial styles of governance in favor of supply-side, market-driven growth. In those successful "competitive cities" in the post-industrial "knowledge-based" age, city-building efforts – both materially and symbolically – have been increasingly directed at creating urban landscapes amenable to wealthy residents, conspicuous consumption, and the so-called creative classes. The prescriptive formula for success rests on "an agglom-erative dynamic involving enterprising subjects, consuming populations, and enabling environments" that promise to deliver both global integration and local prosperity.[46] Mainstream urban geography has traced this dynamic to what might be called economies of proximity (associated with the colocation of interrelated industries, producer services, and knowledge clusters) combined with opportunities for synergies through association and networking. What adds further to the mix of competitive urbanism is a range of other fea-tures, including signature architecture (designed by internationally acclaimed "starchitects"), "smart buildings," attractive amenities, high-end consumer cul-tures, information hubs, innovation districts, start-up business incubators, and streamlined transportation services (refurbished airports, train stations, and high-speed transit corridors) linking the various enclaves that constitute the new postindustrial knowledge, service, and tourist-entertainment economies, while deliberately bypassing abandoned and distressed zones of the urban landscape.[47]

The visual projection of the vibrant city of socioeconomic promise is a highly selective, circumscribed view of urbanism that brings only certain spatial loca-tions into focus: brand new high-rise office complexes ensconced in revital-ized central business districts (CBDs), free enterprise zones, upscale shopping malls, entertainment locations, innovation districts, transport and communica-tions hubs, universities and other centers of creativity, gated residential com-munities, and the kinds of high-end amenities that accommodate the privileged employees and consumers of the creative-entertainment city. The residents who "live, work, and play" in the creative-entertainment city bring qualified skills and training, aspire to upward mobility, are cosmopolitan in outlook, and are highly mobile.[48]

This one-sided vision of urban life – an approach which Ash Amin has called "telescopic urbanism" – focuses only on places that offer the potential and opportunity for future prosperity, while it simultaneously ignores every-thing else, "above all the myriad hidden connections and relational doings that hold together the contemporary city as an assemblage of many types of spatial

[46] Amin, "Telescopic Urbanism," p. 478.
[47] Amin, "Telescopic Urbanism," p. 478. See also Scott, "Emerging Cities of the Third Wave," pp. 289–321; and Allen Scott, "Retrospect," *City* 17, 3 (2013), pp. 384–386.
[48] Amin, "Telescopic Urbanism," p. 478. For the darker underside of urban life, see, Sharon Meagher, "The Darker Underside of Scott's Third Wave," *City* 17, 3 (2013), pp. 395–398.

formation, from economically interdependent neighborhoods to infrastructures, flows and organizational arrangements that course through and beyond
the city."[49] This kind of "telescopic urbanism" conveniently and deliberately
overlooks the everyday lives of ordinary people who inhabit the "multitudinous
city," or what Ricky Burdett and Deyan Sudjic have aptly described as the "endless city."[50] Seen through this optic, those mundane and prosaic spaces – that is,
the ordinary and indistinct terrains occupied by urban dwellers who are simply
"making do" in a social world defined by survivalist economics – just "blurs
out of focus," glossed over as an annoying encumbrance that appears "out of
place." If modernist urban planning, with its utopian aspirations that sometimes over-engineered its flawed promise of shared well-being, took an interest
in the blighted and neglected parts of the city and gestured at the socioeconomic
integration of the urban poor through master plans for public housing, work
programs, social welfare, and mass transit, then the entrepreneurially inclined
visionaries of the "business consultancy city" share no such pretensions and
have no such aspirations.[51]

By validating only those activities and places that offer the potential to
become engines for an imagined future prosperity, telescopic urbanism effectively naturalizes what is in effect a cauterized urbanity – a condition that Rahul
Mehrotra has identified as "one city yet two separate worlds."[52] This blinkered
optic rests on the premise that the world-class aspirations of city builders, on
the one side, and the mundane interstitial spaces of the urban poor, on the
other, have little or no bearing upon each other. In short, it buys into the pre-
tense that these "separate worlds" are hermetically sealed, distanciated environments more or less cut off from one another. This kind of telescopic urbanism is
largely immune to seeing the city in relational terms, that is, as a holistic, interconnected entity constituted out of mutual dependencies and uneven modes
of exploitation. Trapped in its own self-perpetuating mythologies of trickle-
down economics, this entrepreneurial vision of the city is largely disinterested
in the structural conditions that reproduce immizeration and impoverishment.
There is no pretext here of calling for productive integration of the marginalized urban dwellers living in informal, makeshift housing into the mainstream
of urban life. In a fashion similar to the nineteenth-century social construction
of the "deserving poor" versus those social outcasts beyond redemption, the
constricted vision of telescopic urbanism sees only a surplus humanity divided

---

49 Amin, "Telescopic Urbanism," p. 484. See also Ayona Datta, "Encounters with Law and Critical
    Urban Studies: Reflections on Amin's Telescopic Urbanism," *City* 17, 4 (2013), pp. 517–522.
50 See Ricky Burdett and Deyan Sudjic (eds.), *The Endless City: The Urban Age Project by the
    London School of Economics and the Deutsche Bank's Alfred Herrhausen Society* (London:
    Phaidon, 2011).
51 Amin, "Telescopic Urbanism," p. 478 (source of quotation and of ideas).
52 Rahul Mehrotra, "One Space, Two Worlds," *Harvard Design Magazine* (Winter/Spring, 1997),
    pp. 40–41. See Michael Sorkin, "Container Riff," in *Some Assembly Required* (Minneapolis:
    University of Minnesota Press, 2001), pp. 185–190.

between those left to their own logics of survival by means of self-animated microentrepreneurialism and those who cannot be helped, best kept cordoned off and out of sight, left to inhabit the depleted zones of bare life.[53]

To paraphrase Michael Sorkin, the discourse of urbanism that imagines cities only as disaggregated collections of sealed containers rather than as relational assemblages of interconnected parts "participates in a functionalist fantasy of rationalized relations in which a set of predictabilities is offered as a hedge against dysfunction."[54] This kind of functionalist urbanism – the default discourse of mainstream urban studies – "imposes a similar fantasy of prophylaxis," looking to contain what it cannot control. This functional way of thinking falls back upon the belief that scientific rationality (that is, the application of abstract reason) is the normative remedy that can replace the dysfunctionality of the disorderly city with rational order. In short, it denies the underlying realities of the urban social fabric: "the tractability of its edges," its porosity and permeability, where borders represent opportunities and not barriers.[55]

Telescopic urbanism treats the multitudinous city – the hybrid spaces of everyday urbanism – as another world, an anomalous curiosity, an annoying encumbrance, a distressed zone of indistinction, and a dumping ground for (toxic) waste. Two analytic framing devices dominate the discussion of what Amin has referred to as "the existential improvisation in the interstices of the 'endless city.'"[56] The first points to an uplifting narrative of bootstrapping self-help, a rhetorical position that justifies a *laissez-faire*, noninterventionist "hands-off" approach to resolving urban impoverishment. This idea rests on the mistaken view that state interference is the root cause of persistent poverty and that overregulation has held the poor back from taking advantage of their own inventiveness and creative energies. The second calls for a strategy of containment. This *revanchist* approach calls for encouraging alliances among business enterprises, municipal authorities, and middle-class residents "to define and police the boundary between the clean and safe city" with its productive potential and global connectivity, and "the dirty, illegal and threatening city which hinders progress."[57] This strategy of containment also includes allowing powerful coalitions of key stakeholders "to reclaim the faltering and stretched infrastructure of the city" – its transportation and communications networks, its water and electricity supplies, its sanitation and waste disposal systems, and its shared public spaces – by either outright privatization or by surreptitiously

53 Amin, "Telescopic Urbanism," p. 479. See Joäo Biehl, *Vita: Life in a Zone of Social Abandonment* (Berkeley: University of California Press, 2005); and Joäo Biehl, "Vita: Life in a Zone of Social Abandonment," *Social Text* 19,3 (2001), pp. 131–149.

54 Sorkin, "Container Riff," pp. 189–190.   55 Sorkin, "Container Riff," p. 190.

56 Amin, "Telescopic Urbanism," p. 479.

57 Amin, "Telescopic Urbanism," p. 479 [source of quotation]. See also Kate Swanson, "Revanchist Urbanism Heads South: The Regulation of Indigenous Beggars and Street Vendors in Ecuador," *Antipode* 39, 4 (2007), pp. 708–728.

extending their own informal (sometimes illegal or corrupt) practices to secure privileged access to serve their own narrow interests.[58]

Contradictory Spatial Dynamics of Global Urbanism

At the start of the twenty-first century, uneven spatial landscapes are associated with growing socioeconomic inequalities. In the headlong rush to make cities competitive in the ranked hierarchy of alleged urban success, city boosters have disengaged from discussions about how to ensure that urban landscapes function as arenas for the performance of active citizenship and about how to incorporate marginalized residents into the mainstream of urban life.[59] Reshaping the built environment in response to the private demands of "growth coalitions" and large-scale property developers has meant that any serious consideration of the general public interest is lost.[60]

Despite widespread and long-term efforts at obfuscation, denial, and wishful thinking, urban theorists and planning experts across the political spectrum have come to acknowledge that too many work-seekers chasing too few wage-paying jobs in fast-growing cities has generated all sorts of informal practices around self-built housing and survivalist economics.[61] More than a decade ago, in its first concerted effort to calculate the slum population of the world, UN-Habitat painted a rather grim picture. The researchers who produced the highly influential *Slums of the World* forecast that by 2030 at least half of the world's urban population – a figure itself accounting for two-thirds of all humankind – would exist on or under the poverty line, living in slum-like conditions, largely in and around the cities of the so-called Global South. This report indicated that while only 6 percent of the population of the (so-called) "developed world" at the start of the twenty-first century reside in urban slums, the average figure for distressed cities in the "developing world" was 43 percent, with staggering figures for virtually all cities of sub-Saharan Africa (72 percent), impoverished cities of Latin American countries (such as Belize, Bolivia, Guatemala, Haiti, Nicaragua, and Peru), along with a host of rapidly growing cities in Asia and the Middle Eastern countries (all above the 50 percent threshold).[62] The verdict

---

58   Amin, "Telescopic Urbanism," p. 478. See also Stephen Graham, Renu Desai, and Colin McFarlane, "Water Wars in Mumbai," *Public Culture* 25, 1 (2013), pp. 115–141.

59   Faranak Miraftab and Shana Mills, "Insurgency and Spaces of Active Citizenship: The Story of Western Cape Anti-Eviction Campaign in South Africa," *Journal of Planning Education and Research* 25, 2 (2005), pp. 200–217; and Antina von Schnitzler, "Citizenship Prepaid: Water, Calculability, and Techno-Politics in South Africa," *Journal of Southern African Studies* 34, 4 (2008), pp. 899–917.

60   Teddy Cruz, "Rethinking Urban Growth: It's about Inequality, Stupid," in Pedro Gadanho (ed.), *Uneven Growth: Tactical Urbanisms for Expanding Megacities* (New York: The Museum of Modern Art, 2014), pp. 48–55.

61   Davis, *Planet of Slums*, pp. 56–59, 111–113.

62   UN-Habitat, *Slums of the World* (Nairobi: United Nations Human Settlements Programme, 2003). See also UN-Habitat, *State of the World's Cities 2010/2011: Bridging the Urban Divide* (Nairobi: United Nations Human Settlements Programme, 2008).

of the report was unequivocal: "slum life was, and would remain, a life of multiple deprivations, and few rights and reprieves, with inhabitants spending all resources and energies on sheer survival."[63] In this sense, slum life was little better than bare existence, that is, a condition tantamount to social death.[64]

To be sure, there is considerable disagreement in the scholarly literature as to whether terms with negative connotations – such as "slums," "favelas," "barrios," and "ghettoes" – are appropriate signifiers for indicating the ubiquitous and durable presence of impoverished living conditions, primarily in the megacities of hypergrowth concentrated in the (so-called) Global South.[65] Regardless of how one works around such terminological disputes, what is beyond question is the sheer magnitude of worldwide urban poverty and the structural impediments that prevent jobless residents from securing regular wage-paid employment, from acquiring decent housing, and from gaining access to requisite social services – all necessary steps for incorporation into the mainstream of urban life. What these realities bring into sharp focus is the apparent paradox of asymmetric co-dependency between formal economic activities and the entrenchment of informality in many globalizing cities, where "concentrations of 'placeless' capital" sit incongruously side-by-side with informal settlements, which provide cheap labor close to centers of power and production.[66]

Unlike a border that signifies a territorial edge or dividing line, a boundary references a malleable and mutable relationship.[67] Identifying the complexity of the boundaries separating so-called formality and informality divide requires a kind of "forensic examination" that penetrates deeply into the substrata of the urban social fabric at the places where the formal and informal collide and mutate, blending into hybrid concoctions that defy simple classification.[68] Informal settlements function as more than just convenient places of residence: they are also vital life-worlds that accommodate socioeconomic livelihoods, small-scale entrepreneurship and everyday commerce, cultural production, associational life, social interaction, religious worship, political activities, and play. In this sense, informal settlements are inextricably connected – in socioeconomic, infrastructural, and legal terms – to their surrounding or adjacent urban

---

63 Amin, "Telescopic Urbanism," p. 480.

64 See Giorgio Agamben, *Homo Sacer: Sovereign Power and Bare Life* [Trans. Daniel Heller-Roazen] (Stanford: Stanford University Press, 1998); and Nancy Scheper-Hughes, *Death without Weeping: The Violence of Everyday Life in Brazil* (Berkeley: University of California Press, 1992), pp. 384–386.

65 See Alan Gilbert, "The Return of the Slum: Does Language Matter?" *International Journal of Urban and Regional Research* 31 (2007), pp. 697–713; Alan Gilbert, "Extreme Thinking about Slums and Slum Dwellers: A Critique," *SAIS Review* 29, 1 (2009), pp. 35–48; and David Simon, "Situating Slums," *City* 15, 6 (2011), pp. 674–685.

66 See Saskia Sassen, "The Informal Economy: Between New Developments and Old Regulations," *The Yale Law Journal* 103, 8 (1994), pp. 2289–2304.

67 Harel Shapira, "The Border: Infrastructure of the Global," *Public Culture* 25, 2 (2013), pp. 249–260 (esp. p. 257).

68 Ricky Burdett, "Designing Urban Democracy: Mapping Scales of Urban Identity," *Public Culture* 25, 2 (2013), pp. 349–367 (esp. pp. 351–352).

circumstances in varying relationships of dependence.[69] The social and political complexities associated with such volatile juxtapositions partly explain the inability of the planning professions to arrive at credible and sustainable solutions that can effectively uplift informal settlements and unleash the creative potential slum-dwellers.[70]

At the start of the twenty-first century, globalizing cities with world-class aspirations are trapped in a whirlwind of material and visual contradictions that coalesce in highly uneven spatial landscapes of "incredible pluralism."[71] These polarizing dynamics have produced very different and distinctively fragmented social worlds occupying the same physical space. In the contemporary age of globalization, luxury enclaves of overproduction and excess often exist side-by-side with ordinary spaces catering for urban dwellers who struggle to "get by" with inadequate infrastructure and services, indecent housing, and precarious work. This strange juxtaposition of self-enclosed islands of wealth set within rough-edged landscapes of despair challenges our received normative notions of urban modernity. The steady proliferation of sequestered redoubts that cater for wealthy and privileged residents seeking to emulate "first world" amenities of the global economy has produced fragmented urban landscapes marked by visual spatial inequalities. While the basic ideal-typical template for enclave urbanism may have originated in the leading cities of North America and Europe, it is a model for city building that has spread to cities everywhere. In globalizing cities with world-class aspirations, the sheer magnitude of luxury enclaves has rendered the conventional distinction between "first-world" and "third-world" cities obsolete, analytically suspect, and irrelevant.[72]

Sometimes following in the footsteps of leading world-class cities and sometimes jumping far ahead, city builders in aspiring world-class cities have often adopted a *tabula rasa* approach to urban redevelopment, preferring to demolish the existing built environment and start from scratch rather than engage with the messy process of retrofitting incommensurate spaces.[73] The hallmark of this kind of new urbanism at the start of the twenty-first century consists of the abrupt implantation of upscale enclaves that have little or nothing in common with the scale, texture, and fabric of existing neighborhoods. This approach favors abrupt rupture over incremental accretion, that is, starting

[69] Cassim Shepard, "Montage Urbanism: Essence, Fragment, Increment," *Public Culture* 25, 2 (2013) pp. 223–232 (esp. pp. 230–231).

[70] Burdett, "Designing Urban Democracy," pp. 351–352.

[71] Rahul Mehrotra, "The Static and the Kinetic," in Ricky Burdett and Deyan Sudjic (eds.), *Living in the Endless City: The Urban Age Project by the London School of Economics and Deutsche Bank's Alfred Herrhausen Society* (London: Phaidon, 2011), pp. 108–115 (quotation from p. 108).

[72] For one example, see Dick and Rimmer, "Beyond the Third World City," pp. 2303–2321.

[73] Martin J. Murray, "'City Doubles': Re-Urbanism in Africa," in Faranak Miraftab, David Wilson, and Ken Salo (eds.), *Cities and Inequalities in a Global and Neoliberal World* (New York: Routledge, 2015), pp. 92–109.

afresh instead of slow and piecemeal adaptation through a gradual process of organically overlaying usable building typologies onto dis-used or outmoded ones.[74]

While city builders in globalizing cities with world-class aspirations slavishly chase after the holy grail of favorable competitive advantage, new experimental practices have generated novel kinds of everyday urbanism that is at once spontaneous and transgressive, and incremental and stealthy.[75] In seeking to capture these contradictory dynamics, the urban theorist Rahul Mehrotra has distinguished between what he has called the "Static City" and the "Kinetic City." With its roots in the modernist ethos of rational order and spatial coherence, the Static City gestures toward permanence, durability, and monumentality. Its built environment consists of such lasting materials as concrete and steel, glass and brick. Represented as two-dimensional space on conventional city maps, the Static City is constructed in conformity with the prescribed rules of conventional planning practice and in accordance with sound engineering principles – and firmly embedded within formal regulatory regimes of urban governance. With its high-rise buildings and signature architecture, the Static City offers the visual aesthetics of late modernity.[76]

In contrast, the Kinetic City is impermanent, ephemeral, and spontaneous. It is a fluid city of perpetual motion – temporary in nature, haphazard in design, and disorderly in appearance. The Kinetic City is flexible and elastic, and by constantly reinventing itself, it is less a grand vision of what a city should be than a more-or-less random collection of small adjustments that occur not all at once but incrementally over time. Its oversaturated street densities and informal economies produce a sort of three-dimensional land use that collides with the one-dimensional zoning that characterizes the Static City. The Kinetic City consists not of the monumental architectural conceits of the privileged and wealthy, but the mundane architecture of everyday necessity and convenience characterized by incremental building and impermanent structures. The indeterminate spaces of the Kinetic City support the lives and livelihoods of those who use them, and hence, they hold associative values and convey meanings in their local context. The fragile built environment of the Kinetic City rests on an emergent architecture of contingency and malleability that adapts to its circumstances. Patterns of everyday use and occupation determine the form and perception of these indeterminate spaces. The microlevel collaborations and associational life that emerge from the indeterminate spaces of the Kinetic City typically take

---

74 Burdett, "Designing Urban Democracy," p. 353. See also Shepard, "Montage Urbanism," pp. 223–232.

75 Teddy Cruz, "Border Tours: Strategies of Surveillance, Tactics of Encroachment," in Michael Sorkin (ed.), *Indefensible Space: The Architecture of the National Insecurity State* (New York: Routledge, 2008), pp. 111–140 (esp. pp. 121–122).

76 Mehrotra, "The Static and the Kinetic," pp. 108, 110. While Mehrotra may not have explicitly made the connection between the Static City and modernist planning, I have done so here.

the form of informal spatial and entrepreneurial practices that in turn generate different (and sometimes conflicting) ideas about density and land use. The
Kinetic City represents an everyday urbanism that conforms to its own local
logic often at odds with the modernist fixation with rational and efficient order
and with "highest and best use" of buildings and property.[77]

Contrary to conventional wisdom, the Kinetic City is not necessarily or
exclusively the city of the poor, the damned, and the dead.[78] More appropriately, it constitutes "a temporal articulation and occupation of space," which
"suggests how the carefully demarcated spatial limits – both material and symbolic – of formal urbanism are expanded and stretched "to include formally
unimaginable use in dense urban conditions."[79] Nonconforming uses and high
densities in the Kinetic City reshape the social fabric of urban space. Its built
environment consists of discarded materials, recycled and reused in myriad
ways. The Kinetic City consists of a haphazard assemblage of places and connections that appear chaotic and incomprehensible to the untrained eye. What
often seems like a completely random, disaggregated, and improvised world
can actually reveal, upon closer inspection, deliberately planned and structured
activities that are linked with very "elaborate organizational networks."[80]

The nonconforming and self-organizing dynamics of the Kinetic City defy
simple classification. Spaces of inventiveness and opportunity almost always
intersect and blend with spaces of exploitation and despair. The Kinetic
City represents a type of "stealth urbanism" – at once spontaneous and
improvisational.[81] This kind of everyday urbanism is fashioned by urban
dwellers outside the elite property-owning domains of the formal modernity
of state institutions and their conventional regulatory regimes. Instead, it conforms to a kind of "pirate modernity" that has to slip under the legal regulatory
armature of the city "simply in order to survive."[82] The Kinetic City is characterized by small-scale tactics of encroachment that amount to an unofficial
"planning from below." These small acts of transgression and appropriation
invariably cut again the grain of comprehensive, top-down strategies of control and containment. The do-it-yourself (DIY) urbanism of the Kinetic City is
virtually impossible to manage and contain, let alone predict and measure.[83]

[77] Mehrotra, "The Static and the Kinetic," p. 110.
[78] See, for example, Jennifer Mack, "Urban Design from Below: Immigration and the Spatial Practice of Urbanism," *Public Culture* 26, 1 (2014), pp. 153–185.
[79] Mehrotra, "The Static and the Kinetic," p. 110.
[80] This quotation is taken from a description of Lagos. See Rem Koolhaas, "Fragments of a Lecture on Lagos," in Okwui Enwezor et al. (eds.), *Under Siege: Four African Cities: Freetown,
Johannesburg, Kinshasa, Lagos* (Ostfildern-Ruit [Germany]: Hatje Cantz, 2002), pp. 173–183
(quotation from p. 177).
[81] See Cruz, "Border Tours: Strategies of Surveillance, Tactics of Encroachment," p. 121.
[82] Mehrotra, "The Static and the Kinetic," p. 108. See also Ravi Sundaram, *Pirate Modernity:
Delhi's Media Urbanism* (New York: Routlege, 2010).
[83] Cruz, "Border Tours: Strategies of Surveillance, Tactics of Encroachment," p. 134.

Asymmetric Urbanism

The explosive growth of urbanization on a global scale has not only produced new centers of global power outside the core zones of the world economy but also exacerbated spatial divisions and social inequalities in cities everywhere. While rural-to-urban migration may have once offered the promise of amelioration and the opportunity to start afresh, life conditions in the sprawling megacities of hypergrowth have deteriorated for large segments of expanding urban populations. Simultaneously, conventional planning models – with their comprehensive master plans, the installation of ever-expanding infrastructure, and the basic provision of social services – have failed to adequately respond to the contradictory pressures of contemporary urbanism. Both the gentrifying impulses that have produced new luxury enclaves and the tactical urbanism of self-built housing have bypassed and ignored conventional regulatory frameworks, thereby undermining municipal efforts to impose conventional spatial planning rules. It is in this sense that informal practices – that is, activities that take place outside of official sanction – often appeal to the exemption or the "exception" in order to claim legitimacy without appealing to formal regulatory regimes.[84]

Contrary to the roseate projections of free-market advocates of globalization, structural imbalances in the distribution of requisite resources both within and between cities have only become greater over the past three to four decades. Income disparities, socioeconomic divisions, and spatial inequalities have sharply increased not only in leading world-class cities at the core of the world economy but also in the rapidly expanding megacities of hypergrowth.[85] The proliferation of luxury enclaves in globalizing cities with world-class aspirations has proceeded in tandem with the expansion of vast zones of material deprivation. This polarization between enclaves of luxury and zones of hardship has accelerated the asymmetric imbalance at the core of twenty-first-century urbanism.[86]

Looking at globalizing cities as hybrid assemblages of territorial fragments that are incongruously layered over existing urban landscapes enables us to better understand the blurred, fuzzy lines of contemporary asymmetrical urbanism with its contradictory logics and irregular patterns. The unavoidable pressures of globalization have fundamentally reshaped the trajectories of urbanization on a world scale. The increasing concentration of global flows – of finance,

---

[84] Pedro Gadanho, "Mirroring Uneven Growth: A Speculation on Tomorrow's Cities Today," in *Uneven Growth*, pp. 14–25 (esp. p. 15). See also Gabriel Fuentes, "The Real New Urbanism: Engaging Developing World Cities," *The Journal of Spatial Syntax* 4, 2 (2013), pp. 167–178.

[85] See Saskia Sassen, *Cities in World Economy* (Thousand Oaks, CA: Pine Forge Press, 1994), pp. 99–117.

[86] Teddy Cruz, "Rethinking Urban Growth: It's about Inequality, Stupid," in *Uneven Growth*, pp. 48–55.

people, and ideas that insinuate themselves into the social fabric of cities everywhere – have reinforced socioeconomic inequalities.[87]

Exploring the borderlands between the Static City and the Kinetic City
enables us to expose uneven landscapes of contradiction where two distinct
kinds of urbanism collide and overlap – one of difference/unevenness and one
of juxtaposition/similarity.[88] The conflict between the planned city of the modernist imagination and the unplanned city of everyday use is reenacted at the
crossing points between the Static City and the Kinetic City. The excess of
overproduction in the Static City appears as so much ruin and waste. Yet the
reassembly of this cast-off detritus becomes the building blocks of the Kinetic
City, where the recycled "leftovers" create a kind of secondhand urbanism that
insinuates itself in the interstitial spaces of the urban landscape. These largely
invisible, asymmetrical connections reinforce the spatial unevenness of urban
landscapes. The never-ending processes of reshaping and reusing of indeterminate spaces, voids, and unclaimed spaces blur the boundaries between the
Static City and the Kinetic City. These recycling dynamics enact an odd mirroring effect linking the Static City and the Kinetic City in a mutually dependent but strangely choreographed inequality.[89] Compressed into an organic
fabric of overlooked and forgotten spaces of the urban landscape, the Kinetic
City constantly modifies and reinvents itself. By recycling discarded waste and
retrofitting abandoned detritus, it "leaves no ruins."[90] Often operating out of
sight, this kind of intensive, recycled urbanism is emblematic of how informal
settlements and self-built housing in fast-growing cities are expanding much
more rapidly than the historic urban cores they abut and surround, creating
different sets of rules for engagement with local development, and blurring
the distinctions between formality and informality.[91] Salvaged materials and
reclaimed spaces constitute the core of opportunistic urbanism.[92]

The inability to plan and regulate the Kinetic City merely heightens the
contradictions in the enclosed islands of concentrated wealth and privilege.
In those globalizing cities with world-class aspirations, the steady accretion
of new finance centers with global reach, upscale shopping and entertainment
meccas, and gated residential communities has reshaped urban landscapes in
ways unimaginable two to three decades ago. These building typologies are the
visual expression of global integration. The steady profusion of roseate master
plans for new mega-projects, the unveiling of glimmering images of high-rise

---

[87] See Sassen, *Cities in World Economy*, pp. 99–117.

[88] Cruz, "Border Tours: Strategies of Surveillance, Tactics of Encroachment," p. 119.

[89] Cruz, "Border Tours: Strategies of Surveillance, Tactics of Encroachment," p. 124.

[90] Mehrotra, "The Static and the Kinetic," p. 114.

[91] Teddy Cruz, "Tijuana Case Study: Tactics of Invasion – Manufacturing Sites," *Architectural Design* 75, 5 (2005), pp. 32–37.

[92] See Diego Ramirez-Lovering (ed.), *Opportunistic Urbanism* (Melbourne, Australia: RMIT Publishing, 2008).

business districts, and steady stream of strategic visioning exercises are emblematic of the one-dimensional imagination that planners, policymakers, and hired consultants bring to bear on decisions of future development.[93] These calls for remaking the city encapsulate the dreamscape of large-scale property developers seeking to achieve (and optimize) their global aspirations. City builders have locked onto schemes that call for a radical transformation of the physical fabric of urban landscapes. They regard these interventions as most fruitful and immediate way of reconfiguring urban landscapes in order to bring them into conformity with aspiring world-class cities seeking to advance in the rank order of importance. The construction of new airport gateways, high-rise office complexes, corporate business centers, high-speed motorways, bridges and flyovers, and convention centers form the critical building blocks that enable the Static City to announce its "coming-of-age" as a globalizing city. This unbridled optimism for a roseate future of prosperity and international recognition is matched by lingering anxiety about the disorderly effects of permanent poverty.[94]

[93] Mehrotra, "The Static and the Kinetic," p. 114.
[94] Mehrotra, "The Static and the Kinetic," p. 114.

2

The Shape of Cities to Come

Distended Urban Form as the Template for Global Urbanism

At the start of the twenty-first century, haphazard urban growth on a global scale has produced distended, and even bloated, conurbations that bear little resemblance – either structurally or visually – to the classical modern metropolis of the industrial capitalist age.[1] The seemingly boundless patterns of urban growth and expansion around the world have resulted in the breakdown of the kind of compact urban form – with its discrete boundaries, functionally specialized zones, and spatial hierarchies – that characterized city building in Europe and North America throughout most of the twentieth century, if not before. Such conventional binaries as central core and dependent peripheries, city and suburb, and metropolis and hinterland, are no longer appropriate benchmarks through which to grasp the processes of urban transformation at the start of the twenty-first century.[2]

To be sure, the quickening pace of urbanization on a global scale is a matter not just of ballooning population size but also of a fundamental metamorphosis in spatial form. For many older industrial cities in North America and Europe, the corrosive force of deterritorializing suburban sprawl, the declining gravitational pull of the historic downtown core, and the blossoming of "edge cities" at the metropolitan fringe has largely brought an end to the "concentric-circle" patterns of urban development that characterized much

---

[1] My argument here rests on a critical reading of Allen Scott, "Emerging Cities of the Third Wave," *City* 15, 3–4 (2011), pp. 289–321; and Sharon Meagher, "The Darker Underside of Scott's Third Wave," *City* 17, 3 (2013), pp. 395–398.

[2] Laura Taylor, "No Boundaries: Exurbia and the Study of Contemporary Urban Dispersion," *GeoJournal* 76, 4 (2011), pp. 323–339; Andrew Needham and Allen Dieterich-Ward, "Beyond the Metropolis: Metropolitan Growth and Regional Transformation in Postwar America," *Journal of Urban History* 35, 7 (2009), pp. 943–969; and Steef Buijs, Wendy Tan, and Devisari Tunas (eds.), *Megacities: Exploring a Sustainable Future* (Rotterdam: Nai010 Publishers, 2010).

of urban growth in the twentieth century.[3] Urban theorists have looked upon these spatial patterns of peripheral urbanization (or the "urbanization of suburbia") as a new kind of fragmented urban form, one which some have termed the "postsuburban metropolis" or the "decentered city," where powerful centrifugal forces have dispersed traditional central-place functions (corporate headquarter buildings, commercial and retail outlets, and entertainment venues) among different centers struggling with each other for paramountcy within the metropolitan region.[4]

As a general rule, fast-growing cities around the world have become vast, distended, agglomerations without obvious or fixed boundaries, spatially fragmented and increasingly polycentric conurbations on the boundless scale of what urban theorists have variously called the "extended metropolis," "the polycentric metropolis," "polyopolis," "sprawl city," "exopolis," displaced urbanism, "postmetropolis," the "dispersed metropolis," the "limitless city," or the "100-mile city."[5] The social dynamics that have shaped the spatial geography of global urbanism at the start of the twenty-first century require a rethinking of conventional theories of urban morphology that typically begin with the assumption of a structuring central place regulating an adherent landscape around the twin symmetries of density and agglomeration. For all sorts of

[3] Joel Garreau, *Edge City: Life on the New Frontier* (New York: Doubleday, 1991); Robert Beauregard, "Edge Cities: Peripheralising the Centre," *Urban Geography* 16, 8 (1995), pp. 708–721; and Edward Soja, "Regional Urbanization and the End of the Metropolis Era," in Gary Bridge and Sophie Watson (eds.), *New Companion to the City* (Chichester, UK: Wiley-Blackwell, 2011), pp. 679–689. For an early intervention into this discussion, see Carol O'Connor, "Sorting Out the Suburbs: Patterns of Land Use, Class, and Culture," *American Quarterly* 37, 3 (1985), pp. 382–394.

[4] See, *inter alia*, Michael Stern and William Marsh, "Editors' Introduction. The Decentered City: Edge Cities and the Expanding Metropolis," *Landscape and Urban Planning* 36, 4 (1997), pp. 243–246; and Dana Cuff, "Los Angeles: Urban Development in the Postsuburban Megacity," in André Sorensen and Junichiro Okata (eds.), *Megacities: Urban Form, Governance, and Sustainability* (Tokyo: Springer, 2011), pp. 273–287.

[5] See, for example, Peter Hall and Kathy Pain, "From Metropolis to Polyopolis," in Peter Hall and Kathy Pain, (eds.), *The Polycentric Metropolis: Learning from Mega-City Regions in Europe* (New York: Earthscan, 2006), pp. 3–18; Peter Gordon and Harry Richardson, "Beyond Polycentricity: The Dispersed Metropolis, Los Angeles, 1970–1990," *Journal of the American Planning Association* 62, 3 (1996), pp. 289–295; Deyan Sudjic, *The 100-Mile City* (San Diego: Harcourt Brace & Company, 1993); Oliver Gillham, *The Limitless City: A Primer on the Urban Sprawl Debate* (New York: Island Press, 2002); Edward Soja, *ThirdSpace: Journeys to Los Angeles and Other Real-and-Imagined Places* (Oxford: Basil Blackwell, 1996); Edward Soja, "Inside Exopolis: Scenes from Orange County," in Michael Sorkin (ed.), *Variations on a Theme Park: The New American City and the End of Public Space* (New York: Hill & Wang, 1992), pp. 94–122; and Edward Soja, *Postmetropolis: Critical Studies of Cities and Regions* (Malden, MA: Blackwell Publishers, 2000), p. 250. See Catherine Coquery-Vidrovitch, "Review Essays: Is L.A. a Model or a Mess?" *American Historical Review* 105, 5 (2000), pp. 1683–1691. This idea is taken from Martin J. Murray, "City of Layers: The Making and Shaping of Affluent Johannesburg after Apartheid," in Marie Huchzermeyer and Christoph Haferburg (eds.), *Urban Governance in Post-Apartheid Cities* (Stuttgart: Schweizerbart, 2014), pp. 179–196 (esp. p. 179).

reasons, some idiosyncratic and others not, the spatial physiognomy of twenty-first-century urbanism has failed to conform to the classical monocentric image of a singular and vibrant urban central core, characterized by peak concentrations of population, fixed capital investment in premium real estate, and available employment opportunities, surrounded by concentric rings of industrial and residential clusters receding in density toward the periphery, and linked laterally with specialized zones defined by such functions as commercial and manufacturing land use.[6]

The complex processes of urbanization that have shaped global urbanism have fostered contradictory patterns of growth and development that cannot be easily grasped within existing analytic paradigms and conceptual frameworks that seek to make sense of urban transformation and metamorphosis. Instead of the conventional radial-concentric model of urban evolution where intensive concentration of the central core takes place in tandem with the extensive expansion along the dependent suburban fringes, the spatial configuration of new patterns of global urbanism combines high-density concentration of multiple nodal points along with low-density suburbanizing sprawl spread haphazardly across an extended metropolitan zone.[7] This fragmented, decentered pattern of spatial growth and development forces us to transcend the misleading dichotomy between high-density urban core and low-density suburban peripheries.[8] For example, by the end of the twentieth century, suburbs that surrounded cities in the United States contained more office space than the adjoining central cities. As cities experienced decentralization and dispersal into low-density, auto-dependent peripheries, suburban corporate landscapes – particularly in the form of what Louise Mozingo has distinguished as the corporate campus, the corporate business estate, and the office park – triumphed as an American ideal. These white-collar business developments were central elements in reshaping metropolitan settlement patterns, and in defining key (but often ignored) features of postwar urbanism.[9] Without the conventional

[6] These ideas are taken from Martin J. Murray, *City of Extremes: The Spatial Politics of Johannesburg* (Durham, NC: Duke University Press, 2011), pp. 26, 28, 32. For a broader analysis and critique of conventional urban spatial patterns, see Michael Dear, "Los Angeles and the Chicago School: Invitation to a Debate," *City & Community* 1, 1 (2002), pp. 5–32; and Soja, *Postmetropolis*, pp. 84–94.

[7] See Edward Soja, "Regional Urbanization and the End of the Metropolis Era," in Neil Brenner (ed.), *Implosions/Explosions: Towards a Study of Planetary Urbanization* (Berlin: Jovis, 2013), pp. 276–287. For comparative developments, see Michael Dear and Steven Flusty, "Postmodern Urbanism," *Annals of the Association of American Geographers* 88, 1 (1998), pp. 50–72.

[8] See references in previous footnotes, and see Richard Weinstein, "The First American City," in Allen Scott and Edward Soja (eds.), *The City: Los Angeles and Urban Theory at the End of the Twentieth Century* (Berkeley and Los Angeles: University of California Press, 1996), pp. 22–46; and Ian MacBurnie, "The Periphery and the American Dream," *Journal of Architectural Education* 48, 3 (1995), pp. 134–143.

[9] Louise Mozingo, *Pastoral Capitalism: A History of Suburban Corporate Landscapes* (Cambridge, MA: The MIT Press, 2011).

signposts of the modernist city, the seemingly boundless metropolitan agglomerations can only be visualized in discrete fragments, fleeting and sometimes conflicting images that offer little by way of a coherent understanding of the whole.[10]

Seen through the wide-angle lens of epochal transformation, the classic "modern metropolis" that characterized the age of industrial capitalism has virtually ceased to exist as an ideal-typical model of urbanization. For more than a century, the dominant mode of urbanization consisted of the consolidation of high-density core areas surrounded by concentric rings of varying settlement typologies radiating outward away from the center in ever-diminishing densities. By the end of the twentieth century, new patterns of urban growth and development began to emerge, where existing spatial arrangements have started to dissolve, where polycentricity has replaced centrality, and where structured heterogeneity has supplanted spatial homogeneity.[11] The haphazard spread of "edge cities" at the metropolitan periphery have created new kinds of centrality that mimic the functional specializations once reserved for the historic core. The urbanization of suburbia has blurred the once strict distinction between high-density urban core and low-density residential peripheries, the urban and peri-urban, and city and countryside. Vast networks of transportation corridors have produced stretched-out, elongated regional agglomerations that resemble nothing which came before. The spreading tentacles of extensive urbanization have pushed the urban frontier further and further afield, filling in the gaps between cities and engulfed the surrounding hinterlands.[12]

Reflecting on the mutating form of metropolitan regions at the start of the twenty-first century, Gyan Prakash has declared that "the city is dead." In many respects, urban theorists have reached the conclusion that "the city" no longer exists as a coherent and inner-connected whole, that is, as a discrete, distinct entity with more-or-less clearly marked edges and borders, and with a recognizable relationship between high-density center and low-density periphery.[13] The conjoined forces of globalization and peri-urban sprawl have turned cities into "barely legible nodes" spread haphazardly across vast geographical distances.

[10] For comparative purposes, see Sharon Zukin, *Landscapes of Power: From Detroit to Disney World* (Berkeley and Los Angeles: University of California Press, 1991), especially pp. 217–218.

[11] Christian Schmid, "Networks, Borders, Differences: Towards a Theory of the Urban," in *Implosions/Explosions*, pp. 67–80 (esp. p. 67).

[12] Gyan Prakash, "Introduction," in Gyan Prakash and Kevin Kruse (eds.), *The Spaces of the Modern City: Imaginaries, Politics and Everyday Life* (Princeton, NJ: Princeton University Press, 2008), pp. 1–18 (esp. p. 3). See also David Wachsmuth, "City as Ideology: Reconciling the Explosion of the City Form with the Tenacity of the City Concept," *Environment and Planning D* 32, 1 (2014), pp. 75–90.

[13] Gyan Prakash, "Mumbai: The Modern City in Ruins," in Andreas Huyssen (ed.), *Other Cities, Other Worlds: Urban Imaginaries in a Globalizing Age* (Durham, NC: Duke University Press, 2008), pp. 181–204 (quotation from p. 182). See Hillary Angelo and David Wachsmuth, "Urbanizing Urban Political Ecology: A Critique of Methodological Cityism," *International Journal of Urban and Regional Research* 39, 1 (2015), pp. 16–27.

As the divide between urban and rural is perforated almost beyond recognition, the urban form is visible virtually everywhere.[14] These haphazard patterns of extended (and distended) urbanization that have taken hold at the start of the twenty-first century have undermined the idea of the city as something akin to a living organism (where growth and development, and decay and death, are appropriate metaphors). The idea of the "bounded city defined by an internally coherent civic life, organized as a public space inhabited by rational citizens, and structured by clear relationships to the region, nation, and wider world" is increasingly outdated and obsolete.[15]

This wholesale restructuring of urbanization on a global scale has meant that the classic "modern metropolis" of late nineteenth- and early twentieth-century industrial capitalism can no longer serve as the ideal-typical prototype for global urbanism at the dawn of the new millennium. The idealized images of the classical monocentric city of high modernism – always grounded in abstract and exaggerated oversimplifications – are increasingly at odds with the morphological shape of most contemporary cities around the world.[16] The breakdown of the metropolitan ideal of the modernist epoch – defined by a compact, high-density, downtown core radiating outward to low-density suburban edges – has given way to amorphous, horizontally expansive, posturban spatial configurations that are more undefined and fractured, and more fragmented and dispersed than ever before.[17] The unfolding of these new patterns of extensive urbanization have "cast doubt on received understandings of the city as bounded, nodal, and relatively self-enclosed sociospatial condition in favor of more territorially differentiated, morphologically variable, and multiscalar conceptions."[18] The declining significance of a singular historic downtown core as the primary locus for corporate office complexes and upscale commercial activities – coupled with the accelerated pace of peripheral urbanization (or the urbanization of suburbia) – has produced highly uneven, heterogeneous, and incongruous spatial landscapes that consist of a largely unplanned hodgepodge of commercial clusters, business nodal points, and "edge cities" only tangentially connected to each other.[19] No longer tethered to a recognized historic urban core, these multicentric urban agglomerations are defined as much by

---

[14] Neil Brenner and Christian Schmid, "Planetary Urbanism," in Matthew Gandy (ed.), *Urban Constellations* (Berlin: Jovis, 2011), pp. 10–13.

[15] Prakash, "Mumbai: The Modern City in Ruins," p. 184.

[16] Simon Marvin and Steven Graham, *Splintering Urbanism: Networked Infrastructures, Technological Mobilities and the Urban Condition* (New York: Routledge, 2001), pp. 114–115, 116.

[17] Stephen Graham, "Urban Network Architecture and the Structuring of Future Cities," in Henning Thomsen (ed.), *Future Cities – The Copenhagen Lectures* (Copenhagen: Fonden Realdania, 2002), pp. 110–122.

[18] Neil Brenner, "Urban Theory without an Outside," in *Implosions/Explosions*, pp. 14–35 (quotation from p. 15).

[19] For the source of some of these ideas, see Murray, *City of Extremes*, pp. 25–26, 106–107; and Murray, "City of Layers," pp. 179–180.

their edges as by their centers. These highly fragmented, dispersed, and scattered patterns of spatial growth and development have unsettled the conventional understanding of "city" and "suburb" as geographically discrete locations each with their own specific characteristics.[20] These complex processes of spatial restructuring make it increasingly difficult to talk about cities as isolated, independent entities outside of polycentric and extended metropolitan regions. Swirling around office parks, gated estates and residential subdivisions, logistics infrastructures, transportation corridors, and massive shopping malls, and leisure-entertainment sites, these rapidly evolving urban constellations provide an emergent blueprint for contemporary spatial patterns of sprawling urbanism. Haphazard patterns of uneven growth mixed with unruly geographies of territorial expansion represent an ascendant paradigm for the global urbanism of the future.[21]

Eclipse of Modernist City-Building: The Emergence of Privatized Modes of Urban Governance

Modern urban planning in the twentieth century came into existence "to a large extent as a problem-solving discipline," emerging in reaction to the perception that the rapid and haphazard growth of the nineteenth-century industrial metropolis was a "problematic construction" that rested precariously on shaky foundations.[22] At a time when modernist city building and its rational planning models have reached the end of their long reign as the dominant approach to fashioning the "good city," new orientations and frameworks have not yet come into full bloom. This paradox where old models endure as a ghostly presence and emergent approaches remain in their infancy has defined the parameters within which new city-building practices have begun to appear. Because we can no longer ground urban theory on the modernist expectations of a coherent demarcation between dominant central core and dependent peripheries, we need to develop a new critical theory of global urbanism based on the possibility of multiple trajectories of urban transformation operating simultaneously in the same time and space coordinates. The eclipse of modernist city building and its utopian pretenses make it impossible to center urban theory on *a priori* standards of rational order, coherent form, and rapid circulation. Yet the very possibility of developing alternative critical urban theoretical orientations

---

[20] Robert Beauregard, *When America Became Suburban* (Minneapolis: University of Minnesota Press, 2006).

[21] Pierre Veltz, "European Cities in the World Economy," in Arnaldo Bagnasco and Patrick Le Galès (eds.), *Cities in Contemporary Europe* (Cambridge: Cambridge University Press, 2000), pp. 33–47 (esp. p. 34). See also Edward Soja, "Regional Urbanization and Third Wave Cities," *City* 17, 5 (2013), pp. 688–694.

[22] Kees Doevendans and Anne Schram, "Creation/Accumulation City," *Theory, Culture & Society* 22, 2 (2005), pp. 29–43 (p. 29, source of quotations).

largely depends on locating some underlining point of reference, or at least underlying patterns, upon which to ground our thinking.[23]

At the start of the new millennium, the expansive use of public authority as the main mode of urban governance has increasingly been supplanted by a variety of private interests that have steadily asserted their control over the management of urban space. The steady proliferation of regulatory regimes ranging from business improvement districts, community interest developments, and public–private partnerships are merely the visible expression of a wholesale transformation in the public administration and management of urban space. The range of new types and kinds of regulatory regimes have either replaced or greatly undermined public authority. The rapid rise of "privatized planning" where large-scale real-estate interests have increasingly asserted their power to shape the built environment and to construct mega-projects that fall outside the conventional jurisdiction of public authorities.[24]

The expanded role of large-scale private real-estate developers and hybrid (public–private) planning regimes has become the norm in aspiring world-class cities around the globe.[25] These trends find visible expression in the steady accretion of privately owned and managed enclaves (ranging from enclosed shopping malls and shoppertainment extravaganzas to gated residential communities and private satellite towns) and the displacement of low-income urban residents who stand in the way of progress. This gentrifying impulse has given rise to new "generic cities," with their look-alike built environments consisting of a familiar pattern of standardized features, similar ingredients, and stylized aesthetics. Celebrated in an exaggerated way by the well-known "starchitect" Rem Koolhaas and his collaborator Bruce Mau in 1995, these so-called "generic cities" display a variety of shared characteristics, no matter where they appear around the world.[26] These common features typically include a decided preference for large-scale redevelopment projects, an aesthetic attachment to signature "trophy buildings," the private provision of physical infrastructure, mono-functional land uses, standardized and uniform building typologies, unfettered suburban sprawl, a fixation with security, a deliberate disregard for underlying local ecologies, a bland indifference toward cultural heritage (that

---

[23] Jeffrey Alexander, "Robust Utopias and Civil Repairs," *International Sociology* 16 (2001), pp. 579–591.

[24] Shruti Rajagopalan and Alexander Tabarrok, "Lessons from Gurgaon, India's Private City," in David Emanuel Andersson and Stefano Moroni (eds.), *Cities and Private Planning: Property Rights, Entrepreneurship and Transaction Costs* (Northhampton, MA: Edward Elgar, 2014), pp. 199–213.

[25] Clyde Mitchell-Weaver and Brenda Manning, "Public–Private Partnerships in Third World Development: A Conceptual Overview," *Studies in Comparative International Development* 26, 4 (1991–1992), pp. 45–67.

[26] Rem Koolhaas and Bruce Mau [edited by Jennifer Singler], *S, M, L, XL* (Rotterdam and New York: 010 Publishers/The Monacelli Press, 1995); and Maarten Hajer, "The Generic City," *Theory, Culture & Society* 16, 4 (1999), pp. 137–144.

is, building "cities without history"), a neo-Corbusierian disdain for disorderly landscapes, and expanded mechanisms of social exclusion.[27] This trend toward building "generic cities" have gone hand-in-hand with the growing influence of private corporations, philanthropic organizations, and elite "growth coalitions" in what have been conventionally regarded as public processes of urban planning, agenda-setting, and decision-making.[28]

This shift toward privatized planning of urban landscapes represents a significant departure from the modernist vision of city building. As a utopian ideal, modernist principles held that functional efficiency and rational order of urban space were necessary steps required to eliminate the spatial disorder and inefficient land use brought about by the lack of workable regulatory frameworks and unfettered market competition. In its most simplified form, the modernist approach to fashioning the "planned city" rested on the presumption that public authorities operating with little restraint were better able to define and protect the common interests of urban residents.[29]

The shifting place of planning and governance lies at the heart of the future of urbanism. As modernist and high-modernist doctrines of city building have declined in popularity, privatized planning scenarios and entrepreneurial modes of urban governance have increasingly fallen into the hands of private real-estate developers and large-scale property owners. This trend is especially true in fast-growing cities around the world, where public capacities of urban planning agencies are strained to begin with, and where policymakers and middle-class urban residents alike have endorsed and welcomed private intervention and the development of planning initiatives. Even in the postindustrial

---

[27] See Anupama Rao and Paul Rabé, "Workshop Report: 'Public City, Private City'," Institute for Public Knowledge, New York University, 27–28 August 2014. Available at www.rethinking .asia/report/public-city-private-city. In remarking on the decline of the 'historicized city' Rem Koolhaas remarked "the past is too small to inhabit" (Rem Koolhaas, "The Past is too Small to Inhabit," *New Perspectives Quarterly* 30, 4 (2013), 13–18. See also Douglas Baker and Robert Freestone, "Land Use Planning for Privatized Airports: The Australia Experience," *Journal of the American Planning Association* 78, 3 (2012), pp. 328–341.

[28] See Gavin Shatkin, "The City and the Bottom Line: Urban Megaprojects and the Privatization of Planning in Southeast Asia," Environment and Planning A 40, 2 (2008), pp. 383–401; Pedro Pírez, "Buenos Aires: Fragmentation and Privatization of the Metropolitan City," *Environment and Urbanization* 14, 1 (2002), pp. 145–158; Amir Hefetz and Mildred Warner, "Beyond the Market versus Planning Dichotomy: Understanding Privatisation and its Reverse in U.S. Cities," *Local Government Studies* 33, 4 (2007), pp. 555–572; Eugene McCann, "Collaborative Visioning or Urban Planning as Therapy? The Politics of Public–Private Policy Making," *The Professional Geographer* 53, 2 (2001), pp. 207–218; Gavin Shatkin, "Planning Privatopolis: Representation and Contestation in the Development of Urban Integrated Mega-Projects," in Ananya Roy and Aihwa Ong (eds.),.) *Worlding Cities: Asian Experiments and the Art of Being Global* (Malden, MA: Blackwell, 2011), pp. 77–97; and Trevor Hogan, Tim Bunnell, Choon-Piew Pow, Eka Permanasari, and Sirat Morshidi, "Asian Urbanisms and the Privatization of Cities," *Cities* 29, 1 (2012), pp. 59–63.

[29] James Scott, *Seeing Like a State: How Certain Schemes to Improve the Human Condition Have Failed* (New Haven, CT: Yale University Press, 1998), pp. 87–146.

creative-entertainment cities in the (so-called) Global North, where public agencies may still play a significant role in comprehensive land use planning, the
shift toward entrepreneurial modes of urban governance has gone hand-in-
glove with the expanded role of private real-estate interests in shaping urban
policies.[30]

As a general rule, the predominance of private proprietary interests in city
building is deeply rooted in the past.[31] In earlier centuries, urban form assumed
a patchwork pattern where privately owned property and public authority
remained somewhat separate and distinct, each operating in accordance with
their own principles in their own spheres of influence. The rule of *laissez-faire*
economics – what Sam Bass Warner called "privatism" in his historical study of
Philadelphia – played a preponderant role in shaping urban landscapes.[32] The
origins of modern urban planning can be traced to various social movements
for municipal reform that arose in the latter decades of the nineteenth century
as a reaction against the disorder, insalubrity, and unruliness of the industrial
city.[33] Many utopian visionaries active at the turn of twentieth century con-
jured up various versions of an imagined ideal city. Yet the mundane, practical
considerations of adequate sanitation, decent housing, unimpeded movement
of goods and people, and the much-needed provision of social amenities also
animated the desire for planning the city. City and regional planners have long
sought to balance the conflicting demands of economic growth, social equity,
environmental sensitivity, and aesthetic appeal.[34] As a general rule, the planning
process often involves a formal master plan for an entire city or metropolitan
region, a neighborhood plan, a project plan, or a set of policy alternatives. Successful implementation of urban planning proposals usually requires political
astuteness and entrepreneurship on the part of planners and their sponsors,
despite efforts to insulate and shield the planning process from politics. While

[30] Bob Jessop, "The Narrative of Enterprise and the Enterprise of Narrative: Place Marketing and
      the Entrepreneurial City," in Tim Hall and Phil Hubbard, *The Entrepreneurial City: Geogra-
      phies of Politics, Regime, and Representation* (New York: John Wiley & Sons, 1998), pp. 77–
      99. In my view, while the notions of Global North and Global South may function as a useful
      heuristic shorthand referring to broadly distributed patterns of urban life, they have little ana-
      lytic value as epistemological categories that can assist in the production of knowledge.
[31] Georg Glasze, Chris Webster, and Klaus Frantz, "Introduction: Global and Local Perspectives
      on the Rise of Private Neighbourhoods," in Georg Glasze, Chris Webster, and Klaus Frantz
      (eds.), *Private Cities: Global and Local Perspectives* (New York: Routledge, 2010), pp. 1–9. See
      Leonardo Benevolo, *The Origins of Modern Town Planning* (Cambridge, MA: The MIT Press,
      1967).
[32] Sam Bass Warner, *The Private City: Philadelphia in Three Periods of Its Growth* (Philadelphia:
      University of Pennsylvania Press, 1987). See also Richard Foglesong, *Planning the Capitalist
      City: The Colonial Era to the 1920s* (Princeton: Princeton University Press, 2014).
[33] Peter Hall, *Cities of Tomorrow: An Intellectual History of Urban Planning and Design in the
      Twentieth Century* [Third Edition] (Malden, MA: Blackwell, 2002).
[34] See Scott Campbell, "Green Cities, Growing Cities, Just Cities? Urban Planning and the Con-
      tradictions of Sustainable Development," *Journal of the American Planning Association* 62, 3
      (1996), pp. 296–312.

historically rooted in the public administration of urban landscapes, planning has increasingly involved the participation of property owners and real-estate developers in joint arrangements, such as "public–private partnerships."[35]

More than a century ago, the power to shape the direction of city building pitted private real-estate interests against the public administration of the urban landscape. As a reaction to problems associated with the excesses of the late nineteenth-century industrial city, municipal officials turned to modernist planning principles as a way to counteract the deleterious effects of perceived crises in health, sanitation, and infrastructure.[36] For most of the twentieth century, modernist planning in its different permutations and guises shaped city building in the capitalist core of the world economy. Modernist planning principles sought to impose order, coherence, and rationality on the perceived disorder of street life and chaotic urban form of industrial cities in order to bring about much-needed social improvement. The modernist quest for an ordered and rational urban form claimed to offer universal solutions to the myriad problems and perceived chaos of the industrial city. Over time, city-builders exported these planning principles to growing cities in the rest of the world, albeit with mixed results.[37]

The construction of "new towns" gave modernist planners a blank slate on which to create their vision of the ideal urban landscape. Modernist doctrine rested on the conviction that taming the disorderly city depended upon a combination of professional expertise and the deliberate use of public authority to impose solutions on unruly urban landscapes and the people who inhabited them.[38] At root, modernist planning principles were grounded in the faith in the possibility of systematically attacking, and obliterating, the "moving chaos" of urban life, characterized by narrow streetscapes containing a "volatile mixture of people and traffic, businesses and homes, rich and poor."[39] Such comprehensive, holistic goals as efficiency of movement, rational order, and functional

---

35 Stephen Osborne, *Public–Private Partnerships: Theory and Practice in International Perspective* (New York: Routledge, 2002); Tony Bovaird, "Public–Private Partnerships: From Contested Concepts to Prevalent Practice," *International Review of Administrative Sciences* 70, 2 (2004), pp. 199–215; and Roger Wettenhall, "The Rhetoric and Reality of Public–Private Partnerships," *Public Organization Review* 3, 1 (2003), pp. 77–107.

36 Gordon Cherry, "Introduction: Aspects of Twentieth-Century Planning," in Gordon Cherry (ed.) *Shaping an Urban World* (London: Mansell, 1980), pp. 1–21. See also Martin Melosi, *The Sanitary City: Environmental Services in Urban America from Colonial Times to the Present* (Baltimore: The Johns Hopkins University Press, 2000).

37 Robert Home, *Of Planting and Planning: The Making of British Colonial Cities* [Second Edition] (New York: Routledge, 2013); and Will Glover, "The Troubled Passage from 'Village Communities' to Planned New Town Developments in Mid-Twentieth-Century South Asia," *Urban History* 39, 1 (2012), pp. 108–127.

38 Robert Beauregard, "Between Modernity and Postmodernity: The Ambiguous Position of U.S. Planning," *Environment and Planning D* 7, 4 (1989), pp. 381–395.

39 Marshall Berman, *All that is Solid Melts into Air: The Experience of Modernity* (New York: Penguin, 1982), p. 168.

specialization relied on a spatial imaginary of a coherent and legible urban form with clearly demarcated patterns of land use.[40] Modernist planning principles rested on the assumption that detached objectivity, scientific rationality, and expert knowledge could engender a singular,universally correct solution that was superior to other sources of judgement.[41]

The immediate aftermath of World War II signaled the high-water mark of high-modernist city building in North America and Europe with its stress on comprehensive planning and expanded public authority. Seen retrospectively, this relatively short moment in time represented a historically distinct period with limited geographical reach. At this historical conjuncture, single-minded application modernist planning axioms became the international norm, applying objectivity and scientific rationality to city building through decision-making processes regarded as technical (not political) by municipal authorities who were assumed to be neutral and guided by the public interest – which itself was imagined to be the common good. The application of modernist planning principles aimed to "produce a coordinated and functional urban form organized around collective goals."[42] Urban planners successfully institutionalized modernist planning formulas as the basic toolkit of the interventionist state authorities.[43] Public authorities either implicitly or explicitly presumed that the standards of modernist planning served the common good. The implementation of planning goals was a top-down undertaking, because urban planners with technical expertise were considered to have a comprehensive perspective that allowed them to dispassionately recognize the "overall public interest."[44] Rooted in the scientific rationality of positivism, modernist planning doctrine assumed the aura of universal applicability. The theory and practice of modernist planning coalesced around the belief that the concepts, methods, and techniques that had been fashioned and perfected out of the experience of the large industrializing metropolises of North America and Europe were the "social equivalents of natural laws and, as such, universally applicable."[45]

As the assumed universal path to progress, modernization theory became the dominant model for development on a world scale by the second half of the

---

[40] Boyer, *Dreaming the Rational City*, pp. 132, 134, 265.
[41] Sonia Hirt, "Premodern, Modern, Postmodern? Placing New Urbanism in a Historical Perspective," *Journal of Planning History* 8, 3 (2009), pp. 248–2733; and Mariana Valverde, "Seeing Like a City: The Dialectic of Modern and Premodern Ways of Seeing in Urban Governance," *Law and Society Review* 45, 2 (2011), pp. 277–312.
[42] Beauregard, "Between Modernity and Postmodernity," p. 381.
[43] Beauregard, "Between Modernity and Postmodernity," pp. 381–395.
[44] Alan Altshuler, "The Goals of Comprehensive Planning," in Andreas Faludi (ed.), *A Reader in Planning Theory* (Oxford: Pergamon, 1973), pp. 193–210 (esp. p. 193).
[45] Otto Koenigsberger, "Foreword," in Alan Turner (ed.) *Cities of the Poor: Settlement Planning in Developing Countries* (London: Croom Helm, 1980), pp. 11–15 (quotation from p. 13). See also Otto Koenigsberger, "Book Review: *The City in Newly Developing Countries*," *Urban Studies* 8, 1 (1971), pp. 75–76.

twentieth century. Policymakers operated with the assumption that the practice and ideology of modernization represented the universal path to progress.[46] In short order, the tenets of modernist urban planning became thoroughly embedded as major components of modernization theory. Policymakers looked upon the application of these guiding principles as the universal solution to the perceived "disorder" and chaos of (so-called) Third World cities. They justified the export of the modernist planning model overseas as a way of bringing a "benevolent and progressive "modernization process" to a backward Third World."[47] With few exceptions, modernist planning precepts have always revolved around a mixture of politics and moralism: the idea of replacing unpredictable and chaotic activities with an overarching master plan, on the one side; and a prescriptive approach "tied to a utopian project driven by politico-moral ambitions," on the other.[48]

The fundamental flaw of modernist (and high modernist) city building revolved around the mistaken belief that there are universal and exclusive (i.e., necessary and unavoidable) "truths" that are superior to alternative approaches and that legitimately replace and exclude all traditional solutions to urbanism.[49] Modernist thinking rested on a particular narrow and blinkered "way of seeing," which reduced complex phenomena into a set of simplified and calculable variables that produced a highly simplified and stylized image of the city. In other words, the scientific knowledge production of modernist planning thought was premised on the possibility of holding constant those features of urbanism that are indeed always in flux.[50]

In the postwar rush to turn urban planning into an applied science with universal appeal and applicability everywhere, much was lost – the sense of city building as layered palimpsest, the city of collective memory, the enduring importance of place, and the art of place-making. By the final decades of the twentieth century, critics – and especially those with poststructuralist sensibilities – started to question the underlying assumptions regarding the alleged neutrality of the technocratic "rule of experts" that undergirded the modernist planning canon. In time, the once-enduring faith in the power of modernist (and high-modernist) planning to bring order and coherence to urban life

[46] Beauregard, "Between Modernity and Postmodernity," pp. 381–382.

[47] David Harvey, *The Condition of Postmodernity: An Enquiry into the Origins of Cultural Change* (Oxford: Blackwell), pp. 35–36. See also Björn Hettne, *Development Theory and the Three Worlds* (Harlow: Longman, 1995); and Alan Turner, "Urban Planning in the Developing World: Lessons from Experience," *Habitat International* 16, 2 (1992), pp. 113–126.

[48] Léon Krier [interviewed by Nikos Salingaros], "The Future of Cities: The Absurdity of Modernism," *Planetizen* (November 5, 2001).

[49] Leonie Sandercock, *Towards Cosmopolis* (Chichester: John Wiley, 1998). See also Alan Gilbert and Joseph Gugler (eds.), *Cities, Poverty and Development* (Oxford: Oxford University Press, 1981).

[50] See Scott, *Seeing Like a State*, pp. 1–6, 139–146.

began to wane. Modernist planners, architects, and engineers regarded themselves as detached, high-minded experts who could bring scientific objectivity and technical rationality to the goal of providing for the collectively defined public interest. Despite their claims to universality and comprehensiveness, modernist planning models failed to accomplish their goal of constructing the orderly, rational city.[51]

Over time, modernist principles of rational ordering of space through land-use planning, efficiency of movement across the urban landscape, and functional specialization declined as the main driving force behind city-building efforts around the world. The rise of neoliberal urbanism paralleled the retreat of modernist approaches to city building. By promoting market competitiveness as the primary sorting mechanism for the distribution of social services and urban amenities, entrepreneurial modes of urban governance have effectively delivered the *coup de grace* to comprehensive master planning as a public undertaking.[52] Over the past three to four decades, municipal officials have increasingly turned to private companies to provide housing, water, waste disposal, transportation, and a variety of core social services. Private real-estate financing has played an increasing role in the provision of places for social congregation and chance encounter. To a certain degree, the practice of urban planning has become a branch of private enterprise as an increasing number of city administrations work with paid consultants on strategic planning initiatives, rather than conducting comprehensive, holistic planning in-house.[53]

This movement toward expanded corporate influence over entrepreneurial modes of urban governance does not represent a return to premodernist city building where the predominance of private (and parochial) interests was more or less the norm. Instead the steady encroachment of real estate capital in city building and the diminution of public authority have signaled the beginning of a new era where the buying and selling of urban space itself has emerged as a new site for capital accumulation. Globalizing cities with world-class aspirations have become embedded in global flows of financial capital at an unprecedented scale. The resulting competitive rivalry for access to free-floating capital for investment in urban space has resulted in the production of "city-winners" and "city-losers" in the unequal geography of global capitalism.[54]

[51] These ideas are taken from Leonie Sandercock [Images by Peter Lyssiotis], *Cosmopolis II: Mongrel Cities of the 21st Century* (London: Continuum, 2003), pp. 2–3.

[52] Sandercock, *Towards Cosmopolis*, pp. 1–7; and Beauregard, "Between Modernity and Postmodernity," pp. 381–395.

[53] Greg Morrow, "The Privatization of Cities," *Critical Planning* 13 (2006), n.p. (Journal of the UCLA Department of Urban Planning). Available at https://criticalplanning.squarespace.com/volume-13.

[54] See David Harvey, Spaces of Global Capitalism: *Towards a Theory of Uneven Geographical Development* (London and New York: Verso, 2006).

Shifting Fault Lines for Global Urbanism: Privatized Planning and Entrepreneurial Urbanism

Over the past three decades, a key component of the restructuring of urban governance has been a fundamental shift in planning practice from a focus on comprehensive planning (and a primary concern with the location, intensity, form, amount, and harmonization of land use) to a stress on more locally specific strategic projects.[55] One of the principal aims of conventional planning practice has been to use public funding and expertise to direct infrastructure investment in ways that serve as mechanisms for tying the urban fabric together, while simultaneously controlling and guiding private real-estate development through a combination of land-use planning rules, zoning regulations, and financial incentives. What began to take coherent form at the end of the twentieth century was a different type of spatial planning, one that moved away from a largely defensive and reactive approach aimed at controlling land use through the blanket application of zoning regulations to a more flexible, market-oriented, and development-led approach that called for direct and selective intervention. This shift from comprehensive spatial planning to a focus on localized "strategic projects" went hand-in-hand with the replacement of public regulatory regimes and policy instruments with a more *laissez-faire* approach to land use development.[56] The intrusion of an entrepreneurial ethos into the realm of urban planning has not been limited to the direct involvement of large real-estate and property developers, but also includes an entourage of private consulting firms selling "expert" services.[57] Private planning consultants are often hired by public–private coalitions in order to give expert advice on shaping the future of cities. Advocates for this shift to privatized planning frequently claim that the interventions they propose and institute are consensus-based, collaborative, and even inclusionary, rather than elite-centered and expert-driven. Yet on closer inspection, large-scale real-estate developers have been able to manipulate "visioning" processes to serve their own ends with little public oversight.[58]

For more than a century, the term "urban planning" has evoked images of municipal agencies, policymakers, city officials, bureaucrats, and technical experts engaged in the provision of public services, the maintenance of

55 Louis Albrechts, "Bridge the Gap: From Spatial Planning to Strategic Projects," *European Planning Studies* 14, 10 (2006), pp. 1487–1500 (esp. p. 1490). For a wider discussion of the idea of neoliberal planning, see contributions to Tuna Taşan-Kok and Guy Baeten (eds.), *Contradictions of Neoliberal Planning: Cities, Policies, and Politics* (New York: Springer, 2012).

56 Stephan Davies, "Laissez-faire Urban Planning," in David Beito, Peter Gordon, and Alexander Tabarrok (eds.), *The Voluntary City: Choice, Community and Civil Society* (Ann Arbor: University of Michigan Press, 2002), pp. 18–46.

57 David Hayward, "The Privatized City: Urban Infrastructure, Urbanism and Service Provision in the Era of Privatization," *Urban Policy and Research* 15, 1 (1997), pp. 55–56.

58 See McCann, "Collaborative Visioning or Urban Planning as Therapy?" pp. 207–218.

infrastructure, and the introduction of land-use regulations. As Sophie Body-Gendrot, Jacques Carré and Romain Garbaye have suggested, "Planning is traditionally perceived as the paradigmatic product of twentieth-century welfarist urban government, as a technique of land use that was supposed to wrench cities from the clutches of speculators and develop them, hopefully, in the public interest."[59] Yet private real-estate developers and property owners have also engaged in land-use planning, in the regulation of the built environment, in the provision of infrastructure, as well as in the distribution of a variety of social services.[60] These kinds of comprehensive "private planning" were typical in the "company towns" and underresourced cities of the nineteenth century. At the start of the twenty-first century, privatized planning has again become popular in the practice of city building, particularly in so-called "contractual territorial communities," like gated residential estates, homeowners" associations, shopping malls, and office parks.[61] Private planning initiatives have always played a significant role in various types of small-scale infill developments, ranging from single-family housing to multiunit apartment and condominium complexes. But the engagement of these privatized planning interventions has moved far beyond scaled-down additions to the built environment to encompass everything from large-scale redevelopment projects to entirely new satellite cities.[62] The growing popularity of such institutionalized entities as public-private partnerships provides ample evidence that "private developments" do not always exist entirely outside state regulation and control. Nevertheless, privatized urban planning has increasingly resulted in the clustering of upscale mega-projects that are designed as self-enclosed enclaves. Large-scale "private cities" rely upon extraterritorial regulatory regimes operating outside of public jurisdiction.[63]

[59] Sophie Body-Gendrot, Jacques Carré and Romain Garbaye, "Introduction," in Sophie Body-Gendrot, Jacques Carré, Romain Garbaye (eds.), *A City of One's Own: Blurring the Boundaries between Private and Public* (Aldershot, UK: Ashgate, 2008), pp. 1–10 (quotation from p. 3).

[60] Randall Holcombe, "Planning and the Invisible Hand: Allies or Adversaries?" *Planning Theory* 12, 2 (2012), pp. 199–210.

[61] See Stefano Moroni and David Emanuel Andersson, "Introduction: Private Enterprise and the Future of Urban Planning," in David Emanuel Andersson and Stefano Moroni (eds.), *Cities and Private Planning: Property Rights, Entrepreneurship and Transaction Costs* (Northampton, MA: Edgar Elgar, 2014), pp. 1–16.

[62] See, for example, Martin J. Murray, "Waterfall City (Johannesburg): Privatized Urbanism *in Extremis*," *Environment and Planning A* 47, 3 (2015), pp. 503–520; and Claire Herbert and Martin J. Murray, "Building New Cities from Scratch: Privatized Urbanism and the Spatial Restructuring of Johannesburg after *Apartheid*," *International Journal of Urban and Regional Research* 39, 3 (2015), pp. 471–494.

[63] Grazia Brunetta and Stefano Moroni, *Contractual Communities in the Self-Organising City* (Dordrecht, Netherlands: Springer, 2011); and Moroni and Andersson, "Introduction: Private Enterprise and the Future of Urban Planning," pp. 1–16.

One of the defining characteristics of global urbanism at the start of the twenty-first century is the unprecedented shift toward increased corporate influence over regional planning initiatives. Large-scale real-estate developers have conceived of urban development plans on a metropolitan-wide scale, and begun to implement these mega-projects, sometimes with the assistance of municipal authorities and sometimes completely on their own accord without any public oversight.[64] In cities where municipal regulatory regimes have become highly compromised, *the* only true "comprehensive planning" occurs within large-scale, private real-estate development projects.[65] New modes of privatized urban governance have replaced the once sacrosanct commitment of municipal authorities to the public administration of urban space. The breakdown of public administration and holistic spatial planning has produced new regimes of authority in the form of public–private partnerships, privately managed spaces of social congregation, and "common interest developments" with their own rules and regulations governing the use of urban space.[66]

The goal of urban governance is to establish regulatory regimes that can sustain some kind of order, stability, and predictability.[67] Urban governance regimes consist of a vast and complex array of special authorities, extralegal instruments, and quasi-autonomous regulatory agencies charged with decision-making, rulemaking, and the provision of bulk goods and services for collective consumption. At the start of the twenty-first century, large metropolitan regions are often saturated with an overabundance of overlapping and interdependent authorities established to deal with an almost infinite variety of problems and concerns. Despite what might appear at first glance to be an incoherent and messy juridical mosaic, this fragmentation of metropolitan governance is not accidental. The shape of urban governance constantly changes in haphazard ways.[68]

The proliferation of these sometimes intersecting and sometimes parallel governance regimes conforms to underlying logics and competing rationalities

---

[64] Shatkin, "The City and the Bottom Line: Urban Megaprojects and the Privatization of Planning in Southeast Asia," pp. 383–401; Shatkin, "Planning Privatopolis," pp. 77–97.

[65] Pírez, "Buenos Aires: Fragmentation and Privatization of the Metropolitan City," pp. 145–158.

[66] Phil Allmendinger and Graham Haughton, "Soft Spaces, Fuzzy Boundaries and Metagovernance: The New Spatial Planning in the Thames Gateway," *Environment and Planning A* 41, 3 (2009), pp. 617–633. See also Tuna Taşan-Kok, "Entrepreneurial Governance: Challenges of Large-Scale Property-led Urban Regeneration Projects," *Tijdshrift voor Economishe en Sociale Geografie* 101, 2 (2010), pp. 126–149.

[67] Gerry Stoker, "Governance as Theory: Five Propositions," *International Social Science Journal* 50/155 (1998), pp. 17–28.

[68] These ideas are taken directly from Michael Storper, "Governing the Large Metropolis," *Territory, Politics, Governance* 2, 2 (2014), pp. 115–134 (esp. pp. 117, 118, 119). See also Mark Tewdwr-Jones and Donald McNeill, "The Politics of City-Region Planning and Governance: Reconciling the National, Regional and Urban in the Competing Voices of Institutional Restructuring," *European Urban and Regional Studies* 7, 2 (2000), pp. 119–134.

that often arise in response to pressures from powerful property-owning stake-holders who are intent on shaping the cityscape in conformity with their nar-row interests.[69] Governing bodies in metropolitan regions regularly invent new agencies and establish new authorities, often in *ad hoc* fashion, that enable them to address problems as they arise. This ongoing process of tinkering with makeshift governance practices (or what Michael Storper has called "gover-nance bricolage") often takes place without the benefit of sweeping institu-tional reforms and outside of public scrutiny. The forms and types of tinkering varyconsiderably, and include (1) the expansion of classical types of public pro-vision of collective goods and services "through the creation of new agencies or their division or recombination"; (2) the establishment of new special-purpose authorities; (3) "the *ad hoc* invention" of hybrid private–public corporate enti-ties, such as quasi-autonomous nongovernmental organizations or NGOs (so-called *Quangos*), along with other public–private partnerships for supplying goods and services for collective consumption; (4) privatization under pub-lic contract or special charter; (5) regulated private monopolies in the pub-lic service; and (6) intergovernmental agencies that provide services on a cost-recovery basis.[70]

The implementation of more market-oriented planning initiatives has greatly undermined conventional approaches to the public administration of urban landscapes.[71] Impatient property developers have accused conventional land-use planning protocols of creating unnecessary obstacles to real-estate devel-opment and investment because of excessive regulation, costly delays, and uncertainty.[72] As a comprehensive and holistic approach to urban governance, conventional urban planning aims to both facilitate and support market-led growth through private entrepreneurial initiatives, and to regulate and miti-gate the deleterious excesses of unfettered competition. The shift from a reac-tive and defensive planning culture to a proactive and enabling one has sig-naled a dramatic shift in the conventional balance between public authority

[69] See, for example, Gene Desfor and John Jørgensen, "Flexible Urban Governance: The Case of Copenhagen's Recent Waterfront Development," *European Planning Studies* 12, 4 (2004), pp. 479–496.
[70] The ideas in this paragraph are paraphrased from Storper, "Governing the Large Metropolis," pp. 115–134 (esp. p. 124). See also Alan DiGaetano and Elizabeth Strom, "Comparative Urban Governance: An Integrated Approach," *Urban Affairs Review* 38, 3 (2003), pp. 356–395; Philip Booth, "Partnerships and Networks: The Governance of Urban Regeneration in Britain," *Journal of Housing and the Built Environment* 20, 3 (2005), pp. 257–269; and Pauline McGuirk and Andrew MacLaran, "Changing Approaches to Urban Planning in an 'Entrepreneurial City': The Case of Dublin," *European Planning Studies* 9, 4 (2001), pp. 437–457.
[71] John Lovering, "The Relationship between Urban Regeneration and Neoliberalism: Two Pre-sumptuous Theories and a Research Agenda," *International Planning Studies* 12, 4 (2007), pp. 343–366.
[72] Erik Swyngedouw, "Governance Innovation and the Citizen: The Janus Face of Governance-beyond-the-State," *Urban Studies* 42, 11 (2005), pp. 1991–2006; and Jamie Peck and Adam Tickell, "Neoliberalizing Space," *Antipode* 34, 3 (2002), pp. 380–404.

and private initiative. The increasing privatization and devolution of planning processes involves the increasing involvement of private real-estate developers in the preparation and realization of land-use zoning plans, the outsourcing of planning assessments and controls to private consultants and practitioners, and, finally, the management of public spaces and of entire urban areas by private entities.[73]

One important dimension of this ongoing process of transformation is the proliferation of what Phil Allmendinger and Graham Haughton have called the "soft spaces" of governance, particularly evident in multi-scalar spatial planning practices and regeneration initiatives. In contrast to "hard" statutory spaces of public administration with their fixed territorial boundaries, "soft spaces" of spatial governance refer to the "in-between" spaces that exist outside, alongside, or parallel with the formal statutory scales of public regulatory authority.[74] Ranging from small-scale spatial planning to multiregional growth strategies, these "soft spaces" often involve the establishment of new private or quasi-private regulatory regimes that sit alongside and potentially challenge existing territorial arrangements or the dominance of particular scales of governance. As Jonathan Metzger and Peter Schmitt have argued, these "soft spaces" constitute new kinds of nonstatutory vehicles for spatial planning – typically informal or semiformal – "with associations and relations stretching both across formally established boundaries and scalar levels of planning and across previously entrenched sectoral divides." In varying degrees, these emergent soft spaces of spatial governance can sometimes supplement and sometimes supplant existing "hard" (i.e., formally recognized and defined in public statues) spatialities of planning.[75]

Soft spaces with fuzzy boundaries have become new instruments for experiments in neoliberal governmentality. By breaking down the old rigid boundaries that characterized conventional regulatory regimes, new forms of neoliberal governmentality have reworked the very nature of planning itself, rendering it less focused on broad, comprehensive visionary schemes and more

---

73 Phil Allmendinger and Graham Haughton, "Spatial Planning, Devolution, and New Planning Spaces," *Environment and Planning C* 28, 5 (2010), pp. 803–818; Dan Greenwood and Peter Newman, "Markets, Large Projects and Sustainable Development: Traditional and New Planning in the Thames Gateway," *Urban Studies* 47, 1 (2010), pp. 105–119. See also Graham Haughton, Phil Allmendinger, David Counsell, and Geoff Vigar, *New Spatial Planning: Territorial Management with Soft Spaces and Fuzzy Boundaries* (New York and London: Routledge, 2010).

74 Allmendinger and Haughton, "Soft Spaces, Fuzzy Boundaries and Metagovernance," pp. 617–633. See also Graham Haughton and Phil Allmendinger, "The Soft Spaces of Local Economic Development," *Local Economy* 23, 2 (1998), pp. 138–148; and Phil Allmendinger and Graham Haughton, "Critical Reflections on Spatial Planning," *Environment and Planning A* 41, 11 (2009), pp. 2544–2599.

75 Jonathan Metzger and Peter Schmitt, "When Soft Spaces Harden: The EU Strategy for the Baltic Sea Region," *Environment and Planning A* 44, 2 (2012), pp. 263–280 (quotation from pp. 265–266).

concerned with pragmatic negotiations around practical considerations of the "sensible" and the "necessary" in the context of the seeming inevitability of market-oriented kinds of policy rationality. This narrowing of the analytic horizons of planning practice has made it virtually impossible to offer an alternative to what has become the new mainstream paradigm.[76]

The concern for more flexible and responsive planning regimes goes along with the search for a greater involvement of private real-estate developers in the production and implementation of property development plans. The creation of various legal instruments, like planned unit developments (PUDs), tax incremental financing (TIFs), Urban Development Corporations (UDCs), and various other kinds of quasi-autonomous NGOs operating outside of existing municipal regulatory regimes, have in effect institutionalized, and enriched, the practice of privatizing the planning process. At the same time, various exceptions to existing planning regulations, including zoning variances, interim development controls, and incentive zoning, transfer authority from the hands of public authorities to those of private developers.[77] Incorporated into local zoning ordinances, such instruments as PUDs and TIFs give real-estate developers the extraordinary latitude to come forward with their own proposals for street patterns, lot layouts, and land use on any large parcel of land.[78] Such soft space experiments in administrative and spatial deregulation as Enterprise Zones (EZs), empowerment zones and enterprise communities (EZ/ECs), and Simplified Planning Zones (SPZs) have circumvented existing regulatory frameworks, while such entities as Urban Development Corporations (UDCs) have shifted planning powers from elected local authorities to business-led boards, appointed commissions, and special agencies.[79] Finally, a range of financial instruments, like tax credits, bond provisions, and tax exemptions to individuals and businesses, have provided extra incentives that subsidize fresh investments in designated zones of the city while bypassing others.[80]

---

[76] See Graham Haughton, Phil Allmendinger, and Stijn Oosterlynck, "Spaces of Neoliberal Experimentation: Soft Spaces, Postpolitics, and Neoliberal Governmentality," *Environment and Planning A* 45, 1 (2013), pp. 217–234 (esp. p. 231).

[77] Jerold Kayden, *Privately Owned Public Space: The New York City Experience* (New York: Wiley, 2000); and Booth, "Partnerships and Networks," pp. 257–269.

[78] See, for example, Anthony DePalma, David Slade, and Craig Whitaker, *Reclaiming the Waterfront – A Planning Guide for Waterfront Municipalities* (Hoboken, NJ: Fund for a Better Waterfront, 1996).

[79] Graham Haughton, "Trojan Horse or White Elephant? The Contested Biography of the Life and Times of the Leeds Development Corporation," *Town Planning Review* 70 (1999), pp. 173–190; and Graham Haughton and Phil Allmendinger, "Spatial Planning and the New Localism," *Planning Practice and Research* 28, 1 (2013), pp. 1–5; and Phil Allmendinger and Graham Haughton, "The Evolution and Trajectories of English Spatial Governance: 'Neoliberal' Episodes in Planning," *Planning Practice and Research* 28, 1 (2013), pp. 6–26.

[80] Kevin Fox Gotham, "Mechanisms of Mutation: Policy Mobilities and the Gulf Opportunity (GO) Zone," *Urban Geography* 35, 8 (2014), pp. 1171–1195.

This shift toward the creation of experimental deregulatory spaces has meant that practices of exception, both within and beyond the confines of existing legal frameworks, have become a new system of flexible and fuzzy governance that relies on parallel networks, *ad hoc* rule-bending, and informal delivery mechanisms.[81] Public authorities have increasingly turned to making "exceptions" to their legally instituted practices of territorial administration and spatial zoning in order to gain a competitive advantage in the global economy through the selective *ad hoc* management of urban space.[82] Instruments such as "spot zoning," that is, obtaining a site-specific exceptions to the rules that generally govern height, density, parking spaces, uses, and other features of street life, effectively hollow out existing regulatory frameworks.[83] The creation of such coordinating mechanisms as public–private partnerships to oversee the construction of large-scale urban redevelopment projects almost invariably rely upon "exceptionality" measures, such as the relaxation of conventional planning tools, bypassing statutory regulations and institutional bodies, the creation of "project agencies" with special or exceptional powers of intervention and decision-making.[84] These privatized governance regimes "lie at the margins" of conventional statutory planning, and they involve a "significant redistribution of policymaking powers, competencies, and responsibilities to quasi-private and highly autonomous organizations."[85]

The steady accumulation of "spaces of exception" has greatly undermined any reference to a standard benchmark from which exceptionality serves as a deviation. In this sense, exceptionality has become the norm. As Mariana Valverde has argued, zoning regulations are the "state of exception that becomes the rule." The very structure of the legal system, that is, its regulatory architecture, encourages a constant proliferation of discretionary, site-specific exceptions and rules that apply only to micro-spaces. At first glance, this withering array of special allowances creates the Orwellian impression of inconsistency and confusion, while in the long run, they actually conceal deliberate strategies that serve narrow interests outside the glare of public scrutiny. The incredibly cumbersome and geographically limited character of the land use planning and zoning rules "make more general, policy-driven, rational, city-wide change difficult if not impossible."[86]

[81] Idalina Baptista, "Practices of Exception in Urban Governance: Reconfiguring Power inside the State," *Urban Studies* 50, 1 (2013), pp. 37–52 (esp. p. 40). See also Desfor and Jørgensen, "Flexible Urban Governance," pp. 479–496.

[82] Aihwa Ong, *Neoliberalism as Exception: Mutations in Citizenship and Sovereignty* (Durham, NC: Duke University Press, 2006).

[83] Mariana Valverde, "Laws of the Street," *City & Society* 21, 2 (2009), pp. 163–181 (esp. p. 176).

[84] Erik Swyngedouw, Frank Moulaert, and Arantxa Rodriguez, "Neoliberal Urbanization in Europe: Large-Scale Urban Development Projects and the New Urban Policy," *Antipode* 34, 3 (2002), pp. 542–577 (esp. p. 543).

[85] Swyngedouw, Moulaert, and Rodriguez, "Neoliberal Urbanization in Europe," pp. 572, 556 (source of quotations).

[86] Valverde, "Laws of the Street," pp. 175, 176 (source of quotations).

Governing Territory Instead of Disciplining People

At the start of the twenty-first century, the expansion and entrenchment of entrepreneurial modes of urban governance have gone hand-in-hand with a shift of emphasis – sometimes subtle and invisible, and sometimes dramatic and very visible – toward the management and control of space instead of "improving" (and reforming) populations.[87] In the classical Foucauldian formulation, disciplinary tactics focused on fixing people in their proper place, classifying them into discrete populations, and acting upon them via a balance between incentives and "punishments." The adoption of these disciplinary techniques – which Michel Foucault referred to as "transform[ing] the confused, useless or dangerous multitudes into ordered multiplicities" – constituted the primary (yet certainly not exclusive) mode of urban governance that prevailed at the dawn of modernist city building and persisted beyond.[88] For Foucault, the technologies of power were inextricably linked with processes of subjectification – or the constitution of compliant subjects through monitoring of the "conduct of conduct."[89]

This shift in urban governance from the stress on the production of compliant social subjects to the regulation of territory amounts to a wholesale reconfiguration of the relationship between power and place. In what Seth Schindler has referred to as "entering a territorial moment," the management of space, rather than the control of populations, has become "the overriding objective of urban governance."[90] These territory-based urban governance regimes are increasingly geared toward the transformation of urban space itself where material infrastructures, architecture, and the built environment seem to take on a life of their own in regulating the use and occupation of urban landscapes.[91]

The transformation in the logic of urban governance does not necessarily entail a radical break where one disciplinary mode of regulation displaces another.[92] This shift in emphasis in urban governance is not to suggest that the

---

[87] Seth Schindler, "Governing the Twenty-First Century Metropolis and Transforming Territory," *Territory, Politics, Governance* 3, 1 (2015), pp. 7–26 (quotations from p. 7).

[88] Michel Foucault, *Discipline and Punish: The Birth of the Prison* [Translated by Alan Sheridan] (New York: Vintage, 1979), p. 148.

[89] Michel Foucault, "The Subject and the Power," in Hubert Dreyfus and Paul Rabinow (eds.), *Michel Foucault: Beyond Structuralism and Hermeneutics* (Brighton: Harvester, 1982), pp. 208–226. See also Michel Foucault, "Space, Knowledge, and Power (interview with Paul Rabinow)," in Michael Hays (ed.), *Architecture Theory Since 1968* (Cambridge, MA: The MIT Press, 1998), pp. 428–439 (esp. p. 430).

[90] Schindler, "Governing the Twenty-First Century Metropolis and Transforming Territory," pp. 10, 12 (source of quotations).

[91] Tania Murray Li, *The Will to Improve: Governmentality, Development and the Practice of Politics* (Durham: Duke University Press, 2007); Tania Murray Li, "To Make Live or Let Die? Rural Dispossession and the Protection of Surplus Populations," *Antipode* 41, S1 (2009), pp. 66–93.

[92] Schindler, "Governing the Twenty-First Century Metropolis and Transforming Territory," p. 20.

production of populations and the making of subservient social subjects has entirely disappeared, but to argue that these formerly dominant modes of regulation assume a subordinate role in the overall management of space.[93] Put in another way, the instrumentalization of architecture and the built environment as integral features undergirding strategies of urban governance does not replace the management of populations but folds into it as a kind of mutually dependent co-presence.[94] The Foucauldian disciplinary techniques appeared in their most dramatic form during the Industrial Revolution and after, when the creation of docile laboring classes and the stress on mass consumption became the twin pillars of industrial capitalism. In contrast, the governance of territory focuses on aestheticizing urban spaces for affluent urban residents who do not wish to rub shoulders with the unwanted and structurally redundant urban poor.[95]

The Erosion of Territorial Sovereignty and the Emergence of Extraterritorial Modes of Urban Governance

The introduction of legal "practices of exception" has become a useful heuristic device through which to delineate new territorialities of rule, thereby providing a convenient platform for the proliferation of extraterritorial zones within cities.[96] Set loose from conventional administrative protocols that oversee the regulation of urban space, these self-contained enclaves operate as autonomous zones that are temporarily or permanently administered in ways different from the rest of the municipal territory. These extraterritorial zones exist as island-like bubbles outside of the conventional framework of laws, borders, and territories, generating radically new forms of urbanism that undermine and dissolve the conventional regulatory powers of public authorities to administer urban space. These kinds of extraterritorial redoubts are metaphorically (if not functionally) akin to Michel Foucault's concept of heterotopia, spaces of otherness that exist primarily as a counterpoint to the normal order of things. For without the presence of conventional modes of law-abiding territorial governance, these extraterritorial zones could not exist. These extraterritorial "free zones" both stretch and manipulate space in order to work around or evade inconvenient rules and regulations.[97]

In seeking to draw attention to such generic sites as airports and other transitory spaces, Marc Augé distinguished between places and nonplaces.

---

[93] Sally Merry, "Spatial Governmentality and the New Urban Social Order: Controlling Gender Violence through Law," *American Anthropologist* 103, 1 (2001), pp. 16–29.

[94] Łukasz Stanek, "Biopolitics of Scale: Architecture, Urbanism, the Welfare State and After," in Jakob Nilsson and Sven-Olov Wallenstein (eds.), *Foucault, Biopolitics, and Governmentality* (Stockholm: Södertörn Philosophical Studies, 2013), pp. 105–122 (especially p. 115).

[95] Schindler, "Governing the Twenty-First Century Metropolis and Transforming Territory," p. 22.

[96] Ideas here are taken from Baptista, "Practices of Exception in Urban Governance," p. 41.

[97] See Jonathan Bach, "Modernity and the Urban Imagination in Economic Zones," *Theory, Culture, & Society* 28, 5 (2011), pp. 98–122.

In a manner analogous to this distinction, extraterritorial enclaves belong to the netherworld of the nonplace urban realm – outside the jurisdiction and scrutiny of public authorities and spaces formed in relation to certain ends or purposes.[98] In trying to make sense of the breakdown of conventional territorial sovereignty, Keller Easterling has employed the concept of the Zone, and has described the tangled political and economic processes that influence and direct the installation of extraterritorial enclaves as Extrastatecraft – literally, statecraft applied to extraterritoriality, but more figuratively, the process of crafting extraterritorial "free zones."[99]

The proliferation of extraterritorial zones marks a clear departure from the conventional view of sovereign territory that consists of a series of more or less homogenous spatial jurisdictions separated by clearly demarcated borders in a continuous spatial flow. The idea of the "archipelago city" is a useful metaphor for drawing attention to the steady increase in the number of discrete extraterritorial zones. These are the spatial expressions of a multiplicity of "states of exception" that are either created through deliberate withdrawal (whereby public authorities abdicate their exclusive regulatory powers or annul existing legal regimes) or that appear *de facto* outside the official sanction of the law. The existence of these extraterritorial spaces challenges or deposes the sovereign powers of public authorities, and as a consequence marks the eclipse of uniform territorial sovereignty.[100]

In the contemporary postsovereign era, the once vital connection between state-sponsored municipal authority and the territorial integrity of the urban landscape has come apart.[101] The introduction of privatized regulatory regimes has produced new kinds of shared sovereignty where intersecting modes of public and private authority are dispersed and decentered. With the existence of extraterritorial spaces, municipal officials no longer have the exclusive authority to define the public administration of urban space or to monopolize the organization of the field of urban planning. New modes of urban governance in the postsovereign era are part of an *ad hoc* landscape consisting of both uninterrupted flows and hindering barriers that both intersect and overlap in complicated ways. The introduction of new regimes of governance signals a blurring between the inside and the outside of authority. These new modes of governance appear less as the installation of physical barriers but more as the

---

[98] Marc Augé, *Non-Places: Introduction to an Anthropology of Supermodernity* [trans. John Howe] (New York: Verso, 1995), pp. 75–115 (esp. p. 94). For an earlier intervention, see Melvin Webber, "The Urban Place and the Nonplace Urban Realm," in *Explorations into Urban Structure* (Philadelphia: University of Pennsylvania Press, 1964), pp. 79–153.

[99] Keller Easterling, "Zone," in Ilka and Andreas Ruby (eds.), *Urban Transformation* (Berlin: Ruby Press, 2008), pp. 30–45.

[100] Baptista, "Practices of Exception in Urban Governance," pp. 37–52.

[101] Saskia Sassen, *Losing Control? Sovereignty in an Age of Globalization* (New York: Columbia University Press, 1996), pp. 29–30.

decline and undermining of public authority over the administration of urban space.[102]

In aspiring world-class cities around the globe, the adoption of entrepreneurial modes of urban governance has gone hand-in-hand with a significant hollowing out and reduction of municipal functions and responsibilities, including relegating to municipal agencies the truncated role of providing increasingly weak regulatory and coordinating roles for the private- and voluntary-sector delivery of services, and the transfer of the mandate for economic and social policy formulation to a mixture of quasi-autonomous, nongovernmental agencies and other nonstate, business-oriented, stakeholder coalitions.[103] This entrepreneurial stance has led to cutbacks in the municipal provision of social welfare, primary services, and noncommodified objects of collective consumption. In contrast to the inclusive and universal support policies that characterized Keynesian and welfare-state interventionism, city builders now seek to achieve economic regeneration with place-bound and spatially targeted redevelopment schemes and projects.[104]

The neoliberal model for managing the city privileges the unitary logic of market-led entrepreneurial solutions to socioeconomic and environmental problems, where advocacy of supposedly universal cures and one-best-way strategic initiatives is benignly labeled "international best practices."[105] The adoption of entrepreneurial modes of urban governance has marked a shift from an emphasis on seeking ways of delivering public services and local resources fairly, efficiently, and effectively toward a focus on bringing together key stakeholders – particularly large-scale, property-owning elites assembled in pro-growth coalitions – to identify common concerns, develop strategic ideas, and generate the necessary momentum to attract the private investment required for urban revitalization. These new modes of urban governance have largely diminished the role and status of overarching, strategic-development frameworks within urban planning initiatives, at a time when the ideological commitment to the principles of entrepreneurialism and market-led growth has become dominant.[106]

---

[102] Xiangming Chen, *As Borders Blend: Transnational Spaces on the Pacific Rim* (New York: Rowman & Littlefield, 2005); and Keller Easterling, *Enduring Innocence: Global Architecture and Its Political Masquerades* (Cambridge, MA: The MIT Press, 2007), pp. 101–102.

[103] The ideas expressed here and in the following paragraphs are derived (sometimes verbatim) from Martin J. Murray, *City of Extremes: The Spatial Politics of Johannesburg* (Durham, NC: Duke University Press, 2011), pp. 248–249, 277–282.

[104] For a wider view, see Bob Jessop, "From Keynesian Welfare State to Schumpeterian Workfare State," in *Towards a Post-Fordist Welfare State*, ed. Roger Burrows and Brian Loader (London: Routledge, 1994), 13–38; and Swyngedouw, Moulaert, and Rodriguez, "Neoliberal Urbanization in Europe," pp. 547–48, 563–564.

[105] Peck and Tickell, "Neoliberalizing Space," pp. 387–388.

[106] Patsy Healey, Stuart Cameron, Simin Davoudi, Stephen Graham, and Ali Madani-Pour, "Challenges for Urban Management," in Patsy Healey, Stuart Cameron, Simin Davoudi, Stephen

The warm embrace of this kind of civic entrepreneurialism has tended to reinforce the hollowing out of hierarchical and functional governance, with the result that relationships between city government and private business have become increasingly horizontal and network-based, involving cooperative arrangements, compromises, and shifting alliances among stakeholders. Indeed, city government – once the key locus for managing public space, integrating service delivery, and choreographing urban relationships – has increasingly become just one of many influential social actors competing for the control of urban planning agendas and access to scarce resources, in an increasingly competitive world of shared power.[107] Boxed into this market-saturated ethos, urban planning practice has largely abandoned its historic role as the regulating agent that looked upon city building as a holistic exercise in rendering the whole greater than the sum of its parts. Instead of fostering the integration of various communities and the equalization of opportunities across the urban landscape, urban planners have assumed the responsibility for promoting the city's entrepreneurial credentials, managing selective developmental initiatives, and "enforcing distinction" between different parts of the city.[108]

A vast array of "in-between" administrative entities – such as public–private partnerships, nonstatutory regulatory bodies, not-for-profit corporate entities, semiautonomous agencies, stakeholder associations, non-govermental organization (NGOs), incorporated property-owner associations, and even religiously affiliated social-service organizations – have replaced branches of city administration, assuming the functions that public municipalities once monopolized as their exclusive preserve. These semiprivate organizations have assumed a great deal of control over the form, shape, culture, and atmosphere of the congregating spaces that they supply and oversee. They have metamorphosed into a kind of ephemeral shadow state, in which power over the management and use of urban space has become not only fragmented and dispersed, but also localized and horizontal.[109]

Framed within the neoliberal paradigm that guides economic regeneration in the postindustrial metropolis, the creation of public–private partnerships has become the most recent magic elixir for fixing cities: promoting economic growth, providing jobs, expanding tax revenues, and creating a dynamic

Graham, and Ali Madani-Pour (eds.), *Managing Cities: The New Urban Context* (Chichester, England: Wiley, 1995), pp. 273–290 (esp. 283–285).

[107] For a wider discussion, see Katharyne Mitchell, "Transnationalism, Neo- Liberalism, and the Rise of the Shadow State," *Economy and Society* 30, 2 (2001), pp. 165–189; and Rachel Weber, "Extracting Value from the City: Neoliberalism and Urban Redevelopment," *Antipode* 34, 3 (2002), pp. 519–540.

[108] Michael Sorkin, "Introduction," in Michael Sorkin (ed.), *Variations on a Theme Park: The New American City and the End of Public Space* (New York: Hill and Wang, 1992), pp. xi–xv (esp. p. xiv).

[109] See Katharyne Mitchell, "The Culture of Urban Space," *Urban Geography* 21, 5 (2000), pp. 443–449.

new image of a vibrant urban landscape. As semiautonomous agencies, these partnerships have enabled local municipalities to allegedly break free from the old, rigid hierarchies of embedded bureaucratic statism, and to adopt a pragmatic and coalition-based "practical politics" in order to address deep-rooted problems of economic underperformance, poor service delivery, social division and fragmentation, and environmental degradation.[110] As powerful tools for reshaping the urban landscape, public–private partnerships represent the collusion of business interests (which want to protect and even extend their profitable property investments in the city) and municipal authorities (which desire to improve the infrastructure and built environment so as to make the city more attractive to users). Generally speaking, public–private partnerships include a familiar repertoire of subsidies, concessions, and guarantees. These typically fall into four broad categories: land acquisition and condemnation, infrastructure upgrades and additions, financing and tax abatements, and incentive zoning (including relaxation of existing bylaws and building regulations).[111]

As semiautonomous agencies operating outside the bureaucratic structures of local government, public–private partnerships are shielded from public scrutiny and direct electoral accountability. Their implementation enables municipal authorities to mobilize local resources and pool private investments, while at the same time reducing their own role in service delivery.[112] As a particular kind of public–private partnership and "networked local governance," Business Improvement Districts (BIDs) are emblematic of the spatial reorganization of urban governance on a global scale. Large-scale property owners – often in league with compliant municipal authorities – have adopted BIDs as a new model of submunicipal governance as a way of securing private capital for improving the attractiveness of central city spaces. Originating from North America (Canada and the United States), the BID model has become the cornerstone for entrepreneurial approaches to downtown revitalization in aspiring world-class cities around the world.[113] Unlike conventional public–private

---

[110] Allan Cochrane, *Whatever Happened to Local Government* (Milton Keynes, England: Open University Press, 1993), p. 120.

[111] John Hannigan, *Fantasy City: Pleasure and Profit in the Postmodern Metropolis* (London: Routledge, 1998), 129, 134–35; and Anastasia Loukaitou-Sideris and Tridib Banerjee, *Urban Design Downtown: Poetics and Politics of Form* (Berkeley: University of California Press, 1998), pp. 103–104.

[112] Jerry Mitchell, "Business Improvement Districts and the Management of Innovation," *American Review of Public Administration* 31, 2 (2001), pp. 201–217; and Jerry Mitchell, "Business Improvement Districts and the 'New' Revitalization of Downtown," *Economic Development Quarterly* 15, 2 (2001), pp. 115–123.

[113] Richard Briffault, "A Government for Our Time? Business Improvement Districts and Urban Governance," *Columbia Law Review* 99, 2 (1999), pp. 365–477; Malcolm Tait and Ole Jensen, "Travelling Ideas, Power, and Place: The Cases of Urban Villages and Business Improvement Districts," *International Planning Studies* 12, 2 (2007), pp. 107–127; and Ian Cook and Kevin Ward, "Conferences, Informational Infrastructures and Mobile Policies: The Process of Getting Sweden 'BID Ready'," *European Urban and Regional Studies* 19, 2 (2012), pp. 137–152.

partnerships, in which urban redevelopment authorities or other coordinating bodies depend upon municipal funding, BIDs are financed exclusively through (legally mandated) internally generated levies. These semiautonomous bodies operate like updated versions of conventional neighborhood business associations. But they also enjoy a sanctioned legal status that entitles property owners, business enterprises, and merchants in designated precincts to voluntarily tax themselves in order to pay for an expanded repertoire of municipal services normally provided by public bodies.[114]

The creation of such public–private partnerships as BIDs marks the gradual dilution and dispersal of public authority. Such semiautonomous, free-floating agencies effectively function as a surrogate "shadow state" administration, assuming responsibilities conventionally reserved for municipal governmental agencies and initiating urban renewal projects that amount to privatized planning of the cityscape. By carving up the urban landscape into what amounts to parcellized sovereignties, these special precincts are exemplary expressions of splintered street management and the stealthy privatization of the urban realm. These new modes of spatial governance have gone hand-in-hand with the erosion of any real semblance of centralized municipal rule. The creation of such corporate-sponsored entities as public–private partnerships, city improvement districts, and nonelected regulatory bodies, along with the privatization of service delivery, has resulted in the disaggregation of power into rival political rationalities, administrative techniques, and everyday practices in microsettings.[115]

The spread and diffusion of BIDs represents an important innovation in neoliberal urban governance. By allowing for the expanded involvement of local business and property owners in managing urban space, these quasi-independent, corporatized entities have significantly redrawn the boundaries between public and private spheres. Above all, BIDs signify the commodification of urban space. More than simply benign tools of urban revitalization, they illustrate how the balance of power in the "entrepreneurial city" has shifted

---

[114] Elisabeth Peyroux, Robert Pütz, and Georg Glasze, "Business Improvement Districts (BIDs): The Internationalization and Contextualization of a 'Travelling Concept'," *European Urban and Regional Studies* 19, 2 (2012), pp. 111–120; and Sophie Didier, Marianne Morange, and Elisabeth Peyroux, "City Improvement Districts and 'Territorialized Neoliberalism' in South African Cities (Johannesburg, Cape Town)," in Jenny Künkel and Margit Mayer (eds.), *Neoliberal Urbanism and its Contestations: Crossing Theoretical Boundaries* (New York: Palgrave, 2012), pp. 119–136.

[115] Kevin Ward, "'Politics in Motion,' Urban Management and State Restructuring: The Trans-Local Expansion of Business Improvement Districts," *International Journal of Urban and Regional Research* 30, 1 (2006), pp. 54–75. See also Lorlene Hoyt, "Importing Ideas: The Transnational Transfer of Urban Revitalization Strategy," *International Journal of Public Administration* 29, 1–3 (2006), pp. 221–243; and Kevin Ward, "Business Improvement Districts: Policy Origins, Mobile Policies, and Urban Liveability," *Geography Compass* 1, 3 (2007), pp. 657–672.

away from public authorities and into the hands of corporate interests.[116] The formation of BIDs has provided a legal framework that empowers large-scale business enterprises and property owners to assume greater responsibility for refurbishment, maintenance, and security within designated areas. Taken at face value, BIDs are exemplary expressions of the turn toward entrepreneurial modes of urban governance in aspiring world-class cities everywhere. While they are decidedly plugged into local dynamics, the establishment of BIDs reflects the global trend toward using so-called enclave development projects as a way of fostering downtown revitalization.[117]

Yet by separating themselves from the surrounding streetscape, BIDs accentuate processes of spatial polarization and social exclusion. This "privatization of urban governance" has resulted in the extension and consolidation of a fragmented urban landscape – a "patchwork city," primarily cobbled together through elite place-making and imagineering.[118] As they have colonized more and more parts of the urban landscape, BIDs have produced what amounts to an archipelago of extraterritorial sovereign spaces where the ordinary functioning of civil protections under the rule of law is suspended and replaced by the discretionary powers of private ownership. It is their apparent banality and feigned innocence that makes the emergence of these kinds of postpublic space so powerful.[119]

Entrepreneurial modes of urban governance have contributed to a kind of feudalized management of urban space, with separate jurisdictions, impermeable boundaries, and hierarchical divisions. The creation of such incorporated entities as public–private partnerships concentrates the authority to shape the urban environment in the hands of an invisible shadow government of special interests, called stakeholders in the neutral-sounding discourse of "good governance." The division of the urban landscape into fortified

---

[116] Elisabeth Peyroux, "City Improvement Districts in Johannesburg: An Examination of the Local Variations of the BID Model," in *Business Improvement Districts: Ein Neues Governance-Modell aus Perspektive von Praxis und Stadtforschung*, ed. Robert Pütz, Geographische Handelsforschung 14 (Passau, Germany: L. I. S. Verlag, 2008), pp. 139–162.

[117] Peyroux, "City Improvement Districts (CIDs) in Johannesburg," pp. 139–141; M. G. Lloyd, John McCarthy, Stanley McGreal, and Jim Berry, "Business Improvement Districts, Planning and Urban Regeneration," *International Planning Studies* 8, 4 (2003), pp. 295–321; Sophie Didier, Marianne Morange, and Elisabeth Peyroux, "The Spreading of the City Improvement District Model in Johannesburg and Cape Town: Urban Regeneration and the Neoliberal Agenda in South Africa," *International Journal of Urban and Regional Research* 36, 5 (2012), pp. 915–935; and Sophie Didier, Marianne Morange, and Elisabeth Peyroux, "The Adaptative Nature of Neoliberalism at the Local Scale: Fifteen Years of City Improvement Districts in Cape Town and Johannesburg," *Antipode* 45, 1 (2013), pp. 121–139.

[118] Swyngedouw, Moulaert, and Rodriguez, "Neoliberal Urbanization in Europe," p. 573 (source of quotation).

[119] See Keller Easterling, "Siting Protocols," in Peter Lang and Tam Miller (eds.), *Suburban Discipline* (New York: Princeton Architectural Press, 1997), pp. 20–31 (esp. p. 21).

encampments – managed by public–private partnerships under the guise of
BIDs and other semi-autonomous regulatory regimes – marks the erosion of
public authority. This new kind of urban management effectively fragments
municipal government into territorial fiefdoms, thereby subordinating comprehensive land-use planning to a wide variety of place-bound private interests.[120]

As a general rule, BIDs display a spatial organization of power and a form
of domination that escape the control and scrutiny of public administration.
By cocooning themselves within regimes of extraterritorial sovereignty, these
corporate-sponsored entities have shifted the powers of city building exclusively into the hands of property owners and real-estate developers, permitting
these profit-seeking stakeholders to shape the cityscape in accordance with their
particular interests. In carrying out the private appropriation of public space,
these spatial enclosures suppress and marginalize those city dwellers who do
not have the money or a specific reason to enter them. While their goal is
to create cleaner and safer zones in the city, BIDs have often contributed to
the partitioning of the urban landscape into boundary-hardened enclaves.[121]
Even though they subscribe to the consoling myth of political innocence and
even-handedness, they symbolize in microcosm the abandonment of the dream
of an open, inclusive city animated by chance encounter. Rather than serving
the neutral-sounding, technocratic ends of urban revitalization, the spread of
BIDs has anchored a postpublic ideological agenda that values the comfort,
safety, and security of well-to-do residents in their islands of prosperity over
the extension of social safety nets for the truly disadvantaged.[122] Because of
their enhanced role in making infrastructural improvements and in providing
services (including security), BIDs have *de facto* converted publicly administered spaces into privately managed ones. As such, they exemplify a sociospatial strategy that values the regeneration of specific places over the needs of the
urban poor who lack jobs and income.[123]

As the material and symbolic embodiments of a new species of disjointed
urbanism, BIDs and their cloned offspring are the quintessential territorial
nodes of a deterritorialized power. Like gated residential communities and

[120] See David Harvey, "From Managerialism to Entrepreneurialism: The Transformation of Urban
Governance in Late Capitalism," *Geografiska Annaler* 71B, 1 (1989), pp. 1–16; and Mitchell,
"Transnationalism, Neo-Liberalism, and the Rise of the Shadow State," pp. 165–189.

[121] See Volker Eick, "The Co-production of Purified Space: Hybrid Policing in German Business
Improvement Districts," *European Urban and Regional Studies* 19, 2 (2012), pp. 121–136.

[122] Elisabeth Peyroux, "Legitimating Business Improvement Districts in Johannesburg: A Discursive Perspective on Urban Regeneration and Policy Transfer," *European Urban and Regional
Studies* 19, 2 (2012), pp. 181–194; and Randy Lippert, "'Clean and Safe' Passage: Business
Improvement Districts, Urban Security Modes, and Knowledge Brokers," *European Urban
and Regional Studies* 19, 2 (2012), pp. 167–180.

[123] Ward, "'Politics in Motion,'" pp. 70–71; and Nadine Marquardt and Henning Füller,
"Spillover of the Private City: BIDs as a Pivot of Social Control in Downtown Los Angeles,"
European Urban and Regional Studies 19, 2 (2012), pp. 153–166.

enclosed office parks, they "thrive in the legal and juridical limbo of extraterritoriality and political quarantine, enjoying the privileges of isolation and declaring their immunity from municipal oversight."[124] On the one side, these spatial enclaves readily accommodate transnational flows of capital, commodities, ideas, and information. Without a real sense of place derived from their particular locality, they are nevertheless "tightly woven into global networks of cosmopolitan worldliness." In order to facilitate uninterrupted connections catering to international business elites and tourist travelers, they offer flexibility and familiarity. On the other side, in order to function effectively, these extraterritorial spaces require immunity and exclusivity within their immediate geographic surroundings. "Because they operate behind a mask of political innocence and feigned neutrality, they are able to blithely carry out their strategy of carving the urban landscape into an assemblage" of self-contained enclaves.[125]

In this new urban geography of extraterritoriality, BIDs aspire to a condition of existence outside the conventional functioning of the law and its consequences, where their own rules and regulations trump municipal codes, bylaws, and enforcement procedures. In the embryonic "postpublic city," the municipal administration no longer has the ultimate power to legislate, arbitrate, and rule in a bounded space over which it claims nominal sovereignty. Because they override the conventional rules of territoriality that are rooted in mainstream modernist models of public administration, BIDs exemplify the triumph of new postliberal modes of urban governance. They operate as voluntary associations or intentional communities, deliberately programmed to legitimate extralegal transactions that bypass the cumbersome regulations of municipal governance.[126]

Despatialization:[127] The Declining Significance of Public Space

Urbanists have long held the view that the physical and social dynamics of public space play a central role in the formation of a robust civic culture,

---

[124] These ideas for these paragraphs are taken from Martin J. Murray, *City of Extremes: The Spatial Politics of Johannesburg* (Durham: Duke University Press, 2011), pp. 278–283 (pp. 280–281, source of quotations). See also Keller Easterling, "Enduring Innocence" (Presentation at the Symposium "Archipelago of Exceptions. Sovereignties of Extraterritoriality," Centre du Cultura Contemporània de Barcelona (CCCB) November 10, 2005. Available at www .publicspace.org/en/text-library/eng/bo19-enduring-innocence.

[125] These ideas are derived (sometimes almost verbatim) from a careful reading of Keller Easterling, *Enduring Innocence: Global Architecture and Its Political Masquerades* (Cambridge: The MIT Press, 2005), pp. 2–4; and Keller Eastering, "The Zone: The Corporate City is the Zone," in Christine de Baan, Joachim Declerk, and Veronique Patteeuw (eds.), *Visionary Power: Producing the Contemporary City* (Rotterdam: NAi Publishers, 2007), pp. 75–86 (esp. p. 75).

[126] These ideas are taken almost verbatim from Murray, *City of Extremes*, p. 281. See also Peyroux, "City Improvement Districts in Johannesburg," pp. 156–58.

[127] The term "despatialization" comes from William Mitchell, *The City of Bits: Space, Place and the Infobahn* (Cambridge, MA: The MIT Press, 1995), pp. 22, 106.

the forging of collective identities, and the animation of popular democracy. As a normative ideal, meaningful public space has long been associated with unencumbered social congregation, freedom of expression, and political liberty. Urban planners and policy experts have looked upon city streets, parks, squares, and other shared spaces of social congregation as symbolic markers of "collective well-being and possibility," sites of chance encounter, and vibrant places of open political deliberation and debate.[128] While urban scholars and planning practitioners have taken widely divergent views in their assessment of the quality of collective achievement across time and space, they have generally not questioned the assumption that a strong and positive relationship exists among urban public space, civic engagement, and participatory politics.[129]

The urban planning profession has long been motivated by "normative ideals about the city, how it should be planned and the necessity to regulate activities in order to meet desired goals, yet within a process that espoused to be in the 'public interest'."[130] Planning experts have always stressed the management of public space in ways that build a vibrant sociality and civic engagement out of the chance encounter between strangers. Urban planning draws on a long lineage of thought, starting with the idealized notion of *agora* so central in classical Greek philosophy and including such theorists of urban modernity as Walter Benjamin, Georg Simmel, and Louis Mumford, and in later years, Henri Lefebvre and Jane Jacobs. Regardless of their differences, these urbanists all suggested a vital link between the vibrancy of urban public space and strength of civic engagement and the strong bonds of citizenship. This lineage is rooted in the claim that the free and unencumbered mingling of urban residents in open, accessible, and well-managed public space encourages tolerance toward difference, a heightened "pleasure in the urban experience, respect for the shared commons, and an interest in civic and political life."[131]

With the neoliberal turn in urban governance, the boundaries between what is private and what is public have become less clear.[132] The triumph of urban entrepreneurialism has meant that the conjoined logics of commodification and privatization have figured prominently as the main driving forces behind the spatial restructuring of urban landscapes. Under the relentless pressure of

---

[128] Ash Amin, "Collective Culture and Urban Public Space," *City* 12, 1 (2008), pp. 5–24 (source of quotation, p. 6).

[129] Peter Marcuse, "From Critical Urban Theory to the Right to the City," *City* 13, 2–3 (2009), pp. 185–196.

[130] Ronan Paddison and Joanne Sharp, "Questioning the End of Public Space: Reclaiming Control of Local Banal Spaces," *Scottish Geographical Journal* 123, 2 (2007), pp. 87–106.

[131] Amin, "Collective Culture and Urban Public Space," p. 6 (source of quotation). See also Steve Hinchliffe and Sarah Whatmore, "Living Cities: Towards a Politics of Conviviality," *Science as Culture* 15, 2 (2006), pp. 123–138; and Henry Shaftoe, *Convivial Public Spaces: Creating Effective Public Places* (London: Earthscan, 2008).

[132] John Clarke, "Dissolving the Public Realm? The Logics and Limits of Neo-liberalism," *Journal of Social Policy* 33, 1 (2004), pp. 27–48.

laissez-faire market liberalism, the simplistic certainties of the hard-and-fast binary dichotomies separating public and private have come apart.[133] This blurring of boundaries – or hybridization of space – "makes it necessary to develop a flexible definition of public space."[134] As Ronan Paddison and Joanne Sharp have argued, "as neoliberal regeneration redefines more and more spaces as private, it becomes ever more important to attend to the public."[135]

Under the conjoined pressures of globalization and neoliberal orthodoxy, city-building approaches to the future of public space have gravitated in opposite directions. On the one hand, city builders have treated public space as a valuable commercial commodity. In partnership with municipal authorities, corporate real-estate developers have tried to reorder the historic functions of public space through the production of new kinds of sanitized "designer space" that operate as sites of social congregation for appropriate users who can afford to consume. As a general rule, globalizing cities with world-class aspirations have found themselves trapped in intense competition to attract outside investment. Under these circumstances, city builders seek to create environments that are safe and attractive, and which offer the range of amenities and facilities that visitors have come to expect.[136] On the other side, in distressed cities with depleted financial resources and limited capacity to effectively manage their own physical assets, public space often suffers from abandonment and neglect.[137]

A combination of social forces, including privatization, excessive policing, and outright neglect, has contributed to the erosion of public space in cities worldwide. As Setha Low, Don Mitchell, and others have argued, privatization of urban public space has accelerated through the closing and redesign of public parks and plazas, the creation of privatized governance bodies like business improvement districts that replace public authority with their own autocratic control over the monitoring of the surrounding streetscape, and the expansion of aggressive policing that has targeted the urban poor.[138]

---

[133] George Varna and Steve Tiesdall, "Assessing the Publicness of Public Space: The Star Model of Publicness," *Journal of Urban Design* 15, 4 (2010), pp. 575–598 (esp. p. 575).

[134] Margaret Kohn, *Brave New Neighbourhoods: The Privatisation of Public Space* (London: Routledge, 2004), p. 11 (source of quotation). See also Jerold Kayden, *Privately Owned Public Spaces: The New York Experience* (New York: Wiley, 2000); and Z. Müge Akkar Ercan, "Public Spaces of Post-industrial Cities and their Changing Roles," *METU Journal of Faculty of Architecture* 24, 1 (2007), pp. 115–137.

[135] Paddison and Sharp, "Questioning the End of Public Space," p. 92.

[136] Ali Madanipour, *Public and Private Spaces of the City* (London: Routledge, 2003), p. 224.

[137] Matthew Carmona, "Contemporary Public Space, Part Two: Classification," *Journal of Urban Design* 15, 2 (2010), pp, 157–173 (esp. p. 158).

[138] Setha Low, "How Private Interests Take over Public Space: Zoning, Taxes, and Incorporation of Gated Communities," in Setha Low and Neil Smith (eds.), *The Politics of Public Space* (New York: Routledge, 2006), pp. 81–103 (quotation from p. 82); Don Mitchell, *The Right to the City: Social Justice and the Fight for Public Space* (New York: Guilford, 2003); Setha Low, "The Erosion of Public Space and the Public Realm: Paranoia, Surveillance and Privatization

Downsizing of municipal services, off-loading of physical assets, and the shrinking fiscal capacity of municipalities has led to the neglect and abandonment of open and accessible public spaces. These in-between, residual, underutilized, derelict, and deteriorating public spaces – what Anastasia Loukaitou-Sideris has called "cracks in the city" – easily turn into "dead spaces" beyond repair.[139] Often accompanied by fear, suspicion, tension, and even conflict between different social groups, these impoverished public spaces easily become "lost spaces," "danger zones," and "no-go" areas for anxious urban residents.[140]

At the same time, urban regeneration strategies under the sign of neoliberal governance have increasingly turned to such postpublic spatial typologies as enclosed shopping malls, privately managed corporate plazas, "invented" commercialized streetscapes (or what Tridib Banerjee has called "streets created as stage sets"), gated residential estates, and themed entertainment sites as key outposts in the reimagined city.[141] These privately managed "designer spaces" have become so commonplace that they can be considered *de rigueur* "naturalized" components of the tourist-entertainment city. With few other options, these pseudo-public places have become increasingly popular destinations for social congregation and chance encounter.[142] Constituting what Steven Flusty has called "interdictory spaces," they create ordered environments in which conformity is an expectation and in which those deemed "unsuitable" or in some way "threatening" are excluded.[143] But these privately managed commercial spaces appear to lead not to diversification but rather to an inward-looking uniformity and conformist consumption.[144] In the name of safety and security,

in New York City," *City & Society* 18, 1 (2006), pp. 43–49; and Anna Minton, *What Kind of World Are We Building? The Privatisation of Public Space* (London: RICS, 2006).

139 Anastasia Loukaitou-Sideris, "Cracks in the City: Addressing the Constraints and Potentials of Urban Design," *Journal of Urban Design* 1, 1 (1996), pp. 91–103 (p. 91, source of quotation; pp. 100–101). See also Gil Doron, "The Dead Zone and the Architecture of Transgression," *City* 42, 2 (2000), pp. 247–263; and Gil Doron, "'...Those Marvelous Empty Zones on the Edge of our Cities': Heterotopia and the 'Dead Zone'," in Michiel Dehaene and Liven de Cauter (eds.), *Heterotopia and the City: Public Space in a Postcivil Society* (New York: Routledge, 2008), pp. 203–214.

140 Wendy Pullan, "Frontier Urbanism: The Periphery at the Centre of Contested Cities," *The Journal of Architecture* 16, 1 (2011), pp. 15–35.

141 Tridib Banerjee, "The Future of Public Space: Beyond Invented Streets and Reinvented Places," *Journal of the American Planning Association* 67, 1 (2001), pp. 9–24 (esp. p. 14). See also Loukaitou-Sideris and Banerjee, *Urban Design Downtown*, pp. 96–98. See also Matthew Carmona and Filipa Matos Wunderlich, *Capital Spaces: The Multiple Complex Public Spaces of a Global City* (New York: Routledge, 2012).

142 M. Christine Boyer, "The City of Illusion: New York's Public Places," in Paul Knox (ed.), *The Restless Urban Landscape* (Eaglewood Cliffs, NJ: Prentice Hall, 1993), pp. 111–126 (esp. pp. 113–114).

143 Steven Flusty, "The Banality of Interdiction: Surveillance, Control, and the Displacement of Diversity," *International Journal of Urban and Regional Research* 25, 3 (2001), pp. 658–664.

144 Elizabeth Wilson, "The Rhetoric of Public Space," *New Left Review* 1/209 (1995), pp. 146–160 (esp. p. 157).

private real-estate developers – aided and abetted by public agencies – have often planned and built networks of underground tunnels, above-ground "sky bridges," and pedestrian walkways to connect these insular corporate spaces. This web-like network of private connections has created what Trevor Boddy has called the "analogous city," or a city of contrived urban spaces that keeps out the poor and undesirables.[145]

The ascendency of entrepreneurial urbanism, the growing popularity of inward-looking building typologies, and the retreat of the propertied classes into sequestered enclaves has gone hand-in-glove with the erosion of open (and readily accessible) public space. In aspiring world-class cities around the globe, urban landscapes have increasingly come to resemble a jumbled collage of "micro-states," consisting of fortified enclaves and sequestered zones separated from the surrounding cityscape and kept under constant surveillance. Gated residential estates for the wealthy offer a full complement of services, ranging from exclusive private schools, golf courses, and leisure-and-entertainment facilities, protected by private police with around-the-clock securities patrols. It is often the case that these sequestered luxury-enclaves exist side-by-side with illegal settlements without proper sanitation or access to services and where infrastructure is rudimentary or broken down.[146] These fragments of a disjointed urbanity function more or less autonomously, where urban residents across these great social divides have become entrenched in ongoing battles over efforts to maintain their privileged comfortable lives, on the one hand, and the everyday struggle to survive, on the other.[147] Under these circumstances, as David Harvey has put it, "ideals of urban identity, citizenship and belonging – already threatened by the spreading malaise of a neoliberal ethic" – become much more difficult to maintain and sustain.[148]

The proliferation of such post-public spaces as enclosed shopping malls, gated residential estates, and fortified office complexes together with the steady expansion of underground parking and shopping facilities with restricted entry, above-ground skywalks that bypass the streets, interior gardens, landscaped atriums, and other sequestered gathering places, has largely usurped the convention role (in the modernist imagination) of town squares, public parks, and

[145] Trevor Boddy, "Underground and Overhead: Building the Analogous City," in Michael Sorkin (ed.), *Variations on a Theme Park* (New York: Noonday Press, 1992), pp. 123–153.

[146] See, for example, Sonia Hirt, *Iron Curtains: Gates, Suburbs and Privatization of Space in the Post-Socialist City* (New York: John Wiley & Sons, 2012).

[147] Marcello Balbo, "Urban Planning and the Fragmented City of Developing Countries," *Third World Planning Review* 15, 1 (1993), pp. 23–35.

[148] David Harvey, *Social Justice and the City* [Revised Edition] (Athens: University of Georgia Press, 2009), p. 324 (source of quotation). See also David Harvey, "The Right to the City," *International Journal of Urban and Regional Research* 27, 4 (2003), pp. 939–941; David Harvey, "The Right to the City," *New Left Review* 53 (2008), pp. 23–40; and Edésio Fernandes, "Constructing the 'Right to the City' in Brazil," *Social and Legal Studies* 16, 2 (2007), pp. 201–219.

downtown sidewalks as desired sites for everyday social interaction. Barriers, walls, and security perimeters are the visible signs of paranoid urbanism and the growing fortress mentality. The rapid spread of enclosed spaces signifies the expansion of postpublic space in the postliberal city.[149]

Because globalization has accelerated the spread of ideas and influences to cities around the world, real-estate developers, design experts, urban planners, and municipal authorities are no longer tied as they have been in the past to particular localities. Instead they operate with greater degrees of freedom across wider regional and global scales.[150] As a consequence, design formulae are often repeated from place to place with little thought to context. This borrowing, mimicking, or even plagiarizing of generic "globalized" design principles has produced a kind of departicularized urbanism, which in turn has gone hand-in-hand with a form of homogenized public space.[151]

Neoliberal policies and practices operate on the principle that private market mechanisms rather than public authorities can more effectively and efficiently manage urban space. The move toward neoliberal modes of urban governance does not necessarily mean a decrease in the amount of open and accessible places for social congregation and chance encounter, yet it does mean a shift in how these postpublic spaces are produced and regulated. A great deal of scholarly attention has been directed at understanding how municipalities enter into contracts – especially, the popular type of hybrid-joint management-ownership model called "public–private partnerships" – that provide opportunities for the private companies to assume greater authority and discretion over the management of public spaces.[152]

In the roseate imaginary of a world-class city, orderly public space represents a kind of proof of modernity. Yet the transformation of public space into "designer landscapes" that aim to sell the city in the image-conscious world of global neoliberalism has gone hand-in-hand with new mechanisms of social exclusion and marginalization of "unwanted" Others. While appearing to be open and inviting, these post-public spaces have often become sites of conflict,

---

[149] See Martin J. Murray, *Taming the Disorderly City: The Spatial Landscape of Johannesburg after Apartheid* (Ithaca: Cornell University Press, 2008), p. 61.

[150] See, for example, Eugene McCann and Kevin Ward, "Introduction: Urban Assemblages, Territories, and Relations, Practices, and Powers," in Eugene McCann and Kevin Ward (eds.), *Mobile Urbanism: Cities and Policymaking in the Global Age* (Minneapolis: University of Minnesota Press, 2011), pp. xiii–xxxv.

[151] Carmona, "Contemporary Public Space, Part Two: Classification," p. 159.

[152] Jeremy Németh, "Defining a Public: The Management of Privately Owned Public Space," *Urban Studies* 46, 1 (2009): 2463–2490; Tridip Banerjee, "The Future of Public Space: Beyond Invented Streets and Reinvented Places," *Journal of the American Planning Association* 67, 1 (2001), pp. 9–24; Jeremy Németh and Stephan Schmidt, "Toward a Methodology for Measuring the Security of Publicly Accessible Spaces," *Journal of the American Planning Association* 73, 3 (2007), pp. 283–297; Jeremy Németh and Justin Hollander, "Security Zones and New York City's Shrinking Public Space," *International Journal of Urban and Regional Research* 34, 1 (2010), pp. 20–34.

rivalry, and contestation over what is considered their "proper" and "appropriate" use.[153]

In relatively poor cities where high degrees of poverty and class stratification are the norm, mushrooming informal street economies have heightened tensions among various social groupings regarding who is entitled to use the public spaces of the city and for what purposes, pitting property owners, local retail establishments, upscale consumers, and municipal authorities, on the one side, against street vendors, itinerant traders, and ambulant work-seekers, on the other. In those aspiring world-class cities that struggle with high rates of unemployment and widespread impoverishment, affluent urban residents often subscribe to an aesthetic sensibility and an image of social congregating spaces that does not include itinerant street trading and other informal activities.[154] In seeking to "appropriately develop" and to "modernize" the public spaces of their cities, municipal authorities have more often than not imposed strict rules and regulations that place limitations on the legitimate uses of city streets, parks, and other social gathering places.[155] Yet those who depend upon these ostensibly public spaces for their socioeconomic survival have found ways to circumvent deliberate efforts to remove and displace them.[156]

Generally speaking, people who conduct trade on sidewalks and other public gathering places have been subjected to a tightly regulated world of spatial restrictions, bureaucratic challenges, and legal impediments. Because their efforts to eke out a living often fall outside the framework of legal protections, street vendors are vulnerable to harassment and intimidation, and subjected to fines, prosecution, and confiscation of their trading goods.[157] Yet for the most part, these draconian measures have not produced the intended results. The

---

[153] See, for example, Veronica Crossa, "Resisting the Entrepreneurial City: Street Vendors' Vendors' Struggle in Mexico City's Historic Center," *International Journal of Urban and Regional Research* 33, 1 (2009), pp. 43–63.

[154] See, for example, Veronique Dupont, "The Dream of Delhi as a Global City," *International Journal of Urban and Regional Research* 35, 3 (2011), pp. 533–554.

[155] See Ray Bromley, "Street Vending and Public Policy: A Global Review," *International Journal of Sociology and Social Policy* 20, 1 (2000), pp. 1–29; Alfonso Morales, "Conclusion: Law, Deviance, and Defining Vendors and Vending," in John Cross and Alfonso Morales (eds.), *Street Entrepreneurs: People, Place and Politics in Local and Global Perspectives* (New York: Routledge, 2007), pp. 262–269; John Cross and Marina Karides, "Capitalism, Modernity, and the 'Appropriate' Use of Space," in *Street Entrepreneurs*, pp. 19–35 (esp. p. 19); and Mike Douglass and Amrita Danière, "Urbanization and Civic Space in Asia," in Amrita Danière and Mike Douglass (eds.), *The Politics of Civic Space in Asia: Building Urban Communities* (London & New York: Routledge, 2009), pp. 1–18; and Rodrigo Meneses-Reyes and José A Caballero-Juárez, "The Right to Work on the Street: Public Space and Constitutional Rights," *Planning Theory* 13, 4 (2014), pp. 370–386.

[156] Kate Swanson, "Revanchist Urbanism Heads South: The Regulation of Indigenous Beggars and Street Vendors in Ecuador," *Antipode* 39, 4 (2007), pp. 708–728.

[157] John Cross, *Informal Politics: Street Vendors and the State in Mexico City* (Stanford, CA: Stanford University Press, 1998); John Cross, "Pirates on the High Streets: The Street as a Site of Local Resistance of Globalization," in *Street Entrepreneurs*, pp. 125–144; and Lisa

regulation of street-vending activities has contributed to the construction of "an ideal hierarchy of would-be social agents in public spaces by consecrating the distinction between authorized and unauthorized street users." These regulatory strategies seem to condemn them to work at the margins of the places where they are not welcome. However, neither their daily mobility nor their spatial location is restricted to the letter of the law. Yet street traders who have been defined as out of place in the urban realm often manage to circumvent regulatory restrictions, finding ways to reconstitute themselves as "'mobile' actors in order to 'stay' in the spaces from which they were originally displaced."[158] Despite the vigilance of municipal authorities, the filtered spaces of the neoliberal city are porous, permeable, malleable, and pliable.[159] Street vendors in cities as distinct and different as Mexico City and Baguio City (Philippines) have developed strategies to evade, circumvent, or negotiate restrictions on their trade, thereby challenging municipal regulations that privilege the kinds of regular wage-paying work that fits with the boosterist image of progress and development.[160]

In Buenos Aires, for example, shifting modes of municipal governance have converted public space into a sort of visual spectacle, an ethereal space that provides the illusion of genuine social mixing, thereby masking the reality of the space itself as accessible to only a privileged few.[161] Similarly, municipal authorities in Bogota (Columbia) have engaged in concerted efforts to reclaim valued public spaces from ambulant street vendors in order to preserve them as privileged sites for citizen participation. These strategies of urban governance depend upon defining the problem of social congregating space as one of uncertainty and unruliness caused by the "invasion" of unwanted street vendors who bring their disorderly "culture of informality" into places of respectable social interaction and exchange. The use of particular spatial technologies of governance – what Stacey Hunt has called "recuperation-relocation" – has sought to

---

Drummond, "Street Scenes: Practices of Public and Private Space in Urban Vietnam," *Urban Studies* 37, 12 (2000), pp. 2377–2391.

[158] Rodrigo Meneses-Reyes, "Out of Place, Still in Motion: Shaping (Im)Mobility Through Urban Regulation," *Social & Legal Studies* 22, 3 (2013), pp. 335–356 (quotations from p. 335).

[159] Jeremy Németh, "Defining a Public: The Management of Privately Owned Public Space," *Urban Studies* 46,11 (2009), pp. 2463–2490; and Lisa Law, "Defying Disappearance: Cosmopolitan Public Spaces in Hong Kong," *Urban Studies* 39, 9 (2002), pp. 1625–1645.

[160] B. Lynne Milgram, "Reconfiguring Space, Mobilizing Livelihood: Street Vending, Legality, and Work in the Philippines," *Journal of Developing Societies* 27, 3&4 (2011), pp. 261–293; Veronica Crossa, "Reading for Difference on the Street: De-homogenising Street Vending in Mexico City," *Urban Studies* 53, 2 (2016), pp. 287–301; and Meneses-Reyes, "Out of Place, Still in Motion," pp. 335–356.

[161] Emanuela Guano, "Spectacles of Modernity: Transnational Imagination and Local Hegemonies in Neoliberal Buenos Aires," *Cultural Anthropology* 17, 2 (2002), pp. 181–209; Pírez, "Buenos Aires," pp. 145–158; and Garrett Strain, "Neighborhood and Nation in Neoliberal Times: Urban Upheaval, Resistance, and National Identity in Buenos Aires," *intersections* 12, 1 (2012), pp. 14–91.

minimize the threat that street vendors present to upstanding citizens by relocating these unwanted "space invaders" to state-controlled markets in marginal and spatially segregated settings where they are inculcated with the kinds of formalized market discipline necessary to disabuse them of their backward "culture of informality." These technologies, in turn, have created new kinds of urban segregation in which citizens and street vendors are slotted into "differentiated places and rights to mobility."[162] These efforts to maximize the privileged access for socially responsible users to these social gathering places – while simultaneously eliminating the mobility of street vendors – creates a binary conception of citizenship where the rights of the respectable users trump the rights of the unwanted.[163] Invisibility is a crucial feature of modern inequality.[164] Framed as improving the quality of public space in order to make it safe and desirable for citizen participation, this concerted effort to create sanitized places has become a key component in the strategy of selling the city as world class.[165]

In globalizing cities with world-class aspirations, the maintenance of order in post-public spaces of social congregation oscillates between physical force and quiet persuasion. The mechanics of exclusion of the unwanted urban poor from upscale sites of privilege reveal the complicated nature of civic belonging in poor cities with high degrees of class stratification.[166] By using available public space as a site for informal trading and petty entrepreneurship, poor and the marginalized groups encroach upon the aesthetic expectations of respectable and proper urban citizens. Informality and its shadow legality

---

[162] Stacey Hunt, "Citizenship's Place: The State's Creation of Public Space and Street Vendors' Culture of Informality in Bogota, Columbia," *Environment and Planning* D 27, 2 (2009), pp. 331–351 (esp. 332, 337, 340 [p. 331, source of quotation]).

[163] Hunt, "Citizenship's Place," pp. 331–332; and Michael Donovan, "Informal Cities and the Contestation of Public Space: The Case of Bogota's Street Vendors, 1988–2003,",*Urban Studies* 45, 1 (2008), pp. 29–51. For Ho Chi Minh City, see Eric Harms, "Eviction Time in the New Saigon: Temporalities of Displacement in the Rubble of Development," *Cultural Anthropology* 28, 2 (2013), pp. 344–368.

[164] Wilson, "The Rhetoric of Public Space," p. 158.

[165] Rachel Berney, "Pedagogical Urbanism: Creating Citizen Space in Bogotá Colombia," *Planning Theory* 10, 16 (2011), pp. 16–34; and Eric Harms, "Beauty as Control in the New Saigon: Eviction, New Urban Zones, and Atomized Dissent in a Southeast Asian City," *American Ethnologist* 39, 4 (2012), pp. 735–750.

[166] Rachel Berney, "Public Space versus Tableau: The Right-to-the-City Paradox in Neoliberal Bogota, Columbia," in Tony Samara, Shenjing He, and Guo Chen (eds.), *Locating Right to the City in the Global South* (New York: Routledge, 2013), pp. 152–170; Ryan Centner, "Distinguishing the Right Kind of City: Contentious Urban Middle Classes in Argentina, Brazil, and Turkey," in *Locating Right to the City in the Global South*, pp. 247–263; and Christine Hentshel, "City Ghosts: The Haunted Struggles for Downtown Durban and Berlin Neukölln," in *Locating Right to the City in the Global South*, pp. 195–218; David Walker, "Resisting the Neoliberalization of Space in Mexico City," in *Locating Right to the City in the Global South*, pp. 171–194; and Ryan Centner, "Microcitizenships: Fractious Forms of Urban Belonging after Argentine Neoliberalism," *International Journal of Urban and Regional Research*, 36, 2 (2012), pp. 336–362.

undermine the proper use of public space, and thereby trigger the reaction of middle-class citizens who have tried to claim these open places of social congregation as their own.[167] In globalizing cities with world-class aspirations, newly minted "designer landscapes" have become battlegrounds for enacting new dramas of competition between the urban poor who seek a tenuous place in the city as informal street vendors and middle-class groups aspiring to comfortable lifestyles in the newly refurbished public spaces of the city.[168]

The Right to the City: Urban Space and Social Justice

Recent research and writing on cities around the world has substantially unsettled conventional notions of urban space/place, belonging, and citizenship.[169] Once thought of as relatively fixed, stable, and durable, these concepts have been subjected to a significant degree of bending, blending, and stretching. While they may be helpful as convenient points of departure, such binary categorizations as "inclusion" versus "exclusion," "private space" versus "public space," and "citizen" versus "subject" takes us only so far in understanding the complex dynamics that produce everyday precariousness in relatively poor cities around the globe. For instance, the theorization of such fuzzy relationships as "insurgent citizenship,"[170] "flexible citizenship,"[171] "active citizenship," [172] "differential citizenship,"[173] and "microcitizenship"[174] has drawn attention to the malleability of rights and entitlements in the use of urban space. With the shift from (managerial) government to (neoliberal) governance, many of the functions once reserved for public authorities have been absorbed by a burgeoning nonstate sector that largely consists of NGOs and other

[167] Clifton Evers and Kirsten Seale, " Informal Urban Street Markets: International Perspectives," in Clifton Evers and Kirsten Seale (eds.), *Informal Urban Street Markets: International Perspectives* (New York: Routledge, 2015), pp. 1–16.

[168] Emanuela Guano, "The Denial of Citizenship: 'Barbaric' Buenos Aires and the Middle-class Imaginary," *City & Society* 16 (2004), pp. 69–97.

[169] Lynn Staeheli, "Political Geography: Where's Citizenship?" *Progress in Human Geography* 35, 3 (2011), pp. 393–400.

[170] James Holston, "Spaces of Insurgent Citizenship," in James Holston and Arjun Appudurai (ed.), *Cities and Citizenship* (Durham, NC: Duke University Press, 1999), pp. 155–173; James Holston, *Insurgent Citizenship: Disjunctions of Democracy and Modernity in Brazil* (Princeton, NJ: Princeton University Press, 2007); and James Holston, "Insurgent Citizenship in an Era of Global Urban Peripheries," *City & Society* 21, 2 (2009), pp. 245–267.

[171] Aihwa Ong, *Flexible Citizenship: The Cultural Logics of Transnationality* (Durham, NC: Duke University Press, 1999); and Aihwa Ong, *Neoliberalism as Exception: Mutations in Citizenship and Sovereignty* (Durham, NC: Duke University Press, 2006).

[172] Faranak Miraftab and Shana Wills, "Insurgency and the Spaces of Active Citizenship: The Story of the Western Cape Anti-Eviction Campaign in South Africa," *Journal of Planning Education and Research* 25, 2 (2000), pp. 200–217.

[173] Robert Lake and Kathe Newman, "Differential Citizenship in the Shadow State," *GeoJournal* 58, 2–3 (2002), pp. 109–120.

[174] Centnar, "Microcitizenships," pp. 336–362.

not-for-profit entities. Taken together, these organized groups form what amounts to a "shadow state" increasingly responsible for social service delivery and community development. The "shadow state" consists of a wide constellation of NGOs that have assumed duties, responsibilities, and tasks that the retreating state administration has jettisoned under pressure to downsize and offload service provision.[175]

Under circumstances where city officials are really not much more than accomplices of private enterprise, and where urban planning in the public interest is inextricably interlocked with private interests, NGOs have become important tertiary stakeholders in soft planning and service provision. The failure of the market to deliver affordable services and the inability of public authorities to provide for basic needs makes NGOs important secondary agents of caregiving and social development. In this scenario, civil society has become an important third sector outside the realm of private enterprise and the state administration. The "Civil Society Empowerment" initiatives have focused almost entirely on NGOs.[176] By virtue of their relatively independent stance and non-for-profit status (along with and their links to poor communities), NGOs have become key points of entry into civil society.[177] Where downsizing and offloading have effectively reduced the room for maneuver of municipal authorities, non-for-profit organizations have often taken up the slack, engaged in a wide range of activities once reserved for the public administration of the city. The transfer of responsibilities to nonprofit organizations has resulted in uneven accessibility to services and an outright reduction in access to some individuals. The rise of the "shadow state" has produced gaps in the spatial coverage of social services as well as uneven access of citizens to service providers and thus to citizenship.[178]

The dependence of urban residents on the "shadow state" results in differential citizenship or selective disenfranchisement.[179] In theorizing the rupture of

---

[175] Dan Trudeau, "Constructing Citizenship in the Shadow State," *Geoforum* 43, 3 (2012), pp. 442–452.

[176] Md. Manjur Morshed and Yasushi Asami, "The Role of NGOs in Public and Private Land Development: The Case of Dhaka City," *Geoforum* 60 (2015), pp. 4–13.

[177] Kendall Stiles, "International Support for NGOs in Bangladesh: Some Unintended Consequences," *World Development* 30, 5 (2002), pp. 835–846 (esp. 835–836); and Dan Trudeau, "Junior Partner or Empowered Community? The Role of Nonprofit Social Service Providers amidst State Restructuring," *Urban Studies* 45, 13 (2008), pp. 2805–2827.

[178] Brian Turner, "The Erosion of Citizenship," *British Journal of Sociology* 52, 2 (2001), pp. 189–209; Nicholas Fyfe, "Making Space for 'Neo-communitarianism'? The Third Sector, State and Civil Society in the UK," *Antipode* 37, 3 (2005), pp. 536–557; and Nicholas Fyfe and Christine Milligan, "Space, Citizenship, and Voluntarism: Critical Reflections on the Voluntary Welfare Sector in Glasgow," *Environment and Planning A* 35, 11 (2003), pp. 2069–2086.

[179] Lake and Newman, "Differential Citizenship in the Shadow State," pp. 109–120; Dan Trudeau and Luisa Veronis, "Enacting State Restructuring: NGOs as Translation Mechanisms," *Environment and Planning D* 27, 6 (2006), pp. 117–134; and Dan Trudeau, "Towards a Relational View of the Shadow State," *Political Geography* 27, 6 (2008), pp. 669–690.

various forms of social belonging, Robert Castel has developed the concept of "disaffiliation" to unpack the "cumulative logic of deprivation" where "economic insecurity becomes destitution and fragility of relationships becomes isolation."[180] Working with this concept of "disaffiliation" – or the dissociation of the conventional social bonds that tie urban residents to the social worlds around them – enables us to theorize the differential inclusion of the urban poor into the mainstream of urban life along the dimensions of access to regular work, to decent housing, and to the protective shield of state assistance.[181]

The assertive claim of a "right to the city" provides a powerful normative framework to support extralegal occupation of land, unauthorized trading in public streets and thoroughfares, squatting in abandoned buildings, infringement of property rights, idling in public places, and self-built housing outside existing formal building codes by poor urban dwellers.[182] Assertions of a "right to the city" are entangled with questions of citizenship, belonging, and social justice. As David Harvey has argued, "The right to the city is far more than the individual liberty to access urban resources: it is a right to change ourselves by changing the city."[183]

A great deal of urban scholarship has focused attention on how otherwise marginalized and deprived urban residents carve out spaces for themselves in the city through improvisation, stealth and subterfuge, and sheer persistence.[184] James Holston, for example, uses the framework of "insurgent citizenship" to underscore how the urban poor of São Paulo and Brasília engage in a wide variety of clandestine or semiclandestine tactics that place them outside the

---

[180] Robert Castel, "The Roads to Disaffiliation: Insecure Work and Vulnerable Relationships," *International Journal of Urban and Regional Research* 24, 3 (2000), pp. 519–535 (quotations from pp. 534, 520).

[181] Castel, "The Roads to Disaffiliation," p. 520.

[182] Mona Fawaz, "Neoliberal Urbanity: A View from Beirut's Periphery," *Development and Change* 40, 5 (2009), pp. 827–852 (esp. p. 827); Mona Fawaz, "Hezbollah as Urban Planner? Questions to and from Planning Theory," *Planning Theory* 8, 4 (2009), pp. 323–334; Susan Parnell and Edgar Pieterse, "The 'Right to the City': Institutional Imperatives of a Developmental State," *International Journal of Urban and Regional Research* 34, 1 (2010), pp. 146–162; Ananya Roy, "The 21st Century Metropolis: New Geographies of Theory," *Regional Studies* 43, 6 (2009), pp. 819–830; Ananya Roy, "Civic Governmentality: The Politics of Inclusion in Beirut and Mumbai," *Antipode* 41, 1 (2009), pp. 159–179.

[183] Harvey "The Right to the City," p. 23.

[184] Abdoumaliq Simone, "Straddling the Divides: Remaking Associational Life in the Informal African City," *International Journal of Urban and Regional Research* 25, 1 (2001), pp. 102–117; Abdoumaliq Simone, "Resource of Intersection: Remaking Social Collaboration in Urban Africa," *Canadian Journal of African Studies* 37, 2–3 (2003), pp. 513–538; Abdoumaliq Simone, *For the City Yet to Come: Urban Life in Four African Cities* (Durham, NC: Duke University Press, 2004); Abdoumaliq Simone, "People as Infrastructure: Intersecting Fragments in Johannesburg," *Public Culture* 16, 3 (2005), pp. 407–429; Abdoumaliq Simone, "Pirate Towns: Reworking Social and Symbolic Infrastructures in Johannesburg and Douala," *Urban Studies* 43, 2 (2006), pp. 357–370; and Eric Harms, "Knowing into Oblivion: Clearing Wastelands and Imagining Emptiness in Vietnamese New Urban Zones," *Singapore Journal of Tropical Geography* 35 (2014), pp. 312–327.

protections of the law.[185] Along with others, Holston draws on the path-breaking work of Henri Lefebvre who developed the notion of the "the right to the city."[186] The shaping of insurgent public space suggests a mode of city making that is different from institutionalized approaches to city building and their association with master planning and official policymaking. Unlike the conventional practice of urban planning, the making of insurgent public space implies that social groups and individuals can play a distinct role in shaping urban landscapes in defiance of official rules and regulations.[187]

Partha Chatterjee distinguishes between claims for a rightful place in the city that arise from two distinct groups of persons: on the one side, between citizens (i.e., urban residents who operate within the domain of what liberal political theorists call "civil society"), and on the other side, subaltern populations (or urban dwellers whose demands fall outside the realm of legal subjectivity). Well-to-do urban residents who enjoy the full rights and benefits of citizenship have a range of state-legitimated, institutionalized channels open to them through which they are able to pursue their material and symbolic interests. In contrast, subaltern populations have little choice but to transgress the strict lines of legality in their everyday struggles to live and work.[188] Chatterjee argues that this vast domain of political practices that fall outside the hegemonic Western notions of state authority and civil society need to be theorized as a separate category – an arena of contestation which he calls "political society."[189] This sphere of activities, which often take place outside of official legal sanction, nevertheless contribute to popular contestation and hence exert a significant degree of influence over everyday life in ways that fundamentally compromise the goals of modernist rational planning.[190]

While Chatterjee may not have suggested this formulation, making a distinction between citizens (as privileged insiders) and populations (as excluded outsiders) enables us to unpack the hierarchical modalities of urban governmentality, that is, to distinguish between those who have a legitimate right to claim rights and, conversely, those who are suspended in a lawless, extralegal limbo, unable to call upon the law for support yet simultaneously subjected to

---

[185] James Holston, *Insurgent Citizenship: Disjunctions of Democracy and Modernity in Brazil* (Princeton, NJ: Princeton University Press, 2007); and James Holston, "Insurgent Citizenship in an Era of Global Urban Peripheries," *City & Society* 21, 2 (2009), pp. 245–67.

[186] Henri Lefebvre, *Writings on Cities* (Cambridge, MA: Blackwell, 1996); and Henri Lefebvre, *The Urban Revolution* (Minneapolis: University of Minnesota Press, 2003).

[187] Jeffrey Hou, "(Not) your Everyday Public Space," in Jeffrey Hou, (ed.), *Insurgent Public Space: Guerrilla Urbanism and the Remaking of Contemporary Cities* (New York: Routledge, 2010), pp. 1–18 (esp. p. 15).

[188] Partha Chatterjee, *Politics of the Governed: Reflections on Popular Politics in Most of the World* (New York: Columbia University Press, 2004).

[189] Partha Chatterjee, *Lineages of Political Society: Studies in Postcolonial Democracy* (New York: Columbia University Press, 2011), p. 21.

[190] Nissim Mannathukkaren, "The 'Poverty' of Political Society: Partha Chatterjee and the People's Plan Campaign in Kerala, India," *Third World Quarterly* 31, 2 (2010), pp. 295–314 (esp. pp. 295).

its rules and regulations.[191] In post-*apartheid* South Africa, neoliberal reforms in service delivery have employed the rational calculus of marketability in the distribution of prepaid water meters in order to create "calculative citizens" enlisted in their own self-governance.[192] In rapidly growing cities like Yixing (China), city officials have introduced neoliberal policies under the banner of "ecological harmony" as a way of promoting the idea of "green development" and sustainable urbanism. Yet these interventions have worked to entrench socioeconomic inequalities.[193] Working through the wide-angle lens of governmentality, Rachel Berney charts the emergent geographies of spatial governance in Bogota (Columbia), within which poor and marginalized groups seek to make claims upon the municipality. For Berney, these assertions of a "right to the city" assume a fundamentally different tenor than the claims of "citizens," whose bundle of rights and entitlements is affirmed and empowered through constitutional guarantees.[194] In contrast, poor and marginalized groups assert their "right to the city" through their engagement and active participation in extralegal activities outside of official sanction, violating the rules that govern civil society and transgressing the laws of private property.[195]

Acts of insurgency in public space are so complicated that they do not easily fall into the binary oppositions of "top-down" versus "bottom-up." Unconventional efforts to reclaim and remake public space are not always spontaneous, participatory, and inclusive. For example, Ryan Centner contrasts the "right to the city" – which Henri Lefebvre defined as an ontological "right to urban life"[196] – with "the right kind of city," or an imaginary space that reflects a middle-class preoccupation with aesthetically pleasing and safe-and-secure places. In drawing on examples from Istanbul, Rio de Janeiro, and Buenos Aires, he reveals how middle-class urban residents assert exclusionary visions of the right kind of city that, by definition, exclude marginalized groups that threaten their narrow sense of the proper and appropriate use of public space.[197]

---

[191] Giorgio Agamben, *State of Exception* [trans. Kevin Attell] (Chicago: University of Chicago Press, 2005).

[192] Antina von Schnitzler, "Citizenship Prepaid: Water, Calculability, and Techno-Politics in South Africa," *Journal of Southern African Studies* 34, 4 (2008), pp. 899–917.

[193] Jia Ching Chen, "Greening Dispossession: Environmental Governance and Socio-spatial Transformation in Yixing, China," *Locating Right to the City*, pp. 81–104.

[194] Rachel Berney, "Public Space versus Tableau: The Right-to-the-City Paradox in Neoliberal Bogota, Columbia," in *Locating Right to the City*, pp. 152–170.

[195] See, for example, Arjun Appadurai, "Spectral Housing and Urban Cleansing: Notes on Millennial Mumbai," *Public Culture* 12, 3 (2000), pp. 627–651; Asef Bayat, "Uncivil Society: The Politics of the 'Informal People'," *Third World Quarterly* 18, 1 (1997), pp. 53–72; Asef Bayat, "From 'Dangerous Classes' to 'Quiet Rebels': Politics of Urban Subalterns in the Global South," *International Sociology* 15, 3 (2000), pp. 533–556; Asef Bayat, *Life as Politics: How Ordinary People Change the Middle East* (Stanford, CA: Stanford University Press, 2009).

[196] Lefebvre, *Writings on Cities*, p. 158.

[197] Centner, "Distinguishing the Right Kind of City," pp. 247–263.

To a large extent, debates around the "right to the city" have taken for granted the conventional distinction between public space and private space that characterized the birth of the modern capitalist city in the core areas of the world economy. On the one hand, the rights of proprietorship enable the owners of private property to restrict and monitor access to urban spaces to those deemed worthy of admission. In contrast, public space was inextricably linked to the imagined ideal of the public sphere: the arena of modern urban life defined by lively civic engagement, open democratic debate, and popular assembly. The public administration of accessible spaces of the city acted as a counterweight to the powers of private property owners to restrict access and define the use of space. Seen as a shared asset and common resource, public space was governed not by the logic of private property but by the communitarian values of sociability, social interaction, and chance encounter.[198]

The proliferation of all sorts of postpublic spaces has undermined the power of this kind of analytic framework for making claims around "the right to the city." As Aihwa Ong has argued, the emergence of new modes of urban governance adopted in globalizing cities with world-class aspirations have produced new patchwork patterns of "noncontiguous, differentially administered spaces of graduated or variegated sovereignty."[199] The introduction of new zoning practices has created a withering array of regulatory regimes that have undermined the once sovereign power of public authority over the social congregating spaces of the city. Spatial configurations like securitized office parks, gated residential communities, and shopping malls are neither "public" nor "private" in the conventional sense of this distinction. Thus, claiming a "right to the city" through demands for access to public space and the public domain is undermined by the spread of postpublic space where the right to participation and the right to appropriation – the twin pillars of Lefebvre's classical formulation – are increasingly curtailed.[200]

---

[198] See Lilia Voronkova and Oleg Pachenkov, "OPEN/CLOSED: Pubic Spaces in Modern Cities," *Berkeley Planning Journal* 24,1 (2011), pp. 197–207.

[199] Ong, *Neoliberalism as Exception*, p. 7.

[200] Mark Purcell, "Citizenship and the Right to the Global City: Reimagining the Capitalist World Order," *International Journal of Urban and Regional Research* 27, 3 (2003), pp. 564–590; and Mark Purcell, "Excavating Lefebvre: The Right to the City and its Urban Politics of the Inhabitant," *GeoJournal* 58, 2 (2002), pp. 99–108.

PART II

AGGREGATE URBANISM

3

Spatial Restructuring on a Global Scale

Enclave Urbanism and the Fragmentation of Urban Space

At the start of the twenty-first century, the conventional modernist vision of the city and urbanization has lost much of its relevance. Throughout the twentieth century (if not before), the coincidence of two enduring spatial images – sprawling industrial landscapes of factory production, on the one side, and the explosive growth of "big cities" soaring upward (skyscrapers) and expanding outward (via suburban sprawl) – became the most potent visual symbols of the birth of the urban-industrial order (with its historically specific patterns of socioeconomic life) on a global scale. As the spatial expression of the intertwined processes of rapid urbanization and concentrated industrial production, the "modern metropolis" has long stood out as the epitomé of twentieth-century urbanism – the quintessential dreamscape of modernity. As such, the physical form and symbolic characteristics of this type of urbanism became the touchstone and ideal-typical model for mainstream urban theory and planning practice.[1]

"The project of modernity," as Jürgen Habermas has described it, largely stemmed from the eighteenth-century Enlightenment which placed objective reason over superstition, universal values over traditional particularism, and scientific rationality over unfounded belief.[2] As both a movement and an ideology, modernism exerted considerable influence over thinking about cities and urbanism. Originating out of the messiness of rapid urbanization that coincided with mass expansion of industrial production, modern urban planning sought to establish stability and order amid the modernist world of flux, chaos, and incessant change. The theory and practice of modern urban planning, from

---

[1] See, for example, Hans Blumenfeld, *The Modern Metropolis: Its Origins, Growth, Characteristics, and Planning: Selected Essays* (Cambridge, MA: The MIT Press, 1967).

[2] Jürgen Habermas, *The Philosophical Discourse of Modernity* [Translated by Frederick Lawrence] (Cambridge, MA: The MIT Press, 1987).

Baron von Haussmann's creative destruction of Paris starting in the 1860s to
the high-modernist urban renewal schemes of the 1950s and 1960s, sought to
confront and correct the seemingly insurmountable problems associated with
rapid urbanization "within the limits of the language and imagery of modernity." As it solidified its place as a key partner in the practice of city building, modernist planning "bore all the hallmarks of modernity": its core principles rested on a firm belief in unending linear progress toward an optimal end
point, an affection for the technocratic and unitary planning of an ideal social
order, a commitment to objective and standardized conditions of knowledge
and production, and a firm faith in the rational ordering of social and geographic space – all with the overall goal of achieving individual liberty and the
general welfare.[3] In the modernist imagination, the application of the sound
principles of scientific rationality to urban landscapes produced orderly cities
characterized by functional specialization through spatial differentiation, efficiency of movement and circulation, and standardized approaches to planned
interventions aimed at improvements to the built environment.[4]

The Eclipse of Modernism and End of the Modernist Project

Rooted in the "hard technologies" of the late nineteenth-century to early
twentieth-century mechanical revolution, modernist urbanism gave rise to new
urban concepts like the grid and the highway, the superblock and the high-
rise skyscraper, and the central business district and the residential suburb. As
the key ingredients for rapidly industrializing cities, these new infrastructures –
when applied to rebuilding urban landscapes – almost completely undermined
the social fabric of the classical European city of the preindustrial age. Above
all, the technical innovations that produced the hard infrastructure of the modern metropolis allowed for the vertical reach of tall buildings, and the combination of strict separation of land use and increased reliance on automobiles
as the dominant mode of movement created opportunities for suburban sprawl
and single-tract residential housing. In addition, the need for unimpeded and
speedy movement called for the insertion of transportation corridors cutting
through crowded districts of the inner city.[5]

---

[3] Allan Irving, "The Modern/Postmodern Divide in Urban Planning," *University of Toronto Quarterly* 62, 4 (1993), pp. 474–488 (quotations from pp. 475, 476). See David Harvey, *The Condition
of Postmodernity: An Enquiry into the Origins of Cultural Change* (Oxford: Blackwell, 1989),
pp. 9, 10–13, 16–19, 24–28.

[4] M. Christine Boyer, *Dreaming the Rational City: The Myth of American City Planning* (Cambridge: The MIT Press, 1983), 50–51. See also Peter Hall, *Cities of Tomorrow: An Intellectual
History of Urban Planning and Design in the Twentieth Century* (Oxford: Blackwell Publishers,
1988).

[5] Mario Gandelsonas, "Slow Infrastructure," in Dana Cuff and Roger Sherman (eds.), *Fast-
Forward Urbanism: Rethinking Architecture's Engagement with the City* (New York: Princeton
Architectural Press, 2011), pp. 122–131 (esp. p. 123).

Imagined as a singular and coherent whole held together by unitary techno-cratic planning, the "modern metropolis" has long operated as a potent symbol of the modernizing impulse of erasure and reinscription – that is, the physical elimination of the unwanted material objects to pave the way for "blank-slate" renewal, where improvements to the built environment usher into being a radi-ant future.[6] Unquestioned faith in scientific and technical progress endowed modernist planning with "the utopian dream of the rational city."[7] Through-out the twentieth century, the quest for an orderly and rational urban form rested on the unfounded assumption that modernist planning principles offered universal solutions to the problems and perceived chaos of burgeoning indus-trial cities wherever they emerged.[8] Aiming to solve the social crises of rapid urbanization brought about by the rise of industrial capitalism, the project of modernist planning focused on the transformation of "an unwanted present by means of an imagined future."[9] The overarching vision of urban planning and city design became large-scale interventions – what Hildebrand Frey has called "radical surgery" – in the service of modernization.[10]

By the beginning of the second half of the twentieth century, the modernist planning project had crystalized into the international norm, where technocrats sought to apply technical (and universally applicable) solutions to problems associated with rapid urbanization. Modernist planning principles rested on the belief in developing a "comprehensive, rational model of problem-solving and decision-making" with overall aim of producing "a coordinated and coherent urban form" that fulfills the functional necessities of the city. As a normative idea, the application of scientific and technical (and not political) rationality enabled planning experts to remain objective and neutral, to disengage from any hint of "taking sides," to stand above self-interest, and to identify their actions in the public interest.[11]

Yet by the end of the twentieth century, this once enduring faith in the mod-ernist urban planning project as the antidote to urban instability seems to have

---

6   See Robert Fishman, *Urban Utopias in the Twentieth Century: Ebenezer Howard, Frank Lloyd Wright and Le Corbusier* (Cambridge, MA: The MIT Press, 1982); and David Frisby, *Cityscapes of Modernity: Critical Explorations* (Cambridge: Polity Press, 2001).

7   Leonie Sandercock, *Towards Cosmopolis: Planning for Multicultural Cities* (New York: John Wiley, 1998), p. 22 (source of quotation). See also Michael Dear, "Postmodernism and Plan-ning," *Environment and Planning D* 4, 3 (1986), pp. 367–384.

8   See, for example, Guy Baeten, "Clichés of Urban Doom: The Dystopian Politics of Metaphors for the Unequal City – a View from Brussels," *International Journal of Urban Regional Research* 25, 1 (2001), pp. 55–69.

9   James Holston, "Spaces of Insurgent Citizenship," in Leonie Sandercock (ed.), *Making the Invis-ible Visible: A Multicultural Planning History* (Berkeley: University of California Press, 1998), pp. 37–56 (quotation from p. 40).

10 Hildebrand Frey, *Designing the City: Towards a More Sustainable Form* (New York: Spon, 1999).

11 Robert Beauregard, "Between Modernity and Postmodernity: The Ambiguous Position of U.S. Planning," *Environment and Planning D* 7, 4 (1989), pp. 381–395 (quotations from pp. 384, 381).

reached a crisis point, giving way to skepticism and even cynicism.[12] What Jane Jacobs called "the pseudoscience of city planning, and its companion, the art of urban design," had fallen into disfavor, undermined by "the specious comfort of [wishful thinking], familiar superstitions, [and] oversimplifications." For Jacobs, the high-modernist metropolis of the mid-twentieth century exemplified the apotheosis of wrong-headed city building, and the principles of modern urban planning fostered "not the rebuilding of cities, [but] the sacking of cities."[13] In her view, modernist-inspired design motifs that called for order and efficiency above all else failed to take into account the incongruous, the spontaneous, and the unexpected qualities of urban life that gives cities their inherent vibrancy. Her celebration of the unplanned heterogeneity and close-grained spatial diversity of neighborhoods made Jacobs an "antimodernist" in her era, and perhaps a postmodernist today.[14] The once-ardent love affair with top-down, large-scale urban redevelopment programs, the public administration of urban space, and state-sponsored technocratic planning practices designed to stitch the urban fabric together as a coherent and well-functioning whole has given way over time to more incremental approaches to redevelopment, the steady encroachment of privatized corporate planning of the built environment as a substitute for the public management of urban space, and the growing fixation with stand-alone urban enclaves.[15]

Cities have always been highly differentiated spaces expressive of the intertwined process of growth and renewal, on the one side, and decline and ruination, on the other. These contradictory dynamics of fullness imbued with excess and emptiness mixed with deprivation have produced highly uneven spatial landscapes that reflect what Saskia Sassen has termed the "spatalization of power projects."[16] In the current age of neoliberal globalization, healthy cities

---

[12] See David Schuyler, "The New Urbanism and the Modern Metropolis," *Urban History* 24, 3 (1997), pp. 344–358; and Dear, "Postmodernism and Planning," pp. 367–384.

[13] Jane Jacobs, *The Death and Life of Great American Cities* (New York: Vintage, 1961), pp. 13, 4 (source of quotations).

[14] David Hill, "Jane Jacobs Ideas on Big, Diverse Cities: A Review and Commentary," *Journal of the American Planning Association* 54, 3 (1988), pp. 302–314; Linda Hutcheon, "The Politics of Postmodernism: Parody and History," *Cultural Critique* 5 (1986–1987), pp. 179–207; and Scott Larson, "Whose City is it Anyway? Jane Jacobs vs. Robert Moses and Contemporary Redevelopment Politics in New York City," *Berkeley Planning Journal* 22, 1 (2009), pp. 33–41. For a critic of Jane Jacobs that places her work in relation to neoliberalism, see Brian Tochterman, "Theorizing Neoliberal Urban Development: A Genealogy from Richard Florida to Jane Jacobs," *Radical History Review* 112 (2012), pp. 65–87.

[15] See, for example, Gavin Shatkin, "The City and the Bottom Line: Urban Megaprojects and the Privatization of Planning in Southeast Asia," *Environment and Planning A* 40, 2 (2008), pp. 383–401; and Gavin Shatkin, "Planning Privatopolis: Representation and Contestation in the Development of Urban Integrated Mega-Projects," in Ananya Roy and Aihwa Ong (eds.) *Worlding Cities: Asian Experiments and the Art of Being Global* (Malden, MA: Blackwell, 2011), pp. 77–97.

[16] Saskia Sassen, "Reading the City in a Global Digital Age: Between Topographical Representation and Spatialized Power Projects," in Stephen Read, Jürgen Rosemann, and Job van Eldijk (eds.), *Future City* (London and New York: Spon Press, 2006), pp. 145–155.

with world-class aspiration and fragile cities in distress have both been subjected to the polarizing pressures of global integration and local differentiation which, in turn, has led to new kinds of fragmentation, differentiation, and separation. As Erik Swyngedouw has cogently argued, "The parameters of urban life have shifted in new directions, and moved rapidly out of the straightjacket in which modernist urban design and managerial urban practices had tried to capture it."[17] The once visible and strong relationship between downtown urban core and surrounding peripheries – each with their own characteristic speeds, scales, and densities – has not remained tidily fixed in place.[18] On an even broader scale, the domain of what constitutes "the urban" has moved beyond the limits imagined in the blueprints, models, and schemes through which technocratic planning approaches have sought to produce order and stability. The "urban multiplex" – to use Erik Swynegedouw's terminology – has increasingly become a "fragmented kaleidoscope" of disjointed spaces and places, a confusing patchwork of functions and activities, and a mosaic of signs and images that "are nevertheless globally connected in myriad ways."[19] The relentless centrifugal pressures of differentiation and fragmentation that have reshaped contemporary urbanism on a world scale have not only exacerbated existing ruptures and tensions, but also produced new fissures that did not exist before. The resulting montage of diverse settlement patterns consisting of varying densities and building typologies have produced a kind of diffuse urbanism characterized by an ever-changing matrix of edges, borders, and boundaries.[20] Differentiation and fragmentation at all levels of urban life have become the corollary of globalization and the creeping imposition of a near-totalizing commodity culture.[21]

Speaking broadly, global urbanism at the start of the twenty-first century consists of polycentric, amorphous territories defined not by coherence and connection but by discontinuous fragments. This new type of unstructured urbanism, where disjointed aggregation is the dominant mode of urban production, has fractured the metropolitan city of form, undermining its totalizing urban environment and breaking down its strict hierarchies. The power of aggregate urbanism can be found in the serial repetition of disconnected "micropolitan" units, or spatial fragments, spread haphazardly and arbitrarily across vast fields of amorphous and undifferentiated space.[22] The emergence of this kind of fragmented urbanism has produced a jumbled montage of noncontiguous and functionally independent zones of varying intensity and exchange. These discontinuous patterns of urban development have engendered the steady

---

[17] Erik Swyngedouw, "Exit 'Post' – the Making of 'Glocal' Urban Modernities," in *Future City*, pp. 125–144 (quotation from p. 125).

[18] Stephen Reed, "Amsterdam: Beyond Inside and Out," in *Future City*, pp. 194–211 (esp. p. 206).

[19] Swyngedouw, "Exit 'Post' – the Making of 'Glocal' Urban Modernities," p. 125.

[20] Richard Sennett, "Boundaries and Borders," in Ricky Burdett and Deyan Sudjic (eds.), *Living in the Endless City: The Urban Age Project by the London School of Economics and Deutsche Bank's Alfred Herrhausen Society* (London: Phaidon, 2011), pp. 324–341.

[21] Swyngedouw, "Exit 'Post' – the Making of 'Glocal' Urban Modernities," p. 126.

[22] Albert Pope, "From Form to Space," in *Fast-Forward Urbanism*, pp. 143–175 (esp. p. 145).

accretion of enclaves where local autonomies are preferred (in the case of sites of luxury) and enforced (in the case of impoverished zones of abandonment). This kind of assembled urbanism of fragments is only tangentially related to conventional understandings of urban agglomeration as a centralizing process where urban orientation gestures toward a high-density core radiating outward to low-density peripheries.[23]

The forces that have shaped contemporary global city-regions have made it increasingly difficult to make sense of urbanism as anything resembling a continuous whole or coherent shape.[24] In this sense, the future of urbanism imagines remaking cities as assemblages of discrete fragments. In a full-scale reversal of the modernist-inspired obsession with orderly urbanism that dominated planning theory throughout most of the twentieth century, global urbanism at the dawn of the new millennium has broken free from the strictures that characterized the managed capitalism and (centrally) planned modernity of the mid- to late-twentieth century, only to fall victim (ironically, or so it seems) to the siren song of postmodernist ("anything-goes") market-led urban redevelopment and the warm embrace of entrepreneurialism as the best remedies for confronting urban disorder. The modernist straightjacket of the twentieth century – with its technocratic planning apparatuses, its reliance on top-down control, and its *tabula rasa* approach to planned interventions – has given way to the expectant vision of unplanned market competition as the most efficient and reliable platform for triggering growth and for "making the city right." The reinvigorated belief in the enabling powers of the hidden hand of market and the eventual trickling down of wealth shifted the ideological terrain from a collective perspective that celebrated comprehensive and holistic public planning to one heralding the virtues of private initiative and entrepreneurialism.[25] The singular attachment to market-led redevelopment and entrepreneurialism rests on a vision of urbanism where real-estate developers, property owners, architects, urban planners, and city officials join forces to fashion urban "growth machines" with the overall aim of enhancing global competitiveness in the face of the spiraling inter-urban competition that pits aspiring world-class cities one against the other.[26]

Global urbanism at the start of the twenty-first century does not display a forward-looking vision of a humane urban world of the kind that urban reformers and planners at the beginning of the twentieth century imagined

---

[23] Michael Dear, "Cities without Centers and Edges," in *Fast-Forward Urbanism*, pp. 226–242 (esp. pp. 231–232, 234).

[24] Pope, "From Form to Space," pp. 143–144, 145.

[25] David Harvey, "From Managerialism to Entrepreneurialism: The Transformation of Urban Governance in Late Capitalism," *Geografiska Annaler* Series B, Human Geography 71, 1 (1989), pp. 3–17; Stephen Gill, "Globalisation, Market Civilisation, and Disciplinary Neoliberalism," *Millennium* 24 (1995), pp. 399–423; and Tim Hall and Phil Hubbard, "The Entrepreneurial City: New Urban Politics, New Urban Geography?," *Progress in Human Geography* 20, 2 (1996), pp. 153–174.

[26] Swyngedouw, "," Exit 'Post' – the Making of 'Glocal' Urban Modernities," p. 127.

cities to become.[27] A whole range of rather disturbing tendencies have become magnified as cities around the world have increasingly become refuges of last resort for millions of impoverished newcomers seeking a better life. Under circumstances where urban restructuring on a global scale has been subjected to the dissolving powers of market competition, the conjoined forces of global integration and local differentiation have left cities in what amounts to a permanent state of flux and transformation. Wits its roots in an image of functional coherence, the modernist utopian vision of managed urbanism that dominated thinking in the twentieth century has come unglued.[28] In a highly volatile environment in which sociospatial ordering through the disciplinary logic of market competition has become the reigning dogma of the day, metropolitan regions have become, in ways quite different than before, uneven landscapes of power where islands of extreme wealth and social privilege are interspersed with neglected places of deprivation, abandonment, and decline.[29]

In this sense, global urbanism accommodates varying degrees of growth and decline, expansion and shrinkage, and integration and fragmentation, as concurrent and intertwined processes that simultaneously shape cites in sometimes polar opposite ways.[30] Spatially uneven processes of "creative destruction" have led to the physical demolition of blighted areas and the uprooting of communities, while at the same time elevating other areas to "new commanding heights of privilege, money and control."[31] The triumphal entrance of the new epoch of globalization – hailed by the new global urban elite as ushering a new world order of stability, prosperity, and growth – is a double-edged affair. For the privileged, tapping into new sources of wealth and power has enabled them to insulate themselves in virtually hermetically sealed enclaves disconnected from the material deprivations of the everyday urbanism that surrounds them. In contrast, for those at the receiving end of the all-encompassing market tyranny, globalization has enforced new patterns of exclusion and marginalization. The retreat of the wealthy and propertied behind walls and gates has gone hand-in-glove with the relegation of the poor into spaces of confinement at the margins of the mainstream of urban life. This reordering of urban space has intensified the seemingly inexorable movement toward social polarization, which in turn has reinforced ongoing processes of social exclusion and fragmentation.[32]

---

[27] Fishman, *Urban Utopias in the Twentieth Century*, pp. 3–20; and Peter Hall, *Cities of Tomorrow*, pp. 1–13. This idea come from Swyngedouw, ","Exit 'Post' – the Making of 'Glocal' Urban Modernities," p. 134.

[28] See, for example, Susan Buck-Morss, *Dreamworld and Catastrophe: The Passing of Mass Utopia in East and West* (Cambridge, MA: The MIT Press, 2000), pp. 212–215.

[29] Swyngedouw, ","Exit 'Post' – the Making of 'Glocal' Urban Modernities," p. 128.

[30] See, for example, David Scobey, *Empire City: The Making and Meaning of the New York City Landscape* (Philadelphia: Temple University Press, 2002).

[31] Swyngedouw, ","Exit 'Post' – the Making of 'Glocal' Urban Modernities," p. 134.

[32] Swyngedouw, ","Exit 'Post' – the Making of 'Glocal' Urban Modernities," p. 134. See also Don Luymes, "The Fortification of Suburbia: Investigating the Rise of Enclave Communities," *Landscape and Urban Planning* 39, 2–3 (1997), pp. 187–203.

The forces of contemporary globalization that have unleashed the "demand of global competitiveness" have proven to be powerful vehicles for wealthy urban residents to shape urban space in their desired image: the construction of enclaves more closely tethered to the cosmopolitan "global cities" at the commanding heights of the world economy than they are connected to their local surroundings.[33] At the two extremes, wealthy urban residents, on the one side, and impoverished urban dwellers, on the other, consequently bear quite different relationships to global flows of money, capital, technological innovation, and information that become concentrated and condensed in urban enclaves – which themselves have become ever greater containers of all sorts of capital.[34] In the new enclave spaces catering for high finance and their associated business service districts, the gradual accumulation of office towers and smart buildings – "neatly packaged in decorative postmodern architectural jackets" – have begun to act as "pivotal relay centers" in organizing and managing the flows of global capital required to make the world economy function efficiently and effectively.[35]

While modernist approaches to a comprehensively planned urbanism as a strategy and method of intervention has come under severe attack, the modernizing impulses that gesture toward the imagined ideal of a future urban utopia has not disappeared.[36] At this current historical juncture when state-sponsored modernist visions of city building have lost traction around the world, large-scale corporate enterprise has stepped into the breach, promising to start afresh, building new satellite cities that are efficient, sustainable, and well-managed. At the start of the twenty-first century, large-scale corporate enterprises have unveiled a wide range of "audacious [city-building] schemes" that include visions of master-planned, holistically designed "private cities" cocooned under the umbrella of special economic zones (SEZs), massive urban redevelopment projects outfitted with "premium networked infrastructure," and the unprecedented empowerment of real-estate developers in urban governance. These city-building efforts have proceeded in tandem with

---

[33] Alessandro Petti, "Dubai Offshore Urbanism," in Michiel Dehaene and Lieven De Cauter (eds.), *Heterotopia and the City: Public Space in a Postcivil Society* (New York: Routledge, 2008), pp. 287–296; Tom Angotti, "Urban Latin America: Violence, Enclaves, and Struggles for Land," *Latin American Perspectives* 40, 2 (2013), pp. 5–20; R. N. Sharma, "Mega Transformation of Mumbai: Deepening Enclave Urbanism," *Sociological Bulletin* 59, 1 (2010), pp. 69–91; Mike Hodson and Simon Marvin, "Urbanism in the Anthropocene: Ecological Urbanism or Premium Ecological Enclaves?" *City* 14, 3 (2010), pp. 298–313; and Bart Wissink, "Enclave Urbanism in Mumbai: An Actor-Network-Theory Analysis of Urban (Dis) Connection," *Geoforum* 47 (2013), pp. 1–11.

[34] See, for example, Talja Blokland and Mike Savage (eds.), *Networked Urbanism: Social Capital in the City* (Aldershot, UK: Ashgate, 2008).

[35] Swyngedouw, ","Exit 'Post' – the Making of 'Glocal' Urban Modernities," (quotations from p. 135).

[36] Swyngedouw, ","Exit 'Post' – the Making of 'Glocal' Urban Modernities," pp. 127–128.

concerted efforts to demolish poor neighborhoods, evict low-income residents, and cleanse the streets of informal traders.[37]

The dynamics of global urbanism emerging from the current wave of economic and cultural globalization marks an unprecedented radical departure from previous patterns of place-making. Unlike previous moments of global-local interaction and exchange that allowed for a certain degree of hybridization, city-building practices during the present era of global modernity have recast and retrofitted existing vernacular landscapes with little regard for cultural preservation. In the headlong rush to cater for the interests and tastes of a highly influential class of property-holding urban residents, city-building efforts have reshaped urban landscapes in ways that reflect the aesthetics and planning ideals of global capitalism with little relation or regard to values and practices associated with local context.[38] By combining urban reforms with profit-seeking motives, the modernizing impulse has extracted a terrible price, replacing the vernacular with the images of iconic globalism. City builders in globalizing cities with world-class aspirations have begun to replicate pervasive Western building prototypes that exhibit the "hypermodern" or "supermodern" architecture of "nonplaces."[39] As a consequence, urban landscapes in these cities have begun to look increasingly like their Western (and also Far Eastern) counterparts, losing their peculiar identities and distinct urban character.[40]

The Endless City: Extensive Urbanization and the Mutating Urban Form

The conventional conception of the modern metropolis as a coherent topographical entity consisting of a concentrated urban core surrounded by peripheries of ever-diminishing density has given way to a patchwork continuum of built-up spaces interspersed with underutilized areas and connected by varying networks of circulation and movement. This shift corresponds to the transition

---

[37] Gavin Shatkin and Sanjeev Vidyarthi, "Introduction: Contesting the Indian City: Global Visons and the Politics of the Local," in Gavin Shatkin (ed.), *Contesting the Indian City: Global Visions and the Politics of the Local* (Malden, MA: Blackwell, 2014), pp. 1–38 (esp. p. 1). See also Stephen Graham, "Constructing Premium Network Spaces: Reflections on Infrastructure Networks and Contemporary Urban Development," *International Journal of Urban and Regional Research* 24, 1 (2000), pp. 183–200 (p. 183, source of quotation); and Tom Angotti, *The New Century of the Metropolis: Urban Enclaves and Orientalism* (New York: Routledge, 2013).

[38] Jyoti Hosagrahar, *Indigenous Modernities: Negotiating Architecture and Urbanism* (London: Routledge, 2005).

[39] Arif Dirlik, "Architecture of Global Modernity, Colonialism and Places," in Sang Lee and Ruth Baumeister (eds.), *The Domestic and the Foreign in Architecture* (Rotterdam: 010 Publishers, 2007), pp. 37–46. See also Hans Ibelings, *Super-Modernism: Architecture in the Age of Globalization* (Rotterdam: NAi Publishers, 2002), p. 66.

[40] Manish Chalana, "Of Mills and Malls: The Future of Urban Industrial Heritage in Neoliberal Mumbai," *Future Anterior* 9, 1 (2012), pp. a–15 (esp. p. 1).

from the modern industrial era (with industry and manufacturing concentrated in the core areas of the world economy) to the postindustrial global era (with industry and manufacturing dispersed around the globe). The "concentric city" – defined by diminishing densities and dependent peripheries – represented the key nodal point of the industrial era. In contrast, the "polycentric city" – with its web-like sprawl and uneven topography – represents the extended regional metropolis of the global era.[41]

Within the limitations of differing physical geographies, the modern industrial cities of the late nineteenth and early twentieth centuries assumed a surprisingly uniform overall form at a regional scale. In the United States, for example, metropolitan regions tended to converge around the ideal-typical model of the "centralized industrial metropolis" – most clearly expressed in the urban form of Chicago.[42] Writing about the evolution of differential social areas within Chicago in the early twentieth century, the sociologist Ernest Burgess, along with other adherents of the Chicago School, captured the core-to-periphery causality of modernist urbanism in his observation that as the distance between the downtown urban core and its peripheries grew, the city assumed a spatial form that resembled concentric rings of diminishing density.[43]

In modernist urbanism, the main impetus for growth and transformation proceeded outward from the dense urban core to the low-density peripheries.[44] By the late twentieth century, however, the conjoined forces of deindustrialization and suburban sprawl across North America and Europe led to a new urban form that might euphemistically be called the "perforated city."[45] Starting in the early 1960s, deindustrializing cities in North America and Europe experienced population shrinkage in combination with a rapid increase in abandoned and empty spaces. As manufacturing and commercial activities have spread over vast new territories, huge industrial zones along with their outdated infrastructure – the premier sites of nineteenth- and twentieth-century modernity – suddenly became empty and often contaminated wastelands.[46] Edge cities blossomed on the urban fringe with no intrinsic allegiance to the downtown urban core. This wholesale spatial restructuring has been particularly acute with regard to sites of industry. Large numbers of small factories and manufacturing sites that were historically located within older areas of dense urban fabric close

[41] Alex Wall, "Programming the Urban Surface," in James Corner (ed.), *Recovering Landscape* (New York: Princeton Architectural Press, 1999), pp. 233–249 (esp. p. 234).

[42] Robert Fishman, "On Big Beaver Road: Detroit and the Diversity of American Metropolitan Landscapes," *Places* 19, 1 (2007), pp. 42–47.

[43] Ernest Burgess, "The Growth of the City: An Introduction to a Research Project," in Robert Park, Ernest Burgess, and Roderick McKensie (eds.), *The City* (Chicago: University of Chicago Press, 1925 [Reprinted 1987]), pp. 1–14.

[44] Michael Dear, "Cities without Centers and Edges," in *Fast-Forward Urbanism*, pp. 226–242 (esp. p. 230).

[45] See, for example, Daniel Florentin, "The 'Perforated City': Leipzig's Model of Urban Shrinkage Management," *Berkeley Planning Journal* 23, 1 (2010), pp. 83–101.

[46] See, for example, Alan Berger, *Drosscape: Wasting Land in Urban America* (New York: Princeton Architectural Press, 2006).

to the city center disappeared, and their activities were moved to more peripheral areas or relocated outside of North America and Europe. Entire infrastructural networks essential for the movement of commodities – harbors, railways,
and canals – that had accumulated *in situ* over more than two centuries – have
fallen into disuse, suffering from the ill effects of obsolescence, underutilization,
and neglect. The combined effect of this abandonment produced downward
pressure on stable employment, demographic growth, and the social, functional, and symbolic geography of what were once vibrant industrial cities.[47]

Consistent with the long-term evolution of urban form, the classical industrial city of the nineteenth and twentieth centuries has faded into obscurity,
becoming just another layer of what once was.[48] If the modern industrial
metropolis symbolized the modernist vision that brought together an imagined
combination of scientific and technological progress with ideas about public
purpose, collective future, and the common good, then the decline of this type
of urbanism exemplified the failed dreamscapes of modernity.[49] The causes for
the "disappearing industrial city" are multiple, varying from region to region
across the globe. At the risk of oversimplification, it can be said that for once-
vibrant industrial cities of North America and Europe the trends toward decentralization and "deteritorialization" are unmistakable. Enterprises sought to
cut costs by moving to locations with lower transportation costs and where
less expensive labor was available. Simultaneously, technological innovations
in factory production over the past four decades has meant that increased out-
put brought about by automation have required less labor. These wholesale
transformations in the global division of labor and the spatial restructuring
of the world economy were paralleled by dramatic shifts in planning practices.
Starting in the 1980s, municipal authorities – and city builders more generally –
turned away from comprehensive, holistic approaches to land use planning and
adopted instead market-driven solutions (under the guise of the "competitive
city") as an antidote to industrial decline. Under the mantra of "culture-led
redevelopment," new urban growth coalitions sought to use the strategic interventions of museums, theaters, exhibition halls, sports facilities, cultural heritage sites, gambling casinos, airports, and other kinds of leisure-entertainment
venues as substitutes for lost industrial functions and to fill the voids in vacant
land. As Bernardo Secchi has argued, the almost total "absence of a clear and
comprehensive vision of the urban future has led to incoherent choices about
the location, dimensions, and aesthetics of new building projects."[50] While the

---

47 These ideas expressed here are derived from a reading of Bernardo Secchi, "Rethinking and
Redesigning the Urban Landscape," *Places* 19, 1 (2007), pp. 6–11 (esp. p. 6).
48 Berger, *Drosscape*, pp. 63–75.
49 See Sheila Jasanoff, "Future Imperfect: Science, Technology, and the Imaginations of Modernity," in Sheila Jasanoff and Sang-Hyun Kim (eds.), *Dreamscapes of Modernity: Sociotechnical
Imaginaries and the Fabrication of Power* (Chicago: University of Chicago Press, 2015).
50 Secchi, "Rethinking and Redesigning the Urban Landscape," pp. 6, 8 (source of quotations and
ideas).

revitalization of inner-city cores with interchangeable theme stores, entertainment districts, and arts-and-culture zones "may have done wonders for the tax base, and cleaned up areas of blight and decay," it also came at a heavy price in terms of undermining the "unique sense of place and range of experience" for each city. This reshaping of post-industrial landscapes has produced "the synthetic city" where the dominance of corporate enterprise has transformed city spaces into a gigantic "communication mechanism for generating capital."[51]

At the start of the twenty-first century, the revitalized postindustrial landscapes of North America and Europe have metastasized into extended metropolitan conurbations, consisting of porous, fragmented, and dispersed nodes where a heterogeneous mix of building typologies, activities, and people coexist in uneasy alliance. Conventional concepts like land-use zoning for functional specialization, proximity and distance, property hierarchies ("highest and best use"), and the dispersion of density that once guided the building and shaping of the modern industrial city have gradually disappeared as meaningful markers of good urban form. New concepts like ecological compatibility, sustainability, porosity, resilience, and "right distance" (that is, the distance at which people and activities are willing to connect) compel us to rethink the underlying principles guiding the building of contemporary post-industrial landscapes.[52]

Limited by few (if any) physical or environmental impediments, the large-scale metropolises of the twenty-first century have typically responded to increased demand for urban space by expanding outward rather than increasing the density of the built environment close to their historic centers. For the most part, reuse of existing building structures and increasing land-use density are approaches to city building that hold little popular or economic interest. The absence of barriers, physical or otherwise, has meant that urban growth in metropolitan regions around the world has been characterized by an ever-widening expanse of thinly developed and disposable building typologies that lack any of the urban "thickness" fostered by geographic and economic limitations. As Rem Koolhaas observed in *Delirious New York*,the geographic limits of the island of Manhattan and the tight street grid make New York a site of continuous reinvention where "one form of occupancy can only be established at the expense of another. The city becomes a mosaic of episodes, each with its own particular life span, that contest each other through the medium of the Grid."[53] For the most part, rapidly growing metropolitan regions around the world have lacked both expansionary limitations and a grid-like framework

---

[51] Richard Scherr, "The Synthetic City: Excursions into the Real-Not Real," *Places* 18, 2 (2006), pp. 6–15 (quotations from p. 9, 11).

[52] These ideas are derived from Secchi, "Rethinking and Redesigning the Urban Landscape," p. 11.

[53] Rem Koolhaas, *Delirious New York: A Retroactive Manifesto for Manhattan* (New York: Monacelli Press, 1978), p. 21.

to foster the type of urban spatial competition that has characterized vertical cities like New York, Hong Kong, and Singapore.[54]

The End of the Modern Metropolis as Prototype for Global Urbanization

Global urbanism at the start of the twenty-first century, as Stephen Graham has cogently argued, can be characterized by "multiplex" metropolitan regions with multiple (and sometimes rival) centers, tied together by complex flows of capital, trade, people, and ideas.[55] The blurring of high-density core and low-density periphery has blended to create an amorphous and fractured landscape, a kind of posturban hybrid spatial configuration that both expands and grows and shrinks, and contracts, at the same time.[56] Over the past thirty to forty years, the accelerated pace and scale of global urbanization has produced sprawling global city-regions that largely resemble vast, distended, amoeba-like conurbations that have spread over ever-widening geographical distances. Extending more horizontally than vertically, these megalopolises violate every principle of rational planning models of functional specialization of orderly land use, efficient transportation circulation, and rigid enforcement of "highest and best use" of urban space. These patterns of diffuse urbanism, which the urban theorist Thomas Sieverts has called *Zwischenstadt* ("in-between city," or the "urbanized countryside") has become the defining prototype for metropolitan growth and development in the twenty-first century in both rich and poor countries. The idea of the "in-between city" is meant to grasp the emergence of a novel urban form that has largely replaced the conventional idea of the compact and monocentric metropolis. Discontinuous and fragmented, these new conurbations take shape as polycentric webs where lumpy "carpets of settlement" blur the conventional distinction between high-density central cores and low-density peripheral edges.[57] The emergence of what some scholars have termed the "endless city," or the "limitless city," has called into question the continued salience of maintaining a hard-and-fast distinction between a discrete urban zone and its rural hinterlands.[58] With its disorganized and largely unplanned

---

54 Ann Haila, "Real Estate in Global Cities: Singapore and Hong Kong as Property States," *Urban Studies* 37, 12 (2000), pp. 2241–2256.

55 Graham, "Urban Network Architecture," p. 111.

56 See Xaveer de Geyter Architects, *After-Sprawl: Research for the Contemporary City* (Rotterdam: NAi Publishers, 2002).

57 Thomas Sieverts, *Cities without Cities: An Interpretation of the Zwischenstadt* (London: Spon Press, 2003), p. 3.

58 Ricky Burdett and Deyan Sudjic (eds.), *The Endless City: The Urban Age Project by the London School of Economics and Deutsche Bank's Alfred Herrhausen Society* (London: Phaidon, 2011); and Edward Soja and Miguel Kanai, "The Urbanization of the World," in *The Endless City*, pp. 54–68. See also Oliver Gillham, *The Limitless City: A Primer on the Urban Sprawl Debate* (Washington, DC: Island Press, 2002).

patterns of concentrated density interwoven with underutilized *terra incognita*, the "in-between city" evokes the image of posturban space, or what Edward Soja has provocatively called the "postmetropolis."[59] The polycentricity and complex networking of global city-regions has produced sprawling metropolitan landscapes that have become increasingly unbundled, reconfigured, and rescaled. In this concatenation of metropolitan and regional scales, the "globalization of the urban," Edward Soja and Miguel Kanai have suggested, "begins to coincide with the urbanization of the globe."[60] For Soja, the end point of the process of urban restructuring that began in the late twentieth century – what he has called the "postmetropolitan transition" – is a radical transformation in the very nature of the urbanization, "a shift from a long-established metropolitan model of urban development to what needs to be called regional urbanization."[61]

Instead of conceiving of city and countryside as two independent and conflicting social worlds, it is more useful to think of their relationality and integral connectivity. The separation between dense urban core and surrounding periphery has become hopelessly blurred and intertwined, forming strange hybrid mixtures. New amalgamated metropolitan landscapes have come into being where the once-regnant distinctions among city, suburb, and countryside are no longer self-evident or even appropriate as analytic categories.[62] For those who speak of the arrival of "planetary urbanism," the very designation of "the city" – "despite its continued pervasiveness in scholarly and political discourse" – has become outmoded and obsolete as an object of analysis.[63] Metaphorically speaking, contemporary urbanization seems to have no discernible logic, no obvious patterns, and no coherent set of causes or boundaries. Writing about growing megacities in Latin America, the Asia-Pacific, and Africa, scholars have employed a variety of concepts – like "region-based urbanization" (Aguilar and Ward), "extended metropolitan regions" (Drakakis-Smith), "desakota regions" (McGee) – to describe these emergent patterns of polycentric horizontal metropolitan sprawl.[64] Extended metropolitan regions

[59] Edward Soja, *Postmetropolis: Critical Studies of Cities and Regions* (Malden, MA: Blackwell, 2000).
[60] Soja and Kanai, "The Urbanization of the World," p. 67.
[61] Edward Soja, "Regional Urbanization and Third Wave Cities," *City* 17, 5 (2013), pp. 688–694.
[62] Neil Brenner, "Theses on Urbanization," *Public Culture* 25, 1 [69] (2013), pp. 85–114. See also Ivan Turok and Nick Bailey, "The Theory of Polycentric Urban Regions and its Application to Central Scotland," *European Planning Studies* 12, 3 (2004), pp. 371–389.
[63] Neil Brenner and Christian Schmid, "Planetary Urbanization," in Matthew Gandy (eds.), *Urban Constellations* (Berlin: Jovis, 2011), pp. 10–13 (quotation from p. 12). See also Ananya Roy, "Who's Afraid of Postcolonial Theory?" *International Journal of Urban and Regional Research* 40, 1 (2016), pp. 200–209.
[64] T. G. McGee, "The Emergence of *Desakota* Regions in Asia: Expanding a Hypothesis," in Norton Ginsburg, Bruce Koppel, and T. G. McGee (eds.), *The Extended Metropolis: Settlement Transition in Asia* (Honolulu: University of Hawaii Press, 1991), pp. 3–25; Adrián Aguilar and Peter Ward, "Globalization, Regional Development, and Mega-City Development Expansion

represent a fusion of what we commonly understand as urban and rural, where the typical distinction between these two polar extremes has become blurred and increasingly irrelevant.[65] The emergent megalopolis of the twenty-first century expands along corridors of transportation and communication, leapfrogging over or cannibalizing whatever stands in the way, or, as David Drakakis-Smith has argued, "bypassing or surrounding small towns and villages which subsequently experience *in situ* changes in function and occupation."[66]

Properly understood, the "in-between city" refers less to a distinctive spatial form that can be defined in static terms (e.g., fixed average densities, specific constitutive elements, particular mix of land uses, and the like) and more to a set of relationships that realign the elements of urbanity more fundamentally. This realignment includes, first and foremost, the rescaling of sociospatial relationships under circumstances where urban regions are opened up to the centrifugal force fields of globalization. These novel patterns of "diffuse urbanism" – where cities "appear to be formlessly mushrooming urban landscapes" – has become the defining characteristic of twenty-first-century transnational urbanism in rich and poor countries alike.[67] The spatial unevenness of the "in-between" city – where prosperous enclaves are juxtaposed against surrounding impoverished zones – can be traced directly to the contradictory dynamics of contemporary globalization that produces both global integration and connectivity, on the one side, and exclusion and marginalization, on the other.[68]

Planetary Urbanism: The Urbanization of the Whole Globe

In his seminal study called Megalopolis, Jean Gottmann observed in the late 1950s that the extensive transformations in land use and infrastructure

in Latin America: Analyzing Mexico City's Peri-Urban Hinterland," *Cities* 20, 1 (2003), pp. 3–21; and Hamilton Tolosa, "The Rio/São Paulo Extended Metropolitan Region: A Quest for Global Integration," *The Annals of Regional Science* 37, 2 (2003), pp. 479–500; Tommy Firman, "Urban Development in Bandung Metropolitan Region: A Transformation to a Desakota Region," *Third World Planning Review* 18, 1 (1996), pp. 1–22.

65 Alan Gilbert (ed.), *The Mega-City in Latin America* (Tokyo, Paris, and New York: The United Nations University Press, 1996); Gavin Jones and Pravin Visaria (eds.), *Urbanization in Large Developing Countries: China, Indonesia, Brazil, and India* (Oxford: Oxford University Press, 1997); and Gustavo Garza, "Global Economy: Metropolitan Dynamics and Urban Policies in Mexico," *Cities* 16, 3 (1999), pp. 149–170 (esp. p. 154).

66 David Drakakis-Smith, *Third World Cities* [2nd Edition] (New York: Routledge, 2000), p. 21. See T. G. McGee and Ira Robinson (eds.), *Mega Urban Regions of Southeast Asia* (Vancouver: University of British Columbia Press, 1995); and Josef Gugler (ed.), *World Cities beyond the West: Globalization, Development, Inequality* (New York: Cambridge University Press, 2004).

67 Thomas Sieverts, "The In-Between City as an Image of Society: From the Impossible Order towards a Possible Disorder in the Urban Landscape," in Douglas Young, Patricia Burke Wood, and Roger Keil (eds.), *In-Between Infrastructure: Urban Connectivity in a Time of Vulnerability* (Toronto: Praxis(e) Press, 2013), pp. 19–27 (esp. p. 22).

68 Roger Keil and Douglas Young, "In Between Canada: The Emergence of the New Urban Middle," in *In-Between Infrastructure*, pp. 1–18 (esp. pp. 3–4).

systems in the northeast United States were not limited to the densely built areas of cities, but also included transportation corridors, the cultivated zones of agricultural production and managed forestry, hydrological regimes, and irrigation infrastructures. For Gottman, the megalopolis "spreads out far and wide from its original nucleus; it grows amidst an irregularly colloidal mixture of rural and suburban landscapes; it melts on broad fronts with other mixtures, of somewhat similar though different texture." This novel type of urbanization "stands at the threshold of a new way of life."[69]

Building upon Gottman's original ideas, the Greek architect and city planner Constantinos Doxiadis invented the term Ecumenopolis in 1967 to represent his future projection that megalopolitan formations were only intermediate stages that would eventually fuse together. In time, the unfolding of an increasingly continuous urbanizing fabric would eventually culminate in an inevitable future condition of complete urbanization of the globe. In his own research and writing, Doxiadis embarked on a detailed investigation of the patterns, structures, densities, and dimensions of this emergent worldwide web of global urbanization, what he called the "ekistic fabric," or elasticity, of Ecumenopolis.[70] This study of "the inevitable city of the future" revealed in a particularly dramatic way that as urbanization reached its planetary dimensions it engaged with the asymmetries of the natural geography it confronted in new and unprecedented ways. As the projections of futurologists have come to pass, the spread of urbanism on a global scale has become a distinct reality, emerging at the crossroads between what is built and what is connected, and what is controlled and what is yet-to-be-tamed.[71]

The emerging scholarly literature on planetary urbanization provides a promising point of departure to broaden the scope of inquiry concerned with making sense of the multiple trajectories of global urbanism at the start of the twenty-first century.[72] Tracing their source of inspiration to Henri Lefebvre and his claim about the inevitability of "total urbanization," theorists of planetary urbanism contend that urbanization has entered a new phase of unprecedented reach, thereby requiring new theorizations as to what constitutes what is commonly called "the urban." As Edward Soja and Miguel Kanai have suggested,

[69] Jean Gottmann, *Megalopolis: The Urbanized Northeastern Seaboard of the United States* (Cambridge, MA: The MIT Press, 1964), p. 5, 16 (source of quotations).

[70] Constantinos Doxiadis and John Papaioanou, *Ecumenopolis: The Inevitable City of the Future* (New York: Norton, 1974).

[71] Nikos Katsikis, "On the Geographical Organization of World Urbanization," *MONU #20: Geographical Urbanism*, April 2014 [n.p.]. Available at www.terraurbis.com.

[72] Neil Brenner and Christian Schmid, "The 'Urban Age' in Question," *International Journal of Urban and Regional Research* 38, 3 (2013), pp. 731–755; Edward Soja and Miguel Kanai, "The Urbanization of the World," in Ricky Burdett and Deyan Sudjic (eds.), *The Endless City: The Urban Age Project by the London School of Economics and Deutsche Bank's Alfred Herrhausen Society* (London: Phaidon, 2007), pp. 54–69; and Brenner, "Theses on Urbanization," pp. 85–114.

processes of urbanization are not subordinate to globalization, but instead constitute one of the primary vectors directed at the systemic integration of the planet. These processes result in strategically located urban agglomerations exhibiting not only unprecedented size but also increasing complexity and cosmopolitan heterogeneity. New modes of connectivity enable cities to reach virtually everywhere, "thereby spreading spatial impacts of economic, social, cultural, and environmental transformation across ever more extensive territories."[73]

As a general rule, conventional approaches to urban studies focus almost exclusively on processes of growth, agglomeration, and clustering. Yet as Neil Brenner and Christian Schmid have pointed out, what characterizes global urbanism at the start of the twenty-first century are ongoing processes of urbanization that bring together interrelated moments of concentration and extension, expansion and contraction, and growth and decline. The undue stress in mainstream urban studies literature on growth and expansion overlooks the point that urban agglomerations form, expand, shrink, and change continuously, but always via dense webs of relations and connections to other places.[74]

The analytic framework of planetary urbanization highlights the dynamic interdependency of the increasingly continuous web of dense agglomerations with their "operational landscapes" of production, extraction, and circulation that sustain them. As such, it allows for a much more inclusive conceptualization of the actual materialities of urbanization, foregrounding the geographical embeddedness of cities instead of their alleged separateness.[75] This idea of planetary urbanism is premised on the claim that urbanization has extended its tentacles in all directions, swallowing, enclosing, and consuming everything in its path. An infinite array of concepts has been put forward to identify and capture the evolving form of planetary urbanism: the "endless city," the "100-mile city," the "megacity," the "arrival city," and the "indistinguishable city." What constitutes "the urban" is shapeless, formless, and apparently boundless, beset with new contradictions and tensions that make it nearly impossible to discern where borders are and what is "inside" and what is "outside." Planetary urbanism has assumed a "formless form" that is akin to the "chaos...yet underlying order" found in the abstract expressionism of Jackson Pollock, because the process of urbanization tends to break any barriers that seek to fix its limits.[76]

Rapid, explosive processes of urbanization have fundamentally altered the terrain of what it means to theorize the urban realm. Extending the concept of

73 Soja and Kanai, "The Urbanization of the World," p. 54 (source of quotation).

74 Brenner, "Theses on Urbanization," p. 103.

75 Katsikis, "On the Geographical Organization of World Urbanization."

76 Andrew Merrifield, "The Urban Question under Planetary Urbanization," *International Journal of Urban and Regional Research* 37, 3 (2013), pp. 909–922 (esp. 910–911, quotation from p. 913). See also Isabelle Doucet, "[Centrality] and/or Cent][rality: a Matter of Placing the Boundaries," in Giovanni Maciocco (ed.), *Urban Landscape Perspectives* (Berlin and Heidelberg: Springer Verlag, 2008), pp. 93–121.

urbanism as far as it can stretch – as Neil Brenner and Christian Schmid seem to do – has the tendency to flatten and smooth over processes of urbanization that are indeed heterogeneous, uneven, and complex. In the end, they seem to abolish even vague distinctions between the urban and the nonurban realm. As Richard Walker has suggested, what is needed is to "pull back from the brink of totalizing urbanization to look more carefully" at how processes of extensive urbanization "penetrate, exploit and subsume" the rural hinterlands that exist outside the urban realm.[77]

Abolishing all distinction between "the urban" and its "other" limits our analytic capacity to theorize the uneven characteristics of the urbanization process.[78] The challenge for thinking about contemporary processes of extensive urbanization is how to theorize temporal and spatial scales that hold the planetary and the particular in the same frame of reference without losing sight of either. As Monika Krause has argued, "Only if we complement a focus of urbanization with a recognition of ruralization" – that is, "only when we ruralize the way we think" – is it possible to "fully disaggregate the different distinctions that have been subsumed under the categories of urban and rural" and to think about ways of providing broader understanding of variation in sociospatial arrangements and forms of social settlement.[79]

Uneven Spatial Landscapes on a World Scale: Luxury Living in Aspiring World-Class Cities

Writing about ordinary cities at the margins of world economy can easily fall into dystopian caricature, alarmist hyperbole, and one-sided exaggeration.[80] These narrow lenses cloud our understanding about what is actually happening on the ground and why. The undue stress on monochromatic slums and survivalist informality, for example, lends itself to a flattening of metropolitan landscapes and a one-sided impression of homogenized urban life defined primarily by material deprivation and social exclusion. What has been largely overlooked in the scholarly literature on ordinary cities of the Global South – so-called Southern metropolises – is a critical examination of emergent patterns of spatial fragmentation, differentiation, and social division.[81]

---

[77] Richard Walker, "Building a Better Theory of the Urban: A Response to 'Towards a New Epistemology of the Urban?'" *City* 19, 2–3 (2015), pp. 183–191 (quotations from p. 186).

[78] See David Harvey, *Spaces of Global Capitalism: Towards a Theory of Uneven Geographical Development* (New York: Verso, 2006).

[79] Monika Krause, "The Ruralization of the World," *Public Culture* 25, 2 [70] (2013), pp. 233–248 (quotations from p. 234). See also Keith Halfacree, "Rethinking 'Rurality,'" in Anthony Champion and Graeme Hugo (eds.), *New Forms of Urbanization: Beyond the Urban-Rural Dichotomy* (Aldershot, UK: Ashgate, 2004), pp. 285–304.

[80] Jennifer Robinson, "Global and World Cities: A View from Off the Map," *International Journal of Urban and Regional Research* 26, 3 (2002), pp. 531–554.

[81] Charlotte Lemanski, "Global Cities in the South: Deepening Social and Spatial Polarisation in Cape Town," *Cities* 24, 6 (2007), pp. 448–461.

Herein resides a perplexing paradox that cuts against the grain of the homogenizing impulse of the new global age. The explosive growth of cutting-edge economic, transportation, and communications networks has led some analysts to roundly proclaim the "death of distance."[82] Yet as globalization draws the people closer together via time-space compression, accelerated mobility and connectivity among people, and the expansion of virtual communities, great barriers have emerged between neighbors living in close proximity to one another.[83] In contemporary cities, urban residents who are divided not only by class position, but also by racial, religious, ethnic difference, often live what amounts to as "parallel lives": side by side but never really intersecting. While enduring patterns of social segregation in what have been called the dual cities, divided cities, and quartered cities of the so-called Global North are nothing new, great chasms dividing urban dwellers are increasingly playing out at an arguably much greater scale in the "globalizing cities" of the South. Popular (and award-winning) films like *Slumdog Millionaire* (Mumbai), *City of God (Rio de Janeiro)*, and *Tsotsi* (Johannesburg) are not prescient glimpses of a potential urban dystopia in some distant future, but disturbing tales of contemporary realities in cities deeply divided along multiple fault lines.[84]

Debates in the scholarly literature have focused on the extent to which these emergent patterns of spatial fragmentation are an outcome and expression (and ultimately catalyst of) of broader processes of globalization in the age of neoliberalism.[85] Some scholars have stressed the historical continuities with the past, arguing that what were once referred to as Third World cities have always been divided, fragmented, and fractured.[86] In contrast, others have stressed novel kinds of spatial polarization and fragmentation, arguing that these need to be located in the multiscalar processes of political and economic restructuring associated with the neoliberal turn.[87] Looking at these emergent patterns of spatial polarization and fragmentation that have taken root in "globalizing

[82] Frances Cairncross, *The Death of Distance: How the Communications Revolution is Changing our Lives* (Boston: Harvard Business School Press, 1997).

[83] Roland Robertson, "Glocalization: Time-Space and Homogeneity-Heterogeneity," in Mike Featherstone, Scott Lash, and Roland Robertson (eds.), *Global Modernities* (London: Sage, 1995), pp. 25–44.

[84] Andrew Buncombe, "Slumdogs who Seek Success," *The Independent* [London], January 16, 2009.

[85] Gavin Shatkin, "Global Cities of the South: Emerging Perspectives on Growth and Inequality," *Cities* 24, 1 (2007), pp. 1–15; Susan Parnell and Jennifer Robinson, "(Re)theorizing Cities from the Global South: Looking Beyond Neoliberalism," *Urban Geography* 33, 4 (2012), pp. 593–617; Stuart Hodkinson, "The New Urban Enclosures," *City* 16, 5 (2012), pp. 500–518; and Susan Parnell and Sophie Oldfield (eds.), *The Routledge Handbook for Cities of the Global South* (New York: Routledge, 2014).

[86] Marcelo Balbo, "Urban Planning and the Fragmented City of the Developing World," *Third World Planning Review* 15, 1 (1993), pp. 23–55.

[87] For a survey of these issues, see Ryan Bishop, John Phillips, and Wei Wei Yeo, "Perpetuating Cities: Excepting Globalization and the Southeast Asia Supplement," in Ryan Bishop, John Phillips, and Wei Wei Yeo (eds.), *Postcolonial Urbanism: Southeast Asian Cities and Global Processes* (New York: Routledge, 2003), pp. 1–36.

cities" around the world enables us to tease out some conceptual generalizations that will ultimately help us think about what kind of analytic frameworks can best capture the connections between spatial restructuring of cities at a global scale, the reconfiguration of the institutional "rules of the game" exemplified by the triumph of market fundamentalism, and the local dynamics of property markets, real-estate development, and land speculation. At the beginning of the new millennium, urban life has increasingly become the norm for the majority of the world's inhabitants. Under straightened circumstances where sociospatial ordering under the dominance of the capitalist marketplace functions as the main mechanism for differentiating urban residents, cities have become contested sites or battlegrounds for protracted struggles, always bitter and sometimes violent, over who belongs and who does not, that is, who has access to the mainstream of urban life and who is left out.[88]

As a distinctive field of inquiry, mainstream urban studies gained traction in the latter half of the twentieth century when modernization theories and the attendant discourse of developmentalism framed scholarly debate on cities and global processes of urbanization. A strong argument can be made that the differences that existed thirty to forty years ago, between what was then almost universally referred to as First, Second, and Third World cities, while they have not entirely disappeared, have become blurred, as nearly all cities have come under the influence of globalization in the age of neoliberalism. This blurring and bending has meant that cities like Mexico City, Shanghai, and Johannesburg, for example, once considered at the margins of modernity, can be as much sites for cutting-edge innovation and experimentation, as (say) New York, London, or Berlin.[89]

The simultaneous processes of global homogenization and differentiation have not only unsettled the pace and scale of global urbanization, but also fundamentally altered as well as the relations among and between cities and global city-regions. At the start of the twenty-first century, the geographical and functional organization of the world economy has come to revolve around a new power hierarchy of financial command-and-control centers, with three great "capitals of capital" –London, New York, and Tokyo – at the top of the "global cities" rank-order, but supplemented by a second-tier of interconnected and synergistic "globalizing cities."[90] Cities around the world articulate with the global economy and polity in different ways and with varying degrees of intensity, thereby creating strange fusions and hybrid mixtures of similarity and difference, and complex patterns of convergence and divergence. Unpacking

---

[88] Asef Bayat, "From 'Dangerous Classes' to 'Quiet Rebels': Politics of Urban Subalterns in the Global South," *International Sociology* 15, 3 (2000), pp. 533–556. See also Sobia Ahmad Kaker, "Enclaves, Insecurity and Violence in Karachi," *South Asian History and Culture* 5, 1 (2014), pp. 93–107.

[89] Soja and Kanai, "The Urbanization of the World," p. 64.

[90] These ideas are derived from Soja and Kanai, "The Urbanization of the World," p. 64. See Saskia Sassen, "Introduction: Locating Cities on Global Networks," in Saskia Sassen (ed.), *Global Networks, Linked Cities* (New York: Routledge, 2002), pp. 1–36.

how the general features of global urbanization combine with local particulari-
ties requires rigorous and comprehensive comparative analysis that breaks from
a dominant current in mainstream urban studies literature: namely, the sugges-
tion that urbanization can be conceived as a universal process which unfolds in
stages over linear time and converges around a common end point.[91] While the
once-regnant analytic categories like First World and Third World cities are no
longer adequate tools to account for embedded differences, alternative formulations like postcolonial urbanism, cities of the Global South, and "worlding" are
not sufficiently powerful and robust conceptual frameworks that can assist us
in fully comprehending the dynamics of urban unevenness on a global scale.[92]

What Mike Davis has cogently and provocatively called the "planet of
slums" has drawn our attention to the megacities of hypergrowth, fast-growing
metropolitan regions at the periphery of the world economy that have become
vast repositories for impoverished work-seekers, newcomers and old-timers
alike, that is, the jobless legions of urban poor who are trapped in what appears
to be a permanent circumstance of material deprivation.[93] The mass production of slums on a world scale has produced new urban realities that not only
undermine our conventional understandings of cities and urbanization, but also
pose serious challenges for planning theory and practice.[94] The unprecedented
expansion of urban poverty has made "extended" slums, self-built settlements,
and burgeoning informal economies perhaps the most distinctive and distinguishing feature of the rapid pace of urbanization that has produced megacities
of hypergrowth.[95]

In large measure, the globalization of the urban has centered on the massive
expansion of slums and informality, but this reality is only part of the story

[91] For a critique of the mainstream view, see Jennifer Robinson, *Ordinary Cities: Between Modernity and Development* (New York: Routledge, 2006). See also Colin McFarlane, "The Comparative City: Knowledge, Learning, Urbanism," *International Journal of Urban and Regional
Research* 34, 4 (2010), pp. 725–742; Jennifer Robinson, "Urban Geography: World Cities, or a
World of Cities," *Progress in Human Geography* 29, 6 (2005) pp. 757–765; and Jennifer Robinson, "Cities in a World of Cities: The Comparative Gesture," *International Journal of Urban
and Regional Research* 35, 1 (2011), pp. 1–23.

[92] For an engagement with these themes, see Cheryl McEwan, "Material Geographies and Postcolonialism," *Singapore Journal of Tropical Geography* 24, 3 (2003), pp. 340–355; Alan Scott
and Michael Storper, "The Nature of Cities: The Scope and Limits of Urban Theory," *International Journal of Urban and Regional Research* 39, 1 (2015), pp. 1–15; and Roy, "Whose
Afraid of Postcolonial Theory?", pp. 200–209.

[93] Mike Davis, *Planet of Slums* (New York: Verso, 2006).

[94] Faranak Miraftab, "Insurgent Planning: Situating Radical Planning in the Global South," *Planning Theory* 8, 1 (2009), pp. 32–50; Vanessa Watson, "The Usefulness of Normative Planning Theories in the Context of Sub-Saharan Africa," *Planning Theory* 1, 1 (2002), pp. 27–52;
Ananya Roy, "Praxis in the Time of Empire," *Planning Theory* 5, 1 (2006), pp. 7–29; and Edgar
Pieterse, *City Futures: Confronting the Crisis of Urban Development* (Cape Town: UCT Press,
2008).

[95] See, for example, Kees Koonings and Dirk Druijt, "The Rise of Megacities and the Urbanization
of Informality, Exclusion, and Violence," in Kees Koonings and Dirk Druijt (eds.), *Megacities:
The Politics of Urban Exclusion and Violence in the Global South* (London: Zed Press, 2009),
pp. 8–26.

of the spatial restructuring of cities on a world scale. The steady expansion of slums and informality has proceeded in tandem with the emergence and entrenchment of a privileged, property-owning, business-managerial class with varying connections with the leading metropolitan command-and-control centers at the core of the world economy. Seeking to associate themselves with the ethos of cosmopolitan urbanity in cities elsewhere, these globalized neoliberal elites have played an influential role in shaping local city-building processes. This convergence of the global and the local has resulted in uneven spatial landscapes – a new dualism – in "globalizing cities" around the world.[96]

One must be careful, however, not to oversimplify or overemphasize the power of the polarizing impulses toward dualism. Urban spatial restructuring is considerably more complex and multilayered than the kinds of spatial fragmentation and separation that prevailed in earlier times. What is distinctive about these new discontinuous patterns of spatial fragmentation at the start of the twenty-first century is the historically specific dynamics of globalization that have produced inward-looking enclaves for the wealthy juxtaposed against the sprawling wastelands where the vast legions of urban poor are forced by economic necessity to survive in an extralegal limbo.[97]

In the contemporary age of globalization, the proliferation of informal settlements in fast-growing cities around the world has gone hand-in-hand with the accumulating numbers of enclave spaces catering for affluent urban residents. The symmetric development and coexistence of these two quite dissimilar building typologies is a characteristic feature of the rapidly expanding mega-urban regions outside the core areas of the world economy. The substantial expansion of informal settlements and unauthorized squatting are a reflection (and grim reminder) of poor economies and limited opportunities for regular work, the scarcity of affordable housing in the face of rising demand, state incapacity to provide alternative accommodation, and inadequate regulatory authority and lack of zoning controls. In contrast, the declining quality of municipal services and infrastructure provision – combined with increasing fear of crime and the middle-class desire for status – has triggered the steady increase in luxury enclaves for affluent urban residents. Private real-estate developers have filled the void created by the inability (or unwillingness) of fiscally constrained municipalities to provide requisite infrastructure and services. The movement toward self-governance and the private provision of facilities and social amenities has become the corollary of municipal incapacity to deliver public goods and services.[98]

---

[96] Soja and Kanai, "The Urbanization of the World," p. 65.
[97] See James Sidaway, "Enclave Space: A New Metageography of Development?" *Area* 39, 3 (2007), pp. 331–339 (esp. p. 336); and James Sidaway, "Spaces of Postdevelopment," *Progress in Human Geography* 31 3 (2007), pp. 345–361.
[98] See Anaya Roy, "Why India Cannot Plan its Cities: Informality, Insurgence and the Idiom of Urbanization," *Planning Theory* 8, 1 (2009), pp. 76–87.

Bubble Urbanism: A Sprawling Archipelago of Enclaves

Whether growing or shrinking, located at the core of the world economy or at the margins, the variegated patterns of global urbanism that have come into existence at the start of the twenty-first century largely resemble what Maartin Hajer and Arnold Reijndorp have termed an "archipelago of enclaves."[99] As an assemblage of fragments, this new "archipelago city" (or "city within a city") has come to define the geographically uneven field of global urbanism.[100] The proliferation of privatized, single-use building typologies such as gated residential communities, special economic zones, and securitized office parks has "reinvigorated a renewed interest" in enclosed enclaves and their impact on urban form. Characterized by impermeable borders and hard boundaries, island-like enclosures are a kind of "spatial segregation taken to the extreme, a world of fragmentation" where separation and distance triumph over connection and combination.[101]

The archipelago is a compelling metaphor for a distributed network of isolated satellite cities that have been built in or around existing metropolitan landscapes over the past several decades. Since the demise of the modernist-inspired gridiron pattern of city building in the second half of the twentieth century, the inner-connected enclave network, or what technically can be called a "polynuclear conurbation" and otherwise popularly known as the *megalopolis*, has come to fully characterize the production of urban space in the contemporary age of globalization. The spine-based, self-contained enclosures that characterize contemporary urbanism – corporate office parks, residential subdivisions, destination shopping malls, airport-and-logistics complexes, innovation districts, research-and-development campuses, and gated residential estates – "constitute an *ad hoc* flotilla" of building typologies scattered haphazardly across seemingly boundless metropolitan landscapes. Whether such closed urban nodes take the form of high-density clusters or low-density sprawl, and whether they consist of high-rise office towers, condominium complexes, or mass-produced suburban tract housing, the archipelago metaphor allows us to grasp the fragmented character of contemporary urbanism.[102]

Metaphors do matter. As part of an epistemological apparatus, they do more than simply supply the imaginative materials that are required to make sense

---

99 Maarten Hajer and Arnold Reijndorp, *In Search of New Public Domain: Analysis and Strategy* (Rotterdam: NAi Publishers, 2001). See also Paola Viganò, The Contemporary European Urban Project: Archipelago City, Diffuse City and Reverse City," in C. Greig Crysler, Stephen Cairns, and Hilde Heynen (eds.), *The SAGE Handbook of Architectural Theory* (London: Sage, 2012), pp. 657–670.

100 Lara Schrijver, "The Archipelago City: Piercing Together Collectivities," *OASE* 71 [*Journal for Architecture, Urban Formation & Collective Spaces*] (2006), pp. 18–36.

101 Mark Lee, "Two Deserted Islands," *San Rocco Magazine* (2014), pp. 4–10 (esp. p. 4).

102 Albert Pope, "The Island Organism: Hilberseimer in Rockford," in Neeraj Bhatia and Mary Casper (eds.), *The Petropolis of Tomorrow* (New York: Actar, 2013), pp. 92–105 (esp. p. 93).

of what appears to be an incoherent and largely chaotic urban field, but they also provide urban theorizing with a credibility that comes through association with the natural world of physical geology.[103] Planners, designers, and architects have always looked to natural forms and living organisms in order to render arbitrary human constructions seem as obvious and inevitable as the "world of nature" itself. Given this legacy of natural association, the metaphor of the island archipelago appeals to urbanists "because it renders the vagaries of megalopolis" as "enduring as the [deep] geology of the earth."[104]

By employing the logic of association that connects disparate parts into a coherent whole, the archipelago has emerged as a recognized (and useful) metaphor for urban assemblages in the current age of globalization. Unlike the image of *Collage City* (Colin Rowe and Fred Koetter) where "parts combine and collapse through intense juxtaposition," the archipelago metaphor projects a visual impression of the city as something other than an organic whole.[105] Yet despite the indebtedness of the archipelago metaphor to the geographic and geological (and even cartographic) images of islands, what is often missing is an appreciation of the edges and the interfaces that these generate.[106]

The emergent patterns of spatial fragmentation and social polarization are particularly pronounced in aspiring world-class cities like Johannesburg, Cape Town, Mumbai, New Delhi, Istanbul, Singapore, Hong Kong, São Paulo, Rio de Janeiro, Mexico City, and Shanghai – all located outside the historic core areas of the world economy. This fragmentation of urban space consists of fractured morphological patterns, acute socio-spatial polarization, and deepening landscapes of inequality. Ordinary cities at the edge of global capitalism consist of discontinuous parts that do not constitute a homogeneous whole, or a single "organism." These large metropolises are not single, unified entities, but are in fact many different cities, physically contiguous, but quite socially distinct. As Marcelo Balbo has argued, "The city of the Third World is a city of fragments, where urbanization takes place in leaps and bounds, creating a continuously discontinuous pattern." In the city of fragments, the physical environment, social services, infrastructure, sources of income, cultural values, institutional rules, and management and governance systems can vary markedly from neighborhood to neighborhood, and even from street to street. A bird's-eye aerial view of the city reveals spatial structures consisting of many different pieces linked together in a rather haphazard and often quite accidental way.[107]

---

[103] Pope, "The Island Organism," p. 102.   [104] Pope, "The Island Organism," p. 94.

[105] Mary Casper, "On Land, At Sea: Formalizing Public Edges in the Archipelago," in *The Petropolis of Tomorrow*, pp. 106–199 (quotation from p. 108). See also Colin Rowe and Fred Koetter, *Collage City* (Cambridge, MA: The MIT Press, 1979).

[106] Mary Casper, "On Land, At Sea: Formalizing Public Edges in the Archipelago," in *The Petropolis of Tomorrow*, pp. 106–199 (esp. p. 110).

[107] Balbo, "Urban Planning and the Fragmented City of the Developing World," p. 24 (source of quotation).

The geographies of urban enclosure form an integral part of the evolving patterns of neoliberal restructuring of urban space in the contemporary era of globalization. These spatial patterns can be described as a kind of "enclave urbanism" – the segregation of urban residents into self-enclosed "islands" with parallel but distinct realities, physically proximate but institutionally and cognitively estranged from each other. The fragmentation of urban space manifests itself as coexistence and proliferation of barricaded and securitized places juxtaposed against zones of generalized insecurity where the disaggregated fragments appear each in their own way to function autonomously. Following loosely the claim of Nezar Alsayyad and Ananya Roy, it might be argued that the paradigmatic spaces of global urbanism at the start of the twenty-first century are sequestered enclaves, insalubrious slums, and autonomous zones.[108] These fractured and exclusionary microgeographies are constructed through a spectacular diffusion of siege architecture (fences, fortified barriers, high walls), obligatory points of passage (security gates, checkpoints), technologies of social control ("smart" CCTV, biometric recognition techniques), and punitive revanchist policing. Whether catalyzed by class anxieties or paranoid fixations on the "Other," physical partitioning of urban landscapes has become a ubiquitous feature of everyday life in contemporary urbanism.[109]

The ongoing and evolving process of spatial enclosure – what Pedro Pírez has called "microfragmentation" – lies at the heart of global urbanism at the start of the twenty-first century.[110] The erection of walls, gates, and barriers has driven a wedge between the "pleasures of wealth and the desires of the poor."[111] These physical impediments to free movement "constitute the most rudimentary and geographically obvious form of enclosure."[112] As Edward Soja has persuasively argued, "Microtechnologies of social and spatial control infest everyday life," and these accumulate to "produce a tightly meshed and

---

[108] Nezar Alsayyad and Ananya Roy, "Medieval Modernity: on Citizenship and Urbanism in a Global Era," *Space and Polity* 10, 1 (2006), pp. 1–20 (esp. pp. 8, 17).

[109] Anna Minton, *Ground Control: Fear and Happiness in the 21st-Century City* (London: Penguin, 2009); and Anne Bottomley and Nathan Moore, "From Walls to Membranes: Fortress Polis and the Governance of Urban Public Space in 21st-Century Britain," *Law and Critique* 18, 2 (2007), pp. 171–206.

[110] Pedro Pírez, "Buenos Aires: Fragmentation and Privatization of the Metropolitan City," *Environment and Urbanization* 14, 1 (2002), pp. 145–158 (esp. p. 149). See also Alex Vasudevan, Colin McFarlane, and Alex Jeffrey, "Spaces of Enclosure," *Geoforum* 39, 5 (2008), pp. 1641–1646.

[111] Alain Badiou, "The Communist Hypothesis," *New Left Review* 49 (2008), pp. 29–42 (quotation from p. 38). See also Rowland Atkinson and Sarah Blandy, "International Perspectives on the New Enclavism and the Rise of Gated Communities," *Housing Studies* 20, 2 (2005), pp. 177–186.

[112] Alex Jeffrey, Colin McFarlane, and Alex Vasudevan, "Rethinking Enclosure: Space, Subjectivity and the Commons," *Antipode* 44, 4 (2012), pp. 1247–1267 (esp. p. 1250). See Teresa Caldeira, *City of Walls: Crime, Segregation, and Citizenship in São Paulo* (Berkeley: University of California Press, 2000).

prisonlike geography punctuated by protective enclosures and overseen by ubiquitous watchful eyes."[113] Apart from the dissolution of normative notions of shared communal space, solidarity, and mutual responsibility, these new types of spatial enclosure have gone hand-in-hand with a political and institutional fragmentation of urban jurisdiction and spaces of citizenship. In response to their exclusion from the mainstream of urban life, the poor, marginalized, and unwanted have engaged in a variety of tactical maneuvers designed to assert their "right to the city."[114]

The underlying logic of securitization – or what Stephen Graham has termed the "new military urbanism" – has spread to cities around the world.[115] The growing obsession with attaining near-total security – especially around globally connected financial centers, port facilities, upscale residential estates, embassy districts, and tourist-entertainment sites – has resulted in the installation of the kind of passage-point architectures that have become ubiquitous at border crossings, international airports, and other transit hubs. City builders have justified the production of urban enclaves as a tactical response heightened perceptions of vulnerability and violence. In creating safe havens in order to manage everyday insecurities associated with crime and the fear it engenders, enclaves have resulted in shrinking public space, in stifling democratic interaction, and in acerbating tensions over access to space.[116]

Uncertainty in its various guises gives rise to the active ingredients that make the retreat of the comfortable classes into cocooned living and working arrangements both possible and preferable. The transfer of landed property into the willing hands of real-estate capitalists intent on squeezing profit from underutilized buildings and unprofitable public space fits with the neoliberal stress on market competition as the key to renewed cycles of urban growth.[117] Enclave urbanism in the twenty-first century is the pattern of transnational urban

[113] Edward Soja, *Seeking Spatial Justice* (Minneapolis: University of Minnesota Press, 2010), pp. 42–43.
[114] David Harvey, "Right to the City," *International Journal of Urban and Regional Research* 27, 4 (2003), pp. 939–941; Asef Bayat, "Uncivil Society: The Politics of the "Informal People'," *Third World Quarterly* 18, 1 (1997), pp. 53–72; and Asef Bayat, *Life as Politics: How Ordinary People Change the Middle East* (Stanford, CA: Stanford University Press, 2009).
[115] Stephen Graham, *Cities under Siege: The New Military Urbanism* (London and New York: Verso, 2010).
[116] Sobia Ahmad Kaker, "Enclaves, Insecurity and Violence in Karachi," *South Asian History and Culture* 5, 1 (2014), pp. 93–107; and Stephen Graham and Sobia Ahmad Kaker, "Living the Security City: Karachi's Archipelago of Enclaves," *Harvard Design Magazine* 37 (2014), pp. 12–16.
[117] Nicholas Blomley, "Making Private Property: Enclosure, Common Right and the Work of Hedges," *Rural History* 18, 1 (2007), pp. 1–21; Nicholas Blomley, "Enclosure, Common Right and the Property of the Poor," *Social and Legal Studies* 17, 3 (2008), pp. 311–331; Nicholas Blomley, "Making Space for Law," in Kevin Cox, Murray Low, and Jennifer Robinson (eds.), *The Sage Handbook of Political Geography* (London: Sage, 2008), pp. 155–168; and James Ferguson, *Global Shadows: Africa in the Neoliberal World Order* (Durham: Duke University Press, 2006).

development whereby metropolitan city-regions across the globe are becoming agglomerations of spatially separated unequal districts, sharply divided by income, opportunities, and race/ethnicity. Enclave urbanism is not the random outcome of unpredictable structural forces. These new kinds of spatial partitioning reflect the deliberate adoption of practices and policies that inexorably shape the physical and social life of the metropolis. Enclave urbanism does not signify the absence of planning, but the presence of a particular kind of planning.[118] As Ravi Sundaram has suggested, municipal planning agencies have largely shifted their strategic focus to singular mega-projects inserted into existing landscapes rather than unitary visions seeking to stitch parts of the city together. Planners have advocated privatized decoupling of infrastructures where new transportation linkages privilege the uninterrupted and rapid movement between sequestered enclaves.[119]

From Mumbai to São Paulo, from New York to Glasgow, and from Johannesburg to Istanbul, the entrenchment of urban inequality and the increasing fragmentation of the urban landscape has accelerated at an alarming pace.[120] The free-market model of entrepreneurial urbanism that originated in leading North American and European cities toward the end of the twentieth century has spread (albeit unevenly) around the world, producing new patterns of spatial fragmentation and social separation.[121] The construction of self-contained enclaves and satellite cities represents a kind of uncanny return to the core principles of modernist planning, to those utopian experiments of the beginning of the twentieth century when some design specialists and architects thought their projects could establish order in the chaos of rapid industrialization and fast-paced urbanization.[122] Against the sprawling urbanity at the start of the twenty-first century, master-planned, holistically designed urban enclaves offer a predictable uniformity of spatial and aesthetic design, which real-estate developers – sometimes alone and sometimes in concert with public authorities – maintain through the strict enforcement of their own rules and restrictions.[123]

---

[118] Tom Angotti, *The New Century of the Metropolis: Urban Enclaves and Orientalism* (New York: Routledge, 2013), pp. 113–114.

[119] Ravi Sundaram, "Uncanny Networks: Pirate, Urban and New Globalization," *Economic and Political Weekly* 34 (January 3, 2004), pp. 64–71 (quotation from p. 64).

[120] Jeffrey, McFarlane, and Vasudevan, "Rethinking Enclosure: Space, Subjectivity and the Commons," p. 1251.

[121] See David Harvey, *Spaces of Hope* (Berkeley: University of California Press, 2000); and David Harvey, "From Globalization to the New Imperialism," in Richard Appelbaum and William Robinson (eds.), *Critical Globalization Studies* (New York: Routledge, 2005), pp. 91–100.

[122] Robert Fishman, *Urban Utopias in the Twentieth Century: Ebenezer Howard, Frank Lloyd Wright, Le Corbusier* (Cambridge, MA: The MIT Press, 1982); and Peter Hall, *Cities of Tomorrow: An Intellectual History of Urban Planning and Design in the Twentieth Century* [Third Edition] (Malden, MA: Blackwell, 2002), pp. 87–141.

[123] Maria Alvarez-Rivadulla, "Golden Ghettos: Gated Communities and Class Residential Segregation in Montevideo, Uruguay," *Environment and Planning A* 39, 1 (2007), pp. 47–63 (esp. p. 48).

In seeking to achieve global competitiveness through insertion into "knowledge-based" (and information-driven) global circuits of capital, large-scale revitalization projects in aspiring world-class cities often conform to standard formulas that result in generic environments: software office parks, innovation districts, outsourcing hubs, and data-processing centers. The construction of what amounts to "speculative world-city projects" in such cities as Bangalore rests on the assumption that IT (information technology) facilities will become a permanent growth machine.[124] Building typologies like five-star hotels, luxury shopping malls, and gated residential communities are functional places, not usually thought of as particularly unusual or atypical to the casual observer. But without them, everyday life in globalizing cities with world-class aspirations would be unimaginable. Their ubiquitous, parallel existences around the world mean that these places are instantly recognizable, each modeled on similar rules, but typically displaying local specificities. The transformation of globalizing cities into parallel worlds is accompanied by an approximation of urban spaces, regardless of the geographical and cultural distance between them. Even though they reflect the historical specificities of local environments, parallel experiences in globalizing cities have become an integral part of global urbanism at the start of the twenty-first century.[125]

Sequestered enclaves like upscale housing estates, gated residential communities, enclosed shopping malls, themed entertainment destinations, high-rise office towers, and securitized office parks are the signature material form of these evolving patterns of global urbanism. The ongoing accumulation of these distinct building typologies provides ample evidence – certainly in a visual way – of an ongoing spatial restructuring of cities around the world. Yet in seeking to locate common patterns within single explanatory frameworks, mainstream urban studies literature has more often than not portrayed these urban enclaves around the world as general urban forms with similar characteristics. Unfortunately, this approach pays strikingly little attention to dissimilarities between urban enclaves in different places, or for the specific ways in which these relate to and are influenced by local contexts.[126] New urban enclosures at a time of neoliberal restructuring have assumed variegated forms, ranging from extractive enclaves to gated residential communities and from large-scale

---

[124] See, for example, Michael Goldman, "Speculative Urbanism and the Making of the Next World City," *International Journal of Urban and Regional Research* 35, 3 (2011), pp. 555–581; Michael Goldman, "Speculating on the Next World City," in Ananya Roy and Aiwha Ong (eds.), *Worlding Cities: Asian Experiments and the Art of Being Global* (Malden, MA: Wiley-Blackwell, 2011), pp. 229–258.

[125] See, for example, Gavin Shatkin and Sanjeev Vidyarthi, "Introduction: Contesting the Indian City: Global Visions and the Politics of the Local," in Gavin Shatkin (ed.), *Contesting the Indian City: Global Visions and the Politics of the Local* (Malden, MA: Wiley-Blackwell, 2014), pp. 1–38.

[126] Mike Douglas, Bart Wissink, and Ronald Van Kempen, "Enclave Urbanism in China: Questions and Interpretations," *Urban Geography* 33, 2 (2012), pp. 167–182.

mega-projects to "cities-within-cities."[127] While the forces of globalization and economic liberalization have created environments amenable to the emergence of new urban enclaves, local characteristics – like the existing urban landscape and its objects, distinctive topological characteristics, the structure of municipal administration, land and building regulations, informal property relations, and the nexus of business and politics – structure the specific local expression of urban enclaves.[128]

What distinguishes the kinds of spatial fragmentation that has taken place in globalizing cities around the world is a blurring of the boundaries between the public and private realms.[129] Privatization of urban space has gone hand-in-glove with the erosion of the public realm. The expansion of postpublic space – socially congregating space that is in the hands of private management – has replaced the modernist ideal of public space as a site for social congregation, chance encounter, and the mingling of strangers.[130]

Splintering Urbanism and Impermanent Infrastructure

The large-scale infrastructure networks that provide cities with energy, water, transportation facilities, and waste-disposal services have long served as symbols of stability and durability. Designed to last for decades, embedded in the urban substrata, and sustained by complex institutional arrangements, these sociotechnological systems conjure up notions of immobility, obduracy, and resilience.[131] In this sense, infrastructure consists not simply of a collection of physical artifacts and technologies, but also institutional rules and norms for operating these sociotechnical systems, management services to constantly monitor and evaluate their performance, along with a steady supply of material

---

[127] Hodkinson, "The New Urban Enclosures," pp. 500–518.
[128] Bart Wissink, "Enclave Urbanism in Mumbai: An Actor-Network-Theory Analysis of Urban (Dis)connection," *Geoforum* 47 (2013), pp. 1–11 (esp. p. 1).
[129] Z. M. Akkar, "Questioning the 'Publicness' of Public Spaces in Post-Industrial Cities," *Traditional Dwellings and Settlements Review* 16, 11 (2005), pp. 75–91; and Z. Müge Akkar Ercan, "Public Spaces of Post-Industrial Cities and their Changing Roles," *METU Journal of Faculty of Architecture* 24, 1 (2007), pp. 115–137.
[130] Margaret Crawford, "Blurring the Boundaries: Public Space and Private Life," in John Chase, Margaret Crawford, and John Kaliska (eds.), *Everyday Urbanism* (New York: The Monacelli Press, 1999), pp. 22–35.
[131] For the source of these ideas in this paragraph, see Timothy Moss, "Socio-technical Change and the Politics of Urban Infrastructure: Managing Energy in Berlin between Dictatorship and Democracy," *Urban Studies* 51, 7 (2014), pp. 1432–1448 (esp. p. 1434). See also Jane Summerton, "Introductory Essay: The Systems Approach to Technological Change," in Jane Summerton (ed.),.) *Changing Large Technical Systems* (Boulder, CO: Westview Press, 1994), pp. 1–21; Anique Hommels, "Studying Obduracy in the City: Toward a Productive Fusion between Technology Studies and Urban Studies," *Science, Technology, & Human Values* 30, 3 (2005), pp. 323–351; and Anique Hommels, *Unbuilding Cities: Obduracy in Urban Sociotechnical Change* (Cambridge, MA: The MIT Press, 2005), pp. 10–12.

resources to construct and maintain them.[132] Taken together, these attributes interact in a seemingly "seamless web" to create, stabilize, and, subsequently, sustain various sociotechnical configurations. As a consequence, sociotechnical systems become particularly prone to path dependency: once established, they prove intrinsically resistant to radical transformation.[133] Networked infrastructures tend to "coagulate into an amorphous whole," and become fixed in place, "severely anchored in their own history and in the histories of the surrounding structures."[134]

Well-developed infrastructure builds and sustains cities, but its breakdown also fragments the built environment and dissolves the urban social fabric.[135] Up-to-date infrastructure, or the installation of new modes of sociotechnological interconnectivity, has long been integrally linked to the vision of the modern city, the dream of what a decent urban life offers its residents.[136] As Christine Boyer has suggested, urban planning has always extended the promise of fashioning the rational city where infrastructure has provided the material cement binding the parts into a coherent whole.[137] In contrast, the multifaceted processes that Simon Marvin and Stephen Graham have referred to as "splintering urbanism" consist of the unbundling of urban infrastructure as a result of the widespread movement toward liberalization, privatization, and outsourcing of service delivery.[138]

Taking the high-modernist ideal of the ubiquitously networked city as their point of departure, Marvin and Graham documented the decline of the integrated urban form and the rise of a new planning logic characterized by the differential and uneven development of urban and regional spaces.[139] They

[132] Thomas Hughes, "The Evolution of Large Technological Systems," in Wiebe Bijker, Thomas Hughes, and Trevor Pinch (eds.),.) *The Social Construction of Technological Systems: New Directions in the Sociology and History of Technology* (Cambridge, MA: The MIT Press, 1987), pp. 51–82; Susan Leigh Star, "The Ethnography of Infrastructure," *American Behavioral Scientist* 43, 3 (1999), pp. 377–393; and Jochen Monstadt, "Conceptualizing the Political Ecology of Urban Infrastructures: Insights from Technology and Urban Studies," *Environment and Planning A* 41, 8 (2009), pp. 1924–1942.

[133] Moss, "Socio-technical Change and the Politics of Urban Infrastructure," p. 1434.

[134] Hommels, *Unbuilding Cities*, p. 10 (source of quotation).

[135] Keil and Young, "In-between Canada: The Emergence of the New Urban Middle," p. 7.

[136] Kamran Asdar Ali and Martina Rieker, "Introduction: Urban Margins," *Social Text* 95 [26(2)] (2008), pp. 1–12 (esp. p. 4). Some of the ideas for this and the following paragraphs is derived from Martin J. Murray, "Afterword: Re-engaging with Transnational Urbanism," in Tony Samara, Shenjing He, and Guo Chen (eds.), *Locating the Right to the City in the Global South* (New York: Routledge, 2013), pp. 285–310 (esp. pp. 293–295).

[137] M. Christine Boyer, *Dreaming the Rational City: The Myth of American City Planning* (Cambridge, MA: The MIT Press, 1986).

[138] Simon Marvin and Stephen Graham, *Splintering Urbanism: Networked Infrastructures, Technological Mobilities and the Urban Condition* (London: Routledge, 2001). See also Graham, "Constructing Premium Network Spaces," pp. 183–185.

[139] For an excellent critique of the splintering urbanism thesis for its alleged deductive approach and its glossing over of local differences, see Olivier Coutard, "Placing Splintering Urbanism:

begin with the premise that neoliberal modes of urban governance stress economic efficiency and cost recovery instead of social equity, and favor market competition, outsourcing, and privatization over the public provision of shared social services. They argue that the conjoined forces of economic liberalization and the collapse of comprehensive urban planning has resulted in the unbundling of basic urban infrastructure, that is, the segmentation of such requisite urban services as transportation systems, telecommunications, power, and water delivery into different networks and packages.[140] The regulatory regimes that support this unbundling of integrated infrastructure have contributed to a growing chasm in urban landscapes between those globally connected spaces of cosmopolitan urbanity (what Marvin and Graham have called "premium networked spaces") and those "bypassed" areas of abandonment and neglect. No longer saddled with the responsibility to provide comprehensive, integrated, and standardized infrastructure, city builders customize these "premium networked spaces" in order to meet the needs of "valued" users, enabling these powerful urban elites to withdraw from public provision of services and retreat into "secessionary spaces" that are disconnected "from the wider urban fabric," yet connected to similar places, thus forming archipelagos of "globalized enclaves."[141] This unbundling of networked infrastructure reinforces the "vicious cycle" of splintering urbanism, "where attempts at sociotechnical secession lead to greater fear of mixing, so increasing pressure for further secession, and so on."[142] The widening gap between connected and unconnected (or disconnected) places and people has produced splintering urbanism, where "the poverty that matters is not so much material poverty but a poverty of connections," thereby limiting the ability marginalized urban residents "to extend their influence in time and space."[143] Splintering urbanism has contributed not only to the original creation but also to the ongoing "fragmentation of the social and material fabric of cities."[144]

Introduction," *Geoforum* 39, 6 (2008), pp. 1815–1820; and Michelle Kooy and Karen Bakker, "Splintered Networks: The Colonial and Contemporary Waters of Jakarta," *Geoforum* 39, 6 (2008), pp. 1843–1858.

[140] Graham and Marvin, *Splintering Urbanism*, p. 141.

[141] Graham and Marvin, *Splintering Urbanism*, pp. 249, 268, and 389; Graham, "Constructing Premium Network Spaces," pp. 183–200; Stephen Graham, "Interview with Stephen Graham," in Ignatio Farias and Thomas Bender (eds.), *Urban Assemblages: How Actor-Network Theory Changes Urban Studies* (London: Routledge, 2010), pp. 197–206; Stephen Graham, "Flow City: Networked Mobilities and the Contemporary Metropolis," *Journal of Urban Technology* 9, 1 (2002), pp. 1–20; Stephen Graham, "The Spectre of the Splintering Metropolis," *Cities* 18, 6 (2001), pp. 365–368.

[142] Graham and Marvin, *Splintering Urbanism*, p. 383.

[143] Graham and Marvin, *Splintering Urbanism*, pp. 288, 249; and Graham, "Constructing Premium Network Spaces," p. 185.

[144] Graham and Marvin, *Splintering Urbanism*, pp. 33 [source of quotation], 288, 383; Marie-Hélène Zérah, "Splintering Urbanism in Mumbai: Contrasting Trends in a Multilayered Society," *Geoforum* 39, 6 (2008), pp. 1922–1932; Sylvy Jaglin, "The Differentiation of Technical

The partitioning of urban space would not be possible without an accompanying splintering of networked infrastructure. The construction of high-speed highways subsidized automobility, thereby facilitating the suburbanization of wealth in North American cities. Splintering urbanism divided urban landscapes into privileged spaces that are hyperconnected, efficient, and fast, juxtaposed against vulnerable spaces that are disconnected, inefficient, and slow. As Marvin and Graham point out, the privileged, secessionary spaces of splintering urbanism are held together through premium-networked infrastructure that quite literally secede from those surrounding urban environments that are characterized by underserviced infrastructure.[145]

New city-building projects work with design protocols for urban infrastructure that are increasingly premised on the hyperconnectivity, security, and aesthetic sensibility of wealthy urban residents. For example, privately built motorways in Buenos Aires connect wealthy residents with their "country" homes in Pilar.[146] In seeking to counteract the deleterious effects of street congestion and traffic gridlock, municipal authorities approved the construction of a vast expressway built on top of cleared slums in Lagos to facilitate the movement of managers and state officials to and from the wealthy suburbs located on the outskirts of the metropolis.[147] Electronic road pricing systems in Singapore and Hong Kong allow elites to bypass rush-hour traffic jams (a lucid example of space-time compression versus space-time expansion).[148]

In metro Manila (as in other aspiring world-class cities struggling with extreme socioeconomic inequalities), a handful of well-positioned real-estate developers have assumed wide-ranging planning powers in the wake of the retreat of municipal government from proactive engagement in overseeing urban redevelopment. In filling this void, these large-scale real-estate developers have assumed a commanding position in planning the transformation of the built environment, ranging "from the visioning of urban futures to the management of the urban environments that they create."[149] Aiming to circumvent the failures and decay of the existing urban landscape, these privatized planning initiatives have resulted in the construction of an expanding archipelago of

Services in Cape Town: Echoing Splintering Urbanism?" *Geoforum* 39, 6 (2008), pp. 1897–1906; and Ricardo Toledo Silva, "The Connectivity of Infrastructure Networks and the Urban Space of São Paulo in the 1990s," *International Journal of Urban and Regional Research* 24, 1 (2000), pp. 139–164.

[145] Graham, "Constructing Premium Network Spaces," pp. 183–200.

[146] Guy Thuillier, "Gated Communities in the Metropolitan Area of Buenos Aires, Argentina: A Challenge for Town Planning," *Housing Studies* 20, 2 (2005), pp. 255–271 (esp. pp. 258–259).

[147] Matthew Gandy, "Learning from Lagos," *New Left Review* 33 (2005), pp. 37–53; and Matthew Gandy, "Planning, Anti-planning, and the Infrastructure Crisis Facing Metropolitan Lagos," *Urban Studies* 43, 2 (2006), pp. 371–396.

[148] Graham, "The Spectre of Splintering Metropolis," pp. 365–368 (esp. p. 366).

[149] Gavin Shatkin, "The City and the Bottom Line: Urban Megaprojects and the Privatization of Planning in Southeast Asia," *Environment and Planning A* 40, 2 (2008), pp. 383–401 (quotation from p. 388).

integrated urban mega-projects that have been built on a massive scale and are designed to meet the rigorous "international" standards that conform to the aesthetic sensibilities of the consuming middle classes.[150] Large-scale property owners and private real-estate developers have taken the lead in proposing new cutting-edge transportation networks (including light-rail, elevated flyovers, and toll roads) that not only bypass existing congested mass transit systems but also link these privately built, self-contained "new town" enclaves scattered across the urban landscape into something that resembles assemblages of exclusive spaces. By providing public subsidies and relaxing existing land-use zoning regulations, the municipal administration "played an active role in facilitating the privatization of transportation infrastructure" and in fostering land redevelopment. The implantation of these large-scale redevelopment projects into the existing social fabric of the city has depended upon massive land clearances and forcible evictions of the urban poor who stand in the way.[151] The construction of these integrated urban mega-projects has resulted in particular mode of urban development that takes shape as the "privatization of planning."[152]

In their hybrid character, infrastructural projects embed a plurality of symbolic meanings into their material existence. In aspiring world-class cities like Hyderabad, Pune City, and Mumbai, transportation infrastructures like flyovers, bypasses, and expressways have become iconic symbols of urban modernity.[153] But because they cater predominantly to a motorized middle class, these elevated highways – like the PVNR Expressway in Hyderabad, and at 11 kilometers, the longest "flyover" in urban Asia – communicate the values of private markets, individual mobility, and a distinct "western" orientation into the urban landscape much more than public mass transit services do.[154] In Managua, "the ripping out of large swaths of the metropolis" to construct infrastructure projects catering for the sole use of wealthy urbanities, Dennis Rodgers has argued, "encroaches on the public space of the city in a much more extensive way than fortified enclaves do."[155]

---

[150] See Gavin Shatkin, "Colonial Capital, Modernist Capital, Global Capital: The Changing Political Symbolism of Urban Space in Metro Manila, the Philippines," *Pacific Affairs* 78, 4 (2005), pp. 577–600.

[151] See Gavin Shatkin, "Planning to Forget: Informal Settlements as 'Forgotten Places' in Globalising Metro Manila," Urban Studies 41, 12 (2004), pp. 2469–2484; Boris Michel, "Going Global, Veiling the Poor Global City Imaginaries in Metro Manila," *Philippine Studies* 58, 3 (2010), pp. 383–406; and Narae Choi, "Metro Manila through the Gentrification Lens: Disparities in Urban Planning and Displacement Risks," *Urban Studies* 53, 3 (2016), pp. 577–592.

[152] Shatkin, "The City and the Bottom Line," pp. 384, 394, 395 (source of quotations).

[153] Veronique Dupont, "The Dream of Delhi as a Global City," *International Journal of Urban and Regional Research* 35, 3 (2011), pp. 533–554.

[154] C. Ramachandraiah, "Maytas, Hyderabad Metro and the Politics of Real Estate," *Economic and Political Weekly* 44, 3 (January 17–23, 2009), pp. 36–40.

[155] Dennis Rodgers, "'Disembedding' the City: Crime, Insecurity and Spatial Organization in Managua, Nicaragua," *Environment & Urbanization* 16, 2 (2004), pp. 113–123 (quotation from p. 123).

Urban integrated mega-projects (and luxury enclaves more generally) are key components of rebuilding efforts in aspiring world-class cities. These financially costly undertakings are rooted in the pursuit of the holy grail of global connectivity. Because large-scale urban restructuring projects are taking places in cities around the world, their ubiquity suggests that the somewhat faddish fixation on drawing a hard-and-fast distinction between cities of the Global North and those of the Global South is a somewhat false and hence unhelpful dichotomy.[156]

As a general rule, assemblages of large-scale networked infrastructure and sociotechnical systems have played a dominant role in transforming urban space. These infrastructure assemblages consist of both hard physical artifacts and soft policies (modes of governance and institutional systems). In "globalizing cities" with world-class aspirations, the construction of luxury enclaves is often closely linked with the installation of large-scale infrastructure projects like highways, railways, and airports. These infrastructure assemblages of hypermobility are the physical embodiments of urban restructuring.[157] In cities across the Middle East and in North Africa, the installation of major infrastructure projects has become a dominant feature of urban rebuilding, functioning as a substitute for public planning policies and programs often unable to cope with the rapid pace of the urban growth. As physical symbols of mobility and global connectivity, highways, high-speed "super-trains," and dazzling airports seek to promote a carefully manicured image of a vibrant city and a comforting vision of urban life as up-to-date and cosmopolitan – an aspiring equal partner in the global world order.[158]

In Cairo, city builders have engaged in massive road-building exercises since the mid-1990s, constructing a series of arterial ring roads, tunnels, and an impressive number of flyovers that pass above the old medieval city and bypass popular residential quarters close to the inner city, thereby opening up desert peripheries to the development of new satellite cities catering for the affluent.[159] In a similar fashion, the *Malek Faysal* road-building project in Damascus, the Haussmann-like *Avenue Royale* roadway in Casablanca, and a connected series of elevated highways, bridges, and underpasses linking the reconstructed central district of Beirut to the newly expanded International Airport have

[156] Isabelle Berry-Chikhaoui, "Major Urban Projects and the People Affected: The Case of Casablanca's Avenue Royale," *Built Environment* 36, 2 (2010), pp. 216–229.

[157] Agnès Deboulet, "Urban Highways as an Embodiment of Mega and Elite Projects: A New Realm of Conflicts and Claims in Three Middle Eastern Capital Cities," *Built Environment* 36, 2 (2010), pp. 146–161.

[158] Deboulet, "Urban Highways as an Embodiment of Mega and Elite Projects," p. 148. See also Matti Semiaticky, "Message in a Metro: Building Urban Rail Infrastructure and Image in Delhi, India," *International Journal of Urban and Regional Research* 30, 2 (2006), pp. 277–292.

[159] Deboulet, "Urban Highways as an Embodiment of Mega and Elite Projects," pp. 149–150.

fundamentally reshaped existing urban landscapes.[160] These massive transportation infrastructure programs have opened the way new "prestige corridors" that connect noncontiguous luxury enclaves. But these "vanity projects" have come at the price of demolishing low-income housing, dismantling what were once coherent neighborhoods, and uprooting stable communities.[161] For example, the *Navab* regeneration project in central Tehran brought about a major discontinuity in social and physical fabric of the city. As an exemplar of what Jon Lang called a "plug-in urban design" project imposed with little consultation and without much forethought, the Navab motorway broke up the integrity of neighborhoods along its route, undermined any sense of belonging, and disrupted the everyday lives of local residents.[162] As a general rule, these "state-of-the-art" urban integrated mega-projects are built without little thought to their overall social consequences, "amidst a sea of unmet social needs."[163] Rising property prices close to these transportation infrastructure projects effectively drive out everyone but the affluent, thereby reinforcing spatial inequalities.[164]

Rapid urbanization has often gone hand-in-hand with absence of proper planning and preparedness. Faced with the challenges of ballooning cities and haphazard growth, city builders have looked to the construction of "new town" developments with well-defined and well-designed residential, commercial, retail, and recreational precincts. These future satellite cities are self-sufficient, self-managed, and self-governed enclaves with privately owned and created infrastructure, integrated waste management infrastructure, water resource systems, and other amenities in place, thus reducing the pressure on the local governing bodies and the city resources. Constructed under the umbrella of public–private partnerships, these urban enclaves aim to be sustainable cities,

---

[160] Hossein Bahrainy and Behnaz Aminzadeh, "Autocratic Urban Design: The Case of the Navab Regeneration Project in Central Tehran," *International Development Planning Review* 29, 2 (2007), pp. 242–270.

[161] Mona El-Kak Harb, "Postwar Beirut: Resources, Negotiations, and Contestations in the Elissar Project," *Arab World Geographer* 3, 4 (2000), pp. 272–288; Berry-Chikhaoui, "Major Urban Projects and the People Affected: The Case of Casablanca's Avenue Royale," pp. 216–229; and Agnès Deboulet and Mona Fawaz, "Contesting the Legitimacy of Urban Restructuring and Highways in Beirut's Irregular Settlements," in Diane Davis and Nora Libertun de Duren (eds.), *Cities and Sovereignty: Nationalist Conflicts in the Urban Realm* (Bloomington: Indiana University Press, 2010), pp. 117–151.

[162] Bahrainy and Aminzadeh, "Autocratic Urban Design," pp. 264, 267. See also Jon Lang, *Urban Design: A Typology of Procedures and Products* (Amsterdam: Elsevier/Architecture Press, 2005).

[163] Onesimo Flores Dewey and Dianne Davis, "Planning, Politics, and Urban Mega-Projects in Developmental Context: Lessons from Mexico City's Airport Controversy," *Journal of Urban Affairs* 35, 5 (2013), pp. 531–551 (quotation from p. 533).

[164] Bahrainy and Aminzadeh, "Autocratic Urban Design," pp. 241–270.

with intelligent infrastructure, with smart plans, and carefully designed built environments.[165]

Escapist Urbanism: Verticality

Spectacular urban skylines and the striking silhouettes that they create are among the most visible and familiar features of modern cities. The hybrid assemblage of buildings juxtaposed one against the other not only provides a popular tourist image of cities, but also reflects wider urban trajectories, socioeconomic thinking, and power relations.[166] Beginning with the rise of early skyscrapers in the late nineteenth century, the scholarship on tall buildings and building events has assumed myriad forms within urban studies and cultural geography more specifically. At the risk of simplification, it is possible to identify two main currents in this scholarly tradition devoted to understanding "tall buildings" as a distinct building typology. The initial versions of such scholarship privileged the materiality of "tall buildings," often using their physical dimensions (size, height, volume, shape, and scale) "to operate forensically as evidence of wider, more abstract processes or morphological conditions."[167] Working in the North American tradition of settlement geography, a great deal of scholarly writing focused on the economic rationale of constructing taller buildings, sometimes focusing on land values as explanations for the promotion of building skyward and suggesting that high-rise structures are best able to efficiently realize the logic of the highest and best use of urban space. Writing in the same vein, other scholars have stressed exceptionally "tall buildings" as technological achievements and engineering marvels, the physical embodiments of the highest stage in the evolution of human settlement patterns.[168]

The second main current in the scholarly literature has explored "tall buildings" through the lens of urban semiotics and the cultural geography. Seen in this light, the "technical and formal qualities of buildings served [only] as a faint skeletal infrastructure" for scholarly writing more concerned with meaning and the sociocultural politics of representation.[169] This scholarly work has looked

---

[165] Pallavi Tak Rai, "Townships for Sustainable Cities," *Procedia: Social and Behavioral Sciences* 37 (2012), pp. 417–442.

[166] The ideas for this paragraph are taken from Igal Charney and Gillad Rosen, "Splintering Skylines in a Fractured City: High-rise Geographies in Jerusalem," *Environment and Planning D* 32, 6 (2014), pp. 1088–1101 (esp. pp. 1088–1089).

[167] Jane M. Jacobs, "A Geography of Big Things," *Cultural Geographies* 13 (2006), pp. 1–27 (quotation from p. 2). See also Stephen Graham, "Luxified Skies," *City* 19, 5 (2015), pp. 618–645.

[168] Larry Ford, *Cities and Buildings: Skyscrapers, Skid Rows and Suburbs* (Baltimore, MD: Johns Hopkins University Press, 1994); and Carol Willis, *Form Follows Finance: Skyscrapers and Skylines in New York and Chicago* (New York: Princeton Architectural Press, 1995).

[169] Jacobs, "A Geography of Big Things," p. 2. See also Kheir Al-Kodmany, "Tall Buildings, Design, and Technology: Visions for the Twenty-first Century City," *Journal of Urban Technology* 18, 3 (2011), pp. 115–140.

upon tall buildings as landscape artifacts that are expressive of various cultural meanings. By treating tall buildings as signs in a semiotic system of meaning, these socioculturalist interpretations have focused on the ways in which the construction of taller and more distinctive built structures enables city builders to express political and corporate power through urban visibility.[170]

In recent decades, excessively tall buildings that have popped up like so many champagne corks in globalizing cities with world-class aspirations have become ubiquitous symbols of global modernity. As the ultimate figural representations of achievement and success on the world stage, late-twentieth-century tall buildings signaled the "visual announcement of entry into the upper echelons of the global economy," making them "the *sine qua non* of place in the global hierarchy of cities."[171] More precisely, the most spectacular buildings in the most unlikely places have become iconic markers and material embodiments of capitalist modernity, displaying a combination of private entrepreneurialism and the assertion of national identity.[172] "The skyscraper megalomania of Asian cities," Aihwa Ong has argued, "is never only about attracting foreign investment, but fundamentally also about an intensive political desire for world recognition."[173] In an era of hyper-building, the celebration of "tall buildings" made of glass and steel conjures images of the "technological sublime."[174] As a visible sign of what Deyan Sudjic has called the "edifice complex," the steady accumulation of stunning, futuristic high-rise landscapes in aspiring world-class cities represents a kind of over-the-top excess – a gaudy extravagance that distracts the gaze from the seaming underside of urban life.[175] For Anthony

---

[170] Mona Domosh, "The Symbolism of the Skyscraper: Case Studies of New York's First Tall Buildings," *Journal of Urban History* 14, 3 (1998), pp. 320–345 (esp. p. 320); and Gail Fenske, *The Skyscraper and the City: The Woolworth Building and the Making of Modern New York* (Chicago: University of Chicago Press, 2008).

[171] Larry Ford, "World Cities and Global Change: Observations on Monumentality in Urban Design," *Eurasian Geography and Economics* 49 (2008), pp. 237–262 (p. 253, source of first quotation); and Sharon Zukin, "The City as a Landscape of Power: London and New York as Global Financial Capitals," in Lester Budd and Sam Whimster (eds.), *Global Finance and Urban Living: A Study of Metropolitan Change* (New York: Routledge, 1992), pp. 195–223 (p. 203, source of second quotation).

[172] Michelle Acuto, "High-rise Dubai Urban Entrepreneurialism and the Technology of Symbolic Power," *Cities* 27, 4 (2010), pp. 272–284; Tim Bunnell, "Views from Above and Below: the Petronas Twin Towers and/in Contesting Visions of Development in Contemporary Malaysia," *Singapore Journal of Tropical Geography* 20, 1 (1999), pp. 1–23; Carolyn Cartier, "The State, Property Development and the Symbolic Landscape in High-rise Hong Kong," *Landscape Research* 24 (1999), pp. 185–208; and Yasser Elsheshtawy, *Dubai: Behind an Urban Spectacle* (New York: Routledge, 2010).

[173] Aihwa Ong, "Hyperbuilding: Spectacle, Speculation, and Hyperspace of Sovereignty," in Ananya Roy and Aihwa Ong (eds.), *Worlding Cities: Asian Experiments and the Art of Being Global* (Malden, MA: Wiley-Blackwell, 2011), pp. 205–226 (quotation from p. 209).

[174] See David Nye, *American Technological Sublime* (Cambridge, MA: The MIT Press, 1994).

[175] Deyan Sudjic, *The Edifice Complex: How the Rich and Powerful Shape the World* (New York: Penguin, 2005). See also Bruce Grant, "The Edifice Complex: Architecture and the Political

King, the "symbolic functions of architectural giantism" are inextricably linked with "the "globally competitive display of economic virility and political power."[176]

At first glance, tall buildings like skyscrapers and high-rise apartment complexes seem to have little real relevance to the understanding of urban landscapes deeply divided on ethno-national, religious, and political lines. Looking at skyscrapers solely through the lens of architectural practice or real-estate development actually ignores other, equally important latent meanings that they represent. One might think of these tall edifices as vertical storytellers, as they most eloquently narrate the unfolding chronicle of the built form as well as the social, economic, and political trajectories of cities.[177]

Questions of surface, topography, and landscape have functioned as the key analytic points of departure for mainstream urban studies discourses. But as Eyal Weizman has argued, the cartographic, top-down aerial gaze that has long dominated both mainstream and critical geopolitical discourses has worked to flatten their spatial imaginaries. "Geopolitics is a flat discourse," he has suggested, "It largely ignores the vertical dimension and tends to look across rather than to cut through the landscape. This was the cartographic imagination inherited from the military and political spatialities of the modern state."[178] Urban and political theorists have only recently started to grant much greater prominence to the vertical dimensions of urban space.[179] For the most part, this work takes its inspiration from what Eyal Weizman has called the "verticality of power." In writing about the three-dimensionality of urban space, he has sought to expose the complex politics of vertical space that characterize the Orientalist

Life of Surplus in the New Baku," *Public Culture* 26, 3 [74] (2014), pp. 501–528 (esp. p. 506). See also Philipp Meuser, "Astana, Almaty, and Aktau: Architectural Experiments in the Steppes of Kazakhstan," in Alfrun Kliems and Marina Dmitrieva (eds.), *The Post-Socialist City: Continuity and Change in Urban Space and Imagery* (Berlin: Jovis, 2010), pp. 230–247.

[176] Anthony King, "Worlds in the City: Manhattan Transfer and the Ascendance of Spectacular Space," *Planning Perspectives* 11, 2 (1996), pp. 97–114 (quotation from p. 97).

[177] Ford, *Cities and Buildings: Skyscrapers, Skid Rows and Suburbs*, pp. 1–10; Ford, "World Cities and Global Change," pp. 237–262; Jean Gottmann, "Why the Skyscraper?" *Geographical Review* 56, 2 (1966), pp. 190–212; Monika Grubbauer, "Architecture, Economic Imaginaries and Urban Politics: The Office Tower as Socially Classifying Device," *International Journal of Urban and Regional Research* 38, 1 (2014), pp. 336–359; Maria Kaika, "Architecture and Crisis: Re-inventing the Icon, Re-imag(in)ing London and Re-branding the City," *Transactions of the Institute of British Geographers* [New Series] 35, 4 (2010), pp. 453–474; Gillian Rose, Monica Degen, and Begum Basdas, "More on 'Big Things': Building Events and Feelings," *Transactions of the Institute of British Geographers* [New Series] 35, 3 (2010), pp. 334–349; and Michael Short, *Planning for Tall Buildings* (London: Routledge, 2012).

[178] Eyal Weizman, *Hollow Land: Israel's Architecture of Occupation* (London: Verso, 2007). See Eyal Weizman, "Introduction to the Politics of Verticality," Open Democracy (2002), p. 3 (source of quotation). Available at www.opendemocracy.net/ecology-politicsverticality/article_801.jsp.

[179] Stephen Graham and Lucy Hewitt, "Getting Off the Ground: On the Politics of Urban Verticality," *Progress in Human Geography* 37, 1 (2013), pp. 72–92.

and neocolonial architectures of Israeli power in and around the West Bank. In drawing attention to the vertical dimension of power/politics, sovereignty, and space, Weizman has developed what he has called the "revisioning of existing cartographic techniques" in order to create "a territorial hologram in which political acts of manipulation and multiplication transform a two-dimensional surface into a three-dimensional volume."[180]

Focusing on the vertical dimension of urban space draws attention to those built forms in cities notable for their height or depth, "providing a better theoretical understanding of the volumetric nature of particular spaces." This stress on verticality offers valuable conceptual lens for exploring and exposing particular kinds of social and material inequalities embedded in and reproduced in three-dimensional space.[181] Put in theoretical terms, a vertical perspective encourages a broader focus on volume and depth-of-field in place of a two-dimensional (or flat) topographical imagination.[182]

Verticality has ensured that, metaphorically speaking, the "First World" and the "Third World" are spread out in a fragmented patchwork that severs territories into separate and discontinuous layers. The practice of layering produces landscapes that resemble an extended "territorial ecosystem" of externally alienated, but internally homogenized, enclave spaces "located next to, within, above, or below each other."[183] The vertical dimension of urban life naturalizes superiority, reifying privilege by endowing it with certain spatial properties.[184] Urban verticality quite literally means security from the insecurities below.[185] In those sprawling cities of hypergrowth, it is the complex relationship between prevailing networks of urban infrastructure and circulation, the enduring presence of unruly public streetscapes and informal settlements, and the construction of buildings off the ground that currently dominates the politics of the verticality.[186] In Guatemala City, for example, the recent surge in direct overseas investment has triggered a massive real-estate boom that has

[180]   Eyal Weizman, "Introduction to the Politics of Verticality," p. 3 (source of quotation).
[181]   Christopher Harker, "The Only Way is Up? Ordinary Topologies in Ramallah," *International Journal of Urban and Regional Research* 38, 1 (2014), pp. 318–335 (esp. 319, source of quotation). See Jeffrey Hou, "Vertical Urbanism, Horizontal Urbanity: Notes from East Asian Cities," in Vinayak Bharne (ed.), *The Emerging Asian City: Concomitant Urbanites and Urbanisms* (New York: Routledge, 2013), pp. 234–243.
[182]   Graham and Hewitt, "Getting Off the Ground," pp. 72–73); and Stuart Elden, "Secure the Volume: Vertical Geopolitics and the Depth of Power," *Political Geography* 34 (2013), pp. 35–51.
[183]   Eyal Weizman, "The Politics of Verticality," in Malkit Shoshan (ed.), *Territoria: Illustrations of the Israeli-Palestinian Conflict* [First Edition, Volume 1] (Haifa: Association of Forty, 2002), pp. 43–68 (p. 43, source of quotation).
[184]   See Andrew Harris, "Vertical Urbanism: Flyovers and Skywalks in Mumbai," in Matthew Gandy (ed.), *Urban Constellations* (Berlin: Jovis, 2011), pp. 118–123.
[185]   Peter Adey, "Vertical Security in the Megacity: Legibility, Mobility and Aerial Politics," *Theory, Culture, & Society* 27, 6 (2010), pp. 51–67 (esp. p. 58).
[186]   Graham and Hewitt, "Getting Off the Ground," pp. 72–92.

resulted in a fundamental alteration of the skyline. With more than 100 new office towers and condominium complexes – each over ten stories – constructed in the last decade or so, Guatemala City represents a "vivid and visually stunning example of how the rich" have managed to "lift themselves above the rest." Height has produced a new kind of vertical segregation. Verticality has metastasized into a new kind of spatial strategy that elevates wealthy urban residents above the problematic streetscape and away from its unruly public space. The construction of high-rise buildings has enabled propertied elites to create distance between themselves and "the poor, the marginalized, and the violent." Verticality has become a new mode of public culture where disengagement and detachment are the norm. High-rise buildings "stand not so much as monuments to modernity but to impunity." In "cities striated by verticality," it has become virtually impossible to realize the modernist ideals of openness, social mixing, and collective use of public space.[187]

Similarly, Mumbai presents a stark contrast between the emergent "vertical city" of hypermodernity with the "horizontal city" of dense streetscapes, broken down infrastructure, and informal settlements. The construction of this new archipelago of high-rise towers, as Vyjayanthi Rao suggests, "has added a three-dimensional twist to the drama of hierarchy, exclusion, and dispossession." The "emerging vertical city" thus renders these derelict landscapes of surrounding informal urbanism obsolete and increasingly irrelevant. "The city of the future is a floating world which is being built on space that has to be created by being unlocked from a labyrinth of regulations," Rao has argued. "This detached social world of new wealth goes hand-in-hand with a floating population of persons" subject to displacement and removal – categories of persons who need to be moved in order to make urban space more "efficient" and "rational" – and hence open to predatory property speculation.[188]

Perhaps the most extreme and notorious Mumbai example of the vertical secession of the super-rich elite is the construction of a colossal 27-story, 400,000-square-foot tower named Antilia, worth more than U.S. $1 billion and owned by Mukesh Ambani. The U.S. $1 billion tower – shown in Figure 3.1 – includes a six-story vertical parking garage for 168 cars, three helipads, a fully outfitted cinema, a staff of servants that exceeds 600, a series of airborne swimming pools, and an independent health club for each of the five family members.[189] Such high-rise buildings soar uncomfortably above the deprivation and violence below. In Mumbai and other "globalizing" cities of the South, the widespread construction of vertical "islands within cities" are

---

187 Kevin O'Neill and Benjamin Fogarty-Valenzuela, "Verticality," *Journal of the Royal Anthropological Institute [N.S.]* 19, 2 (2013), pp. 378–389 (quotations from pp. 378, 379).
188 Vyjayanthi Rao, "Proximate Distances: The Phenomenology of Density in Mumbai," *Built Environment* 33, 2 (2007), pp. 227–248 (quotation from p. 245).
189 Mark Magnier, "Mumbai Billionaire's Home Boasts 27 Floors, Ocean and Slum Views," *The Los Angeles Times*, October 24, 2010.

FIGURE 3.1. Atilia Tower, private residence, Mumbai.
(Photograph courtesy of INDRANIL MUKHERJEE /AFP/Getty Images.)

marketed to wealthy urban residents as solutions to perceived problems of insecurity, infrastructural failure, and environmental degradation.[190]

Taking a three-dimensional frame of spatial analysis as our point of departure enables us to grasp the complex fluidities of urban space. Verticality has
produced parallel but unequal worlds where the processes of splintering urbanism occur not just horizontally across space but along the dimensions of above
and below. The installation of a plethora of new urban prosthetics – pedestrian
skywalks, heliports, elevated highways, bridges, private toll roads, air corridors, tunnel bypasses – has often led to the wholesale spatial restructuring of
modern cities, a brutal process that Marshall Berman (in writing about the
Robert Moses-inspired Cross-Bronx Expressway) once referred to as "urbicide" and Eyal Weizman (in investigating the architecture of occupation in
Israel/Palestine) has termed the "politics of verticality."[191] In São Paulo, for
example, wealthy urban residents have abandoned the street level altogether,
and taken to the skies with the use of the largest fleet of private helicopters

[190] Adey, "Vertical Security in the Megacity," p. 58 (source of quotation). See also Wissink,
"Enclave Urbanism in Mumbai," pp. 1–11; and Shubhangi Athalye, "Rebuilding Mumbai –
Dreams and Reality," *Ethnographic Praxis in Industry Conference Proceedings* 1 (2012),
pp. 350–353.
[191] Marshall Berman, *All that is Solid Melts into Air*, pp. 328–329 (source of quotation); and
Weizman, *Hollow Land*, pp. 12–16.

in the world.[192] In Managua, a whole urban layer has been ripped out of the social fabric of the metropolis for exclusive use by wealthy elites with profound implications for urban social relations.[193] Instead of following the conventional pattern of enclave urbanism where urban landscapes are fragmented into an archipelago of isolated and noncontiguous "fortified enclaves," city builders have constructed a viable and secure network of interconnected high-speed roadways that have effectively "disembedded" a whole layer of the metropolis from the social fabric of the city.[194] The introduction of these new modes of circulation and connection does more than simply provide technical solutions to persistent problems of overcrowded streetscapes and time-consuming traffic congestion. Speed enhances mobility, thereby opening some places to global connections while simultaneously closing off others.[195]

In a similar vein, Andrew Harris has shown that Mumbai is encircled by more than sixty above street-level ("flyovers") highways and more than fifty elevated pedestrian walkways ("skywalks"). These flyovers and skywalks can be understood as key components in the world-class aspirations of city builders to reimagine Mumbai as an emergent global city by "emphasizing predictability, efficiency, and linearity over the fluid choreography and illegibility" of the chaotic streetscape. Inspired by ideas and techniques from around the world, these infrastructure networks have "acted to stitch together and connect a new polycentric landscape of suburban business districts, shopping malls, and residential colonies."[196] Rather than operating simply as a technological (engineering) remedy for relieving congestion, these infrastructural prosthetics perform an invidious sociopolitical function as highly visible premium networked space inserted into the unplanned social fabric of the city.[197] The design and location of these flyover and skywalk projects in Mumbai have come to not only symbolize "splintering urbanism" but also have acted to demarcate, spatialize, and normalize "categories of informal/formal and citizen/noncitizen, thereby fostering both a literal and metaphorical underclass."[198] This three-dimensional fracturing of urban space has not only reinforced existing social inequalities but also produced new vertical relations of power.[199] Paying attention to these

[192] Martin J. Murray, "The Evolving Spatial Form of Cities in a Globalizing World Economy: Johannesburg and Sao Paulo" (Democracy and Governance Programme, Occasional Paper #5. Human Sciences Research Council, Cape Town, 2005).
[193] Rodgers, "'Disembedding' the City," p. 123.   [194] Davis, Planet of Slums, p. 118.
[195] See Paul Virilio, Speed and Politics [Translated by Marc Polizzotti] (Los Angeles: Semiotext[e], 1977).
[196] Harris, "Vertical Urbanism: Flyovers and Skywalks in Mumbai," p. 115 (source of both quotations).
[197] Andrew Harris, "Concrete Geographies: Assembling Global Mumbai through Transport Infrastructure," City 17, 3 (2013), pp. 343–360; and Andrew Harris, "The Metonymic Urbanism of Twenty-first-century Mumbai," Urban Studies 49, 13 (2012), pp. 2955–2973.
[198] Harris, "Vertical Urbanism: Flyovers and Skywalks in Mumbai," p. 116 (source of quotation).
[199] Harris, "Vertical Urbanism: Flyovers and Skywalks in Mumbai," p. 116.

vertical dimensions of power enables us to grasp how the installation of seem-ingly innocuous infrastructure has led to a "fundamental reorganization of metropolitan space, involving a drastic diminution of the intersections between the lives of the rich and the poor."[200]

In writing about Israel/Palestine, Eyal Weizman and Rafi Segal, for example, conceptualize the carving up of urban landscapes into separate spheres of circu-lation as a "politics of verticality."[201] They argue that Israeli settlements rang-ing from small-scale encampments to entire New Towns strategically located in the West Bank constitute the most effective weapon in the war for territory. The origins of this civilian occupation can be traced to early frontier expan-sion sponsored by the Zionist state apparatus (the post-1948 Sharon Plan) that begin with transit camps, outpost agrarian settlements, and the resettlement of Palestinian villages with new Israeli immigrants coming from outside.[202] By occupying elevated locations, these cocooned enclaves are not only physically separated from the much poorer Palestinian neighbors but they also enjoy a vertical sovereignty of surveillance.[203] This architecture of civilian occupation has been almost entirely dependent on the infrastructure networks (roadways, electricity, and water services) provided by the Israeli military as the repressive arm of the state apparatus.[204]

Examining high-rise geographies in Jerusalem can assist in highlighting two key facets of city building: entrenched spatial divisions and the (re)production of contested spaces. As Igal Charney and Gillad Rosen have argued, Jerusalem consists of a heterogeneous landscape divided into three distinct archetypal zones: the Old City, Arab Jerusalem, and Israeli Jerusalem. Taken together, these "three Jerusalems" constitute a spatial configuration of spatially differ-entiated but interconnected "mini-cities" shaped by deeply entrenched dynam-ics of suspicion and mistrust, antagonistic mindsets, and conflicting values. Distinct paradigms and legacies (colonial, postcolonial, and neoliberal) have been responsible for forging the diverse planning policies and practices behind

---

[200] Davis, *Planet of Slums*, p. 119.

[201] See Weizman, "Introduction to the Politics of Verticality." See contributions to Eyal Weizman, Rafi Segal, and David Tartakover (eds.), *A Civilian Occupation: The Politics of Israeli Archi-tecture* (London: Verso, 2003).

[202] Marco Allegra, The Politics of Suburbia: Israel's Settlement Policy and the Production of Space in the Metropolitan Area of Jerusalem," *Environment and Planning A* 45, 3 (2013), pp. 497–516; Eyal Weizman, "Strategic Points, Flexible Lines, Tense Surfaces, Political Volumes: Ariel Sharon and the Geometry of Occupation," *The Philosophical Forum* 35, 2 (2004), pp. 221–244; and Joe Painter, "Prosaic Geographies of Stateness," *Political Geography* 25, 7 (2006), pp. 752–774.

[203] Elia Zureik, David Lyon, and Yassem Abu-Laban, *Surveillance and Control in Israel/Palestine: Population, Territory and Power* (London: Routledge, 2010).

[204] See Weizman, *Hollow Land*, pp. 87–110. See also Aleen Noble and Elisha Efrat, "The Geog-raphy of the Intifada," *Geographical Review* 80, 3 (1990), pp. 288–307; and Elisha Efrat, *Geography of Occupation* (Jerusalem: Carmel Publications, 2002).

the patterns of urban development that have produced these three mini-cities.[205]

To be sure, examining these "three Jerusalems" does not provide an exhaustive cartographic inventory of the microdimensions of spatial conflict in Israel/Palestine, yet it can help in drawing attention to several of the dominant features of the exceptional political geography of the city. The ongoing contestation over high-rise geographies in Jerusalem reflects the different dimensions of city building as it relates to ethno-national divisions, to economic ambitions of an entrepreneurial kind, and to formal and informal processes of reproduction and transformation. The Old City has remained a protected space of immense significance as a sacred site with a sociocultural heritage identity all its own. The strict enforcement of building codes and height restrictions were intended to preserve the built environment of the Holy City as if it were frozen in time.[206] In Arab Jerusalem, urban development and land-use planning has been subordinated to the predominance of Israeli ethno-national aspirations and territorial claims. The unilateral imposition of discriminatory land regimes and the deliberate misuse of planning policies and procedures have systematically delegitimized the rights of Palestinian residents, and, at the same time, entrenched Israeli control over urban space.[207] In Arab Jerusalem, enduring exclusion and discrimination against the Palestinian residents makes taller buildings possible, provided that they are built within the informal development path.[208] These

---

[205] Charney and Rosen, "Splintering Skylines in a Fractured City," pp. 1088–1101 (quotation from p. 1089). See Andreas Faludi, "A Planning Doctrine for Jerusalem?" *International Planning Studies* 2, 1 (1997), pp. 83–102; Shahd Wari, "Jerusalem: One Planning System, Two Urban Realities," *City* 15, 3–4 (2011), pp. 457–472; Shlomo Hasson, "Local Politics and Split Citizenship in Jerusalem," *International Journal of Urban and Regional Research* 20, 1 (1996), pp. 116–133; Anne Shlay and Gillad Rosen, *Jerusalem: The Spatial Politics of a Divided Metropolis* (London: Polity Press, 2015); and Nir Gazit, "Boundaries in Interaction: The Cultural Fabrication of Social Boundaries in West-Jerusalem," *City & Community* 9, 4 (2010), pp. 390–413.

[206] Rassem Khamaisi, "Resisting Creeping Urbanization and Gentrification in the Old City of Jerusalem and its Surroundings," *Contemporary Arab Affairs* 3 (2010), pp. 53–70. See also Sarah Kaminker, "For Arabs Only: Building Restrictions in East Jerusalem," *Journal of Palestine Studies* 26, 4 (1997), pp. 5–16.

[207] Charney and Rosen, "Splintering Skylines in a Fractured City," p. 1089. See also Michael Dumper, *Jerusalem Unbound: Geography, History and the Future of the Holy City* (New York: Columbia University Press, 2014); Yosef Rafeq Jabareen, "The Politics of State Planning in Achieving Geopolitical Ends: The Case of the Recent Master Plan for Jerusalem," *International Development Planning Review* 32, 1 (2010), pp. 27–43; Haim Yacobi, "God, Globalization, and Geopolitics: On West Jerusalem's Gated Communities," *Environment and Planning A* 44 (2012), pp. 2705–2720; Oren Yiftachel, *Ethnocracy: Land and Identity in Israel/Palestine* (Philadelphia: University of Pennsylvania Press, 2006); and Oren Yiftachel and Haim Yacobi, "Planning a Bi-national Capital: Should Jerusalem Remain United?" *Geoforum* 33, 1 (2002), pp. 137–145.

[208] Charney and Rosen, "Splintering Skylines in a Fractured City: High-rise Geographies in Jerusalem," p. 1089. See also Francesco Chiodelli, "Planning Illegality: The Roots of Unauthorized Housing in Arab East Jerusalem," *Cities* 29, 2 (2012), pp. 99–106; and Kaminker, "For Arabs Only," pp. 5–16.

unequal relations provide Israeli authorities with the formal capacity to restrict growth both in horizontal and vertical directions in Palestinian settlement areas, thereby triggering local responses through informal urban development in what Oren Yiftachel has called "gray spaces."[209]

The construction of the Separation Wall, an approximately 700 kilometer-long barrier erected in the first decade of the twenty-first century between Israel and the Palestinian Authority, physically splintered Palestinian territories, creating enclaves spatially separated from each other.[210] Built for security reasons inspired by and geopolitical motivations, this highly disputed Israeli project, has in effect redrawn municipal boundaries, disconnecting some areas of Arab Jerusalem from the rest of the city.[211] The unofficial recasting of municipal boundaries has produced a bifurcated planning regime: restrictive on one side of the Separation Wall and lax on the other. Whereas Palestinian neighborhoods that have remained under Israeli jurisdiction have been subjected to formal planning height restrictions, neighborhoods disconnected from the rest of the city – as a kind of "no man's land" – have been able to evade strict adherence to planning restrictions and zoning laws.[212] The hegemonic use of power by Israeli authorities and their systematic manipulation of planning procedures to strengthen control over annexed territories and to disenfranchise significant

[209] Oren Yiftachel, "Critical Theory and 'Gray Space': Mobilization of the Colonized," *City* 13, 2 (2009), pp. 246–263. See also Ravit Hananel, "Planning Discourse versus Land Discourse: The 2009–12 Reforms in Land-use Planning and Land Policy in Israel," *International Journal of Urban and Regional Research* 37, 5 (2013), pp. 1611–1637.

[210] Marco Allegra, "The Politics of Suburbia: Israel's Settlement Policy and the Production of Space in the Metropolitan Area of Jerusalem," *Environment and Planning* A 45, 3 (2013), pp. 497–516; Oren Yiftachel and Haim Yakobi, "Barriers, Walls, and Diacritics: The Shaping of 'Creeping Apartheid' in Israel/Palestine," in Michael Sorkin (ed.), *Against the Wall: Israel's Barrier to Peace* (New York: The New Press, 2005), pp. 138–157; Franceso Chiodelli, "Re-shaping Jerusalem: The Transformation of Jerusalem's Metropolitan Area by the Israeli Barrier," *Cities* 31 (2013), pp. 417–424; Ariel Handel, "Gated/Gating Community: The Settlement Complex in the West Bank," *Transactions of the Institute of British Geographers* 39, 4 (2014), pp. 504–517; Francesco Chiodelli, "The Next Jerusalem: Potential Futures of the Urban Fabric," *Jerusalem Quarterly* 53 (2014), pp. 50–60; Wendy Pullan, Philipp Misselwitz, Rami Nasrallah, and Haim Yacobi, "Jerusalem's Road 1: An Inner City Frontier? *City* 11, 2 (2007), pp. 176–198; and Ronald Rael, "Border Wall as Architecture," *Environment and Planning D* 29, 3 (2011), pp. 409–420.

[211] Polly Pallister-Wilkins, "The Separation Wall: A Symbol of Power and a Site of Resistance?" *Antipode* 43, 5 (2011), pp. 1851–1882; and Rami Nasrallah, "The Jerusalem Separation Wall: Facts and Political Implications," in Robert Brooks (ed.), *The Wall Fragmenting the Palestinian Fabric in Jerusalem* (Jerusalem: The International Peace and Cooperation Center, 2007), pp. 13–26.

[212] Abdalla Owais, "Transformations between East Jerusalem and its Neighborhoods," in Omar Yousef, Abdalla Owais, Rasseem Khamaisi, and Rami Nasrallah (eds.), *Jerusalem and its Hinterland* (Jerusalem: International Peace and Cooperation Center, 2008), pp. 53–65. See also Christopher Harker, "New Geographies of Palestine/Palestinians," *The Arab World Geographer* 13, 3–4 (2010), pp. 199–216; Handel, "Gated/gating Community," pp. 504–517; and Haim Yacobi, "The NGOization of Space: Dilemmas of Social Change, Planning Policy, and the Israeli Public Sphere," *Environment and Planning D* 25, 4 (2007), pp. 745–758.

local populations exhibits the characteristic features of what Oren Yiftachel has called the "dark side" of planning.[213]

In contrast, an entirely different trajectory of city building has occurred in Israeli Jerusalem. The adoption of a more permissive approach allowing for tall-building development has gone hand-in-hand with the transition from an ethno-national emphasis on state-sponsored spatial expansion – that is, territorial expansion via horizontal growth – to an agenda that favors intensification and densification embodied in the development of large-scale, high-rise buildings. This shift corresponds to the exhaustion of territorial gains within municipal boundaries and the growing international discontent with the construction of Israeli settlements on disputed lands. In response to these limitations, city-builders have adopted a new approach that reroutes development inward by promoting densification and infill development along with high-rising building.[214]

Seen through a topographical lens, Jerusalem is neither a uniform territory nor a flat space. To a large extent, the mushrooming of tall buildings across Israeli Jerusalem reflects the steady encroachment of entrepreneurial approaches to city-building strategies at the dawn of the twenty-first century. Shifting planning ideologies have brought about rethinking of height limitations on buildings. Verticality was once regarded as a major threat to the traditional image and picturesque landscape of Jerusalem. But the triumph of the entrepreneurial vision for Israeli Jerusalem has dovetailed with the relaxation of height restrictions, thereby setting the stage for the "normalization" of tall urban developments under the sway of real-estate capitalism.[215] High-rise buildings represent, in fact, a condensed version of power relations between those who rule and decide and those who are subordinated, excluded, and marginalized.[216]

City builders have contributed to the production of pockets of urban poverty by converting land-use patterns into real-estate development zones that push the urban poor to its peripheries. It is often the case that these real-estate development zones subscribe to a particular kind of appropriate building typology – the high-rise office building or apartment bloc – to validate its insertion into

---

[213] Oren Yiftachel, "Planning and Social Control: Exploring the Dark Side," *Journal of Planning Literature* 12, 4 (1998), pp. 395–406; and Anne Shlay and Gillian Rosen, "Making Place: The Shifting Green Line and the Development of 'Greater' Metropolitan Jerusalem," *City & Community* 9, 4 (2010), pp. 358–389.

[214] Charney and Rosen, "Splintering Skylines in a Fractured City: High-rise Geographies in Jerusalem," p. 1089.

[215] Charney and Rosen, "Splintering Skylines in a Fractured City: High-rise Geographies in Jerusalem," p. 1089. See also Yosef Rafeq Jabareen, "The Politics of State Planning in Achieving Geopolitical Ends: The Case of the Recent Master Plan for Jerusalem," *International Development Planning Review* 32, 1 (2010), pp. 27–43.

[216] Charney and Rosen, "Splintering Skylines in a Fractured City: High-rise Geographies in Jerusalem," p. 1090.

the urban fabric. In cities like Mumbai, São Paulo, and Rio de Janeiro, this built-form invariably results in escalating costs for land and construction, pushing the urban poor further away into deprived zones with inadequate or non-existent infrastructure and poor services. In globalizing cities with world-class aspirations, the simplifying binary – the sprawling slum and the multistoried building – has become the dominant rhetoric describing the built environment of the city.[217] The stark contrast between these building typologies has effectively erased the diversity that exists in the "in-between" places that constitute the built-form of the city. The globalizing aspiration of becoming a vertically oriented city has triggered a process of creative destruction that aims at eliminating all irregular settlements and ambiguous habitats, especially those that have catered for and sustained informal livelihoods and living conditions. Real estate developers have continued to promote a "blank slate" approach to urban redevelopment, an approach inspired by grand modernist planning traditions, and clearly detrimental to the continuity of the vernacular built environments and the local communities that created them. This kind of global modernity has espoused some of the same ideals of comprehensive modern planning practice, but is distinctive both in its use of what has been termed "hypermodern" architecture of hallucinogenic spectacle and in the leading role that private property owners play in its implementation.[218] In catering for the interests of the propertied middle classes and appealing to the global aesthetics of super-modernity, real-estate developers have retrofitted or simply eliminated vernacular environments, home to most working-class residents.[219]

Put theoretically, while it might seem that high-rise buildings provide a possible solution to the problems of density, this building typology has in reality only produced more slums. Slum-making happens because the construction of high-rise buildings is accompanied by increased costs of building and a new economy of land use, one that depends significantly on wider streets, more space for car-parking, and in the final order of things, fewer people occupying available land. In sum, building on the vertical plane satisfies the interests of real-estate developers for profitable investments and contributes to the self-satisfaction of conventional planners, but it also results in the further production of slums.[220]

---

217 Rahul Mehrotra, "Constructing Historic Significance: Looking at Bombay's Historic Fort Area," *Future Anterior* 1, 2 (2004), pp. 25–32.

218 Manish Chalana, "Slumdogs vs. Millionaires: Balancing Urban Informality and Global Modernity in Mumbai, India," *Journal of Architectural Education* 63, 2 (2010), pp. 25–37 (esp. p. 25). See also Arif Dirlik, "Architecture of Global Modernity, Colonialism and Places," in Sang Lee and Ruth Baumeister (eds.), *The Domestic and the Foreign in Architecture* (Rotterdam: 010 Publishers, 2007), pp. 37–46.

219 Neera Adarkar, "Gendering the Culture of Building," *Economic & Political Weekly* 38 [Number 43], 25–31 October 2003), pp. 4527–4534.

220 See Rahul Srivastava and Matias Eshanove, "Why Mumbai's Slums are Villages," *Airoots* (November 26, 2006) Available at www.airoots.org/why-mumbai%E2%80%99s-slums-are-villages.

Spatial Strategies of Enclosure: Fortification

The continued accumulation of new enclosed enclaves for the well-to-do has proceeded in tandem with the rapid expansion of informal settlements, self-building housing, and slums.[221] The increasing popularity of such building typologies as gated residential communities, securitized office complexes, and enclosed shopping malls reflect an "architecture of fear" where property-owning urban elites have retreated behind the protective shield of walls, gates, and private security policing.[222] The commodification and closing-off of urban space has engendered a wide array of regulatory regimes and architectural strategies designed to discipline the unwanted "Others". The language of "siege architecture," "zero tolerance" policing, and "preventative crime control" has found a welcome foothold in the privileged enclaves that have proliferated in "globalizing" cities everywhere.[223]

In the contemporary age of neoliberal globalization, what is striking is the extent to which the mixture of fear and disdain of wealthy urban residents for the urban poor remains such a powerful social force in the making of the cosmopolitan image of aspiring world-class cities.[224] The proliferation of urban enclaves and the clearing away of informal settlements have become two sides of the same coin. Even in such liberal and "Enlightened" cities as Amsterdam, private real-estate developers have joined forces with middle-class residents to safe and secure environments free from "undesirable" groups.[225] From London to Mumbai, and from New York to São Paulo, urban economies geared toward providing services and amenities for the well-to-do residents require a vast legions of cheap labor in order to function efficiently, yet the "consuming classes" prefer to limit their social contact with those they consider beneath their status. Too many architects, design specialists, and urban planners acquiesce in the face of pressures to support property-led redevelopment above all else and to become complicit in the demands of the urban wealthy seeking to retreat into their opulent sanctuaries. All too often, they willingly collaborate in city-building efforts to transform urban spaces into playgrounds for the rich and allow their "professional ethics" to be suffocated by property

---

[221] Tayyab Mahmud, "Slums, Slumdogs, and Resistance," *Journal of Gender, Social Policy, & the Law* 18, 3 (2010), pp. 685–710 (esp. p. 694).

[222] Teresa Caldeira, "Fortified Enclaves: The New Urban Segregation," *Public Culture* 8, 2 (1996), pp. 303–328; Teresa Caldeira, "Building Up Walls: The New Pattern of Spatial Segregation in São Paulo," *International Social Science Journal* 147 (1996), pp. 55–66; Teresa Caldeira, *City of Walls: Crime, Segregation and Citizenship in São Paulo* (Berkeley: University of California Press, 2000); and Jon Connell, "Beyond Manila: Walls, Malls and Private Spaces," *Environment and Planning A* 31, 3 (1999), pp. 417–439.

[223] Mahmud, "Slums, Slumdogs, and Resistance," p. 694.

[224] Matthew Gandy, "Urban Flux," *Architectural Design* 79, 5 (2009), pp. 12–17 (esp. p. 14).

[225] Manuel Aalpers, "The Revanchist Renewal of Yesterday's City of Tomorrow," *Antipode* 43, 5 (2011), pp. 1696–1724 (esp. p. 1696).

speculation, expanding gentrification, and the profit-seeking interests of real-estate capital.[226]

In a context of enduring class inequalities where the regulatory capacities of public authorities are relatively weak, private corporate planning represents a desirable "spatial fix" for the propertied classes. For large-scale real-estate developers, the capacity to plan, regulate, and manage large-scale redevelopment projects has provided them with a convenient way to "wall out the unwanted disorder of the public city and, at the same time, to preserve [inside these newly-minted urban enclaves] a standard of spatial order commensurate with the sense [of those wealthy propertied classes] of their social position as being equal, or more precisely, coeval, with their cosmopolitan urban counterparts" in the world-class cities of North America and Europe.[227] It is important to recognize that demands for sequestered enclaves with their premium networked infrastructures are premised on an assessment – inspired by a sense of class superiority – about the unredeemed qualities of existing urban landscapes.[228] For the urban wealthy with ties to the leading world-class cities at the core of the world economy, "disorder" has come to signify more than just crumbling infrastructure, poor public services, and overcrowded streetscapes, but also crime, squatting, unwanted density, noise, unsavory smells, unsanitary conditions, and general backwardness – that is, abject spaces "associated with, and adulterated by," the unwanted Others.[229]

In the "globalizing" cities at the margins of the world economy, the ways in which wealthy urban residents are uprooted from local circumstances and linked into (seemingly) a-territorial and ethereal global networks and circuits are only made possible by a distinctly territorial, if fragmented and fractured, fortification and securitization of space. In looking at global urbanism at the start of the twenty-first century, urban theorists have increasingly turned their attention to the relationship between crime (and the fear it engenders), insecurity, and risk management, on the one side, and spatial enclosures, defensive landscapes, and military urbanism, on the other.[230] In writing on contemporary urbanism, Zygmut Bauman rightly links the "city of fear" to an evolving architecture of deliberate enclosure. In a disturbing reversal of a progressive movement toward integration and inclusion, cities have reached "the

---

226 John Joe Schlichtman and Jason Patch, "Gentrifier? Who, Me? Interrogating the Gentrifier in the Mirror," *International Journal of Urban and Regional Research* 38, 4 (2014), pp. 1491–1508; and Gandy, "Urban Flux," p. 14.

227 Garrido, "The Ideology of the Dual City," pp. 168, 169 (source of quotation).

228 See, for example, Marco Garrido, "Civil and Uncivil Society: Symbolic Boundaries and Civic Exclusion in Metro Manila," *Philippine Studies* 56, 4 (2008), pp. 443–466.

229 Garrido, "The Ideology of the Dual City," p. 169 (source of quotation).

230 Jon Coaffee, *Terrorism, Risk and the City: The Making of a Contemporary Urban Landscape* (Burlington, VT: Ashgate, 2003); Stephen Graham (ed.), *Cities, War, and Terrorism: Towards an Urban Geopolitics* (Malden, MA: Blackwell, 2004); Paul Virilio, *Bunker Archeology* (New York: Princeton Architectural Press, 1994).

point where they are characterized, instead of by the one-time external wall that protected residents against external enemies, by a multiplicity of internal walls protecting some residents against others within the city."[231] The technologies that produce the built form of enclosed space – or what can be called "bunker architecture" – evoke images of hilltop fortresses, impenetrable redoubts, and trench warfare.[232] Spatial typologies like citadel office complexes, enclosed shopping malls, gated residential communities, elaborate security gates, checkpoints, and high walls have become a common feature of new city-building efforts around the world.[233] The fortification of individual buildings has expanded to the securitization of entire neighborhoods, zones, and districts within cities. Urban scholars have observed the increasing popularity of physical or symbolic boundaries and territorial closures. Access restrictions limit the use of such social congregating places as airports, civic buildings, financial districts, and tourist-entertainment precincts.[234] More and more, cities have become partitioned into luxury enclaves and derelict "no-go" areas, where strategically placed "obligatory passage points" maintain their separation.[235]

Scholars like Mike Davis, Teresa Caldeira, and Dennis Rodgers, for example, have called attention to an emergent "security-obsessed urbanism," where municipal authorities either directly engage in or legitimate the use of force and violence to remove undesirable people from places where they are not wanted.[236] As Mike Davis has argued, "the old liberal paradigm of social control, attempting to balance repression with reform, has long been superseded by a rhetoric of social warfare that calculates the interest of the urban

[231] Zygmut Bauman, "Seeking Shelter in Pandora's Box," *City* 9, 2 (2005), pp. 161–168 (quotation from p. 161).

[232] Eduardo Mendieta, "The Axle of Evil: SUVing through the Slums of Globalizing Neoliberalism," *City* 9, 2 (2005), pp. 195–204; and Nan Ellin, "Fear and City Building," *The Hedgehog Review* V, 3 (2003), pp. 43–61.

[233] Samer Bagaeen and Ola Uduku (eds.), *Gated Communities: Social Sustainability in Contemporary and Historical Gated Developments* (London: Earthscan, 2010).

[234] See Jon Coaffee, "Urban Renaissance in the Age of Terrorism: Revanchism, Automated Social Control or the End of Reflection," *International Journal of Urban and Regional Research* 29, 2 (2005), pp. 447–454 (esp. p. 449).

[235] Graham, "The Specter of Splintering Metropolis," pp. 365–368 (esp. p. 366). See also Stephen Graham, "Cities and the 'War on Terror'," in Michael Sorkin (ed.), Indefensible Space: The Architecture of the National Insecurity State (New York: Routledge, 2007), pp. 1–28; and Stephen Graham, "Switching Cities Off," *City* 9, 2 (2005), pp. 169–194. For a literary treatment of the bordering processes, see Ana Manzanas and Jesús Benito Sanchez, "Unbound Cities, Concentric Circles: Karen Tai Yamashita's *Tropic of Orange*," *Cities, Borders and Spaces in Intercultural American Literature and Film* (New York: Routledge, 2011), pp. 49–64 [Chapter 3].

[236] Caldeira, "Fortified Enclaves: The New Urban Segregation," pp. 303–328; Caldeira, *City of Walls*; and Rodgers, "'Disembedding' the City," pp. 113–123. Edward Soja uses the term "security-based urbanism" but attributes it to Mike Davis. See Edward Soja, *Postmetropolis: Critical Studies of Cities and Regions* (Malden, MA: Blackwell, 2000), pp. 303, 304.

poor and the middle classes as a zero-sum game."[237] The architecture of fear and intimidation has spilled over into public spaces, transforming them into closely guarded, and carefully monitored, privately managed places of social congregation. In aspiring world-class cities from Mexico City to Buenos Aires, and from Istanbul to Beirut, historic downtown centers have emerged as key sites for market-led redevelopment and renewal projects. Under the guise of "urban renaissance," these market-led mega-projects have stressed such hyper-modern *accoutrements* of good urbanism as walkable streetscapes, mixed-use development, sustainable infrastructure, improved aesthetically pleasing designs, cultural vitality, convenient accessibility with an emphasis on place-marketing marketing and safety.[238] As key traveling ideas, metaphors of urban renaissance have become increasingly influential in urban policymaking circles, with its particular emphasis on "quality-of-life" issues founded on the principles of social mixing, sustainability, connectivity, higher densities, walkability and high-quality streetscapes, and accessibility.[239] In aspiring world-class cities, urban revitalization policies are discursively linked, in large measure, to urban fears and risk management.[240] Yet these efforts at revitalization have gone hand-in-hand with new management strategies designed to cleanse spaces of unwanted and undesirable figures as informal traders, beggars, and idlers.[241] Market-led regeneration and neoliberal management strategies have blurred the distinction between "renaissance" and "revanchism," giving rise to "the enactment of [new policies] intended to exclude, displace and disperse 'dangers,' 'risks,' and 'threats,' and even particular activities," which city managers perceive as "disorderly" and "disruptive."[242] The genuine public realm of chance encounter has slowly eroded, giving way to what Michael Walzer famously

[237] Mike Davis, *City of Quartz: Excavating the Future of Los Angeles* (New York: Verso, 1990), p. 223.

[238] Taner Oc and Steve Tiesdell (eds.), *Safer City Centres: Reviving the Public Realm* (London: Paul Chapman, 1997); Ali Madanipour, *Public and Private Spaces of the City* (London: Routledge, 2003); Ian Gordon, "The Resurgent City: What, Where, How, and for When?" *Planning, Theory and Practice* 5, 3 (2004), pp. 371–379.

[239] Coaffee, "Urban Renaissance in the Age of Terrorism," p. 454.

[240] Leslie Kern, "Selling the 'Scary City': Gendering Freedom, Fear and Condominium Development in the Neoliberal City," *Social & Cultural Geography* 11, 3 (2010), pp. 209–230.

[241] Steven Flusty, "The Banality of Interdiction: Surveillance, Control and the Displacement of Diversity," *International Journal of Urban and Regional Research* 25, 3 (2001), pp. 658–664; Mike Raco, "Remaking Place and Securitizing Space: Urban Regeneration and the Strategies, Tactics, and Practices of Policing in the UK," *Urban Studies* 40, 9 (2003), pp. 1869–1887; Alan Reeve, "The Private Realm of the Managed Town Centre," *Urban Design International* 1, 1 (1996), pp. 61–80; Andrew Merrifield, "Public Space: Integration and Exclusion in Urban Life," *City* 5, 6 (1996), pp. 57–72; and Gordon MacLeod, "From Urban Entrepreneurialism to a "Revanchist City"? On the Spatial Injustices of Glasgow's Renaissance," *Antipode* 34, 3 (2002), pp. 602–624.

[242] Coaffee, "Urban Renaissance in the Age of Terrorism," p. 448 (source of quotation; rest of the sentence paraphrased). See also Tony Roshan Samara, "Policing Development: Urban Renewal as Neoliberal Security Strategy," *Urban Studies* 47, 1 (2010), pp. 197–214.

referred to as "single-minded spaces," and what urban theorists have called post-public space.[243]

This "ecology of fear" often assumes a life of its own. Risk management strategies and efforts to create safer cities through architectural design have served to further fragment the urban landscape, establishing complex rules of inclusion and exclusion that have resulted in increasingly complex patterns of segregation and displacement.[244] A global security-and-control paradigm has increasingly become the dominant logic behind practices of urban governance. In what amounts to the everyday militarization of the city, the massive deployment of surveillance technologies has become integral and embedded part of the planning toolkit with the aim of reducing crime and preventing antisocial behavior.[245]

Beyond conventional CCTV, digital imaging, and facial recognition systems, a plethora of new technologies borrowed from the military have come to play a wider role in colonizing "the civilian sphere" with power not only to deter but also to classify people and sort them into categories.[246] These technologies are key components in the expanding exercise of power in urban space. For theorists like Gilles Deleuze, contemporary urbanism is crisscrossed with rapidly deployed, free-floating forms of control, where advances in computerized information technologies are capable of tracking individuals across physical and virtual space.[247] In a similar vein, Stephen Graham has argued that "biased use of new technologies can support new extremes of inequality and a splintering of previously homogenous infrastructural experiences."[248] Advances in computerized information technology clearly embody the tension between increased convenience, on the one side, and expanded surveillance and control, on the other.

Characteristic Features of Urban Enclaves

The construction of urban enclaves catering to the affluent residents and global business enterprises reveals three features of city building in the contemporary era of neoliberal globalization. The first feature is that these large-scale

---

[243] Michael Walzer, "Pleasures and the Cost of Urbanity," *Dissent* 33, 4 (1986), pp. 470–475. See Adam Holden and Kurt Iveson, "Designs on the Urban: New Labour's Urban Renaissance and the Spaces of Citizenship," *City* 7, 1 (2003), pp. 57–72.

[244] Jon Coaffee, "Urban Renaissance in the Age of Terrorism," p. 449.

[245] Coaffee, "Urban Renaissance in the Age of Terrorism," p. 454; and Stephen Graham, "Cities as Battlespace: The New Military Urbanism," *City* 13, 4 (2009), pp. 383–402; and Roy Coleman, "Images from a Neoliberal City: The State, Surveillance and Social Control," *Critical Criminology* 12, 1 (2004), pp. 21–42.

[246] Coaffee, "Urban Renaissance in the Age of Terrorism," p. 454.

[247] Gilles Deleuze, "Postscript on the Societies of Control," *October* 59 (1992), pp. 3–7.

[248] Graham, "The Specter of Splintering Metropolis," p. 366. See also Stephen Graham, "Spectres of Terror," in Philipp Misselwitz and Tim Rieniets (eds.), *City of Collision: Jerusalem and the Principles of Conflict Urbanism* (Basel, Switzerland: Birkhauser, 2006), pp. 156–162.

urban enclaves resemble "cities-within-the-city" in that they bring together a full range of urban amenities from business office complexes to residential housing, and from leisure and entertainment venues to outdoor lifestyle options. Yet these master-planned, holistic redevelopment projects hide the fact that their existence is only possible within the city that provides them with the means of tapping into services and infrastructure. A reliable supply of high-quality services and infrastructure for those who live there means that it is almost unnecessary for residents to leave the confines of the sequestered redoubts, except for excursions to similar "elsewheres."[249]

The second feature is that the types of privatized planning that underpins the production of these self-contained enclaves leaves the rest of the city in a sort of limbo, virtually unaffected and untouched by metropolitan-wide planning policy decisions. A distinctive kind of "entrepreneurial governance" has taken shape in these enclaves where the administration of postpublic space has largely fallen into private hands. In this way, the city has come to reflect the logic of the global marketplace: "messy competition outside and heavy rational planning inside."[250] This state of affairs has reinforced social segregation and social inequalities not as a consequence of deliberate policies but largely as the result of marketplace bargaining power.[251]

Third, the urban chaos that results from the private production of fragmented space has reinforced the marginalization and social exclusion of the urban poor. The imposition of strict zoning regulations, land-use standards, and building guidelines has often fragmented and undermined public places and place life by establishing a strict demarcation between partitioned affluent zones and the surrounding unplanned and unregulated cityscape.[252] Shifting modes of municipal governance have converted existing public places into a sort of visual spectacle that function as playgrounds for the consuming classes. Under these circumstances, pedestrian streets, squares, plazas, parks, and promenades are

[249] See, for example, Dennis Rodgers, "'Nueva Managua': The Disembedded City," in Mike Davis and Daniel Monk (eds.), *Evil Paradises: Dreamworlds of Neoliberalism* (New York: New Press, 2007), pp. 127–139; and Dennis Rodgers, "Haussmannization in the Tropics: Abject Urbanism and Infrastructural Violence in Nicaragua," *Ethnography* 13, 4 (2012), pp. 413–438.

[250] Pedro Pírez, "Buenos Aires: Fragmentation and Privatization of the Metropolitan City," *Environment & Urbanization* 14, 1 (2002), pp. 145–158 (p. 155, source of quotation).

[251] See Choon-Piew Pow, "Constructing a New Private Order: Gated Communities and the Privatization of Urban Life in Post-Reform Shanghai," *Social & Cultural Geography* 8, 6 (2007), pp. 813–833.

[252] Trevor Boddy, "Underground and Overhead: Building the Analogous City," in Michael Sorkin (ed.), *Variations on a Theme Park* (New York: Noonday Press, 1992), pp. 123–153; Jack Byers, "The Privatization of Downtown Public Space: The Emerging Grade-separated City in North America," *Journal of Planning Education and Research* 17, 3 (1998), pp. 189–205; Anastasia Loukaitou-Sideris, "Privatization of Public Open Space: Los Angeles Experience," *Town Planning Review* 64, 2 (1993), pp. 139–167; and Don Mitchell, "The Annihilation of Space by Law: The Roots and Implications of Anti-homeless Laws in the United States," *Antipode* 29, 3 (1997), pp. 303–335.

squeezed so much they become almost obsolete and unrecognizable.[253] This process of what might be called "despatialization" has produced something akin to ethereal space – locations that provide the illusion of genuine social mixing yet mask the reality of the space itself as accessible to only a privileged few.[254] Metaphorically at least, those enclaves inserted into the existing urban fabric are often located between continued obscurity of the city and a potential future of grandiosity. In other words, while urban enclaves serve as potent – if only indeterminate – claims to the achievement of world-class status, they also can just as easily represent unfulfilled ambition and unrealized fantasy.[255]

[253] See Rachel Berney, "Public Space versus Tableau: The Right-to-the-City Paradox in Neoliberal Bogotá, Columbia," in Tony Samara, Shenjing He, and Guo Chen (eds.), *Locating the Right to the City in the Global South* (New York: Routledge, 2013), pp. 152–170; Akkar Ercan, "Public Spaces of Post-industrial Cities and their Changing Roles," pp. 115–137; and Carolyn Cartier, "Megadevelopment in Malaysia: From Heritage Landscapes to 'Leisurescapes' in Melaka's Tourism Sector," *Singapore Journal of Tropical Geography*, 19, 2 (1998), pp. 151–176.

[254] Donald Crilley, "Megastructures and Urban Change: Aesthetics, Ideology and Design," in Paul Knox (ed.), *The Restless Urban Landscape* (Englewood Cliffs, NJ: Prentice Hall, 1993), pp. 127–164. For "despatialization," see William Mitchell, *City of Bits: Space, Place, and the Infobahn* (Cambridge, MA: The MIT Press, 1995), p. 106; and Lawrence Herzog, *Return to the Center: Culture, Public Space, and City Building in the Global Era* (Austin: University of Texas Press, 2006), p. 27.

[255] These sentences are taken almost verbatim from Seth Schindler, "Governing the Twenty-First Century Metropolis and Transforming Territory," *Territory, Politics, Governance* 3, 1 (2015), pp. 7–26 (especially p. 16).

4

Cities as an Assemblage of Enclaves

Realizing the Expectations of Late Modernity

Conventional urban studies literature has largely framed the understanding of the struggling cities at the margins of modernity almost exclusively through the distorting lens of so-called "Third World" urbanization where overburdened cities – swamped by large numbers of people without regular wage-paying work, lacking up-to-date infrastructure, and hampered by lax planning guidelines – lag behind the developed, globally ambitious, and mature cities of the West.[1] In part, it is this neo-orientalist framework – restricting imaginings of sprawling megacities of hypergrowth to a stereotypical litany of slums, squalor, informality, and overcrowding – that have made it difficult to theorize the global unevenness of spatial landscapes, particularly the dynamics of extreme socioeconomic inequalities and their relationship to urban form.[2] This *problematique*

---

[1] While the actual term "third world city" has largely fallen out of favor, its original connotations of backward and underdeveloped cities – poor cities in poor countries – has remained a salient way of thinking in mainstream urban theory. See Jennifer Robinson, *Ordinary Cities: Between and Modernity* (New York: Routledge, 2006), pp. 1–12, 116–140. Generally speaking, conventional approaches to urban studies treat struggling cities in (so-called) "developing countries" as "only good for describing absences and wanting" (Edgar Pieterse, "Cityness and African Urban Development" (Working Paper No. 42 [2010], World Institute for Development Economics Research), quotation from p. 2 [ISBN 978–92–9230–279–5]. Available at http://hdl .handle.net/10419/54110. See also Alan Gilbert, "Housing in Third World Cities: The Critical Issues," *Geography* 85, 2 (2000), pp. 145–155.

[2] Tom Angotti, *The New Century of the Metropolis: Urban Enclaves and Orientalism* (New York: Routledge, 2013), pp. 113–114. See also Tim Bunnell, Daniel Goh, Chee-Kien Lai and Choon-Piew Pow, "Introduction: Global Urban Frontiers? Asian Cities in Theory, Practice and Imagination," *Urban Studies* 49, 13 (2012), pp. 2785–2793; Trevor Hogan, Tim Bunnell, Choon-Piew Pow, Eka Permanasari, and Sirat Morshidi, "Asian Urbanisms and the Privatization of Cities," *Cities* 29, 1 (2012), pp. 59–63; and Tim Bunnell and Anant Maringanti, "Practicing Urban and Regional Research beyond Metrocentricity," *International Journal of Urban and Regional Research* 34, 2 (2010), pp. 415–420; and Daniel Goh and Tim Bunnell, "Recentring Southeast Asian Cities," *International Journal of Urban and Regional Research* 37, 3 (2013), pp. 825–833.

of "backward cities" in poor countries is no longer a helpful way of making sense of what is actually happening on the ground. Binary oppositions like First World and Third World cities (or "developed" and "developing") cities – categorical distinctions that achieved a great deal of popularity in the "development decades" after World War II – have long provided key points of reference and starting points for analysis for conventional urban studies and planning theory. But these outdated and redundant conceptual distinctions have proven themselves to be ill-equipped to make sense of the proliferation of the "enclave spaces" and the resulting spatial unevenness that increasingly characterize urban landscapes in China, India, Southeast Asia, Africa, Latin America, and the Middle East.[3]

One strong current in the scholarly literature has suggested that the globalizing impulses unleashed at the end of the twentieth century – especially the shifts driven by the revolution in information and communication technologies (ICTs) – heralded the "end of geography," the "death of distance," and the emergence of a "borderless world."[4] This line of reasoning has suggested that the new age of connectivity, characterized primarily by the deregulation of market competition and increased economic integration in an emergent friction-less capitalism, have contributed to a marked space–time compression of socioeconomic processes.[5] The consensus among these commentators in this subfield of globalization studies is that technological progress has effectively detached the socioeconomic activities from the "spatial fix" that tied them to specific locations.[6] Deterritorialization – a term coined "to describe the rearranging and restructuring of spatial relations as a consequence of the technological, material, and geopolitical transformations of the late twentieth century" – implies that location and place – that is, territory – have lost their significance and power in everyday life. To speak of deterritorialization in the discourse of contemporary globalization is to suggest "a generalized dismantling of the

[3] James Sidaway, "Enclave Space: a New Metageography of Development?" *Area* 39, 3 (2007), pp. 331–339 (esp. p. 336); and James Sidaway, "Spaces of Postdevelopment," *Progress in Human Geography* 31, 2 (2007), pp. 345–361.

[4] Richard O'Brien, *Global Financial Integration: The End of Geography* (London: Pinter Publishers, 1992); Frances Cairncross, *The Death of Distance: How the Communications Revolution is Changing our Lives* (Boston: Harvard Business School Press, 1997); and Kenichi Ohmae, *The Borderless World: Power and Strategy in the Interlinked Economy* [Revised Edition] (New York: Harper Business, 1999).

[5] See David Newman and Anssi Passi, "Fences and Neighbors in the Postmodern World: Boundary Narratives in Political Geography," *Progress in Human Geography* 22, 2 (1998), pp. 186–207; Anssi Passi, "Boundaries as Social Processes: Territoriality in the World of Flows," *Geopolitics* 3, 1 (1998), pp. 69–88; David Newman, "Geopolitics Renaissant: Territory, Sovereignty, and the World Political Map," *Geopolitics* 3, 1 (1998), pp. 1–16; and H. W. Yeung, "Capital, State, and Place: Contesting the Borderless World," *Transactions of the Association of British Geographers* NS 23, 3 (1998), pp. 291–309.

[6] Stephen Graham, "The End of Geography or the Explosion of Place? Conceptualising Space, Place, and Information Technology," *Progress in Human Geography* 22, 2 (1998), pp. 165–185.

complex of geography, power, and identity that supposedly defined and delimited everyday life in in the developed world for most of the twentieth century." As a spatial trope, deterritorization acquires its distinctive catchet by reference to a new condition of speed and information flows, the transgression (and hence porosity) of inherited (fixed and stable) borders, the transcendence of taken-for-granted divides, and the advent of a more interconnected "globalized" world. While regimes of territoriality are constantly in flux and subject to negotiation, the various "discourses of deterritorialization tend to ascribe a unique transcendency to the contemporary condition, defining it as a moment of overwhelming newness."[7]

The rhetoric of deterritorialization rests, of course, on "sweepingly superficial representations of boundaries, borders, and territories" at the start of the twenty-first century. These celebrations of the inevitable borderless world marked by the unimpeded movement of capital, ideas, and goods tend to operate with normative prescriptions that promote neoliberal visions of what the emergent "information age" (or the "telecommunications revolution") should create, namely, a "friction-free" capitalist marketplace that knows no barriers or limitations. Yet despite its widespread and popular rhetorical appeal, the supposed "transcendence of territoriality" has overlooked and ignored asymmetrical concentrations of flows, informational disparities, the spatial unevenness of networked infrastructures, and nodal connections that are layered upon and embedded within existing territorial relations of power.[8] In the contemporary age of globalization, the hyper-mobility of capital, information, and commodities has gone hand-in-hand with a deepening of social inequalities across the globe, rearranging rather than abolishing borders, boundaries, and territories.[9]

At the start of the twenty-first century, metropolitan regions are quickly becoming agglomerations of unequal districts and precincts, sharply divided by race, class, and other social distinctions that mark difference, and often physically separated by a combination of "hard" and "soft" barriers. This type of enclave urbanism is not a random occurrence. "Enclaving" reflects the deliberate adoption of policies that shape the physical and social life of the metropolis. As Tom Angotti has argued, these enclaves are not the unintended outcome of the lack of planning regulations, but the intentional consequence of new kinds of privatized planning.[10] While cities have always consisted of splintered and fractured spaces, the current spatial geography of enclave urbanism is

---

7 Ideas for this paragraph derived from Gearóid Ó Tualthail (Gerald Toal), "Borderless Worlds? Problematising Discourses of Deterritorialization," in Nurit Kliot and David Newman (eds.), *Geopolitics at the End of the Twentieth Century: The Changing World Political Map* (London: Frank Cass, 2000), pp. 139–154 (quotations from p. 139, 140).

8 Ó Tualthail (Gerald Toal), "Borderless Worlds?" pp. 149–151 (quotation from p. 142).

9 Deljana Iossifova, "Searching for Common Ground: Urban Borderlands in a World of Borders and Boundaries," *Cities* 34 (2013), pp. 1–5.

10 Angotti, *The New Century of the Metropolis*, p. 113.

significant because of the ways in which these largely self-contained entities are "superimposed upon existing patterns of human settlements."[11]

The Limits of "Imitative" Urbanism

Generally speaking, most scholarly work looking at the rising tide of *corporate-led* urban development in aspiring world-class cities over the past several decades has tended to attribute the visible patterns of spatial polarization to be "wholly the outcome of contemporary globalization." Yet in looking at Metro Manila, for example, Marco Garrido has suggested that the enduring patterns of segregation commonly associated in conventional urban studies literature with polarization – that is, "urban landscapes fragmented into networks of privatized elite spaces overlaying the public city" – actually has as much to do with modernist-inspired city building under colonialism as it has with the contemporary era of globalization. In short, in order to genuinely understand the nature of the postcolonial "dual city," it is necessary to look behind and beyond the contemporary manifestations of globalization, and consider as well "the enduring influences" of city building under colonialism, particularly its modernist ethos of progress.[12]

The production of enclaves and the proliferation of slums are increasingly blended together in new hybrid forms of city building that resemble nothing like what came before. The (so-called) "super-gentrification" of leading world-class cities in the Global North, which has produced heightened sociospatial disparities and sites of exclusivity, has spilled over to cities large and small around the world.[13] Yet instead of conceiving of the global spread of gentrifying impulses solely through the lens of "imitative urbanism" (or the idea that struggling cities of the so-called Global South simply copy, or plagiarize, from the Global North), it is more productive to think relationally, that is, to adopt the conceptual frameworks of comparative and "cosmopolitan urbanism," which view the conjoined processes of redevelopment and displacement not in terms of universalizing one-size-fits-all models but in the context of their local specificities.[14]

---

[11] Newman and Paasi, "Fences and Neighbours in the Postmodern World," p. 190 (source of quotation).

[12] Marco Garrido, "The Ideology of the Dual City: The Modernist Ethic in the Corporate Development of Makati City, Metro Manila," *International Journal of Urban and Regional Research* 37, 1 (2013), pp. 165–185 (quotations from p. 167, 182). For a similar argument, see Janet Abu-Lughod, "Tale of Two Cities: The Origins of Modern Cairo," *Comparative Studies in Society and History* 7, 4 (1965), pp. 429–457.

[13] Tim Butler and Loretta Lees, "Super-Gentrification in Barnsbury, London," *Transactions of the British Institute of Geographers* 31, 4 (2006), pp. 467–487; Loretta Lees, "Super-Gentrification: The Case of Brooklyn Heights, New York City," *Urban Studies* 40, 12 (2003), pp. 2487–2509; and Loretta Lees, Tom Slater, and Elvin Wyly, *Gentrification* (New York: Routledge, 2013).

[14] Loretta Lees, "The Geography of Gentrification: Thinking through Comparative Urbanism," *Progress in Human Geography* 36, 2 (2012), pp. 155–171; and Andrew Harris, "From London

One key aspect of how globalization and planning practice are inextricably linked together is that the traveling of policy recommendations across borders has accelerated and gained momentum, reaching "historically unprecedented" levels of intensity.[15] In the current age of globalization, planning ideas and practices have not just spread along a single pathway from the "West to the rest," or the "developed" to the "developing" world, or the "Global North" to the "South." Comingling and blending of policy recommendations have produced cross-fertilizing movements that represent the "synthesized products of an international planning community."[16] The worldwide proliferation and cross-border circulation of strategic planning has meant that ideas and practices have become detached from their origins, and thus from their "original" identities and sources of inspiration.[17] The "transnationality" of "policy tourism" has meant that these ideas and practices can both be locally anchored but also easily flow across borders, decisively shaping the adoption of strategic planning interventions in a variety of locations.[18]

"Urban policy mobilities" have become an integral part of transnational norm-making. The showcasing of best-practice cases of strategic planning has created viable channels for the dissemination of ideas and the global circulation of expert knowledge.[19] Yet this making of transnational urban policy interventions is an uneven process in which only specific ideas on urban development are chosen to become a new global standard. Instead of holistic morphological planning that aims to stitch the urban fabric into a coherent whole, the revitalization strategies that have become the most popular have laid particular stress on the construction of attention-getting (but

to Mumbai and Back Again: Gentrification and Public Policy in Comparative Perspective," *Urban Studies* 45, 12 (2008), pp. 2407–2428.

[15] Malcolm Tait and Ole Jensen, "Travelling Ideas, Power and Place: The Cases of Urban Villages and Business Improvement Districts," *International Planning Studies* 12, 2 (2007), pp. 107–127 (p. 107, source of quotation). See also Farokh Afshar and Keith Pezzoli, "Introduction: Integrating Globalization and Planning," *Journal of Planning Education and Research* 20, 3 (2001), pp. 277–280.

[16] Stephen Ward, "Transnational Planners in a Postcolonial World," in Patsy Healey and Robert Upton (eds.), *Crossing Borders: International Exchange and Planning Practices* (London: Routledge, 2010), pp. 46–72 (p. 66, source of quotation). See also Patsy Healey, "Introduction: The Transnational Flow of Knowledge and Expertise in the Planning Field," in Patsy Healey and Robert Upton (eds.), *Crossing Borders: International Exchange and Planning Practices* (London: Routledge, 2010), pp. 1–26.

[17] Louis Albrechts, "In Pursuit of New Approaches to Strategic Spatial Planning: A European Perspective," *International Planning Studies* 6, 3 (2001), pp. 293–310 (esp. p. 294).

[18] Christof Parnreiter, "Commentary: Toward the Making of a Transnational Urban Policy?" *Journal of Planning Education and Research* 31, 4 (2011), pp. 416–422. See also Sara González, "Bilbao and Barcelona 'in Motion': How Urban Regeneration 'Models' Travel and Mutate in the Global Flows of Policy Tourism," *Urban Studies* 48, 7 (2011), pp. 1397–1418.

[19] Eugene McCann, "Urban Policy Mobilities and Global Circuits of Knowledge: Toward a Research Agenda," *Annals of the Association of American Geographers* 101, 1 (2011), pp. 107–30.

sometimes ill-fitting) mega-projects inserted incongruously into the existing urban fabric.[20]

Scholars in urban studies have become increasingly intrigued by the ways that urban policy and planning ideas travel from city to city, particularly when they gravitate to cities outside the "heartlands" of the capitalist core of the world economy.[21] To paraphrase Idalina Baptisa, one must take great care not to engage in an over-investment in the hegemonic status of key "traveling ideas" (such as neoliberalism) as uniformly applicable theoretical concepts and as unassailable analytical frameworks as they take root in fragile cities at the borderlands of core zones of the world economy.[22] Instead of stressing the diffusion (i.e., the straightforward mimicry, borrowing, and copying) of urban policies as they move from city to city, it is more instructive to emphasize the translation (i.e., open to multiple interpretations) of these "traveling ideas" that assume hybrid "lives of their own" as they mutate and evolve under place-specific circumstances. In short, emulation is not identical to unidirectional imitation or unilineal replication. The epistemological break from simplistic diffusionist accounts enables us to see that "traveling ideas" do not operate as stable artifacts of "policy-on-the-move" that effectively colonize diversity and difference through their homogenizing effects, but instead are produced relationally in historically specific contexts. Within the framework of serial repetition that seem to identify the patterns of spatial fragmentation and enclave format, there exist certain underlying logics of differentiation and difference-making. Within the broad contours of global urbanism at the start of the twenty-first century, one can observe that luxury enclaves and autonomous zones have appeared "everywhere." The steady proliferation of luxury enclaves in globalizing cities with world-class aspirations – specifically, struggling cities outside the "heartlands" of the core zones of the world economy – has become both a visible sign of being cutting-edge and hypermodern, and, at the same, time symbolic

---

[20] Patsy Healey, *Making Better Places: The Planning Project in the Twenty-first Century* (New York: Palgrave Macmillan, 2010), p. 170. See also Bent Flyvbjerg, Nils Bruzelius, and Werner Rothengatter, *Megaprojects and Risk: An Anatomy of Ambition* (Cambridge, UK: Cambridge University Press, 2003).

[21] Patsy Healey, "The Universal and the Contingent: Some Reflections on the Transnational Flow of Planning Ideas and Practices," *Planning Theory* 11, 2 (2012), pp. 188–207; Patsy Healey, "Introduction: The Transnational Flow of Knowledge and Expertise in the Planning Field," in Patsy Healey and Robert Upton, *Crossing Borders: International Exchange and Planning Practices* (London: Routledge, 2010), pp. 1–26; Jennifer Robinson, "2010 Urban Geography Plenary Lecture – The Travels of Urban Neoliberalism: Taking Stock of the Internationalization of Urban Theory," *Urban Geography* 32, 8 (2011), pp. 1087–1109; and Ananya Roy, "Urbanisms, Worlding Practices and the Theory of Planning," *Planning Theory* 10, 1 (2011), pp. 6–15; and Patsy Healey, "Circuits of Knowledge and Techniques: The Transnational Flow of Planning Ideas and Practices," *International Journal of Urban and Regional Research* 37, 5 (2013), pp. 1510–1526.

[22] Idalina Baptista, "The Travels of Critiques of Neoliberalism: Urban Experiences from the 'Borderlands'," *Urban Geography* 34, 5 (2013), pp. 590–611. (esp. pp. 590–591).

markers of becoming different, that is, more independent and less peripheral and marginal.[23]

Globalization of Urbanization: The Emergence of "New Urbanisms"

Aspiring world-class cities at the margins of capitalist modernity cannot be treated as merely sites where the contradictions of globalization, neoliberal economic reforms, and the outside imposition of structural adjustment are simply played out in exaggerated ways. Rather these cities actualize these contradictions by inventing "new urbanisms" that bring the "global" into direct contact with the "local." These "new urbanisms" depend on the adoption of new regulatory regimes, the creation of "new" spaces of luxury consumption, the proliferation of "new" microeconomies, and the forging of "new" arenas for land speculation and property investment. New urbanisms function as social mechanisms for the management of urban residents through a hybrid mixture of unrelenting market discipline and vigilant state monitoring. The disappearance of formal employment opportunities, the promotion of subcontracting and outsourcing, the establishment of special economic zones, the suffocation of labor unions, the enabling the production of enclosed enclaves for the wealthy, the carrying out of slum clearances, and the displacement of informal trading all contribute to the production of new urban environments that favor the well-to-do, affluent residents of the city. These new patterns of social exclusion, spatial partition, and marginalization reflect the desire of new urban property-owning elites to both manage the disorderly effects of urban informality and to insert themselves favorably into global financial and commodity circuits. These "new urbanisms" are also contested sites of negotiation and compromise, and conflict and resistance. Social movements, political coalitions, and cooperative associations of all kinds engage in efforts, through organized collective action or unorganized forms of resistance, to reclaim the city.[24]

What has been too often overlooked in the existing scholarly literature on aspiring world-class cities outside the core areas of the world economy are the ever-changing dynamics of spatial fragmentation and social polarization.[25] From Shanghai to Saigon (Ho Chi Minh City), from Delhi to Mumbai, and from Manila to Managua, cities scattered across the rapidly urbanizing world have become experimental sites for improvisational engagements with modernity, cosmopolitanism, and globalization. Whether triggered by a massive influx

---

[23] For the inspiration behind these ideas, see Jane M. Jacobs, "A Geography of Big Things," *Cultural Geographies* 13, 1 (2006), pp. 1–27 (esp. p. 1, 2, 7).

[24] Tony Samara, Shenjing He, and Guo Chen, "Introduction: Locating the City in the Global South," in Tony Samara, Shenjing He, and Guo Chen (eds.), *Locating the Right to the City in the Global South* (New York: Routledge, 2013), pp. 1–20.

[25] Some of the ideas in the following paragraphs are taken from Martin J. Murray, "Afterword: Re-engaging with Transnational Urbanism," in Tony Samara, Shenjing He, and Guo Chen (eds.), *Locating the Right to the City in the Global South* (New York: Routledge, 2013), pp. 285–310.

of overseas capital investment in real estate or driven by "home-grown" local propertied interests (or some hybrid combination of the two), city builders in "globalizing cities" around the world have turned to large-scale redevelopment schemes as a way to achieve world-class status and to carve out a distinctive identity for themselves. These mega-projects typically take the form of large-scale, iconic, and expensive office complexes, cutting-edge infrastructure, commercial and tourist-entertainment sites, and luxury housing.[26]

In aspiring world-class cities around the globe, self-sufficient, sequestered enclaves have become a common template for new city-building projects that cater to corporate business clients and wealthy residents.[27] As a distinctive mode of spatial organization, the enclave format includes a variety of building typologies, ranging from large-scale mega-projects, securitized office complexes, leisure-and-entertainment sites, vacation getaways, and even entire satellite cities built at the edges of existing metropolitan landscapes. As spatially demarcated zones physically detached from the surrounding urban fabric, urban enclaves have unsettled the classic modernist paradigm of the integrated and holistic city organized around functional specializations. In contrast to the modernist vision of integrated and holistic cities, the enclave format has produced fragmented urban landscapes, where the city comes to resemble an assemblage of discrete parts. Essential to this emerging "enclave urbanism" is the introduction of social, legal, and physical boundaries, often relating to differentiated regimes of governance.[28] While the enclosure of public and private space in cities is nothing new, the rationale that has accompanied the formation of these luxury enclaves and autonomous zones at a time of neoliberal restructuring has a historical specificity all its own. The choice of building typologies, the mechanics of land-use planning, and the aesthetics of architectural design reflect the dominant logic of marketplace competition for landed property and the power of real-estate capital to shape the built environment.[29]

---

[26] Saree Makdisi, "Laying Claim to Beirut: Urban Narrative and Spatial Identity in the Age of *Solidère*," *Critical Inquiry* 23, 3 (1997), pp. 660–705; Gavin Shatkin, "The City and the Bottom Line: Urban Megaprojects and the Privatization of Planning in Southeast Asia," *Environment and Planning A* 40, 2 (2008), pp. 383–401; Christopher Silver, *Planning the Megacity: Jakarta in the Twentieth Century* (New York: Routledge, 2008); Choon-Piew Pow and Lily Kong, "Marketing the Chinese Dream Home: Gated Communities and Representations of the Good Life in (Post-) Socialist Shanghai," *Urban Geography*, 28, 2 (2007), pp. 129–159; and Choon-Piew Pow, "Securing the 'Civilized' Enclaves: Gated Communities and the Moral Geographies of Exclusion in (Post-)Socialist Shanghai," *Urban Studies*, 44, 8 (2007), pp. 1539–1558.

[27] Choon-Piew Pow, "Urban Entrepreneurialism, Global Business Elites and Urban Mega-Development: A Case Study of Suntec City," *Asian Journal of Social Science* 30, 1 (2002), pp. 53–72.

[28] See David Harvey, *The Condition of Postmodernity: An Enquiry into the Origins of Cultural Change* (Cambridge: Blackwell, 1989).

[29] Teresa Caldeira, "Fortified Enclaves: The New Urban Segregation," *Public Culture* 8, 2 (1996), pp. 303–328; Don Luymes, "The Fortification of Suburbia: Investigating the Rise of Enclave Communities," *Landscape and Urban Planning* 39, 2–3 (1997), pp. 187–203; and Martin Coy,

Urban enclaves typically rely on a combination of architectural design (walls, gates, and barriers) along with elaborate technologies of surveillance and policing to maintain their separateness. Not only are these sequestered enclaves protected from unwanted intrusion, but they are also linked to other spaces of exclusion such as urban mega-projects and upscale leisure-and-entertainment venues through dedicated transit corridors, pedestrian skyways, and highway bypasses. Looking at elevated flyovers, underground passageways, skywalks, and fortified high-rise buildings enables us to see cities as assemblages of three-dimensional spaces. The horizontal and vertical extension of modes of spatial governmentality has produced three-dimensional landscapes of inclusion and incorporation, on the one side, and exclusion and polarization, on the other.[30]

Urban enclaves are spaces of both global engagement and entanglement. As such, they are vehicles through which city-builders in "globalizing cities" seek to realize the "expectations of [late] modernity."[31] In aspiring world-class cities around the world, real-estate developers – acting either alone or in concert with municipal authorities – have launched ambitious schemes designed to lure international investments and global tourists.[32] City boosters have stressed public–private partnerships, place-marketing, and culture-led development as the key components of competition-based and market-led strategies to jump-start revitalization projects. This "fight for the global catwalk" (to borrow a useful metaphor from Monica Degen) has typically involved the sponsorship of flagship property-led redevelopment projects where "cities compete with each other by parading made-up images of different areas of the city which advertise these spaces as favorable and attractive to business and leisure."[33] Faced with the imperatives of global competitiveness, city builders in so-called "developing countries" have turned to up-to-date mega-projects with modern infrastructure as a way of "securing optimal productive platforms for mobile and local capital."[34] This frantic race to fashion world-class cities on the

"Gated Communities and Urban Fragmentation in Latin America: The Brazilian Experience," *GeoJournal* 66, 1–2 (2006), pp. 121–132.

[30] Simon Marvin and Steven Graham, *Splintering Urbanism: Networked Infrastructures, Technological Mobilities and the Urban Condition* (New York: Routledge, 2001), p. 284. See also Eyal Weizman, *Hollow Land: Israel's Architecture of Occupation* (New York: Verso, 2007).

[31] James Ferguson, *Expectations of Modernity: Myths and Meanings of Urban Life on the Zambian Copperbelt* (Berkeley: University of California Press, 1999), p. 1.

[32] See, for example, Lisa Weinstein, Neha Sami, and Gavin Shatkin, "Contested Developments: Enduring Legacies and Emergent Political Actors in Contemporary Urban India," in Gavin Shatkin (ed.), *Contesting the Indian City: Global Visions and the Politics of the Local* (Malden, MA: Wiley-Blackwell, 2014), pp. 38–64.

[33] Monica Degen, "Fighting for the Global Catwalk: Formalizing Public Life in Castlefield (Manchester) and Diluting Public Life in el Raval (Barcelona)," *International Journal of Urban and Regional Research* 27, 4 (2003), pp. 867–880 (esp. pp. 867–868).

[34] Edgar Pieterse, *City Futures: Confronting the Crisis of Urban Development* (London: Zed Books, 2008), pp. 37–38 (p. 38, source of quotation).

margins of modernity recasts city-building efforts into a business operation, where privately led strategic initiatives undermine holistic planning under the watchful eye of a vigilant public administration, and where "profitability replaces the public good."[35]

Perhaps the most emblematic symbols of spatial fragmentation in the ordinary cities at the edge of global capitalism are the juxtaposed polarities of gated residential communities and slums – physically proximate sites that nevertheless produce (and reproduce) fundamentally dissimilar social worlds.[36] It is possible to sketch an urban topography in the megacities of hypergrowth that is marked by the exponential growth of slums and entrenched patterns of social and class segregation. Slums constitute a pervasive and diverse ecology with multiple processes of development and consolidation, constituting a significant portion of the built environment in poor cities characterized by extreme socioeconomic inequalities.[37] What has often been overlooked is that the proliferation of slums and informal settlements has proceeded in tandem with the steady growth of sequestered enclaves like gated residential communities, upscale shopping complexes, and securitized office buildings catering to the affluent residents. Urban enclaves ranging from sequestered residential estates to new suburban towns and full-sized satellite cities are increasingly embraced as spectacular, technical signifiers of global cosmopolitanism and urban economic progress – the material symbols of late modernity.[38] These self-contained precincts for the wealthy function as "pivots" between spaces and flows, providing leverage and connection with the core financial centers of the world economy.[39]

The spatial logic of neoliberal globalization has reproduced extreme patterns of social segregation and zoned consumption. These urban enclaves signal the voluntary segregation of the rich.[40] If the celebrated iron-and-glass arcades of the mid-nineteenth century were the glimmering "enchanted forests" of early consumer capitalism, then the luxury-themed environments of twenty-first-century urbanism – including "city-sized supermalls, gated residential estates, "*faux* downtown 'lifestyle centers,'" along with similar artificial island-like enclosures – aptly "function as alternative universes for privileged

[35] Janice Perlman, *Favela: Four Decades of Living on the Edge in Rio de Janeiro* (Oxford and New York: Oxford University Press, 2010), p. 249 (source of quotation).

[36] Renaud Le Goix, "Gated Communities: Sprawl and Social Segregation in Southern California," *Housing Studies* 20, 2 (2005), pp. 323–343 (esp. 336–337).

[37] Nezar Alsayyad and Ananya Roy, "Medieval Modernity: On Citizenship and Urbanism in a Global Era," *Space and Polity* 10, 1 (2006), pp. 1–20 (esp. p. 8, 17).

[38] Rowland Atkinson and Sarah Blandy, "Introduction: International Perspectives on The New Enclavism and the Rise of Gated Communities," *Housing Studies* 20, 2 (2005), pp. 177–186.

[39] Pow, "Urban Entrepreneurialism, Global Business Elites and Urban Mega-Development," pp. 53–72.

[40] Emanula Guano, "The Denial of Citizenship: 'Barbaric' Buenos Aires and the Middle-class Imaginary," *City and Society* 16, 1 (2004), pp. 69–97.

forms of human life."[41] The proliferation of these "theme park" landscapes for the wealthy testifies to the rootlessness of the new urban middle class across the world. The patterns of spatial fragmentation – produced by the dual processes of deliberately planned (sequestered) enclaves, on the one hand, and unplanned "peripheral informality," on the other – starkly represent the accelerating spatial polarization and social cleavage that has engulfed the "globalizing" cities outside the core areas of the world economy.[42]

Off-Worlds: Surreal Dreamscapes of Late Modernity

In the contemporary discourse on globalization, such building typologies as gated residential communities, securitized office parks, retail precincts, export processing zones, and tourist resorts stand out as concrete manifestations of urban fragmentation.[43] As a general rule, the scholarly literature has identified these exclusive urban enclaves as the iconic spaces of neoliberal urbanism that are largely disconnected from the existing urban social fabric and facilitate the steady encroachment of private management of the cityscape.[44] Peter Marcuse, for example, had similar relationships between spatial fragmentation and social disparities in mind when he distinguished residential "enclaves," "citadels," and "ghettoes."[45] Surely, as Marcuse argued a long time ago, there is nothing particularly new about divided cities.[46] Historically speaking, spatial clustering

---

[41] Mike Davis and Daniel Bertrand Monk, "Introduction," in Mike Davis and Daniel Bertrand Monk (eds.), *Evil Paradises: Dreamworlds of Neoliberalism* (New York: The New Press, 2007), pp. ix–xvi (quotation from p. xv).

[42] Asef Bayat and Eric Denis, "Who is Afraid of *Ashwaiyyat?*" *Environment and Urbanization* 12, 2 (2000), pp. 185–199 (esp. p. 199). See also Engin Esin and Kim Rygiel, "Of Other Global Cities: Frontiers, Zones, Camps," in Barbara Drieskens, Franck Mermier, and Heiko Wimmen (eds.), *Cities of the South: Citizenship and Exclusion in the 21st Century* (Beirut/London: Saqi Books, 2007), pp. 169–176.

[43] Werner Breitung, "Enclave Urbanism in China: Attitudes towards Gated Communities in Guangzhou," *Urban Geography* 33, 2 (2012), pp. 278–294.

[44] Robyn Dowling, Rowland Atkinson, and Pauline McGuirk, "Privatism, Privatisation and Social Distinction in Master-planned Residential Estates," *Urban Policy and Research* 28, 4 (2010), pp. 391–410; Renaud Le Goix, "Gated Communities as Predators of Public Resources: The Outcomes of Fading Boundaries between Private Management and Public Authorities in Southern California," in Georg Glasze, Chris Webster, and Franz Klaus (eds.), *Private Cities: Global and Local Perspectives* (New York: Routledge, 2006), pp. 76–91; and Carolyn Thompson, "Master-Planned Estates: Privatization, Socio-Spatial Polarization and Community," *Geography Compass* 7, 1 (2013), pp. 85–93.

[45] Peter Marcuse, "The Enclave, the Citadel, and the Ghetto: What has Changed in the Post-Fordist U.S. City," *Urban Affairs Review* 33, 2 (1997), pp. 228–264.

[46] Peter Marcuse, "What's So New about Divided Cities?" *International Journal of Urban and Regional Research* 17, 3 (1993), pp. 355–365. See also Peter Marcuse, "'Dual City': A Muddy Metaphor for a Quartered City," *International Journal of Urban and Regional Research* 13, 4 (1989), pp. 697–708.

and partitioning seem to be an enduring feature of urban life.[47] Michael Dear and Steven Flusty identified the formation of enclaves as a general tendency of what they called postmodern urbanism. In introducing the term "patchwork city," they sought to draw attention to the patterns of urban fragmentation.[48] What is new about urban fragmentation at this time of contemporary globalization is that city builders seem to be under no illusions about the need to gesture toward urban coherence through comprehensive master-planning, or adhering to holistic visions of urban landscapes – ideas that they often regard as hindering their freedom to improvise. Polarization and division of modernist city building have thus been superseded by intensified fragmentation and segregation in the current age of globalization, not only in the overall functional patterns of land use but also in the agglomeration and clustering of infrastructure, the proliferation of enclosed building typologies, and the microsocial fabric of cities (namely, the expansion of walls, gates, and other barriers).[49] As a general rule, the territorial restructuring of metropolitan landscapes that has unfolded at the start of the twenty-first century has replaced the polycentric metropolis of the high-modernist era with a reticular pattern and diffuse network of interconnected nodes. The resulting fragmentation of urban landscapes has ring-fenced some territories inside the functional networks of the city while leaving others outside.[50]

Inspired by glimpses of global cosmopolitanism, the wealthy classes of the highly unequal cities of the world have attached themselves to a utopian view on the future that projects an image of globally connected social world consisting of hypermodern central business districts, gated residential communities, and luxury shopping malls juxtaposed against the messy spatial realities of slums, informality, and stalled development. These sequestered enclaves, or what Mike Davis has called "off-worlds," are often carefully designed to replicate, mimic, or even plagiarize the suburban landscapes of North American (but specifically

---

[47] Peter Marcuse, "Not Chaos but Walls: Postmodernism and the Partitioned City," in Sophie Watson and Katherine Gibson (eds.), *Postmodern Cities and Spaces* (Oxford: Blackwell, 1994), pp. 243–253; Peter Marcuse, "The Ghetto of Exclusion and the Fortified Enclave: New Patterns in the United States," *American Behavioral Scientist* 41, 3 (1997), pp. 311–326; and Peter Marcuse, "Space in the Globalizing City," in Neil Brenner and Roger Keil (eds.), *The Global Cities Reader* (New York: Routledge, 2006), pp. 26–269.

[48] Michael Dear and Steven Flusty, "Postmodern Urbanism," *Annals of the Association of American Geographers* 88, 1 (1998), pp. 50–72. See also Michael Dear, "The Urban Question after Modernity," in Heiko Schmid, Wolf-Dietrich Sahr, and John Urry (eds.), *Cities and Fascination: Beyond the Surplus of Meaning* (Burlington, VT: Ashgate, 2011), pp. 17–32.

[49] Pedro Pírez, "Buenos Aires: Fragmentation and Privatization of the Metropolitan City," *Environment & Urbanization* 14, 1 (2002), pp. 145–158. See also Axel Borsdorf and Rodrigo Hidalgo, "The Fragmented City: Changing Patterns in Latin American Cities," The Urban Reinventors Paper Series. *The Urban Reinventors Online Journal*, Issue 3/09, pp. 1–18. Available at www.urbanreinventors.net.

[50] See, for example, Martin Coy, "Gated Communities and Urban Fragmentation in Latin America: The Brazilian Experience," *GeoJournal* 66, 1–2 (2006), pp. 121–132.

Southern Californian) cities.⁵¹ These "imagineered" lifestyle spaces have become a distinctive trope in an emergent culture of conspicuous consumption in such cities as Hong Kong and Singapore, and Jakarta and Cairo.⁵² As a general rule, upscale housing estates in new Chinese cities bear a striking resemblance to gated residential communities in the United States.⁵³ Similar to their U.S. counterparts, "sealed residential quarters" are master-planned precincts: walled compounds with guarded entry gates, sometimes supplemented by high-tech surveillance equipment, such as closed-circuit cameras and infrared alarm systems at the edges.⁵⁴ The high-end versions have unabashedly imitated the architecture and design stylistics of gated residential communities in North America. For example, the *nouveau riche* in Beijing commute north by freeway to gated residential estates with names like "Beverly Hills," "Sun City," and "Orange County" (designed by a Newport Beach architect with Martha Stewart décor).⁵⁵ These gated suburban subdivisions of sprawling million-dollar California-style homes draw their inspiration from a *faux* Los Angeles imaginary and attract upper income residents who desire the luxuriating image of a leisurely American lifestyle.⁵⁶

These urban enclaves represent a kind of inverse (self-)ghettoization and the physical fortification of privilege and wealth. Like slums, these urban enclaves exhibit some regularity in spatial design, but there are marked differences in the processes of their development as well as their implications for wider urban place-making.⁵⁷ There remains a nuanced and complex interweaving of an elite

⁵¹ Mike Davis, *Planet of Slums* (New York: Verso, 2006), p. 114.

⁵² Laura Ruggeri, "'Palm Springs': Imagineering California in Hong Kong," in *Evil Paradises: Dreamworlds of Neoliberalism*, pp. 102–113 (esp. p. 102). See also Harald Leisch, "Gated Communities in Indonesia," *Cities* 19, 5 (2002), pp. 341–350.

⁵³ Fulong Wu, "Rediscovering the 'Gate' under Market Transition: From Work-Unit Compounds to Commodity Housing Enclaves," *Housing Studies* 20, 2 (2005), pp. 235–254.

⁵⁴ Pu Miao, "Deserted Streets in a Jammed Town: The Gated Community in Chinese Cities and its Solution," *Journal of Urban Design* 8, 1 (2003), pp. 45–66; Chris Webster, Fulong Wu, and Janjing Zhao, "China's Modern Walled Cities," in Georg Glasze, Chris Webster, and Klaus Frantz (eds.), *Private Cities: Local and Global Perspectives* (London and New York: Routledge, 2005), pp. 153–169; and Youqin Huang, "Collectivism, Political Control, and Gating in Chinese Cities," *Urban Geography* 27, 6 (2006), pp. 507–535.

⁵⁵ Davis, *Planet of Slums*, p. 115. See Fulong Wu and Klaire Webber, "The Rise of Foreign Gated Communities in Beijing: Between Economic Globalization and Local Institutions," *Cities* 21, 3 (2004), pp. 203–213; Fulong Wu, "Transplanting Cityscapes: The Use of Imagined Globalization in Housing Commodification in Beijing," *Area* 36, 3 (2004), pp. 227–234; Xiuhong Hu and David Kaplan, "The Emergence of Affluence in Beijing: Residential Social Stratification in China's Capital City," *Urban Geography* 22, 1 (2001), pp. 54–77; and Guillaume Giroir, "The Purple Jade Villas (Beijing): A Golden Ghetto in Red China," in Georg Glasze, Chris Webster, and Klaus Frantz (eds.), *Private Cities: Global and Local Perspectives* (London: Routledge, 2005), pp. 142–152.

⁵⁶ Christian Aaen, "North of Beijing, California Dreams Come True," *New York Times*, February 3, 2003.

⁵⁷ Georg Glasze, Klaus Frantz, and Chris Webster, "The Global Spread of Gated Communities," *Environment & Planning B: Planning and Design* 29, 3 (2002), pp. 315–320.

global urban repertoire – of which fortified enclaves are an established and integral part – and local circumstances.[58] Nevertheless, as Teresa Caldeira has suggested, the forms of enclosure and exclusion under which current spatial transformations have occurred are so common that it is indeed tempting to treat them as a shared formula adopted by real-estate developers, architects, and urban designers in aspiring world-class cities everywhere.[59]

Perhaps not so surprisingly, conventional urban studies literature tends to focus either on privileged spaces of wealth, on the one side, or on distressed spaces of decay, on the other. Yet in the "globalizing cities" where socioeconomic inequalities are deeply entrenched, new patterns of spatial fragmentation have become normalized (and even "naturalized") features of everyday life, where insulated compounds for the wealthy and depleted zones of urban marginality reproduce and expand in an interdependent manner, both intersecting and dependent upon each other. On the one side, inward-looking and self-contained enclaves, where the privatization of management and provision of services is the typical mode of urban governance, have become showcases of a new kind of cosmopolitan urbanity indifferent to local surroundings. On the other side, deprived sites of involuntary isolation bring together concentrated forms of economic vulnerability and neglect. Looking at the interdependence between these seemingly diametrically opposed poles gives us clues as to how city building under the sign of neoliberal globalization has left its mark on global urbanism at the start of the twenty-first century. Processes of spatial restructuring have divided urban landscapes into socially distinct zones where separation, insulation, and containment constitute the key operative principles governing city building. Yet unlike the walled cities of premodern Europe, porous membranes instead of insurmountable barriers allow for the selective inclusion – and not the enforcement of total exclusion – of the laboring poor to provide services and amenities requisite for the luxury-lifestyles of affluent urban residents. Correlatively, with the adoption of neoliberal modes of urban governance, the privatization of provision of social services has gone hand-in-hand with limited access to public resources.[60] These kinds of layered cities have become harbingers of a new urbanity at the start of the twenty-first century.[61]

---

[58] For a more nuanced view that pushes back against an all-encompassing neoliberal agenda, see Pauline McGuirk and Robyn Dowling, "Neoliberal Privatization? Remapping the Public and Private in Sydney's Master-planned Residential Estates," *Political Geography* 28, 3 (2009), pp. 174–185; Pauline McGuirk, "Neoliberalist Planning? Re-thinking and Re-casting Sydney's Metropolitan Planning," *Geographical Research* 43, 1 (2005), pp. 59–70; and Pauline McGuirk and Robyn Dowling, "Master-Planned Residential Developments: Beyond Iconic Spaces of Neoliberalism?" *Asia Pacific Viewpoint* 50, 2 (2009), pp. 120–134.

[59] Tersa Calderia, *City of Walls: Crime, Segregation and Citizenship in Sao Paolo* (Oakland, CA: University of California Press, 2000), p. 1.

[60] Ayfer Bartu-Candan and Biray Kolluoğlu, "Emerging Spaces of Neoliberalism: A Gated Town and a Public Housing Project in Istanbul," *New Perspectives on Turkey* 39 (2008), pp. 37–38.

[61] Bartu-Candan and Kolluoğlu, "Emerging Spaces of Neoliberalism," pp. 5, 9, 41.

Enclave Urbanism: Spatial Fragmentation and the Splintering of Urban Landscapes

The explosive growth of super-sized mega-urban regions in the Asia Pacific Rim, the Middle East, and coastal Africa over the past three to four decades is inseparable from the intensifying processes of contemporary globalization.[62] As the magnitude of global flows of capital has expanded in quantum leaps and bounds over the same timeframe, megalopolises with world-class aspirations have become more open to the impulses of globalization. With each decade, the folding of additional circuits of global capital into these aspirant world-class cities have brought about the reconfiguration of urban landscapes, transforming them from dependent "colonial cities" that primarily served as *entrepots* for primary commodity transfers to distant markets in the core areas of the capitalist world economy, to industrializing cities absorbing direct investment in assembly operations and manufacturing in the 1970s, and, finally, to centers of global consumption beginning in the mid-1980s.[63]

With a population that has already surpassed the 20-million threshold, Jakarta is one of the largest and fastest growing megacities in the world, the biggest metropolis by a wide margin in Southeast Asia. The spatial form of Jakarta (the Dutch colonial historic center called Batavia) has expanded outward, and has become integrated with the bordering areas (Tangerang in the west, Bekasi in the east, and Bogar in the south), forming a new megalopolis that is generally known as *Jabodetabek*. The indigenous settlements (known as "old-kampong") that were once on the agricultural fringe of Jakarta have increasingly become isolated and marginalized, hemmed in by superhighways, industrial sites, and gated housing estates, and squeezed by newer informal settlements (known as "squatter-kampong"). The mushrooming of satellite cities, new gated housing estates, and enclosed shopping complexes on the ex-urban fringe has created a patchwork metropolis, a lattice-like mosaic of highly differentiated and unequal urban spaces. This reticular pattern of urban development has produced uneven growth through polarization.[64]

---

[62] Michael Douglass, "Globalization, Mega-projects and the Environment: Urban Form and Water in Jakarta," *Environment and Urbanization Asia* 1, 1 (2010), pp. 45–65 (esp. p. 47). See also Gavin Jones, "Southeast Asian Urbanization and the Growth of Mega Urban Regions," *Journal of Population Research* 19, 2 (2002), pp. 119–136.

[63] Douglass, "Globalization, Mega-projects and the Environment: Urban Form and Water in Jakarta," p. 47. See also Howard Dick and Peter Rimmer, "Beyond the Third World City: The New Urban Geography of South-east Asia," *Urban Studies* 35, 12 (1998), pp. 2303–2321.

[64] Andrea Peresthu, "Questioning the JABOTABEK Growth Centre Strategies," in Marisa Carmona, Devisari Tunas, and Marinda Schoonraad (eds.), *Globalization, Urban Form and Governance: Globalization and the Return of the Big Plans* [Volume 7] (Delft: Delft University Press, 2003), pp. 57–75. See also Charles Goldblum and Tai-Chee Wong, "Growth, Crisis and Spatial Change: A Study of Haphazard Urbanisation in Jakarta, Indonesia," *Land Use Policy* 17, 1 (2000), pp. 29–37.

According to a popular slogan, "Jakarta is not really a city, but a conglomeration of villages." This claim conveys the image of a fragmented metropolis characterized by haphazard and irregular sprawl.[65] Conceiving of Jakarta as a loose assemblage of discrete parts suggests that the urban form is an amorphous pastiche of districts, neighborhoods, and precincts, where the city is not adequately equipped with proper infrastructure and social amenities, and municipal authorities lack sufficient regulatory mechanisms to manage land development through careful zoning.[66] The greater Jakarta metropolitan region exemplifies an overburdened megalopolis struggling with problems of rapidly expanding population, overstretched infrastructure, poor-quality housing, high unemployment, inadequate defective public transportation, and extensive environmental degradation.[67]

At the same time, like many other megalopolises with world-class aspirations, Jakarta at the start of the new millennium is a city infused with the global ambitions of a new generation of enterprising, corporate, and professional middle-class urban residents. Luxury enclaves like mega-malls, high-rise apartment complexes, clustered office parks, and new private cities have begun to appear with increasing regularity across the broader metropolitan region.[68] The realization of these class-based aspirations is almost always synonymous with the commodification of urban space. The (re-)valoration of urban space makes city life more attractive to property owners and affluent users. The conjoined processes of redevelopment and revitalization – otherwise known as gentrification – have become an aggressive force, reclaiming the city for those affluent urban residents by excluding the poor through a combination of rising property values and land values, forcible evictions, and the introduction of regulatory regimes that work against the poor. Large-scale real-estate interests have accomplished this aggressive valorization of the inner city of Jakarta through a combination of rising property values and land prices, forcible evictions, and the introduction of new regulatory regimes hostile to the urban poor.[69]

[65] Manasse Malo and P. J. M. Nas, "Queen City of the East and Symbol of the Nation: The Administration and Management of Jakarta," in Jürgen Rüland (ed.), *The Dynamics of Metropolitan Management in Southeast Asia* (Singapore: Institute of Southeast Asian Studies, 1996), pp. 99–132 (esp. p. 100, source of quotation).

[66] Silver, *Planning the Megacity*, pp. 19–20, 22.

[67] Roman Cybriwsky and Larry Ford, "City Profile Jakarta," *Cities* 18, 3 (2001), pp. 199–210. See also Tommy Firman, "The Restructuring of Jakarta Metropolitan Area: A 'Global City' in Asia," *Cities* 15, 4 (1998), pp. 229–243.

[68] Tunggul Yunianto, "On the Verge of Displacement: Listening to Kampong Dwellers in the Emotional Economy of Contemporary Jakarta," *Thesis Eleven* 121, 1 (2014), pp. 101–121. See also Tim Bunnell and Michelle Ann Miller, "Jakarta in Post-Suharto Indonesia: Decentralisation, Neoliberalism and Global City Aspiration," *Space and Polity* 15, 1 (2011), pp. 35–48.

[69] Yunianto, "On the Verge of Displacement," p. 102. See also Abidin Kusno, *Behind the Postcolonial: Architecture, Urban Space and Political Cultures in Indonesia* (New York: Routledge, 2000).

The absence of effective state regulatory regimes in the management of urban development has resulted in the dual process of urbanization where unauthorized settlements and self-built housing coexist with large-scale, self-contained "new towns" scattered across the sprawling metropolitan landscape. The majority of urban dwellers in the Jakarta metropolitan region, notably lower middle-income groups and the poor, still reside in unplanned and unregulated settlements, particularly urban slums (known as *"kampungs"*) close to the city center and semirural settlements on the periphery.[70] Although master plans and land-use zoning instruments have long been in place, there has been little if no effective spatial planning in Jakarta, and nonexistent building regulations for most residential quarters and *kampungs* has meant that construction has been haphazard, unregulated, and uncontrolled.[71] Rapid population growth has meant that state management of physical space has been beyond the capacity of the poorly equipped and financiallystrapped municipal authorities. For the most part, city officials have employed the formal rules of land-use planning and building codes in order to achieve their grand development visions, and they have not used these tools for the regulation of microspaces of the city. State funding has largely been directed at key priority areas like new business districts, civic centers, expressways, and face-lifting mega-projects. In spite of efforts to improve conditions in informal settlements, *kampong* life is still largely concealed by a thin veneer of modern commercial buildings constructed along major roadways.[72]

The paucity of affordable housing has meant that unauthorized land subdivision has become the main source of supply for households to construct dwellings for themselves outside of municipal regulation. Unregistered title deeds have gone hand-in-hand with informal housing developments and the expansion of *kampongs*. Persistent demand for low-cost housing has meant that land subdivision has become unstoppable. Because of ongoing fragmentation of land holdings that results in miniscule-sized plots, the practice of informal self-built housing has tended to ignore planning guidelines in order to maximize the built-up floor space. The lack of effective regulation has produced substandard, inferior, and poor quality habitation. High population densities have induced great land scarcity, thereby giving rise to intensive competition over access to limited resources. The installation of urban infrastructure and social amenities has not kept pace with rising land-use intensification.

---

[70] Tommy Firman, "New Town Development in Jakarta Metropolitan Region: A Perspective of Spatial Segregation," *Habitat International* 28, 3 (2004), pp. 349–368 (esp. p. 353). See Yunianto, "On the Verge of Displacement," pp. 101–121.

[71] Jieming Zhu, "Symmetric Development of Informal Settlements and Gated Communities: Capacity of the State: The Case of Jakarta, Indonesia," (Asia Research Institute, National University of Singapore, Working Paper Series No. 135, February 2010), [25 pp.]; and AbdouMaliq Simone, *City Life from Jakarta to Dakar: Movements at the Crossroads* (New York: Routledge, 2010).

[72] Zhu, "Symmetric Development of Informal Settlements and Gated Communities," p. 13.

Once a certain tipping point has been reached, *kampongs* have slipped into slums.[73]

Ambiguous property regimes go hand-in-hand with inconsistent tenancy rights. A significant majority of poor urban residents lack formal (that is, legally recognized) title to the land upon which they have built rudimentary housing, but instead occupy unregistered plots that exist largely outside state regulatory and corporate financial systems. This dualism in land markets goes a long way toward explaining the hyper-fragmented character of the patterns of land-use development in Jakarta.[74] The failure of public regulatory regimes to provide for rigorous land-use planning has created a void that private real-estate developers have filled. Despite the conspicuous absence of municipal planning regulations, land assembly for private "new town" developments was unable to succeed without the visible helping hand of municipal officials in facilitating the acquisition of property and development permits. In the greater Jakarta metropolitan region, real-estate developers and property speculators have gobbled up sizeable amounts of prime agricultural land on the fringes of the historic downtown core, converting these sites into expansive satellite cities on the urban edge.[75] The construction of privately built "new towns" like Lippo Karawaci [Lippo Village], Lippo Cikarang [City], and BSD [Bumi Serpong Damai] City on the outskirts of Jakarta exemplify this trend toward enclave development and urban fragmentation.[76] This corporate mode of city building has facilitated the transfer of urban infrastructure and services into the hands of private real-estate developers who in turn have taken charge of providing the kinds of amenities needed to fulfill the aspirations of affluent urban residents for upscale residential housing, luxury leisure and entertainment sites, and high-quality work environment. Municipal planning authorities have not only failed to perform a regulatory role over informal urban development, but also have turned over its regulatory functions to corporate real-estate developers in the planning of new towns, gated residential communities, and other

[73] Zhu, "Symmetric Development of Informal Settlements and Gated Communities," pp. 15–17.

[74] See Michael Leaf, "Land Rights for Residential Development in Jakarta, Indonesia: The Colonial Roots of Contemporary Urban Dualism," *International Journal of Urban and Regional Research* 17, 4 (1993), pp. 477–499; and Michael Leaf, "The Suburbanisation of Jakarta: A Concurrence of Economics and Ideology," *Third World Planning Review* 16, 4 (1994), pp. 341–356. Special thanks to Gavin Shatkin for pointing out the dualism in land markets to me in personal correspondence.

[75] Tommy Firman, "Demographic and Spatial Patterns of Indonesia's Recent Urbanization," *Population, Space and Place* 10, 6 (2004), pp. 421–434.

[76] Tommy Firman, "The Continuity and Change in Mega-urbanization in Indonesia: A Survey of Jakarta–Bandung Region (JBR) Development," *Habitat International* 33, 4 (2009), pp. 327–339. See also Mike Douglass, "Globalization on the Edge: Fleeing the Public Sphere in the (Peri-)urban Transition in Southeast Asia," in Tôn Nữ Quỳnh Trân, Fanny Quertamp, Claude de Miras, Nguyễn Quang Vinh, Lê Văn Năm, Trương Hoàng Trương (eds.), *Trends of Urbanization and Suburbanization in Southeast Asia* (Ho Chi Minh City: General Publishing House, 2012), pp. 101–118.

luxury enclaves.[77] These satellite cities reflect the world-class aspirations of the real-estate developers who have built them and the corporate elites who inhabit them.[78] These privatized "corporate cities" are virtually self-governing entities that have seceded from the public administration of the greater Jakarta metropolitan region.[79]

More than simply monochromatic suburban residential estates, these multi-functional "new towns" were modeled on the design principles of the Garden City movement. Originating as an imagined radically utopian alternative to the overcrowded, unplanned, and insalubrious modern industrial city, the Garden City movement promised a reconnection of nature to the city and the establishment of alternating rhythms of work and leisure through the planned integration of industrial, commercial, residential, and recreational activities in a self-contained setting. Privately built corporate cities like Lippo Karawaci, Lippo Cikarang, and BSD City bear a striking resemblance to nineteenth-century "company towns" incubated in the largely unregulated managerial culture of paternalistic capitalism. As a general rule, these "new towns" have conformed to carefully planned spatial designs, bringing together up-to-date infrastructure along with high-rise office buildings, skyscraper apartment blocks, leisure and entertainment amenities, upscale shopping malls, and themed residential estates that have cloned similar ones in Orange County, Irvine, and other corporate city developments in Southern California.[80]

Variations among these new towns, satellite cities, and gated residential communities obviously exist. Yet as a general rule, these luxury enclaves all tend to draw upon the same utopian imaginaries: they aspire to reach the promised land of becoming truly world class. By offering global connections and a new urban cosmopolitan culture, they wish to remain private, exclusive, secure, and self-contained.[81] Together with related services and infrastructure connecting them with each other, they form "interdictory spaces" that

---

77 Zhu, "Symmetric Development of Informal Settlements and Gated Communities," pp. 19–20.
78 Bunnell and Miller, "Jakarta in Post-Suharto Indonesia," pp. 35–48. See also Tom Percival and Paul Waley, "Articulating Intra-Asian Urbanism: The Production of Satellite Cities in Phnom Penh," *Urban Studies* 49, 13 (2012), pp. 2873–2888.
79 Trevor Hogan, Tim Bunnell, Choon-Piew Pow, Eka Permanasari, and Sirat Morshidi, "Asian Urbanisms and the Privatization of Cities," *Cities* 29, 1 (2012), pp. 59–63.
80 Trevor Hogan and Christopher Houston, "Corporate Cities – Urban Gateways or Gated Communities against the City? The Case of Lippo, Jakarta," in Tim Bunnell, Lisa Drummond and K. C. Ho (eds.), *Critical Reflections on Cities in Southeast Asia* (Singapore: Times Academic, 2002), pp. 243–264 (esp. pp. 248–254).
81 See, for example, Mike Douglass and Liling Huang, "Globalizing the City in Southeast Asia: Utopia on the Urban Edge – The Case of Phu My Hung, Saigon," in Ronan Paddison, Peter Marcotullio, and Mike Douglass (eds.), *Connected Cities: Histories, Hinterlands, Hierarchies and Networks and Beyond. Volume III* (Thousand Oaks, CA: Sage, 2010), pp. 287–319; and William Paling, "Planning a Future for Phnom Penh: Mega Projects, Aid Dependence and Disjointed Governance," *Urban Studies* 49, 13 (2012), pp. 2889–2912.

systematically exclude people who do not fit the targeted market profile of desirable residents.[82]

What made BSD City a watershed in the history of city building in Indonesia was because private real-estate developers – and not state authorities – originally conceived of its master plan and have carried out the actual construction and management of this sprawling mega-project. The spatial plan for this 6,000-hectare "new town" development includes residential, commercial, and industrial land uses with an expected population of 600,000 residents. In order to bypass heavy traffic congestion, real-estate developers constructed a 13-kilometer private toll road linking a number of upscale "new towns" (Bintaro Jaya, BSD, Citra Raya, Puri Jaya, Teluk Naga, and Pantai Papuk Indah). The proliferation of luxury enclaves around the greater Jakarta metropolitan region has resulted in the displacement of disenfranchised residents who literally have had no choice but to build informal dwellings wherever land was available. Without legal title or official permits (the symbolic currency of the institutional order), these informal squatters have become vulnerable in the extreme.[83]

The Shift from Holistic Master Planning to Strategic Planning through Mega-Projects

In the urban Middle East, it is clearly the case that "stand-alone" mega-projects are at the core of contemporary city planning.[84] These large-scale interventions into the urban fabric are laboratories for experiments in engineering and design, platforms for the introduction of new technologies for urban governance and management, and visible expressions of "composite models and hybrid ideologies embedded in these planning processes."[85] Like master-planned mega-projects elsewhere in the contemporary urban world, the challenge for city builders is to produce holistically designed urban enclaves that both gesture toward local specificity – thereby making claims to "uniqueness" – and incorporate building typologies, design motifs, and aesthetic standards that reflect familiar packages found in world-class cities. Many mega-projects, such as *City of Silk* in Kuwait, *Al-Abdali* in Amman, *Solidère* in Beirut, *Saphira* and *Bou Regreg* in Rabat, represent a clear movement away from holistic urban

---

[82] Steven Flusty, "The Banality of Interdiction: Surveillance, Control and the Displacement of Diversity," *International Journal of Urban and Regional Research* 25, 3 (2001), pp. 658–664.

[83] Trevor Hogan and Julian Potter, "Big City Blues," *Thesis Eleven* 121, 1 (2014), pp. 3–8 (esp. p. 7). See also Yunianto, "On the Verge of Displacement," p. 102.

[84] See Rod Burgess and Marisa Carmona, "The Shift of Master Planning to Strategic Planning," in Marisa Carmona (ed.), *Planning through Projects: Moving from Master Planning to Strategic Planning. 30 Cities* (Amsterdam: Techne Press, 2009), pp. 12–42.

[85] Pierre-Arnaud Barthel, "Arab Mega-Projects: Between the Dubai Effect, Global Crisis, Social Mobilization and a Sustainable Shift," *Built Environment* 36, 2 (2010), pp. 133–145 (p. 133, source of quotation).

planning on a grand scale and the adoption instead of a city-building model that stresses the assemblage of discrete "stand-alone" fragments.[86]

Urban integrated mega-projects in the Middle East and North Africa have largely converged around stylized models of city building that include mixed-use business districts, high-end residential accommodation, and the predictable range of "playscapes" (such as upscale malls, leisure parks, and entertainment sites).[87] These pre-packaged "spatial products" are designed for successful performance in the capitalist marketplace.[88] As such, they reflect neoliberal urban planning principles whose mission is to put on the market new "globalized spaces" that acquire world-class status.[89]

The greater Cairo metropolitan region consists of a relentlessly expanding, distended, and bloated conurbation spread haphazardly across vast geographical space. Low-density sprawl, combined with automobile dependency and the lack of reliable public transit, has produced a formless, unplanned, and uncontrolled megalopolis where the peripheries have become detached from the historic downtown core. Starting in the late 1970s, Western aid agencies, particularly the U.S. Agency for International Development (AID) and the World Bank, stepped in to assist Egyptian state authorities in planning the future growth of Cairo in order to accommodate population oversaturation. The aim was to foster a competent Egyptian state administration capable of responding to informal urbanization that was rapidly gobbling up the agricultural periphery. However, these initiatives that sought to channel the city's growth into planned and serviced desert sites were almost entirely unsuccessful. The projects became enmeshed in bureaucratic struggles over control of valuable state-owned desert land. In large measure, these ambitious planning exercises failed to achieve their goals because of the authoritarian nature of state power and the exclusionary political order that constrained independent action by spatial planners.[90]

---

[86] Bent Flyvbjerg, "Machiavellian Megaprojects," *Antipode* 37, 1 (2005), pp. 18–22. See also Philip Boland, "Sexing Up the City in the International Beauty Contest: The Performative Nature of Spatial Planning and the Fictive Spectacle of Place Branding," *Town Planning Review* 84, 2 (2013), pp. 251–274.

[87] Rami Farouk Daher, "Amman: Disguised Genealogy and Recent Urban Restructuring and Neoliberal Threats," in Yasser Elsheshtawy (ed.), *The Evolving Arab City: Tradition, Modernity and Urban Development* (London: Routledge, 2008), pp. 37–68 (esp. p. 60). See also Yasser Elsheshtawy, "The Middle East City: Moving beyond the Narrative of Loss," in Yasser Elsheshtawy (ed.), *Planning Middle Eastern Cities: An Urban Kaleidoscope in a Globalizing World* (London: Routledge, 2004), pp. 1–21.

[88] Fernando Diaz Orueta and Susan Fainstein, "The New Mega-projects: Genesis and Impacts," *International Journal of Urban and Regional Research* 32, 4 (2009), pp. 759–767.

[89] Yasser Elsheshtawy, "Urban Dualities in the Arab World: From a Narrative of Loss to Neoliberal Urbanism," in Michael Larice and Elizabeth MacDonald (eds.), *Urban Design Reader* (London: Routledge, 2013), pp. 475–496.

[90] W. J. Dorman, "Exclusion and Informality: The Praetorian Politics of Land Management in Cairo, Egypt," *International Journal of Urban and Regional Research* 37, 5 (2013), pp. 1584–1610 (esp. p. 1584).

In order to absorb the population overspills from the densely packed and overcrowded residential precincts closer to the older central city, various government ministries began in the 1970s to adopt a "desert development strategy" that aimed to create far-flung galaxy of satellite cities and new desert towns built on the fringes of Cairo City. Despite these efforts to relieve the housing crisis, informal settlements and unauthorized squatting has continued unabated. The failure of various policies (Greater Cairo Regional Master Plan, "new settlements" schemes, new town plans) to accommodate the housing needs of middle- and low-income people has resulted in the paradoxical imbalance between the expansion of exclusive gated residential communities for the wealthy, on the one hand, and the construction of nearly empty new satellite cities for middle-income residents, on the other.[91] Since the 1990s, inordinate amounts of human and financial resources have been directed at building these new satellite cities in order to provide public housing, private compounds, individual subdivisions, and, in some instances, manufacturing complexes. However, the overall success in attracting new residents has been insignificant. Not even a fraction of the target twelve million residents has been absorbed. This pattern of unplanned growth has merely aggravated social injustice and housing inequality.[92]

Cairo is a diverse city of stark contrasts – a chaotic megalopolis on the verge of careening out of control.[93] The steady, incremental expansion of unplanned housing and unauthorized squatting in the interstices of the built environment has continued to be the dominant mode of urbanization. State-led relocation programs and emergency housing development converted large parts of publicly owned desert land to informal settlements. The absence of adequate programs for affordable housing triggered unauthorized encroachment on state-owned desert lands, the massive expansion of informal settlements on privately owned agricultural land on the peri-urban fringes of the city, and the illegal extension of existing buildings in the already overcrowded, low-income resident precincts.[94]

[91] Wael Fahmi and Keith Sutton, "Greater Cairo's Housing Crisis: Contested Spaces from Inner City Areas to New Communities," *Cities* 25, 5 (2008), pp. 277–297.

[92] Janet Abu-Lughod, "The Desert City Today," in David Sims (ed.), *Understanding Cairo: The Logic of a City out of Control* (Cairo: American University in Cairo, 2010), pp. 169–210 (esp. p. 171).

[93] Regina Kipper, "Cairo: A Broader View," in Regina Kipper and Marion Fischer (eds.), *Cairo's Informal Areas: Between Urban Challenges and Hidden Potentials. Facts. Voices. Visions* (Cairo: German Technical Cooperation [GTZ], 2009), pp. 13–17. See also Diane Singerman and Paul Amar, "Contesting Myths, Critiquing Cosmopolitanism, and Creating the Cairo School of Urban Studies," in Diane Singerman and Paul Amar (eds.), *Cairo Cosmopolitan: Politics, Culture and Urban Space in the New Middle East* (Cairo: American University in Cairo Press, 2006), pp. 1–43.

[94] David Sims and Janet Abu-Lughod, "A History of Modern Cairo: Three Cities in One," in *Understanding Cairo*, pp. 45–90 (esp. p. 86).

Despite thirty years of attempts by state authorities to limit unplanned growth and urban expansion on agricultural land around Cairo, informal settlements around Cairo sheltered an estimated 65 percent of the total metropolitan population (or 10.5 out of 16.2 million inhabitants) by the first decade of the twentieth century, with numbers increasing an estimated 2 percent per annum.[95] These residential neighborhoods consisting of unauthorized housing differ in size, shape, and living conditions. Yet what they all have in common is that they were not officially planned, but rather grew spontaneously without municipal oversight. Despite circumstances where this informal housing is *de facto* illegal, municipal authorities have more or less tolerated the autoconstruction of housing units. The adoption of policies of brutal eradication has never been a realistic option.[96]

The metamorphosis of Cairo over the past three or four decades from the classic European model of a "compact city" radiating outward from an historic urban core (akin to, say, Brussels or Amsterdam) to the North American pattern of horizontally oriented spatial diffusion on a vast scale (resembling Los Angeles or Tucson/Phoenix) has produced a hybrid urban form, where new private (satellite) cities have lured the super-rich escaping from high densities, traffic congestion, air and noise pollution by offering a rich plethora of opulent amenities. Starting in the last quarter of the twentieth century, the greater Cairo metropolitan region has experienced what Asef Bayat and Eric Denis have called "a trend in urbanization outside the [conventional] administrative definition of cities, a sort of spontaneous urbanization of agglomerations" at the outer edges of the historic urban core.[97] The emergence and subsequent development of this new pattern of "diffuse urbanization" has signaled a shift from the conventional expectation of a universal, state-managed, and incrementally planned urbanization to a more spontaneous, unplanned, and privately led process of urban transformation. This "postmetropolitanization" signifies a "diffusion of urbanity" over vast geographical space, incorporating "agro-towns" (where agricultural activities continue to dominate), urban villages, new industrial zones, and satellite cites (catering for the wealthy) into an extended and interconnected agglomeration of discontinuous fragments. The accompanying car-dependent mobility system that these diffuse residential settlement patterns

---

95 Marion Séjourné, "The History of Informal Settlements," in Kipper and Fischer, *Cairo's Informal Areas: Between Urban Challenges and Hidden Potentials*, pp. 17–20; and Janet Abu-Lughod, "Informal Cairo Triumphant," in *Understanding Cairo*, pp. 91–138.

96 Julia Gerlach, "Three Areas: Manshiet Nasser, City of the Dead, Boulaq al-Dakrour," in Kipper and Fischer, *Cairo's Informal Areas: Between Urban Challenges and Hidden Potentials*, pp. 49–52. See also Julia Elyachar, "Mappings of Power: The State, NGOs, and International Organizations in the Informal Economy of Cairo," *Comparative Studies in Society and History* 45, 3 (2003), pp. 571–605; and Julia Elyachar, *Markets of Dispossession: NGOs, Economic Development and the State in Cairo* (Durham, NC: Duke University Press, 2005).

97 Bayat and Denis, "Who is Afraid of *Ashwaiyat*?" pp. 199, 195 (source of quotation).

brought into being not only reflects but also intensifies the onerous inequalities that characterize contemporary Cairo.[98]

Although informal housing has become the dominant mode of residential accommodation, there are very few shantytowns and horrific "slums" in Cairo. Apart from some inner pockets and some of the more remote urbanized fringes, the overall quality of construction in informal areas is reasonably decent, especially in areas where it has been incrementally consolidated over time. Nevertheless, because of their unplanned and "random" construction – from which they derive their name in Egyptian Arabic, *ashwa'iyyat* (meaning "disordered" or "haphazard"), these areas of informal shelter suffer greatly from problems associated with accessibility, narrow streetscapes, the absence of vacant land and open spaces, very high residential densities, and woefully inadequate infrastructure and municipal services. Although it contravenes the building standards established by the state authorities, informal urbanization cannot be regarded as totally clandestine and invisible.[99] Long aware of what was happening outside formal regulations, city officials and planning authorities have for decades adopted a *laissez-faire* approach, supported by a well-consolidated system of clientelism and corruption that has ensured the *de facto* tolerance of the administration. Yet at the same time, official pronouncements have aimed at "pathologizing" informal housing by presenting it as social threat and a disease that should be removed from the city.[100] In the official discourse of municipal authorities and policymakers, "unplanned" and spontaneously built settlements are often described as "cancer cells," "devilish expansions," "ugly deformities," "shelters for criminals," and "breeders of terrorists."[101]

Some places have acquired a certain degree of notoriety because of their distinctiveness and historical peculiarity. At the bottom end of the informal settlement called Manshiet Nasser, where most of rubbish of Cairo is brought to be sorted and recycled, there is a large cemetery, also known as the "City of the Dead."[102] It is here in this funerary space among the tombs where the very poor have carved out accommodation for themselves. There is a long tradition of illicit occupation of abandoned or rarely visited funeral courtyards. Some of the mausoleums date back hundreds of years. Egyptians bury their dead in chambers under the earth. A small house with an open yard is usually constructed above this chamber. This arrangement allows the relatives to mourn

[98] Bayat and Denis, "Who is Afraid of *Ashwaiyat*?" pp. 185–199 (p. 195, for source of quotations).
[99] Elena Piffero, "Beyond Rules and Regulations: The Growth of Informal Cairo," in Kipper and Fischer, *Cairo's Informal Areas: Between Urban Challenges and Hidden Potentials*, pp. 20–27.
[100] Bayat and Denis, "Who is Afraid of *Ashwaiyat*?" pp. 185–199.
[101] Farha Ghannam, "Two Dreams in a Global City: Class and Space in Urban Egypt," in Andreas Huyssen (ed.), *Other Cities, Other Worlds: Urban Imaginaries in a Globalizing Age* (Durham: Duke University Press, 2008), pp. 267–287 (p. 278, source of quotations).
[102] Jeffrey Nedoroscik, *The City of the Dead: A History of Cairo's Cemetery Communities* (Westport, CT: Greenwood Press, 1997).

in peace, and take shelter in case they wish to spend the night. This cemetery district has been restructured by shifting modes of occupation.[103] From the start, poor people have always lived in the mausoleums and have taken care of the graves. Since the 1950s, more and more of these caretakers began to bring their families to live with them, and had children and grandchildren. These residents usually do not pay rent. Instead, they care for and keep guard over the graves in return for permission to stay. Many mausoleums have electricity, and some have access to water. In some sections of the cemetery, residents have built actual apartment blocks. Over time, this cemetery has acquired new meaning with the addition of a medical center, a post office, and two schools.[104]

Perhaps not so surprising, by transferring the responsibility for the production of lower middle class housing to "irregular" (and hence unauthorized) constructors, state officials have discovered a convenient way to exempt themselves from what has become nearly impossible obligations to provide decent resident accommodation. This disengagement of the authorities is indeed only too apparent. This "policy of negligence" toward informal neighborhoods has actually reinforced the political dependence of the urban residents.[105] Knowing the impossibility of relying upon legal housing rights since informality is by definition outside the laws), the inhabitants of informal accommodation largely depend on the "concessions" and the "benevolence" of municipal authorities. Consequently, clientelism and patronage networks become the singular vehicle through which local communities can negotiate the tolerance of the government and the partial provision of the necessary infrastructure. Rather than guiding these informal building processes through the supply of serviced sites, state authorities relied upon a series of decrees aimed at increasing the fines and penalties for illegal construction on agricultural land.[106]

For at least the last two decades, property developers have gobbled up vast expanses of the public domain on the desert plateaus bordering the city to the east and to the west, where private building contractors have produced

[103] Anna Tozzi Di Marco, "The Reshaping of Cairo's City of the Dead: Rural Identity versus Urban Arena in the Cairene Cultural Narrative and Public Discourse," *Anthropology of the Middle East 6*, 2 (2011), pp. 38–50 (for the source of these ideas, see pp. 38–40).

[104] Gerlach, "Three Areas," in *Cairo's Informal Areas: Between Urban Challenges and Hidden Potentials*, pp. 49–52.

[105] Cilja Harders, "The Informal Social Pact: The State and the Urban Poor in Cairo," in Eberhard Kienle (ed.), *Politics from Above, Politics from Below: The Middle East in the Age of Economic Reform* (London: Saqi, 2003), pp. 91–213; and J. W. Dorman, *The Politics of Neglect: The Egyptian State in Cairo, 1974–98* (Unpublished Ph.D. Thesis, School of Oriental and African Studies, University of London, 2007). See also Farha Ghannam, "The Visual Re-Making of Urban Space: Relocation and the Use of Public Housing in 'Modern' Cairo," *Visual Anthropology* 10, 2–4 (1998), pp. 264–280; and Farha Ghannam, "Mobility, Liminality, and Embodiment in Urban Egypt," *American Ethnologist* 38, 4 (2011), pp. 790–800.

[106] Piffero, "Beyond Rules and Regulations: The Growth of Informal Cairo," in Kipper and Fischer, *Cairo's Informal Areas: Between Urban Challenges and Hidden Potentials*, pp. 20–27; and Ghannam, "The Visual Re-Making of Urban Space," pp. 264–280.

countless numbers of apartment blocks and commercial clusters. To conform
to the new national "ethics" of neoliberalism, corporate builders who once
produced massive amounts of public housing at the behest of state authorities
have become private contractors, constructing luxury properties while benefit-
ing from easy credit furnished by state-owned banks. This financing is gauged
according to the speculative and overvalued worth of land purchased at a very
low price, under conditions where state authorities have ensured minimal costs
for property developers.[107]

Along with upscale shopping malls, dozens of luxury gated residential communities (accompanied by golf courses, amusement parks, private schools,
and health clinics) have proliferated along the arterial beltways. In contrast
to the ideal model of a dense, compact, organic historic urban core (which
orientalist geographers have long celebrated as the traditional "Asiatic" city),
the greater Cairo metropolitan region has grown and expanded by leaps and
bounds, resembling the nonlinear patterns of a new city more akin to Los
Angeles or Las Vegas, where distance is gauged according to the speed of
the automobile.[108] This new "horizontal city" is marked by the steady exodus of urban elites away from the historic downtown core and to the rapidly
developing edges. Sprawling mixed-used precincts like New Cairo City (nearly
three times the size of Manhattan Island and consisting of high-end residential accommodation, leisure-entertainment sites, and private hospitals, international schools, and universities) represent the apotheosis of escapist urbanism.
Upscale residential districts like Masr El Gedida, postcolonial Nasr City (with
pseudo Bauhaus-Nasserite matchbox housing units), Heliopolis (with its neo-
Mamluk apartment architecture), and Maadi have been rebuilt in the image
of cosmopolitan modernity where wealthy residents can escape traffic congestion, overcrowded streetscapes, and visible expressions of enduring poverty.[109]
In what Mona Abaza has termed "nomadism of the rich," the mass exodus
of wealthy urban residents have abandoned decaying districts close to the
historic downtown core, leaving behind them run-down derelict spaces that
once housed mansions and palaces. They have decamped to new satellite cities

[107] Eric Denis, "Cairo as Neoliberal Capital? From Walled City to Gated Communities," in Singer-
       man and Amar, *Cairo Cosmopolitan*, pp. 47–72 (esp. pp. 58–59). See Diane Singerman, "The
       Contested City," in Dianne Singerman (ed.), *Cairo Contested: Governance, Urban Space, and
       Global Modernity* (Cairo: American University in Cairo Press, 2009), pp. 3–38; and Thanassis
       Cambanis, "To Catch Cairo Overflow, 2 Megacities Rise in Sand," *New York Times*, August
       24, 2010.
[108] Denis, "Cairo as Neoliberal Capital?" in Singerman and Amar, *Cairo* Cosmopolitan," pp. 48–
       49. See also Khaled Adham, "Globalization, Neoliberalism, and New Spaces of Capital in
       Cairo," *Traditional Dwellings and Settlements Review (TDSR)* 17, 1 (2005), pp. 19–32.
[109] Mona Abasa, "Egyptianizing the American Dream? Nasr City's Shopping Malls, Public Order,
       and Privatized Military," in Singerman and Amar, *Cairo Cosmopolitan*, pp. 193–220. See also
       Petra Kuppinger, "Exclusive Greenery: New Gated Communities in Cairo," *City & Society*
       16, 2 (2004), pp. 35–61.

created on both sides of the desert. These "islands of luxury" consist mainly of the serial repetition of gated residential communities, landscaped compounds, and high-rise condominium complexes, connected by highways that are easily accessible to upscale shopping malls. The imagined landscape of a new up-market Disneyfied Cairo, with Dubai as its ideal model, offers an escape route to *faux* suburbia, "together with endless private cars with chauffeurs and servants commuting with public transport, and multiple ring-roads surrounding Cairo, flying over unwanted hidden slums." Despite the hard-branding exercises mounted to advertise these places as the high point of urban living, these new satellite cities that have been built without sound planning principles and with woefully inadequate infrastructure, including public transport, which deliberately excludes the underprivileged.[110] A far-flung network of highways and arterial ring roads has tethered these self-contained enclaves into an expansive inland empire of privilege.[111]

This radical reconfiguration of the metropolitan landscape – which its promoters invite us to celebrate as an urban renaissance (or *nahda umraniya*) – is completely in line with the parameters of economic liberalization and market-driven property development. Property-holding elites have placed themselves at the center of this new way of life, stitching together this vast "archipelago of 'microcity communities' that they administer as if they were so many experimental accomplishments of a private democracy to come." Functioning like a large-scale experimental land-use plan almost completely in private hands, the proliferation of gated residential communities – along with the attendant sequestered leisure sites – has literally "authorize[d] the elites who live there to continue the forced march for economic, oligopolistic liberalization, without redistribution," while shielding themselves from the deleterious ill effects of environmental pollution and overdevelopment.[112] With such fancy-sounding names as Utopia, Qatamiya Heights, Beverly Hills, Palm Hills, Jolie-Ville, Mena Garden City, New Cairo City, and Dreamland, these places appeal to the escapist fantasies of the well-to-do who wish to emulate the global phantasmagoric idea of "California-living" in a semiarid desert setting that resembles the eponymous Los Angeles. These self-enclosed "villas of the desert" epitomize the trend toward the fragmenting postmetropolitan ideal of sprawling

[110] Mona Abaza, "Critical Commentary: Cairo's Downtown Imagined: Dubaisation or Nostalgia?" *Urban Studies* 48, 6 (2011), pp. 1075–1087 (esp. p. 1077 and 1081 [source of quotations]). See also Kuppinger, "Exclusive Greenery," pp. 35–61.

[111] Denis, "Cairo as Neoliberal Capital? From Walled City to Gated Communities," p. 52 (source of quotations). See also Mohamed Elshahed, "From Tahrir Square to Emaar Square: Cairo's Private Road to a Private City," *The Guardian*, April 7, 2014.

[112] Denis, "Cairo as Neoliberal Capital? From Walled City to Gated Communities," p. 52 (source of both quotations). See also David Sims, *Egypt's Desert Dreams: Development or Disaster?* (New York and Oxford: Oxford University Press, 2015); and Abu-Lughod, "The Desert City Today," in *Understanding Cairo*, pp. 169–210.

satellite cities that connect the twin imaginaries of fortress urbanism and utopian Valhalla.[113]

Sprouting out of the desert west of the Giza pyramids and only minutes from central Cairo on the newly constructed ring road, "Dreamland" has brought together all the *accoutrements* of a luxury-themed environment in an enclosed setting. Copied from Celebration, the private residential community built by the Walt Disney Corporation in Orlando, Florida, "Dreamland" is more than simply a collection of luxury residences. This gated community complex also includes a *faux*-California theme park, horse-racing tracks, conference facilities, a hospital and health clinics, state-of-the art fitness center, schools catering to foreign diplomats, and an upscale hotel. Dreamland provides unimpeded views of the plateau of the pyramids of Giza, access to a private amusement park, and membership privileges at a golf course.[114] Along with similar self-contained domiciliary sites constructed for those wealthy urbanites fleeing the central precincts of Cairo, Dreamland offers what Farha Ghannam has called "flexible urbanity," that is, a means of bringing together the benefits of urban life while avoiding actually living in the city. As a kind of malleable strategy, this mode of escapist urbanism means that wealthy residents can acquire all the benefits of resources and facilities linked to everyday life in Cairo (sports and entertainment venues, healthcare, schools, retail shopping), and yet, at the same time, providing the means to evade its crowded streetscapes, environmental pollution, and broken-down infrastructure. Above all, Dreamland promises to regulate and limit social interactions with the urban poor and their "informal" way of life.[115]

This rejection of the metaphorical "chaotic city" conforms to an antiurban "risk management discourse" that naturalizes the accumulated anxieties about urban living and, by identifying them with poverty, criminality, and violent protests, incorporates them into a single story of uncertainty and danger. In the mindscape of wealthy Cairenes, "old Cairo" has become a complex of unsustainable nuisances and aggravations "against which nothing more can be done, except to escape or to protect oneself."[116] The word *ashwa'iyyat*, which derives from the Arabic root that signifies "chance," appeared in popular discourse at the beginning of the 1990s to designate slums, shantytowns, self-made settlements housing the influx of newcomers from the rural provinces. Seen through

[113] This idea is taken almost verbatim from Denis, "Cairo as Neoliberal Capital? From Walled City to Gated Communities," pp. 51, 52. See also Karim Kesseiba, "Cairo's Gated Communities: Dream Houses or Unified Houses," *Procedia: Social and Behavioral Sciences* 170 (2015), pp. 728–738.
[114] Ghannam, "Two Dreams in a Global City," in *Other Cities, Other Worlds*, p. 271; and Timothy Mitchell, "Dreamland," in Mike Davis and Daniel Monk (eds.), *Evil Paradises: Dreamlands of Neoliberalism* (New York: Verso, 2007), pp. 1–33.
[115] Ghannam, "Two Dreams in a Global City," p. 272.
[116] Denis, "Cairo as Neoliberal Capital? From Walled City to Gated Communities," [quotations from pp. 50, 52, 53].

the dystopian lens of the unwanted "Other," the designation *ashwa'iyyat* came to signify "unnatural communities" that were "ruralizing" urban centers and thereby transforming metropolitan Cairo into a "city of peasants." These informal settlements signified a "Hobbesian locus of lawlessness and extremism, producing a 'culture of violence' and an 'abnormal' way of life."[117] By the end of the 1990s, the term *ashwa'iyyat* came to describe not just illegitimate and illegal places, but the peoples who inhabited them, thereby labeling a near majority of urban dwellers as risky, "hazardous," shiftless wanderers. For long-term residents, these peasant newcomers represented anomie, poverty, disease, criminality, and political extremism. This errant figure of the wayward nomad is that which has most unsettled the cosmopolitan image of Cairo as a "globalizing" city with world-class aspirations. Seen as "the invading silhouette of the decidedly peasant migrant" slowing surrounding and strangling the city, the *fellah* [fellahin] (peasants) came to represent all that was wrong with urban life in "old Cairo." This designation also reanimates the classic Muslim opposition between the *fellah* (nonmodern, illiterate outsider) and the *hadari* (modern, civilized, and literate insider).[118]

As a globalizing metropolis at the time of neoliberal globalization, Cairo exists at the intersection of competing ideological fault lines: on the one side, the headlong rush into the hypermodernity of global connectivity; and on the other, an enduring crisis of failed dreams and broken promises. The old modernization solutions are no longer tenable, because religious radicalism and authoritarian state practices have produced a kind of stalemate where a shared vision of the future has literally disappeared. The proliferation of cocooned urbanoid enclaves like gated residential communities, upscale malls, and private leisure sites for the wealthy represent perhaps the most striking and revealing outcomes of "this new ecology of risk and the monopolization of politics." These building typologies reveal processes disorganizing and reorganizing conventional modes of living and cohabiting in the city. In short, these spatial assemblages expose the underlying dynamics of a new neoliberal "moral order" that is justified through escapist discourse of risk aversion.[119]

These new building typologies have mimicked the globalized "traveling idea" of the self-contained "protected city," that is, an assemblage of "desert colonies" encircled by high walls and offering a totally managed autonomy.

---

[117] Bayat and Denis, "Who is Afraid of *Ashwaiyat*?" p. 185 (source of quotation). *International Affairs* 65, 2 (2012), pp. 171–186. See also Nada Tarbush, "Cairo 2050: Urban Dream or Modernist Delusion?" *Journal of International Affairs* 65, 2 (2012), pp. 171–186.

[118] Denis, "Cairo as Neoliberal Capital? From Walled City to Gated Communities," [quotations from p. 54]. See also Diane Singerman, "Cairo Cosmopolitan: Citizenship, Urban Space, Publics, and Inequality," in Barbara Drieskens, Franck Mermier, and Heiko Wimmen (eds.), *Cities of the South: Citizenship and Exclusion in the 21st Century* (London: Al-Saqi Books, 2007), pp. 82–111.

[119] Denis, "Cairo as Neoliberal Capital? From Walled City to Gated Communities," (quotation from p. 54); and Mitchell, "Dreamland," in *Evil Paradises*, p. 33.

But these spatial products represent something more than the straightforward importation of a universal model as a kind of one-to-one correspondence between originating source and eventual outcome. What is also visible is the influence of the Persian Gulf oil monarchies and their extravagant taste for luxurious living. Stylized fashions borrowed from the Persian Gulf have appeared in the grand reinforcements of baroque guilding, imposing balconies, and neoclassic colonnades. The architectural stylistics and built form of upscale villas and mansions reveal clear gestures toward the appropriation of worldwide trends, but in a "hybridized" form mixing local and Arab-regional motifs.[120]

This tendency to think of informality, or the informal city, and the "aswaii way of life" as producing unwanted outsiders has proceeded in tandem with the steady expansion of newly minted and privately managed satellite cities on the metropolitan edge. Wealthy urban residents have joined the silent march to the urban periphery, escaping high densities, overcrowded streets, traffic congestion, air and noise pollution, and the spatial constraints of living close to the historic urban core. Once the status symbols of cosmopolitan urban living, the old spacious villas in the Zamalek and Maadi inner suburbs of Cairo have been slowly demolished and replaced by densely packed high-rise apartment blocks. The new ring roads around the city have enabled the wealthy to retreat to the new opulent private satellite cities at the peri-urban fringe. This duality of peripheral informalization, on the one hand, and privately planned exclusive suburbanization, on the other, is a "stark manifestation of the urban polarization and social cleavage" that has come to characterize the greater Cairo metropolitan region at the start of the twenty-first century.[121]

In early 2014, Emaar Properties PJSC (the real-estate developers behind the world's tallest building, the Burj Khalifa in Dubai) reached an agreement with the Egyptian defense ministry. The agreement cleared the way for the construction of Emaar Square (referred to as a "city within a city"), the commercial-retail centerpiece of a mixed-use real-estate development called Uptown Cairo. Promoted as an isolated island disconnected from the urban headaches of downtown Cairo, the 4.5 million square meter Uptown Cairo complex includes amenities ranging from open-air shopping for specializing in global luxury brands, exclusive residential accommodation (including townhouses, penthouses, and villas featuring Italian, Mediterranean, Spanish, and Arabian architectural stylistics), and leisure and entertainment venues. The defense ministry, which owns the massive tract of land upon which the planned

---

[120] Denis, "Cairo as Neoliberal Capital? From Walled City to Gated Communities," (quotations from p. 54); and Nezar Alsayyad, "Hybrid Culture/Hybrid Urbanism: Pandora's Box of the 'Third Space'," in Nezar Alsayyad (ed.), *Hybrid Urbanism: On the Identity Discourse and the Built Environment* (Westport, CT: Praeger, 2001), pp. 1–18; and Farha Ghannam, *Remaking the Modern: Space, Relocation, and the Politics of Identity in a Global Cairo* (Berkeley: University of California Press, 2002), pp. 25–42.

[121] Bayat and Denis, "Who is Afraid of *Ashwaiyat*?" p. 199 (source of quotation). See also Ghannam, *Remaking the Modern*, pp. 25–42, 43–66.

Uptown Cairo will be built, is largest landowner and property manager in Egypt. In 1997, a presidential decree gave the military establishment the right to manage all undeveloped nonagricultural land. By one estimate, this right to ownership amounted to an incredible 87 percent of the land mass of the country. In the city of Cairo, this pattern of ownership has translated to "massive, walled plots of land in lucrative locations, monitored from watchtowers."[122] For the most part, these tracts of land have remained vacant, awaiting their turn to be magically transformed into upscale shopping malls, fancy hotels, or exclusive housing for military officers. Emaar Square is one of the latest (and perhaps the largest) of these military-secured real-estate developments.[123] A system of private roads will link this private city to the main ring-road network, and in all likelihood requiring the removal of poor homeowners in the Jabal al-Ahmar area.[124]

Under the political regime led by Hosni Mubarak (1981–2011), the state administration and its business cronies initiated a development plan called Cairo 2050. This redevelopment scheme called for the mass eviction of thousands of families in order to transform the metropolitan landscape into pockets of high-end shopping complexes, leisure sites, and gated residential communities for the wealthy. Real estate developers and corporate financiers from Kuwait, Saudi Arabia, and the UAE were the primary source of investment capital. Despite the interruption brought about by the 2011 popular protests in Cairo and elsewhere, the large-scale real-estate projects that characterized the "Dubai-zation" of Cairo are back on track, including the Maspero Triangle and Uptown Cairo.[125]

As Mohamed Elshahed has argued, those city builders who celebrate Dubai's urban model and seek its expansion across the middle east region make the unethical choice of ignoring the fact that the "instant cities" of the Persian Gulf emerged out of a very specific relationship between political power and real-estate capital: namely, that they are often one and the same. The expansion of this model into cities such as Cairo, where the military establishment has unchallenged access both to politics and capital (land, resources, construction), has already had a disastrous impact on the urban majority – those who

[122] Mohamed Elshahed, "From Tahrir Square to Emaar Square: Cairo's Private Road to a Private City," *The Guardian*, April 7, 2014 (source of quotation).

[123] Abaza, "Egyptianizing the American Dream?" in *Cairo Cosmopolitan*, pp. 193–220. See also Mona Abaza, "Shopping Malls, Consumer Culture and the Reshaping of Public Space in Egypt," *Theory, Culture & Society* 18, 5 (2001), pp. 97–122.

[124] Mohamed Elshahed, "From Tahrir Square to Emaar Square: Cairo's Private Road to a Private City," *The Guardian*, April 7, 2014.

[125] Pierre-Arnaud Barthel and Leïla Vignal, "Arab Mediterranean Megaprojects after the 'Spring': Business as Usual or a New Beginning?" *Built Environment* 40, 1 (2014), pp. 52–71; Mohamed Elshahed, "From Tahrir Square to Emaar Square: Cairo's Private Road to a Private City," *The Guardian*, April 7, 2014; and Abaz, "Critical Commentary: Cairo's Downtown Imagined," pp. 1075–1087.

have been marginalized, "moved out of the way when necessary, and put to work under unacceptable conditions, with no power to mobilize and with little pay."[126]

"Going Global": Rebuilding Istanbul in the Image of a World-Class City

In seeking to achieve its globalist aspirations of becoming a genuine 'world-class' city, Istanbul has undergone an accelerated process of urban transformation since the end of the last century that has not only reconfigured the historic downtown core but also fundamentally reshaped the metropolitan fringe.[127] As the built environment has been subjected to the powerful force of real-estate capitalism, the evolving metropolitan landscape has experienced feverish and unprecedented expansion – both upward and outward.[128] Following in the footsteps of other globalizing cities with world-class aspirations, city builders in Istanbul have set out to re-build central areas of the city, both in the historic downtown core and at the edges, to conform to the global image of cosmopolitan modernity. Ironically, these isolated enclaves have blossomed at a time when Istanbul has rapidly become a sprawling metropolis without easily recognizable limits. New roadways, bridges, subway lines, and tunnels have cut through tightly knit (if not largely claustrophobic) neighborhoods, bulldozing the last remaining barriers to market exchange. Huge mega-projects, gated residential estates, and other introverted spaces represent – at least symbolically – efforts to maintain the semblance of order amidst this growing urban maelstrom, places walled off from the discord of a seemingly endless and rapidly evolving city in the throes of unprecedented transformation.[129]

For the past half century, urban redevelopment in Istanbul has largely consisted of highly heterogeneous pattern of differentiated land ownership, combined with various building typologies, architectural styles, and building heights tied to narrow streetscapes. This complex, idiosyncratic layering of form and function – what Jesse Honsa has called a "dense and pixelated urban form" – was able to easily absorb dramatic shifts in economic activities and in

[126] Mohamed Elshahed, "From Tahrir Square to Emaar Square: Cairo's Private Road to a Private City," *The Guardian*, April 7, 2014 (source of quotation).

[127] Ozan Karaman, "Urban Pulse – (Re)Making Space for Globalization in Istanbul," *Urban Geography* 29, 6 (2008), pp. 518–525; and Tuna Kuyucu and Özlem Ünsal, "'Urban Transformation' as State-led Property Transfer: An Analysis of Two Cases of Urban Renewal in Istanbul," *Urban Studies* 47, 7 (2010), pp. 1479–1499.

[128] Binnur Öktem, "The Role of Global City Discourses in the Development and Transformation of the Buyukdere–Maslak Axis into the International Business District of Istanbul," *International Planning Studies* 16, 1 (2011), pp. 27–42; and Ozan Karaman, "Urban Renewal in Istanbul: Reconfigured Spaces, Robotic Lives," *International Journal of Urban and Regional Research* 37, 2 (2013), pp. 715–733.

[129] Tan Yigitcanlar and Melih Bulu, "Dubaization of Istanbul: Insights from the Knowledge-based Urban Development Journey of an Emerging Local Economy," *Environment and Planning A* 47, 1 (2015), pp. 89–107.

urban land use.[130] But the current process of urban transformation has consolidated these loosely interconnected cells into monochromatic, monopolistic
pockets. Lacking uniformity, these self-enclosed parcels have become the foundation for a latticework of highly uneven urban development characterized by
social polarization and spatial segregation.[131]

The explosive growth of high-rise building construction over the past several decades has dwarfed the once picturesque scenographic *tableau* of historic mosques with their shiny domes and slender minarets – a panoramic view
that, along with presence of water, oriented the distinctive skyline of the city
until the late 1970s. As part-and-parcel of ongoing efforts to integrate Istanbul into global circuits of capital, city builders have engaged in a two-pronged
strategy involving not only the construction of numerous showcase mega-
projects that reflect the global ambitious of a new propertied elite but also the
erasure of much of the fine-grained fabric of older residential neighborhoods
close to the city center.[132] The redevelopment program for Istanbul – what John
Lovering and Hade Türkmen has called "neoliberal modernization," or a historically distinct kind of free-market modernity – has assumed "a highly authoritarian form of neoliberalism, in which global discourses and policy models
are combined with local traditions and institutions to rationalize a radical–
conservative project to rebuild the city and its sociocultural characteristics."[133]
With the adoption of a more entrepreneurial and market-driven outlook, Istanbul has become less inclusive and less accommodating of the urban poor and
new immigrants.[134] The symbolic markers of globalization – such as glam-
orous sites of entertainment and high-end consumption, the commodification of urban real estate and subsequent gentrification – have become ever
more visible throughout the city, resulting in accelerating conflict and contestation over urban space.[135] The kind of urban restructuring that Istanbul has

---

[130] Jesse Honsa, "Istanbul's Fading Metabolism," *Failed Urbanism*, October 17, 2014 (source of
quotation). Available at www.failedarchitecture.com/istanbuls-fading-metabolism.

[131] Asu Aksoy, "Riding the Storm: 'New Istanbul'," *City* 16, 1–2 (2012), pp. 93–111 (esp. p. 93).

[132] Ozan Karaman, "Resisting Urban Renewal in Istanbul," *Urban Geography* 35, 2 (2014),
pp. 290–310.

[133] John Lovering and Hade Türkmen, "Bulldozer Neoliberalism in Istanbul: The State-led Construction of Property Markets, and the Displacement of the Urban Poor," *Urban Geography*
16, 1 (2011), pp. 73–96 (quotation from p. 73).

[134] Çaglar Keyder, "Globalization and Social Exclusion in Istanbul," *International Journal of
Urban and Regional Research*, 29, 1 (2005), pp. 124–134; Zeynep Merey Enlil, "The Neoliberal Agenda and the Changing Urban Form of Istanbul," *International Planning Studies* 16, 1
(2011), pp. 5–25; and İclal Dinçer, "The Impact of Neoliberal Policies on Historic Urban Space:
Areas of Urban Renewal in Istanbul," *International Planning Studies* 16, 1 (2011), pp. 43–
60.

[135] Mine Eder and Özlem Öz, "Neoliberalization of Istanbul's Nightlife: Beer or Champagne?"
International Journal of Urban and Regional Research 39, 2 (2015), pp. 284–304. See also
Özlem Ünsal and Tuna Kuyucu, "Challenging the Neoliberal Urban Regime: Regeneration
and Resistance in Başıbüyük and Tarlabaşı," in Deniz Göktürk, Levent Soysal and Ipek Türeli
(eds.), *Orienting Istanbul: Cultural Capital of Europe?* (New York: Routledge, 2010), pp. 51–
70.

experienced reflects the neoliberal agenda of improving the city's competitive advantage and enhancing its visible profile.[136] The resulting sharp increase in social polarization has produced new sites of wealth, on the one hand, and burgeoning squatter settlements and their declining opportunities for socioeconomic improvement on the other. In promoting their vision of property-led redevelopment, municipal authorities have portrayed their efforts to install new regulatory regimes that formalize land markets and property sales as a necessary and inevitable means required to achieve the end goal of becoming a world-class megacity.[137] Acting to aid and abet large-scale real-estate developers, municipal authorities have used urban renewal and regeneration projects as a convenient tool of dispossession, expropriating vulnerable residents from prime lands and uprooting them from their long-standing social networks. Under the cover of housing improvement, state officials have introduced various "transformation projects" grounded in private homeownership schemes in order to incorporate the urban poor into new "property regimes" that employ strict market criteria to allocate differentiated access to housing in the city.[138]

Like other globalizing cities with world-class aspirations, Istanbul remains trapped between two competing logics: on the one side, the top-down political ambitions to globalize the city have succeeded through their rebuilding efforts to transform many parts of the city into the cosmopolitan and secular image of late modernity. In seeking to achieve an outward-oriented "competitive image" for Istanbul, a loose coalition of large-scale real-estate developers, property financiers, architects, urban designers, and local politicians have virtually turned entire sections of the city into a gigantic construction site in itself. The cityscape has been subjected to significant interventions that aim to re-shape many of the major cultural sites, historical landmarks, and natural ecological zones of the city.[139] As Istanbul has entered the new millennium, virtually every part of the city has been exposed to radical transformation, as more and more underutilized and noncommodified land is pulled into the

---

[136] Ökyü Potuoğlu-Cook, "Beyond the Glitter: Belly Dance and Neoliberal Gentrification in Istanbul," *Cultural Anthropology* 21, 4 (2006), pp. 633–60; Bartu-Candan and Kolluoğlu, "Emerging Spaces of Neoliberalism," pp. 5–46; Kuyucu and Ünsal, "'Urban Transformation' as State-led Property Transfer," pp. 1479–99; Asuman Türkün, "Urban Regeneration and Hegemonic Power Relationships," *International Planning Studies* 16, 1 (2010), pp. 61–72; and Aksoy, "Riding the Storm," pp. 93–111.

[137] Ozan Karaman, "Urban Neoliberalism with Islamic Characteristics," *Urban Studies* 50, 16 (2013), 3412–3427.

[138] Ozan Karaman, "Urban Renewal in Istanbul," p. 716, 719–723; and Ayca Zayim, "Differentiated Urban Citizenship and Housing Rights: Analysing the Social Impacts of Urban Redevelopment in Globalizing Istanbul," *International Planning Studies* 19, 3–4 (2014), pp. 268–291.

[139] Evren Aysev Deneç, "The Reproduction of the Historical Center of Istanbul in the 2000s: A Critical Account on Two Projects in Fener-a Balat," *METU JFA* 31, 2 (2014), pp. 163–188. See also Feyzan Erkip, "Global Transformations versus Local Dynamics in Istanbul: Planning in a Fragmented Metropolis," *Cities* 17, 5 (2000), pp. 371–377.

FIGURE 4.1. Zorlu Center, multiuse complex, Istanbul.
(Photo Credit: Thomas Mayer.)

market for landed property, catapulting the whole of the city into an irreversible
process of large-scale urban redevelopment. In short, İstanbul has undergone a
series of mega-scale construction operations – such as the mixed-use complex
called the Zorlu Center, shown in Figure 4.1 – that have unalterably reconfigured the social fabric of the city.[140] In anticipation of the future, large-scale
real-estate developers have engaged in speculative investment in high-rise office

---

[140] Asu Aksoy, "The Violence of Change," in Ricky Burdett and Deyan Sudjic (eds.), *Living in the
Endless City: The Urban Age Project by the London School of Economics and Deutsche Bank's
Alfrde Herrhausen Society* (London: Phaidon Press, 2011), pp. 232–239 (esp. pp. 232, 234).

towers, luxury hotels, and high-rise apartment complexes. The construction of mass housing projects has created ribbons of high-rise, high-density suburbs in the peri-urban periphery, not only creating more socially homogeneous residential environments and fundamentally altering the social geography of the city.[141]

On the other hand, the particular brand of pious free-market conservatism that has come to dominate the property-led redevelopment agenda has been unable to deal adequately with unplanned metropolitan growth. Istanbul has become a patchwork of very different building typologies, fueled in part by property speculation and in part by spontaneous self-built accommodation. Municipal authorities have no serious strategy to deal with further expansion, as the city has continued "to swallow the forests around it." Current plans for dealing with the growing congestion caused by the insertion of new mega-projects, towering office buildings, and sprawling shopping malls close to the city center calls for an ambitious program of large-scale demolitions around highway exits, in order to make way for the construction of brand new avenues and arterial roadways. Informal residential districts are particularly vulnerable to such clearances, and disgruntled residents have organized militant resistance campaigns against such demolitions in several neighborhoods.[142]

First- and second-generation squatters, who register more than half the population of Greater Istanbul, have constituted a double problem for the "world-city" image to which city boosters have aspired in the neoliberal era. Sensing their own marginalization and abandonment, these poor residents have not only mounted impromptu militant campaigns against the highways and other infrastructural "improvements" scheduled to be driven through their neighborhoods but also provided a vast "vote bank" for Islamic political parties that have proclaimed their opposition to "the architectural pretensions of global capital" – high-rise condominium buildings and skyscrapers, conspicuous consumption, and luxurious lifestyles for the aspiring wealthy.[143]

The shift toward a top-down kind of property-led urban redevelopment unfolded over time in stages.[144] Starting in the mid-twentieth century, a half-century-long period of unplanned and uncontrolled urbanization – brought about by rapid influx of rural-to-urban migrants and coupled with

---

See also Nur Bahar Sakizlioglu and Justus Uitermark, "The Symbolic Politics of Gentrification: The Restructuring of Stigmatized Neighborhoods in Amsterdam and Istanbul," *Environment and Planning A* 46, 6 (2014), pp. 1369–1385.

[141] Enlil, "The Neoliberal Agenda and the Changing Urban Form of Istanbul," pp. 5–25 (esp. p. 18).

[142] Cihan Tugal, "The Greening of Istanbul," *New Left Review* 51 (2008), pp. 65–80 (quotation from pp. 79); and Enlil, "The Neoliberal Agenda and the Changing Urban Form of Istanbul," pp. 19–21.

[143] Tugal, "The Greening of Istanbul," p. 65 (source of quotation); and Zayim, "Differentiated Urban Citizenship and Housing Rights," pp. 268–291.

[144] Enlil, "The Neoliberal Agenda and the Changing Urban Form of Istanbul," pp. 5–25; and Lovering and Türkmen, "Bulldozer Neoliberalism in Istanbul," pp. 73–96.

inefficient urban management – produced a chaotic urban landscape that defied any real sense of order or stability. Beginning in the 1950s, municipal authorities allowed newcomers who were migrating from rural areas to construct self-built housing – squatter settlements known as *gecekondu* (literally, "built overnight") – on illegally occupied (largely state-owned vacant) land on the fringes of Istanbul. Without official permission or any form of state legitimacy, this kind of informal housing became a habitus deeply ingrained in the social fabric of everyday life.[145] Built either by the settlers themselves or by land speculators, this officially tolerated mode of informal urbanization quickly became the dominant means of gaining access to residential accommodation.[146] Istanbul was literally "a city without slums," where virtually penniless new arrivals could easily find inexpensive housing and tap into opportunities for making a living. The city was a place where successive waves of new migrants could gradually and incrementally integrate themselves into the social and economic mainstream of urban life, albeit always at the precarious margins.[147] In the absence of planned (formal) social housing policies, the widespread reliance upon self-built housing and informal markets became the only mechanisms through which the urban poor could be absorbed into makeshift residential neighborhoods. The particular solution to the "housing problem" that municipal authorities adopted in the 1980s revolved around legalizing unauthorized land appropriations and inner-city squatting.[148] This mode of "crude urbanization" – epitomized by the *gecekondu* –resulted in irregular patterns of urban growth, inadequate urban infrastructure, disorderly public spaces, unsafe build practices, and low-quality housing stock.[149] The retroactive extension of private ownership rights to unauthorized squatters by means of several "building amnesties" helped to sustain a populist coalition between industrialists in need of cheap labor, political parties seeking to obtain the loyalty of the urban poor, and lower-class residents in search of affordable housing.[150]

---

[145] İlhan Tekeli, "Bridging Histories," in *Living in the Endless City*, pp. 210–217 (esp. p. 213).

[146] Türkün, Urban Regeneration and Hegemonic Power Relationships," pp. 61–72; and Ayşe Öncü, "The Politics of Urban Land Market in Turkey: 1950–1980," *International Journal of Urban and Regional Research* 12, 1 (1988), pp. 38–64.

[147] Cem Başlevent and Meltem Dayıoğlu, "The Effect of Squatter Housing on Income Distribution in Urban Turkey," *Urban Studies* 42, 1 (2005), pp. 31–45.

[148] Çaglar Keyder, "Liberalization from Above and the Future of the Informal Sector: Land, Shelter, and Informality in the Periphery," in Faruk Tabak and Michaeline Crichlow (eds.), *Informalization: Process and Structure* (Baltimore: The Johns Hopkins University Press, 2000), pp. 119–132; Ayşe Buğra, "The Immoral Economy of Housing in Turkey, *International Journal of Urban and Regional Research* 22, 2 (1998), pp. 282–302; and Öncü, "The Politics of Urban Land Market in Turkey: 1950–1980," pp. 38–64.

[149] Derya Özkan, *The Misuse Value of Space: Spatial Practices and the Production of Space in Istanbul* (Unpublished Ph.D. Dissertation, University of Rochester, 2008), p. 33.

[150] Kuyucu and Ünsal, "'Urban Transformation' as State-led Property Transfer," p. 1483; and Utku Balaban, "The Enclosure of Urban Space and Consolidation of the Capitalist Land Regime in Turkish Cities," *Urban Studies* 48, 10 (2011), pp. 2162–2179.

By the end of the twentieth century, housing provision to low-income residents moved from the phase of *de facto* occupation to *de jure* legalization, and from financialization to speculation.[151] Municipal authorities gave squatters permission to build four-story residential units, thereby enabling these new property owners to expand their makeshift houses into low-quality apartment blocks, sometimes for the use of their children but sometimes for rent to provide extra income. Such investments in property improvements were usually beyond the means of newly arrived immigrants, so building contractors (*yapsatçılar*) filled the void, collecting the lion's share of the burgeoning rental income, and thereby creating a multilayered class hierarchy among the squatters "that was partially distinct from their position in the labor force." These building contractors upgraded these makeshift shanties on small irregular plots of land into concrete-built apartment blocks, often using cheap and inadequate materials that left them exposed to periodic flooding and highly vulnerable to unexpected earthquakes. The new lax zoning regulations imposed few restrictions on choice of building materials or standards. The result of this largely unregulated building process has been "to create an uncanny architectural cityscape," where the poor have continued to live in their own unfinished multistory concrete buildings and renters squeeze into overcrowded upstairs units. This new type of dwelling is informally called an *apartkondu* – a hybrid term combining *gecekondu* (squatter residence) and *apartman* (middle-class apartments).[152]

After decades of relatively slow and incremental transformation, Istanbul has undergone a largely privately planned, neoliberal restructuring of metropolitan space at the start of the twenty-first century. Ever-taller and multiplying high-rise office blocks, bank buildings, elite residential towers, and colossal luxury hotels compete for attention in the increasingly crowded skyline. The multistory towers that provide the vertical definition of the Zorlu Center – as shown in Figure 4.2 – epitomize this trend. Rapidly increasing numbers of exclusive shopping malls, restaurants, cafes, and night clubs have crowded the downtown urbanscape.[153] Along with other culture-led redevelopment projects involving the regeneration of abandoned factory and warehousing sites, the wholesale retrofitting of the disused waterfront zone has brought Istanbul into the global spotlight.[154]

These large renewal projects – or what Tuna Kuyucu and Özlem Ünsal refer to as large "urban transformation projects" (UTPs) – have become the principal mechanisms by which real-estate developers and municipal authorities have imposed a capitalist logic on urban land and housing markets, especially in only

[151] Türkün, Urban Regeneration and Hegemonic Power Relationships," pp. 63–66.
[152] Tugal, "The Greening of Istanbul," p. 69 (source of quotations).
[153] Bartu-Candan and Kolluoğlu, "Emerging Spaces of Neoliberalism: a Gated Town and a Public Housing Project in Istanbul," pp. 5–46 (esp. p. 6).
[154] Zeynep Gunay and Vedia Dokmeci, "Culture-led Regeneration of Istanbul Waterfront: Golden Horn Cultural Valley Project," *Cities* 29, 4 (2012), pp. 213–222.

FIGURE 4.2. High-rise buildings, Zorlu Center, Istanbul.
(Photo Credit: Thomas Mayer.)

partially commodified informal housing areas and "rundown" inner-city neighborhoods not fully subject to the logic of market exchange. Real-estate developers look upon *gecekondu* neighborhoods as underutilized spatial resources that can be mobilized in commodified as the key building blocks for urban renewal. By redefining the rules of private ownership and instituting market dynamics, these UTPs – or "neoliberal market-making tools" – achieve two main goals: the "physical and demographic "upgrading" of particular localities within the city and the construction of a neoliberal regime of governance that no longer tolerates the legal ambiguities and the incompletely commodified market structure" that prevails in these areas. These radical interventions into the management of urban space disproportionately benefit loosely aligned coalitions of real-estate developers, banking and credit institutions, and state officials with an interest in accelerating urban transformation via the institutionalization of a neoliberal regulatory regime. Yet this process has subjected highly vulnerable urban residents, those whose livelihoods depend in large measure on populist redistributive mechanisms, to the logic of the capitalist marketplace.[155]

Given a free rein to bypass the regulatory frameworks of comprehensive planning and rely instead on project-based fragmented interventions,

[155] Kuyucu and Ünsal, "'Urban Transformation' as State-led Property Transfer," pp. 1478–1480 (source of ideas for this paragraph; and p. 1479, source of quotations).

FIGURE 4.3. Batishir mega-project, Istanbul.
(Photo Credit: Artist Rendition, DB Architects Istanbul.)

prominent real-estate developers have valorized this process of urban redevelopment through large-scale, property-led renewal schemes. As can be seen in the
artist rendition of the Batishir mega-project depicted in Figure 4.3, these fast-
paced efforts at urban redevelopment have transformed disused waterfronts,
industrial wastelands, existing public spaces, historic inner-city neighborhoods,
unauthorized self-help (squatter) housing, and natural protection zones into the
gigantic construction sites that have blossomed haphazardly across the urban
landscape. Large-scale redevelopment programs have targeted "neighborhoods
with low-quality housing or derelict but historically valuable properties."[156]
Demolition and land clearances have gone hand-in-hand with profit-seeking
investments in land property and widespread land speculation.[157] In seeking
to resolve problems associated with rapid and unplanned urbanization, these

[156] Aksoy, "The Violence of Change," p. 234 (source of quotation).
[157] Ibrahim Gundogdu and Jamie Gough, "Class Cleansing in Istanbul's World Class Project," in
Libby Porter and Kate Shaw (eds.), *Whose Urban Renaissance? An International Comparison of Urban Regeneration* (New York: Routledge, 2009), pp. 16–24; and Elvan Gülöksüz,
"Negotiation of Property Rights in Urban Land in İstanbul," *International Journal of Urban
and Regional Research* 26, 3 (2002), pp. 462–476.

large-scale, property-led renewal schemes have become the model of urban redevelopment: they function as instruments of what amounts to a kind of "urbicide," or self-inflicted destruction of the built environment.[158]

The "new Istanbul" consists in the main of four distinct housing typologies: gated residential estates, clusters of high-rise condominium towers, serially reproduced ranks of nondescript apartment slabs, and suburban tracts of individual homes serving a range of income groups. Despite their ostensible differences, the common denominator "seems to be precisely the fear of openness." The force fields of globalization have shaped the urban landscape, but in ways that appear in the guise of a deeply conservative approach to fundamentalist neoliberalism.[159]

Urban space has been subjected to large-scale private investments in real estate. Spatial transformation has occurred not only at the metropolitan fringes but also in the central neighborhoods in the historic urban core. In what amounts to a snowball effect, gated residential communities and their attendant comfortable lifestyles have become widespread among the new upper and middle classes of the city.[160] Since the 1980s, enclosed enclaves ranging from the ubiquitous gated residential communities and luxury housing estates to self-contained islands of modern office space and commercial enterprises in the inner city, and to new suburban towns and entirely new satellite cities at the peri-urban periphery, have been the driving force behind urban real-estate markets and housing development.[161] Unlike earlier "self-building" phases, the production of mass housing in Istanbul has largely been organized predominantly through the Housing Development Agency, or the Toplu Konut İdaresi Başkanlığı (TOKI). As a general rule, TOKI has employed a single urban typology: gated residential complexes of repetitive tower clusters on open land on the peri-urban fringe. These patterns of TOKI development have paralleled the emergence of a new middle class in Istanbul for whom a TOKI flat is an integral

---

[158] See Zeynep Gunday, "Renewal Agenda in Istanbul: Urbanisation vs. Urbicide" (49th ISOCARP Congress 2013, Brisbane, Australia). See also Zeynep Gunay, T. Kerem Koramaz, and A. Sule Ozuekren, "From Squatter Upgrading to Large-scale Renewal Programmes: Housing Renewal in Turkey," in Richard Turkington and Christopher Watson (eds.), *Renewing Older Housing: A European Perspective* (Bristol: Policy Press, 2014), pp. 215–244.

[159] Aksoy, "The Violence of Change," in Burdett and Sudjic, *Living in the Endless City:* pp. 232–239 (quotation from p. 232). See also Basak Tanulku, "Gated Communities: From 'Self-Sufficient Towns' to 'Active Urban Agents," *Geoforum* 43, 3 (2012), pp. 518–528.

[160] Serife Geniş, "Producing Elite Localities: The Rise of Gated Communities in Istanbul," *Urban Studies* 44, 4 (2007), pp. 771–798; and Bartu-Candan and Kolluoğlu, "Emerging Spaces of Neoliberalism," pp. 5–46.

[161] Ayşe Öncü, "The Politics of Istanbul's Ottoman Heritage in the Era of Globalism: Refractions through the Prism of a Theme Park," in Barbara Drieskens, Franck Mermier, and Heiko Wimmen (eds.), *Cities of the South: Citizenship and Exclusion in the 21st Century* (Beirut/London: Saqi Books, 2007), pp. 233–264.

part of the dream of home and automobile ownership, even if these scenarios bring social isolation, long commute times, and long-term debt.[162]

Ongoing practices of neoliberal restructuring has fundamentally recast the urban landscape by producing a steady increase in high-rise residential towers, colossal office buildings, luxury hotels, and spacious shopping malls. The evolving urbanscape has continued to be filled in with new residential compounds sequestered behind gates and walls. At the same time, new spaces of production, consumption, and leisure are kept under constant surveillance through strict security measures. Put simply, what has emerged is an ongoing *gating of the cityspace*, enclosing new forms of wealth and luxury lifestyles. New modes of governance and social relations have taken root in these enclosed enclaves.[163]

While North American-style tract housing and fenced-in suburbs have long been a stable feature of Istanbul's periphery, gated residential estates have evolved into a new building typology that has increasingly begun to encroach upon the high-density urban core. Smaller parcel sizes and higher Floor-Area Ratio (FAR) have resulted in distinct enclaves that appear as densely packed clusters of high-rise buildings that bear little or no relationship to their immediate surroundings. While estimates vary, it can be said with a high degree of certainty that more than one thousand gated residential estates have been built in Istanbul in the new millennium, ranging from dense clusters with few social amenities to huge complexes with multiple lifestyle options. Marketed for their safety and ample social facilities, their hidden agenda for status-conscious middle-class residents is their exclusivity.[164]

The logic of the ex-urban gated residential estates has invaded the urban core. If the utopian dreamscape of the modern city revolved around the monumentality of public space, the kind of building typologies that have come to characterize the built environment of Istanbul offer a different vision for contemporary urbanism: clusters of high-rise buildings wrapped around an enclosed garden space, detached from the surrounding urban landscape by their self-imposed autonomy. Recalling the walled spaces of the Ottoman Era, this contemporary iteration of an *enclosed paradise* has emerged as a new, and almost universally applied, building and architectural typology. For architects and real-estate developers, interior garden space has become the single most preferred stylistic feature regardless of building typology: gated residential estates, schools, luxury hotels, office complexes, and government facilities all follow a similar principle. This kind of introverted space is an *accoutrement*

[162] Aksoy, "Riding the Storm: 'New Istanbul'," pp. 93–111; Karaman, "Urban Renewal in Istanbul: Reconfigured Spaces, Robotic Lives," pp. 715–733; and Türkün, "Urban Regeneration and Hegemonic Power Relationships," pp. 61–72.

[163] Bartu-Candan and Kolluoğlu, "Emerging Spaces of Neoliberalism," p. 7; and Aliye Ahu Akgün and Tüzin Baycan, "Gated Communities in Istanbul: The New Walls of the City," *Town Planning Review* 83, 1 (2011), pp. 87–109.

[164] Bartu-Candan and Kolluoğlu, "Emerging Spaces of Neoliberalism: A Gated Town and a Public Housing Project in Istanbul," pp. 5–46 (esp. p. 6).

that offers a simulation of shared community and collective living while simultaneously utterly denying genuine plurality.[165]

Real-estate developers routinely advertise and market multiuse complexes "as cities unto themselves." Like prepackaged tourist vacations, they contain all the essential ingredients of what it seems urban life should be, but they invariably lack the sense of belonging and community that comes with actual community. Advertised as "creating an unequalled living space at the heart of Istanbul" and the "new meeting venue in the city," the multiuse Zorlu Center is only one of many high-profile projects close to the downtown city center that exemplify the "continued dynamism of the high-end real estate market."[166] Close to the financial district and with easy access to major transportation corridors, this mixed-use project, with its wide interior spaces and grand-scale buildings, brings together five separate but inner-connected components – world-class retail shopping, high-rise office facilities, elite residences, luxury hotel accommodation, and a state-of-the-art multipurpose theater for the performing arts. Despite its hermetically enclosed setting, the architects who designed the site somehow refer to the expansive interior courtyard as a "public space" and a historic "town square." Surrounded on all sides by highways, the most convenient way to reach the complex is by an underground tunnel that connects to the city metro system. This method of connecting to the city exemplifies the pattern of how up-to-date transportation infrastructure links isolated, standalone architectural building sites, while flagrantly bypassing the less-luxurious streetscape that surrounds it.[167]

At one and the same time and in parallel fashion, informal *gecekondu* housing (informal squatter accommodation), which historically absorbed and housed the successive waves of massive rural-to-urban migration required to fill the labor needs of national developmentalist project since the 1950s, has lost its original *raison d'etre*.[168] Expected to fade away as the project of modernization deepened, *gecekondu* have come to be seen as impediments blocking the path of urban redevelopment.[169] In the neoliberal discourse of market triumphalism, these vast, informally developed *gecekondu* neighborhoods are eyesores and

---

[165] Karaman, "Urban Pulse – (Re)Making Space for Globalization in Istanbul," pp. 518–525; Aksoy, "Riding the Storm: 'New Istanbul'," pp. 93–111; and Barku-Candan and Kolluoğlu, "Emerging Spaces of Neoliberalism: A Gated Town and a Public Housing Project in Istanbul," pp. 5–46.

[166] Jon Gorvett, "Mixed-Use Zorlu Center Raises Stakes in Istanbul," *New York Times*, July 14, 2011 (source of quotations).

[167] Jon Gorvett, "Mixed-Use Zorlu Center Raises Stakes in Istanbul," *New York Times*, July 14, 2011 (source of quotations). See also Suha Özkan and Philip Jodidio, *A Vision in Architecture: Projects for the Istanbul Zorlu Center* (New York: Rizzoli International Publications, 2012).

[168] Kemal Karpat, *The Gecekondu, Rural Migration, and Urbanization* (Cambridge: Cambridge University Press, 1976).

[169] Tahire Erman, "The Politics of Squatter (*Gecekondu*) Studies in Turkey: The Changing Representations of Rural Migrants in the Academic Discourse," *Urban Studies* 38, 7 (2001), pp. 983–1002; and Deniz Yonucu, "A Story of a Squatter Neighborhood: From the Place of the

breeding grounds for crime and drugs. The creation of the "new stigmatizing topographic lexicon" has renamed these places *varofl*, thereby denoting a permanent marginality and trapping them in new forms of poverty. Official discourses have routinely portrayed *gecekondu* residents as unwanted "invaders" and illegitimate occupiers, thereby justifying the withdrawal of services.[170] This language distress and decay has rendered these neighborhoods vulnerable to all sort of repressive interventions, including physical destruction and forced removal.[171]

With little or no interference from public authorities, these largely self-contained, proprietary enclaves (defined by the private provision of requisite services) have shaped the urban macro-form, not only fostering suburban sprawl but also radically transforming the historic inner core.[172] Mass middle-class housing projects have formed ribbons of high-rise, high-density suburbs along the periphery. While these have created more socially homogeneous residential environments, they have developed in tandem with the emergence of sprawling informal settlements on the metropolitan fringe.[173] The incongruous juxtaposition of new shopping malls and high-rise apartment blocks, old *gecekondu* districts, and empty lands has produced a bizarre kind of uneven, patchy landscape. Urban enclaves like gated residential estates have become the new symbols of global consumerist culture and an ideal lifestyle formula for the emergent propertied classes to display their economic and cultural capital. Creating distance from the crowded, unhygienic, and violent city life has crystallized in the formation of a new middle-class identity. Private ownership of residential housing in a natural environment with perfectly designed living spaces and set apart from the urban poor have become symbolic markers that correspond to a class ideology of modernizing urban elites seeking to find their rightful place in the global space of flows.[174]

From the start of the new millennium, there has been a radical shift in the governance of urban land and housing markets in Turkey from a "populist" to a "neoliberal" mode. Large-scale UTPs are the main mechanisms through which neoliberal modes of urban governance are instituted in incompletely commodified urban areas.[175] These emergent patterns of urban restructuring

'Dangerous Classes' to the 'Place of Danger'," *The Berkeley Journal of Sociology* 52 (2009), pp. 50–72; and Lovering and Türkmen, "Bulldozer Neoliberalism in Istanbul," pp. 73–96.

[170] Bartu-Candan and Biray Kolluoğlu, "Emerging Spaces of Neoliberalism," p. 7 (source of quotation). See Zayim, "Differentiated Urban Citizenship and Housing Rights," pp. 275–276.

[171] See Ozan Karaman and Tolga Islam, "On the Dual Nature of Intra-urban Borders: The Case of a Romani Neighborhood in Istanbul," *Cities* 29, 4 (2012), pp. 234–243.

[172] Akgün and Baycan, "Gated Communities in Istanbul," p. 107.

[173] Enlil, "The Neoliberal Agenda and the Changing Urban Form of Istanbul," pp. 5–25.

[174] Ayse Öncü, "The Myth of the 'Ideal Home' Travels across Cultural Borders to Istanbul," in Ayse Öncü and Petra Weyland (eds.), *Space Culture and Power: New Identities and Globalizing Cities* (London: Zed Books, 1997), pp. 56–72; and Keyder, "Globalization and Social Exclusion in Istanbul," pp. 124–134.

[175] Kuyucu and Ünsal, "'Urban Transformation' as State-led Property Transfer," p. 1479.

has meant that anonymous housing projects (that could be anywhere in the world) have steadily replaced long-standing "finely meshed street patterns of the *gecekondu* (informal squatter housing) and *yap-sat* districts, with their intricate social and microeconomic structures, their vibrant street activities and their small-scale character."[176] The resulting functional segregation brought about by these new modalities of urban development does not allow for small-scale economic improvisation and investment that take the form of street guilds and bazaars specializing in particular types of goods – the everyday lifelines of the poor. The competition engendered by the proliferation of street trading and hawking has created "an orientation toward public spaces – and greater visibility – in front of the buildings," thereby forcing commercial activity onto the sidewalks and into the streets. This spatial condition depends upon mobility of people and goods while at the same time it brings congestion and oversaturation of markets. This vibrant situation contrasts sharply with upscale shopping centers and gated residential estates with their stress on order and predictability. These building typologies represent an entirely different concept of the city and the commercial goods and everyday experiences it produces. "Precisely tailored to the specific needs" of a restricted range of privileged user groups, enclosed shopping malls and gated enclaves contradict the uncertainties, ambiguities, and openness that define informal urban life. As "secluded islands [of exclusivity], they orient themselves in opposition" to the small-scale entrepreneurialism and informal commercialism that thrive in the interstices of public space.[177]

In the new global imaginary, the "projected city" consists of an assemblage of gentrified spaces that conform to the logic of the marketplace and respond to the expectations of cosmopolitan modernity.[178] Instead of maximizing permeability within a specific enclosed space, such *faux*-public spaces as luxury shopping centers and gated residential communities turn the actually existing spatial codes of the city inside out, by minimizing points of intersection and operating in isolation. Organized events at distinct destinations have replaced chance encounters and unexpected interactions. Instead of the vibrancy of urban life generated by serendipitous street activities, the focus has shifted to one of "convenience and composed interior spaces." The negative consequence of these patterns of deliberate segregation into urban enclaves is as obvious as it is as unavoidable: while isolated islands use private investment capital to "hide themselves in ever-more grandiose stage-set-like pieces of architecture,"

---

[176] Kees Christiaanse, Mark Michaeli, and Tim Rieniets, "Istanbul's Spatial Dynamics," *Urban Age* (Cities Programme, London School of Economics, 2009), pp. 1–2 (quotation from p. 1).

[177] Christiaanse, Michaeli, and Rieniets, "Istanbul's Spatial Dynamics," pp. 1–2 (quotations from p. 2).

[178] Aksoy, "The Violence of Change," pp. 236–237. See also C. Nil Uzun, "The Impact of Urban Renewal and Gentrification on Urban Fabric: Three Cases in Turkey," *Tijdschrift voor economische en sociale geografie* 94, 3 (2003), pp. 363–375; and Ayşegül Can, "Neo-Liberal Urban Politics in the Historical Environment of Istanbul – The Issue of Gentrification," *Planning* 23, 2 (2013), pp. 95–104.

the actual city fades into the background, and the real-life dynamism and plurality of urban living dwindle.[179]

Metro Manila: Building the Partitioned City of Enclaves

Mega-project real-estate development has long been an integral feature of the explosive growth of Metro Manila in the post–World II era.[180] Looking at the long arc of corporate-led city-building efforts in Metro Manila over the past half-century reveals a longer story that complicates conventional understandings of spatial restructuring in the contemporary age of globalization.[181] First unveiled in the 1950s, the development of the Makati central business district (CBD) was an early prototype for the corporate master-planned "new city" projects that originated well before the contemporary era of globalization. Built and operated by the powerful Ayala Land Corporation, Makati quickly became the financial and commercial center for the Manila metropolitan region. Inspired by a modernist ethic of progress, the urban planners behind this early mega-project conceived of it as a self-contained (i.e., bundled) and nominally integrated space that offered a solution to the problematic features of "backward" Manila – with its overcrowded streetscape, broken-down infrastructure, and weak public regulatory authority. Seen in this light, "by embodying the highest standards of development, New Makati constituted a space of progress."[182]

But this trend toward carving up the metropolitan landscape of Metro Manila into large-scale real-estate projects has expanded significantly in recent years.[183] While Makati City has remained *primus inter pares* as a premier financial center because it has continued to house the lion's share of headquarters office complexes for leading global corporations, a number of rival mega-projects have emerged. One of the most notable exemplars is Bonifacio Global City (BGC), a master-planned, mixed-use, real-estate development that can trace its origins to the sale of development rights to a 214-hectare portion of Fort Bonifacio, a former military base, to a consortium of businesses for U.S. $1.6 billion in 1995. Originally an American fort built during the

---

[179] Christiaanse, Michaeli, and Rieniets, "Istanbul's Spatial Dynamics," pp. 1–2 (quotations from p. 2).

[180] Gavin Shatkin, "Colonial Capital, Modernist Capital, Global Capital: The Changing Political Symbolism of Urban Space in Metro Manila, the Philippines," *Pacific Affairs* 78, 4 (2006), pp. 577–600 (esp. p. 591).

[181] Garrido, "The Ideology of the Dual City," p. 167. See also Arnisson Andre C. Ortega, "Desakota and Beyond: Neoliberal Production of Suburban Space in Manila's Fringe," *Urban Geography* 33, 8 (2012), pp. 1118–1143.

[182] Garrido, "The Ideology of the Dual City," pp. 168–169, source of quotation).

[183] Shatkin, "Colonial Capital, Modernist Capital, Global Capital," p. 591; and Jana Marie Kleibert and Lisa Kippers, "Living the Good Life? The Rise of Urban Mixed-Use Enclaves in Metro Manila," *Urban Geography* 37, 3 (2016), pp. 373–395.

American colonial period that served as a detention center for political dissidents under the Ferdinand Marcos regime, BGC is located 11 kilometers (6.8 miles) southeast of the center of Manila in an area disputed between the cities of Makati and Taguig. An interlocking network of private corporations, property-holding companies, and public agencies managed by a public–private partnership including Ayala Lands, Evergreen Holdings, and the Bases Conversion Development authority (a state corporation with public authority to release military properties for real-estate development), Fort Bonifacio Development Corporation has taken control of "master planning" operations for Bonifacio Global City. Nicknamed "the Fort," this corporate-led real-estate mega-project has become a highly stylized high-rise financial center replete with corporate office space, upscale shopping districts, and upscale residential accommodation. The real-estate developers behind Bonifacio Global City have tried to create a planned environment that is the antithesis of the congestion of central Manila and the somewhat old-fashioned stylistics of Makati City, bringing together an assemblage of global corporations, public facilities (schools and universities), retail and leisure facilities (gigantic shopping malls and high-end restaurants) and high-rise condominium complexes for the well-to-do. The master plan of Bonifacio Global City bears an undeniable resemblance to both the classical layout of the city-states of the Italian Renaissance with their formal circulation grids and separate precincts integrated into a seemingly coherent whole.[184]

The serial reproduction of these new urban mega-projects has brought to light the significant role of public–private partnerships in facilitating the process of place-making for the benefit of corporate enterprise. As a general rule, these large-scale real-estate developments have followed the template that originated with the Makati CBD, using the tools of land-use planning, setting limits to vehicle entry points, carefully controlling setbacks and floor-area ratios, and employing "a variety of other mechanisms to create an attractive environment for foreign investors and consumers."[185] Each of these mega-projects offers corporate tenants and residents a full palate of social amenities: an integrated environment with opportunities for corporate investment, shopping and entertainment, and residence.[186] In essence, what has occurred is the privatization of planning where public authorities increasingly act as facilitators of private real-estate investment in city-building projects, providing inexpensive land, enabling development, and financing infrastructure linkages.[187]

New Makati became the dominant prototype for real-estate development characterized by a deliberated strategy of spatial enclosure: the steady accretion

---

[184] Shatkin, "Colonial Capital, Modernist Capital, Global Capital," pp. 591–592.
[185] Shatkin, "Colonial Capital, Modernist Capital, Global Capital," p. 593 (source of quotation). See also Kleibert and Kippers, "Living the Good Life?" pp. 373–395.
[186] Jon Connell, "Beyond Manila: Walls, Malls, and Private Spaces," *Environment and Planning A* 31, 3 (1999), pp. 417–439.
[187] Shatkin, "Colonial Capital, Modernist Capital, Global Capital," p. 594.

of corporate mega-projects bundling social services within exclusive spaces and the rapid expansion of walled residential subdivisions euphemistically called "villages" that proliferated throughout the 1990s. Like Makati, these enclaves were developed according to standards aimed at class exclusivity. Yet unlike Makati, these corporate mega-projects have emerged "within a network of elite spaces," with proliferating citadels (such as gated residential estates, luxury condominium complexes, and high-rise office buildings) linked to such upscale spaces of luxury consumption as exclusive shopping malls and elite recreational sites through a network of high-speed toll highways and elevated flyovers, and outfitted with up-to-date telecommunications, power grids, and water infrastructures that barely extend into the surrounding public city.[188]

Set within the context of entrenched class inequalities, and where the regulatory capacity of the state administration is relatively weak, privatized corporate planning represents a spatial fix for the propertied classes, "a way to wall out the disorder of the public city and, at the same time, preserve within its perimeter a standard of spatial order" equivalent to the imagined cosmopolitan urbanity found in the leading cities of North America, Europe, and the Asia Pacific Rim. In the urban imaginary of the propertied classes, "disorder" signified more than just unregulated building, overcrowded streets, and clogged patterns of traffic circulation, but also crime, density, noise, noxious smell, illegal squatting, "unsanitary conditions, and general backwardness – that is, spaces associated with, and adulterated by, the masses."[189]

Spatial segregation in Metro Manila is largely characterized by latticework patterns of world-class business enclaves and upscale residential neighborhoods interspersed with deteriorating building stock and impoverished slums, where aspiring middle-class residents and urban poor live virtually side-by-side in separate (and distinct) spaces divided by physical and symbolic boundaries.[190] Safely cocooned inside these upscale enclaves, wealthy residents have come to "experience the city as an archipelago of carefully planned spaces," ranging from spacious shopping malls, luxury condominiums, gated residential estates, and leisure sites, connected by elevated, climate-controlled transport corridors.[191] The expanded role for privatized planning has transformed the

---

[188] Garrido, "The Ideology of the Dual City," p. 182 (source of quotation). See also Gavin Shatkin, "Planning to Forget: Informal Settlements as 'Forgotten Places' in Globalising Metro Manila," *Urban Studies* 41, 12 (2004), pp. 2469–2484.

[189] Garrido, "The Ideology of the Dual City," pp. 168–169 (quotation from p. 169). See also Marco Garrido, "Civil and Uncivil Society: Symbolic Boundaries and Civic Exclusion in Metro Manila," *Philippine Studies* 56, 4 (2008), pp. 443–466.

[190] Marco Garrido, "The Sense of Place behind Segregating Practices: An Ethnographic Approach to the Symbolic Partitioning of Metro Manila," *Social Forces* 91, 4 (2013), pp. 1343–1362.

[191] Shatkin, "Colonial Capital, Modernist Capital, Global Capital," p. 593 (source of quotation). See also Gavin Shatkin, "The City and the Bottom Line: Urban Megaprojects and the Privatization of Planning in Southeast Asia," *Environment and Planning A* 40, 2 (2008), pp. 383–401; and Neferti Tadiar, "Manila's New Metropolitan Form," *Differences: A Journal of Feminist Cultural Studies* 5, 3 (1993), pp. 154–178 (esp. p. 154).

urban landscape of Metro Manila into a postcolonial "dual city," where rich and poor live in proximity, but in urban environments that separate and unequal. These distinguishable social worlds consist of a largely planned "private city" thoroughly embedded in an ethos of world-class aspirations, on the one side, and a "public city" characterized by a degraded built environment suffering from neglect and abandonment, on the other.[192]

Enclosures within Enclosures

The opportunistic intervention of real-estate developers and property speculators in urban reconstruction often becomes visible in distressed cities in the aftermath of catastrophic events like (so-called) natural disasters, war-related devastation, and industrial ruination, especially at moments when the destruction of the material and social fabric of cities gives rise to a "state of exception" discourse.[193] By calling for the suspension of conventional regulatory frameworks, this rhetoric of "exceptionality" seeks to legitimize extraordinary (and extralegal) spatial interventions in postdisaster reconstruction, typically in the name of the public good, quick recovery, and restoring economic growth.[194] As Jane Schneider and Ida Susser have suggested, "The necessity or opportunity for reconstruction exposes a city immediately and powerfully" to market-driven pressures, namely, through the demand "to generate profits for transnational corporate interests associated with finance, name-brand shopping, and tourism."[195]

The building and rebuilding of the world-famous resort enclave at Cancún, Mexico, as a main destination in the global tourist market provides a telling example of the dynamics of enclosure and the catalytic role that natural disasters can play in them.[196] The reconstruction efforts undertaken after Hurricanes Gilbert (1988) and Wilma (2005) facilitated the creation of an evolving logic of "enclosures within enclosures," whereby real-estate developers and hotel owners – always aided and abetted by municipal authorities – carried out the privatization of public lands, particularly ocean beaches and shorelines, for

---

[192] Garrido, "The Ideology of the Dual City," p. 182; and Shatkin, "Colonial Capital, Modernist Capital, Global Capital," p. 594. See also Emma Porio, "Decentralisation, Power and Networked Governance in Metro Manila," *Space and Polity* 16, 1 (2012), pp. 7–27.

[193] Neil Smith, "Disastrous Accumulation," *South Atlantic Quarterly* 106, 4 (2007), pp. 769–787.

[194] See James Ferguson, *Global Shadows: Africa in the Neoliberal World Order* (Durham: Duke University Press, 2006); and Alex Vasudevan, Colin McFarlane, and Alex Jeffrey, "Spaces of Enclosure," *Geoforum* 39, 5 (2008), pp. 1641–1646.

[195] Jane Schneider and Ida Susser, "Wounded Cities: Destruction and Reconstruction in a Globalized World," in Jane Schneider and Ida Susser (eds.), *Wounded Cities: Destruction and Reconstruction in a Globalized World* (Oxford, UK: Berg, 2003), p. 4 (source of quotation).

[196] Vasudevan, McFarlane, and Jeffrey, "Spaces of Enclosure," pp. 1641–1646; and Alex Jeffrey, Colin McFarlane, and Alex Vasudevan, "Rethinking Enclosure: Space, Subjectivity and the Commons," *Antipode* 44, 4 (2012), pp. 1247–1267.

exclusive use of the global tourism market. In practice, this process took shape as a far-reaching, spatial, aesthetic, and socioeconomic reconfiguration of the Hotel Zone in Cancún from a low-density luxury resort to a mass tourism, all-inclusive entertainment destination after Hurricane Gilbert, and the emergence of a timeshare high-rise condominium model after Hurricane Wilma. With this successive unfolding of new business models, real-estate developers strategically took advantage of "posthurricane reconstruction to redefine space, displace risk, and reposition themselves and the city in global circuits of capital accumulation."[197]

The strategic appropriation of catastrophic events like tsunamis, hurricanes, and floods as destructive but creative occasions by real-estate developers is not unique to such places as Cancún, Aceh (Indonesia), and other tourist zones of what has been called the "pleasure periphery."[198] Unexpected devastation often provides real-estate developers and property speculators with sufficient justification to create "regimes of exception" that give them virtually *carte blanche* authority to rebuild in disaster-devastated spaces. Suspension of conventional regulatory regimes and substitution of *ad hoc* exceptional measures facilitate the exemption of real-estate developers from conventional planning and legal protocols.[199]

A great deal of scholarly research has shown that cities such as New York after 9/11 and New Orleans after Hurricane Katrina became important laboratories for real-estate developers and municipal officials to experiment with post-disaster rebuilding as an opportunity to advance far-reaching neoliberal policy reforms. This one-sided emphasis on the use of market-centered approaches for urban recovery and rebuilding in New York and New Orleans should be seen not as coherent or sustainable responses to urban disaster, but rather as flawed and contradictory restructuring strategies that have only intensified the inequities they have claimed to remedy.[200]

---

[197] Matilde Córdoba Azcárate, Idalina Baptista, and Fernando Domínguez Rubio, "Enclosures within Enclosures and Hurricane Reconstruction in Cancún, Mexico," *City & Society* 26, 1 (2014), pp. 96–119 (quotation from p. 96).

[198] Nicholas Phelps, Tim Bunnell, and Michelle Ann Miller, "Post-Disaster Economic Development in Aceh: Neoliberalization and Other Economic-Geographical Imaginaries," *Geoforum* 42, 2 (2011), pp. 418–426; and Michelle Ann Miller and Tim Bunnell, "Post-Disaster Urban Renewal: Memories of Trauma and Transformation in an Indonesian City," *Asia Research Institute Working Papers Series, No. 154* (National University of Singapore, 2011) [19 pages].

[199] Kevin Fox Gotham, "Re-anchoring Capital in Disaster Devastated Spaces: Financialisation and the Gulf Opportunity (GO) Zone Programme," *Urban Studies* (2014) 53, 7 (2016), pp. 1362–1383.

[200] Kevin Fox Gotham, "From 9/11 to 8/29: Post-Disaster Recovery and Rebuilding in New York and New Orleans," *Social Forces* 87, 2 (2008), pp. 1039–1062; and Jamie Peck, "Liberating the City: Between New York and New Orleans," *Urban Geography* 27, 8 (2006), pp. 681–713. See also Nandini Gunewardena and Mark Schuller (eds.), *Capitalizing on Catastrophe: Neoliberal Strategies in Disaster Reconstruction* (Lanham, MD: Alta Mira, 2008); Cedric Johnson (ed.), *The Neoliberal Deluge: Hurricane Katrina, Late Capitalism, and the Remaking of*

Kevin Fox Gotham and Miriam Greenberg have suggested that New York City and New Orleans have emerged as paradigmatic "crisis cities," where free-market approaches to postdisaster recovery have increasingly become the dominant models for crisis-stricken cities around the world. These *laissez-faire* strategies of rebuilding – which Gotham and Greenberg have appropriately labeled "crisis-driven urbanization" – emphasize the privatization of disaster aid, the devolution of recovery responsibility to local administrative bodies, and the generous use of corporate tax incentives, federal grants, and financial subsidies to underwrite market-centered revitalization and undertake aggressive branding campaigns designed to market the redeveloped city for business and tourism.[201] Rather than target the residential populations and ecosystems where the impact of the disasters were most acute, the kinds of monetary assistance designed to aid in recovery has actually subsidized luxury development and urban rebranding campaigns that accelerated incipient gentrification and displacement of the most vulnerable residents. By critically examining both the pre- and posthistory of the devastating events in New York and New Orleans, it is possible to see how long-neglected landscapes of potential risk and vulnerability combine with starkly inequitable redevelopment strategies to turn sudden disaster into long-term crises. Such uneven and contradictory postdisaster recovery and rebuilding not only impeded community recovery efforts but also exacerbated risk of future crisis.[202] These market-centered policies remove public accountability and oversight from the decision-making and implementation process, thereby shielding private real-estate developers from unwanted scrutiny.[203]

Faced with dwindling public funds and with no choice but to downsize functions and outsource services, city officials around the world have backed away from their once dominant role in overseeing the management of urban space. In those struggling cities faced with dwindling revenues combined with overstretched social services and neglected infrastructure, what scholars have called "austerity urbanism" has produced its own set of historically specific conditions that have become a "new operational matrix for urban politics."[204] For

New Orleans (Minneapolis: University of Minnesota Press, 2011); Vincanne Adams, Taslim Van Hattum, and Diana English, "Chronic Disaster Syndrome: Displacement, Disaster Capitalism, and the Eviction of the Poor from New Orleans," *American Ethnologist* 36, 4 (2009), pp. 615–636.

[201] Kevin Fox Gotham and Miriam Greenberg, *Crisis Cities: Disaster and Redevelopment in New York and New Orleans* (New York: Oxford University Press, 2014), pp. xi, 11–16.

[202] Kevin Fox Gotham and Miriam Greenberg, "Post-Disaster Recovery and Rebuilding in New York and New Orleans," *Social Forces* 87, 2 (2008), pp. 1039–1062.

[203] Gotham and Greenberg, "Post-Disaster Recovery and Rebuilding in New York and New Orleans," p. 18.

[204] Jamie Peck, "Austerity Urbanism: American Cities under Extreme Economy," *City* 16, 6 (2012), pp. 626–655 (p. 626, source of quotation); Fran Tonkiss, "Austerity Urbanism and the Makeshift City," *City* 17, 3 (2013), pp. 312–324; Jamie Peck, "Pushing Austerity: State Failure, Municipal Bankruptcy and the Crises of Fiscal Federalism in the USA," *Cambridge*

at least the past three decades, neoliberal modes of urban governance have repeatedly demanded strict market discipline as a defining feature of restoring prosperity by kick-starting growth.[205] In times of financial and economic crisis, cities that have suffered from loss of manufacturing and jobs have become sites of austerity measures, such as permanent fiscal restraint, making do with declining tax revenues, bankruptcies, retrenchment of public expenditures, and deep cuts to municipal services.[206] "Austerity urbanism" has produced its own repertoire of juridical regimes that bypass conventional approaches to land-use planning, service delivery, and electoral democratic governance. In distressed cities undergoing bankruptcy, the outside imposition of top-down governance regimes clustered under the rubric of "emergency management" have dispensed with conventional electoral-democratic process of local government and generally closed off avenues for public participation.[207] At the level of local municipal administration, this approach to restoring competitiveness has translated into "fiscal discipline, local-government downsizing, and privatization."[208]

Journal of Regions, Economy and Society 7, 1 (2014), pp. 17–44; and Lee Pugalis and David McGuinness, "From a Framework to a Toolkit: Urban Regeneration in an Age of Austerity," *Journal of Urban Regeneration and Renewal* 6, 4 (2013), pp. 339–353; and Stewart Williams, "The Temporary City," *Australian Planner* 50, 3 (2013), pp. 278–279.

[205] Margit Mayer, "First World Urban Activism: Beyond Austerity Urbanism and Creative City Politics," *City* 17, 1 (2013), pp. 5–19; and Jamie Peck, Nik Theodore, and Neil Brenner, "Neoliberal Urbanism Redux?" *International Journal of Urban and Regional Research* 37, 3 (2013), pp. 1091–1099; and William Tabb, "The Wider Context of Austerity Urbanism," *City* 18, 2 (2014), pp. 87–100.

[206] Peck, "Austerity Urbanism: American Cities under Extreme Economy," pp. 626–655; Mark Davidson and Kevin Ward, "'Picking up the Pieces': Austerity Urbanism, California and Fiscal Crisis," *Cambridge Journal Regions, Economy and Society* 7, 1 (2014), pp. 81–97; Lee Pugalis and Joyce Liddle, "Austerity Era Regeneration: Conceptual Issues and Practical Challenges, Part 1," *Journal of Urban Regeneration and Renewal* 6, 4 (2013), pp. 333–338; and Stephen Hall and Andrew Jonas, "Urban Fiscal Austerity, Infrastructure Provision and the Struggle for Regional Transit in 'Motor City'," *Cambridge Journal of Regions, Economy and Society* 7, 1 (2014), pp. 189–206.

[207] Carolyn Loh, "The Everyday Emergency: Planning and Democracy under Austerity Regimes," *Urban Affairs Review* 52, 5 (2016), pp. 832–863.

[208] Jamie Peck, "Pushing Austerity," p. 18 (source of quotation). See also Mark Purcell, "Resisting Neoliberalization: Communicative Planning or Counter-hegemonic Movements?" *Planning Theory* 8, 2 (2009), pp. 140–165.

PART III

ZONE FORMATS AND THE URBANISM
OF EXCEPTION

5

Autonomous Zones and the Unbundling of Territorial Sovereignty

The neoliberal discourse of developmentalism provides its own self-serving justification through a vigorous appeal to the structural imperatives of globalization. Similar to the focus of modernization theory in the post–World War II era, development discourse presents globalization as "a force external to, and hence beyond the scope of, political agency articulated at any particular point on the globe."[1] This urgent talk of the need to adjust to an alleged inevitability resembles the Thatcherite "there is no alternative" (TINA) rhetoric of the 1980s.[2] As such, the discourse of developmentalism provides a convenient background against which the construction of urban enclaves in odd places can be made to seem as not only politically neutral technical exercises but also inevitable outcomes of the inexorable forces of globalization. As a dominant "ideological project," the discourse of entrepreneurial urbanism "has absorbed the [charismatic appeal] of popular, post–Cold War accounts of globalization to make its claims appear" necessary, reasonable, and (at the end of the day) effective. Cities have become convenient and "useful platforms" for enabling the globally connected "ambitions" of new growth coalitions, which are themselves intent on spreading the message of market-led redevelopment and entrepreneurial modes of municipal governance. Urban settings provide a "malleable spatial container" within which to experiment with new modalities of urban management that prioritize market-based solutions as the main mechanisms for "expressing, aggregating, and informing public choices."[3]

---

[1] Christopher Parker, "Tunnel-bypasses and Minarets of Capitalism: Amman as Neoliberal Assemblage," *Political Geography* 28, 2 (2009), pp. 110–120 (quotation from p. 113).

[2] See, for example, Ronaldo Munck, "Neoliberalism, Necessitarianism and Alternatives in Latin America: There is no Alternative (Tina)?" *Third World Quarterly* 24, 3 (2003), pp. 495–511.

[3] These ideas are borrowed almost verbatim from Parker, "Tunnel-bypasses and Minarets of Capitalism," pp. 113–114 (p. 113–114, source of quotations).

One striking feature of the current phase of urban restructuring – involving both the rebuilding of physical space and introduction of new privately managed regulatory regimes – is the unprecedented scale of private (as opposed to public) influence and control over urban and regional planning processes. The triumph of neoliberal modes of urban governance has gone hand-in-hand with new kinds of privatized planning. Over the past three decades, if not longer, "a cult of privatization" has mesmerized city builders with promises of "quick-fixes" and spectacular makeovers as the singular pathway for inching up in the global hierarchy of aspiring world-class cities. This wholesale transfer of decision-making power over the management of urban space from public authorities to private real-estate developers has strongly influenced the shape and design of the urban landscape. City building under the sign of neoliberal globalization has shifted the terrain of responsibility for the administration of urban space out of the public realm and into the hands of private stakeholders in ways that appreciably narrow the terrain of decision-making and yet without any "discernible collective advantage."[4] This redistribution of policymaking power that favors private interests has taken place "in the name of greater flexibility," cost-effectiveness, and enhanced efficiency.[5]

A steady growth in the kinds of quasi-private and largely autonomous organizations – like business improvement districts, public–private partnerships, and a host of independent agencies – compete with and often replace local and regional authorities as the principal entities in charge of urban management and land-use planning. However, this shift does not necessarily imply an actual weakening or diminution of state power, but merely its reformulation as enabling agent and facilitator of private enterprise.[6] Planning thus becomes the business of clearing away legal obstacles and onerous regulatory frameworks that stand in the way of private proprietary interests, and task of allocating and adjudicating property rights among large-scale real-estate coalitions.[7] The proliferation of urban redevelopment projects undertaken by large-scale real-estate capitalists has effectively replaced the modes of comprehensive and statutory planning that prevailed under the sign of modernism. The scarcity of prime real estate in the face of growing demand offers the prospect of high returns.

---

[4] Tony Judt, "What Is Living and What Is Dead in Social Democracy," *New York Review of Books*, December 17, 2009 [source of quotations]. Available at www.nybooks.com/articles/archives/2009/dec/17

[5] David Harvey, "From Managerialism to Entrepreneurialism: The Transformation in Urban Governance in Late Capitalism," *Geografiska Annaler: Series B, Human Geography* 71, 1 (1989), pp. 3–17.

[6] Ozlem Guzey, "Neoliberal Urbanism Restructuring the City of Ankara: Gated Communities as a New Life Style in a Suburban Settlement," *Cities* 36, 1 (2014), pp. 93–106 (quotation from p. 95).

[7] See, *inter alia*, John Lovering, "The Relationship between Urban Regeneration and Neoliberalism: Two Presumptuous Theories and a Research Agenda," *International Planning Studies* 12, 4 (2007), pp. 343–366.

Under these circumstances, landed property has become the main source of capital accumulation, and municipal authorities have increasingly turned to large-scale redevelopment projects – high-rise office buildings, convention centers, shopping malls, luxury housing developments, and leisure-entertainment sites – to satisfy planning and policy objectives that have focused on reinforcing the competitive position of metropolitan economies.[8]

The proliferation of master-planned, holistically designed, and privately owned enclaves for wealthy urban residents has made conventional comprehensive planning approaches – spearheaded by public authorities and directed at the enhancement of collectively consumed social services and facilities – increasingly anachronistic and irrelevant.[9] Urban redevelopment has increasingly taken shape as project-focused and market-led initiatives. In this sense, "signature" mega-projects have become the emblematic tools of urban regeneration policies.[10] Privatized planning through large-scale redevelopment projects has emerged as the main strategy to stimulate economic restructuring where attention to holistic design, stylistic detail, morphology, the global gesturing of iconic architecture, and pleasing aesthetics is paramount.[11] Seen in this light, strategic planning is important for facilitating the room-for-maneuver for private investment. Planning initiatives and policies function to regulate these large-scale private redevelopment schemes by allowing existing legal frameworks and regulatory regimes to follow the demands of market forces.[12]

Privatized Planning

In the wake of the retreat of municipal authorities from the management of urban space, large-scale real-estate developers and their coterie of assisting agents – financial institutions, architecture firms, design consultancies, transportation engineers, and the like – have largely filled the void, assuming new comprehensive planning powers (once exclusively reserved for city officials).

---

[8] İclal Dinçer, "The Impact of Neoliberal Policies on Historic Urban Space: Areas of Urban Renewal in Istanbul," *International Planning Studies* 16, 1 (2011), pp. 43–60; Asuman Türkün, "Urban Regeneration and Hegemonic Power Relationships," *International Planning Studies* 16, 1 (2011), pp. 61–72; and Erik Swyngedouw, Frank Moulaert, and Arantxa Rodriguez, "Neoliberal Urbanization in Europe: Large-scale Urban Development Projects and the New Urban Policy," *Antipode* 34, 3 (2002), pp. 542–577.

[9] Colin McFarlane, "Infrastructure, Interruption, and Inequality: Urban Life in the Global South," in Stephen Graham (ed.), *Disrupted Cities: When Infrastructure Fails* (New York: Routledge, 2010), pp. 131–144 (especially p. 134).

[10] Susan Fainstein, "Mega-projects in New York, London and Amsterdam," *International Journal of Urban and Regional Research* 32, 4 (2008), pp. 768–785; and Fernando Diaz Orueta and Susan Fainstein, "The New Mega-Projects: Genesis and Impacts," *International Journal of Urban and Regional Research* 32, 4 (2008), pp. 759–767.

[11] Jamie Peck and Adam Tickell, "Neoliberalizing Space," *Antipode* 34, 3 (2002), pp. 380–404; Swyngedouw, Moulaert, and Rodriguez, "Neoliberal Urbanization in Europe," pp. 542–577.

[12] Guzey, "Neoliberal Urbanism Restructuring the City of Ankara," p. 95.

Acquiring leverage over key decision-making about city building has enabled powerful coalitions of property owners, real-estate developers, and financiers to take the lead in reshaping the urban landscape. In increasing numbers of aspiring world-class cities, the only effective land use and spatial planning occurs within large-scale private real-estate developments, including new office parks, gated residential communities, and tourist enclaves.[13]

This emergent approach to city building is not simply the uninterrupted outcome of the blind adoption of conventional "Western" planning models, but reflects the incentives, constraints, and opportunities put into motion in aspiring world-class cities around the world during the current phase of globalization.[14] This new model of urban redevelopment is largely dependent upon regressive state subsidies for profit-driven, private-sector development, the abandonment of the very idea of "public purpose" and the "common good" by municipal planning agencies, and the adoption instead of neoliberal modes of urban governance that idealize entrepreneurial solutions to city management.[15] Large-scale property owners do not just oversee the construction of integrated mega-projects, but they take command over the conceptualization and implementation of entire infrastructural systems that are layered onto the existing metropolitan form. The kind of public–private partnerships that typically emerge reflect the dominant position of corporate real-estate developers in every stage of the planning process, from the initial visioning exercises in creating an imagined future of what they expect their redevelopment projects to accomplish to the final stage of leaving in place management companies to oversee the new urban enclaves that they implant in the urban social fabric.[16] This model of urban development contrasts sharply modernist and high-modernist approaches to holistic, comprehensive planning.[17]

Regardless of the reasons for the failure of planning theory and practice to address the pressing problems associated with rapid growth in distressed

---

[13] See Pedro Pírez, "Buenos Aires: Fragmentation and Privatization of the Metropolitan City," *Environment & Urbanization* 14, 1 (2002), pp. 145–158 (esp. p. 145); and David Wilson, "Spaces of Neoliberalism: Urban Restructuring in North America and Western Europe," *Annals of the Association of American Geographers* 94, 3 (2004), pp. 676–678.

[14] Gavin Shatkin, "The City and the Bottom Line: Urban Megaprojects and the Privatization of Planning in Southeast Asia," *Environment and Planning A* 40, 2 (2008), pp. 383–401 (esp. p. 384).

[15] See Stephen Graham, "Constructing Premium Network Spaces: Reflections on Infrastructure Networks and Contemporary Urban Development," *International Journal of Urban and Regional Research* 24 (2000), pp. 183–200.

[16] Shatkin, "The City and the Bottom Line," p. 388.

[17] See David Harvey, "From Managerialism to Entrepreneurialism: The Transformation of Urban Governance in Late Capitalism," *Geografiska Annaler* 71B (1989), pp. 3–17; and Bob Jessop, "The Entrepreneurial City: Re-Imaging Localities, Redesigning Economic Governance, or Restructuring Capital?" in Nick Jewson and Susanne MacGregor (eds.), *Transforming Cities: Contested Governance and New Spatial Divisions* (London and New York: Routledge, 1997), pp. 28–41.

metropolitan regions experiencing rapid population increases, city builders have pushed ahead with large-scale mega-projects that have transformed the urban landscape of cities in India, China, Southeast Asia, Latin America, Africa, and elsewhere. In constructing luxury enclaves for affluent urban residents, private real-estate developers have successfully taken control over the installation and regulation of infrastructure and the private management of services. This "privatization of planning" embodies a distinctive kind of instrumental rationality that "underwrites a frontier of metropolitan expansion."[18]

In his study of Metro Manila, Gavin Shatkin has identified a privatized planning strategy – which he calls "bypass-implant urbanism" – that involves abandoning (or "bypassing") congested and decaying spaces of the existing "public city" to their own devices, and focusing instead on "implanting" large-scale, integrated mega-projects in strategic locations with easy access to up-to-date infrastructure.[19] This mode of urban redevelopment fosters the construction of privately built, self-contained enclaves that are connected to one another via streamlined transportation systems laid out largely for the convenience of wealth residents.[20] Similarly, Dennis Rodgers has suggested that wealthy elites in Managua (Nicaragua) have extended the logic of fortified enclaves beyond the patterns of fragmentation that can be found in other cities throughout the world. Rather than breaking the urban landscape into an archipelago of discontinuous and isolated "fortified enclaves," city builders in Managua have effectively "disembedded" a whole layer of the metropolis from the existing fabric of the city through the construction of an exclusive "fortified network" for the urban elites protected by private security and connected by means of the insertion of high-speed roadways.[21]

This kind of spatial planning is largely the result of the expansion of the power of private real-estate operations on a grand scale where state authorities and city officials participate in the restricted capacity as facilitators and enabling agents. The subordination of urban spatial production to private real-estate interests has taken place largely because of the inability of public authorities to shape land-use planning in a real way. In struggling cities where regulatory regimes severely weakened or are virtually nonexistent, the physical expansion of the urban landscape lies beyond the control of local authorities. Large-scale real-estate developers have often adopted the principles and models

[18] Anaya Roy, "Why India Cannot Plan its Cities: Informality, Insurgence and the Idiom of Urbanization," *Planning Theory* 8, 1 (2009), pp. 76–87 (esp. p. 86).

[19] Gavin Shatkin, "Planning Privatopolis: Representation and Contestation in the Development of Urban Integrated Mega-Projects," in Ananya Roy and Aihwa Ong (eds.), *Worlding Cities: Asian Experiments and the Art of Being Global* (Malden, MA: Blackwell, 2011), pp. 77–97.

[20] Gavin Shatkin, "Coping with Actually Existing Urbanisms: The Real Politics of Planning in the Global Era," *Planning Theory* 10, 1 (2011), pp. 79–87 (quotation from p. 81). See also Shatkin, "The City and the Bottom Line," pp. 383–401.

[21] Dennis Rodgers, "'Disembedding' the City: Crime, Insecurity and Spatial Organization in Managua, Nicaragua," *Environment & Urbanization* 16, 2 (2004), pp. 113–124.

of urban planning, not as operational tools to serve the public interest, but as a means to produce and shape the built environment in ways that satisfy private profitable investment.[22] This new approach to city building, embedded on the prevailing logic of private project planning, primarily obeys the laws of the capitalist marketplace. This haphazard approach to city building has produced an uneven agglomeration of disconnected places lacking coherence, unity, and a sense of wholeness.[23] The overall shape of the urban built environment has increasingly come to resemble the sum (or aggregate) of the steady accumulation of private real-estate developments and their spillovers.[24]

There are, of course, notable exceptions to the ascendant power of real-estate capitalism to shape urban redevelopment projects in aspiring world-class cities around the world. The active and powerful role of state agencies (operating in the framework of a regulated market economy) is particularly evident in urban development projects in China, Vietnam, and elsewhere where the party–state apparatus has played a dominant role in establishing the administrative governance structures with authority to build new cities, expand and merge existing ones, and even eliminate others.[25]

In such high-profile projects as special economic zones, high-tech campuses, and refurbished central business districts in existing cities, newly minted state agencies in China in particular have taken the lead in cobbling together joint-venture (public and private) development projects with the aim of improving the global image of aspiring world-class cities and "boosting property values."[26] The creation of entirely new satellite cities corresponds to neither simple market capitalism nor to planned socialism, but to the initiative of state enterprises that supply resources (including land, financing, and expertise), establish pricing mechanisms, offer incentives to attract outside investment, and determine what is to be built and where. Philip Huang has called this practice the "third hand" – not the "invisible hand" of self-regulating market rationality (so celebrated in Adam Smith), nor the nonmarket planned interventions ("visible hand") of socialist bureaucrats.[27] City-building efforts in urban China have

---

[22] Shatkin, "The City and the Bottom Line: Urban Megaprojects and the Privatization of Planning in Southeast Asia," pp. 383–401.

[23] Martin J. Murray, "The City in Fragments: Kaleidoscopic Johannesburg after Apartheid," in Gyan Prakash and Kevin Kruse (eds.), *The Spaces of the Modern City* (Princeton: Princeton University Press, 2008), pp. 144–178 (esp. p. 172).

[24] Pírez, "Buenos Aires," p. 155.

[25] See Carolyn Cartier, "Transnational Urbanism in the Reform-era Chinese City: Landscapes from Shenzhen," *Urban Studies* 39, 9 (2002), pp. 1513–1532; and Carolyn Cartier, "Territorial Urbanization and the Party-State in China," *Territory, Politics, Governance* 3, 3 (2015), pp. 294–320.

[26] You-tien Hsing, *The Great Urban Transformation: Politics of Land and Property in China* (New York and Oxford: Oxford University Press, 2010), p. 9 (source of quotation).

[27] Philip C. C. Huang, "Chongqing Equitable Development Driven by a 'Third Hand'?" *Modern China* 37, 6 (2011), pp. 569–622 (esp. pp. 572–574, 576–577).

responded to specific queues: state enterprises have the enabling powers to requisition requisite land, demolish existing built structures, and relocate residents. Local municipalities can assign land-use rights to private real-estate developers for extended periods of time. This mode of using land to finance development represents the peculiar fusion of state enterprise with private real-estate developers. State agencies used access to land as a means of acquiring marketplace bargaining power toward achieving its primary spatial objective of fostering urban growth and development.[28] In Shenzhen, for example, municipal authorities and state enterprises have taken the lead in the planned transformation of what was once a collection of high-growth industrial zones into a world-class city built around "business services and high-technology industries [and] distinguished by international standard architecture and urban cultural amenities."[29] This "state-led" approach to the construction of free trade zones and other zonal formats undermines broad generalizations that suggest that these spatial products exclusively serve narrow corporate interests and are almost totally free from state interference.

The Enclave Format: Autonomous Zones and Concessionary Urbanism

As an exemplary expression of an extraterritorial "legal habitat," the enclave format is a mutable and mutating formula for blending unrestrained free enterprise within an overarching framework of strict management controls.[30] Though its origins can be traced back to the independent city-states and free ports of classical antiquity, the autonomous zone has only emerged in last several decades as a promiscuous and powerful extraterritorial global form, evolving rapidly from an out-of-way precinct for warehousing custom-free goods, to an aggressive postwar strategy for jump-starting stalled local economies of what was then termed the "third world," to a tax-free haven for large-scale corporate enterprises to evade labor regulations and avoid financial oversight, and eventually to a paradigm for building such glittering world-class cities as Hong Kong, Singapore, and Dubai.[31]

---

[28] See Hsing, *The Great Urban Transformation*, pp. 5–29.

[29] Cartier, "Transnational Urbanism in the Reform-era Chinese City," p. 1520 (source of quotation). See also Carolyn Cartier, "Neoliberalism and the Neoauthoritarian City in China – Contexts and Research Directions: Commentary in Conversation with Jennifer Robinson's Urban Geography Plenary Lecture," *Urban Geography* 32, 8 (2011), pp. 1110–1121.

[30] This idea is derived from Keller Easterling, *Enduring Innocence: Global Architecture and Its Political Masquerades* (Cambridge, MA: The MIT Press, 2005), pp. 2–3; Keller Easterling, "Zone," in Ilke and Andreas Ruby (eds.), *Urban Transformation* (Berlin: Ruby Press, 2008), pp. 30–45 (esp. pp. 30–31); and Keller Easterling, "The Corporate City is the Zone," in Christina de Baan, Joachim Declerk, and Veronique Patteeuw (eds.), *Visionary Power: Creating the Contemporary City* (Rotterdam: NAi Publishers, 2007), pp. 75–85 (esp. p. 75, source of quotation).

[31] These ideas (and some phraseology) are taken from Keller Easterling, "Zone: The Spatial Softwares of Extrastatecraft," *Places: Forum of Design for the Public Realm* [Posted June

Whatever else, the zone provides the perfect extralegal format for sheltering corporate enterprise from unwanted scrutiny and for ensuring immunity from outside interference.[32] As a legally sanctioned instrument for promoting and sheltering private enterprise, the zone format "presides over a laundry list of exemptions and exceptions," coupled with the imposition of a host of restrictive covenants, internal guidelines, and tight regulatory regimes.[33] The urban enclaves that have proliferated at the edges of cities around the world are skillfully designed to legally legitimate and sanction a new kind of entrepreneurial governance. Operating outside the reach of public oversight, these new urban enclaves are spatial manifestations of the kinds of extraterritoriality that have accompanied the unfolding of global urbanism at the start of the twenty-first century.[34]

As self-contained spatial products with lives of their own, urban enclaves have increasingly become a variant of the free zone or autonomous region. As an integral feature of global urbanism at the start of the new millennium, the free zone or autonomous region is a highly contagious and globalized spatial format that reflects the evolving power of what Keller Easterling has termed *extrastatecraft*. A portmanteau concept that conveys meaning *outside of* and *in addition to* statecraft, extrastatecraft represents the peculiar assemblage of power, finance, and deception that provide the "perfect legal habitat" for legitimating nonstate transactions. The practice of *extrastatecraft* refers to urban enclaves, special economic zones, and business improvement districts governed by private business interests operating more or less independently of local, national, and international law.[35]

The autonomous zone – sometimes referred to as the Free Trade Zone (FTZ), Foreign Trade Zone, Special Economic Zone (SEZ), Export Processing

11, 2012]. Available at http://places.designobserver.com/feature/zone-the-spatial-softwares-of-extrastatecraft/34528/html. See also Keller Easterling, *Extrastatecraft: The Power of Infrastructure Space* (New York: Verso, 2014), pp. 27–37; and Robert McCalla, "The Geographical Spread of Free Zones Associated with Ports," *Geoforum* 21, 1 (1990), pp. 121–134.

[32] Easterling, "The Corporate City is the Zone," p. 75. See also Ronan Palen, *The Offshore World: Sovereign Markets, Virtual Places, and Nomad Millionaires* (Ithaca, NY: Cornell University Press, 2003); Dara Orenstein, "Foreign Trade Zones and the Cultural Logic of Frictionless Production," *Radical History Review* 109 (2011), pp. 36–61; and Xiangming Chen, "The Evolution of Free Economic Zones and the Recent Development of Cross-National Growth Zones," *International Journal of Urban and Regional Research* 19, 5 (1995), pp. 593–621.

[33] See Easterling, "The Spatial Softwares of Extrastatecraft," [n.p.] (source of quotation); and Keller Easterling, "Extrastatecraft," in Kanu Agrawal, *et al.* (eds.), *Perspecta 39: Re-Urbanism Transforming Capitals* (Cambridge, MA: The MIT Press, 2007), pp. 4–16.

[34] Eyal Weizman, Anselm Franke, and Thomas Keenan, *Archipelago of Exception – Sovereignties of Extraterritoriality* (Barcelona: Centro de Cultura Contemporánea [CCCB] November, 2005); and Anselm Franke, Eyal Weizman, and Ines Geisler (Ines Weizman), "Islands: The Geography of Extraterritoriality," *ARCHIS* 6 (2003), pp. 18–54.

[35] Easterling, "Zone," in *Urban Transformation*, p. 31 (source of quotation); Easterling, "Extrastatecraft," p. 16; and Easterling, *Extrastatecraft: The Power of Infrastructure Space*, p. 15.

Zone (EPZ), Free Enterprise Zone, Empowerment Zone, Exclusionary Security Zones, or an almost limitless variety of labels drawn from the dozens of variants – represents a dynamic crossroads and destinations of global trade, corporate finance, skilled management, and nearly instantaneous communication.[36] If the steady accretion of urban enclaves signals the ways in which building typologies have become repeatable on a global scale, then it is the autonomous zone that demonstrates the ways in which global urbanism at the start of the twenty-first century it seeks to be more global and open, yet at the same time, has become more private and insular.[37]

While perhaps stretching the analogy beyond its analytic capacity, the historical antecedents of autonomous zones can be found in the independent city-states of Medieval Europe, the loose alliance of perhaps 60 to 160 merchant towns forming the Hanseatic League that flourished from the thirteenth to the fifteenth century along the Baltic and North Sea coasts, the eighteenth-century frontier-settlements of the New World, the "treaty ports" of nineteenth-century colonialism, and the resource-extraction concessions of the imperialist age.[38] These early historical roots of the contemporary zone format originated from the need of merchandising-commercial enterprises to "maintain strategically ambiguous spaces" that would enable them to facilitate "more fluid circulation of capital, commodities, and people, in ways that "might not otherwise be permissible" under the political constraints of empires and, later, of sovereign nation-states.[39] In the past, "garrison-*entrepôts*" from Hong Kong to Singapore, and Zanzibar to Bridgetown (Barbados), as Janet Roitman has stressed, functioned as trans-shipment hubs that merged trading and military functions in ways that both circumscribed and strengthened the imperial projects of the colonial (and later postcolonial) nation-states, while simultaneously embedding them in regional and global circuits of capital and commodity circulation.[40]

---

[36] Easterling, "Zone: Spatial Softwares for Extrastatecraft" [n.p.]; Easterling, "Extrastatecraft," p. 6; and Easterling, *Extrastatecraft: The Power of Infrastructure Space*, p. 15.

[37] Easterling, *Enduring Innocence*, pp. 2–3; and Easterling, "Extrastatecraft," pp. 4–16.

[38] The merchant towns of the Hanseatic League that lasted from the thirteenth to the seventeenth century in northern Germany and the surrounding areas had their own legal system and furnished their own armies for collective diplomatic protection and mutual aid. Despite these shared features, the organization itself was not actually a confederation of city-states. Only a very small number of the merchant towns within the league enjoyed the full autonomy and liberties comparable to those of a free imperial city. See Hendrik Spruyt, *The Sovereign State and Its Competitors* (Princeton: Princeton University Press, 1994), pp. 109–129; and Alexander Fink, "The Hanseatic League and the Concept of Functional Overlapping Competing Jurisdictions," *Kyklos* 65, 2 (May 2012), pp. 194–217.

[39] The ideas in this paragraph are derived from Jonathan Bach, "Modernity and the Urban Imagination in Economic Zones," *Theory, Culture & Society* 28, 5 (2011), pp. 98–122 (esp. pp. 99–100 [source of quoted phrases]).

[40] Janet Roitman, "Garrison-Entrepôt," *Cahiers d'études Africaines* 38, 150 (1998), pp. 297–329; Janet Roitman, "Modes of Governing: The Garrison-Entrepôt," in Aihwa Ong and Stephen Collier (eds.), *Global Anthropology: Technology, Politics, and Ethics as Anthropological Problems* (Malden, MA: Blackwell, 2005), pp. 417–436; and Janet Roitman, *Fiscal Disobedience: An*

As the formation of coherent international system of sovereign nation-states national space became perhaps the singularly most important project of the nineteenth and most of the twentieth centuries, it was necessary for these medieval or colonial trading depots to become formally codified in order to conveniently fit into the overriding logic of the sovereign international state system.[41] This codification took the legal form of "jurisdictional exception" – a practice made possible by the same principles that allowed nation-states to exert exclusive jurisdiction within a territory. In addition, sovereign nation-states could also determine which regulations applied to which parts of its territory. As Ronen Palan has argued, the power of territorial sovereignty allowed nation-states to unilaterally alter their regulatory regimes not only to attract economic activities but also to restrict trade and investment, using a logic that echoed Carl Schmitt's often-quoted dictum: the sovereign is he who can decide the exception.[42]

Current controversies over autonomous zones and regimes of privatized authority can be located within a longer genealogy of concessionary urbanism that includes model company towns, resource-extractive enclaves, and enclosed manufacturing estates. The company towns of the nineteenth-century age industrial capitalism were archetypical "privatized spaces" where particular business enterprises functioned as the single owners of manufacturing facilities, the sole proprietors of company stores, exclusive employers of workers, monopolistic landlords for residential housing, and the solitary town planners with the power to exclude local political authority.[43] Company towns were thus paradigmatic expressions of an earlier era of concessionary urbanism that combined business enterprise with a heavy dose of paternalism, social engineering, and autocratic control.[44] What distinguishes the production of company towns

Anthropology of Economic Regulation in Central Africa (Princeton, NJ: Princeton University Press, 2005).

[41] John Agnew, *Geopolitics: Re-visioning World Politics* (London: Routledge, 2003).

[42] This idea is taken from Bach, "Modernity and the Urban Imagination in Economic Zones," p. 100. See also Ronen Palan, *The Offshore World: Sovereign Markets, Virtual Places, and Nomad Millionaires* (Ithaca, NY: Cornell University Press, 2003).

[43] Oliver Dinius and Angela Vergara (eds.), *Company Towns in the Americas: Landscape, Power, and Working-Class Communities* (Athens: University of Georgia Press, 2011); Masahiro Tokunaga, "Enterprise Restructuring in the Context of Urban Transition: Analysis of Company Towns in Russia," *The Journal of Comparative Economic Studies* 1 (2005), pp. 79–102; Marcelo Borges and Susana Torres (eds.), *Company Towns: Labor, Space, and Power Relations across Time and Continents* (New York: Palgrave Macmillan, 2012); and Michael Levien, "Special Economic Zones and Accumulation by Dispossession in India," *Journal of Agrarian Change* 11, 4 (2011), pp. 454–83.

[44] Dion Kooijman, "Company Towns: Between Economic Dominance and Mass Media: A Review of Rassenga 70 (1998)," *Space and Culture* 3, 4–5 (2000), pp. 244–245; John Garner, *The Model Company Town Urban Design through Private Enterprise in Nineteenth-Century New England* (Amherst: University of Massachusetts Press, 1984); Robert Fogelsong, *Planning the Capitalist City* (Princeton, NJ: Princeton University Press, 1986); Linda Carlson, *Company Towns of the Pacific Northwest* (Seattle: University of Washington Press, 2003); Margaret Crawford, *Building*

from city building more generally is that they are able to reconcile global infrastructures of production with local resources and a captive labor force. Quite literally, company towns – yesterday and today – function as machines for production. Constructed on a privatized model of development, they make use of comprehensive planning models that allow for the production of a distinctive morphological place-identity.[45]

The more recent origins of the distinctive zonal format can be traced to the establishment of export processing zones close to half a century ago. These export-oriented business incubators consisted of showering corporate enterprises with a host of incentives (including the elimination of custom duties and tariffs, relation of labor regulations, and tax holidays) in exchange for the establishment of manufacturing "start-ups" in then out-of-the-way places like frontier-borders (*maquiladoras* of northern Mexico), the enclosed manufacturing hubs that gave rise to the so-called "Asian Tigers," and the coastal city-regions of postsocialist China.[46] Export-oriented processing zones grew with extraordinary rapidity from a handful of experiments in the first decades after the Second World War (notably Shannon in Ireland, Operation Bootstrap and the Puerto Rico Industrial Development Company [PRIDO] in Puerto Rico, Kandla in India, Kaohsiung in Taiwan, Maan in South Korea) to more than 100 in the mid-1980s and to more than 5,000 in 135 countries at the start of the twenty-first century.[47]

the *Workingman's Paradise: The Design of American Company Towns* (London and New York: Verso, 1995); John Garner, *The Company Town: Architecture and Society in the Early Industrial Age* (Oxford: Oxford University Press, 1992); and Hardy Green, *The Company Town: The Industrial Edens and Satanic Mills That Shaped the American Economy* (New York: Basic Books, 2010).

45 See Neerag Bhatia, "Introduction: Floating Frontiers," in Neeraj Bhatia and Mary Casper (eds.), *The Petropolis of Tomorrow* (New York: Actar, 2013), pp. 12–19.

46 Chen, "The Evolution of Free Economic Zones and the Recent Development of Cross-National Growth Zones," pp. 593–621. See also N. L. Sum, "Theorizing the Development of East Asian Newly-Industrializing Countries: A Regulationist Perspective," in Bob Jessop (ed.), *Regulation Theory and the Crisis of Capitalism* (Cheltenham: Edward Elgar, 2001), pp. 354–390; See also Kee-Cheok Cheong and Kim-Leng Goh, "Hong Kong as Charter City Prototype – When Concept Meets Reality," *Cities* 35 (2013), pp. 100–103; and James Wang and Daniel Olivier, "Port-FEZ Bundles as Spaces of Global Articulation: The Case of Tianjin, China," *Environment and Planning* A 38, 8 (2006), pp. 1487–1503.

47 Palan, *The Offshore World*, pp. 51–52; 118–120; Nicolas Papadopoulos and Shavin Malhotra, "Export Processing Zones in Development and International Marketing: An Integrative Review and Research Agenda," *Journal of Macromarketing* 27, 2 (2007), pp. 148–161; World Bank Group, "Special Economic Zones: Performance, Implications and Lessons Learned for Zone Development," #45869 (Washington, DC: World Bank, 2008); Bae Gyoon Park, "Spatially Selective Liberalization and Graduated Sovereignty: Politics of Neoliberalism and 'Special Economic Zones' in South Korea," *Political Geography* 24, 7 (2005), pp. 850–873; Triyakshana Seshadri, "An Analysis of the Feasibility of Private Land Assembly for Special Economic Zones in India," *Urban Studies* 49, 10 (2012), pp. 2285–2300; and Jamie McCallam, "Export Processing Zones: Comparative Data from China, Honduras, Nicaragua, and South Africa" [Working paper No. 21] (Geneva: International Labour Office, 2011), p. 2.

The autonomous zones that have spread incongruously across the globe at the start of the twenty-first century represent a radically new mutation of this old spatial form.[48] Over the past half century, the zone as a distinctive kind of spatial typology has proliferated in number, expanded in size, and evolved in form. At the start of the twenty-first century, export processing zones have become the near-ubiquitous spatial expressions of the globalized nature of production and trade on a world scale. The proliferating numbers and types of zones over the last half-century makes any single definition, let alone a standardized nomenclature, increasingly difficult if not impossible to arrive at. This lack of clarity signals a shift in the sociospatial formation of late modernity as export processing zones turn from pragmatic spaces for the unregulated production of exports into actual places, both imagined and lived.[49]

As a particular kind of spatial product, the autonomous zone originated from a logic of exception at the heart of the evolving relationship between state sovereignty and territorial integrity. As the embodiment of the evolving practices of territorial sovereignty, autonomous zones establish what Jonathan Bach has termed "nested exceptionalisms": that is, the complex interplay of exemptions to the rule of law that creates points of contact where organized networks, market exchanges, and political power intersect in all sorts of different permutations.[50] As key locations for the production of space in response to evolving modalities of capitalist accumulation and circulation, these points of contact turn the autonomous zone into a kind of a "new urban imagination that recombines scales, functions, and identities."[51]

As an idealized formula for sponsoring all sorts of activities outside the glare of public oversight, the zone "has begun to breed promiscuously with other enclave formats," merging with offshore financial sanctuaries, tourist and entertainment getaways, knowledge villages, high-technology campuses, corporate business parks, factory compounds, transportation hubs, museums, and even universities. Rather than functioning solely as catalysts for private enterprise and simply dissolving into the general business climate of its host site, the zone has become a durable yet malleable instrument, evolving and mutating as it has grown, and absorbing more and more functional specializations and activities within its boundaries. In the past several decades, the zone has become a kind of experimental "petri dish for the cultivation of a host of spatial products," ranging from global "call centers" to software production facilities, and from business incubators to securitized office parks – "that easily migrate around

[48] Easterling, "Zone: Spatial Softwares for Extrastatecraft" [n.p.]; Easterling, "Extrastatecraft," p. 6; and Easterling, *Extrastatecraft: The Power of Infrastructure Space*, pp. 15, 40.

[49] See Bach, "Modernity and the Urban Imagination in Economic Zones," pp. 99–122. Easterling, "Zone: Spatial Softwares for Extrastatecraft" [n.p.]; and Easterling, "Extrastatecraft," pp. 6–9.

[50] Bach, "Modernity and the Urban Imagination in Economic Zones," p. 99 (source of quotation).

[51] Bach, "Modernity and the Urban Imagination in Economic Zones," p. 99 (source of quotation). See also Jamie Cross, *Dream Zones: Anticipating Capitalism and Development in India* (London: Pluto, 2014).

the world and that thrive in legal lacunae and political quarantine, enjoying the insulation and lubrication of zone exemptions."[52]

The hallmark of the zone format – that is, the capacity to legally redefine and configure activities within a designated space – has brought about multiple variations, ranging from IT production facilities to high-tech research clusters, and from offshore tax havens to innovation districts. It is difficult to privilege one of the countless manifestations of the zonal prototype, since it is this ambiguity and malleable capacity that enables all sorts of hybrid combinations to come into being. What gives the zone format its special qualities is its mutability and malleability, allowing it to blend promiscuously with existing networks in novel and anomalous ways.[53] Despite their different aims and purposes that these sites serve, they are homologous in how they employ territorial strategies of inclusion and exclusion for modulating relations between connectivity and disconnectivity.[54]

As a template for city building, the autonomous zone as corporate business enclave is a primary aggregate unit of the globalizing cities everywhere, offering a "clean slate," "one-stop" entry into local economies around the world.[55] Indeed, as Keller Easterling has argued, "having swallowed the city whole, the zone is now the germ of a city-building epidemic that reproduces glittering mimics of Dubai, Singapore, and Hong Kong."[56] Rather than following a progressive evolution, zone development resembles more a "proliferation of mutations," somewhat akin to a haphazard, zigzag pattern along multiple pathways. Indeed, operating as it does in a more or less frictionless realm of legal and other exemptions, the autonomous zone, as it merges with other enclave formats, "perhaps most naturally adopts the scripts – the aura of fantasy – of the vacation resort and theme park." Taken together, corporate business travelers, upscale tourists, itinerant workers imported from elsewhere create what amount to transient populations that, "like temporary agreements and shifting identities, are good for business."[57] As it has multiplied and spread around the world, the autonomous zone has assumed hybrid forms that defy simple classification. The increasing complexity of the zone – its constant shape-shifting – has made it more difficult if not impossible to define, classify, and label. As it has mutated on the ground, the zone has oscillated between visibility and invisibility, identity and anonymity.[58]

[52] Easterling, "Zone: The Spatial Softwares of Extrastatecraft," [n.p.] (source of quotations). See also Easterling, *Extrastatecraft: The Power of Infrastructure Space*, pp. 37–41.
[53] Bach, "Modernity and the Urban Imagination in Economic Zones," p. 100.
[54] See Sven Opitz and Ute Tellmann, "Global Territories: Zones of Economic and Legal Dis/connectivity," *Distinktion: Scandinavian Journal of Social Theory* 13, 3 (2012), pp. 261–282 (esp. p. 261).
[55] Easterling, "The Corporate City is the Zone," p. 75 (source of quotation).
[56] Easterling, *Extrastatecraft: The Power of Infrastructure Space*, p. 26 (source of quotation).
[57] Easterling, "Zone: The Spatial Softwares of Extrastatecraft," [n.p.] (source of quotations).
[58] Easterling, "The Corporate City is the Zone," pp. 75–76.

The emergence of autonomous zones – special economic zones, free trade areas, export manufacturing zones, construction sites populated by imported workers, and gated tourist resorts catering to foreign visitors, offshore finance centers – represent the opening wedge of what has become a trend that has accelerated around the world. Drawing on the innovative approach of Giorgio Agamben, Aihwa Ong has described these autonomous zones as "spaces of exception" – places that are integral to the smooth and efficient functioning of flexible capitalism and in which rights are suspended. Autonomous zones operate in an extralegal limbo, making "exceptions" to existing legally instituted practices of territorial administration and spatial zoning in order to gain a competitive advantage in the global economy through the selective management of space. The deployment of extralegal practices of exception (and exemption) delineates new spaces of rule, temporarily or permanently administered in ways different from existing territorial regimes of governance.[59] More specifically, Thomas Blom Hansen and Finn Stepputat have identified these special zones as the "return of the concession in a new form."[60] Indeed, Eileen Scully's description of nineteenth-century territorial concessions in China as "anomalous zones" in which governing bodies suspend fundamental norms reads remarkably like what Agamben has called the "state of exception."[61]

Zone Typologies

The proliferation of "zone typologies" undermines the ontological presumption that links state sovereignty with territorial space.[62] Autonomous zones have insinuated themselves in the gaps, voids, and in-between spaces brought about by the breakdown of territorial sovereignty. The zone format represents a complex mixture of old, new, hybrid forms – territorial, trans-territorial, extraterritorial forms of association and authority that coexist and overlap in nested

---

[59] Aihwa Ong, *Neoliberalism as Exception: Mutations in Citizenship and Sovereignty* (Durham, NC: Duke University Press, 2006). Indeed, Jamie Cross, for example, has pushed back against this characterization of zones as singularly exceptional spaces. See Jamie Cross, "Neoliberalism as Unexceptional: Economic Zones and the Everyday Precariousness of Working Life in South India," *Critique of Anthropology* 30, 4 (2010), pp. 355–373.

[60] Thomas Blom Hansen and Finn Stepputat, "Sovereignty Revisited," *Annual Reviews of Anthropology* 35 (2006), pp. 295–315 (quotation from p. 308).

[61] Eileen Scully, "Taking the Low Road to Sino-American Relations: Open Door Expansionists and the Two China Markets," *Journal of American History* 82, 1 (1995), pp. 62–83. See also Eileen Scully, *Bargaining with the State from Afar: American Citizenship in Treaty Port China* (New York: Columbia University Press, 2001). See Giogio Agamben, *State of Exception* [trans. Kevin Attell] (Chicago: University of Chicago Press, 2005). For a well-formulated critique of Agamben, see Derek Gregory, "The Black Flag: Guantánamo Bay and the Space of Exception," *Geografiska Annaler* 88 B, 4 (2006), pp. 405–427.

[62] John Agnew, "The Territorial Trap: The Geographical Assumptions of International Relations Theory," *Review of International Political Economy* 1, 1 (1994), pp. 53–80. For a critique, see Stuart Elden, "Thinking Territory Historically," *Geopolitics* 15, 4 (2010), pp. 757–761.

hierarchies.[63] Autonomous zones do not share the formal characteristics of sovereign nation-states within bounded territory, but they "appear [to act] in state-like ways" and strive to assert their authority vis-à-vis surrounding territorial sovereignties.[64] Operating and interacting at different levels and scales, they function as highly mobile (and hence slippery) modes of social organization and control.[65]

The steady accretion of autonomous zones has brought about an accelerated unbundling of sovereign territoriality and the consequent dispersal and sharing of authority. The territories that the zone format creates do not rest on "permanences," or spatial fixes, but remain "contingent on the relational processes that create, sustain, and dissolve them."[66] Autonomous zones constitute a hidden matrix of spatialized power. The zone format enables powerful nonstate actors "to enact state-like functions and the modalities of sovereignty." As a kind of performance, autonomous zones engage in the quotidian practices of sovereignty: making, applying, and enforcing rules of conduct.[67]

Conventional (and semiabsolute) definitions of sovereignty include the requirement of effective political control, or the capacity to exert the "monopoly of legitimate physical violence" over clearly demarcated territory. Without this right to govern through the establishment and enforcement of the law, sovereignty is no more than contingent and conditional.[68] While conventional thinking has invariably linked questions of sovereignty with state-making (statecraft), recent scholarship has shifted to more ambiguous spatial arrangements, or indeterminate "gray zones" through which sovereign power operates and is produced.[69] If we broaden our understanding of the notion of sovereignty "to include other forms of power that are not strictly juridical,"[70] then it is possible to speak of the idea of "*de facto* or 'effective' sovereignty."[71] Understood as the ability and capacity to exercise power, this revised notion of sovereignty is delinked from purely legal definitions. Constituting a far broader concept

---

[63] James Sidaway, "On the Nature of the Beast: Re-charting Political Geographies of the European Union," *Geografiska Annaler, Series B* 88, 1 (2006), pp. 1–14 (quotation from p. 10).

[64] Fiona McConnell, "The Fallacy and the Promise of the Territorial Trap: Sovereign Articulations of Geopolitical Anomalies," *Geopolitics* 15, 4 (2010), pp. 762–768 (quotation from p. 763).

[65] Anderson, "The Shifting Stage of Politics," pp. 149–150.

[66] David Harvey, *Cosmopolitanism and the Geographies of Freedom* (New York: Columbia University Press, 2009), p. 190.

[67] McConnell, "The Fallacy and the Promise of the Territorial Trap," p. 764 (source of quotation).

[68] Stuart Elden, "Contingent Sovereignty, Territorial Integrity and the Sanctity of Borders," SAIS Review 26, 1 (2006), pp. 11–24 (esp. pp. 15 [source of quotation], 19).

[69] Alison Mountz, "Political Geography I: Reconfiguring Geographies of Sovereignty," *Progress in Human Geography* 37, 6 (2013), pp. 829–841 (esp. p. 830).

[70] Aihwa Ong, *Flexible Citizenship: The Cultural Logic of Transnationality* (Durham, NC: Duke University Press, 1999), p. 216 (source of quotation).

[71] John Agnew, "Sovereignty Regimes: Territoriality and State Authority in Contemporary World Politics," *Annals of the Association of American Geographers* 95, 2 (2005), pp. 437–461 (esp. pp. 438 [source of quotation], 456).

applicable beyond conventional statehood, *de facto* sovereignty can therefore be disentangled from a necessary connection to bounded territory. Such a distinction between *de jure* and *de facto* sovereignty is not simply an academic exercise.[72] Autonomous zones constitute what Fiona McConnell has termed "geopolitical anomalies."[73] Geopolitical anomalies like zones, camps, and concessions are spatialized entities engaged in processes of territorialization. The zone format enables powerful actors to deploy sovereignty in extraterritorial ways. Autonomous zones exercise various kinds of "effective" or "de facto" sovereignty outside the bounds of the sovereign nation-state. They typically rely on fuzzy borders and unclear boundaries to carve out extraterritorial enclaves for themselves.[74]

Rethinking Territorial Sovereignty

In our conventional understanding, sovereignty refers to the ultimate formal authority over demarcated territory. Put simply, mainstream approaches have looked upon sovereignty as centralized, monolithic, and coterminous with the territorial borders of the nation-state.[75] Yet these conventional depictions of sovereignty as an idealized and stable "singular condition" leads us to overlook many of the hybrid modes of inclusion and exclusion that operate across space. The breakdown of territorial sovereignty has signaled the opening of a new era of flexible, fragmented, and rescaled jurisdictions. The fragmentation (and shattering) of sovereign power opens the door for a plethora of local, trans-local, and regional spatio-political experiments. Rather than a clear, stable, dichotomous legal-juridical boundary between inside and outside, one encounters ensembles of variegated sovereignty and an undulating, uneven terrain of rights, entitlements, and privileges. Sovereignty should no longer be treated "as a uniform effect of state rule but as the contingent outcomes of various strategies." The theoretical understanding of sovereignty as a singular wellspring from which power, authority, and order spring forth has given way to alternative modes of flexible, splintered, and multiscaled rule.[76]

In the contemporary age of globalization, the proliferation of autonomous zones has brought about the "material deconstruction of existing territorial frameworks, the excision of conventional boundaries, and the simultaneous

---

[72] See, for example, Stephen Krasner, *Sovereignty: Organized Hypocrisy* (Princeton, NJ: Princeton University Press 1999); Stephen Krasner (ed.), *Problematic Sovereignty: Contested Rules and Political Possibilities* (New York: Columbia University Press 2001); and James Sidaway, *Imagined Regional Communities: Integration and Sovereignty in the Global South* (London: Routledge, 2002).

[73] McConnell, "The Fallacy and the Promise of the Territorial Trap: Sovereign Articulations of Geopolitical Anomalies," p. 762.

[74] Agnew, "The Territorial Trap," p. 72.

[75] See John Agnew, "Still Trapped in Territory?" *Geopolitics* 15 (2010), pp. 779–784.

[76] Ong, *Neoliberalism as Exception*, p. 100 (source of quotations).

creation of mobile spaces and spaces of enclosure" intended to simultaneously facilitate the movement of capital and commodities, and "limit the mobility of populations judged to be superfluous." The functioning and viability of autonomous zones depends upon the unbundling of territorial sovereignty. The zone format embodies new territorial configurations that promote both the elimination of public authority and the exit of sovereign statecraft, along with the emergence of novel technologies of domination grounded in new modes of privatized governance and new mechanisms producing and reinforcing social stratification. Autonomous zones engage in the production of boundaries, "whether by moving already existing ones or by doing away with them, fragmenting them, decentering or differentiating them."[77]

The proliferation of autonomous zones has placed conventional understanding of state sovereignty under strain. If the centralization of legal, political, and economic functions in a bounded territory have historically made the nation-state the essential unit (i.e., a unified political entity) across the globe, the proliferation of autonomous zones has signaled the partial undoing of these processes and the emergence of a new political topography of extraterritoriality, strongly connected to the spaces of global flows of capital, goods, information, and people. As Ann Stoler has suggested, such extraterritorial enclaves have precedents in the "legal and political fuzziness of dependences, trusteeships, protectorates and unincorporated territories" that were "part of the deep grammar of partially restricted rights in the nineteenth- and twentieth-century imperial world."[78] Autonomous zones are sites where the mutations of sovereign power become particularly apparent.[79] As Sven Opitz and Ute Tellmann have shown, zones increasingly exist not simply as spaces for the exclusive exercise of sovereign power, but as complex political technologies that organize social and economic relations in complex spatial and nonspatial ways. As a peculiar "global form" of high modernity, zones neither imply a "strict uniformity" nor suggest a predictable conformity with specific normative prescriptions.[80] They are in practice quite versatile technologies, serving different aims and have very different effects. As flexible spatial products, zones can easily host a range of very different practices: they operate as production regimes aimed at export processing, as much as they can serve as logistical hubs and function as knowledge and technology centers. They constitute border sites that range from offshore financial clearinghouses to detention centers. Whatever their special functional use, zones "are constructed, maintained, and championed in light

---

77 Achille Mbembe, "At the Edge of the World: Boundaries, Territoriality, andSovereignty in Africa" [Trans. Steven Rendall] *Public Culture* 12, 1 (2000), pp. 259–284 (quotations from p. 284, 261).

78 Ann Laura Stoler, "On Degrees of Imperial Sovereignty," *Public Culture* 18, 1 (2006), pp. 125–146 (quotation from p. 137).

79 Brett Neilson, "Zones: Beyond the Logic of Exception?" *Concentric: Literary and Cultural Studies* 40, 2 (2014), pp. 11–28.

80 Opitz and Tellmann, "Global Territories," pp. 263–264 (quotation from p. 263).

of a liberal planetary horizon of circulation that they intend to serve."[81] While they are not exclusive to them, zones belong to the fuzzy nexus of power relations that can be called our contemporary "global assemblages" in particular ways.[82] To understand the changing face of power embedded in zones "we need a less monolithic conception of sovereignty" – one that accounts for the overall effects of globalization, moves beyond conventional notions of mutually exclusive territories, and recognizes increasing incapacity of sovereign regimes, as Saskia Sassen puts it, "to legitimate and absorb all legitimating power, to be the source of law."[83] Autonomous (or semiautonomous) zones are bounded spaces defined by juridical borders. While they are largely exempt from the legal regimes that operate in the jurisdictions within which they are embedded, they "constitute differential regulatory spaces."[84]

Autonomous zones constitute spaces of exception because they typically operated through exemptions to law and the relaxation of other forms of normative regulation. These exceptions, however, are almost always partial. Exceptional forms of rule in autonomous zones typically operate alongside local civil laws, "opportunistic applications of international law, and diverse norms and standards promulgated by corporate [enterprise]." Zones can at once function as spaces of exception, existing in a kind of lawless limbo, "and spaces saturated by competing norms and calculations."[85]

As a normative concept, state sovereignty is increasingly challenged, especially by the functional view in which public authorities lose their conventional privileged position of exclusive powers of governance and are forced to compete with supranational, private, and local actors over the allocation of regulatory authority that enables them to manage urban space. Dispensing with the conventional normative concept of territorial sovereignty in favor of a functional approach only intensifies inequalities, weakening restraints on coercive intervention and diminishing critical roles of the public administration of cities as a locus of identity and an integral site of politics.[86]

Rethinking conventional urban theory means that we need to develop new conceptual frameworks and new vocabularies attuned to the production of new enclosed urban enclaves and the spatial dynamics of graduated sovereignty. New modalities of privatized planning and management systems create discontinuous territorial fragments (or extraterritorial enclaves) that preempt and displace municipal governance. These new privatized zoning practices that

---

[81] Opitz and Tellmann, "Global Territories," p. 263 (source of quotation).

[82] See, for example, Aiwha Ong and Stephen Collier (eds.), *Global Assemblages: Technology, Politics, and the Ethics of Anthropological Problems* (Malden, MA: Blackwell, 2004).

[83] Saskia Sassen, *Territory•Authority•Rights: From Medieval to Global Assemblages* [Updated Edition] (Princeton, NJ: Princeton University Press, 2008), p. 415 (source of quotation).

[84] Opitz and Tellmann, "Global Territories," p. 266 (source of quotation).

[85] Brett Neilson, "Zones: Beyond the Logic of Exception?" *Concentric: Literary and Cultural Studies* 40, 2 (2014), pp. 11–28 (quotations from p. 11).

[86] Benedict Kingsbury, "Sovereignty and Inequality," *European Journal of International Law* 9, 4 (1998), pp. 599–625.

produce noncontiguous and differently administered spaces force us to reconsider liberal conceptions of state sovereignty and public authority not as uniform and homogeneous, but as disaggregated, variegated, and graduated.[87]

In the prevailing view of mainstream international relations theory, territorial sovereignty rests on the presupposition that spatial landscapes are divided into fixed, mutually exclusive, and geographically defined jurisdictions enclosed by discrete and meaningful borders.[88] Seen from this angle of vision, territorial sovereignty – at least in metaphorical terms – resembles something akin to a container, holding something inside while simultaneously keeping something outside. At root, territorial sovereignty is a legal-juridical concept that entails the Weberian presumption of ultimate law-making and law-enforcing authority within a clearly defined territory: the absence of competing claims to legitimacy and independence from external authorities. In the conventional understanding, sovereignty linked with territory implies exclusive authority over a discrete geographic jurisdiction where bundles of laws, rules, and regulations apply unambiguously within the space encompassed by its borders. In short, territorial sovereignty is a mode of governance and means of organizing and defining political authority. The modernist fantasy of unambiguous state sovereignty and "absolute" space ultimately rests on the "undisputed right to determine the framework of rules, regulations and policies within a given territory and to govern accordingly."[89]

Yet as a mounting number of scholars have argued, this conventional thinking that posits fixed and secure territorial units of sovereign space as its analytic point of departure is increasingly problematic for understanding the geopolitical complexities of contemporary globalization.[90] In seeking to expose what he has called the "territorial trap," John Agnew has challenged the conventional view that postulates the invariable overlap between territory and sovereignty.[91] In arguing against the supposition that sovereignty is absolute and indivisible, he opened up ways of exploring the "complex territorial configurations

---

[87] Ong, *Neoliberalism as Exception*, pp. 88–96; 99–104; James Sidaway, "Enclave Space: A New Metageography of Development?" *Area* 39, 3 (2007), pp. 331–339; Anne-Marie Slaughter, "Disaggregated Sovereignty: Towards the Public Accountability of Global Government Networks," *Government and Opposition* 39, 2 (2004), pp. 159–190; and Saskia Sassen, "Toward a Multiplication of Specialized Assemblages of Territory, Authority, and Rights," *Parallax* 13, 1 (2007), pp. 87–94.

[88] John Ruggie, "Territoriality and Beyond: Problematizing Modernity in International Relations," *International Organization* 47, 1 (1993), pp. 139–174 (esp. p. 151).

[89] David Held and Anthony McGrew, "Globalization and the Liberal Democratic State," *Government and Opposition* 28, 2 (1993), pp. 261–278 (quotation from p. 265).

[90] James Anderson, "The Shifting Stage of Politics: New Medieval and Postmodern Territorialities?" *Environment and Planning D* 14, 2 (1996), pp. 133–153; Tuomas Forsberg, "Beyond Sovereignty, Within Territoriality: Mapping the Space of Late-Modern (Geo)Politics," *Cooperation and Conflict* 31, 4 (1996), pp. 355–386; and Gearoid Ó Tuathail and Timothy Luke, "Present at the (Dis)integration: Deterritorialization and Reterritorialization in the New Wor(l)d Order," *Annals of the Association of American Geographers* 84, 3 (1994), pp. 381–398.

[91] Agnew, "The Territorial Trap," pp. 53–80.

of authority."[92] Such alternative readings of territoriality effectively "denaturalize and problematize sovereignty and conceptually unbundle its constituent elements of territory, authority, and statehood."[93]

In conventional thinking, territory is a fixed, unmovable, unchanging, geopolitical entity, whose finite limits determine the beginnings and ends of sovereignty, political authority, and statehood. Challenging this reductionist conception of spatially fixed and mutually exclusive territorial sovereignties enables us to expand our horizons and recognize the multifaceted dimensions of territoriality – treating it not just as a tangible, fixed object, but equally as a flexible construct of social and political power.[94] If the mutually constitutive relationship between territoriality and sovereign statehood could not in any way be conceived of as an *a priori* one, then it certainly follows that the connection between the two is historically contingent and ought to be treated as a historical construction.[95]

By stretching the boundaries of existing legal regimes based on territorial sovereignty, the zone format breaks down the unambiguous relationship between authority and territory. Autonomous zones reside outside the territorial logic of "de jure" sovereignty and operate in the "gaps" or voids between and across recognized national territorial boundaries.[96] This "unbundling" of formal (rational-legal) authority has resulted in "new and hybrid" forms of territoriality.[97]

Looking at the fragmentation of territorial sovereignty that characterizes Israel/Palestine provides a lens into thinking, at least analogically, about the variegated modes of governance that have accompanied contemporary city building on a global scale. For Israel/Palestine, conventional understandings of territorial sovereignty fail to adequately capture the complex, multitudinous, and fragmentary nature of sovereignty that can be observed on the ground.[98] The sovereign authority that the Israeli state security apparatus has produced

---

[92] This phrase is taken from Sidaway, "On the Nature of the Beast," p. 1 (source of quotation).

[93] McConnell, "The Fallacy and the Promise of the Territorial Trap," p. 762 (source of quotation).

[94] David Newman, "Territory, Compartments and Borders: Avoiding the Trap of the Territorial Trap," *Geopolitics* 15, 4 (2010), pp. 773–778 (esp. p. 773).

[95] Simon Reid-Henry, "The Territorial Trap Fifteen Years On," *Geopolitics* 15, 4 (2010), pp. 752–756 (esp. pp. 753).

[96] McConnell, "The Fallacy and the Promise of the Territorial Trap," p. 764.

[97] Sidaway, "On the Nature of the Beast," p. 10 (source of quotation). See also C. Murray Austin and Mukesh Kumar, "Sovereignty in the Global Economy: An Evolving Geopolitical Concept," *Geography Research Forum* 18 (1998), pp. 49–64; and Agnew, "Sovereignty Regimes," pp. 440–441.

[98] For the source of these ideas, see Nir Gazit and Robert Latham, "Spatial Alternatives and Counter-Sovereignties in Israel/Palestine," *International Political Sociology* 8, 1 (2014), pp. 63–81 (esp. pp. 67–68). See also Eyal Weizman, *Hollow Land: Israel's Architecture of Occupation* (New York: Verso Books, 2007); and Yehouda Shenhav and Yael Berda, "Juxtaposing the Israeli Occupation of the Palestinian Territories with Colonial Bureaucratic History," in Adi Ophir, Michal Givoni, and Sari Hanafi (eds.), *The Power of Inclusive Exclusion: Anatomy of Israeli Rule in the Occupied Palestinian Territories* (Cambridge, MA: The MIT Press; and New York: Zone Books, 2009), pp. 337–374.

along the borders and within the designated Occupied Territories is "under-institutionalized," that is, it tends "to lack a firm bureaucratic administration or a formalized legal system that affixes authoritative control." Instead of a singular, uniform, and comprehensive institutionalized military or civilian administration," there are "multiple, localized and temporal cores of [institutionalized] political power."[99]

These transitory, mobile, and disjointed kinds of sovereign coding – what Adi Ophir, Michal Givoni, and Sari Hanafi have called the "logic of inclusive exclusion" – are typically associated the topographies of power along frontiers, but they can just as easily be applied to understanding new modes of governance found in cities.[100] The "state of exception" that the Israeli security apparatus has endorsed for the Occupied Territories constitutes a distinctive political logic of inclusive exclusion – a means by which "the occupied territories are excluded from the state of Israel in order that Israel can include Palestine under it system of control."[101]

Medieval Urbanism Redux

Nezar AlSayyad and Ananya Roy have evoked the idea of "medieval urbanism" as a trans-historical analytic category through which to make sense of contemporary cities in the age of neoliberal globalization. As they suggest, "the medieval city reminds us that the relationship between cities and globalization is not new." "But perhaps more importantly," they continue, "the medieval city reminds us of the paradoxes, exclusions and segmentations that have always been associated with city form and urban organization."[102] This kind of analogical reasoning enables us to draw attention to the points of convergence between medieval cities and transnational urbanism at the start of the twenty-first century. The metaphorical construct of the medieval city is a valuable analytical tool for examining contemporary urban geographies and the multiple and competing sovereignties through which they are constituted. While the concept of modern citizenship was initially conceived of as a set of abstract individual rights embedded in the sovereignty of the nation-state, the modes of belonging and attachment to place associated with contemporary urbanism assume many different forms. In the current phase of globalization, citizenship

99 Nir Gazit, "Social Agency, Spatial Practices and Power: The Micro-Foundations of Fragmented Sovereignty in the Occupied Territories," *International Journal of Politics, Culture and Society* 22, 1 (2009), pp. 83–103 (quotation from p. 84).

100 Adi Ophir, Michal Givoni and Sari Hanafi, "Introduction," in *The Power of Inclusive Exclusion*, pp. 15–30.

101 Stephen Morton, *States of Emergency: Colonialism, Literature, and the Law* (Liverpool: Liverpool University Press, 2013), p. 174.

102 Nezar Alsayyad and Ananya Roy, "Medieval Modernity: on Citizenship and Urbanism in a Global Era," *Space and Polity* 10, 1 (2006), pp. 1–20 (esp. p. 2, source of quotation). I have used some of the ideas here, but shaped them to fit my own understanding and my own purposes.

is "flexible," as Aihwa Ong has argued.[103] As in medieval cities, these new kinds of "flexible citizenship" are linked not to the "imagined community" of the nation-state, but to either dependent patronage or to associational membership (as in the guild), and in both cases, it is fundamentally about gaining access to protection.[104]

By historicizing what they regard as ostensibly "new" urban practices, Alsayyad and Roy seek to explain the rescaling of citizenship and exclusionary power not from the conventional analytic perspective of singular regimes of sovereign nation-states embedded in an international system but through the wide-angle lens of the fragmented domains of partitioned cities. They break away from linear periodizations of history and teleological understandings of modernity by mobilizing the concept of the "medieval urbanism" as a transhistorical analytical category.[105] In a fashion similar to Marshall Berman, they argue that modernity should be understood as an essentially and inevitably fractured, divided, and contradictory project.[106] The seemingly oxymoronic phrasing of "medieval modernity" can thus reveal "the inherent paradoxes of the modern: fiefdoms of democracy, the materialist immediacy of religious fundamentalism, the simultaneity of war and humanitarianism."[107]

Alsayyad and Roy have suggested that their conceptual reframing of "medieval urbanism" is helpful in exposing the deeply fragmented character of urban life. They identify three main aspects of contemporary citizenship that highlight congruence between medieval and contemporary cities. First, the emergence of new forms of citizenship located in urban enclaves comes at the expense of the ideal notion of modern citizenship, which is conventionally conceived of as a set of abstract individual rights embedded in the concept of the sovereign nation-state. Second, extralegal, private systems of governance create new kinds of "rights-bearing individuals" that substitute for the state authority guaranteeing the equality of citizenship. Grounded in notions of natural liberty, self-actualizing autonomous subjects, and person freedom, the idea of "rights-bearing individuals" rests on a commitment to securing private property rights over the consolidation of public law and shared citizenship.[108] Third, this emerging logic of rule has territorial manifestations where the modern city displays a kind of medieval "ordering of space" with perforated jurisdictions consisting of intersecting, irregular, and diverse memberships.[109]

---

[103] Ong, *Flexible Citizenship*, p. 6.   [104] Alsayyad and Roy, "Medieval Modernity," p. 2.
[105] Alsayyad and Roy, "Medieval Modernity," pp. 8, 16, 17.
[106] Marshall Berman, *All that is Solid Melts into Air: The Experience of Modernity* (New York: Penguin, 1982), pp. 15–36.
[107] Alsayyad and Roy, "Medieval Modernity," pp. 8, 16–17 (source of quotation).
[108] See, for example, Mireille Abelin, "'Entrenched in the BMW': Argentine Elites and the Terror of Fiscal Obligation," *Public Culture* 24, 2 [67] (2012), pp. 329–356 (esp. p. 349).
[109] Alsayyad and Roy, "Medieval Modernity," pp. 5, 8, 16 (source of phrase). See also James Holston and Arjun Appadurai, "Introduction: Cities and Citizenship," in James Holston

Alsayyad and Roy draw attention to the profound and reciprocal relationship between new modalities of governmentality and new spatial expressions of citizenship. The patchwork patterns and fragmented geography of discontinuous enclaves produces multiple, imbricated, and differentiated landscapes of sovereignty. These fundamental shifts in the regulatory regimes – what Aihwa Ong has called "variegated sovereignty" – have serious consequences for the normative ideals embedded in the notion of the "promise of the city" as the locus of freedom and tolerance, conviviality, and serendipity.[110] For some, the advent of extraterritorial sovereignties seems to suggest the beginnings of a kind of frontier urban geography in which the continuous and linear divides associated with conventional nation-state territoriality are steadily replaced by more flexible, patchy, and elastic (even if less permeable) demarcations of the inside/outside binary.[111]

Taking seriously the modalities of medieval urbanism makes possible an understanding of the embedded paradoxes of global urbanism at the start of the twenty-first century. Whereas medieval towns sought to achieve local insularity above all else, new cities aspire to global connectivity unencumbered by locality. The steady accretion of all sorts of new spatial configurations ranging from gated residential communities, business improvement districts, special economic zones, and the like, have produced their own sets of rules and regulations, restrictive covenants, and statutory exclusions that contribute to the dissolution, fragmentation, and localization of comprehensive citizenship rights.[112] New forms of belonging and attachment to place sometimes substitute for, or are even hostile, to comprehensive citizenship rights associated with the sovereign nation-state. New kinds of privatized governance structures like common interest developments, neighborhood homeowners' associations, and the embryonic Charter Cities movement operate in a fashion somewhat akin to medieval fiefdoms, imposing privately sanctioned rules and regulations that replace outside public regulatory authority. These variegated and shifting sovereignties have produced their own perverse logics of extraterritorial modes of urban governance. These new modes of graduated sovereignty have transformed contemporary cities into what James Holston and Arun Appadurai have

and Arjun Appudurai (eds.), *Cities and Citizenship* (Durham: Duke University Press, 1999), pp. 1–18.

110   See Aihwa Ong, "The Chinese Axis: Zoning Technologies and Variegated Sovereignty," *Journal of East Asian Studies* 4 (2004), 69–96; Aihwa Ong, "Graduated Sovereignty in Southeast Asia," *Theory, Culture, and Society* 17, 4 (2000), pp. 55–75. See also Kian Tajbakhsh, *The Promise of the City: Space, Identity, and Politics in Contemporary Social Thought* (Berkeley: University of California Press, 2001).

111   Stephen Graham, "The Spectre of Splintering Metropolis," *Cities* 18, 6 (2001), pp. 365–368; and Eyal Weizman, *Hollow Land: Israel's Architecture of Occupation* (London: Verso, 2007), pp. 6–7, 116–117, 200–201.

112   See AlSayyad and Roy, "Medieval Modernity," p. 4. See also Michael Correa-Jones, "The Origins and Diffusion of Racial Restrictive Covenants," *Political Science Quarterly* 115, 4 (2000), pp. 541–568 (esp. p. 543).

termed a "honeycomb of jurisdictions," a "medieval body" of "overlapping, heterogeneous, nonuniform, and increasingly private memberships."[113]

Arising out of legal loopholes that offer immunity from municipal jurisdiction, these new satellite cities built on the edge of existing metropolis are self-governing islands that resemble the independent city-states and autarkic "free ports" of yesteryear. As a distinctive kind of extraterritorial space, these urban mega-projects are highly specialized assemblages of territory, authority, and rights/entitlements that have effectively established their own modes of governance outside of the conventional institutional framework of public administration.[114] As a general rule, these processes of deterritorialization have resulted in an institutional vacuum that has enabled real-estate developers to effectively delink from the existing normative order of the "public city" and to establish their own privatized regimes of centralized control. The planned rollout of these new satellite cities signals how extraterritorial power can produce and justify a new kind of enclave urbanism (or what Keller Easterling has called "zone urbanism") that bears little relation to conventional practices of city building. This process of radical reurbanism has fundamentally recast the conventional balance between municipal governance and public authority, on the one side, and corporate real-estate interests and private proprietorship, on the other.[115]

In the contemporary age of globalization, the meaning and significance of juridical borders, as well as their geographical location, can change significantly and dramatically over space and time. The recognition of the complexity, diversity, and plurality of territorial sovereignty has spawned a new conceptual vocabulary – neomedievalism, "new medieval" territorialities, postmodern territorialities, postcolonial sovereigntyscapes – as a way of capturing what is actually happening on the ground.[116] Similarly, the introduction of novel concepts like variegated or "graduated" sovereignties enables us to adopt a critical perspective that allows for different and multiform sovereign visions without an original and pure reference point.[117] The exercise of variegated sovereignty

[113] Holston and Appadurai, "Introduction: Cities and Citizenship," p. 13 (source of quotation). For the idea of "graduated sovereignty," see Ong, *Flexible Citizenship*, pp. 215–224. See Sidaway, "Enclave Space," pp. 331–339.

[114] Sassen, *Territory•Authority•Rights*, pp. 34–37, 45–48; and Saskia Sassen, "Neither Global nor National: Novel Assemblages of Territory, Authority, and Rights," *Ethics & Global Politics* 1, 1–2 (2008), pp. 61–79.

[115] Easterling, *Extrastatecraft: The Power of Infrastructure Space*, p. 41. See also Keller Easterling, "The Corporate City is the Zone," pp. 75–85.

[116] Stephen Kobrin, "Back to the Future: Neomedievalism and the Postmodern Digital World Economy," *Journal of International Affairs* 51, 2 (1998), pp. 361–386; and Anderson, "The Shifting Stage of Politics," pp. 140–141; James Sidaway, "Sovereign Excesses? Portraying Postcolonial Sovereigntyscapes," *Political Geography* 22, 2 (2003), pp. 157–178 (esp. p. 160); and Jörg Friedrichs, "The Meaning of New Medievalism," *European Journal of International Relations* 7, 4 (2001), pp. 475–501.

[117] Sidaway, "Sovereign Excesses?" p. 160.

increasingly depends on a more complicated geography of transnational assemblages, flows, and enclaves.[118]

Variegated sovereignty posits something akin to a medieval system of rule, consisting of a "patchwork" of overlapping and incomplete basket of rights and authorities superimposed and inextricably entangled. Some time ago, John Ruggie labeled this institutional framework "heteronomous," connoting a "lattice-like network of authority relations."[119] These overlapping, interwoven, and incomplete systems of authority often result in competing claims about who possesses the power to impose rules and regulations over the same geographic territory.[120]

The early theorists of globalization went too far in positing borderless worlds and frictionless space leading inevitably to deterritorialization.[121] As Neil Brenner has persuasively argued, globalization is best understood in terms of a distinctive kind of reterritorialization.[122] The physicality of borders, along with territorial compartmentalization, has not disappeared under the relentless corrosive pressures of globalization.[123] The reconfiguration and reordering of fixed territories takes place at one and the same time as the corrosive dynamics of cross-border flows and networks[124] If territoriality has remained a central feature of contemporary geopolitical and geo-economic practice, so too must we take into account the deployment of extraterritorial forms of power.[125] Looking at extraterritoriality through the lens of "effective" or "*de facto*" sovereignties enables us not only to avoid fixed and stable conceptions of territorial

---

[118] Alex Jeffrey, Colin McFarlane, and Alex Vasudevan, "Rethinking Enclosure: Space, Subjectivity and the Commons," *Antipode* 44, 4 (2012), pp. 1247–1267 (esp. p. 1250).

[119] John Ruggie, "Review: Continuity and Transformation in World Politics: Towards a Synthesis," *World Politics* 35, 2 (1983), pp. 261–285 (p. 274, source of quotation).

[120] See Peter Gratton, *The State of Sovereignty: Lessons from the Political Fictions of Modernity* (Albany: State University of New York Press, 2012).

[121] Newman, "Territory, Compartments, and Borders," p. 774.

[122] Neil Brenner, "Globalisation as Reterritorialisation: The Re-scaling of Urban Governance in the European Union," *Urban Studies* 36, 3 (1999), pp. 431–451.

[123] See, for example, David Newman and Anssi Paasi, "Fences and Neighbours in the Post-Modern World: Boundary Narratives in Political Geography," *Progress in Human Geography* 22, 2 (1998), pp. 186–207; Vladimir Kolossov, "Border Studies: Changing Perspectives and Theoretical Approaches," *Geopolitics* 10, 4 (2005), pp. 606–632; Anssi Paasi, "Generations and the Development of Border Studies," *Geopolitics* 10, 4 (2005), pp. 663–671; and David Newman, "The Lines that Continue to Separate Us: Borders in a Borderless World," *Progress in Human Geography* 30, 2 (2006), pp. 1–19.

[124] Newman, "Territory, Compartments, and Borders," p. 775. See also David Newman, "The Resilience of Territorial Conflict in an Era of Globalization," in Miles Kahler and Barbara Walter (eds.), *Globalization, Territoriality, and Conflict* (Cambridge: Cambridge University Press, 2006), pp. 85–110.

[125] Simon Reid-Henry, "The Territorial Trap Fifteen Years On," pp. 754–755. See, for instance, Anssi Paasi, "Boundaries as Social Processes: Territoriality in the World of Flows," *Geopolitics* 3, 1 (1998), pp. 69–88.

sovereignty but also to see how spaces acquire concrete meanings at their edges, on their borders, and along their frontiers.[126]

Regimes of Exception: Extraterritoriality

The idea of *"regimes of exception"* can provide a useful way to theorize about governance innovations that complicate conventional understandings of territorial sovereignty. Broadly defined, *"regimes of exception"* refer to practices of governance that rely on the suspension of conventional regulatory protocols and the substitution of extraordinary measures designed to exempt key players from existing protocols. Put in another way, the adoption of exceptional measures establishes an alternative set of procedural rules to deliver policies, programs, and projects. It can be said that every *ad hoc* governance practice that seeks to alter organizational capacity – through a combination of various formal agreements and informal practices –operates as an *exception* to existing standards of rule and oversight. Regimes of exception are extra-juridical, that is, they depend on the suspension of the juridical order itself, thereby blurring the distinction between public and private, legality and illegality, and norm and exception.[127]

Organized under the auspices of the zone format, regimes of exception have increasingly become the principal paradigm of governance. Autonomous zones seek to redefine the field of governance and the territoriality of rule through a redistribution of power.[128] They produce sites that are ambiguous, "gray," exceptional, and asymmetrical expressions of authority. Autonomous zones embody juridical fragmentation where modes of governance are marked by duplication, overlap, or gaps in authority. What always remain contested are questions about jurisdiction and control of territory: "Who governs a site, polices its borders, [and] regulates mobility in the form of entry and exclusion?"[129]

The formation of autonomous zones creates new kinds of relationality and mediation. The rhetorical (and hence normative) aim of what Andrew Barry has called "zones of qualification" is to forge a clear separation between a well-governed "inside" and an unpredictable "outside."[130] Autonomous zones are the embodiment of heterogeneous and dynamic topologies of power. The

---

[126] John Agnew, "Sovereignty Regimes: Territoriality and State Authority in Contemporary World Politics," *Annals of the Association of American Geographers* 95, 2 (2005) pp. 437–461; and Newman, "Territory, Compartments, and Borders," p. 773.

[127] Idalina Baptista, "Practices of Exception in Urban Governance: Reconfiguring Power Inside the State," *Urban Studies* 50, 1 (2013), pp. 37–52.

[128] Baptista, "Practices of Exception in Urban Governance," p. 49.

[129] Mountz, "Political Geography I," p. 834 (source of quotation).

[130] Andrew Barry, "Technological Zones," *European Journal of Social Theory* 9, 2 (2006), pp. 239–253 (esp. pp. 245–250).

"necessary fiction" of territorial sovereignty provides autonomous zones with sufficient cover to maintain feigned innocence.[131]

The conventional way of thinking about extraterritoriality has focused on identifying a designated space or special status that lies outside territorial boundaries, and either benefits or suffers from the suspension of jurisdiction overruling the existing sovereignty.[132] Atypical places like embassies, refugee camps, detention centers, internment facilities, and free trade zones are some key examples that operate in this way. Yet over time, the number and *genres* of extraterritorial spaces have greatly increased, diversified, and crystalized into a dense and opaque configuration of exception and exemption that superimposes its own rules and, as a consequence, erodes and undermines the very notion of territorial sovereignty.[133]

As a general rule, urban enclaves operate under the umbrella of shared sovereignty. They acquire their privileged status as extraterritorial enclaves by virtue of a bargain with the machinery of the local municipal administration. The installation of new regulatory regimes enables urban enclaves to enjoy a degree of territorial and administrative autonomy. They operate a kind of joint, parallel, or shadow administration. The organizational logics undergirding the management of these new urban enclaves suggest that a different paradigm of power that rules through differential hierarchies has replaced prevailing state-centered notions of territorial governance with what some scholars have referred to as "shared," "graduated," "variegated," or even "disaggregated" sovereignty.[134]

In new city-building efforts around the world, real-estate developers extol the virtues of the enclave format because it enables them to build a city according to their own specifications without outsider oversight or interference. Yet even as the enclave format has replaced conventional municipal governance with private management, it has itself become an instrument of corporate domination and market manipulation. The enclave format provides a distinctive

---

[131] Elden, "Contingent Sovereignty, Territorial Integrity and the Sanctity of Borders," pp. 11–24; Krasner, *Sovereignty: Organized Hypocrisy*; and Easterling, "Extrastatecraft," pp. 6, 11.

[132] See, for example, Choon-Piew Pow, "Living it Up: Super-rich Enclave and Transnational Elite Urbanism in Singapore," *Geoforum* 42, 3 (2011), pp. 382–393; and Trevor Hogan, Tim Bunnell, Choon-Piew Pow, Eka Permanasari, and Sirat Morshidi, "Asian Urbanisms and the Privatization of Cities," *Cities* 29, 1 (2012), pp. 59–63.

[133] Jeffrey Winters, *Power in Motion: Capital Mobility and the Indonesian State* (Ithaca, NY: Cornell University Press, 1996); Easterling, "Extrastatecraft," pp. 4–16; and Easterling, "Zone," in *Urban Transformation*, pp. 30–45.

[134] Stephen Krasner, "Sharing Sovereignty: New Institutions for Collapsed and Failing States," *International Security* 29, 1 (2004), pp. 85–120; Ong, "Graduated Sovereignty in Southeast Asia," pp. 55–75; Ong, "The Chinese Axis: Zoning Technologies and Variegated Sovereignty," pp. 69–96; and Sidaway, "Enclave Space," pp. 331–339; Slaughter, "Disaggregated Sovereignty: Towards the Public Accountability of Global Government Networks," pp. 159–190; and Park, "Spatially Selective Liberalization and Graduated Sovereignty," pp. 850–873.

kind of distributive protocol for serial repetition of similar building typologies and a code of procedures that shapes separate precincts into "more uniform networks of organization."[135]

As exemplary expressions of entrepreneurial urbanism, "corporate cities" may indeed represent a harbinger of twenty-first-century urbanism.[136] The holistic, master-planned model provides for a prepackaged urbanity – instantly whole, integrated, and connected. Operating outside conventional jurisdiction of municipal administration, privatized urban enclaves – with their repetitive commercial formats that combine office complexes, mixed-use lifestyle centers, exclusive residential components, and leisure activities – aspire to be self-contained worlds unto themselves, self-reflexive, and innocent of political entanglements.[137]

Fluid Frontier Geography

One way of conceptualizing these evolving patterns of spatial partitioning in globalizing cities is to think in terms of what Eyal Weizman described as "frontier geography."[138] Rather than rigid and fixed, the borders that define urban enclaves are elastic and mutable. These borders belong more to a fluid conception of frontier geography rather than to fixed state of permanence. Weizman outlined the principles of frontier geography in the context of the architecture of the Israeli occupation of Palestine. But these principles can be extended to analyze the everyday life-spaces of the "globalizing cities" everywhere.[139] Frontier geography, as Weizman has argued, is characterized by a nonlinear, non-continuous, and noncontiguous demarcation of space that is antithetical to fixed lines and stationary points. Whereas conventional borders are linear and fixed, frontiers are malleable and flexible – with temporary lines of engagement and confrontation that are marked by makeshift boundaries and irregular divides. Unlike a borderland that separates and divides territories, a frontier is

135 Keller Easterling, "Siting Protocols," in Peter Lang and Tam Miller (eds.), *Suburban Discipline* (New York: Princeton Architectural Press, 1997), pp. 21–31 (quotation from p. 21).

136 For entrepreneurial urbanism, see Tim Hall and Paul Hubbard, "The Entrepreneurial City: New Urban Politics, New Urban Geography?" *Progress in Human Geography* 20, 2 (1996), pp. 153–174; Tim Hall and Paul Hubbard (eds.), *The Entrepreneurial City: Geographies of Politics, Regime, and Representation* (London: John Wiley, 1998); and Kevin Ward, "Entrepreneurial Urbanism, State Restructuring and Civilizing 'New' East Manchester," *Area* 35, 2 (2003), pp. 116–127. For corporate cities, see Anoya Datta, "India's Ecocity? Environment, Urbanisation, and Mobility in the Making of Lavasa," *Environment and Planning C* 30, 10 (2012), pp. 982–996.

137 Easterling, *Enduring Innocence*, p. 3.

138 Eyal Weizman, "Principles of Frontier Geography," in Philipp Misselwitz and Tim Rieniets (eds.), *City of Collision: Jerusalem and the Principles of Conflict Urbanism* (Basel: Birkhäuser Publishers for Architecture, 2006), pp. 84–92.

139 Henk Van Houtum and Ton Van Naerssen, "Bordering, Ordering and Othering," *Tijdschrift voor economische en sociale geografie* [TESG] 93, 2 (2002), pp. 125–136.

inherently unstable and contested, in its simplest form, "a territory for two dreams," but in more complicated situations, subject to pressures both inside and outside.[140]

Frontier geographies, according to Weizman, can be found in varying degrees wherever one looks at the geographical expansion of power. There is no doubt that these principles characterize the enclave spaces of aspiring world-class cities at the edge of the world economy. As a general rule, contemporary geopolitical space has incorporated frontier characteristics. Rather than being demarcated by continuous lines, urban landscapes have come to closely resemble a territorial patchwork of self-contained, introverted enclaves.[141] These urban enclaves are protected behind mobile, nonlinear borders and barriers that can expand and constrict across the infrastructural capillaries of urban space. Put bluntly, the mobile barrier replaces the fixed border. "The border is in fact everywhere," Weizman has argued, "around every public and private property and infrastructure, taking the form of local and regional fortifications and security apparatuses" made visible by roadblocks, checkpoints, fences, walls, CCTV surveillance, and sentry posts.[142]

Rather than the smooth and borderless space celebrated in the overly romanticized versions of globalization, urban landscapes have been subjected to new kinds of fragmentation, separation, and division.[143] Borders (or boundaries) are "fundamental structuring elements" of space-making, and their relevance reaches beyond their power to mark territories, define edges, and designate thresholds. Without exception, urban space consists of various boundaries created by administrative interventions, by calculated policy decisions, by processes of sociocultural segregation, by urban design, or by discursive constructions enabled via imaginary representations and cognitive mapping.[144] Borders are dynamic spatial features of urban landscapes. They do not simply mark "a fixed point in space or time, [but] rather symbolize social practices of spatial differentiation." Their existence, location, and actual impact are most fruitfully understood as outcomes (anticipated or unanticipated) of social processes of marking, ordering, and othering.[145] Borders protect against unwanted

---

[140] Wendy Pullan, "Frontier Urbanism: The Periphery at the Centre of Contested Cities," *The Journal of Architecture* 16, 1 (2011), pp. 15–35 (esp. p. 15, source of quotation). See also Joël Kotek, "Divided Cities in the European Cultural Context," *Progress in Planning* 52, 3 (1999), pp. 227–237 (quotation from p. 228).

[141] Weizman, *Hollow Land*, p. 7.

[142] Weizman, "Principles of Frontier Geography,'" p. 86 (source of quotation).

[143] See Liam O'Dowd, "From a 'Borderless World' to a 'World of Borders': 'Bringing History Back In'," *Environment and Planning D* 28, 6 (2010), pp. 1031–1050.

[144] Werner Breitung, "Borders and the City: Intra-Urban Boundaries in Guangzhou (China)," *Quaestiones Geographicae* 30, 4 (2011), pp. 55–61 (p. 55 [source of quotation], 56 [source for my ideas]).

[145] Van Houtum and Van Naerssen, "Bordering, Ordering and Othering," pp. 125–136 (p. 125, source of quotation).

intrusion, ensure control over territory, allocate power of decision-making, facilitate administration, and foster secrecy.[146]

In this geographical imagining, the unwanted urban poor are never really contained behind fixed lines. The fluidity of social contact has transformed urban landscapes into battle grounds where slum-dwellers, informal traders, and itinerant work-seekers function as contemporary proxies for the "dangerous classes" of the modern metropolis of the industrial capitalist age. It is the everyday presence of these unwanted, dangerous, and implacable urban "Others" that motivates what amounts to a perverse kind of elite retreat. The imaginative geographies of enclave urbanism operate by "fold[ing] distance into difference" through a wide array of spatial strategies. The "architectures of enmity" operate by "multiplying partitions and enclosures that serve to demarcate the 'same' from the 'other.'"[147]

Frontier geographies depend on a complex matrix of points and lines. Lines of transport and communication "function as wedges that open up "alien terrain" for further colonization." They also create effective physical barriers that break localities into a plethora of isolated enclaves with highly circumscribed habitats.[148] The most obvious example, and the one upon which Weizman focuses his attention, is the West Bank where a serpentine network of "Israeli-only" bypass roadways not only connect the heavily fortified settlement enclaves but also serves to encircle and carve up the social and political space of the Palestinian territories.[149]

This concept of "frontier geography" can be extended to other examples where the installation of infrastructure acts to fragment urban landscapes. In Managua, for example, new road networks have connected elite enclaves but also served to justify slum clearances.[150] In the frontier imaginary, space and time intersect and overlap. The fragmentation of space is mirrored by "temporal non-sequentiality" where social action unfolds in an inconsistent manner.[151] The dislocation and distortion of temporal rhythms appear most evidently in marking the time of informal livelihoods and irregular work. The creation of informal settlements and slums acts, in effect, as a "precarious process of urbanization in reverse," where slum dwellers, work-seekers, and newcomers actually "live in a constant state of transience and temporariness."[152] The material

---

[146] Breitung, "Borders and the City," pp. 57–58.
[147] Derek Gregory, *The Colonial Present* (Oxford: Blackwell, 2004), p. 17, 20 (source of quotations).
[148] Weizman, "Principles of Frontier Geography," p. 89 (source of quotation).
[149] Eyal Weizman, *Hollow Land*, pp. 179–184.
[150] Dennis Rodgers, "Haussmannization in the Tropics: Abject Urbanism and Infrastructural Violence in Nicaragua," *Ethnography* 13, 4 (2012), pp. 413–438.
[151] Weizman, "Principles of Frontier Geography," p. 91.
[152] For the source of this idea and other ideas in earlier paragraphs, see Nasser Abourahme, "Contours of the Neoliberal City: Fragmentation, Frontier Geographies, and the New Circularity," *Occupied London*, No. 4 (2009) [n.p.]. Available at www.occupiedLondon.org/contours

foundations of their lives are contingent on unpredictable circumstances that range from the spontaneous eruption of social catastrophes brought on by fickle weather to the disruptive interventions of state authorities.[153]

Frontiers and zones are designed with the intention of maintaining separation. The logic behind frontier geography can also be found in the assemblage of autonomous zones.[154] Yet unlike frontiers, whose logic is to keep out and away those who are unnecessary and hence unwanted, zones are deliberately demarcated places nestled within (alien) sovereign nation-states and city territories. Above all else, autonomous zones operate through the production and maintenance of irregularity. Overlapping jurisdictions typically result in competing forms of social control and modes of regulation. They are extraterritorial places where the logic of exception suspends conventional rules and regulations and substitutes its own. The kinds of autonomous zones that have accompanied global urbanism at the start of the twenty-first century represent a new paradigm for organizing corporate enterprise and for protecting those inside from unwanted scrutiny. Like cruise ships and island paradises, autonomous zones are useful platforms for conspicuous consumption in an idyllic setting. Rather than working with a system of continuous, discrete, and exclusive sovereignties, what is happening is the emergence of a patchwork of overlapping spaces of greater or lesser degrees of rights and rightlessness, where cocooned enclaves that restrict access are juxtaposed against abject spaces of neglect and abandonment.[155]

---

[153] See, for example, Martin J. Murray, "Fire and Ice: Unnatural Disasters and the Disposable Urban Poor in Post-Apartheid Johannesburg," *International Journal of Urban and Regional Research* 33, 1 (2009), pp. 165–192.

[154] Engin Isin and Kim Rygiel, "Abject Spaces: Frontiers, Zones, Camps," in Elizabeth Dauphinee, and Cristina Masters (eds.), *The Logics of Biopower and the War on Terror: Living, Dying, Surviving* (London: Palgrave Macmillan, 2007), pp. 178–203 (esp. p. 193, 199).

[155] Isin and Rygiel, "Abject Spaces: Frontiers, Zones, Camps," p. 199.

6

Typologies of Zones

At the current phase of neoliberal globalization, three key components – private ownership of landed property and real-estate investment, organizational networks, and regulatory (or governance) regimes – have blended together to shape the (*de jure* or *de facto*) sovereign space of autonomous zones. Whatever their hybrid combinations, these components provide autonomous zones with distinct modes of discipline that enable them to establish a clear distinction between a well-governed "inside" and an unpredictable "outside." The formation of extraterritorial zones resembles what Ghazi-Walid Falah has labeled the geopolitical dynamics of "enclaving" and "exclaving."[1] Put simply, the formation of enclaves and exclaves "bears strong similarity to spatial partitioning familiar under labels such as gerrymandering, zoning and redlining when applied to discriminatory manipulation of space and its allocation for the benefit and power enhancement of a given social class or ethnic group in the population."[2] Like enclaves and exclaves that depend upon rebordering, autonomous zones represent new spatial regimes that violate conventional understandings of territorial sovereignty.[3]

---

[1] Ghazi-Walid Falah, "Dynamics and Patterns of the Shrinking of Arab Lands in Palestine," *Political Geography* 22, 2 (2003), pp. 179–209. See also Stefan Berger, "The Study of Enclaves – Some Introductory Remarks," *Geopolitics* 15, 2 (2010), pp. 312–328; and Evgeny Vinokurow, *A Theory of Enclaves* (Lanham, MD: Lexington Books 2007).

[2] Falah, "Dynamics and Patterns of the Shrinking of Arab Lands in Palestine," p. 185 (source of quotation). The spatial metaphor of exclaves refers to "small pockets of land lying outside the main territory [but] within the territory of neighboring States" [Martin Ira Glassner, *Political Geography* (New York: John Wiley, 1993), p. 69].

[3] Emmanuel Brunet-Jailly, "Theorizing Borders: An Interdisciplinary Perspective," *Geopolitics* 10, 4 (2005), pp. 633–649.

Because the zone format is subject to so many permutations and variations, it is difficult to identify a single type that can serve as a paradigmatic exemplar in spatial terms. In some instances, the zone format coincides with city boundaries (for example, Shenzhen, Songdo City, and Lavasa). As such, it lays claim to being a specific kind of city (for example, Techno-City, Eco-City, and CyberCity). In other instances, the zone is an appendage to an existing city, serving as a kind of prosthetic device with special functions and distinctive characteristics that sets it apart its surroundings. In other iterations, it is a subset of the city itself (for example, Dubai), where the urban landscape consists of the serial repetition of distinct zones. In yet others, the zone is restricted to particular functional specifications – like port facilities, warehousing, and light manufacturing.[4]

As legal instruments, zones are as diverse as there are many types. In the most extreme cases, extraterritorial zones are completely exempt from civil law and local governmental control. They are not part of the territory of the state administration that houses them: instead, they are governed by a legal entity or independent authority that can freely negotiate with corporations and foreign governmental bodies. In most instances, however, they are hybrid concoctions of exception and exemptions.[5] More specifically, the regulatory regimes governing zones are partial or, as Keller Easterling has argued, they are blended "with domestic civil law, manipulated by business to create opportunistic mixtures of international law, and sometimes adopted fully by the host nation."[6] Whatever the extraterritorial legal arrangements that operate within zones, they usually function as para-state proxies with the power to negotiate exemptions to international laws or global compacts pertaining to labor, environment, sanitation, health and safety, and human rights. What these circumstances suggest is that "they are often sites of carceral labor discipline, unsafe work practices, environmental degradation, dispossession, exploitation, and the dominance of market logics over territorial rights." More importantly, the existence of such conditions in zones cannot be attributed entirely to lax regulatory regimes in the host country. They are also the result and responsibility of the corporate enterprises that operate in these spaces and those that connect to them through global supply chains. These are often transnational corporations that are headquartered in cities far from the specific location of zones themselves.[7]

---

[4] Ideas for this paragraph are derived from a reading of Jonathan Bach, "Modernity and the Urban Imagination in Economic Zones," *Theory, Culture & Society* 28, 5 (2011), pp. 98–122 (esp. p. 102).

[5] Bach, "Modernity and the Urban Imagination in Economic Zones," p. 102.

[6] Keller Easterling, "Zone: The Spatial Softwares of Extrastatecraft," *Places: Forum of Design for the Public Realm*, June 11, 2012. Available at http://places.designobserver.com/feature/zone-the-spatial-softwares-of-extrastatecraft/34528/html.

[7] Brett Neilson, "Zones: Beyond the Logic of Exception?" *Concentric: Literary and Cultural Studies* 40, 2 (2014), pp. 11–28 (esp. p. 21, source of quotation).

Zone Typologies

The ubiquity and diversity of these autonomous zones calls for a typology of distinct types.[8] Put broadly, the zonal format "achieves its physical form along an ideal-typical continuum." While seeking to distinguish between different types of zones can be useful for analytical purposes, the existence of hybrid forms "on the ground" can easily blur these hard-and-fast distinctions. At one end of this continuum, there are temporary assemblages – what Jonathan Bach has called "modular zones" – that rely upon mobility, flexibility, and impermanence to function efficiently and effectively.[9] As a general rule, these modular zones have a particular relationship to space (usually small-scale and molecular) and time (temporary and even ephemeral). All too often, these temporary zones aspire to become permanent sites of sovereign exception. At the other end of the spectrum, there are durable "autonomous zones" that have become permanently embedded in place. In some cases, they have become literally indistinguishable from cities to the point of either dissolving their zone designation (e.g., Shenzhen) or assembling and integrating multiple mini "zone-lets" into a wider urban landscape (e.g., Dubai).[10]

Temporary encampments housing displaced persons fleeing famine, low-intensity war, and other catastrophic events epitomizes the ideal-typical imaginary of the modular zone. With so many people on the move, emergency settlement areas for temporary sojourners are emerging as perhaps the quintessential geographies of the modern condition at a time of great uncertainty.[11] As "non-communities of the excluded," refugee camps exemplify, as Zygmunt Bauman has argued, an impermanent condition symbolized by a frozen state of transience and an "ongoing, lasting state of temporariness" – denoting circumstances where past and future blend into a seemingly never-ending "permanent present."[12] Yet these provisional spaces on occasion turn the immediacy of emergency circumstances, born of exception and necessity, into permanent mutations.[13]

---

[8] See Charlie Hailey, *Camps: A Guide to 21st Century Space* (Cambridge, MA: The MIT Press, 2009).

[9] Bach, "Modernity and the Urban Imagination in Economic Zones," p. 102 (source of quotations).

[10] Bach, "Modernity and the Urban Imagination in Economic Zones," p. 102.

[11] Romola Sanyal, "Urbanizing Refuge: Interrogating Spaces of Displacement," *International Journal of Urban and Regional Research* 38, 2 (2014), pp. 558–572 (esp. p. 558).

[12] For the first quotation, see John Hyndman, *Managing Displacement: Refugees and the Politics of Humanitarianism* (Minneapolis: University of Minnesota Press, 2000), p. 183. See Zygmunt Bauman, *Society under Siege* (London: Polity, 2002), p. 114 (source of second quotation).

[13] Deborah Gans and Matthew Jelacic, "The Refugee Camp: Ecological Disaster of Today, Metropolis of Tomorrow," *Architectural Design* 74, 2 (2004), pp. 82–86; Allen Armstrong, "Evolving Approaches to Planning and Management of Refugee Settlements: the Tanzanian Experience," *Ekistics* 57, 342–343 (1990), pp. 195–204; and Peter Nyers, "Emergency or

In the scholarly literature, there is a frequent tendency to juxtapose the camp (as exception) and the city (as norm) as discrete places (and bounded spaces) in contradiction with one another. Framed in this way, "camps are thought of as mimetic spaces" that gradually appropriate urban characteristics "to become *camp-villes* or city-camps where a unique form of enduring organization of space, social life and system of power is created that exists nowhere else." In analytic terms, the problem with creating dichotomous conceptions and neat binaries to refer to such hybrid spaces, particularly in relation to refugee camps, is that these dualistic understandings are incapable of recognizing the fluidity of relationships (spatial and political) and the social agency of displaced people.[14]

Security zones, refugee camps, "tent cities," ("black ops") prison complexes, Olympic Villages, labor compounds, protest occupations, humanitarian "safe havens," and transit encampments of all kinds often begin as makeshift arrangements arising from emergency situations, but these sometimes evolve unexpectedly into "virtual cities" in their own right, that is, self-governing entities with their own rules and regulations.[15] While they may remain in a liminal state for extended periods of time, refugee camps exist at the intersections of multiple layers of governance and legality that makes them difficult to classify in any unambiguous way.[16] In short, it is necessary to theorize these provisional spaces in ways that go beyond treating them as only temporary interruptions or

Emerging Identities? Refugees and Transformations in World Order," *Millennium* 28, 1 (1999), pp. 1–26.

[14] Romola Sanyal, "Squatting in Camps: Building and Insurgency in Spaces of Refuge," *Urban Studies* 48, 5 (2011), pp. 877–890 (quotation from p. 879).

[15] See, for example, Jenny Edkins, "Sovereign Power, Zones of Indistinction, and the Camp," *Alternatives* 25, 1 (2000), pp. 3–25. See also Lindsay Weiss, "Exceptional Space: Concentration Camps and Labor Compounds in Late 19th Century Southern Africa," in Adrian Myers and Gabriel Moshenka (eds.), *Archaeologies of Internment* (New York: Springer, 2010), pp. 21–32; Rutvica Andrijasevic, "From Exception to Excess: Detention and Deportations across the Mediterranean Space," in Nicholas De Genova and Nathalie Peutz, (eds.) *The Deportation Regime: Sovereignty, Space, and the Freedom of Movement* (Durham, NC: Duke University Press, 2010) pp. 147–165; Stavros Stavrides, "Occupied Squares and the Urban 'State of Exception': In, Against and Beyond the City of Enclaves," in Estela Schindel and Pamela Colombo (eds.), *Spaces and Memories of Violence: Landscapes of Erasure, Disappearance and Exception* (New York: Palgrave Macmillan, 2014), pp. 231–243; Stuart Elden, "Spaces of Humanitarian Exception," *Geografiska Annaler B* 88, 4 (2006), 477–485; and Peter Bishop and Lesley Williams, *The Temporary City* (New York: Routledge, 2012), pp. 2–9. As Achille Mbembe has put it, the refugee camp "ceases to be a provisional place, a space of transit that is inhabited while awaiting a hypothetical return home. From the legal as well as the factual point of view, what was supposed to be an exception becomes routine and the rule within an organization of space that tends to become permanent. In these human concentrations with an extraterritorial status, veritable imaginary nations henceforth live" ("At the Edge of the World: Boundaries, Territoriality, and Sovereignty in Africa," [Trans. Steven Rendall] *Public Culture* 12, 1 (2000), pp. 259–284 (quotation from p. 270).

[16] Sanyal, "Squatting in Camps," p. 877.

unusual aberrations – or even as variants of what might be termed "emergency urbanism."[17]

Perhaps the quintessential exemplar of the gradual mutation from temporary situation into semipermanent condition are the Palestinian refugee camps that have existed for close to sixty years in Lebanon.[18] In these and other encampments, displaced persons are sometimes forced to languish in limbo for years, if not generations, while awaiting the right circumstances to "return home." Prolonged exile has often become the norm rather than the exception, thereby requiring us to "rethink" refugee spaces not simply as temporary, impermanent, "transitional settlements" that are fixed within the neat and bounded geographies, but perhaps as evolving spaces that resemble embryonic cities, cities-in-formation, or stunted cities not-yet-made, thereby constituting a kind of unfinished, frustrated urbanization.[19]

As a distinct type of rule, "modularity" – the driving force behind the formation of modular zones – seeks frictionless disentanglement and withdrawal from existing regulatory regimes. The architecture of modularity tends not toward "external standardization" and engagement with the social world that surrounds them, but rather "internal self-containment." Modular zones seek above to remain detached from the place in which they happen to find themselves. Understood in this way, the practice of modularity creates the conditions for modular zones that are malleable, "mobile, without foundation, impermanent, and disposable or reusable elsewhere."[20] As exemplars of contested geographies, modular zones have precarious and unstable boundaries.[21]

Modular zones are discontinuous territorial fragments that are set apart from the world around them. They tend to be mobile and transient, protected by makeshift barriers, provisional boundaries, or largely invisible security apparatuses. Modular zones are largely the result of a variety of corrosive processes

---

[17] This term is taken from Sanyal, "Urbanizing Refuge," p. 561, who in turn borrows it from Jim Lewis, "Phenomenon: The Exigent City," *The New York Times Magazine*, June 8, 2008. Available at www.nytimes.com/2008/06/08/magazine/08wwln-urbanism-t.html.

[18] Hassan Ismae'l Sheikh, "An Urbanity of Exile: Palestinian Refugee Camps," *A10: New European Architecture* 27 (2009), pp. 60–62; Julie Peteet, *Landscape of Hope and Despair: Palestinian Refugee Camps* (Philadelphia: University of Pennsylvania Press, 2009); Sari Hanafi, "Palestinian Refugee Camps in Lebanon As a Space of Exception," *REVUE Asylon(s)* N°5 (2008), [n.p.]; and Diana Martin, "From Spaces of Exception to 'Campscapes': Palestinian Refugee Camps and Informal Settlements in Beirut," *Political Geography* 44 (2015), pp. 9–18.

[19] Michel Agier, "Between War and City: Towards an Urban Anthropology of Refugee Camps," *Ethnography* 3, 3 (2002), pp. 319–341 (esp. pp. 336–337). See also Liisa Malkki, "News from Nowhere: Mass Displacement and Globalized 'Problems of Organization'," *Ethnography* 3, 3 (2002), pp. 351–360.

[20] Hannah Appel, "Offshore Work: Oil, Modularity, and the How of Capitalism in Equatorial Guinea," *American Ethnologist* 39, 4 (2012), pp. 692–709 (quotations from pp. 697, 698). See also Andrew Barry, "Technological Zones," *European Journal of Social Theory* 9, 2 (2006), pp. 239–253.

[21] Gabriel Giorgi and Karen Pinkus, "Zones of Exception: Biopolitical Territories in the Neoliberal Era," *Diacritics* 36, 2 (2006), pp. 99–108 (esp. p. 99).

that have caused the splintering of preexisting political surfaces and boundaries. They are extraterritorial because they are positioned outside of the sovereignty and jurisdiction that surrounds them.[22]

Like offshore resource platforms and mining concessions temporarily staged for the extraction of raw materials, modular zones resemble mobile capsules that cultivate few if any enduring ties with their local environment. This lack of attachment to place them gives them a great deal of room for maneuver.[23] Their impermanence can sometimes provide these transient places with claims to legitimacy. These kinds of makeshift experiments with modularity range from confined spaces like military bases and embassies, to spaces of confinement and quarantine like clandestine prisons and detention facilities.[24] These modular zones tend to reference exceptional sites – liminal places where conventional rules do not apply or laws are suspended.[25] They are places where sovereignty is contested, undermined, evaded, called into question, or – conversely – asserted more strenuously.[26] Modular zones operate at the blurry intersection between territoriality and legality, thereby giving rise to all sorts of paradoxes regarding legal status, jurisdiction, and the intensification of precarity.[27] Benefitting from the "resourcefulness of jurisdiction," they offer unique opportunities to experiment with novel and idiosyncratic forms of governance that are both a

---

[22] See Eyal Weizman, "On Extraterritoriality." Lecture at the symposium "Archipelago of Exception. Sovereignties of Extraterritoriality," November 10–11, 2005. Available at www .publicspace.org/en/text-library/eng/bo11-on-extraterritoriality. See also Anselm Franke and Eyal Weizman, *Territories: Islands, Camps and Other States of Utopia* (Berlin and Cologne: Kunst Werke and Walter Koenig Press, 2003).

[23] See Pádraig Carmody, "Cruciform Sovereignty, Matrix Governance and the Scramble for Africa's Oil: Insights from Chad and Sudan," *Political Geography* 28, 6 (2009), pp. 353–361.

[24] Sasha Davis, "The U.S. Military Base Network and Contemporary Colonialism: Power Projection, Resistance and the Quest for Operational Unilateralism," *Political Geography* 30, 4 (2011), pp. 215–224; Rachel Woodward, "Military Landscapes: Agendas and Approaches for Future Research," *Progress in Human Geography* 38, 1 (2014), pp. 40–61. For prisons, see Derek Gregory, "The Black Flag: Guantanamo Bay and the Space of Exception," *Geografiska Annaler* 88, 4 (2006), pp. 405–427; Derek Gregory, "Vanishing Points: Law, Violence, and Exception in the Global War Prison," in Derek Gregory and Alan Pred (eds.), *Violent Geographies: Fear, Terror, and Political Violence* (New York: Routledge, 2007), pp. 205–236; Simon Reid-Henry, "Exceptional Sovereignty? Guantanamo Bay and the Re-colonial Present," *Antipode* 39, 4 (2007), pp. 627–648; James Sidaway, "'One Island, One Team, One Mission': Geopolitics, Sovereignty, 'Race' and Rendition," *Geopolitics* 15, 4 (2010), pp. 667–683; Lauren Martin and Matthew Mitchelson, "Geographies of Detention and Imprisonment: Interrogating Spatial Practices of Confinement, Discipline, Law, and State Power," *Geography Compass* 3, 1 (2009): 459–477; and Nicholas Mirzoeff, "The Empire of Camps," *Situation Analysis* 1 (2002), pp. 20–25.

[25] Stuart Elden, *Terror and Territory: The Spatial Extent of Sovereignty* (Minneapolis: University of Minnesota Press, 2009).

[26] Alison Mountz, "Political Geography I: Reconfiguring Geographies of Sovereignty," *Progress in Human Geography* 37, 6 (2013), pp. 829–841 (esp. p. 832).

[27] Mathew Coleman, "Immigration Geopolitics beyond the Mexico-U.S. Border," *Antipode* 38, 1 (2007), pp. 54–76; and Alison Mountz, "The Enforcement Archipelago: Detention, Haunting, and Asylum on Islands," *Political Geography* 30, 3 (2011), pp. 118–128.

part of, and apart from, national boundaries. Through zoning, niching, out-bordering, insulating, quarantining, unbundling, dislocating, and offshoring, modular zones are jurisdictional enclaves often at the forefront of efforts at pioneering some of the most inventive – and shadowy – forms of sovereignty and governance in the modern world.[28]

Floating Cities: Nomadic Offshore Urbanism

One particularly intriguing venture that perhaps epitomizes the ideal "modular zone" is the promotion of extraterritorial "floating cities," or island-like "seast-eads," that operate offshore in international waters. The lynchpin of these imag-ined places is the idea of popular sovereignty and self-rule. In the utopian fan-tasy world of anarcho-libertarians, "seasteading" refers to the establishment of permanent "off-world" settlements living at sea – self-governing colonies that are located outside the auspices and juridical reach of established governing bodies and sovereign nation-states. In a real sense, these *flotilla fiefdoms* repre-sent the geographical extension of artificial islands located closer to shore.[29] The seasteading movement promotes their visionary *faux*-island schemes as experiments in libertarian utopian living – self-sustaining communities of indi-vidualists who can rage against the state machine.[30] Like artificially constructed island spaces, floating cities hold out the promise of transforming "the bland-ness or failures of the *status quo* by making the contemporary even more up-to-date and cutting edge."[31]

"Islomania," or the fascination (or some might say even an obsession) with islands, has long and deep roots in the European cultural imagination.[32] For

---

[28] See Godfrey Baldacchino, *Island Enclaves: Offshoring Strategies, Creative Governance, and Subnational Island Jurisdictions* (Montreal: McGill-Queen's Press-MQUP, 2010), pp. xxi–xxii (p. xxvi, source of quotation). See also Godfrey Baldacchino and David Milne (eds.), *Lessons from the Political Economy of Small Islands: The Resourcefulness of Jurisdiction* (New York: Palgrave Macmillan, 2010).

[29] Philip Steinberg, Elizabeth Nyman, and Mauro Caraccioli, "Atlas Swam: Freedom, Capital, and Floating Sovereignties in the Seasteading Vision," *Antipode* 44, 4 (2012), pp. 1532–1550.

[30] Joe Lonsdale and Peter Thiel, two successful venture capitalists and hedge fund managers behind the influential online businesses Facebook and PayPal, launched the *Seasteading Institute* (TSI), whose stated mission it is to "establish permanent, autonomous ocean communities to enable experimentation and innovation with diverse social, political, and legal systems." The institute explicitly invokes an escapist rhetoric of withdrawal "because the world needs a new frontier, a place where those who are dissatisfied with our current civilization can go to build a different (and hopefully better) one." [Quoted in Mark Jackson and Veronica della Dora, "'Dreams so big only the Sea can hold Them': Man-made Islands as Anxious Spaces, Cultural Icons, and Travelling Visions," *Environment and Planning A* 41, 9 (2009), pp. 2086–2104 (quotation from p. 2100).

[31] Jackson and della Dora, "'Dreams so big only the Sea can hold Them'," p. 2100 (source of quotation).

[32] The term 'islomania' was coined for contemporary use by Lawrence Durrell in *Reflections on a Maritime Venus* (Mount Jackson, VA: Axios Press, 1953). Vanessa Smith and Ron Edmond,

centuries, islands have been identified in European discourses as places of simplicity, carefree innocence, peaceful coexistence, and abundant bounty. They
resemble "a blank canvas, on which solitary, independent individuals can paint
whatever they desire most." As such, utopian discourses idealize the island "as
the perfect site for autonomous actors to exert their freedom as they try out
new ideas."[33] Swept away from the problems of the real world, island living is
inundated with Edenic imaginings and Arcadian and Picturesque imagery without the corrupting influence of the modern world.[34] Islands are often regarded
as eccentric anachronisms, the "scattered remnants" of old colonial empires,
retrofitted to conform to a variety of contemporary purposes. Among other
things, islands can be exotic "get-away" tourist destinations, wildlife sanctuaries, vacation sites, nature preserves, military bases, and isolated scientific
research stations.[35] Dreamers and schemers have long drawn on utopian fantasies of colonizing marine and island spaces as models for idealized libertarian commonwealths. Like the Garden of Eden, island-like settlements signify
a finite, concentrated world, complete in and of themselves with fixed boundaries and territorial integrity. "Floating cities" are material spaces for enclave
escapism that operate on a double register: utopian dreamscapes of communitarian self-governance combined with cynical retreat from unwanted "Big
Government."[36] These artificially constructed landforms combine principles

"Introduction," in Vanessa Smith and Ron Edmond (eds.), *Islands in History and Representa-
tion* (London: Routledge, 2003), pp. 1–18; John Gillis, *Islands of the Mind: How the Human
Imagination Created the Atlantic World* (New York: Palgrave Macmillan, 2004); Françoise
Peron, "The Contemporary Lure of the Island," *Tijdschrift voor Economische en Sociale
Geografie* 95, 3 (2004), pp. 326–339; Timothy Beatley, *Blue Urbanism: Exploring Connections
between Cities and Oceans* (Washington, DC: Island Press, 2014); David Lowenthal, "Islands,
Lovers, and Others," *The Geographical Review* 97 (2007), pp. 202–229; T. G. Baum, "The Fas-
cination of Islands: The Tourist Perspective," in Douglas Lockhart and Daivd Drakakis-Smith
(eds.), *Island Tourism: Problems and Perspectives* (London: Pinter, 1996), pp. 21–35; Russell
King, "The Geographical Fascination of Islands," in Douglas Lockhart, David Drakakis-Smith,
John Schembri (eds.), *The Development Process in Small Island States* (London: Routledge,
1993), 13–37; and Klaus Dodds and Stephen Royle, "Introduction: Rethinking Islands," *Journal of Historical Geography* 29, 4 (2003), pp. 487–498.

[33] Steinberg, Nyman, and Caraccioli, "Atlas Swam," p. 1534 (source of both quotations).

[34] Alexander Hugo Schulenburg, "'Island of the Blessed': Eden, Arcadia, and the Picturesque in
the Textualizing of St Helena," *Journal of Historical Geography* 29, 4 (2003), pp. 535–553.

[35] Peter Noland, "Imperial Archipelagos: China, Western Colonialism and the Law of the Sea,"
New Left Review 80 (2013), pp. 77–95. See also Philip Steinberg, *The Social Construction
of the Ocean* (Cambridge: Cambridge University Press, 2001); Philip Steinberg, "Insularity,
Sovereignty and Statehood: The Representation of Islands on Portolan Charts and the Con-
struction of the Territorial State," *Geographiska Annaler* 87, 4 (2005), pp. 253–265; Philip
Steinberg, "Sovereignty, Territory, and the Mapping of Mobility: A View from the Outside,"
Annals of the Association of American Geographers 99, 3 (2009), pp. 467–495; and Philip
Steinberg, "The Deepwater Horizon, the Mavi Marmara, and the Dynamic Zonation of Ocean
Space," *Geographical Journal* 177, 1 (2011), pp. 12–16.

[36] Patri Friedman and Brad Taylor, "Seasteading: Competitive Governments on the Ocean," *Kyklos* 65, 2 (2012), pp. 218–235.

of both seasteading and instant "start-up cities" built holistically from scratch. A plethora of visionary schemes like Charter Cities, StartUp Cities, Free Zones, and Seasteading have appropriated and reappropriated this utopic tradition that combines individualist (entrepreneurial) self-reliance and "anti-statist" self-governance.[37]

The seasteading movement seeks to "further the establishment and growth of permanent, autonomous ocean communities [by] enabling innovations with new political and social systems" on semistationary, floating platforms.[38] A hybrid mixture of ideologies, including techno-optimism, libertarian secession theories, and strains of anarcho-capitalism, have fueled the seasteading movement. The proponents of extraterritorial "floating cities" have promoted these offshore platforms as the newest frontier in creative thinking, entrepreneurial enterprise, and social engineering. For free-market libertarians, seasteads represent insular and uncorrupted city-states where free-market capitalism can regain its original energy and where the spirit of individual entrepreneurship can flourish without burden or hindrance.[39]

A host of modern-day visionaries have sought to apply engineering prowess and technical expertise in ways that join the heterotopia of the oceangoing cruise ship with the historic idealization of the island, enabling permanent habitation in the "free medium" of the sea.[40] For these political idealists, the island utopia is less an escape and retreat than the forward wedge and harbinger of a wider political project.[41] According to its libertarian promoters, seasteading offers a platform through which to test for the viability of private-property anarchism or anarcho-capitalism, at least in their nascent forms.[42] As

---

[37] Parag Khanna, "Beyond City Limits," *Foreign Policy* (August 16, 2010), pp. 120–123 and 126–128; Michael Strong and Robert Himber, "The Legal Autonomy of the Dubai International Financial Centre: A Scalable Strategy for Global Free-Market Reforms," *Economic Affairs* 29, 2 (2009), pp. 36–41; Elizabeth Nyman, "Island Exceptionalism and International Maritime Conflicts," *The Professional Geographer* 65, 2 (2013), pp. 221–229; and Jackson and della Dora, "'Dreams so big only the Sea can hold Them'," pp. 2086–2104.

[38] Jackson and della Dora, "'Dreams so Big only the Sea can hold Them'," p. 2100 (source of quotation). See Patri Friedman and Brad Taylor, "Seasteading: Institutional Innovation on the Open Ocean" (Paper presented at the Australasian Public Choice Society Conference, December 9–10, 2010, University of Canterbury, Christchurch, New Zealand), Seasteading Institute, December 2010.

[39] Steinberg, Nyman, and Caraccioli, "Atlas Swam," p. 1533, 1535.

[40] Kent Keith, "Floating Cities: A New Challenge for Transnational Law," *Marine Policy* 1, 3 (1977), pp. 190–204; and Philip Steinberg, "Liquid Urbanity: Re-engineering the City in a Post-Terrestrial World," in Stanley Brunn (ed.), *Engineering the Earth: The Impacts of Mega-Engineering Projects* (Berlin: Springer 2011), pp. 2113–2122.

[41] Steinberg, Nyman, and Caraccioli, "Atlas Swam," p. 1535.

[42] "Developing the technology to create settlements in international waters, which we refer to as seasteading, changes the technological environment rather than attempting to push against the incentives of existing political systems. As such, it sidesteps the problem of reform and is more likely than more conventional approaches to significantly alter the policy equilibrium" (Friedman and Taylor, "Seasteading: Competitive Governments on the Ocean," p. 235).

self-governing mini-states, floating cities are the perfect laboratories to experiment with new forms of urban governance. From the libertarian perspective, seasteads mean freedom from taxes and the oppressive imposition of burdensome regulation, plus the ability to pursue enterprises that would not be possible onshore. These self-governing ocean-colonies enable residents to avoid unnecessary public bureaucracy or unwanted oversight.[43] Seasteads are offshore places where, as their proponents contend, "profit-seeking entrepreneurs" are able to "establish permanent settlements with the power to set their own rules."[44]

Miniature maritime prototypes that resemble functioning seasteads already exist. The offshore island-world of the United Arab Emirates (UAE) exemplifies this archipelago-enclave model that blends extraterritorial immunity with complete social programming and physical security-isolation. In what Pernilla Ouis has insightfully called "modernizing nature – naturalizing modernity," the seven mini-states that constitute the UAE began in the 1990s to construct artificial islands built on reclaimed land in close proximity to the shoreline.[45] This practice of the mega-engineering of *faux* islands started with the larger Emirates, but quickly spread to the coastal areas of the smaller and poorer northern shiekhdoms.[46] With its assorted jumbo-size ephemera (including fantasy theme parks and indoor sky slopes), Dubai has become the "global icon of imagineered urbanism."[47] In Dubai, the island-state of Burj Al Arab is a small artificial island connected to the mainland via a private curving bridge – a kind of umbilical cord that tethers a cloned offspring to the mothership. Its ultramodern urban landscape includes the iconic Burj Al Arab (seven-star) Hotel, soaring to a height of 210 meters, and is designed to mimic the sail of a floating ship. The *Jumeira* Islands, an archipelago of fifty artificial islands built in such odd shapes as palm trees and whole world maps, combine what Heiko Schmid has called a libertine, playful "economy of fascination" with the tight access

---

43 Jon White, "Floating Cities could redefine Human Existence," *New Scientist* 215/2883 (September 22, 2012), pp. 26–27.

44 Friedman and Taylor, "Seasteading: Competitive Governments on the Ocean," p. 224 (source of quotation).

45 Pernilla Ouis, "Engineering the Emirates: The Evolution of a New Environment," in Stanley Brunn (ed.), *Engineering Earth: The Impacts of Megaengineering Projects* (Amsterdam: Springer Netherlands, 2011), pp. 1409–1423 (p. 1409, source of quotation); and Pernilla Ouis, "'And an Island Never Cries': Cultural and Societal Perspectives on the Mega Development of Islands in the United Arab Emirates," in Viorel Badescu and Richard Cathcart (eds.), *Macroengineering Seawater in Unique Environments* (Berlin Heidelberg: Springer, 2011), pp. 59–75.

46 Ouis, "Engineering the Emirates," pp. 1409–1423; and Pernilla Ouis, "'Greening the Emirates': The Modern Construction of Nature in the United Arab Emirates," *Cultural Geographies* 9, 3 (2002), 334–347.

47 Mike Davis, "Fear and Money in Dubai," *New Left Review* 41 (2006), pp. 47–68 (quotation from p. 47); Richard Smith, "Dubai in Extremis," *Theory, Culture & Society* 31, 7–8 (2014), pp. 291–296; and Martin Hvidt, "Public–Private Ties and their Contribution to Development: The Case of Dubai," *Middle Eastern Studies* 43, 4 (2007), pp. 557–577.

controls of gated residential estates.[48] The instantly recognizable, palm-shaped island called Palm Jumeirah (with its frond-like extensions surrounded by a eleven-kilometer protective breakwater) is an offshore extension of Dubai that has attracted a great deal of international attention as a luxury "get-away" for the super-rich.[49] These fantasy "paradise islands" are linked by a causeway to a "Miami-like beachfront crammed with mega-hotels, apartment skyscrapers and yachting marinas."[50] The *faux* mini-state of Burj Al Arab, less than one thousand feet offshore, marks a departure from the conventional regulatory frameworks.[51] This artificial maritime redoubt was the first experimental laboratory for testing "the potential of *offshore urbanism*: [a separated territory] with its own sovereignty, its own laws," and its own internally consistent regulatory frameworks, where excessive spectacle is a kind of performance art. Burj Al Arab is an exemplary expression of "the conciliatory and pragmatic attitude of the Emirate," in which conservative Islam (with its pious religiosity with draconian sociocultural restrictions) coexists with radical "free market" capitalism (where virtually "anything goes" and foreign nationals can buy property on freehold ownership).[52]

In the same vein, Philip Steinberg has explored three examples of mega-engineering advances that enable settlements to span the land-water divide: *Maasbommel*, a residential community of floating houses in The Netherlands; *The World*, a permanent residency condominium cruise ship; and *SeaCode*, a proposed floating laboratory for computer engineers.[53] For centuries, the nomadic boat people of Southeast Asia have lived an itinerant life hunting and gathering in and around the ocean. These so-called "sea gypsies" around Thailand, Myanmar, Malaysia, the Philippines, and Indonesia have lived entirely on their boats and have come ashore only to trade, repair their boats, and gather

---

[48] Heiko Schmid, "Economy of Fascination: Dubai and Las Vegas as Examples of Themed Urban Landscapes [Ökonomie der Faszination: Dubai und Las Vegas als Beispiele thematisch inszenierter Stadtlandschaften]," *Erdkunde* 60, 4 (2006), pp. 346–361 (p. 346, source of quotation).

[49] Allessandro Petti, "Dubai Offshore Urbanism," in Michiel Dehaene and Lieven De Cauter (eds.), *Heterotopia and the City: Public Space in a Postcivil Society* (New York: Routledge, 2008), pp. 287–296; Jackson and della Dora, "'Dreams so big only the Sea can hold Them'," pp. 2086–2104; and Christian Steiner, "From Heritage to Hyper-reality? Tourism Destination Development in the Middle East between Petra and the Palm," *Journal of Tourism and Cultural Change* 8, 4 (2010), pp. 240–253.

[50] Davis, "Fear and Money in Dubai," p. 47 (source of quotation).

[51] Yasser Elsheshtawy, "Redrawing Boundaries, Dubai an Emerging Global City," in Yasser Elsheshtawy (ed.), *Planning Middle Eastern Cities: An Urban Kaleidoscope* (New York: Routledge, 2004), pp. 169–199.

[52] Petti, "Dubai Offshore Urbanism," in *Heterotopia and the City: Public Space in a Postcivil Society*, pp. 287–296 (quotations from p. 288).

[53] Steinberg, "Liquid Urbanity," in *Engineering the Earth*, pp. 2113–2122; and Roland Atkinson and Sarah Blandy, "A Picture of the Floating World: Grounding the Secessionary Affluence of the Residential Cruise Liner," *Antipode* 41, 1 (2009), pp. 92–110.

materials from seaside jungles that the ocean did not provide.[54] Giant cruise liners carry thousands of guests on lengthy voyages in luxurious surroundings. Offshore oil platforms provide floating accommodation for hundreds of workers amid harsh weather and dangerous conditions. The Principality of Sealand, a concrete sea fort constructed off the Suffolk coast of Great Britain during World War II, is occupied by a family who has introduced various lawsuits to try to get the artificial island recognized as a sovereign state.[55] Each of these examples, however, falls some way short of the permanent, self-governing and radically innovative ocean-based colonies imagined by the seasteaders. To realize their utopian dreams, they must overcome a host of tricky technical, legal, and cultural problems. They must work out how to build seasteads in the first place. They must discover a way to escape the legal shackles of sovereign states. Finally, they must give people sufficient reason to inhabit their floating cities.[56]

Although seasteading is a highly speculative, and perhaps an impractical if not utterly impossible project, the thinking behind the establishment of permanent, autonomous ocean settlements, or self-actualizing communities of aggregated individuals, reflects efforts to resolve contradictions within capitalism: between, on the one hand, the need for predictable order and planning, and, on the other hand, the desire to foster personal freedoms and enable self-actualizing entrepreneurship. As a general rule, this tension often enters mainstream discourse through ideological constructs that combine "adherence to classical liberal ideals about individual entrepreneurship with hostility toward government intervention."[57] Schemes such as Charter Cities, StartUp Cities, Voluntary Cities, Free Zones, and the Seasteading movement share a common belief in "the seemingly paradoxical ideal" that individual freedom and self-determination can only be fostered through the deliberate engineering and rational ordering of a carefully planned, insular environment.[58]

Contemporary modular zones can assume a variety of forms and shapes. Their distinctive capacity is their malleability, that is, their ability to adjust to changing circumstances. Visionary models for social transformation are no longer aimed at the broad canvass of social life, but they take shape as small

---

54 Clifford Sather, *The Bajau Laut: Adaptation, History, and Fate in a Maritime Fishing Society of Southeastern Sabah* (Oxford: Oxford University Press, 1997); David Sopher, *The Sea Nomads: A Study of the Maritime Boat People of Southeast Asia* (Singapore: National Museum Press, 1977); and Ismail Ali, "Since Birth Till Death, What is their Status: A Case Study of the Sea Bajau in Pulau Mabulo, Semporna," *Journal of Arts Science & Commerce* 1, 1 (2010), pp. 156–166.

55 China Miéville, "Floating Utopias," in Mike Davis and Daniel Bertrand Monk (eds.), *Evil Paradises: Dreamworlds of Neoliberalism* (New York: New Press, 2008), pp. 251–261.

56 Patri Friedman, a former Google software engineer who is grandson of famed economist Milton Friedman and son of even more radical economic theorist David Friedman, founded the Seasteading Institute in 2010. See Jessa Gamble, "Has the Time Come for Floating Cities?" *The Guardian*, March 18, 2014.

57 Steinberg, Nyman, and Caraccioli, "Atlas Swam," p. 150 (source of quotation).

58 Steinberg, Nyman, and Caraccioli, "Atlas Swam," p. 1550.

secessions from the larger social order of things. The mystic anarchist Hakim Bey (his real name is Peter Lamborn Wilson) used the analogy of eighteenth-century "pirate utopias" to evoke an image of what he called the Temporary Autonomous Zone (TAZ). Turning away from modern utopianism and the grand idea of social revolution, and taking cues from the celebration of nomadism (Deleuze and Guattari), Bey explored the potential of miniature enclaves, impromptu gatherings, and small groups to create and sustain temporary alternatives to the impersonal and hierarchical social order that he so distained.[59] His overall aim was to highlight indeterminate zones existing within late capitalism, "everyday occurrences that refuse, whether by accident or design, to be incorporated into dominant narratives." These enclaves can take a variety of ephemeral and sometimes mobile forms, ranging from annual festivals to temporary occupations of public squares. They can also exist for longer periods of time – as long as they remain out of sight of state regulation.[60]

The mark of *de jure* territorial sovereignty is the capacity to establish the rule of law and enforce compliance. Seen in this light, the high seas, transoceanic shipping, the seashore, and airspace are quintessential embodiments of non-sovereign spaces, existing in a kind of legal limbo or state of exception. It is here where legal conundrums abound and where jurisdiction is highly contested. These nonsovereign spaces constitute awkward geopolitical geographies that are difficult to classify in conventional terms.[61]

As a general rule, the travel, leisure, and tourism industries have gone a long way toward carving out completely privatized enclaves for tourist consumption in exotic places around the world. The privatization of these enclosed spaces depends upon the subordination of land and resource management, labor relations, and the provision services and infrastructure to regulatory regimes entirely in private hands. What perhaps best exemplifies the creation of entirely private space are pleasure cruises on oceangoing vessels traveling to the Caribbean, the Mediterranean, and the Adriatic coastline.[62]

---

[59] Hakim Bey, *T. A. Z. The Temporary Autonomous Zone, Ontological Anarchy, Poetic Terrorism* (Brooklyn, NY: Autonomedia, 1991), pp. 95–134. See also Gilles Deleuze and Félix Guattari, *A Thousand Plateaus: Capitalism and Schizophrenia* (Minneapolis: University of Minnesota Press, 1987).

[60] See Simon Sellars, "Hakim Bey: Repopulating the Temporary Autonomous Zone," *Journal for the Study of Radicalism* 4, 2 (2010), pp. 83–108 (quotation from p. 84).

[61] Noland, "Imperial Archipelagos," pp. 77–95. See A. Clair Cutler, *Private Power and Global Authority: Transnational Merchant Law and the Global Political Economy* (Cambridge: Cambridge University Press, 2003).

[62] Paul Wilkinson, "Caribbean Cruise Tourism: Delusion? Illusion?" *Tourism Geographies: An International Journal of Tourism Space, Place and Environment* 1, 3 (1999), pp. 261–282; Adam Weaver, "Spaces of Containment and Revenue Capture: 'Super-Sized' Cruise Ships as Mobile Tourism Enclaves," *Tourism Geographies: An International Journal of Tourism Space, Place and Environment* 7, 2 (2005), pp. 165–184; Robert Wood, "Caribbean Cruise Tourism: Globalization at Sea," *Annals of Tourism Research* 27, 2 (2000), pp. 345–370; Adam Weaver, "The McDonaldization Thesis and Cruise Tourism," *Annals of Tourism Research* 32, 2 (2005),

Offshore Resource Platforms and Onshore Concessionary Sites

Semipermanent production platforms like offshore oil rigs, oceangoing fish-processing vessels, and transoceanic supertankers also constitute a distinct kind of modular zone. These mobile production units can be easily moved to other locations to accommodate market conditions of supply and demand. In the contemporary age of globalization, they function as convenient laboratories for political engineering and entrepreneurial experimentation.[63] The "flag of convenience" (FOC) system of ship registration globalized labor markets in maritime shipping by providing a legal excuse enabling corporate ship-owners to create offshore "spaces of exception."[64] Similarly, offshore financial centers effectively commodify sovereignty by creating mechanisms for tax avoidance, and questionable business dealings, money laundering, and facilitating the unrestricted movement of footloose capital.[65]

Yet what distinguishes "extraction enclaves" from highly mobile modular zones is that they have to be located only where commodified resources can be found.[66] This dependence on place – or "spatial fix" – sets limits on the room for maneuver for mineral-extraction enterprises engaged not only in the production of commodities but also the protection of their assets. These place-based enclaves of mineral extractive investment represent an important contemporary manifestation of intensified processes and patterns of uneven spatial development that have come into existence alongside the wider proliferation of export processing zones, gated residential estates, sequestered tourist resorts, and enclosed shopping malls.[67] Offshore oil concessions, for example, demarcate territorial units "allocated for the extraction of wealth [from the

---

pp. 346–366; and George Foster, "South Seas Cruise a Case Study of a Short-lived Society," *Annals of Tourism Research* 13, 2 (1986), pp. 215–238.

[63] See Godfrey Baldacchino, "Islands and the Offshoring Possibilities and Strategies of Contemporary States: Insights on/for the Migration Phenomenon on Europe's Southern Flank," *Island Studies Journal* 9, 1 (2014), pp. 57–68.

[64] Nathan Lillie, "Bringing the Offshore Ashore: Transnational Production, Industrial Relations and the Reconfiguration of Sovereignty," *International Studies Quarterly* 54, 3 (2010), pp. 683–704 (esp. p. 689).

[65] See, for example, William Vlcek, "Behind an Offshore Mask: Sovereignty Games in the Global Political Economy," *Third World Quarterly* 30, 8 (2009), pp. 1465–1481; Ronen Palan, "Tax Havens and the Commercialization of State Sovereignty," *International Organization* 56, 1 (2002), pp. 151–176; John Urry, *Offshoring* (Malden, MA: Polity Press, 2014); William Brittain-Catlin, *Offshore: The Dark Side of the Global Economy* (New York: Picador, 2005); and Jason Sharman, "Offshore and the New International Political Economy," *Review of International Political Economy* 17, 1 (2010), pp. 1–19.

[66] James Ferguson, "Seeing Like an Oil Company: Space, Security, and Global Capital in Neoliberal Africa," *American Anthropologist* 107, 3 (2005), 377–382. See also Neerag Bhatia, "Introduction: Floating Frontiers," in Neeraj Bhatia and Mary Casper (eds.), *The Petropolis of Tomorrow* (New York: Actar, 2013), pp. 12–19.

[67] See, for example, Joshua Kirshner and Marcus Power, "Mining and Extractive Urbanism: Postdevelopment in a Mozambican Boomtown," *Geoforum* 61 (2015), pp. 67–78 (esp. p. 70).

sea floor] in the form of raw materials." The singular image of the isolated oil platform has typically dominated the narrative construction of the energy extractive industry, "both as an icon of technological progress and as a site of postoperational ecological reclamation, punctured throughout by the occasional though obsessive media events of operational failures."[68] Yet rather than isolated objects floating in the wilderness-like sea, oil production platforms are more appropriately understood as nodes in an expansive network of offshore logistics devoted to resource extraction. In this sense, oil rigs are not insular technological objects but rather the most visible expression of the territorial imperative that links the gridded concessionary field of oil blocks with the mainland political structures which regulate the offshore proprietary regime.[69]

The world's first offshore oil platform was built in the Caspian Sea, off the coast from the city of Baku in 1947. What began as the single route to a drilling site 35 kilometers from shore became *Neft Daşlari*, or the *Oil Rocks*, a fully functional town constructed above the sea. With a population of 5,000 workers and overseers, the city was comprised of more than 200 kilometers of bridges joining a network of artificially created "hub islands" that spanned an area of approximately seven hectares.[70] While its importance declined in the 1990s, the *Oil Rocks* has recently experienced a renaissance due to expanded oil exploitation.[71]

On a broader scale, it is often the *permanence* of the infrastructures that extraction processes require, often in isolated or remote areas, which give rise to the production urban settlements that acquire an "afterlife" in the shadow of resource depletion. The appropriation and adaption of extraction sites and their gradual transformation into new urban outposts have taken the form of what Filipe Correa has called the "postoil city." In this sense, production platforms become prototypes for microcities where logistics and infrastructure required for resource extrication operate as the skeletal underbelly for new cities. As Felipe Correa has put it, "The metrics of the oil camp have become the template for a new type of postoil city," one that is a direct spinoff of the oil production process itself.[72]

Positioned outside of the sovereignty and jurisdiction that surrounds them, enclaves of mineral extraction function as extraterritorial entities. Such discrete extraterritorial zones are spatial expressions of the rollout of a series of "states of exception." For Hannah Appel, the offshore enclave is a framing device, a site of intentional disengagement, on behalf of which resource-extraction companies do a great deal of work not only to extricate the production of

---

[68] See Rania Ghosn, "The Expansion of the Extractive Territory," in *The Petropolis of Tomorrow*, pp. 228–237 (quotations from pp. 233, 232).

[69] Ghosn, "The Expansion of the Extractive Territory," pp. 229, 233, 237.

[70] Maya Pryzbylski, "Re-Rigging Transborder Logics across the Bounded Site," in *The Petropolis of Tomorrow*, pp. 258–271 (esp. 260).

[71] Alex Webb, "Oil Rocks," in *The Petropolis of Tomorrow*, pp. 192–223.

[72] Felipe Correa, "Forward: Alternative Post-Oil Cities," in *The Petropolis of Tomorrow*, pp. 8–9.

profit from the place in which it happens to find itself, but also to structure risk, liability, and responsibility in such a way that corporate enterprises can seem to remove themselves from local social, legal, political, and environmental entanglements.[73] These are work-intensive efforts designed to create juridical and even geographic spaces in which corporate enterprises can abide by their own rules, import their own technologies, infrastructures, standardized procedures, labor regimes, legal guidelines, forms of expertise, and people – laborers, lawyers, technicians, consulting firms, specialist experts, and managers.[74] These kinds of offshore boundary-making projects allow large-scale, resource-extraction companies to bemoan poverty, pollution, instability, and kleptocracy beyond their borders, "as if they have nothing to do with it, while they work furiously to disentangle their operations, residential footprints, corporate practices, legal presence, shareholder value, and moral identities from life 'outside their walls.'"[75]

As Appel has argued, "offshore" is not an *a priori* given in the order of things, either as a distinct geographic location, or as a particular industrial site, or even as an evocative metaphor of "placeless economic interaction."[76] Rather, "the offshore" is a social construction that is deliberately "brought into being, sustained, or allowed to wither away [through] common, day-to-day socio-material practices."[77] The phenomena of "offshore" is linked with the existence and development of extraterritorial spatial jurisdictions beyond the reach of "onshore" regulatory authorities. It is in this sense that "offshore" entails the reworking of sovereignty, or more precisely, the "unbundling of sovereignty."[78]

---

[73] Appel, "Offshore Work: Oil, Modularity, and the How of Capitalism in Equatorial Guinea," p. 693. See also Suzana Sawyer, "Commentary: The Corporation, Oil, and the Financialization of Risk," *American Ethnologist* 39, 4 (2012), pp. 710–715.

[74] Appel, "Offshore Work: Oil, Modularity, and the How of Capitalism in Equatorial Guinea," pp. 693, 697, 702. See also Anna Zalik, "Zones of Exclusion: Offshore Extraction, the Contestation of Space and Physical Displacement in the Nigerian Delta and the Mexican Gulf," *Antipode* 41, 3 (2009), pp. 557–582.

[75] Appel, "Offshore Work: Oil, Modularity, and the How of Capitalism in Equatorial Guinea," p. 694 (source of quotation). See also Abigail Ackah-Baidoo, "Enclave Development and 'Offshore Corporate Social Responsibility': Implications for Oil-rich Sub-Saharan Africa," *Resources Policy* 37, 2 (2012), pp. 152–159.

[76] Appel, "Offshore Work: Oil, Modularity, and the How of Capitalism in Equatorial Guinea," p. 693 (source of quotation). For the source of this last phrase, see Angus Cameron and Ronen Palan, *The Imagined Economies of Globalization* (London: Sage, 2004), p. 105.

[77] Annemarie Mol, *The Body Multiple: Ontology in Medical Practice* (Durham, NC: Duke University Press, 2002), p. 6 (source of quotation). See Saulesh Yessenova, "The Tengiz Oil Enclave: Labor, Business, and the State," *PoLAR: Political and Legal Anthropology Review* 35, 1 (2012), pp. 94–114; and Brenda Chalfin, "Governing Offshore Oil: Mapping Maritime Political Space in Ghana and the Western Gulf of Guinea," *South Atlantic Quarterly* 114, 1 (2015), pp. 101–118.

[78] Alan Hudson, "Offshoreness, Globalization and Sovereignty: A Postmodern Geo-Political Economy?" *Transactions of the Institute of British Geographers* 25, 3 (2000), pp. 269–283 (quotation from p. 269). See also Alan Hudson, "Offshores Onshore: New Regulatory Spaces

Such entities as offshore financial centers (OFCs), export processing zones, and special economic zones – which are located legally, but not necessarily always physically, outside the jurisdiction of onshore regulation – have increasingly played a central role in the restructuring of sovereignty as an ordering principle of the global political economy.[79] The self-sufficient quality of these kinds of modular units encapsulate extraterritoriality, appropriated sovereignty, suspension of the law, and multiple transgressions on human rights that take place in a fixed and self-contained space.[80] In an era of "softened sovereignty," ungoverned spaces fill in the gaps, undermining the rule of law by providing alternative kinds of shadowy governance.[81]

The term "offshore" evokes images of exceptionality, that is, the enjoyment of extraterritorial administrative autonomy outside of the territorial sovereignty of "onshore" political regimes. But this distinction between "offshore" and "onshore" as distinct sites is actually not much more than a convenient fiction.[82] The geographical spread of "onshore" mineral-extraction enclaves have proliferated over the past three decades. These sites or extractive production are umbilically tied to global circuits of capital, while simultaneously detached from the economically "useless" spaces in between.[83] This integration of these extractive clusters into hierarchically structured production

and Real Historical Places in the Landscape of Global Money," in Ron Martin (ed.), *Money and the Space Economy* (London: Wiley, 1999), pp. 139–195; and John Allen, "Powerful Geographies: Spatial Shifts in the Architecture of Globalization," in Stewart Clegg and Mark Haugaard (eds.), *The SAGE Handbook of Power* (London: Sage, 2008), pp. 157–174.

79 Ronan Palan, "Trying to Have your Cake and Eat It: How and Why the State System has Created Offshore," *International Studies Quarterly* 42, 4 (1998), pp. 625–44; Ronan Palan, "The Emergence of an Offshore Economy," *Futures* 30, 1 (1998), pp. 63–67; Ronan Palan, "Offshore and the Structural Enablement of Sovereignty," in Mark Hampton and Jason Abbott (eds.), *Offshore Finance Centres and Tax Havens: The Rise of Global Capital* (London: Macmillan, 1999); John Gerard Ruggie, "Territoriality and Beyond: Problematizing Modernity in International Relations," *International Organization* 47, 1 (1993), pp. 139–174; Alan Hudson, "Placing Trust, Trusting Place: on the Social Construction of Offshore Financial Centres," *Political Geography* 17, 8 (1998), pp. 913–937; Bill Maurer, "Islands in the Net: Rewiring Technological and Financial Circuits in the 'Offshore' Caribbean," *Society for Comparative Study of Society and History* 43, 3 (2001), pp. 467–501; and Bill Maurer, "Re-regulating Offshore Finance," *Geography Compass* 2, 1 (2008), pp. 155–75.

80 See Camillo Boano and Ricardo Martén, "Agamben's Urbanism of Exception: Jerusalem's Border Mechanics and Biopolitical Strongholds," *Cities* 34, 1 (2013), pp. 6–17 (esp. p. 8); and Jason Sharman, "Offshore and the New Political Economy," *Review of International Political Economy* 17, 1 (2010), pp. 1–19.

81 Anne Clunan and Harold Trinkunas, "Conceptualizing Ungoverned Spaces: Territorial Statehood, Contested Authority, and Softened Sovereignty," in Anne Clunan and Harold Trinkunas (eds.), *Ungoverned Spaces: Alternatives to State Authority in an Era of Softened Sovereignty* (Stanford: Stanford University Press, 2010), pp. 17–33.

82 See Lillie, "Bringing the Offshore Ashore," pp. 683–704.

83 Jana Hönke, *Transnational Companies and Security Governance: Hybrid Practices in a Postcolonial World* (New York: Routledge, 2013); and Hannah Appel, "Walls and White Elephants: Oil Extraction, Responsibility, and Infrastructural Violence in Equatorial Guinea." *Ethnography* 13, 4 (2012), pp. 439–465.

networks has resulted in re-scaling processes in which state-based territorial sovereignty does not completely disappear, but declines in importance in favor of a re-territorialization of rule at the local and the regional level.[84] The limited territorial reach of the central state apparatuses often combines with a multiplicity of parallel, overlapping, and sometimes competing spatial orders and sovereignties.[85]

Rather than relying on classical approaches that focused exclusively on maintaining rigid discipline within the confines of their own territorial enclaves, mineral extraction enterprises have begun to experiment with advanced models of security risk management. The industrial mining enclaves of the Copperbelt in Katanga (Democratic Republic of the Congo), for example, have adopted new topographies of security governance that are considerably more flexible and malleable than the rigid model of disciplinary social control via coercive paternalism that prevailed in earlier times. These new regulatory regimes combine the fortress-like protection of narrow pockets of production with selective development interventions in neighboring communities in the vicinity of the mining operations "to transform them into a kind of 'protection belt.'"[86] Within this zone, mineral-extraction enterprises flexibly cooperate with local political authorities, community representatives, NGOs, state agents, and international organizations in an attempt to minimize local risks to the physical security of their operations.

This mode of indirect governance, what Jana Hönke has termed "a policy of discharge" – operates indirectly through the "quasi-delegation" of state functions to private companies.[87] Rather than necessarily weakening the powers of central state authorities, this outsourcing of governance functions to private agents is a means for consolidating state rule over the periphery. This policy of discharge involves the indirect delegation or outsourcing of normal state functions to private companies, such as enforcing property rights, adjudicating disputes, and managing conflict and social (dis)order, as a way of ensuring stability in the pockets of extraction.[88]

---

[84] Jana Hönke, "Transnational Pockets of Territoriality: Governing the Security of Extraction in Katanga (DRC)" (Working Paper Series of the Graduate Centre Humanities and Social Sciences of the Research Academy Leipzig, Leipzig, 2009), 26 pp. (esp. p. 5).

[85] Janet Roitman, "New Sovereigns? Regulatory Authority in the Chad Basin," in Thomas Callaghy, Ronald Kassimir, and Robert Latham (eds.), *Intervention and Transnationalism in Africa: Global-local Networks of Power* (Cambridge: Cambridge University Press, 2010), pp. 240–263. See Ulf Engel and Andreas Mehler, "Under Construction: Governance in Africa's New Violent Social Spaces," in Ulf Engel and Gorm Rye Olsen (eds.), *The African Exception* (Burlington, VT: Ashgate, 2005), pp. 87–102.

[86] Hönke, "Transnational Pockets of Territoriality: Governing the Security of Extraction in Katanga (DRC)," p. 4.

[87] Jana Hönke, "New Political Topographies: Mining Companies and Indirect Discharge in Southern Katanga (DRC)," *Politique africaine* N° 120, 4 (2011), pp. 105–127 (esp. pp. 105, 106–107, 122).

[88] Hönke, "Transnational Pockets of Territoriality," p. 14.

Miniature Cities

At a broader scale, the zonal format represents a new kind of *faux*-urbanism, one in which deliberately planned enclaves are created as an autonomous refuge (or retreat) from the larger social world that surrounds them. These kinds of "make-believe" cities function as heterotopian space because they interrupt and disrupt the apparent continuity of everyday urban life. They acquire their meaning and significance through their extraordinariness.[89]

Company towns exemplify this movement toward deliberate isolation and separation. One of the most famous (if not for all the wrong reasons) company towns was the experimental outpost on a 25,000-square kilometer tract of land dedicated to rubber manufacturing carved out of the remote Amazon jungle called *Fordlândia*. Originally conceived by Henry Ford and the Ford Motor Company, *Fordlândia* (along with its nearby counterpart called *Belterra*) was a company town constructed around plantation agriculture inspired by the image of efficient industrial production and the idealized model of the streamlined assembly line. Ford established an entire city with full amenities for the 10,000 residents – complete with modest clapboard houses laid out in rows, manicured lawns, sidewalks, indoor plumbing, a state-of-the-art power plant, hospitals, central squares, movie theaters, golf courses, and, of course, "Model As and Model Ts rolling down the paved streets." Yet upon arrival, the company management "encountered unforeseen challenges linked to the attempted export of the Ford way of thinking and doing business – practices that had worked so well at home in Michigan – into the remote and underdeveloped Amazon basin."[90] From the start, this hybrid experiment with industry and urbanism was "plagued by waste, violence, and vice." The eventual downfall of *Fordlândia* was brought about by a woeful lack of knowledge of the local setting and circumstances. Without the expert advice of botanists or geologists, the rubber trees never really flourished as planned. Further, as a social experiment, Ford imposed community standards on all residents (both American and Brazilian), or what he called "the healthy lifestyle," including a complete prohibition on alcohol consumption and smoking, and compulsory wholesome activities on the weekends, such as poetry readings and group singalongs. These strict teetotaling rules were completely at odds with local expectations. Disgruntled employers engaged in continuous bouts of fighting, rioting, and work stoppages. After less than two decades in existence, this dystopian experimental oasis eventually closed in 1945 at considerable financial loss. Even today,

---

[89] Michiel Dehaene and Lieven De Cauter, "The Space of Play: Toward a General Theory of Heterotopia," in Michiel Dehaene and Lieven De Cauter (eds.), *Heterotopia and the City: Public Space in a Postcivil Society* (New York: Routledge, 2008), pp. 86–102.

[90] Ralf Barkemeyer and Frank Figge, "Fordlândia: Corporate Citizenship or Corporate Colonialism," *Corporate Social Responsibility and Environmental Management* 19, 2 (2012), pp. 69–78.

overgrown ruins of this abandoned American town still exist, a striking out-of-place *tableau* of a failed utopia.[91]

If sovereign nation-states have become unmanageable, then smaller, more predictable enclaves must be created for those who want to make their own rules.[92] The self-proclaimed anarchist commune in Copenhagen called Free-town Christiania (*Fristaden Christiania*) exemplifies this idea of spatial auton-omy. Christiania is the 84-acre village-enclave founded in 1971 when a brigade of youthful squatters and aspiring artists took over an abandoned military base on the edge of town and proclaimed it a "free zone" beyond the reach of Dan-ish law. This self-governed neighborhood of about 850 residents is perhaps the largest and longest-lasting commune in history. Over time, resident built an "entire settlement of spare, humble, Hobbit-like homes that surrounds a lake and runs along gravel paths and cobblestone roads that wind through woods to the seaside." They restored older buildings and covered these in colorful murals. There are bars, cafés, grocery shops, a fully outfitted building-supply store, health clinics, a museum, art galleries, a concert hall, a skateboard park, a recycling center, and even a recording studio (built inside an old shipping container).[93]

In 2011, Christiania residents reached an agreement with the municipal authorities. On the one side, the agreement seemed to guarantee the survival of Christiania, but on the other, it enabled city officials to extend their regula-tory powers into domains that used to be self-regulated by the residents alone. Under these changed circumstances, Christiania has come to represent a pecu-liar case of hybrid blending of forces of autonomy and of forces of neoliberaliza-tion. The evolving tensions between these two contending forces could poten-tially lead to different outcomes that challenge conventional understandings of both autonomy and neoliberalism.[94] At the end of the day, these historically contingent experiments in alternative lifestyles like Christiania and Exarcheia (a neighborhood in Athens that is renowned for its anticapitalist ethos and

91 Greg Gandin, *Fordlândia: The Rise and Fall of Henry Ford's Forgotten Jungle City* (New York: Metropolitan Books, 2009), pp. 9, 10 (source of quotations); Gary Leggett, "Playgrounds: Rad-ical Failure in the Amazon." *Architectural Design* 81, 3 (2011), pp. 68–75; and John Galey, "Industrialist in the Wilderness: Henry Ford's Amazon Venture," *Journal of Inter-American Studies and World Affairs* 21, 2 (1979), pp. 261–289.

92 Sven Lütticken, "Parklife," *New Left Review* 10 [NS] (2001), pp. 111–118. See Andrew Heben, *Tent City Urbanism: From Self-Organized Camps to Tiny Villages* (Eugene, OR: The Village Collaborative, 2014).

93 Tom Freshton, "'You are now Leaving the European Union,'" *Vanity Fair*, September 12, 2013 (source of quotations); and Kim Christian Moeller, "Police Crack Down on Christiania in Copenhagen," *Crime, Law, and Social Change* 32, 4 (2009), pp. 337–345.

94 Alberto Vanolo, "Alternative Capitalism and Creative Economy: The Case of Christiania," *International Journal of Urban and Regional Research* 37, 5 (2013), pp. 1785–1798; and Alessandro Coppola and Alberto Vanolo, "Normalising Autonomous Spaces: Ongoing Trans-formations in Christiania, Copenhagen," *Urban Studies* 52, 6 (2015), pp. 1152–1168.

its capacity for revolt) function as a kind of performative enactment of "safe spectacle."[95]

The physical destruction in May 2015 of the migrant encampment known as Ponte Mammolo (or *Comunità la Pace*) highlights the ephemerality and unpredictability of sites of temporary refuge. Despite the fact that this migrant enclave had survived various efforts to remove its occupants for nearly two decades, bulldozers reduced its whitewashed prefabricated dwellings and ramshackle lodgings to rubble in a matter of hours. Located near a metro station on the eastern side of Rome, Ponte Mammolo provided refuge for earlier waves of immigrants and asylum seekers who arrived and never left. Most of the permanent residents of the camp had been there so long that they had achieved legal immigration status. According to city officials, it was the upsurge of newcomers – particularly from Eritrea – that tipped the balance in favor of the decision to demolish the camp. New arrivals swelled the population of the camp, spilling out onto a parking lot in front. Ponte Mammolo was only one of several makeshift encampments in Rome. Though in principle they may have occupied the illegal shantytown only temporarily, for many of the immigrants who found refuge there, the impromptu dwellings had become home.[96] Ponte Mammolo is only one of a number of impromptu encampments housing refugees, asylum seekers, and job-seeking immigrants in Rome and elsewhere in Italy.[97]

While these self-declared "free zones" are inherently unstable and under constant threat of extinction, contemporary city-states like Singapore, Monaco, and Vatican City have long-standing claims to territorial sovereignty. While there are historical precedents like Rome, Athens, Carthage, and the Italian city-states during the Renaissance, only a handful of sovereign city-states exist today, with some disagreement as to which places should (and should not) be included in the category. While a great deal of consensus exists that the term properly applies to Singapore, Monaco, and Vatican City, other places that are often referred to as modern city-states include Malta, San Marino, Liechtenstein, Andorra, and Luxembourg.[98]

[95] Andrew Wood, "Managing the Lady Managers: The Shaping of Heterotopian Spaces in the 1893 Chicago Exposition's Woman's Building," *Southern Communication Journal* 69, 4 (2004), pp. 289–302. See Andreas Chatzidakis, Pauline Maclaran, and Alan Bradshaw, "Heterotopian Space and the Utopics of Ethical and Green Consumption," *Journal of Marketing Management* 28, 3–4 (2012), pp. 494–515.

[96] Elisabetta Povoledo, "Migrants' Lives in Ruin as Camp is Razed in Rome," *New York Times*, May 17, 2015.

[97] Maria Bethke and Dominik Bender, *The Living Conditions of Refugees in Italy* (Frankfurt am Main: Förderverein PRO ASYL e.V., February 28, 2011).

[98] Geoffrey Parker, *Sovereign City: The City-state through History* (Chicago: University of Chicago Press, 2005). See also Godfrey Baldacchino, "A Nationless State? Malta, National Identity and the EU," *West European Politics* 25, 4 (2002), pp. 191–206.

Free Trade Zones as Hypermodern Mobile Cities

As a general rule, autonomous zones cannot be tethered to any particular purpose or ideology. For Hakim Bey, the TAZ is an invisible "free enclave" that temporarily evades and escapes state oversight and regulation. These indeterminate zones represent fleeting pocket-like capsules of anarchy that provide transient alternatives for small groups and gatherings seeking respite from the normal state of affairs. Yet unlike these small-scale "pop-up" utopias, enclave spaces like export processing zones constitute a highly visible and autonomous "free states," where the relaxation of the rule of law enables private authority to replace public regulation and oversight.[99]

In exploring what they call the archeology of the future, John Armitage and Joanne Roberts have argued that in the contemporary age of hypercapitalism and "globalaritariansm" such secessionary spaces as free trade zones and their franchised spinoffs have come to resemble hypermodern "mobile cities" that are disconnected from any temporal or territorial moorings and cut loose from all forms of social responsibility. These self-governing enclaves are primarily concerned with creating pockets of freedom outside of public regulation and interference, while they simultaneously seek to evade taxes and squeeze as much as they can out of their captive work force. Free trade zones typically operate like highly securitized, floating factory islands. By virtue of the imposition of military-like management practices where workers enjoy few rights and no job security, they represent the total mobilization of everyday life in the pursuit of profit maximization. Like detention camps and prison complexes, free trade zones rely on a "mentality of the emergency" where conventional rule of law is suspended and where fear and intimidation have become the main mechanisms to enforce strict discipline.[100] The malleability of export processing zones, business parks, and other self-governing enclaves enables them to expand or shrink in accordance with the vagaries of the world economy. They are mobile entities that can be easily dismantled and moved from one place to another in search of better conditions.[101] Corporate enterprises operating on a global scale are, after all, the true nomads: over the past half century, it seems that only capital has lived up to rhizomatic theory of Deleuze and Guattari – always on the move, not subject to any definitive territorialization. Simply put, corporate enterprises that operate under the umbrella of export processing zones have "neither beginning nor end, but always a middle (*milieu*)" from which they

---

99 Lütticken, "Parklife," pp. 111–118.
100 John Armitage and Joanne Roberts, "From the Hypermodern City to the Gray Zone of Total Mobilization in the Philippines," in Ryan Bishop, John Phillips, and Wei Wie Yeo (eds.), *Postcolonial Urbanism: Southeast Asian Cities and Global Processes* (New York: Routledge, 2003), pp. 87–101 (p. 100, source of quotation).
101 Armitage and Roberts, "From the Hypermodern City to the Gray Zone of Total Mobilization," p. 89 (source of quotation).

overspill their original boundaries and expand laterally across space.[102] As they move around the world economy, corporate enterprises function like nomadic forms of super-affluence that rely on a kind of networked extraterritoriality.[103]

Armitage and Roberts single out the Cavite Export Processing Zone (CEPZ), a 276-hectare site located approximately thirty kilometers south of Manila in the town of Rosario, as an exemplar of what they call hypermodern "mobile cities" that marks the "advent of the time-space of the grey zone of total mobilization."[104] The CEPZ has grown exponentially from just a few enclosed factories at an enclosed site employing less than a hundred people in 1986 to a major center for electronics and garments manufacturing comprised of more than 300 enterprises with close to 65,000 employees.[105] According to Naomi Klein, the CEPZ can be characterized as a "fantasyland for foreign investors," nothing short of "a tax free economy sealed off from the local government of both town and province – a miniature military state within a democracy."[106]

In this dystopian image, modular zones are mobile entities that create amorphous, opaque, and parallel networks of extraterritorial sovereignty.[107] These obscure networks of extraterritorial sovereignty are mobile and fungible in the sense of what Bruno Latour has termed the "immutable mobile," that is, networks that maintain their physical shape as they move through space (e.g., ocean liners, oil tankers, and high-speed trains).[108] Such mobile zones as export processing zones have mutated into camp-like organizations, where an ethic of streamlined efficiency has come to dominate unequal transactions, and "where being nonproductive equals being a nonperson, and accountable not to their respective state but to the corporate networks."[109] By virtue of their disconnection from the surrounding territory and its regulatory regimes, microenclosures like cloistered business parks and free trade zones are "test sites for the hypermodern city of the future."[110]

Autonomous zones are the ultimate neoliberal spaces of exception, allowing for the relaxation of regulatory regimes and enabling the free play of market forces. By exploiting situations where territorial sovereignty is little more

[102] Gilles Deleuze and Félix Guattari, *A Thousand Plateaus: Capitalism and Schizophrenia* (Minneapolis: University of Minnesota Press, 1987), p. 21 (source of quotation).

[103] Atkinson and Blandy, "A Picture of the Floating World," pp. 92–110.

[104] Armitage and Roberts, "From the Hypermodern City to the Gray Zone of Total Mobilization," p. 89 (source of quotation).

[105] Rogelio Limpin, "Cavite Ecozone Slams Manila Truck Ban," *Manila Times*, March 3, 2014.

[106] Naomi Klein, *No Logo: Taking Action against the Brand Bullies* (London: Flamingo, 2000), pp. 195–229 (quotations from p. 204, 206).

[107] Caroline Nordstrom, "Shadows and Sovereigns," *Theory, Culture & Society* 17, 4 (2000), pp. 35–54.

[108] See Bruno Latour, *Science in Action* (Cambridge, MA: Harvard University Press, 1987).

[109] Bach, "Modernity and the Urban Imagination in Economic Zones," p. 103 (source of quotation).

[110] Armitage and Roberts, "From the Hypermodern City to the Gray Zone of Total Mobilization," pp. 99–100 (quotation from p. 100).

than a convenient fiction, corporate enterprise has been able to create "off-shore" or nonterritorial regulatory regimes that best correspond to their inter-ests. The expansive logic of capitalism, when faced with constraints imposed by strict enforcement of territorial sovereignty, seeks out bifurcated or varie-gated sovereignty.[111] Mobile elements of corporate capital can operate in areas of limited regulation by "bracketing" their activities, without challenging the right of the sovereign state administrations to "carry on discharging traditional roles as if nothing had happened."[112] This "unbundling" and deterritorializa-tion of territorial sovereignty is a way for corporate capital to escape oversight and unwanted attention.[113]

Fortified Redoubts

The Spanish exclaves of Ceuta and Melilla are two small autonomous port cities located on the north coast of Africa bordering on Morocco.[114] Because they are on the front line of key migration routes between Europe and Africa, these two coastal enclaves have come to play a significant role as European Union border "lockouts" in the western Mediterranean region. Local authori-ties loyal to Spain erected multiple rings of security fences (topped with barbed wire) around both these miniscule city-states in a desperate effort to halt the increasing influx of (mainly) sub-Saharan migrants seeking to enter "Fortress Europe."[115] The complex security systems also include armed patrols, motion detectors, video surveillance cameras with infrared capabilities, long lines of stationary watchtowers, and powerful halogen spotlights for nighttime illumi-nation. The state administration Morocco considers these redoubts to be "occu-pied towns" – exemplary expressions of the anachronistic legacies of colonial rule – and has repeatedly called for Spain to transfer sovereignty. Yet despite these territorial claims, the Moroccan state administration has continued to "protect" the perimeters of both enclaves.[116] The rebordering and fortification policies that have come into existence at Cueta and Melilla stand in stark con-trast to those globalization narratives that dismiss the significance of borders in the twenty-first century.[117] The exponential growth of worldwide "walling

[111] Ronen Palan, *The Offshore World: Sovereign Markets, Virtual Places, and Nomad Millionaires* (Ithaca, NY: Cornell University Press, 2003), pp. 3–4.
[112] Palan, "Trying to Have Your Cake and Eating It," pp. 625–644 (quotation from p. 627).
[113] Lillie, "Bringing the Offshore Ashore," p. 683.
[114] Peter Gold, *Europe or Africa? A Contemporary Study of the Spanish North African Enclaves of Ceuta and Melilla* (Liverpool: Liverpool University Press, 2000).
[115] Yosefa Loshitzky, "Fortress Europe. Introduction," *Third Text* 20, 6 (2006), pp. 629–634.
[116] Jaume Castan Pinos, "Assessing the Significance of Borders and Territoriality in a Globalized Europe," *Regions & Cohesion* 3, 2 (2013), pp. 47–68.
[117] Thomas Christiansen and Knut Erik Jørgensen, "Transnational Governance above and below the State: The Changing Nature of Borders in Europe," *Regional and Federal Studies* 10, 2 (2000), pp. 62–77.

practices" signals how processes of re-bordering and reterritorialization have produced "global landscapes of flaws and barriers."[118]

Put broadly, the contradictory practices of deterritorialization and reterritorialization, that is, communication and interaction, on the one hand, and fortification and securitization, on the other, coexist in uneasy tension. The dual function of borders, that is, separation and contact, cannot be reduced to a "simplistic binary in which they operate in opposition to each other, as these functions occur simultaneously." By combining a highly securitized border fence with a significant interaction with the neighboring Moroccan hinterland, the Spanish enclaves of Ceuta and Melilla illustrate this dichotomous relationship.[119] Similarly, the tiny Italian island of Lampedusa functions at once as a sleepy tourist outpost in the middle of the Mediterranean Sea and a prime destination for irregular migrants and asylum seekers fleeing on rickety boats from Northern Africa to the European Union.[120]

As the forces of globalization undermine state sovereignty, the installation of new kinds of borders – walls, fences, and barricades – serve as prophylaxes against desperate migrants, mobile labor, contagious disease, terror, and the innumerable other sociopolitical forces real and unreal that threaten to undermine and expose the enduring myth of the sovereign nation-state. Borders bolster fantasies of self-sufficiency, reconfiguring "dependency as autonomy," concealing from view the interdependency that has become the norm in the contemporary age of globalization.[121]

Concessionary Urbanism: The City as Zone, the Zone as City

The autonomous zone has become a contagious paradigm for contemporary city building around the world. It is here where "city" and "zone" intersect and blend together. The zone format has become a platform for attracting and shaping of fantasies and aspirations of modernity, especially in the Global South where the majority of zones are located. In fact, the attractiveness of the autonomous zone for city-builders draws from its "discursive power as a [hypermodernist] fantasy of rationality and new beginnings" – constructed *de novo* on blank slate platforms. In this sense, the zone has become an integral part of a normative political "discourse about urban futures" in which the zonal format functions as the embryonic form of cities-yet-to-come.[122]

---

[118] Wendy Brown, *Walled States, Waning Sovereignty* (New York: Zone Books, 2010), p. 24.
[119] Gabriel Popescu, *Bordering and Ordering the Twenty-first Century: Understanding Borders* (Plymouth: Rowland & Littlefield, 2012), p. 11 (source of quotation).
[120] Rutvica Andrijasevic, "Lampedusa in Focus: Migrants Caught between the Libyan Desert and the Deep Sea," *Feminist Review* 82, 1 (2006), pp. 120–125.
[121] Brown, *Walled States, Waning Sovereignty*, p. 123 (source of quotation), 130.
[122] Bach, "Modernity and the Urban Imagination in Economic Zones," p. 99 (source of quotations).

Urban enclaves form the basic, functional building-blocks for what Keller Easterling has called "the zone city." Yet even as the autonomous zone has traded conventional state bureaucracy and public oversight for potentially more complex layers of privatized, para-state governance, "it has itself become an instrument of market manipulation and a perverse tool of economic liberalism."[123] In its most recent incarnations, the zone format has swallowed the whole of the city, and sometimes even calls itself a "city."[124] The term has become a source of pride, an exaggerated validation of the evolution of the zone beyond its original identity as a remote locale for warehousing and transshipment. In some places, the "city" refers to the actual zone enclave, as is the case in numerous "cyber cities," "techno-cities," or "logistics cities."[125] The Science Industrial Parks of the IT industry seem especially keen to acquire the "city" designation. The examples of this kind of self-designation can be multiplied almost endlessly: Konza Techno City (south of Nairobi), Ebene CyberCity on the island of Mauritius, HITEC City (Hyderabad Information Technology Consultancy City) in India, Dubai Logistics City, or Global Gateway Logistics City (Clark Free Port Zone, Philippines). Yet the term "city" can also refer to an actual metropolis, a recognizable city-state, or urban agglomeration of zones tethered together to form an integrated whole. While the zone format enables private owners and managers to banish as many of the unwanted frictions of urbanity as possible, it nevertheless welcomes a range of social amenities associated with world-class cities.[126]

Performance and Masquerade: The Zone as Urban Form and Fantasy

The large-scale private real-estate development called Songdo City (adjacent to the Incheon International Airport 35 miles west of Seoul) illustrates Keller Easterling's observation that the zone has become the "new urban paradigm."[127] Hailed as a cutting-edge, high-tech "green city," New Songdo City is the most ambitious master-planned, holistically designed "instant city" since the celebrated construction of Brasília 50 years ago. Located on an artificial island arising from the Yellow Sea, Songdo City is constructed on a grand scale to rival downtown Boston, only with a much taller skyline and a denser built

123 Keller Easterling, "Zone: The Spatial Softwares of Extrastatecraft," Places: Forum of Design for the Public Realm [2012] (Posted June 11, 2012) [n.p.], (source of quotation). Available at http:/Places.designobserver.com/about.html.

124 Keller Easterling, "The Corporate City is the Zone," in Christina de Baan, Joachim Declerk, and Veronique Patteeuw (eds.), *Visionary Power: Creating the Contemporary City* (Rotterdam: NAi Publishers, 2007), pp. 75–85 (esp. p. 76).

125 See, for example, M. Christine Boyer, *CyberCities: Visual Perception in the Age of Electronic Communications* (New York: Princeton Architectural Press, 1996).

126 Easterling, "Zone: The Spatial Softwares of Extrastatecraft," n.p.

127 Keller Easterling, "Zone," in Ilka and Andreas Ruby (eds.), *Urban Transformation* (Berlin: Ruby Press, 2008), pp. 30–45 (quotation from p. 31).

environment. Built almost entirely from scratch on land reclaimed from the sea, this visionary city-building scheme consists of a carefully pieced together assemblage of high-rise office buildings clustered together in a central business district, an assortment of upscale residential building typologies catering to a range of lifestyles and incomes, and luxurious tourist and entertainment venues that mimic highly stylized aesthetics in vogue in leading world-class cities elsewhere.[128]

New Songdo City is an exemplar of "test-bed urbanism," a living laboratory for testing corporate deregulation.[129] City boosters have promoted New Songdo as a brand new type of multifunctional city: at once an "aerotropolis" that provides transport linkages to the world economy, a "ubiquitous city" (or "U-city") that connects all aspects of urban life to centralized information systems through up-to-date wireless technologies, and a sustainable city that reduces resource consumption.[130] The blend of city and zone thus becomes the latest version of the "city of tomorrow," to use a phrase borrowed from Peter Hall, in a long line of efforts at planned and imagined cities for the improvement of urban living, greater efficiency, and more freedom.[131]

The zone becomes a city, alternately appended to, isolated from, or set within the boundaries of an existing urban landscape. Sometimes it becomes the whole city itself, blurring the categories. Above all else, the zone copies the city, mimicking its shape, mirroring its image, and plagiarizing its experiences.[132] In

---

[128] C.-G. Kim, "Place Promotion and Symbolic Characterization of New Songdo City, South Korea," *Cities*, 27, 1 (2010), pp. 13–19; and Jung In Kim, "Making Cities Global: The New City Development of Songdo, Yujiapu and Lingang," *Planning Perspectives* 29, 3 (2014), pp. 329–356.

[129] Orit Halpern, Jesse LeCavalier, Nerea Calvillo, and Wolfgang Pietsch, "Test-Bed Urbanism," *Public Culture* 25, 2 [70] (2013), pp. 272–306. See Arthur Segel, "New Songdo City," Harvard Business School Occasional Paper 9–206–019 (2006), pp. 1–20; and Kim Jun-Woo and Young-Jin Ahn, "Songdo Free Economic Zone in South Korea: A Mega-Project Reflecting Globalization?" *Journal of the Korean Geographical Society* 46, 5 (2011), pp. 662–672.

[130] Anne Galloway, "Intimations of Everyday Life: Ubiquitous Computing and the City," *Cultural Studies* 18, 2–3 (2004), pp. 384–408; Germaine Halegoua, "The Policy and Export of Ubiquitous Place: Investigating South Korean U-Cities," in Marcus Foth, Laura Forlano, Christine Satchell, and Martin Gibbs (eds.), *From Social Butterfly to Engaged Citizen: Urban Informatics, Social Media, Ubiquitous Computing, and Mobile Technology to Support Citizen Engagement* (Cambridge, MA: The MIT Press, 2011), pp. 315–334; and Sofia Shwayri, "A Model Korean Ubiquitous Eco-city? The Politics of Making Songdo," *Journal of Urban Technology* 201 (2013), pp. 39–55.

[131] Peter Hall, *Cities of Tomorrow: An Intellectual History of Urban Planning and Design in the Twentieth Century*, 3rd edition (Malden, MA: Blackwell, 2002).

[132] Mary Anne O'Donnell, "Becoming Hong Kong, Razing Baoan, Preserving Xin'An: An Ethnographic Account of Urbanization in the Shenzhen Special Economic Zone," *Cultural Studies* 15, 3–4 (2001), pp. 419–443 (esp. pp. 419–421). See also David Bell and Mark Jayne (eds.), *City of Quarters: Urban Villages in the Contemporary City* (Burlington, VT: Ashgate, 2004).

borrowing so much from the city, the zone becomes its simulacrum: a copy that ironically subverts the legitimacy and authority of its original.[133] In so doing, the zone subverts and appropriates urban forms, functions, and practices, turning these into a hybrid zone/city entity.[134] The best-known hybrid zone/cities have attracted a great deal of attention: Navi Mumbai (New Bombay), Dubai, and Shenzhen.[135] But there are dozens more in various stages of development scattered haphazardly around the world from Clark Special Economic Zone on the site of a former U.S. airbase in the Philippines, to Lekki Free Trade Zone and Eko-Atlantic (Lagos), and Kish Island (Iran).[136]

As urban paradigm, the zonal format for city building corresponds to what Kees Doevendans and Anne Shram have called the "creation city," an archetype of urban form constructed out of whole cloth as a *tabula rasa* experiment, ideally on an unencumbered and empty site. As an expression of hypermodernity, the "creation city" originates *de novo*, constructed precisely as designed, purely geometrical, and "deterritorialized," that is, not related to its location and historically independent of its *"genius loci."*[137] The zone-as-city resembles the "creation city" *par excellence*, designed according to the basic needs of logistics and infrastructure, where form and function are subordinated to "the ideal physical space where production and circulation logics meet and intersect."[138] To function as a transit node that connects the local economic activities to global production chains, autonomous zones must privilege efficient transport and rapid mobility. As the material embodiment of the creation city, the autonomous zone emerges as "a true infrastructure city." The utopian fantasy of a genuine "creation city" gathers its inspiration from an imaginary frictionless space where enterprising individuals can perform optimally with minimal interference from public authorities. This image of self-reliance underlies the incessant self-promotion of autonomous zones as "business paradises"

---

133 Scott Durham, *Phantom Communities: The Simulacrum and the Limits of Postmodernism* (Stanford, CA: Stanford University Press, 1998), pp. 1–10.

134 O'Donnell, "Becoming Hong Kong," pp. 419–443.

135 Michael Pacione, "Mumbai," *Cities* 23, 3 (2006), pp. 229–238; Annapurna Shaw, *The Making of Navi Mumbai* (Hyderabat: Orient Longman Private Limited, 2004); and Annapurna Shaw, "Planning and Local Economies in Navi Mumbai: Processes of Growth and Governance," *Urban Geography* 24, 1 (2003), pp. 2–15.

136 See, for example, Pelu Awofeso, "One Out of Every Two Nigerians Now lives in a City There are many Problems but Just One Solution," *World Policy Journal* 27, 4 (2010), pp. 67–73; and Vanessa Watson, "African Urban Fantasies: Dreams or Nightmares?" *Environment and Urbanization* 26, 1 (2014), pp. 215–231.

137 Kees Doevendans and Anne Schram, "Creation/Accumulation City," *Theory Culture & Society* 22, 2 (2005), pp. 29–43 (esp. pp. 29–31 [p. 31, source of quotation]).

138 James Wang and Daniel Olivier, "Port-FEZ Bundles as Spaces of Global Articulation: The Case of Tianjin, China," *Environment and Planning* A 38, 8 (2006), pp. 1487–1503 (quotation from p. 1487).

that come as close as possible to achieving the elusive effortless space of unimpeded free enterprise.[139]

Taken together, the Cartesian "creation city" and the uninterrupted "smooth space" sought by corporate capital produce a new kind of autonomous zone as a "seductively experimental space" that primarily functions as a blank slate upon which to construct the city as pure business enterprise.[140] This fundamentally ahistorical understanding of the city is as deliberately purposeful as it is stridently functional. Without the burden of the historical past, the zone becomes "pure possibility" where what is imagined can become real. The creation of self-contained cities without history has engendered a kind of anonymous modernity that has allowed corporate enterprises the free rein to shape urban landscapes in whatever ways they see fit. As geographic locations unburdened by existing urban infrastructure and blighted built environments, autonomous zones represent the proverbial "fresh start" and "clean slate" experiment where anything can happen.[141]

The zonal format enables real-estate developers to build entire cities from scratch: not only factories, dormitories, warehouses, and port facilities, but also iconic skyscrapers, state-of-the-art office buildings, commercial-retail complexes, upscale residential areas with California-style villas, multiple golf courses, luxury hotels, theme parks, health clinics and hospitals, and universities and private schools. All these features are endowed with a sense of newness and "nowness," and a relentless orientation to the future. Within the autonomous zone as a pure (unimpeded) space of real-estate development and speculation, private planning agencies, design specialists, and architects hope to erase the messiness and inconvenience often attached to historical tradition and cultural heritage, and look forward to reinventing something entirely new out of whole cloth.[142]

In this new frictionless space, the autonomous zone assumes the aura of a utopian community: a "model city" without the stress and accompanying social vices associated with contemporary urbanism. The zone/city hybrid has clear historical antecedents in holistically planned cities of the past. With its carefully designed residential and commercial spaces set among sprawling industrial landscapes, the "zone-as-city" has cobbled together an odd assemblage of nineteenth-century Owenite utopianism, the back-to-nature ethos of early twentieth-century Garden Cities (Ebenezer Howard), vague traces of Soviet "totally planned" cities, the paternalist legacy of company towns, the security

---

[139] See both Bach, "Modernity and the Urban Imagination in Economic Zones," p. 107 (source of quotation); and Doevendans and Schram, "Creation/Accumulation City," pp. 29–31.

[140] Ideas for this and some following paragraphs derived from Bach, "Modernity and the Urban Imagination in Economic Zones," p. 108 (source of quotation).

[141] Bach, "Modernity and the Urban Imagination in Economic Zones," p. 108 (source of quotation).

[142] Bach, "Modernity and the Urban Imagination in Economic Zones," p. 108.

fixation associated with late twentieth-century gated residential communities, and even the environmental determinism of New Urbanism.[143]

The zone/city hybrid embodies the tension between constructing from scratch an entirely new type of metropolis, and offering an alternative to something that already exists. On the one side, the zone/city hybrid embodies the "creation city" image of infrastructural utopia. The futurist thinking around what are referred to as cyber-cities, eco-cities, smart cities, U-cities, or sentient cities have fixated on a forward-looking hypermodernist vision of cities as neo-organicist hybrids that combine material objects and synthetic sentience – or what Matthew Gandy has called "cyborg urbanism."[144] The fantasy-scape of engineers, architects, and futurologists is to build "smart cities" where information-processing capabilities are embedded inside the operational systems of urban infrastructure.[145] The sentient city is one that can remember, correlate, and anticipate.[146] There are many competing definitions of intelligent cities, but all tend to converge on cutting-edge information and communication technologies coupled to local computation capacities embedded in the physical artifacts of urban infrastructures. A U-city – or ubiquitous city – is one is where all main information systems share data in real time, and computers are built into the residential units, utilities, streetscapes, and office buildings.[147] Engineers and planners speak enthusiastically about "u-life in the U-city," meaning that everything is seamlessly connected to everything else, thereby enabling the city to literally "think for itself" in real time.[148]

---

[143] Bach, "Modernity and the Urban Imagination in Economic Zones," p. 108. See also Karen Till, "Neotraditional Towns and Urban Villages: The Cultural Production of a Geography of 'Otherness,'" *Environment and Planning D* 11, 6 (1993), pp. 709–732; and Marcelo Borges and Susana Torres, "Company Towns: Concepts, Historiography, and Approaches," in Marcelo Borges and Susana Torres (eds.), *Company Towns: Labor, Space, and Power Relations across Time and Continents* (New York: Palgrave Macmillan, 2012), pp. 1–40.

[144] Matthew Gandy, "Cyborg Urbanization: Complexity and Monstrosity in the Contemporary City," *International Journal of Urban and Regional Research* 29, 1 (2005), pp. 26–49 (esp. p. 33).

[145] Michael Weinstock with Mehran Gharleghi, "Intelligent Cities and the Taxonomy of Cognitive Scales," *Architectural Design* 83, 4 (3013), pp. 56–65.

[146] Mark Shepard (ed.), *Sentient City: Ubiquitous Computing, Architecture, and the Future of Urban Space* (Cambridge, MA: The MIT Press, 2011); Mike Crang and Stephen Graham, "SENTIENT CITIES Ambient Intelligence and the Politics of Urban Space," *Information, Communication & Society* 10, 6 (2007), pp. 789–817; David Beer, "Thoughtful Territories: Imagining the Thinking Power of Things and Spaces," *City* 11, 2 (2007), pp. 229–238; and Milind Naphade, Guruduth Banavar, Colin Harrison, Jurij Paraszczak, and Robert Morris, "Smarter Cities and their Innovation Challenges," *Computer* 44, 6 (2011), pp. 32–39.

[147] Pamela Licalzi O'Connell, "Korea's High-Tech Utopia, Where Everything Is Observed," *The New York Times*, October 5, 2005.

[148] Dong-Hee Shin, "Ubiquitous City: Urban Technologies, Urban Infrastructure and Urban Informatics," *Journal of Information Science* 35, 5 (2009), pp. 515–526 (esp. p. 515); Sang Ho Lee, Tan Yigitcanlar, Jung-Hoon Han, and Youg-Taek Leem, "Ubiquitous Urban Infrastructure: Infrastructure Planning and Development in Korea," *Innovation: Management, Policy & Practice* 10, 2–3 (2008), pp. 282–292.

On the other hand, the city/zone hybrid functions as a heterotopia: an alternative "other space" that seeks to compensate for the untidy realities that planners strive to consign to the borders beyond the zone itself. In short, the zone-as-heterotopia seeks to create, as Michel Foucault put it, "another real space, as perfect, as meticulous, as well arranged as ours is mess, ill-constructed, and jumbled."[149] These efforts to compensate for untidy realities of contemporary urban life create an excess that cannot be adequately contained within the magical thinking of the rationally planned "creation city."[150] As heterotopia, the zone/city hybrid rests on a fantasy-excess that mixes the grandiosity of over-the-top architectural marvels, the aspirations of nineteenth-century world exhibitions, and playfulness of the miniature theme park. Enclosed, overdesigned, and divided into distinct subzones (under the mantra of "live, work, and play"), the zone/city hybrid has come to resemble what Richard Scherr has called the "synthetic city": a programmed environment of themed entertainments that simulates real urbanism.[151]

This fixation on the art of spectacle has transformed the city/zone hybrid into an inverted version of the nineteenth-century world exposition – the exhibition city on display. Yet instead of "authentic" reproductions of colonized lands with their strange and exotic customs, visitors encounter the hypermodern fantasy of cosmopolitan urbanity in the stylized form of a planned theme park. The zone/city hybrid uses various representational strategies – what might be called "imagineering" or "hard branding" – to provide an illusionary field on which to symbolically imagine a common future tied into global cosmopolitanism.[152]

In contrast to cultural heritage sites that reify lived spaces of the historical past by locating them in the present, the zone/city hybrid objectifies not a carefully crafted version of earlier times but a simulated image of future that is grounded in a fantasy of the hypermodern city as orderly space that is rationally planned and efficiently used. The zone/city hybrid is a miniature utopia, a self-contained island that derives its power from its exceptional status and from its aspirational ambition to become a genuine model for the future.[153]

As a general rule, the zone/city hybrid does not constitute an integrated metropolitan landscape in the ideal imagination of modernist city building, but forms instead a disconnected patchwork or assemblage of small-scale "zone-lets." In turn, these mini-zones break the urban social fabric into distinct

[149] Michel Foucault, "Of Other Spaces?" *Diacritics* 16, 1 (1986), pp. 22–27 (quotation from p. 26).
[150] Bach, "Modernity and the Urban Imagination in Economic Zones," p. 109.
[151] Richard Scherr, "The Synthetic City: Excursions into the Real-Not Real," *Places* 18, 2 (2005), pp. 6–15.
[152] Ipek Türeli, "Modeling Citizenship in Turkey's Miniature Park," *Traditional Dwellings and Settlements Review* 17, 2 (2006), pp. 55–69 (esp. p. 123). See also Anna Kligmann, *Brandscapes: Architecture and the Experience Economy* (Cambridge, MA: The MIT Press, 2007), pp. 55–56, 278–281.
[153] Ideas here and next derived from Bach, "Modernity and the Urban Imagination in Economic Zones," pp. 111, 114.

districts, precincts, and parks defined by their functional specializations. The attachment of such "cartoonish names" as Biopolis, Technopolis, Fusionpolis, Infracity, and Technocity to these places symbolically anoints these "zone-lets" with the artificial status of "miniature cities" nestled within real cities. This assemblage of districts blurs the line between residential suburbs, satellite cities, gated residential communities, and special zones – most notably as knowledge production (biotechnology, information technologies, research and development) replaces manufacturing as the *raison d'etre* for city building.[154]

If the nineteenth-century "exhibition complex" sought to inculcate middle-class values and a sense of national identity in their visitors, the contemporary zone/city hybrid has similarly pursued this goal "with citizenship embedded in a neoliberal context of entrepreneurship and innovation contributing to economic competitiveness."[155] Aspiring world-class cities like Singapore, Shenzhen, and Dubai, where intense competition for investment has shifted from cheap labor to skilled expertise, contend with each other over how to offer the best conditions for innovation and research and development.[156] In their investigation of the "new (knowledge-based) economy" discourse in Singapore, Kai Wen Wong and Tim Bunnell have described how the various strands of zonal logic materialize in the story of "one north," a planned "technopole" for biomedical, IT, and the media industry located in the southwestern part of city-state.[157] For those city boosters seeking to push forward the developmentalist trajectory of Singapore, "one north" (deliberately written in lowercase in official representations of the mega-project) has become an iconic symbol of the shift toward the new "knowledge-based economy." At first, this high-tech "innovation incubator" that became known as "one north" was conceived as a "science habitat" or "business park" in the original concept plan for a technology corridor located in the southwestern part of Singapore. Construction work began in 2001 on the two key "nodes" in "one north": a biotechnology hub called Biopolis and a location for the ICT and media industries called Fusionpolis. Fostering this "knowledge economy" depended upon attracting both local and foreign creative talent and establishing an environment where business interactions, technology exchanges, and informal social networking could flourish with the aim of creating a breeding ground for innovation and techno-entrepreneurship. State authorities in Singapore transformed the two residential estates into refurbished "bohemian" enclaves for skilled workers who commute

---

[154] Bach, "Modernity and the Urban Imagination in Economic Zones," p. 111 (source of phrase).

[155] Bach, "Modernity and the Urban Imagination in Economic Zones," p. 111 (source of quotation).

[156] See also Brenda Yeoh and Tou Chuang Chang, "Globalising Singapore: Debating Transnational Flows in the City," *Urban Studies* 38, 7 (2001), pp. 1025–1044.

[157] Kai Wen Wong and Tim Bunnell, "'New Economy' Discourse and Spaces in Singapore: A Case Study of 'one north,'" *Environment and Planning A* 38, 1 (2006), pp. 69–83. (I have borrowed this example from Bach, "Modernity and the Urban Imagination in Economic Zones," pp. 111–112).

to nearby Biopolis and Fusionopolis, where they generate the knowledge and innovative capacity necessary for economic growth in Singapore. This reinvention of these residential areas as "little bohemias" served two seemingly contradictory ideological agendas of the ruling party called the People's Action Party (PAP). On one hand, these bohemian spaces were key components in the developmentalist strategy of fostering the new-economy culture of entrepreneurship, creativity, and innovation. The aim of transforming knowledge-based industries into a developmentalist trajectory of sustained economic growth has formed the basis of the political legitimacy of the PAP for quite some time. On the other hand, despite wanting to encourage these "values" and "cultures" of entrepreneurship and innovation in order to spur scientific collaboration and cutting-edge research and development, the PAP remained concerned about the introduction of outside influences that they deemed inconsistent with the social order.[158] These "little bohemias" are marked out as spaces in which "alternative" lifestyles, values, and ideas may be tolerated, yet without contaminating the conservative Asian values of a supposed silent majority living in public housing estates, which constitute much of the electoral support for the PAP.[159]

The Zone as Experimental City: The Case of Shenzhen

Few cities anywhere in the world have created wealth faster than the Shenzhen city-region, but the social costs of its apparent phenomenal success appear at every corner: environmental destruction, soaring crime rates, and the disillusionment and degradation of its vast labor force of migrant workers. Shenzhen was a languid fishing village in the Pearl River delta, next to Hong Kong, when paramount leader Deng Xiaoping decreed the area a special economic zone in 1980.[160] As the first Special Economic Zone (SEZ) in China, the establishment of Shenzhen represented a novel experiment in a market-led growth path that was deliberately designed to jump-start economic growth after the near collapse of the socialist centrally planned economy. Located on the border between mainland China and Hong Kong, Shenzhen has developed from what was at first an industry-led, outward processing SEZ to an aspiring world-class city of the twenty-first century with the highest per-capita income levels in the country.[161] As dozens of small rural villages were demolished to make way for its construction, the Shenzhen Special Economic Zone (SSEZ) became a living laboratory for applying free market economic principles and *laissez-faire*

---

[158] Quotation taken from Wong and Bunnell, "'New Economy' Discourse and Spaces in Singapore: A Case Study of 'one-north,'" p. 77.

[159] Wong and Bunnell, "'New Economy' Discourse and Spaces in Singapore: A Case Study of 'one-north,'" p. 78.

[160] Howard French, "Chinese Success Story Chokes on its own Growth," *New York Times*, 19 December 2006.

[161] Ya Ping Wang, Yanglin Wang, and Jiansheng Wu, "Urbanization and Informal Development in China: Urban Villages in Shenzhen," *International Journal of Urban and Regional Research* 33, 4 (2009), pp. 957–973.

FIGURE 6.1 Shenzhen free trade zone.
(Photograph courtesy of Fotosearch/ Getty Images.)

practices that were alien under socialist command economy. As a place where new economic freedoms of private enterprise were first incubated, Shenzhen – as shown in Figure 6.1 – quickly outgrew this early identity as "quarantined capitalist enclave," and has ballooned into a booming twenty-first-century metropolis with aspirations to become a "world-class" city centered on finance and business services supporting the surrounding manufacturing economy of the larger Pearl River delta economic region.[162] The physical growth and restructuring of the city reflect the imagination and experimentation of the government and urban planners who had no prior experience of planning for the

[162] This phrase is taken from Easterling, "Zone: The Spatial Softwares of Extrastatecraft," [n.p.]. See Carolyn Cartier, "Transnational Urbanism in the Reform-era Chinese City: Landscapes from Shenzhen," *Urban Studies* 39, 9 (2002), pp. 1513–1532.

growth of the invisible hand in a fledgling socialist market economy.[163] With a phenomenal rate of population growth (ranging from 15 to 28 percent per annum), Shenzhen has a resident population of close to ten million and a transient population of around 14 million. The SEZ comprises four of the seven districts of the city and approximately 150 square miles. There are plans to expand the zone to include other districts for a total of approximately 700 square miles.[164]

In taking what can be considered a "strong" position on global convergence, business strategist and McKinsey partner Kenichi Ohmae has argued that the "nation-state has become an unnatural, and even dysfunctional, unit for organizing human activity and managing economic endeavor in a borderless world." In place of the outmoded sovereign nation-state, he has called for the formation of "region states" as "free enterprise havens" with relaxed controls and *laissez-faire* economics. The meteoric rise of Shenzhen as an economic powerhouse prompted Ohmae to identify it as an exemplar of a successful neoliberal "region-state."[165] As a paean to hypermodernity, Shenzhen owes its meteoric growth to the mixture of its insertion into globalized circuits of production and free market liberalism. As Jonathan Bach has put it, Shenzhen "is in its own way, the very equivalent of 1920s Berlin or New York in its urban intoxication, its inexorable newness, its multiple, overlapping fantasies of progress, promises, and peril." City boosters often bundle together its component parts – its factories, residential settlements, migrant workers, skyscrapers, urban villages, and parks – into a tidy narrative of progress and embrace of market forces, hurdling ahead at "Shenzhen speed."[166] As the city grew at an astonishing rate of more than 27 percent from 1980 to 2006, it experienced a meteoric ascent from rural fields and agricultural production to a booming metropolis outfitted with up-to-date infrastructure, high-tech innovation zones, skilled manufacturing plants, and airfreight and container ports.[167]

What accounts for the alleged success' of the Shenzhen model?[168] At a glance, the simple formula of cheap land, proximity to port facilities, lax

---

[163] Mee Kam Ng, "Shenzhen," *Cities* 20, 6 (2003), pp. 429–441.

[164] Keller Easterling, "Zone: The Spatial Softwares of Extrastatecraft," n.p.

[165] Kenichi Ohmae, "The Rise of the Region State," *Foreign Affairs* 72, 2 (Spring 1993), pp. 78–87 (quotations from p. 78); and Kenichi Ohmae, *The End of the Nation State: The Rise of Regional Economies* (New York: The Free Press, 1995).

[166] Jonathan Bach, "'They Come in as Peasants and Leave Citizens': Urban Villages and the Making of Shenzhen," *Cultural Anthropology* 25, 3 (2010), pp. 421–458 (both quotations from p. 421).

[167] Jonathan Bach, "Shenzhen: City of Suspended Possibility," *International Journal of Urban and Regional Research* 35, 2 (2011), pp. 414–420; Xiangming Chen and Tomas de'Medici, "Research Note – The 'Instant City' Coming of Age: Production of Spaces in China's Shenzhen Special Economic Zone," *Urban Geography* 31, 8 (2010), pp. 1141–1147.

[168] See Jun Zhang, "From Hong Kong's Capitalist Fundamentals to Singapore's Authoritarian Governance: The Policy Mobility of Neoliberalising Shenzhen, China," *Urban Studies* 49, 13 (2012), pp. 2853–2871.

environmental regulations and ineffective enforcement, and an inexpensive (and largely compliant) migrant labor force have meant that Shenzhen has managed to attract huge investment ($3–5 billion per annum in recent years) from abroad, including legions of foreign corporations that have built export-based manufacturing industries. With 7 million migrant workers in an overall population of about 12 million (compared with Shanghai's 2–3 million migrants out of a population of 18 million), by the late twentieth century Shenzhen became the literal and symbolic heart of the Chinese market-driven economic miracle.[169]

The foundational myth of Shenzhen lays particular stress on opportunity, economic freedom, and upward mobility. Everyday stories about Shenzhen are replete with "rags-to-riches" stories that, as Jonathan Bach has argued, "All contain the same tropes of poor folk making good, of cleverness trumping education, of opportunity awaiting those who act, and the validation of the self through large amounts of money."[170] Put in another way, these narratives function to produce what Roland Barthes called cultural codes, whose "utterances" are "implicit proverbs" that "insert the dominant discourse into personal and collective stories, dreams, advertisements and fantasies, all of which serve to perpetuate the meta-fantasy of self-improvement through getting rich."[171] Yet these apocryphal stories of success effectively gloss over a catalogue of big-city problems, including increasing pollution, lack of affordable housing, and poor public planning. The seamy side of urbanism is often ignored.[172]

The explosive growth of the Shenzhen city-region has produced contradictory results. Boomtowns or "instant cities" vary in their growth trajectories, but all seem sooner or later to have to face their limitations. Municipal authorities have been forced to confront an accumulation of economic, social, and political challenges that stem from its super-fast growth.[173] The enormous expansion of infrastructure, the rapid construction of distinct industrial sites and

---

[169] Howard French, "Chinese Success Story Chokes on its own Growth," *New York Times*, December 19, 2006.

[170] Bach, "Shenzhen: City of Suspended Possibility," p. 415 (source of quotation).

[171] Roland Barthes, *S/Z* (New York: Hill and Wang, 1974), p. 100. For the source of this idea, see Bach, "Shenzhen: City of Suspended Possibility," p. 415 (source of quotation).

[172] Bach, "Shenzhen: City of Suspended Possibility," pp. 414–420; and Lin Ye, "State-led Metropolitan Governance in China: Making Integrated City Regions," *Cities* 41 (Part B) (2014), pp. 200–208. For newspaper report on the disastrous December 2015 landslide that resulted in scores of deaths and leveled dozens of low-income apartment buildings, see Neil Gough, "The Overnight Metropolis," *New York Times*, December 24, 2015.

[173] Chen and de'Medici, "Research Note – The 'Instant City' Coming of Age," pp. 1141–1147; and Xiangming Chen, "The Evolution of Free Economic Zones and the Recent Development of Cross-national Growth Zones," *International Journal of Urban and Regional Research* 19, 4 (1995), pp. 593–621.

overbuilt residential settlements, and inadequate environmental regulations have profoundly altered the local environment.[174]

As an early experimental prototype for the "zone-as-city," Shenzhen has long led a double rhetorical life that has careened back and forth between an image of a vibrant place of opportunity and an infamous zone of danger and crime. Ironically, Shenzhen has been a victim of its own success. Rapid economic growth and a reputation as the richest city in mainland China have only enhanced its magnetic appeal to desperate migrants seeking a better life in urban China. With real opportunities for upward mobility quite limited, newcomers are left to fend for themselves and as a consequence can be drawn into the criminal underground. As restrictions on entry into Shenzhen are increasingly relaxed, city officials have found the problem of policing a floating population of about 5.8 million people more difficult to handle. The city has long operated as a popular destination for wealthy tourists and ambitious entrepreneurs, as well as "bargain shoppers" and roving pleasure-seekers from neighboring Hong Kong. But these tourists, in turn, act as a lure for criminal gangs who prey on them.[175]

This circle of circumstances has provided a fertile breeding ground for criminality. Lo Wu Station is the northern terminus of the East Rail Line (Kowloon-Canton Railway) of Hong Kong. The station serves as a primary checkpoint for rail passengers between Hong Kong and Shenzhen. The large department store connected to the Lo Wu border train station on the Shenzhen side of the border crossing is colloquially known as the "house of *faux*" because of its wide selection of illegally produced "knockoffs." But beyond the almost ubiquitous existence of this rather mundane copyright infringement practices, the "in-between" places of Shenzhen have become sites for criminal activities, ranging from widespread pickpocketing and auto theft, to kidnapping, extortion, and murder.[176] Often disguised in karaoke joints and massage parlors, but increasingly in the open, prostitution has become one of the most lucrative shadow businesses.[177] As elsewhere in what amounts to frontier zones, overextended municipal authorities blame crime on migrants and mafias, both of which exist in overabundance. Yet despite its tough reputation as a crime

---

[174] Xiaozi Liu, Gerhard K. Heilig, Junmiao Chen, and Mikko Heino, "Interactions between Economic Growth and Environmental Quality in Shenzhen, China's First Special Economic Zone," *Ecological Economics* 62, 3 (2007), pp. 559–570.

[175] Howard French, "Chinese Success Story Chokes on its own Growth," *New York Times*, December 19, 2006; and Adrian Blackwell, "Shenzhen – Topology of a Neoliberal City," in Rodolphe El-Khoury and Edward Robbins (eds.), *Shaping the City: Studies in History, Theory and Urban Design* (New York: Routledge, 2013), pp. 278–311.

[176] Bach, "Modernity and the Urban Imagination in Economic Zones," p. 113.

[177] Howard French, "Chinese Success Story Chokes on its own Growth," *New York Times*, December 19, 2006.

mecca, much of the urban landscape of Shenzhen consists of bland, look-alike housing complexes for legions of white-collar employees.[178]

Yet at the start of the twenty-first century, Shenzhen has begun to look less like a successful model than an ominous warning sign of the social limitations of a growth-above-all-else approach.[179] While grueling labor conditions exist in many cities in China, gigantic manufacturing plants, employing as many as 200,000 workers each, have established a particular reputation for harshness among workers and labor rights advocates in Shenzhen. Managers routinely have neglected occupation health and safety concerns, and have stretched the working day from 9 to 14 hours, with no weekends or holidays off. A considerable proportion of the labor force has complained that they received less the minimum wage. Labor advocacy groups have argued that monthly turnover rates of 10 percent or more are not uncommon.[180] The poor working conditions, in turn, have helped spawn large-scale wildcat strikes and smaller job actions for better hours and wages.[181] For economic planners in China, the Shenzhen recipe for success is increasingly seen as all but irrelevant: "too harsh, too wasteful, too polluted, [and] too dependent on the churning, ceaseless turnover of migrant labour." For the most part, equity has been sacrificed for growth. According to Zhao Xiao, an economist and former advisor to the Chinese State Council, "this path is now a dead end." Cities like Shenzhen cannot "count on the beauty of investment covering up 100 other kinds of ugliness."[182]

The newcomers who have flocked to Shenzhen are largely illegal migrants because they lack official authorization to live in the city. These unauthorized migrants have typically found accommodation in what amount to "spatial holes" created by an anomalous fissure in the system of "urban villages." When Shenzhen first started to explode in size, these "urban villages" were able to retain their customary designation as "rural." As a consequence, these spatial pockets were able to circumvent the legal land-use regulations of the city while they became increasingly enclosed within the boundaries of the municipality.[183] Functioning literally as miniature "spaces of exemption" within a much larger visible space of exception, urban villages have become increasingly dense sites

[178] Bach, "Modernity and the Urban Imagination in Economic Zones," p. 113; and Howard French, "Chinese Success Story Chokes on its own Growth," *New York Times*, December 19, 2006.

[179] John Zacharias and Yuanzhou Tang, "Restructuring and Repositioning Shenzhen, China's New Mega City," *Progress in Planning* 73, 4 (2010), pp. 209–249.

[180] Howard French, "Chinese Success Story Chokes on its own Growth," *New York Times*, December 19, 2006.

[181] Bach, "Modernity and the Urban Imagination in Economic Zones," p. 113.

[182] Howard French, "Chinese Success Story Chokes on its own Growth," *New York Times*, December 19, 2006 (source of quotation and paraphrase).

[183] Bach, "'They Come in as Peasants and Leave Citizens': Urban Villages and the Making of Shenzhen," pp. 421–458.

crowded with high-rise residential units that are rented to migrants who arrive in the city without proper authorization. These "urban villages" have also operated as platforms for the kinds of quasi-legal and "black market" commerce that contradict the image of the rationally ordered city. The unauthorized migrants who have crowded into these high-rise apartment complexes have little or no legal protection from the predations of criminal hustlers and police alike. Like illegal migrants in cities elsewhere, they are "largely reduced to invisible and expendable inhabitants who are nonetheless instrumental in the construction and menial service sector industries." If the figure of the "invisible" migrant functions metaphorically as the "open secret" in the success story that accompanied the establishment of the SSEZ, then the displaced farmer who once tilled the land is the figure that signifies the primitive or original accumulation – captured by the "rude processes of land transfer" (or what David Harvey has called "accumulation by dispossession") – that jump-started the autonomous zone in the first place.[184]

Postcolonial Hong Kong (with its animating ethos of entrepreneurial capitalism) and Shenzhen (with its core ideology of capitalist industrialism within the socialist market economy) have both adopted pro-growth strategies to cope with challenges imposed by a globalizing world economy.[185] This developmentalist philosophy of fast-paced modernization has exerted tremendous pressure on both cities, pushing them further away from the desired path of sustainable urbanism. Despite the shared policy rhetoric of pursuing sustainable development, both city administrations have largely refrained from identifying and analyzing the costs and benefits of policy choices. Without a critical rethinking of the "growth-first" mentality, sustainability principles – such as an ethical utilization of natural resources and meeting the aspirations for intra- and intergenerational equity – have been sidelined as part of the core policy agenda.[186]

[184] Bach, "Modernity and the Urban Imagination in Economic Zones," pp. 113–114 (first quotation from p. 113; second from p. 114). See David Harvey, "The 'New' Imperialism: Accumulation by Dispossession," *Socialist Register* 40 (2004), pp. 63–87. See also Carolyn Cartier, "'Zone fever,' the Arable Land Debate, and Real Estate Speculation: China's Evolving Land Use Regime and its Geographical Contradictions," *Journal of Contemporary China* 10, 28 (2001), pp. 445–469; Deborah Brautigam and Tang Xiaoyang, "African Shenzhen: China's Special Economic Zones in Africa," *Journal of Modern African Studies* 49, 1 (2011), pp. 27–54; and Pál Nyíri, "Enclaves of Improvement: Sovereignty and Developmentalism in the Special Zones of the China-Lao Borderlands," *Comparative Studies in Society and History* 54, 3 (2012), pp. 533–562.

[185] Mee Kam Ng and Wing-Shing Tang, "Land-use Planning in 'One Country, Two Systems': Hong Kong, Guangzhou and Shenzhen," *International Planning Studies* 4, 1 (1999), pp. 7–27; and Xiaolong Luo and Jianfa Shen, "The Making of New Regionalism in the Cross-boundary Metropolis of Hong Kong–Shenzhen, China," *Habitat International* 36, 1 (2012), pp. 126–135.

[186] Mee Kam Ng, "Sustainable Urban Development Issues in Chinese Transitional Cities: Hong Kong and Shenzhen," *International Planning Studies* 7, 1 (2002), pp. 7–36 (especially p. 7).

Zone Cities

Global urbanization is accelerating at a faster pace than ever before, and while urban growth and development may appear to replicate what came before, fundamental shifts in thinking about building new cities is taking place just beneath the surface. Over the past several decades, hundreds of new master-planned, holistically designed "private cities" have been constructed or are in the advanced planning stages in various locations around the world. Brand new "satellite cities" like New Songdo near Incheon (South Korea), Lavasa near Pune (India), Strand East in London (United Kingdom), PlanIT Valley near Porto (Portugal), and Waterfall City (Johannesburg) exemplify this trend toward building private cities from scratch. This growing privatization of city building has led to changing dynamics between real-estate developers, urban designers and architects, construction engineering firms, public authorities, and eventual end-users. Shifting alliances between financiers, builders, and clients make it impossible to identify any single organizational model for the shift toward privatized urbanism.[187]

City builders in the United Arab Emirates have employed the zone format to distinct advantage – to dilute and control foreign influence, to elevate and protect the status of privileged nationals, and to leverage existing oil and gas resources to create diversified industries. Much like Shenzhen, Dubai is nothing other than "the city as zone and the zone as city."[188] While it operates as an off-shore financial center and a global trans-shipment hub, Dubai actually consists of an assemblage of relatively autonomous zones, most of which have acquired the name "city."[189] The first free trade zone, named the Jebel Ali Free Zone, was established in 1985 and has expanded to 48 square kilometers. Since that time, Dubai has spawned a variety of zones for almost every imaginable program and function: Dubai Internet City, Dubai Waterfront City, Dubai Health Care City, Dubai Maritime City, Dubai Silicon Oasis, Dubai Knowledge Village, Dubai Techno Park, Dubai Media City, Dubai Outsourcing Zone, Dubai Academic City, Dubai Studio City, Dubai International Humanitarian City, Dubai Industrial City, Dubai Textile Village, and Dubai Auto Parts City.[190] Each precinct offers a different cocktail of incentives that include easy-to-obtain visas,

---

187 Paul Goldberger, "The Rise of the Private City," in Julia Vitullo-Martin (ed.), *Breaking Away: The Future of Cities* (New York: The Twentieth Century Fund Press, 1996), pp. 135–147. For a review of some of the extant literature, see Martin J. Murray, "Waterfall City (Johannesburg): Privatized Urbanism *in Extremis*," *Environment and Planning A* 47, 3 (2015), pp. 503–520.

188 Easterling, "Zone: The Spatial Softwares of Extrastatecraft," n.p. (source of quotation).

189 Ahmed Kanna, "Flexible Citizenship in Dubai: Neoliberal Subjectivity in the Emerging "City-Corporation" *Cultural Anthropology* 25, 1 (2010), pp. 100–129; and David Bassens, Ben Derudder, and Frank Witlox, "The Making and Breaking of Dubai: The End of a City–state?" *Political Geography* 29, 6 (2010), pp. 299–301.

190 Jacques Horovitz and Anne-Valérie Ohlsson, "Dubai Internet City: Serving Business," *Asian Journal of Management Cases* 2, 2 (2005), pp. 163–209.

streamlined customs processing, cheap labor from South Asia and Africa, tax write-offs, and foreign ownership of property (including the right to own real estate in such upscale residential districts as the Palm Islands and other projects developed by the powerful Nakheel Properties group).[191] What complicates thinking about Dubai as a single city is the fact that different zones are enveloped in their own peculiar legal status. For instance, Dubai Media City, the headquarters for major global news outlets, allows freedoms of speech that are not technically permitted elsewhere in Dubai.[192]

Similarly, King Abdullah Economic City, located on the Red Sea near Jedda (Saudi Arabia), consists of an assemblage of zones that taken in the aggregate constitute what amounts to a full-blown city. Launched in 2006 by the Saudi government and the Dubai-based real-estate developer called Emaar Properties, King Abdullah Economic City, when it is finished, will encompass 168 square kilometers – a city about the size of Brussels. The Saudi ruling elite also plan to build a host of other "instant cities," including Knowledge Economic City (in Medina), Jazan Economic City (in Jazan), and Prince Abdulaziz bin Mousaed Economic City (in Hail).[193] The first precinct planned for King Abdullah Economic City is a vast industrial zone covering one-third of the city, consisting of a combination of factory space, dormitories for foreign workers, and a mosque. The original plans call for a manufacturing zone, named "Plastics Valley," designed to take advantage of auxiliary petrochemical resources; a globally connected deepwater container seaport with up-to-date logistics, warehousing and trans-shipment facilities; and, located some distance away from these areas, various "city districts" with residential, educational, tourist, healthcare, and cultural areas. The architectural design of the Bay La Sun district envisions a large upscale shopping mall, a business park, a mosque, a five-star hotel, and tall office buildings, all carefully arranged around artificial canals and connected by a signature bridge. The promotional materials advertising the distinctiveness of King Abdullah Economic City lay particular stress on a "high-class" and "prosperous" lifestyle, with a range of high-end residential options. King Abdullah Economic City is situated on the Mecca-Medina rail line, part of a high-speed rail network that Saudi Arabia is still in the planning stages. The city permits foreign ownership and offers a variety of tax exemptions from import duties. Residents pay no personal income tax and corporate taxes are minimal. In architectural renderings, King Abdullah Economic City appears as a pristine, shimmering "golden city" knitting together skyscrapers

[191] Ahmed Kanna, *Dubai: The City as Corporation* (Minneapolis: University of Minnesota Press, 2011).

[192] Easterling, "Zone: The Spatial Softwares of Extrastatecraft," n.p.

[193] J. E. Peterson, "Life after Oil: Economic Alternatives for the Arab Gulf States," *Mediterranean Quarterly* 20, 3 (2009), pp. 1–18; Jad Mouawad, "The Construction Site Called Saudi Arabia," *New York Times*, January 20, 2008; and Waleed Abdullah Abdulaal, "Large Urban Developments as the New Driver for Land Development in Jeddah," *Habitat International* 36, 1 (2012), pp. 36–46.

and traditional Islamic buildings in a way intended to symbolically monumentalize the state administration and its "wise leadership."[194]

Like the "company towns" of nineteenth-century America, and maybe even like the utopian experiments of protestant pilgrims in the New World, the free zone can be understood as a peculiar variant of an "intentional community."[195] Although structured to avoid the messy unpredictability of the conventional city, the autonomous zone nevertheless generates its own particular brand of modern enclave urbanism. Indeed, after multiple cycles of mutation and adaptation, the zone has developed a multiplicity of variations. Masdar City, located on the outskirts of Abu Dhabi and established by the Abu Dhabi Future Energy Company, has established itself as a free zone for green energy enterprises and sustainable urbanism. Originally advertised as the world's first carbon-neutral and zero-waste city, Masdar has yet to overcome sceptics who derided it as a gimmick.[196] Master planned by the architectural firm Foster and Partners, the overall spatial design resembles something akin to the ideal city of antiquity. Laid out in the pattern of a square grid, Masdar City consists of distinct sections designed to maximize shading, collect solar energy, and promote natural airflow. Personal-rapid-transit electric vehicles are restricted to underground maze of roadways, thereby promoting pedestrian traffic above. Combining research clusters with enterprise incubators, universities have become one of "the newest species to join the zone habitat." Qatar Education City, for instance, located just outside Doha, uses the campus park/zone model to host the satellite campuses of eight universities, six from the United States and one each from the United Kingdom and France. This type of public–private sponsorship – Education City is funded by a foundation that is in turn supported by the Emirate – seeks to transform the advantages of the Western university into a kind of "zone incubator" sponsoring a mix of scientific thinking, research and development, and private enterprise.[197]

The case of the city-state of Macau – the first and last Western settlement in China – provides ample evidence that the old fixation on international borders, as hard lines between sovereign nation-states, does not actually fit the reality of a sociocultural world with global flows and graduated sovereignties.[198] In the post-Westphalian era of fragmented territorialities, traditional notions

---

[194] Easterling, "Zone: The Spatial Softwares of Extrastatecraft," n.p. (source of quotations).

[195] See Linda Carlson, *Company Towns of the Pacific Northwest* (Seattle: University of Washington Press, 2003).

[196] Nicholai Ouroussoff, "In Arabian Desert, a Sustainable City Arises," *New York Times*, September 25, 2010; and Anonymous, "Urban Dreamscapes: Starting from Scratch," *Economist*, September 7, 2013.

[197] Easterling, "Zone: The Spatial Softwares of Extrastatecraft," n.p. (source of quotation). See also Agatino Rizzo, "Rapid Urban Development and National Master Planning in Arab Gulf Countries: Qatar as a Case Study," *Cities* 39 (2014), pp. 50–57.

[198] Werner Breitung, "Macau Residents as Border People: A Changing Border Regime from a Socio-cultural Perspective," *Journal of Current Chinese Affairs* 38, 1 (2009), pp. 101–127.

of monolithic state sovereignty have come unglued, replaced by ambiguous regimes of authority that are less fettered by norms and practices centered on the state rule as the supreme power within its territorial boundaries.[199] The hybrid sovereignty at work in Macao is a particularly vivid example of what Hedley Bull as early as 1979 called "new medievalism," by which he meant a secular version of the medieval "system of overlapping authority and multiple loyalty."[200] Once a Portuguese colony, Macau is a Special Administrative Region of the People's Republic of China (PRC) strategically situated within the sprawling megacity region of the Pearl River Delta. Since its return to the PRC in 1999, this semiautonomous city-state has replaced Las Vegas as the world's most lucrative site of casino gaming revenue.[201] Macao has become a key financial site in the restructuring of global capitalism in East Asia, analogous to the autochthonous role of the Italian city-states of Venice and Genoa in the historical origins of merchant capitalism.[202]

With its special regime of legal exceptionalism and strategic management of cross-border flows of people and capital, Macau is a "globally connected and locally disconnected" territory whose phantasmagoric glass cityscape mimics themed tourist destinations and entertainment environments in aspiring world-class cities around the world.[203] In shedding its once-dominant image as a colonial backwater, and a seedy, decaying "city of sin" that languished under inept Portuguese rule, this island-like city-state used a massive influx of foreign

[199] Susan Henders, "So What If It's Not a Gamble? Post-Westphalian Politics in Macau," *Pacific Affairs* 74, 3 (2001), pp. 342–360. On the demise of the Westphalian state system, see Mark Zacher, "The Decaying Pillars of the Westphalian Temple: Implications for International Order and Governance," in James Rosenau and Ernest-Otto Czempiel, (eds.), *Governance without Government: Order and Change in World Politics* (Cambridge: Cambridge University Press, 1992), pp. 58–101.

[200] Hedley Bull, *The Anarchical Society: A Study of Order in World Politics*, 2nd Edition (London: Macmillan, 1995), pp. 245–246 (source of quotations).

[201] Tim Simpson, "Macau Metropolis and Mental Life: Interior Urbanism and the Chinese Imaginary," *International Journal of Urban and Regional Research* 38, 3 (2014), pp. 823–842; Sonny Lo and Herbert Yee, "Legitimacy-Building in the Macau Special Administrative Region: Colonial Legacies and Reform Strategies," *Asian Journal of Political Science* 13, 1 (2005), pp. 51–79; and Carlos Balsas, "Gaming Anyone? A Comparative Study of Recent Urban Development Trends in Las Vegas and Macau," *Cities* 31 (2013), pp. 298–307. For an historical account, see Richard Louis Edmonds, "Macau: Past, Present and Future," *Asian Affairs* 24, 1 (1993), pp. 3–15.

[202] Tim Simpson, "Scintillant Cities: Glass Architecture, Finance Capital, and the Fictions of Macau's Enclave Urbanism," *Theory, Culture & Society* 30, 7–8 (2013), pp. 343–371. See also Wing Tong Ip, "Casino Capitalism and Social Polarization in Macao," *Asian Education and Development Studies* 1, 3 (2012), pp. 276–293; and Cathy H. C. Hsu and Zheng Gu, "Ride on the Gaming Boom: How Can Hong Kong, Macau and Zhuhai Join Hands to Develop Tourism in the Region?" *Asia Pacific Journal of Tourism Research* 15, 1 (2010), pp. 57–77.

[203] Manuel Castells, *The Rise of the Network Society*, Volume 1, [2nd edition] (Cambridge, MA: Blackwell, 2000), p. 436 (source of quotation).

capital to reimagine itself as a grand tourist mecca akin to Las Vegas and Dubai. In contrast to the usual view of Macau as a washed-up, second-rate Hong Kong with a tarnished history as a European trading *entrepôt*, this self-governing territory has developed a worldwide reputation as the "Monte Carlo of the Orient."[204]

Yet casino capitalism has generated contradictory outcomes in Macau. On the one hand, the gaming industry has stimulated rapid economic growth, provided employment, and strengthened the postcolonial state apparatus in Macau during periods of socioeconomic boom. On the other hand, casino capitalism has fostered the widening of the income gap between the rich and the poor, given rise to serious environmental degradation (including poor air quality, wasteful water supply, noise pollution, and inadequate solid waste disposal), contributed to addictive gambling practices, and delegitimized the postcolonial state administration during times of global and regional socioeconomic downturn.[205]

Zone Masquerade

As exemplary expressions of the zone format, urban enclaves have adopted an organizational and political language that relies quite heavily on terms like *openness, relaxation,* and *freedom.* Yet the actual reality that accompanies the creation of urban enclaves is often quite the opposite. In order to distinguish itself from its surroundings, the zone typically offers what appears to be a cleaner, smarter, and more beautiful urbanism than what exists around it. Yet this promise of openness often turns out to be a clever masquerade. Autonomous zones aspire to be the perfect spatialized utopias for the neoliberal age.[206] They create their own "rules of the game," seeking exemption from whatever laws that might apply to them, just as maritime city-states for centuries tipped the scales in their own favor. Yet unlike the old city-states that set their sights on breaking from the customs and prejudices of their time, the

---

[204] For the use of this term, see Fanny Vong Chuk Kwan, "Gambling Attitudes and Gambling Behavior of Residents of Macao: The Monte Carlo of the Orient," *Journal of Travel Research* 42, 3 (2004), pp. 271–278. See also Tim Simpson, "Materialist Pedagogy: The Function of Themed Environments in Post-Socialist Consumption in Macau," *Tourist Studies* 9, 1 (2009), pp. 60–80; and William Vlcek, "Taking *Other* People's Money: Development and the Political Economy of Asian Casinos," *The Pacific Review* 28, 3 (2015), pp. 323–345.

[205] Sonny Lo, "Casino Capitalism and Its Legitimacy Impact on the Politico-administrative State in Macau," *Journal of Current Chinese Affairs* 38, 1 (2009), pp. 19–47; Lo Shiu Hing, "Casino Politics, Organized Crime and the Postcolonial State in Macau," *Journal of Contemporary China* 14, 43 (2005), pp. 207–224; and Xiaojiang Yu, "Growth and Degradation in the Orient's 'Las Vegas': Issues of Environment in Macau," *International Journal of Environmental Studies* 65, 5 (2008), pp. 667–683.

[206] Keller Easterling, *Enduring Innocence: Global Architecture and Its Political Masquerades* (Cambridge, MA: The MIT Press, 2005), pp. 4–5.

"zone city" is not yet the scene of forward-looking genuine urbanity, but rather the setting for hypercontrol, exclusion, and private gain.[207]

As both the logical platform for a capital accumulation strategy and a city-in-its-own-right, the autonomous zone gives rise to an apparent disjuncture: it functions simultaneously as an enclosed "space of exception" and as a proto-type for a new type of city *writ large*. As a space of exception, the autonomous zone is made possible only by strict enforcement of its own internal rules and regulations. Yet as an experimental prototype for a new kind of urbanity, the autonomous zone mediates as much as it segments, functioning as a platform for bridging relations between local and global and for restructuring the relationship of local propertied elites to global capital. While it originated as tax-free factory sites connected to transnational port facilities, the export processing zone has mutated in seemingly surprising and magical ways. By transforming itself into a miniature city, or perhaps an assemblage of miniature cities, the city/zone hybrid represents a concentrated experiment in hypermodern urbanism. In this sense, city/zone hybrids are key locations for understanding the impact of globalization on urban form in the era of hypermodernity.[208]

---

[207] Easterling, "Zone: The Spatial Softwares of Extrastatecraft" (n.p.). See also James Sidaway, "Spaces of Postdevelopment," *Progress in Human Geography* 31, 3 (2007), pp. 345–361.

[208] Bach, "Modernity and the Urban Imagination in Economic Zones," p. 115.

7

Hybrid Zones and the Breakdown of Conventional Modalities of Urban Governance

The kinds of global urbanism emerging from the current wave of hypermodernist city building marks "an unprecedented radical departure from existing patterns of place."[1] As redevelopment projects have progressively refashioned cityscapes into assemblages of urban enclaves outfitted in a glittering new global image, existing land-use patterns and long-standing spatial connections are disrupted, if not eliminated outright. The steady accumulation of enclosed enclaves has transformed urban landscapes into a multitude of relatively autonomous "sovereignscapes," or discontinuous territorial fragments where the administrative rules through which they are governed are "free of any incumbent bureaucracy."[2]

The proliferation of autonomous zones complicates the complex territorial configurations of singular sovereign authority. In conventional thinking, sovereignty (i.e., the singular and centralized capacity to make rules and enforce them) represents the ultimate or last-resort power of decision-making over a carefully demarcated territory and the population which inhabits it.[3] The formation of autonomous zones breaks down the strict imbrication between sovereignty and territory, a largely symbiotic relationship where reliance upon a singular authority establishes a governance structure carved out of the same set of rules. This unbundling of territorial sovereignty is a highly selective process, and does not conform to any overriding logic that suggests a single route.

---

[1] Manish Chalana, "Slumdogs vs. Millionaires: Balancing Urban Informality and Global Modernity in Mumbai, India," *Journal of Architectural Education* 63, 2 (2010), pp. 25–37 (quotation from p. 25).

[2] James Sidaway, "Sovern Excesses? Portraying Postcolonial Sovereignityscapes," *Political Geography* 22, 2 (2003), pp. 157–178. See also Keller Easterling, *Extrastatecraft: The Power of Infrastructure Space* (New York: Verso, 2014), p. 48 (source of quotation).

[3] See Tom Nairn, "Sovereignty after the Election," *New Left Review* 1/224 (1997), 3–18 (esp. p. 3), for the source of this idea.

The zone format operates through the enactment of variegated, truncated, or compromised sovereignties.[4]

At a time of hypermodernity, new conceptualizations that refer to the decoupling of territoriality and sovereignty – sometimes called "new medievalism," "neomedievalism," or "postmodern territorialities" – recognize that geographic space has become more complex, fluid, and "relational" where overlapping authorities disrupt singular systems of monolithic control. As a general rule, conventional concepts based on idealized notions of "absolute" space are increasingly problematic for understanding the spatial complexities of city building at the present historical conjuncture.[5]

The zone format converges around the peculiar nexus of global modernity, investment capital, and exception. The steady multiplication of autonomous zones means that power is no longer identified in the singular sovereignty of state-sanctioned authority, but is distributed across the entirety of urban landscapes. This devolution from centralized authority creates bifurcated sovereignty regimes.[6]

Operating as an emergent strategy of city building, the zone format has increasingly filtered through urban landscapes as sites of both production and consumption. As extralegal habitats that nurture and grow their own sources of power, autonomous zones possess an organizational logic that favors stealth and camouflage over transparency and openness. These innovations in governance appear in strange disguises and under unexpected circumstances, sometimes by adopting various kinds of imitative or "simulated sovereignty." The zone format has become a persistent yet mutable instrument, adapting to new circumstances and changing shape in ways that could not have been imagined at the start. Autonomous zones can turn temporary exceptions – sometimes created out of the immediacy of emergency situations – into permanent mutations.[7]

As the zone format has multiplied and spread, it has also evolved and mutated, mixing with other increasingly popular spatial typologies like tourist-entertainment sites, business hubs, office parks, warehousing precincts, logistics centers, facilities for light assembly, innovation districts, and gated residential estates, to become the basic template, or building block, for fashioning

---

4 For a wider view, see Stephen Krasner, *Sovereignty: Organized Hypocrisy* (Princeton, NJ: Princeton University Press, 1999); Stephen Krasner, "Abiding Sovereignty," *International Political Science Review* 22, 3 (2001), pp. 229–251; and Wendy Brown, *Walled States, Waning Sovereignty* (Cambridge, MA: The MIT Press, 2010).

5 Jörg Friedrichs, "The Meaning of New Medievalism," *European Journal of International Relations* 7, 4 (2001), pp. 475–501; and Juliet Fall, Drawing the Line: *Nature, Hybridity and Politics in Transboundary Spaces* (Burlington, VT: Ashgate Press, 2005).

6 Easterling, Extrastatecraft, pp. 49, 148.

7 Keller Easterling, "Zone: The Spatial Softwares of Extrastatecraft," *Places: Forum of Design for the Public Realm* (June 11, 2012), [n.p.]. Available at http://places.designobserver.com/feature/zone-the-spatial-softwares-of-extrastatecraft/34528.

emergent "cities of tomorrow."[8] This new "free zone" paradigm provides new kinds of socio technical infrastructures that are grafted onto, transplant, and extend existing ideas about city building at a time of rapid globalization. As a distinctive socio spatial formation of late modernity, the zone format has adapted and consolidated into a new prototype for fast-track urbanism. Employing the rhetoric of freedom and openness, autonomous zones operate as a kind of "shadow state" existing parallel with, but beyond the reach of public administration. As undeclared constellations of private authority, they are actively engaged in transforming extraterritorial spaces into profit-making machines for corporate enterprise.[9]

As built manifestations of prescriptive commercial formulas enabling corporate enterprise, autonomous zones are hybrid assemblages of hard and soft infrastructures, generic design blueprints, and administrative rules. The zone format is as much a distinctive social practice as it is a physical place. As repeatable spatial templates that constitute the architecture of the city itself, autonomous zones act as a distinctive kind of aspirant "global space" through the convergence of three intersecting and overlapping practices: jurisdictional envelopes (or "rule-through-exception"), technological hardwares and softwares (logistics and infrastructure), and imaginative aesthetics (the unencumbered "free spaces" of frictionless movement of capital, goods, and information). By combining infrastructure and information technology, the zone format has become the very operating system for constructing the city itself.[10]

Concessionary Urbanism

Concessions – that is, territorial spaces within which some aspects of state sovereignty are either permanently or temporarily transferred to private corporate interests – have a long history. Most notably, concessions were especially significant for the extractive and developmental functions they performed during late colonialism and, notably in China, as treaty ports, *entrepôts*, and administrative outposts of free trade imposed under imperialism.[11] While many concessions disappeared with the end of colonialism, they survive today in the form of resource-extractive enclaves managed by such powerful entities as multinational oil companies or mining giants. These large-scale corporate

---

[8] Easterling, Extrastatecraft, pp. 36, 12.

[9] Easterling, *Extrastatecraft*, pp. 32–36, 42–48. See Ahmed Kanna, "The 'State Philosophical' in the 'Land without Philosophy': Shopping Malls, Interior Cities, and the Image of Utopia in Dubai," *Traditional Dwellings and Settlements Review*, 16, 2 (2005), pp. 59–73.

[10] Keller Easterling, "Zone: The Spatial Softwares of Extrastatecraft," *Places: Forum of Design for the Public Realm* (June 11, 2012), [n.p.]. See also Keller Easterling, "The Corporate City is the Zone," in Christina de Baan, Joachim Declerk, and Veronique Patteeuw (eds.), *Visionary Power: Creating the Contemporary City* (Rotterdam: NAi Publishers, 2007), pp. 75–85.

[11] Pál Nyíri, "Guest Editorial: The Renaissance of Concessions," *Political Geography* 31 (2012), pp. 195–196.

enterprises have continued to exercise state-like coercive and sometimes wel-fare activities that replicate state functions, most recently in the new guise of corporate social welfare programs that appear under the discourse of social responsibility.[12]

The proliferation of new modes of urban governance – such as free trade zones, business improvement districts, gated residential communities, spe-cial enterprise concessions, tax-free havens, investment corridors, community empowerment initiatives, redevelopment projects, and public-private partner-ships – have effectively broken urban landscapes into spatial fragments that reflect emergent configurations of accumulated wealth and power. Exploring these sites of neoliberal policy innovation enables us to uncover a story of urban fragmentation that has largely been elided in both statist-institutional perspectives of mainstream comparative politics and conventional urban stud-ies. The insertion of these hybrid regulatory regimes into the urban social fabric marks the start of efforts to bring market-oriented solutions to bear on such conventional problems of urban management like provision of services, safety and security, and maintenance and repair – all of which were once the exclusive mandate of public authorities.[13]

City building has increasingly taken place through the logic of exception, whereby real-estate developers demand exemptions from existing regulatory regimes, including tax write-offs, relaxation of land-use regulations, zoning variances, and accelerated approval processes. Real-estate developers legitimate to the suspension of the rule of law by reference to nagging "red tape," bureau-cratic slowness, and the need for haste. Taken together, these dispensations, concessions, and negotiated compromises amount to what Idalina Baptista has called a "regime of exception," that is, a tractable system of governance estab-lished by extraordinary measures that create and enforce alternative sets of procedural rules and institutional structures to deliver a desired outcome. The anomalies that autonomous zones create are not inconsistent aberrations or abnormal deviations, but instead their precise objectives.[14]

This shift toward flexible governance has opened a terrain of administra-tive malleability, where conventional planning protocols lose their power to enforce strict conformity to uniform standards. Practices of exception provide the conditions of possibility to bypass and abrogate existing practices of gov-ernance. What is clear is that city building increasingly takes place under cir-cumstances characterized by pliant, *ad hoc* decision-making, or what Ananya

---

[12] Marina Welker, "'Corporate Security Begins in the Community': Mining, the Corporate Social Responsibility Industry, and Environmental Advocacy in Indonesia," *Cultural Anthropology* 24, 1 (2009), pp. 142–179; and James Ferguson, "Seeing Like an Oil Company: Space, Security, and Global Capital in Neoliberal Africa," *American Anthropologist* 107, 3 (2005), pp. 377–382.

[13] Nyíri, "Guest Editorial: The Renaissance of Concessions," pp. 195–196.

[14] Idalina Baptista, "Practices of Exception in Urban Governance: Reconfiguring Power Inside the State," *Urban Studies* 50, 1 (2013), pp. 39–54 (quotation from p. 43).

Roy has described as the *informalization* of the planning process.[15] This permissive approach consistently provides real-estate developers with more flexibility in bending the rules in their favor. Seen in this light, improvised decision-making does not represent a failure in planning practice or the inability of urban planners to shape the built environment. On the contrary, informality in planning "appears to be a deliberate planning strategy that best fits the interests of those decision-makers who find in the flexibility it provides the leeway needed to regulate and organize the development of the city according to their own interests."[16] While it may be mandated by law, public oversight is rarely implemented. In the end, flexibility can more often than not come under the dominance of powerful private interests. To be sure, informality as a planning practice – or the existence of *ad hoc*, case-by-case processes of decision-making within the planning process – amounts to a regime of exception.[17] Large-scale urban redevelopment projects are planned and executed as exceptionalities, that is, produced on an improvised basis outside of conventional planning regimes with their standardized regulations and procedures.[18]

The logic of exception marks a shift from fixed forms of sovereignty (and its law-bound regularities) to graduated forms of sovereignty, with its "sliding and contested scales of differential rights." Unlike the dreamscape of modernist planning, exceptionality signals "processes of becoming, not fixed things."[19] Put bluntly, regimes of exception are constitutive of a new mode of privatized planning that enables real-estate developers to abrogate the rule of law and substitute their own regulatory guidelines.[20]

Hybrid Zones as Template for New Modes of Urban Governance

Over the past several decades, the sheer numbers and genres of extraterritorial spaces have expanded, diversified, and consolidated into dense configurations of exception and exemption that superimpose themselves and act to undermine the very notion of territorial sovereignty. Seen in this light, territories are no longer (strictly speaking) confined to a clearly demarcated bounded shape,

[15] Ananya Roy, "Why India Cannot Plan its Cities: Informality, Insurgence and the Idiom of Urbanization," *Planning Theory* 8, 1 (2009), pp. 76–87.

[16] Marieke Krijnen and Mona Fawaz, "Exception as the Rule: High-End Developments in Neoliberal Beirut," *Built Environment* 36, 2 (2010), pp. 245–259 (quotation from p. 255).

[17] Krijnen and Fawaz, "Exception as the Rule: High-End Developments in Neoliberal Beirut," pp. 245–259.

[18] Marieke Krijnen, *Facilitating Real Estate Development in Beirut: A Peculiar Case of Neoliberal Public Policy* (Unpublished Master's Thesis, Department of Arab and Middle East Studies, American University of Beirut, 2010), pp. 21–23.

[19] Ann Laura Stoler, "Imperial Debris: On Ruins and Ruination," *Cultural Anthropology* 23, 2 (2008), pp. 191–219. See also Ann Laura Stoler, "On Degrees of Imperial Sovereignty," *Public Culture* 18, 1 (2006), pp. 125–146.

[20] Baptista, "Practices of Exception in Urban Governance," pp. 43–44.

but become – in addition – complex systems of relationships and large-scale structural networks.[21]

In Amman (Jordan), the conjoined efforts of city builders, including real-estate developers and political power-brokers, have remade Amman in the image of a "new city" by way of the introduction of globalized benchmarks of speed, efficiency, and connectivity. This production of new systems of movement and connection represents the deliberate intervention into urban space in ways that conform to the interests of corporate business interests. Yet instead of accepting at face value the conventional understanding of property markets and the production of space under contemporary capitalism as rooted in the economic rationality of the market, the reshaping of the urban landscape in Amman reflects the continued ability of oligarchic networks at the heart of spatial production "to turn economic reform discourses, including that of contemporary market urbanism, to their own decidedly illiberal purposes."[22] Regimes of exception engage in the production of territory. The steady accretion of private regulatory authorities ranging from Special Economic Zones, Poverty Pocket schemes, development corridors, community empowerment initiatives, urban regeneration projects, gated residential communities, to planned satellite cities have reconfigured the landscapes of power. These spaces of exemption have privileged well-to-do urban residents who can bypass and circumvent the neglected areas of the city.[23]

In short, the changing cityscape of Amman reflects efforts to empower private agencies and to bring market-oriented solutions to bear on conventional problems of urban governance. The introduction and deployment of new regulatory regimes built around infrastructural ensembles have effectively created

---

[21] Easterling, *Extrastatecraft: The Power of Infrastructure Space*, pp. 42–44.

[22] Najib Hourani, "Urbanism and Neoliberal Order: The Development and Redevelopment of Amman," *Journal of Urban Affairs* 36, s2 (2014), pp. 634–649 (p. 634, source of quotation). See also Najib Hourani and Ahmed Kanna, "Arab Cities in the Neoliberal Moment," *Journal of Urban Affairs* 36, s2 (2014), pp. 600–604.

[23] From the airport, the main highway traverses the desert toward the Aqaba Special Economic Zone Authority, an administratively independent and state-owned corporation that governs 400 km² and some 100,000 people in and around the only seaport in Jordan. Before reaching the airport, the north–south highway intersects with the Amman Development Corridor Project. Co-financed by the Country Assistance Program of the World Bank and the European Investment Bank, the project promises, according to a World Bank report, to act as "a catalyst for economic development and expansion" by "enhancing conditions for growth led by the private sector." The axis of this large-scale initiative is a 40 km stretch of highway that will serve as the southern-most segment of the Greater Amman Ring Road, thereby improving communications to the existing Qualifying Industrial Zone (QIZ) facilities at Sahab, and opening a further 300 km² of land for private real-estate development. State authorities have offered a variety of tax holidays and other incentives to encourage investment. This description is borrowed from Christopher Parker, "Tunnel-bypasses and Minarets of Capitalism: Amman as Neoliberal Assemblage," *Political Geography* 28, 2 (2009), pp. 110–120 (esp. p. 113, source of quotation).

"a social reality that [neoliberal discourse] suggests already exists."[24] These regulatory regimes enable private interests to leverage their newly acquired authorities to defend "market requirements" (i.e., the necessity of cost recovery) against the claims of deliberative citizenship.[25] As the neoliberal development discourse of development celebrates the involvement of entrepreneurial initiative and private agencies in the "governance" of places and populations, it remains silent on the possible authoritarian implications of this shift.[26]

In Johannesburg, the lateral extension of privately managed precincts known as city improvement districts (CIDs) has largely replaced public authorities in the historic downtown core. In their formal operations, CIDs form an "archipelagic network of power" that has replaced the public management of urban space. By amassing powers conventionally reserved for municipal administrative bodies, CIDs are the primary aggregate units of the entrepreneurial city and neoliberal governance. More than merely reinforcing existing divisions in the already splintered urban landscape, "CIDs have effectively gone their own way," producing a new spatial order that marks "not just an insular retreat" from the social fabric of the city, "but the deliberate construction of an extended network of fortified enclaves disconnected from the rest of the urban landscape." This wholesale withdrawal from the public modes of urban governance "amounts to a new kind of transcendent enclave urbanism, marked by the shift toward a form of autarkic urban development that leads inevitably to the creation of an archipelago of self-reliant, [self-contained island-like enclosures] with little or no organic connection to the surrounding cityscape."[27]

Informality as a Mode of Urban Governance

The evolving metropolis of the twenty-first century is a paradoxical space of contradiction and contestation. On the one hand, what characterizes the contemporary age of global urbanism are deepening inequalities, ongoing displacements and removals, and the entrenchment of separations that territorialize urban identities in enclave geographies. On the other hand, city building is shaped by grassroots expressions of citizenship, civil society engagement,

---

[24] Thomas Lemke, "Foucault, Governmentality, and Critique," *Rethinking Marxism* 14, 3 (2000), pp. 49–64 (quotation from p. 59). This idea is borrowed from Parker, "Tunnel-Bypasses and Minarets of Capitalism," p. 110.

[25] Parker, "Tunnel-Bypasses and Minarets of Capitalism," p. 111. See also Rami Farouk Daher, "Amman: Disguised Genealogy and Recent Urban Restructuring and Neoliberal Threats," in Yasser Elsheshtawy (ed.), *The Evolving Arab City: Tradition, Modernity and Urban Development* (London: Routledge, 2008), pp. 37–68.

[26] Parker, "Tunnel-Bypasses and Minarets of Capitalism," p. 117. See also James Sidaway, "Spaces of Postdevelopment," *Progress in Human Geography* 31, 3 (2007), pp. 345–361; and Claudio Minca, "Agamben's Geographies of Modernity," *Political Geography* 26, 1 (2007), pp. 78–97.

[27] Martin J. Murray, *City of Extremes: The Spatial Landscape of Johannesburg* (Durham: Duke University Press, 2011), pp. 260–282 (quotations from p. 282).

and social mobilizations. These populist sentiments create platforms that insist upon "participatory" frameworks of collaborative planning.[28]

As a general rule, the core principles of modernist planning have long extolled the virtues of officially sanctioned, formal regulation as a vital instrument for bringing order to the disorderly city.[29] Seen from this angle, informality – or the persistence of unregulated (and hence chaotic) practices and irregular spaces that operate outside official authorization and control – appears to be antithetical to formal planning. Contrary to this conventional way of thinking, Nezar AlSayyad and Ananya Roy have convincingly argued that informality constitutes, in fact, a distinct (and disguised) mode of regulation, that is, "a set of tactics" that establish "rules of the game" that shape interactions between and among individuals and social groups.[30] If formality stresses the fixing of exchange relationships, then informality operates through the constant negotiability of transactions. Properly understood, then, informality is not marginal or exceptional, but on the contrary, an organizing logic of everyday life – or a distinct mode of urbanism.[31]

In contrast to the conventional thinking that treats formality and informality as hermetically sealed, distinct spheres of activity, they are actually inextricably entangled in myriad ways. Because municipal authorities have the discretionary power to effectively extend, or conversely suspend, the protections of the law (i.e., to establish the legal "inside" and the illegal "outside"), they can effectively determine what is formal and what is not. By defining what is legitimate and what is illegitimate, they effectively "determine which forms of informality will thrive and which will disappear."[32]

Cast in this light, informality in all its manifestations can thus be understood as a mode of urban governance that is "in fact produced through intricate webs of norms and regulations" that do not involve the participation or exercise of official sanction.[33] The unauthorized practices and irregular spaces of the

---

[28] Ananya Roy, "Civic Governmentality: The Politics of Inclusion in Beirut and Mumbai," *Antipode* 41, 1 (2009), pp. 159–179. See also Martin Webb, "Meeting at the Edges: Spaces, Places and Grassroots Governance Activism in Delhi," *South Asia Multidisciplinary Academic Journal* 8 (2013), pp. 1–14.

[29] Frank Gaffikin and David Perry, "The Contemporary Urban Condition: Understanding the Globalizing City as Informal, Contested, and Anchored," *Urban Affairs Review* 48, 5 (2012), pp. 701–730 (esp. p. 723).

[30] Nezar AlSayyad and Ananya Roy, "Medieval Modernity: On Citizenship and Urbanism in a Global Era," *Space and Polity* 10, 1 (2006), pp. 1–20 (p. 8, source of quotation). See also Neema Kudva, "The Everyday and the Episodic: The Spatial and Political Impacts of Urban Informality," *Environment and Planning A* 41, 7 (2009), pp. 1614–28.

[31] Nezar AlSayyad and Ananya Roy, "Urban Informality: Cross Borders," in Ananya Roy and Nezar AlSayyad (eds.), *Urban Informality: Transnational Perspectives from the Middle East, Latin America, and South Asia* (Lanham, MD: Lexington Books, 2004), pp. 1–6 (esp. p. 5).

[32] Ananya Roy, "Urban Informality: Toward an Epistemology of Planning," *Journal of the American Planning Association* 71, 2 (2005), pp. 147–158 (esp. p. 149).

[33] AlSayyad and Ananya Roy, "Medieval Modernity," p. 9.

informal city jostle uncomfortably with the abstract spaces of the planned city with its land-use zoning and building codes. Under circumstances where formal regulatory regimes are either weak or entirely absent, key power-brokers, civic and community-based associations, faith-based groups, and NGOs often fill in the void, dispensing patronage and adjudicating disputes, and making rules and enforcing compliance.[34]

As numerous scholars have demonstrated, religious groups and political organizations often play pivotal roles in providing much-needed social services in the vast informal settlements that surround depressed cities.[35] Faced with the deprivation of everyday life and the neglect if not outright hostility of state authorities, these social groups and organizations have effectively established themselves as an effective "shadow state," thereby producing "a fragmented domain of multiple and competing sovereignties."[36] Unlike the politics of interest-group liberalism, with "its democratic system of checks and balances," these competing sovereignties often represent "a hardening of ever-fragmenting fundamentalisms and parochialisms – the politics of fiefdoms negotiated through modes of visible and invisible regulations."[37] Rather than operating as positive vehicles of empowerment and upliftment, community-based organizations (CBOs) and their leadership often block progress, controlling or capturing benefits aimed at the poor and misusing them for private gain. As Joop De Wit and Erhard Berner have shown in their study of community-based projects in the slums of three large Indian cities, municipal agencies, international donors, and NGOs "cannot easily escape the logic of patronage, and often themselves become part of a system of vertical dependency relations."[38]

In Mumbai, Hindu fundamentalist (and xenophobic) groups like the Shiva Sena party have gained popular support by promising to acquire and transfer habitable land under conditions of highly restrictive land markets and extreme housing scarcity. Over the course of the past four decades, the Shiva Sena "has sutured a specific form of regional chauvinism with a national message about Hindu power through the deployment of the figure of the Muslim as the archetype of the invader, the stranger, and the traitor."[39] The massive, nationwide campaign of ethnocidal mob violence directed against impoverished

---

[34] AlSayyad and Ananya Roy, "Medieval Modernity," p. 10.

[35] Mike Davis, *Planet of Slums* (New York: Verso, 2006), pp. 195–196. See also Asef Bayat, "Activism and Social Development in the Middle East," *International Journal of Middle East Studies* 34, 2 (2002), pp. 1–28.

[36] AlSayyad and Roy, "Medieval Modernity," p. 12.

[37] AlSayyad and Roy, "Medieval Modernity," p. 12.

[38] Joop De Wit and Erhard Berner, "Progressive Patronage? Municipalities, NGOs, CBOs and the Limits to Slum Dwellers' Empowerment," *Development and Change* 40, 5 (2009), pp. 927–947 (quotation from p. 927).

[39] Arun Appadurai, "Spectral Housing and Urban Cleansing: Notes on Millennial Mumbai," *Public Culture* 12, 3 (2000), pp. 627–651 (quotation from p. 646).

Muslims in 1992–1993 coincided with the spatial geography of urban overcrowding, intense competition over street commerce, and housing shortage
nightmares in Mumbai. In a "bizarre utopia of urban renewal," Hindu extrem-
ists seeking to reclaim land for their own religious followers engaged in a
violent outbreak of "ethnic cleansing" designed to destroy Muslim-owned
shops and residential dwellings, and to push Muslims out of streets and public spaces in those neighborhoods "where the two groups lived cheek by
jowl."[40]

In the sprawling slums of many Latin American cities, Pentecostal Christian
churches have emerged as key power-brokers in local politics, in part because
of their ability to supply the much-needed social services municipal authorities
have largely failed to deliver, and to offer a modest "safety net" for the poor-
est of the poor.[41] Like populist Islam, Pentecostal and charismatic Christian-
ity conveys a powerful message of spiritual redemption through engagement
and participation in community service.[42] Gang membership often provides a
secular route to resist the humiliations imposed by living in stigmatized sites
of deprivation. In contrast, religious conversion can be a "gendered form of
oppositional culture" that emerges in response to the male oppositional culture of gang membership. For women, the "flight into a religious world that
prohibits drinking, advocates moral redemption, and still believes in honest
hard work" signifies a disillusionment and disenchantment with the secular
world of political parties and municipal authorities who fail to deliver on their
promises of providing social services.[43] In slums, the municipal officials, political parties, religious associations, civic organizations, and NGOs all compete
for power and influence, offering different territorialized forms of association
and patronage.[44] Even when religious groups are not directly involved, slum
dwellers develop their own distinct politics, regimes of rule, and institutional
dynamics. In Villa el Salvador, a famous *barricada* of Lima, transformed from
an informal squatter settlement into a well-ordered, working-class neighborhood, the estimated 350,000 residents have more or less adopted "a set of

---

[40] Appadurai, "Spectral Housing and Urban Cleansing," p. 649 (source of quotations). See also
Arun Appadurai, "Sovereignty without Territoriality: Notes for a Postnational Geography," in
Setha Low and Denise Lawrence-Zúñiga (eds.), *The Anthropology of Space and Place* (Cam-
bridge: Blackwell, 2003), pp. 337–349.

[41] AlSayyad and Roy, "Medieval Modernity," p. 11. See Mike Davis, "Planet of Slums," *New
Left Review* 26 (2004), pp. 5–34 (esp. pp. 31–32). See also Adedamola Osinulu, "The Road
to Redemption: Performing Pentecostal Citizenship in Lagos," in Mamadou Diouf and Rosalind Fredericks (eds.), *The Arts of Citizenship in African Cities: Infrastructures and Spaces of
Belonging* (New York: Palgrave Macmillan, 2014), pp. 115–136.

[42] Eric Kremer, "Spectacle and the Staging of Power in Brazilian Neo-Pentecostalism," *Latin American Perspectives* 32, 1 (2005), pp. 95–120.

[43] Donna Goldstein, *Laughter Out of Place: Race, Class, Violence and Sexuality in a Rio Shantytown* (Berkeley: University of California Press, 2003), p. 219).

[44] AlSayyad and Roy, "Medieval Modernity," p. 12.

norms and "laws" of local bosses over which the state has hardly any control" under circumstances where the presence of public police is minimal.[45]

Under circumstances where local power-brokers replace the formal authority of the state administration with their own modes of governance, the distribution of patronage becomes the *de facto* logic of rule. Yet, the logic of rule is never monolithic: the terrain always consists of uneasy alliances and shifting sovereignties. The political economy of patronage can vary from a mediated role of brokerage between formal regimes of governance and local communities to the relatively autonomous condition of "free space."[46]

Beirut, City of Mirrors: The Imbrication of Formal and Informal Planning Practices

Sometimes the selection of extreme cases that illustrate the unbundling of territory and sovereignty can help us to bring into sharp relief the actual workings of global urbanism on the ground. While they may appear as outliers (or "limit cases") located at the far edges of the spectrum, these extraordinary expressions of deterritorialization allow us to imagine the form that the "urbanism of exception" might take if these emergent patterns of nested sovereignties were generalized across urban landscapes. Seen from this perspective, the exceptional case offers prescient clues as to where global urbanism may be going.

In Beirut (Lebanon), the striking contrast between the spectacular rebuilding of the devastated historic core, on the one side, and the incremental rehabilitation of the southern suburbs after the end of the 1975–1990 civil war on the other, illustrates the clash of competing rationalities that split along the lines of top-down formal planning versus laterally extended informal interventions at the grassroots. From the start, the commercial resurrection of downtown Beirut and its deliberate rebranding as a leading metropolis of the Arab world triggered a great deal of controversy and hotly contested debate over the nature and scope of urban reconstruction in the aftermath of war-related devastation.[47]

---

[45] Marcelo Balbo, "Urban Planning and the Fragmented City of the Developing World," *Third World Planning Review* 15, 1 (1993), pp. 23–55 (p. 25, source of quotation). See also Daniella Gandolfo, *City at Its Limits: Taboo, Transgression, and Urban Renewal in Lima* (Chicago: University of Chicago Press, 2009).

[46] AlSayyad and Roy, "Medieval Modernity," p. 12.

[47] Caroline Nagel, "Ethnic Conflict and Urban Redevelopment in Down Town Beirut," *Growth and Change* 31, 2 (2000), pp. 211–234; Caroline Nagel, "Reconstruction Space, Re-creating Memory: Sectarian Politics and Urban Development in Postwar Beirut," *Political Geography*, 21, 5 (2002), pp. 717–725; Aseel Sawalha, *Reconstructing Beirut: Memory and Space in a Postwar Arab City* (Austin: University of Texas Press, 2010); Sara Fregonese, "The Urbicide of Beirut? Geopolitics and the Built Environment in the Lebanese Civil War," *Political Geography* 28, 5 (2009), pp. 309–318; and Hashim Sarkis and Peter Rowe, "The Age of Physical Reconstruction," in Peter Rowe and Hashim Sarkis (eds.), Projecting Beirut: Episodes in the Construction and Reconstruction of a Modern City (Munich: Prestel, 1998), pp. 275–284.

This urban redevelopment project became the virtual dreamscape of visual consumption, a platform for the hoped-for insertion into global and cosmopolitan circuits of power. Conducted under the aegis of a joint stock real-estate company known by its French acronym *Solidère*, the rebuilding process was a historically singular event of postwar rebuilding when a lone company assumed ownership and management control of a highly symbolic place.[48] In a bold move, Rafik Hariri, the millionaire ex-politician and founder of *Solidère*, engineered the adoption of a controversial amendment that created an exception to the 1977 planning legislation. So-called "law 117" (through special powers of compulsory purchase) enabled *Solidère* to expropriate land and property from existing owners, who were compensated with stock-shares in the company, at what many claimed fell far short of the true market value of their properties. Owners had the option to keep their properties, but only on condition they had sufficient funds to restore their buildings in line with strict preservation guidelines determined by the Company. As part of this sweetheart reconstruction scheme, *Solidère* acquired "exceptional powers" over conventional land-use planning functions, including determining building typologies and supervising the installation of its own "[*faux*] public" infrastructure works. In what critics lambasted as akin to highway robbery, an act of piracy, or even a kind of vigilantism conducted deceitfully under the cover of law, this *carte blanche* mandate cleared the way for *Solidère* to manage the city center like its own private mini-fiefdom. To secure protection from any challenges from rival real-estate developers, *Solidère* exercised control over the entire project via a network of business allies and high-ranking city officials. In order to implement the reconstruction effort, the Company systematically razed the war-torn urban fabric, creating a virtual *tabula rasa* right at the heart of the historic city.[49]

This master-planned, privately owned flagship reconstruction project marked a decisive moment where, in the words of Saree Makdisi, "state projects end and private projects begin can no longer be determined – not because this is a strong state organizing a command economy but because [real estate] capital has *become* the state."[50] This large-scale mega-project constituted and

---

[48] Yasmeen Arif, "Impossible Cosmopolises: Dislocations and Relocations in Beirut and Delhi," in Shail Mayaram (ed.), *The Other Global City* (New York: Routledge, 2009), pp. 101–128 (esp. p. 127). See also Ghenwa Hayek, *Beirut, Imagining the City: Space and Place in Lebanese Literature* (London: I. B. Taurus, 2015); and Najib Hourani, *Capitalists in Conflict: A Political Economy of the Life, Death, and Rebirth of Beirut* (Unpublished Ph.D. dissertation, New York University, 2005).

[49] Reinhoud Leenders, "No Body Having too Much to Answer For: *Laissez-faire*, Networks, and Postwar Reconstruction in Lebanon," in Steven Heydeman (ed.), *Networks of Privilege in the Middle East: The Politics of Economic Reform Revisited* (New York: Palgrave MacMillan, 2004), pp. 169–200 (esp. pp. 184–185); and Oliver Wainwright, "Is Beirut's Glitzy Downtown Redevelopment all that it Seems?" *Guardian* [UK], January 22, 2015.

[50] Saree Makdisi, "Laying Claim to Beirut: Urban Narrative and Spatial Identity in the Age of *Solidère*," *Critical Inquiry* 23, 3 (1997), pp. 660–705 (p. 688, source of quotation). See also Joe Nasr and Eric Verdeil, "The Reconstruction of Beirut," in Salma Jayyusi, Renata Holod, Attilio

defined the "formal" approach to planning and real-estate redevelopment in Beirut after the devastating civil war. Although *Solidère* initially planned for the heritage preservation of some older iconic buildings, it demolished most of the original historic core and built modern buildings on top of the ruins, displacing small-scale business owners and inhabitants in the process. In the process of rebuilding, Beirut became "perhaps the world's largest laboratory for postwar reconstruction," or what two scholars have called a "permanent (re)construction site," that was subjected to the globalizing forces of consumerism, privatization, and *laissez-faire* entrepreneurialism.[51]

The *Solidère* postwar reconstruction project reinvented the city's historic core of Beirut, transforming the downtown center into a separate enclave of high-end exclusivity, abruptly severed from the rest of the city by a network of highways that constitute solid physical barriers. A new landscape of high-rise buildings and immaculately rebuilt streets stands in stark contrast with the dense morphology of the somewhat ramshackle neighborhoods that surround the area. Perhaps not so surprisingly, the rehabilitated city center preserved and perpetuated the isolation of the historic core of the city in abiding to the boundaries forged during the civil war. *Solidère* transformed the battle-zone of downtown Beirut from an abject space of military violence into a ludic space of free flow of capital without altering in any fundamental way the spatial detachment of the downtown core from the rest of the city.[52]

Widely considered as the embodiment of a new political and economic era associated with the neoliberal project of the late Prime Minister Rafik Hariri (1995–2005), *Solidère* sought to establish Beirut as a global destination for international capital and investors, in line with other (so-called) neoliberal (market-driven) urban interventions in the Arab Middle East and elsewhere. Wrapped in nostalgia and wishful thinking, *Solidère* fashioned an uplifting narrative that imagined a "reborn Beirut" by mobilizing a stylized image of cosmopolitanism tailored for place-branding and for attracting foreign direct investment.[53] By drawing on a simplistic recollection of the alleged Lebanese

---

Petruccioli and André Raymond (eds.), *The City in the Islamic World*. Volume 2 (Leiden and Boston: Brill, 2008), pp. 1116–1141.

[51] First quotation is from Esther Charlesworth, *Architects without Frontiers: War, Reconstruction and Design Responsibility* (Oxford and Burlington: Architectural Press Elsevier, 2006), p. 54. Second quotation is from Krijnen and Fawaz, "Exception as the Rule: High-End Developments in Neoliberal Beirut," p. 245.

[52] Marwan Ghandour and Mona Fawaz, "Spatial Erasure: Reconstruction Projects in Beirut," *ArteEast Quarterly* (Spring, 2010). Available at www.arteeast.org. See Najib Hourani, "From National Utopia to Elite Enclave: The Selling of the Beirut Souqs," in Gary McDonogh and Marina Peterson (eds.), *Global Downtowns* (Philadelphia: University of Pennsylvania Press, 2012), pp. 136–159; and Hadi Makarem, "Actually Existing Neoliberalism: The Reconstruction of Downtown Beirut in Post-Civil War Lebanon" (Unpublished Ph.D. dissertation, London School of Economics and Political Science, 2014).

[53] Sara Fregonese, "Between a Refuge and a Battleground: Beirut's Discrepant Cosmopolitanisms," *Geographical Review* 102, 3 (2012), pp. 316–336 (esp. p. 317).

traditions of entrepreneurialism, cultural pluralism, and innovation, this effort to construct an idealized "layered city of memory" was remarkably selective in the historical narrative it reproduced and the collective memory it evoked. Stitching together sanitized references to restored Roman baths, reconstructed Ottoman "historic buildings," and French colonial promenades, *Solidère* fashioned the carefully manicured motto – "Beirut, Ancient City of Future" – to re-brand the city in ways that erased the reminders of the more recent traumatic and violent events that led to the destruction of the historic downtown center, and replaced these bitter memories with a romanticized appeal to a more glorious and heroic past.[54]

Like the proverbial phoenix rising, the city builders behind the reconstruction effort have sought to transform the ravaged core of Beirut into the premier seaside destination for luxury living and recreation in the Middle East. The ambitious master plan, spearheaded from the beginning by British architect Angus Gavin, who previously worked with the London Docklands Development Corporation, is an odd assortment of careful urban design and historic preservation, interspersed with "showy outbursts by big name global architects." Many streetscapes "have been impeccably restored to their *beaux-arts* glory, with colonnaded pavements and beautifully carved stonework along cornices and window reveals, reviving the fusion of French colonial and Levantine vernacular."[55]

From the start, the rebuilding project was harnessed to a vision of a post civil war Beirut that aligned the commercial recovery of the city to the entrepreneurial interests of large-scale capital of Lebanese and Arab Gulf origins. The rebuilding project benefited from a wide array of public subsidies, such as tax exemptions and financial assistance to offset costs of infrastructure, and generous dispensation enshrined in special regulations designed *à la carte*

---

[54] Phrases and slogans are from the original master plan of *Solidère*. See Craig Larkin, "Speaking in the Silence: Youthful Negotiations of Beirut's Postwar Spaces and Memories," in Wendy Pullan and Britt Bailie (eds.), *Locating Urban Conflicts: Ethnicity, Nationalism and the Everyday* (New York: Palgrave Macmillan, 2013), pp. 93–114 (p. 98 for source of quotations). See also Miriam Cooke, "Beirut Reborn: The Political Aesthetics of Auto-Destruction," *The Yale Journal of Criticism* 15, 2 (2002), pp. 393–424; Craig Larkin, "Remaking Beirut: Contesting Memory, Space, and the Urban Imaginary of Lebanese Youth," *City & Community* 9, 4 (2010), pp. 414–442; Ghada Masri, "Reconstructing Phoenicia: Tourist Landscapes and National Identity in the Heart of the Lebanese Capital," in Robert Maitland and Brent Ritchie (eds.), *City Tourism: National Capital Perspectives* (Cambridge, MA: CAB International, 2009), pp. 225–238; Adrienne Fricke, "Forever Nearing the Finish Line: Heritage Policy and the Problem of Memory in Postwar Beirut," International Journal of Cultural Property *12*, 2 (2005), pp. 163–181; Oussama Kabbani, "Public Space as Infrastructure: The Case of the Postwar Reconstruction of Beirut," in *Projecting Beirut*, pp. 68–82; and Craig Larkin, "Beyond the War? The Lebanese Postmemory Experience," *International Journal of Middle East Studies* 42, 4 (2010), pp. 615–635.

[55] Oliver Wainwright, "Is Beirut's Glitzy Downtown Redevelopment all that it Seems?" *Guardian* [UK], January 22, 2015 (source of quotations).

FIGURE 7.1. *Solidère* project, Beirut.
(Photo Credit: Marieke Krijnen.)

to fit the needs and interests of the private real-estate developers.[56] *Solidère* redrew the original streetscape of the old city, demolishing many of its architectural and urban landmarks and replacing these with new building typologies that enhance the "commercial trading value" of the new landscape. The historic buildings that remained were brought into line with the refurbished image of the city – as displayed in Figure 7.1, a kind of "Disneyfied" imitation of a real city preserved in a *faux* time warp for the feigned aesthetic pleasure of wealthy globe-trotting tourists.[57] As Oliver Wainwright has argued, "these new pseudo-historic streets recall their former selves, but they have been reincarnated as upmarket *doppelgängers*, precious replicas of what had been the well-worn and well-loved blocks of these lower-class neighborhoods." Under the guiding hand of *Solidère*, Beirut has inexorably become a skyscraper city of

[56] Makdisi, "Laying Claim to Beirut," pp. 661–705; and Sofia Shwayrik, "From Regional Node Backwater and Back to Uncertainty: Beirut, 1943–2006," in *The Evolving Arab* City, pp. 69–98.
[57] See Suzanne Kassab, "On Two Conceptions of Globalization: The Debate around the Reconstruction of Beirut," in Ayçe Oncu and Petra Weylande (eds.), Space, Culture and Power: *New Identities in Globalizing Cities* (London: Zed Books, 1997), pp. 42–55.

lofty office towers and "floating villages" of penthouses stacked one atop the other – "vertical extrusions of inflated land values."[58]

Operating on the basis of a new faith in economic liberalism and a *laissez-faire* approach to city building, *Solidère* reconstructed the devastated downtown core into a hypermodern and socioeconomically isolated district that is intended to serve as a new playground for a global, and especially rich Arab elite.[59] Indeed, this new sanitized and purified Beirut has become an exportable model for urban redevelopment in other cities of the Arab world, like Amman (Jordan), Riyadh and Jeddah (Saudi Arabia), and Hazmieh (Lebanon). Large-scale construction and real-estate companies from the Arab Gulf, like Sama Dubai, have begun to build cities in its image elsewhere in the region.[60]

This remaking and reimagining of war-torn Beirut through an elaborate assemblage of downtown mega-projects took place in tandem with the emergence of Hezbollah (the "party of God") as the *de facto* state administration in the impoverished suburban neighborhoods south of the central city.[61] In Beirut, the designation "southern suburbs" has a negative connotation, often used interchangeably with anarchy, unauthorized squatting, illegality, and poverty. The southern suburbs–created at first by a permanent flow of rural migrants and later by both urban and rural refugees from the 1975–1991 civil war and the Israeli occupation (1978–2000) – are homogenous and impoverished quarters of Beirut, consisting mostly of Shi'a Muslim residents and by the second decade of the twenty-first century comprised one third of the population of the greater Beirut metropolitan region. As such, this vast catchment area has been stigmatized as an uninviting belt of misery, a vast zone of rural migrants, displaced peoples, and Palestinian refugees – all squeezed into temporary encampments without proper services or infrastructure.[62] The southern outskirts of Beirut became spatially fragmented into militia-controlled "mini-states," home

---

[58] Oliver Wainwright, "Is Beirut's Glitzy Downtown Redevelopment all that it Seems?" *Guardian* [UK], January 22, 2015.

[59] Shwayrik, "From Regional Node Backwater and Back to Uncertainty: Beirut, 1943–2006," in *The Evolving Arab City*, pp. 69–98.

[60] Hilary Silver, "Divided Cities in the Middle East," *City & Community* 9, 4 (2010), pp. 34–357 (esp. 351). See also Fricke, "Forever Nearing the Finish Line," pp. 163–181; and Larkin, "Remaking Beirut: Contesting Memory, Space, and the Urban Imaginary of Lebanese Youth," pp. 414–442.

[61] Sara Fregonese, "Beyond the 'Weak State': Hybrid Sovereignties in Beirut," *Environment and Planning D* 30, 4 (2012), pp. 655–674 (esp. p. 667); Steven Seidman, "The Politics of Cosmopolitan Beirut from the Stranger to the Other," *Theory, Culture & Society* 29, 2 (2012), pp. 3–36; and Najib Hourani, "Capitalists in Conflict: The Lebanese Civil War Reconsidered," *Middle East Critique* 24, 2 (2015), pp. 137–160.

[62] Aseel Sawalha, "'Healing the Wounds of the War': Placing the War-Displaced in Postwar Beirut," in Jane Schneider and Ida Susser (eds.), *Wounded Cities: Destruction and Reconstruction in a Globalized World* (Oxford: Berg, 2003), pp. 271–290 (esp. p. 272).

to all sorts of newcomers to the city.[63] Over time, these newcomers became permanent inhabitants, and these "camp-cities" became an integral part of the southern precincts of Beirut.[64]

Despite the uncertainly produced by the long civil war, Beirut was far from an insular "closed city": its urban landscape was subjected to an odd globalization all of its own, consisting of transnational flows of capital organized under the watchful eye of warlords, informal economies of social and infrastructural services provided by militias, and real-estate development in spite of the ongoing violence. For celebrants of the neoliberal global order, the micro managed "militia economy" operated in "the realm of pathology, infected by politics and cultural traditionalism, by predatory gangsterism and transnational criminality." Its backwardness "prevented Beirut from taking its rightful place as the primary regional driver of the Arab world toward integration with global markets." Yet as Najb Hourani has argued, the "militia economy" was never fully outside larger processes of financial globalization, but instead was integrated into a global field consisting not of formal financial enterprises operating according to a universal capitalist rationality, but rather one of similarly constituted networks of entrepreneurs, private companies, and other institutional actors working within and alongside a variety of global networks in pursuit of politico-economic power.[65]

Just as elaborate urban mega-projects such as *Solidère* and Elyssar have remade Beirut in the radiant image of a world-class cosmopolitan city, Hezbollah (the political party best known for its role as the "Islamic Resistance" against Israel) has emerged as the main mediator of social rights for the Shi'a poor.[66] Its rise to power can only be understood in the context of civil-war Beirut where the city was divided into various zones, each governed by well-armed religious militias. What is striking is the maturation and subsequent

---

[63] Nadine Khayat, *Case Studies: The Elyssar Reconstruction Project; The Ministry of the Displaced; The Economic and Social Fund for Development, Lebanon 2007* (Beirut: Lebanese Center for Policy Studies (LCPS); and London: Tiri, 2007), pp. 7–8.

[64] Michel Agier, "From Refugee Camps to the Invention of Cities," in Barbara Drieskens, Franck Mermier, and Heiko Wimmen (eds.), *Cities of the South: Citizenship and Exclusion in the 21st Century* (Beirut: SAQI, 2007), pp. 169–175; and Mona Fawaz, "Neoliberal Urbanity and the Right to the City: A View from Beirut's Periphery," *Development and Change* 40, 5 (2009), pp. 827–852.

[65] Najib Hourani, "Transnational Pathways and Politico-Economic Power: Globalisation and the Lebanese Civil War," *Geopolitics* 15, 2 (2010), pp. 290–311 (p. 291, source of quotations).

[66] Roula Majdalani, "The Governance Paradigm and Urban Development: Breaking New Ground?" in Seteney Shami (ed.), *Capital Cities: Ethnographies of Urban Governance in the Middle East* (Ottawa: University of Toronto Press, 2001), pp. 135–140; Shwayri, "From Regional Node to Backwater and Back to Uncertainty, Beirut, 1943–2006," in *The Evolving Arab City*, pp. 69–98; Mona el-Kak Harb, "Transforming the Site of Dereliction into the Urban Culture of Modernity: Beirut's Southern Suburb and Elisar Project," in *Projecting Beirut*, pp. 173–182; and Mona El-Kak Harb, "Postwar Beirut: Resources, Negotiations, and Contestations in the Elissar Project," *Arab World Geographer* 3, 4 (2000), pp. 272–288.

transformation of Hezbollah from a popular paramilitary "war machine" into a competent apparatus of service provision and urban development. Its development programs in the southern suburbs of Beirut include the provision of housing, education, medical services, water, sewage systems, and electricity.[67]

What is critical to understanding post–civil war Beirut are the ways in which a complex and hybrid mix of non state actors have actively engaged in the production of mundane spaces (including such installations as roads, industrial zones, housing, and social service centers), which have resulted in the reconfiguration of existing geographies of power and control. Along with other religious-political organizations, Hezbollah provided infrastructure services to informal settlements in the almost total absence of state services, thereby transforming the southern peripheries of Beirut into frontiers of sectarian conflict through territorial battles over land, housing, and available resources.[68] In the wake of the summer 2006 Israeli invasion and bombardment, Hezbollah took charge as the main planning actor in the reconstruction of the southern suburban neighborhoods of Beirut. Hezbollah became a full partner for all relief agencies and reconstruction donors, and played a dominant role in the rehabilitation of damaged road networks and bridges as well as the development of design schemes for the reconstruction of a number of ravaged villages and neighborhoods.[69]

Depending on one's particular perspective, Hezbollah can be considered at one and the same time an NGO, a Lebanese political party, a resistance movement, and an armed militia.[70] Such social categories, however, selectively emphasize or blur Hezbollah's various activities in the arenas of politics, military organization, resistance to occupation, and service provision – all of which characterize its diverse functions. The hybrid character of the two main religious-political organizations in southern Beirut – the Shi'a-led Hezbollah and the Druze Progressive Socialist Party (PSP) – makes their spatial interventions difficult to categorize in any unambiguous way. Each organization is a

[67] Mona el-Kak Harb, "Postwar Beirut: Resources, Negotiations, and Contestations in the Elyssar Project," in *Capital Cities*, pp. 111–133; and Asef Bayat, "Activism and Social Development in the Middle East," *International Journal of Middle East Studies*, 34, 2 (2002), pp. 1–28.

[68] Agnès Deboulet and Mona Fawaz, "Contesting the Legitimacy of Urban Restructuring and Highways in Beirut's Irregular Settlements," in Diane Davis and Nora Libertun de Duren (eds.), Cities and Sovereignty: Identity Politics in Urban Spaces (Bloomington: Indiana University Press, 2011), pp. 117–151.

[69] Mona Fawaz, "Hezbollah as Urban Planner? Questions to and from Planning Theory," *Planning Theory* 8, 4 (2009), pp. 323–334. See also Augustus Richard Norton, *Hezbollah: A Short History* (Princeton, NJ: Princeton University Press, 2007); Jim Quilty and Lysandra Ohrstrom, "The Second Time as Farce: Stories of Another Lebanese Reconstruction," *MERIP* 37, 2 (2007), pp. 31–41; Fawaz, "Neoliberal Urbanity and the Right to the City," pp. 827–852; and Mona Fawaz, "An Unusual Clique of City-Makers: Social Networks in the Production of a Neighborhood in Beirut (1950–75)," *International Journal of Urban and Regional Research* 32, 3 (2008), pp. 565–585.

[70] Hussain Abdul-Hussain, "Hezbollah: A State within a State," *Current Trends in Islamist Ideology* 8 (2009), pp. 68–81.

complex mixture of public and private activities, combining local militias with transnational networks. They cannot be confined to the simplifying categories of "non state actors" or NGOs, since they function simultaneously inside the state administration and outside it. Neither can they be considered political parties in the conventional sense, since they are involved in a wide range of diverse "state-like" activities.[71] Put concretely, these organizations maintain armed militias, serve as philanthropic charities, function as NGOs that manage transnational donations, administer social services, and deliver public works.[72]

The spatial practices of Hezbollah have transformed what used to be a depressed peripheral area into a religiously contested frontier zone, where spatial contestation has become less about war maneuvering and more about the social production of a spatial order of political difference through property markets, building and infrastructure construction, and urban regulations and land-use zoning.[73] Rather than introducing an innovative model of land-use planning that decisively breaks with the reigning neoliberal approaches, Hezbollah has adopted a language of proprietary rights that corresponds closely with the conception of property rights advocated by neoliberal planning, that is, one that enshrines private, individual ownership as sacrosanct and desirable. According to Mona Fawaz, the "neoliberal planning regime" that Hezbollah has adopted is not the accidental outcome of unreflective policy choices; rather, it is necessary step that has enabled the party to consolidate control over its territory in the city and to fix the future of land-use planning in accordance with its own political calculations.[74]

Over time, Hezbollah mutated from a political organization providing social welfare services in the low-income neighborhoods and informal settlements in the southern peripheries of Beirut during the civil war into a proto-state agency (a virtual "shadow state") providing shelter for internally displaced families. After the July 2006 war between Israel and Lebanon, this religious-political organization underwent a further transformation, becoming an aggressive top-down property development agency with a vision for a future world-class city. Hezbollah has used a variety of different tools – such as intervention into housing and real-estate markets, contestation over infrastructure and property rights, war compensation policies, urban planning and design

---

[71] Hiba Bou Akar, "Contesting Beirut's Frontiers," *City & Society* 24, 2 (2012), pp. 150–172. These sentences are taken almost verbatim from p. 151.

[72] Mona Harb, "Faith-Based Organizations as Effective Development Partners? Hezbollah and Postwar Reconstruction in Lebanon," in Gerald Clarke and Michael Jennings (eds.), *Development, Civil Society and Faith-Based Organizations* (New York: Palgrave Macmillan, 2008), pp. 214–239. See also Ananya Roy, "Civic Governmentality: The Politics of Inclusion in Beirut and Mumbai," *Antipode* 41, 1 (2009), pp. 159–179.

[73] Akar, "Contesting Beirut's Frontiers," p. 150 (source of quotation).

[74] Mona Fawaz, "The Politics of Property in Planning: Hezbollah's Reconstruction of Haret Hreik (Beirut, Lebanon) as Case Study," *International Journal of Urban and Regional Research* 38, 3 (2014), pp. 922–934.

practices, and land-use zoning policies and building laws – to carve out a distinctive "fiefdom,"[75] or a space-in-the-making that Hiba Bou Akar has termed "Hezbollah City."[76]‖

Spatial landscapes in deeply divided cities like Beirut (or Belfast, Nicosia, and Jerusalem) often become oversaturated with conflicting meanings. In the words of journalist Monika Borgman, "Beirut is a city of camps, full of blocked thoroughfares. The visible city is not the city. The city is invisible. Everything is a screen."[77] The spatial reconstruction strategies of *Solidère* and Hezbollah can be seen as two sides of the same coin: in going about embedding their competing visions of the urban future, they have both set themselves on a collision course against the city.[78] In other words, they both act with limited public affirmation, and independently of public oversight or municipal control. Whether commercial or sectarian, they both represent interests that are partially sectarian, private, and narrowly focused on particular goals. These crystallized interests are a telling symptom of the hybrid sovereignties that operate in parallel universes in Beirut. *Solidère* and Hezbollah each have a different vision of the city and its future. Proponents of each vision marshal support from within their own constituencies, thereby setting in motion platforms involving coercive urban politics. Both visions draw on different historical narratives: on the one side, Hezbollah has tapped into a history of resistance to external oppression; on the other side, *Solidère* has identified with a long history of commercial integration at the heart of the Arab Mediterranean.[79] In fashioning an image of itself as pious and incorruptible, Hezbollah seeks to stand above the corrupt city.[80] In contrast, *Solidère* presents a sanitized, elitist version of Beirut as a cosmopolitan world-class city: a clean, orderly, and regulated enclave as opposed to the chaotic, run-down parts of the city, with their crumbling infrastructure and overcrowded streetscapes.[81]

---

[75] Mona el-Kak Harb, "Postwar Beirut: Resources, Negotiations, and Contestations in the Elyssar Project," in *Capital Cities*, p. 117; and Fawaz, "An Unusual Clique of City-Makers," pp. 565–585.

[76] Akar, "Contesting Beirut's Frontiers," pp. 150–172; and Hiba Bou Akar and Mohamad Hafeda (eds.), *Narrating Beirut from the Borderlines* (Beirut: Heinrich Böll Foundation, 2011).

[77] Lieven De Cauter provides the quotation from Monika Borgman. See Lieven De Cauter, "Towards a Phenomenology of Civil War: Hobbes Meets Benjamin in Beirut," *International Journal of Urban and Regional Research* 35, 2 (2011), pp. 221–230.

[78] Edward Randall, "Reconstruction and Fragmentation in Beirut" (Conflict in Cities and the Contested State: Everyday Life and the Possibilities for Transformation in Belfast, Jerusalem and other divided cities. *Divided Cities/Contested States*), Working Paper No. 29 (2014), pp. 17–18. See also Akar, "Contesting Beirut's Frontiers," pp. 150–172; Fawaz, "Neoliberal Urbanity and the Right to the City," pp. 827–852; and Fawaz, "An Unusual Clique of City-Makers," pp. 565–585.

[79] Krijnen and Fawaz, "Exception as the Rule," pp. 245–259.

[80] Fawaz, "Hezbollah as Urban Planner?" pp. 323–334.

[81] Scott Bollens, *City and Soul in Divided Societies* (New York and London: Routledge, 2012), p. 185.

To be sure, Hezbollah is not the only organizational entity – religious, political, or otherwise – involved in informal planning practices outside formal juridical administration of state authorities. Always and everywhere, urban landscapes are "marked, crisscrossed, and fragmented by demarcation lines which are simultaneously real and virtual." At any moment, these virtual demarcation lines can become real, brought to life by agencies and organizations without formal authorization to make these sorts of deliberate decisions.[82]

Fragmented Regimes of Territorial Governance

Informal settlements and slums, on the one side, and exclusive urban enclaves like gated residential communities and other deliberately sequestered landscapes, on the other, occupy the polar extremes in cities divided by deep sociocultural cleavages. They are both governed by the logic of exception, which acts to suspend the conventional rule of law. Both operate under extralegal rules and regulations beyond the capacity of municipal authorities to effectively manage or even officially intervene. Gated residential communities and other sequestered landscapes embody a "distinctive territorialisation of citizenship"[83] – or what Setha Low and Steven Robins have termed a new "spatial governmentality."[84] The key characteristic of these spatial regimes is the formation of cocooned compounds that are governed by private bodies that largely escape public scrutiny. Such collective entities as common interest communities (CICs), common interest developments (CIDs), and "community/neighborhood associations" typically operate as the private governance bodies for gated residential communities. These self-governing enclaves rely on covenants, conditions, and restrictions to privately govern and control land use, design decisions, services, and even social conduct. As incorporated collective entities, they own, operate, and manage the common properties within their boundaries, including open space, parking, recreational facilities, and open-access streets. These private governing bodies have the legal authority to enforce "reciprocal rights and obligations." They are "contractual associations" that deliver some type of neighborhood-level governance in the form of rules and regulations and the provision of local services (e.g., safety and security, road maintenance, landscaping) on the basis of assessments (fees) collected from members.[85]

---

[82] Lieven De Cauter, "Towards a Phenomenology of Civil War," p. 424 (source of quotation).

[83] Alsayyad and Roy, "Medieval Modernity," p. 6 (source of quotation).

[84] Setha Low, "The Edge and the Center: Gated Communities and Urban Fear," in Setha Low and Denise Lawrence Zuniga (eds.), *The Anthropology of Space and Place* (Cambridge, MA: Blackwell, 2003), pp. 387–407 (esp. p. 390); and Steven Robbins, "At the Limits of Spatial Governmentality: A Message from the Tip of Africa," *Third World Quarterly* 23, 4 (2002), pp. 665–689.

[85] Chris Webster, Georg Glasze, and Frantz Klaus, "Guest Editorial: The Global Spread of Gated Communities," *Environment and Planning B* 29, 3 (2002), pp. 315–320 (esp. p. 315).

Codified as specialized covenants, legally binding contracts, and deed restrictions, this governance structure creates new types of private governance in the form of "home-owner" or neighborhood associations.[86] As Evan McKenzie has argued (following Robert Reich), these "privatopias" signal the "secession of the successful."[87] In this sense, gated residential estates, with their own internal regulations and codes, represent a new kind of privatized governance where contract law in defense of restrictive covenants functions as the supreme authority, where property values are the foundational pillars of community life, and where exclusion is the driving force behind social organization.[88] Although the individual rights associated with private property have historically been the legal domain that has protected affluent residents from spatial encroachment, collective agreements with formal legal standing have increasingly become the prototype for urban residential development. Taking the form of condominiums, cooperatives and single- and multi family homes, private residential communities (gated and non gated) are spreading worldwide across diverse socioeconomic classes.[89]

As such, these self-governing enclaves are more than just the resultant outcome of neoliberal urban governance policies. They are also active agents that produce new technologies of spatial governance, generate new kinds of sovereignty largely independent of public authority, and manufacture subjectivities and identities.[90] Gated residential communities epitomize supply-driven residential segregation, that is, they are the embodiment of security gates in search of a residential community to inhabit them. As Jeremy Seabrook has put it in a particularly sardonic rhetoric, the super-wealthy elite of the "globalizing" cities at the margins of modernity occupy a liminal place of "gilded captivity": they "cease to be citizens of their own countries and become nomads belonging to, and owing allegiance to, a super terrestrial topography of money; they become patriots of wealth, nationalists of an elusive and golden nowhere."[91]

The political logic of the exception creates "a pattern of noncontiguous, differently administered spaces of "graduated" or "variegated sovereignty.'"[92]

---

[86] Low, "The Edge and the Center," p. 390; and Mike Davis, *City of Quartz: Excavating the Future of Los Angeles* (New York: Vintage, 1992).

[87] Evan McKenzie, *Privatopia: Homeowner Associations and the Rise of Residential Private Government* (New Haven: Yale University Press, 1994), pp. 186–187. McKenzie quotes Robert Reich, "Succession of the Successful," *New York Times Magazine*, January 20, 1991 (p. 42).

[88] Alsayyad and Roy, "Medieval Modernity," p. 8. See also Michael Dear and Steven Flusty, "Postmodern Urbanism," *Annals of the Association of American Geographers* 90, 1 (2000), pp. 50–72; and Michael Dear and Steven Flusty, "Engaging Postmodern Urbanism," *Urban Geography* 20, 5 (1999), pp. 393–416.

[89] Eran Ben-Joseph, "Double Standards, Single Goal: Private Communities and Design Innovation," *Journal of Urban Design* 9, 2 (2004), pp. 131–151.

[90] Alsayyad and Roy, "Medieval Modernity," p. 8.

[91] Jeremy Seabrook, *In the Cities of the South: Some Scenes from a Developing World* (London: Verso, 1996), p. 211 (source of quotation)

[92] Aiwha Ong, *Neoliberalism as Exception: Mutations in Citizenship and Sovereignty* (Durham: Duke University Press, 2006), p. 7.

Some of these zones have well-defined and heavily policed borders, while others have porous and fluid boundaries. Some zones grant formal benefits and exact formal obligations, while others operate in accordance with informal rules and moral persuasion. Because they both exist in a liminal space outside existing regulatory frameworks, gated residential communities and slums are the opposite extremes of a singular process that carves the city into different orders of mottled citizenship where the mechanisms of patronage become the principles of rule. Seen from this angle of vision, neither slums nor gated residential communities fall wholly under the exclusive domain of state regulation and public authority. They both straddle a liminal border-zone of extraterritorial sovereignty.[93]

Autonomous zones operate as complex and dynamic systems of exception. As exemplary expression of autonomous zones, Free Trade Zones (FTZs) have a juridical status, as a matter of legal exemption, that considers them as not part of the sovereign territory of nation-states, such that goods moving through them enjoy exemptions from tariffs and duties (along with various other state and local tax obligations). FTZs function as storage and trans-shipment areas, but also host all sorts of production activities – such as assembling, repackaging, and the like – which take place in a legal limbo outside of jurisdiction of the sovereign territories within which they are embedded. Furthermore, users of FTZs are exempt from regulatory oversight that enables them to bypass inspection and avoid civil law and even international law. FTZ authorities are not only able to override government ministries, local courts, revenue offices, central banks, and planning authorities, but replace them with their own administrative and logical systems of rule. As a matter of course, FTZs have acquired the power to grant exemptions from laws regulating unfair labor practices, environment standards, sanitation codes, and even human rights abuses.[94] As "parastatal proxies," FTZ authorities are able to employ wide legal-juridical discretion to claim exceptions. For users of these zones, these exceptions translate into enhanced entitlements, rights, and privileges. The activities of FTZs constitute not merely a matter of rolling back the power of public administration, but involves "the thickening of the regulatory functions of quasi-state authorities which set the legal and social forms of control."[95]

Postliberal Urbanism

In the postliberal city, new modes of governance – a vast array of pseudo-public authorities, public–private partnerships, redevelopment agencies, special-purpose commissions, and unelected organizations and entities operating outside of public oversight – have become the primary mechanisms for

93 Alsayyad and Roy, "Medieval Modernity," pp. 11–12.
94 Keller Easterling, "Zone: The Spatial Softwares of Extrastatecraft," [n.p.].
95 Ong, *Neoliberalism as Exception*, p. 90 (source of quotation).

administering fragmented metropolitan landscapes.[96] These quasi-private entities, and the spaces they control, have become detached (in varying degrees)
from the governing principles and the regulatory reach of public authorities.
In ever-expanding ways, cities increasingly consist of a kaleidoscopic mélange
of distinct sociopolitical spaces that have divided urban landscapes into hybrid
assemblages of distinct enclaves and autonomous zones – each defined by a distinct package of rights, entitlements, and protections.[97] These modes of flexible
sovereignty enable these proto-state agencies and organizations to both fragment and extend the space of rule/authority.[98]

The logic of exception has evolved into corrosive force vis-à-vis the rule of
law. The rich and powerful claimants to private property are able to use exceptionality as a way of creating flexible, splintered, and rescaled legal regimes. The
deployment of regimes of exception in a geographically targeted fashion enables
quasi-private entities to suspend the conventional rule of law.[99] The powers of
exception, that is, the capacity to rescind the normal palate of rules, provides
powerful social actors with wide discretion to shape the form and functions of
the splintered city. These private actors and agencies enjoy (to varying degrees)
the capacity to unbundle and rebundle regulatory regimes in particular configurations in ways that allow them both to do what they please and to conceal their
actions from public scrutiny. This unbundling of public regulatory regimes with
their single-purpose mandate has produced a layered tableau of proliferating
exceptions and polymorphous forms of governance.[100]

The logic of the exception fragments unified and singular conceptions of
territorial sovereignty. Suspended sovereignty provides for creation of extraterritorial jurisdictions. Sketched in bold strokes, *sovereignty* can no longer
be usefully thought of as emanating from a coherent "political singularity."
Rather, "sovereignty is manifest in multiple, often contradictory strategies that
encounter diverse claims and contestations, and produce diverse and contingent
outcomes."[101]

---

[96] L. Owen Kirkpatrick and Michael Peter Smith, "The Infrastructural Limits to Growth:
Rethinking the Urban Growth Machine in Times of Fiscal Crisis," *International Journal of
Urban and Regional Research* 35, 3 (2011), pp. 477–503 (esp. p. 481).

[97] Saskia Sassen, *Territory•Authority•Rights: From Medieval to Global Assemblages* [Updated
Edition] (Princeton: Princeton University Press, 2008), pp. 264–268.

[98] Ong, *Neoliberalism as Exception*, p. 7.

[99] Stephen Humphreys, "Legalizing Lawlessness: On Giorgio Agamben's State of Exception,"
The European Journal of International Law 17, 3 (2006), pp. 677–687.

[100] See Alan Hudson, "Beyond the Borders: Globalisation, Sovereignty and Extraterritoriality,"
Geopolitics 3, 1 (1998), pp. 89–105.

[101] Ong, *Neoliberalism as Exception*, p. 19 (quotation from p. 7).

8

An Urbanism of Exception

Contrary to the exaggerated and unfounded rhetorical claims that the dissolving powers of globalization has left a borderless, fluid, and deterritorialized social world in their wake, the hard edges of geographical boundaries have proliferated, embedding themselves in new ways from the microscopic and local to the macroscopic and global.[1] Globalization in all its manifold forms has coincided with its loosening of older territorial boundaries of political power and cultural identity, yet it has also triggered the emergence of new and different forms of boundary-making at every geographical scale. Boundaries and borders originate intrinsically from the constant and often conflict-laden social production of the nodes, regions, scales, and territories that shape, and are shaped by, asymmetrical relations of power and opportunity.[2]

At the start of the twenty-first century, urban landscapes have been subjected to the twin pressures of spatial fragmentation and social segregation. While old modes of spatial demarcation have not faded away, new asymmetric mechanisms of bordering have arisen, not only superimposing themselves (and hence reinforcing) on what came before, but also creating new borderlines of separation.[3] In the current phase of globalization, urban borderlands

[1] Henk van Houtum, Olivier Kramsch and Wolfgang Zierhofer, "Prologue: B/ordering Space," in Henk van Houtum, Olivier Kramsch, and Wolfgang Zierhofer (eds.), *B/ordering Space* (Burlington, VT: Ashgate, 2005), pp. 1–13 (esp. p. 1); and Liam O'Dowd, "From a 'Borderless World' to a 'World of Borders': 'Bringing History Back In,'" *Environment and Planning D* 28, 6 (2010), pp. 1031–1050.

[2] Edward Soja, "Borders Unbound: Globalization, Regionalism, and the Postmetropolitan Transition," in *B/ordering Space*, pp. 33–46 (esp. pp. 34, 35).

[3] Emmanuel Brunet-Jailly, "Theorizing Borders: An Interdisciplinary Perspective," *Geopolitics* 10 (2005), pp. 633–649; Henk van Houtum, Ton van Naerssen, "Bordering, Ordering and Othering," *Tijdschrift voor economische en sociale geografie [TESG]* 93, 2 (2002), pp. 125–136; Anssi Paasi, "The Changing Discourses on Political Boundaries Mapping the Backgrounds, Contexts

have increasingly become not just territorial lines demarcated in space or boundary-markers that signal some sort of geographical distinction, but rather powerful measures of selection – functional instruments or tools of systematic exclusion.[4] Cities have increasingly come to resemble patchwork agglomerations of bounded spaces – consisting of "insular cells," "fortified enclaves," and similar corporatized "privatopias" – where the social construction of an assortment of walls, gates, and barriers are the visible symptom of the growing obsession with maintenance of secure boundaries.[5] The enclave format acts as a microcosm of contemporary urban realities. Practices of urban enclosure have become the "modus operandi of neoliberal urbanism," constructing privatized spaces for wealthy urban residents, undermining social cohesion, and displacing and excluding the urban poor from places where they are not wanted.[6]

The serial reproduction of these self-contained sequestered spaces has become one of the most salient and dominant features of the contemporary urban condition on a global scale.[7] At the start of the twenty-first century, the ongoing restructuring of urban space, which is at least partly a result of the pressures of globalization, has produced complex patterns of spatial sorting that are organized around newly emergent "varieties and scales of engagement and disengagement."[8] Luxurious enclaves catering to the privileged and wealthy have proliferated in aspiring world-class cities everywhere. Arranged under a variety of guises, these enclaves function as sites of production, financial

and Contents," in *B/ordering Space*, pp. 17–32; and Ron Rael, "Border Wall as Architecture," *Environment and Planning D* 29, 3 (2011), pp. 409–420.

[4] Camillo Boano and Ricardo Martén, "Agamben's Urbanism of Exception: Jerusalem's Border Mechanics and Biopolitical Strongholds," *Cities* 34 (2013), pp. 6–17. "Borderlands are spatial manifestations of inclusion and exclusion" [Deljana Iossifova, "Searching for Common Ground: Urban Borderlands in a World of Borders and Boundaries," *Cities* 34 (2013), pp. 1–5 (quotation from p. 4)]. See also Deljana Iossifova, "Borderland Urbanism: Seeing between Enclaves," *Urban Geography* 36, 1 (2015), pp. 90–108.

[5] Edward Soja, "Borders Unbound: Globalization, Regionalism, and the Postmetropolitan Transition," in *B/ordering Space*, p. 43; Teresa Caldeira, "Fortified Enclaves: The New Urban Segregation," *Public Culture* 8 (1996), pp. 303–328; and Evan McKenzie, *Privatopia: Homeowner Associations and the Rise of Residential Private Government* (New Haven: Yale University Press, 1994).

[6] Stephen Hodkinson, "The New Urban Enclosures," *City* 16, 5 (2012), pp. 500–518 (esp. p. 505, source of quotation). See also Peter Aning Tedong, Jill Grant, and Wan Nor Azriyati Wan Abd Aziz, "The Social and Spatial Implications of Community Action to Enclose Space: Guarded Neighbourhoods in Selangor, Malaysia," *Cities* 41 (Part A) (2014), pp. 30–37; Peter Aning Tedong, Jill L. Grant, Wan Nor Azriyati Wan Abd Aziz, "Governing Enclosure: The Role of Governance in Producing Gated Communities and Guarded Neighborhoods in Malaysia," *International Journal of Urban and Regional Research* 39, 1 (2015), pp. 112–128.

[7] See also Ayfer Bartu-Candan and Biray Kolluoğlu, "Emerging Spaces of Neoliberalism: A Gated Town and a Public Housing Project in Istanbul," *New Perspectives on Turkey* 39 (2008), pp. 5–46 (esp. p. 8).

[8] Nick Ellison and Roger Burrows, "New Spaces of (dis)engagement? Social Politics, Urban Technologies and the Rezoning of the City," *Housing Studies* 22, 3 (2007), pp. 295–312 (quotation from p. 295).

clearinghouses, logistics centers, residential estates, transportation hubs, tourism getaways, and speculative ventures.[9] Such evocative images as "splintering urbanism,"[10] "quartered cities,"[11] "city of walls,"[12] "enclave urbanism,"[13] and "bypass urbanism"[14] provide a range of useful lenses through which to view these newly emergent patterns of spatial sorting that enable privileged social groups with the capacities and resources to remove themselves, physically or virtually, from the perceived threats posed by various "others" and to withdraw into their own secure redoubts. For aspiring world-class cities seeking to position themselves as viable hubs of operation for transnational capital and business, one visible manifestation of the impact of contemporary globalization – and the attendant neoliberal reorganization of urban governance regimes – has been the partitioning of urban landscapes into well-serviced and gated settlements for the newly emergent urban elites, on the one side, and the confinement of the urban poor into abject spaces of neglect, on the other.[15] Enclave spaces are the material expressions of intensified processes and patterns of uneven development. They typically "operate under regulatory and

---

9 Stephen Graham and Sobia Ahmad Kaker, "Living the Security City: Karachi's Archipelago of Enclaves," *Harvard Design Magazine* 37 (2014), pp. 12–16. See also Stephen Graham, *Cities under Siege: The New Military Urbanism* (New York and London: Verso, 2010), pp. 9–10; and Sobia Ahmad Kaker, "Enclaves, Insecurity and Violence in Karachi," *South Asian History and Culture* 5, 1 (2014), pp. 93–107.

10 Stephen Graham and Simon Marvin, *Splintering Urbanism: Reworked Infrastructures, Technological Mobilities and the Urban Condition* (London: Routledge, 2001).

11 Peter Marcuse, "Space and Race in the Post-Fordist City: The Outcast Ghetto and Advanced Homelessness in the United States Today," in Enzo Mingione (ed.), *Urban Poverty and the Underclass* (Oxford: Blackwell, 1996), pp. 176–217; and Peter Marcuse, "The Ghetto of Exclusion and the Fortified Enclave: New Patterns in the United States," *American Behavioral Scientist* 41, 3 (1997), pp. 311–326; and Peter Marcuse, "The Enclave, the Citadel, and the Ghetto: What has Changed in the Post-Fordist U.S. City," *Urban Affairs Review* 33, 2 (1997), pp. 228–264.

12 Teresa Caldeira, *City of Walls: Crime, Segregation and Citizenship in São Paulo* (Berkeley and Los Angeles: University of California Press, 2000).

13 Shenjing He, "Evolving Enclave Urbanism in China and its Socio-spatial Implications: The Case of Guangzhou," *Social & Cultural Geography* 14, 3 (2013), pp. 243–275; Bart Wissink, "Enclave Urbanism in Mumbai: An Actor-Network-Theory Analysis of Urban (Dis)connection," *Geoforum* 47 (2013), pp. 1–11; and Mike Douglass, Bart Wissink, and Ronald van Kempen, "Enclave Urbanism in China: Consequences and Interpretations," *Urban Geography* 33, 2 (2012), pp. 167–182.

14 Viktor Ramos, *The Continuous Enclave: Strategies in Bypass Urbanism* (Unpublished Masters Thesis, School of Architecture, Rice University, 2009). For the notion of "bypass-implant urbanism," see Gavin Shatkin, "Coping with Actually Existing Urbanisms: The Real Politics of Planning in the Global Era," *Planning Theory* 10, 1 (2011), pp. 79–87; and Gavin Shatkin, "The City and the Bottom Line: Urban Megaprojects and the Privatization of Planning in Southeast Asia," *Environment and Planning A* 40, 2 (2008), pp. 383–401.

15 R.N. Sharma, "Mega-Transformation of Mumbai: Deepening Enclave Urbanism," *Sociological Bulletin* 59, 1 (2010), pp. 69–91 (esp. p. 69).

legal bubble-domes" that suspend the normal juridical order and are tailored to the specific needs of special interests.[16]

As a particular mode of territorialization, the enclave format is the paradigmatic form of spatial organization that has fundamentally reshaped city-building efforts at the start of the twenty-first century. Cities have increasingly come to resemble hybrid assemblages of segregated and discontinuous island-like enclosures that are maintained through elaborate techniques of surveillance, regulatory controls, and architectural design. Not only are these enclaves physically separated from the surrounding urban landscape, but they are also linked to similar spaces of exclusion that vary in size, purpose, and aesthetic orientation.[17] As the most common prescriptive template for organizing city building in the age of hyper-globalization, the enclave format functions as embodiment of specific power relationships within the city. By seeking frictionless freedom to operate with impunity via exemption from existing legal regulations, urban enclaves have redefined the specific modalities of spatial governance.[18]

Island-like enclosures are the basic aggregate units for city building in the contemporary age of late modernity. Born under the sign of global high finance, the enclave format functions as a scalar surrogate – a shadowy substitute – for "both the nation-state that organized and regulated the Fordist economy and the modernist city that was the locus of industrial production and collective consumption."[19] The defining feature of urban enclaves is their discontinuous and disjunctive social geography, that is, they both gesture toward firm global connections while they simultaneously seek disengagement with their local settings[20] As a self-contained "spatial products" with varying degrees of administrative autonomy, urban enclaves resemble something like foreign alien bodies implanted within the urban social fabric.[21]

---

[16]   Mike Davis, "Fear and Money in Dubai," *New Left Review* 41 (2006), pp. 47–68 (quotation from p. 63).

[17]   Nezar AlSayyad and Ananya Roy, "Medieval Modernity: On Citizenship and Urbanism in a Global Era," *Space and Polity* 10, 1 (2006), pp. 1–20 (esp. p. 5). See also Bülent Diken, "From Refugee Camps to Gated Communities: Biopolitics and the End of the City," *Citizenship Studies* 8, 1 (2004), pp. 83–106; and James Sidaway "Enclave Space: A New Metageography of Development?" *Area* 39, 3 (2007), pp. 331–339.

[18]   Pier Vittorio Aureli, "City as Political Form: Four Archetypes of Urban Transformation, "*Architectural Design* 81, 1 (2011), pp. 32–37 (esp. p. 32).

[19]   Tim Simpson, "Scintillant Cities: Glass Architecture, Finance Capital, and the Fictions of Macau's Enclave Urbanism," *Theory, Culture & Society* 30, 7–8 (2013), pp. 343–371 (quotation from p. 345).

[20]   See Manuel Castells, *The Rise of the Network Society, Volume 1* [2nd edition] (Cambridge, MA: Blackwell, 2000), p. 436.

[21]   Frederic Jameson, *Archaeologies of the Future: The Desire Called Utopia and Other Science Fictions* (London: Verso, 2005), p. 15.

In their many guises and masquerades ranging from special economic zones to gated residential estates, and from securitized office parks to virtually complete satellite cities, urban enclaves weave together capital and power in the particular spatial settings.[22] As Tim Simpson has argued, the zone-enclave can be understood "as a commodified and derivative urban form."[23]

Much like those derivative financial instruments at the center of the subprime mortgage crisis that wreaked havoc on financial capitalism at the start of the twenty-first century, the value of enclaves stems from a potent speculative package of assets and indices, forming what Keller Easterling has called a "real estate cocktail."[24] In the era of speculative capitalism, urban enclaves have become privileged sites for the conversion of "opaque and illiquid assets into liquid and transparent securities."[25] Whether offshore or onshore, the enclave format offers a safe haven for corporate enterprises seeking anonymity at a time of financial volatility and political uncertainty. These aggregate units – variously referred to as corporate cities, Special Administrative Regions (SARs), quasi-states, and various other names for autonomous zones characterized by "encapsulated urbanity or juridical exception" – provide a placeless disassociation from what surrounds them.[26]

More broadly, when we once thought of cities as remarkably singular, one-of-a-kind material expressions of incremental building undertaken in fits and starts over long periods of time, city building in the first decades of the twenty-first century has increasingly (but by no means exclusively) taken shape as the assemblage of a predictable collection of similar components built at a fast pace. Put bluntly, new city building efforts have produced urban landscapes that consist of mélange of a repeatable spatial products, which conform to commercial formulas and infrastructural logics, and appear as if they originate out of nowhere.

States of Exception

The scholarly work of Giorgio Agamben – particularly his observations on the "state of exception" and the ideological foundation of "biopolitics" – has introduced a distinctly spatial approach to understanding the relational dynamics

[22] Keller Easterling, "The Corporate City is the Zone," in Christina de Baan, Joachim Declerk, and Veronique Patteeuw (eds.), *Visionary Power: Creating the Contemporary City* (Rotterdam: NAi Publishers, 2007), pp. 75–85.

[23] Simpson, "Scintillant Cities," p. 346 (source of quotation).

[24] Keller Easterling, *Enduring Innocence: Global Architecture and its Political Masquerades* (Cambridge, MA: The MIT Press, 2005), pp. 1–5 (p. 1, source of quotation).

[25] Kevin Fox Gotham, "Creating Liquidity out of Spatial Fixity: The Secondary Circuit of Capital and the Subprime Mortgage Crisis," *International Journal of Urban and Regional Research* 33, 2 (2009), pp. 355–371 (p. 357, source of quotation).

[26] Simpson, "Scintillant Cities," p. 346 (source of quotation).

between enclosure and partitioning, on the one side, and new typologies of territorial governance, on the other.[27] By elaborating and refining a set of axiomatic
propositions about sovereign power and the rule of law, Agamben is able to
show how the suspension of normal juridical practice opens up the conditions
of possibility for the creation of a "state of exception" – a zone of indistinction
where the legal and extralegal "cross over into one another."[28] For Agamben,
the paradigmatic exemplar of the "state of exception" is "the camp," a distinct kind of emergency situation, or a zone of lawlessness and anomie, where
the rule of law no longer holds and sovereign power has produced both an
intensification and a proliferation of bare life. Agamben depicts the "state of
exception" as a permanent, immutable, and lawless void that falls outside the
normal exercise of juridical conventions – a situation that allows for anything
to happen within its borders. Those trapped inside the state of exception are
summarily "reduced to bare life, stripped of all political and legal status at the
mercy of the sovereign."[29]

Agamben focused his analysis on "the camp" as the privileged space of
exception.[30] His account of the relations between sovereign power, the state
of exception, and bare life provides an invaluable guide for understanding such
phenomena as detention centers and prison camps that exist outside the boundaries of conventional legal authority. But his narrow focus on the isolated territory of "the camp" as the singular expression of exceptionality limits the analytic power of his framework. Against this view, it is more fruitful to conceive
of these spaces of exception as, in fact, saturated with rules and regulations
(i.e., with laws) rather than devoid of them, the result of a meticulously orches-
trated dynamic designed to create alternative regulatory regimes rather than to
escape from them altogether. In short, spaces of exception signal not simply the
suspension of the law but the imposition of alternative "rules of the game" or
normative prescriptions.[31]

Agamben has suggested that the state of exception is, in fact, a "normal technique" of governance that radically alters the structure and meaning of legal-
istic and political forms of governing everywhere.[32] Just as Foucault's reading

---

[27] Giorgio Agamben, *State of Exception* [trans. Kevin Attell] (Chicago: University of Chicago
    Press, 2005), pp. 23, 50–51.
[28] See Derek Gregory, "The Black Flag: Guantánamo Bay and the Space of Exception,"
    Geografiska Annaler [Series B] 88, 4 (2006), pp. 405–427 (quotation from p. 412).
[29] Ideas derived from Codi Hauka, "Spaces of Exception and Suspended Logic: Redefining Agam-
    ben's Biopolitical Paradigm on Sovereignty, Law and Space," *Hemispheres* 36 (2013), pp. 67–80
    (quotation from p. 67).
[30] Boano and Martén, "Agamben's Urbanism of Exception, p. 7 (source of quotation).
[31] These ideas are derived from Hauka, "Spaces of Exception and Suspended Logic," p. 67. See also
    Oliver Belcher, Lauren Martin, Anna Secor, Stephanie Simon, and Tommy Wilson, "Everywhere
    and Nowhere: The Exception and the Topological Challenge to Geography," *Antipode* 40, 4
    (2008), pp. 499–503; and Bülent Diken and Carsten Bagge Laustsen, *The Culture of Exception:
    Sociology facing the Camp* (New York: Routledge, 2005).
[32] Agamben, *State of Exception*, p. 14.

of the panopticon interrogated a singular phenomenon that opens up ways
to indicate wider apparatuses of surveillance and control, so too focusing on
"the camp" as the exemplar of state of exception can reveal broader processes
of the suspension of the rule of law that operate at multiple spatial scales.[33]
Reworking and expanding upon Agamben's "juridico-political paradigm" of
exceptionality – or the suspension of the normal (and expected) operations of
the rule of law – to the broader and (hence more blurry) scale of the metropolis
enables us to move beyond the narrow focus on singular places and isolated territories. By stretching the idea of exceptionality in ways that extend and bend
across space, it is possible to conceive of an "urbanism of exception" where
urban landscapes consist of interlocking, overlapping, and intersecting spatial
topographies of "exceptional spaces," all of which operate in accordance with
their own rules of the game and do not depend upon a singular, *a priori* conception of the rule of law. In this way, these spaces of exception cannot be seen
as deviations from a shared conventional standard, but as the normal *modus
operandi* that characterizes urban governance at the start of the twenty-first
century.[34]

For Agamben, "the camp" signals the basic molecular unit – the elemen-
tary building block – of modern life, where its micro scalar quality encapsu-
lates extraterritoriality, appropriated sovereignties, the suspension of the rule
of law, and multiple transgressions of human rights in a bounded, fixed, and
contained space.[35] In contrast, urban spaces of exception are harder to analytically separate from the wider social fabric because they are imbued with other
signs and meanings (and conventions and practices) intrinsic to urban environments. In cities, spaces of exception are not segregated in absolute terms or
encapsulated with fixed boundaries, but instead continuously respond, adapt,
and "shape-shift" in relation to their adjacent environments. The urbanism of
exception is an ever-mutating response to changing circumstances. Seen in this
light, the logic behind the camp has prefigured the grafting of exceptionality
onto the much broader and more diffuse terrain of urban space. City-building
processes have extrapolated exceptionality beyond static units, extending the
logic of exception into urban realm.[36] The lens of the state of exception provides a particularly useful vantage point from which to observe the increasingly routine and normal suspension of the rule of law and the "unexceptional"
relaxation of conventional regulatory regimes, where the use of the rhetoric of
emergency, necessity, and the "common good" typically serve as the grounds
for legitimation.[37]

---

[33] Richard Ek, "Giorgio Agamben and the Spatialities of the Camp," *Geografiska Annaler B* 88,
   4 (2006), pp. 363–386 (esp. pp. 372, 374).
[34] Iossifova, "Borderland Urbanism," pp. 90–108.
[35] Boano and Martén, "Agamben's Urbanism of Exception," p. 8.
[36] Boano and Martén, "Agamben's Urbanism of Exception," p. 9.
[37] For the source of ideas for the following paragraphs, see Fernanda Sánchez and Anne-Marie
   Broudehoux, "Mega-Events and Urban Regeneration in Rio de Janeiro: Planning in a State of

The state of exception is based on the relaxation, suspension, or outright abolition of the preexisting normal juridical order. The enclave format effectively relies on the unofficial declaration of a state of exception, that is, the creation of extraordinary decision-making frameworks that depend upon the suspension of the normal juridical order. Rather than a provisional and extraordinary measure, the state of exception has become a technique of governance, increasingly used in ways that allow for the proliferation of urban enclaves outside existing regulatory frameworks.[38] Defined as the suspension of law by extraordinary means, the state of exception produces an opaque (albeit, not empty) space, a zone of indeterminacy in which normal regulatory authorities are set aside. The *de facto* suspension of the conventional regulatory authority and the adoption of extraordinary measures has proven to be highly effective, to the extent that the calculated creation of a permanent state of exception enables "special interests" to construct urban enclaves outside public scrutiny and oversight.[39] Isolated legally and physically from their immediate surroundings, urban enclaves are analogous to Agamben's concept of the "camp," where the power of exceptional regulation displaces the normal rule of law.[40]

Enclave Urbanism

Enclave urbanism – a term analogous to what has been sometimes called "zone urbanism," "offshore urbanism," "modular urbanism," "bubble urbanism," and "archipelago urbanism" – denotes a hardening of the borders and boundaries that separate, divide, and fragment urban space.[41] This crystallization of urban landscapes into separate and discontinuous island-like enclosures resonates with what Mike Davis called the "city of quartz" (a reference to the hard edges of Los Angeles) in which the mirage of urban permeability, open flows, and unimpeded social interaction masks an archipelago of secessionary

---

Emergency," *International Journal of Urban Sustainable Development* 5, 2 (2013), pp. 132–155. For a treatment of the social construction of "emergency" in relationship to Detroit, see Jamie Peck, "Framing Detroit," in Michael Peter Smith and L. Owen Kirkpatrick (eds.), *Reinventing Detroit: The Politics of Possibility* (New Brunswick, NJ: Transaction, 2015), pp. 145–165.

[38] See L. Owen Kirkpatrick, *Sovereignty and the Fragmented City: The Many Citizenships of Detroit, Michigan* (Detroit, MI: Wayne State University Press, 2016); and L. Owen Kirkpatrick, "Graduated Sovereignty and the Fragmented City: Mapping the Political Geography of Citizenship in Detroit," In Cherstin Lyon (ed.), *Place, (Dis)Place, and Citizenship* (Detroit: Wayne State University Press, forthcoming).

[39] Isaac Marrero-Guillamón, "Olympic State of Exception," in Hilary Powell and Isaac Marrero-Guillamón (eds.), *The Art of Dissent: Adventures in London's Olympic State* (London: Marshgate Press, 2012), pp. 20–29 [290–291 footnotes] (esp. pp. 21–22).

[40] Isaac Marrero-Guillamón, "Olympic State of Exception," p. 29.

[41] Werner Breitung, "Borders and the City: Intra-Urban Boundaries in Guangzhou (China)," *Quaestiones Geographicae* 30, 4 (2011), pp. 55–61. For a wider view, see Brunet-Jailly, "Theorizing Borders – An Interdisciplinary Perspective," pp. 633–649.

spaces that are largely segregated, inaccessible, and insulated.[42] The proliferating numbers of urban enclaves has produced an urban landscape that resembles a dispersed archipelago of isolated island-like enclosures. The "archipelago city" consists of a hybrid assemblage of discontinuous territorial fragments or exceptional spaces. These discrete extraterritorial zones are the spatial expressions of the serial reproduction of multiple states of exception (or "states of emergency"), that are either created through the process of law (through which the law is in fact severely undermined or annulled) or that appear *de facto* within them.[43] The social production of "states of exception" through the suspension of the law effectively transforms exceptional spaces into routinized topographical forms of spatiality.[44]

Because they owe their existence to the suspension of conventional regulatory frameworks of governance, urban enclaves are spatial materializations of the logic of exception. As Nezar AlSayyad and Ananya Roy have argued, urban enclaves "are the forms of exceptionalism that constitute the normal. They lie not at the extraterritorial periphery of city-space, but are instead the very modalities" of space-making and boundary-marking that "produce the city."[45] Urban enclaves have become places of permanent exception, with their own territorial sovereignty, their own laws, and their own rules of inclusion-exclusion. These enclaves are neither completely "inside" the city, nor completely "outside" existing governance frameworks. Instead, they constitute a kind of "third space," operating in a legal limbo or void where conventional regulatory regimes are suspended.[46]

While social exclusion and spatial segregation have always been associated with urban form, the emergence of new kinds of enclave urbanism at the start of the twenty-first century has marked a fundamental shift in how we conceive of the fundamental components and building blocks of urban landscapes. These novel circumstances require us to think about new kinds of city building where the paradigm is not the city taken as a whole – not even the exclusionary neoliberal city – but rather an *urbanism of exception*.[47] The model of the urbanism

[42] John Flint, "Cultures, Ghettos and Camps: Sites of Exception and Antagonism in the City," *Housing Studies* 24, 4 (2009), pp. 417–431 (ideas taken from p. 418). See also Mike Davis, *City of Quartz: Excavating the Future in Los Angeles* (New York: Vintage, 1992).

[43] Eyal Weizman, "On Extraterritoriality." Lecture at the symposium "Archipelago of exception. Sovereignties of extraterritoriality" (November 10–11, 2005). Available at www.publicspace .org/en/text-library/eng/bo11-on-extraterritoriality. See Eyal Weizman, "Principles of Frontier Geography," in Philipp Misselwitz and Tim Rieniets (eds.), *City of Collision: Jerusalem and the Principles of Conflict Urbanism* (Basel: Birkhäuser Publisher for Architecture, 2006), pp. 84–92.

[44] Boano and Martén, "Agamben's Urbanism of Exception, pp. 6–17 (esp. p. 6, 13–14).

[45] Alsayyad and Roy, "Medieval Modernity," p. 16 (source of quotations).

[46] Alessandro Petti, "Dubai Offshore Urbanism," in Michiel Dehaene and Lieven de Cauter (eds.), *Heterotopia and the City: Public Space in a Postcivil Society* (New York: Routledge, 2008), pp. 287–296 (esp. p. 292).

[47] These ideas originate with Alsayyad and Roy, "Medieval Modernity," pp. 2–3, 18.

of exception provides a new prototype of city building, a hybrid urban land-scape consisting of discontinuous fragments spread haphazardly across a broad spatial expanse and fall outside the rule of law and function independently of juridical regularity. Multilayered cities consisting of multiple intersecting, overlapping, and interlocking "spaces of exception" have produced elastic and shifting spatial geographies. These multiple spaces of exception are woven into the social fabric of the city, not as isolated territories but as integral features of contemporary urbanism itself. As the quintessential "exceptional spaces," urban enclaves have their own "specific rules and rhythms of use, where each is controlled through a localized 'regime of exceptionality' in which certain general laws and [conventional] rights are suspended."[48]

The formation of urban enclaves represents a kind of spatial ordering outside the façade of sovereign state institutions and public authority. Self-contained urban enclaves are the inverse of the camp precisely because they reinforce rather than suspend legal norms – that is, they are saturated with regulatory prescriptions rather than devoid of them. Instead of operating in radically dif-ferent ways from the regulatory regimes that exist outside them, urban enclaves and autonomous zones often make obvious and bring into the open "that which is often obscured or hidden in wider economic or social domains."[49]

In his essay "What is a Paradigm?" Giogio Agamben explains that the paradigm "is excluded from the rule not because it does not belong to the nor-mal case, but, on the contrary, because it exhibits belonging to it."[50] It is in this way that urban enclaves and autonomous zones can be considered paradig-matic expressions of contemporary urbanism. They belong to the "normal case," because they embody the embryonic entrepreneurial tendencies of neolib-eral urbanism. But because the conflictual and overlapping normative regimes that crystallize within them also often exceed their borders, urban enclaves and autonomous zones display their belonging to the "normal case" in an excessive and exaggerated way.[51]

The Practice of Exceptional Urbanism

Mobilizing theories of exception enables us to identify not only the unbundling of conventional urban regulatory regimes but also shifts in legal mechanisms

---

[48] Stavros Stavrides, "Contested Urban Rhythms: from the Industrial City to the Post-Industrial Urban Archipelago," *The Sociological Review* 61 [Issue Supplement S1] (2013), pp. 34–50 (p. 34, source of quotation). See also Pier Carlo Palermo and Davide Ponzini, *Place-making and Urban Development: New Challenges for Contemporary Planning and Design* (New York: Routledge, 2015), pp. 17–18.

[49] Brett Neilson, "Zones: Beyond the Logic of Exception?" *Concentric: Literary and Cultural Stud-ies* 40, 2 (2014), pp. 11–28 (p. 25, source of quotation).

[50] Gioggio Agamben, *The Signature of All Things: On Method* [Trans. Luca D'Isanto and Kevin Attell] (New York: Zone Books, 2009), p. 14 (source of quotation).

[51] Neilson, "Zones: Beyond the Logic of Exception?, p. 25.

that facilitate the normative suspension of standard planning and governance procedures.[52] Such widely divergent circumstances as the hosting of world-class mega-events, abrupt ruination brought on by (so-called) natural disasters, and other extraordinary circumstances create the conditions for declarations of state of emergency, thereby establishing seemingly unusual and unique, but always exceptional circumstances. The "state of emergency" always carries with it a call to action, and thus becomes a convenient excuse to legitimize the adoption of exceptional politico-administrative frameworks that authorize the relaxation of existing rules in order to speed up implementation of interventions and facilitate large-scale interventions into the built environment that take place outside the normal rule of law.[53] It is through their capacity to generate a sense of urgency – what might be called "planning in a state of emergency" – that financial failure and bankruptcy, catastrophic ruination, and assorted other out-of-the-ordinary occasions create unique, exceptional conditions that facilitate and accelerate the realization of large-scale urban projects.[54] The progressive normalization of the state of exception has eroded rule-bound procedures that give substance to conventional regulatory regimes. It is in this sense that the state of exception has become a core technique of routine urban governance, mobilized at a time of (real or imagined) crisis under the sign of neoliberal urbanism.[55]

Calling upon this "state of emergency" enables real-estate developers – in alliance with compliant city officials – to bypass established procedures, to lift existing restrictions and controls over what can be built and how, to ignore conventional social norms, to suspend civic participation and democratic accountability, to reformulate established planning regulations, to circumvent existing laws, to relax safety standards, and to introduce highly flexible regulatory instruments that facilitate the implementation of urban renewal projects.[56]

52 Neil Gray and Libby Porter, "By Any Means Necessary: Urban Regeneration and the 'State of Exception' in Glasgow's Commonwealth Games," *Antipode* 47, 2 (2015), pp. 380–400 (esp. p. 381).

53 Sánchez and Broudehoux, "Mega-events and Urban Regeneration in Rio de Janeiro: Planning in a State of Emergency," pp. 132–155; and Idalina Baptista, "Practices of Exception in Urban Governance: Reconfiguring Power Inside the State," *Urban Studies* 50, 1 (2013), pp. 39–54.

54 Sánchez and Broudehoux, "Mega-Events and Urban Regeneration in Rio de Janeiro: Planning in a State of Emergency," pp. 132–155. See also John Rennie Short, "Globalization, Cities and the Summer Olympics," *City* 12, 3 (2008), pp. 321–340; Chris Gaffney, "Mega-Events and Socio-Spatial Dynamics in Rio de Janeiro, 1919–2016," *Journal of Latin American Geography* 9, 1 (2010), pp. 7–29; and Stephen Essex and Brian Chalkley "Mega-Sporting Events in Urban and Regional Policy: A History of the Winter Olympics," *Planning Perspectives* 19, 2 (2004), pp. 201–232; Marrero-Guillamón, "Olympic State of Exception," in *The Art of Dissent*, pp. 20–29; Hyun Bang Shin, "Unequal Cities of Spectacle and Mega-Events in China," *City* 16, 6 (2012), pp. 728–744; and Mike Raco, "The Privatisation of Urban Development and the London Olympics 2012," *City* 16, 4 (2012), pp. 452–460.

55 Gray and Porter, "By Any Means Necessary," p. 383.

56 This litany of 'exceptions' is taken from a reading of Sánchez and Broudehoux, "Mega-Events and Urban Regeneration in Rio de Janeiro: Planning in a State of Emergency," p. 136; Graeme

This "state of exception" allows for imposition of extralegal forms of governance, particularly the transfer of extraordinary powers into the hands of large-scale property developers or quasi-private agencies "to carry out massive urban transformations without any form of accountability."[57] Employed on an ever-widening basis, the exception has literally become the rule. Such exceptional circumstances result "in the creation of self-governing extraterritorial enclaves, constituted as special autonomous zones – a kind of a state within the state – where political and ethical responsibilities are blurred and sovereign law is suspended." These "privatized planning" interventions that remake the city create "archipelagos of extraterritoriality," which function as virtual parallel universes, with their own distinct kinds of exceptional governance and their own brand of juridical autonomy. These market-friendly planning orientations associated with mega-projects almost always promote the concentration of political power and investment capital, along with the privatization of public services and the erosion of public space.[58] The *ad hoc* nature of these interventions signal a total disregard for long-term comprehensive master-planned development and a lack of concern for the local social and material context.[59] This exceptionalism associated with the relaxation of conventional regulatory regimes is marked by the accelerated demise of a holistic planning vision in the service of the public interest and its replacement with improvised "strategic planning" initiatives. It is under these circumstances where competitive, entrepreneurial, and economistic conceptualizations of the city, characterized by private intervention in the service of regeneration, have replaced the conventional modernist paradigm of the public administration of urban space.[60] This form of privatized planning in a "state of emergency" has effectively "inscribed new forms of

Hayes and John Horne, "Sustainable Development: Shock and Awe? London 2012 and Civil Society," *Sociology* 45, 5 (2011), pp. 749–764 (esp. pp. 759, 760); Bülent Diken and Carsten Bagge Laustsen, "Sea, Sun, Sex, and the Discontents of Pleasure," *Tourist Studies* 4, 2 (2004), pp. 99–114; and Willem Schinkel and Marguerite van den Berg, "City of Exception: The Dutch *Revanchist* City and the Urban *Homo Sacer*," *Antipode* 43, 5 (2011), pp. 1911–1938.

57 Sánchez and Broudehoux, "Mega-Events and Urban Regeneration in Rio de Janeiro," p. 136 (source of quotation). See also Anne-Marie Broudehoux, "Neoliberal Exceptionalism in Rio de Jainero's Olympic Port Redevelopment," in Michael Leary and John McCarthy (eds.), *The Routledge Companion to Urban Regeneration* (London: Routledge, 2013), pp. 558–568.

58 Sánchez and Broudehoux, "Mega-Events and Urban Regeneration in Rio de Janeiro: Planning in a State of Emergency," p. 136 (source of quotation). See also Anne-Marie Broudehoux, "Spectacular Beijing: The Conspicuous Construction of an Olympic Metropolis," *Journal of Urban Affairs* 29, 4 (2007), pp. 383–399.

59 Sánchez and Broudehoux, "Mega-Events and Urban Regeneration in Rio de Janeiro," p. 138. See also Greg Andranovich, Matthew Burbank, and Charles Heying, "Olympic Cities: Lessons Learned from Mega-Event Politics," *Journal of Urban Affairs* 23, 2 (2001), pp. 113–131.

60 Sánchez and Broudehoux, "Mega-Events and Urban Regeneration in Rio de Janeiro," p. 148.

power relations in the urban landscape, giving extraordinary powers" to corporate real-estate developers and public–private partnerships to transform the urban environment.[61]

Enhanced exceptional measures are routinely legitimated under the guise of some combination of necessity and urgency: these function as a moralizing groundwork that justify the relaxation of the application of the law and the suspension of normal procedures. Powerful groups supporting relaxed regulatory frameworks justify their actions by reference to temporal and budgetary pressures, by making fraudulent claims to serve the "public good," by offering promises about "legacy" rewards, and by pointing to "job creation" and other spillover benefits. Only by virtue of the emphasis on the "good common" does the exception effectively become the force of reason. As Neil Gray and Libby Porter have persuasively argued, "What the public interest justification offers to the acquiring authority and the urban growth coalitions maneuvering behind the scenes is an almost water-tight discursive framework from behind which defense of almost any necessary action can be made."[62]

This largely expedient process consistently provides real-estate developers more flexibility in the construction of their mega-projects, even if these situations require *more* bending of the rules than would be normally allowed within the framework of the law. These circumstances are what Ananya Roy has described as the *informalization* of the planning process, a process that, she has argued, stems from the capabilities of neoliberal modes of urban governance to shape spaces according to their ever-changing logics.[63] In aspiring world-class cities, such *informalization* is appealing because of the pliant elasticity it provides elite decision-makers in allowing particular exemptions or circumventions of existing regulations – but not others. Thus, *ad hoc* decision-making does not signify a failure in planning or the inability of municipal authorities to organize the production of the urban built environment. On the contrary, informality – or the bending of official rules to create "exceptions" – "appears to be a deliberate planning strategy that best fits the interests of those decision-makers who find in the flexibility it provides the leeway needed to regulate and organize the development of the city according to their own interests."[64] The advantages of informality rests in its malleability to bend official rules to create "exceptions" under circumstances in what otherwise might be termed "the

---

[61] Sánchez and Broudehoux, "Mega-Events and Urban Regeneration in Rio de Janeiro," p. 149 (source of quotation).

[62] Gray and Porter, "By Any Means Necessary," p. 385, 381 (quotation from p. 391). See also Baptista, "Practices of Exception in Urban Governance," pp. 39–54.

[63] Anaya Roy, "Why India Cannot Plan its Cities: Informality, Insurgence and the Idiom of Urbanization," *Planning Theory* 8, 1 (2009), pp. 76–87.

[64] Marieke Krijnen and Mona Fawaz, "Exception as the Rule: High-End Developments in Neoliberal Beirut," *Built Environment* 36, 2 (2010), pp. 245–259 (quotation from p. 255).

art of speculative governance."[65] Informality as a planning practice depends upon the existence of *ad hoc*, case-by-case processes of decision-making embedded within the formal planning process. This unbundling of existing rules and regulations corresponds with neoliberal technologies of urban governance. By adopting extraordinary measures and suspending the normal rule of law, the logic of exception has become an important technique of governance in its own right.[66]

---

[65] Michael Goldman, "Speculative Urbanism and the Making of the Next World City," *International Journal of Urban and Regional Research* 35, 3 (2011), pp. 555–581 (esp. pp. 561, 575). See Judith Innes, Sarah Connick, and David Booher, "Informality as a Planning Strategy," *Journal of the American Planning Association* 73, 2 (2007), pp. 195–210.

[66] Krijnen and Fawaz, "Exception as the Rule," pp. 255–256.

Bibliography

Secondary Sources

Aalpers, Manuel, "The Revanchist Renewal of Yesterday's City of Tomorrow," *Antipode* 43, 5 (2011), pp. 1696–1724.

Abaza, Mona, "Shopping Malls, Consumer Culture and the Reshaping of Public Space in Egypt," *Theory, Culture & Society* 18, 5 (2001), pp. 97–122.

"Egyptianizing the American Dream? Nasr City's Shopping Malls, Public Order, and Privatized Military," in Diane Singerman and Paul Amar (eds.), *Cairo Cosmopolitan: Politics, Culture and Urban Space in the New Middle East* (Cairo: American University in Cairo Press, 2006), pp. 193–220.

"Critical Commentary. Cairo's Downtown Imagined: Dubaisation or Nostalgia?" *Urban Studies* 48, 6 (2011), pp. 1075–1087.

Abbott, Andrew, "Of Time and Space: The Contemporary Relevance of the Chicago School," *Social Forces* 75, 4 (1997), pp. 1149–1182.

Abdulaal, Waleed Abdullah, "Large Urban Developments as the New Driver for Land Development in Jeddah," *Habitat International* 36, 1 (2012), pp. 36–46.

Abdul-Hussain, Hussain, "Hezbollah: A State within a State," *Current Trends in Islamist Ideology* 8 (2009), pp. 68–81.

Abelin, Mireille, "'Entrenched in the BMW': Argentine Elites and the Terror of Fiscal Obligation," *Public Culture* 24, 2 [67] (2012), pp. 329–356.

Abu-Lughod, Janet, "Tale of Two Cities: The Origins of Modern Cairo," *Comparative Studies in Society and History* 7, 4 (1965), pp. 429–457.

"The Desert City Today," in David Sims (ed.), *Understanding Cairo: The Logic of a City out of Control* (Cairo: American University in Cairo, 2010), pp. 169–210.

"Informal Cairo Triumphant," in David Sims (ed.), *Understanding Cairo: The Logic of a City out of Control* (Cairo: American University in Cairo, 2010), pp. 91–138.

Ackah-Baidoo, Abigail, "Enclave Development and 'Offshore Corporate Social Responsibility': Implications for Oil-rich Sub-Saharan Africa," *Resources Policy* 37, 2 (2012), pp. 152–159.

Acuto, Michelle, "High-rise Dubai Urban Entrepreneurialism and the Technology of Symbolic Power," *Cities* 27, 4 (2010), pp. 272–284.

Adams, Laura, and Asel Rustemova, "Mass Spectacle and Styles of Governmentality in Kazakhstan and Uzbekistan," *Europe-Asia Studies* 61, 7 (2009), pp. 1249–1276.

Adams, Vincanne, Taslim Van Hattum, and Diana English, "Chronic Disaster Syndrome: Displacement, Disaster Capitalism, and the Eviction of the Poor from New Orleans," *American Ethnologist* 36, 4 (2009), pp. 615–636.

Adey, Peter, "Vertical Security in the Megacity: Legibility, Mobility and Aerial Politics," *Theory, Culture & Society* 27, 6 (2010), pp. 51–67.

Adham, Khaled, "Globalization, Neoliberalism, and New Spaces of Capital in Cairo," *Traditional Dwellings and Settlements Review (TDSR)* 17, 1 (2005), pp. 19–32.

Afshar, Farokh, and Keith Pezzoli, "Introduction: Integrating Globalization and Planning," *Journal of Planning Education and Research* 20, 3 (2001), pp. 277–280.

Agamben, Giorgio, *Homo Sacer: Sovereign Power and Bare Life* [Trans. Daniel Heller-Roazen], (Stanford: Stanford University Press, 1998).

State of Exception [trans. Kevin Attell], (Chicago: University of Chicago Press, 2005).

The Signature of All Things: On Method [Trans. Luca D'Isanto and Kevin Attell], (New York: Zone Books, 2009).

Agier, Michel, "From Refugee Camps to the Invention of Cities," in Barbara Drieskens, Franck Mermier, and Heiko Wimmen (eds.), *Cities of the South: Citizenship and Exclusion in the 21st Century* (Beirut: SAQI, 2007), pp. 169–175.

Agnew, John, "The Territorial Trap: The Geographical Assumptions of International Relations Theory," *Review of International Political Economy* 1, 1 (1994), pp. 53–80.

Geopolitics: Re-visioning World Politics (London: Routledge, 2003).

"Sovereignty Regimes: Territoriality and State Authority in Contemporary World Politics," *Annals of the Association of American Geographers* 95, 2 (2005), pp. 437–461.

"Still Trapped in Territory?" *Geopolitics* 15 (2010), pp. 779–784.

Aguilar, Adrián, and Peter Ward, "Globalization, Regional Development, and Mega-City Development Expansion in Latin America: Analyzing Mexico City's Peri-Urban Hinterland," *Cities* 20, 1 (2003), p. 3–21.

Akar, Hiba Bou, "Contesting Beirut's Frontiers," *City & Society* 24, 2 (2012), pp. 150–172.

Akar, Hiba Bou, and Mohamad Hafeda (eds.), *Narrating Beirut from the Borderlines* (Beirut: Heinrich Böll Foundation, 2011).

Akgün, Aliye Ahu, and Tüzin Baycan, "Gated Communities in Istanbul: The New Walls of the City," *Town Planning Review* 83, 1 (2011), pp. 87–109.

Akkar Ercan, Z. Müge, "Questioning the 'Publicness' of Public Spaces in Post-industrial Cities," *Traditional Dwellings and Settlements Review* 16, 11 (2005), pp. 75–91.

"Public Spaces of Post-industrial Cities and their Changing Roles," *METU Journal of Faculty of Architecture* 24, 1 (2007), pp. 115–137.

Aksoy, Asu, "The Violence of Change," in Ricky Burdett and Deyan Sudjic (eds.), *Living in the Endless City: The Urban Age Project by the London School of Economics and Deutsche Bank's Alfrde Herrhausen Society* (London: Phaidon Press, 2011), pp. 232–239.

"Riding the Storm: 'New Istanbul,'" *City* 16, 1–2 (2012), pp. 93–111.

Albrechts, Louis, "In Pursuit of New Approaches to Strategic Spatial Planning: A European Perspective," *International Planning Studies* 6, 3 (2001), pp. 293–310.
  "Bridge the Gap: From Spatial Planning to Strategic Projects," *European Planning Studies* 14, 10 (2006), pp. 1487–1500.
Alexander, Jeffrey, "Robust Utopias and Civil Repairs," *International Sociology* 16 (2001), pp. 579–591.
Agier, Michel, "Between War and City: Towards an Urban Anthropology of Refugee Camps," *Ethnography* 3, 3 (2002), pp. 319–341.
Ali, Ismail, "Since Birth Till Death, What is their Status: A Case Study of the Sea Bajau in Pulau Mabulo, Semporna," *Journal of Arts Science & Commerce* 1, 1 (2010), pp. 156–166.
Al-Kodmany, Kheir, "Tall Buildings, Design, and Technology: Visions for the Twenty-first Century City," *Journal of Urban Technology* 18, 3 (2011), pp. 115–140.
Allegra, Marco, "The Politics of Suburbia: Israel's Settlement Policy and the Production of Space in the Metropolitan Area of Jerusalem," *Environment and Planning A* 45, 3 (2013), pp. 497–516.
Allen, John, "Powerful Geographies: Spatial Shifts in the Architecture of Globalization," in Stewart Clegg and Mark Haugaard (eds.), *The SAGE Handbook of Power* (London: Sage, 2008), pp. 157–174.
Allmendinger, Phil, and Graham Haughton, "Soft Spaces, Fuzzy Boundaries and Metagovernance: The New Spatial Planning in the Thames Gateway," *Environment and Planning A* 41, 3 (2009), pp. 617–633.
  "Critical Reflections on Spatial Planning," *Environment and Planning A* 41, 11 (2009), pp. 2544–2599.
  "Spatial Planning, Devolution, and New Planning Spaces," *Environment and Planning C* 28, 5 (2010), pp. 803–818.
  "The Evolution and Trajectories of English Spatial Governance: 'Neoliberal' Episodes in Planning," *Planning Practice and Research* 28, 1 (2013), pp. 6–26.
AlSayyad, Nezar, "Hybrid Culture/Hybrid Urbanism: Pandora's Box of the 'Third Space,'" in Nezar Alsayyad (ed.), *Hybrid Urbanism: On the Identity Discourse and the Built Environment* (Westport, CT: Praeger, 2001), pp. 1–18.
AlSayyad, Nezar, and Ananya Roy, "Urban Informality: Cross Borders," in Ananya Roy and Nezar AlSayyad (eds.), *Urban Informality: Transnational Perspectives from the Middle East, Latin America, and South Asia* (Lanham, MD: Lexington Books, 2004), pp. 1–6.
AlSayyad, Nezar, and Ananya Roy, "Medieval Modernity: On Citizenship and Urbanism in a Global Era," *Space and Polity* 10, 1 (2006), pp. 1–20.
Altshuler, Alan, "The Goals of Comprehensive Planning," in Andreas Faludi (ed.), *A Reader in Planning Theory* (Oxford: Pergamon, 1973), pp. 193–210.
Alvarez-Rivadulla, Maria, "Golden Ghettos: Gated Communities and Class Residential Segregation in Montevideo, Uruguay," *Environment and Planning A* 39, 1 (2007), pp. 47–63.
Amin, Ash, "Spatialities of Globalization," *Environment and Planning A* 34, 3 (2002), pp. 385–399.
  "Collective Culture and Urban Public Space," *City* 12, 1 (2008), pp. 5–24.
  "Telescopic Urbanism and the Urban Poor," *City* 17, 4 (2013), pp. 476–492.

"The Urban Condition: A Challenge to Social Science," *Public Culture* 25, 2 (2013), pp. 201–208.

Anderson, James, "The Shifting Stage of Politics: New Medieval and Postmodern Territorialities?" *Environment and Planning D* 14, 2 (1996) pp. 133–153.

Andranovich, Greg, Matthew Burbank, and Charles Heying, "Olympic Cities: Lessons Learned from Mega-Event Politics," *Journal of Urban Affairs* 23, 2 (2001), pp. 113–131.

Andrijasevic, Rutvica, "Lampedusa in Focus: Migrants Caught between the Libyan Desert and the Deep Sea," *Feminist Review* 82, 1 (2006), pp. 120–125.

"From Exception to Excess: Detention and Deportations across the Mediterranean Space," in Nicholas De Genova and Nathalie Peutz, (eds.), *The Deportation Regime: Sovereignty, Space, and the Freedom of Movement* (Durham, NC: Duke University Press, 2010) pp. 147–165.

Angelo, Hillary, and David Wachmuth, "Urbanizing Urban Political Ecology: A Critique of Methodological Cityism," *International Journal of Urban and Regional Research* 39, 1 (2015), pp. 16–27.

Angotti, Tom, "Urban Latin America: Violence, Enclaves, and Struggles for Land," *Latin American Perspectives* 40, 2 (2013), pp. 5–20.

The New Century of the Metropolis: Urban Enclaves and Orientalism (New York: Routledge, 2013).

Appardurai, Arjun, "Here and Now," in Arjun Appadurai (ed.), *Modernity at Large: Cultural Dimensions of Globalization* (Minneapolis: University of Minnesota Press, 1996), pp. 1–11.

"Spectral Housing and Urban Cleansing: Notes on Millennial Mumbai," *Public Culture* 12, 3 (2000), pp. 627–651.

"Sovereignty without Territoriality: Notes for a Postnational Geography," in Setha Low and Denise Lawrence-Zúñiga (eds.), *The Anthropology of Space and Place* (Cambridge: Blackwell, 2003), pp. 337–349.

Appel, Hannah, "Offshore Work: Oil, Modularity, and the How of Capitalism in Equatorial Guinea," *American Ethnologist* 39, 4 (2012), pp. 692–709.

"Walls and White Elephants: Oil Extraction, Responsibility, and Infrastructural Violence in Equatorial Guinea." *Ethnography* 13, 4 (2012), pp. 439–465.

Arif, Yasmeen, "Impossible Cosmopolises: Dislocations and Relocations in Beirut and Delhi," in Shail Mayaram (ed.), *The Other Global City* (New York: Routledge, 2009), pp. 101–128.

Armitage, John, and Joanne Roberts, "From the Hypermodern City to the Gray Zone of Total Mobilization in the Philippines," in Ryan Bishop, John Phillips, and Wei Wie Yeo (eds.), *Postcolonial Urbanism: Southeast Asian Cities and Global Processes* (New York: Routledge, 2003), pp. 87–101.

Armstrong, Allen, "Evolving Approaches to Planning and Management of Refugee Settlements: The Tanzanian Experience," *Ekistics* 57, 342–343 (1990), pp. 195–204.

Asdar Ali, Kamran, and Martina Rieker, "Introduction: Urban Margins," *Social Text* 95 [26(2)] (2008), pp. 1–12.

Atkinson, Roland, and Sarah Blandy, "Introduction: International Perspectives on The New Enclavism and the Rise of Gated Communities," *Housing Studies* 20, 2 (2005), pp. 177–186.

"A Picture of the Floating World: Grounding the Secessionary Affluence of the Residential Cruise Liner," *Antipode* 41, 1 (2009), pp. 92–110.

Augé, Marc, *Non-Places: Introduction to an Anthropology of Supermodernity* [trans. John Howe] (New York: Verso, 1995), pp. 75–115.

Aureli, Pier Vittorio, "City as Political Form: Four Archetypes of Urban Transformation, "*Architectural Design* 81, 1 (2011), pp. 32–37.

The Possibility of an Absolute Architecture (Cambridge, MA: The MIT Press, 2011).

Austin, C. Murray, and Mukesh Kumar, "Sovereignty in the Global Economy: An Evolving Geopolitical Concept," *Geography Research Forum* 18 (1998) pp. 49–64.

Awofeso, Pelu, "One Out of Every Two Nigerians Now Lives in a City There are many Problems but Just One Solution," *World Policy Journal* 27, 4 (2010), pp. 67–73.

Azcárate, Matilde Córdoba, Idalina Baptista, and Fernando Domínguez Rubio, "Enclosures within Enclosures and Hurricane Reconstruction in Cancún, Mexico," *City & Society* 26,1 (2014), pp. 96–119.

Bach, Jonathan, "'They Come in as Peasants and Leave Citizens': Urban Villages and the Making of Shenzhen," *Cultural Anthropology* 25, 3 (2010), pp. 421–458.

"Shenzhen: City of Suspended Possibility," *International Journal of Urban and Regional Research* 35, 2 (2011), pp. 414–420.

"Modernity and the Urban Imagination in Economic Zones," *Theory, Culture & Society* 28, 5 (2011), pp. 98–122.

Badiou, Alain, "The Communist Hypothesis," *New Left Review* 49 (2008), pp. 29–42.

Baeten, Guy, "Clichés of Urban Doom: The Dystopian Politics of Metaphors for the Unequal City – A View from Brussels," *International Journal of Urban Regional Research* 25, 1 (2001), pp. 55–69.

Bagaeen, Samer, and Ola Uduku (eds.), *Gated Communities: Social Sustainability in Contemporary and Historical Gated Developments* (London: Earthscan, 2010).

Bahrainy, Hossein, and Behnaz Aminzadeh, "Autocratic Urban Design: The Case of the Navab Regeneration Project in Central Tehran," *International Development Planning Review* 29, 2 (2007), pp. 241–270.

Baigent, Elizabeth, "Patrick Geddes, Lewis Mumford and Jean Gottmann: Divisions over 'Megalopolis,'" *Progress in Human Geography* 28, 6 (2008), pp. 687–700.

Baker, Douglas, and Robert Freestone, "Land Use Planning for Privatized Airports: The Australia Experience," *Journal of the American Planning Association* 78, 3 (2012), pp. 328–341.

Baker, Steve, "The Sign of the Self in the Metropolis," *Journal of Design History* 3, 4 (1990), pp. 227–234.

Balaban, Utku, "The Enclosure of Urban Space and Consolidation of the Capitalist Land Regime in Turkish Cities," *Urban Studies* 48, 10 (2011), pp. 2162–2179.

Balbo, Marcello, "Urban Planning and the Fragmented City of Developing Countries," *Third World Planning Review* 15, 1 (1993), pp. 23–35.

Baldacchino, Godfrey, "A Nationless State? Malta, National Identity and the EU," *West European Politics* 25, 4 (2002), pp. 191–206.

Island Enclaves: Offshoring Strategies, Creative Governance, and Subnational Island Jurisdictions (Montreal: McGill-Queen's Press-MQUP, 2010).

"Islands and the Offshoring Possibilities and Strategies of Contemporary States: Insights on/for the Migration Phenomenon on Europe's Southern Flank," *Island Studies Journal* 9, 1 (2014), pp. 57–68.

Baldacchino, Godfrey, and David Milne (eds.), *Lessons from the Political Economy of Small Islands: The Resourcefulness of Jurisdiction* (New York: Palgrave Macmillan, 2010).

Balsas, Carlos, "Gaming Anyone? A Comparative Study of Recent Urban Development Trends in Las Vegas and Macau," *Cities* 31 (2013), pp. 298–307.

Banerjee, Tridip, "The Future of Public Space: Beyond Invented Streets and Reinvented Places," *Journal of the American Planning Association* 67, 1 (2001), pp. 9–24.

Baptista, Idalina, "Practices of Exception in Urban Governance: Reconfiguring Power Inside the State," *Urban Studies* 50, 1 (2013), pp. 37–52.

"The Travels of Critiques of Neoliberalism: Urban Experiences from the 'Borderlands,'" *Urban Geography* 34, 5 (2013), pp. 590–611.

Barkemeyer, Ralf, and Frank Figge, "Fordlândia: Corporate Citizenship or Corporate Colonialism," *Corporate Social Responsibility and Environmental Management* 19, 2 (2012), pp. 69–78.

Barry, Andrew, "Technological Zones," *European Journal of Social Theory* 9, 2 (2006), pp. 239–253.

Barthel, Pierre-Arnaud, "Arab Mega-Projects: Between the Dubai Effect, Global Crisis, Social Mobilization and a Sustainable Shift," *Built Environment* 36, 2 (2010), pp. 133–145.

Barthel, Pierre-Arnaud, and Leïla Vignal, "Arab Mediterranean Megaprojects after the 'Spring': Business as Usual or a New Beginning?" *Built Environment* 40, 1 (2014), pp. 52–71.

Barthes, Roland, *S/Z* (New York: Hill and Wang, 1974).

Bartu-Candan, Ayfer, and Biray Kolluoğlu, "Emerging Spaces of Neoliberalism: A Gated Town and a Public Housing Project in Istanbul," *New Perspectives on Turkey* 39 (2008), pp. 5–46.

Başlevent, Cem, and Meltem Dayıoğlu, "The Effect of Squatter Housing on Income Distribution in Urban Turkey," *Urban Studies* 42, 1 (2005), pp. 31–45.

Bassens, David, Ben Derudder, and Frank Witlox, "The Making and Breaking of Dubai: The End of a City-state?" *Political Geography* 29, 6 (2010), pp. 299–301.

Baum, T. G. "The Fascination of Islands: The Tourist Perspective," in Douglas Lockhart and David Drakakis-Smith (eds.), *Island Tourism: Problems and Perspectives* (London: Pinter, 1996), pp. 21–35.

Bauman, Zygmunt, *Society under Siege* (London: Polity, 2002).

"Seeking Shelter in Pandora's Box," *City* 9, 2 (2005), pp. 161–168.

Bayat, Asef, "Uncivil Society: The Politics of the 'Informal People,'" *Third World Quarterly* 18, 1 (1997), pp. 53–72.

"From 'Dangerous Classes' to 'Quiet Rebels': Politics of Urban Subalterns in the Global South," *International Sociology* 15, 3 (2000), pp. 533–556.

"Activism and Social Development in the Middle East," *International Journal of Middle East Studies*, 34, 2 (2002), pp. 1–28.

Life as Politics: How Ordinary People Change the Middle East (Stanford, CA: Stanford University Press, 2009).

Bayat, Asef, and Eric Denis, "Who is Afraid of *Ashwaiyyat*?" *Environment and Urbanization* 12, 2 (2000), pp. 185–199.

Beatley, Timothy, *Blue Urbanism: Exploring Connections between Cities and Oceans* (Washington, DC: Island Press, 2014).

Beauregard, Robert, "Between Modernity and Postmodernity: The Ambiguous Position of U.S. Planning," *Environment and Planning D* 7, 4 (1989), pp. 381–395.

"Without a Net: Modernist Planning and the Postmodern Abyss," *Journal of Planning Education and Research* 10, 3 (1991), pp. 189–194.

"Edge Cities: Peripheralising the Centre," *Urban Geography* 16, 8 (1995), pp. 708–721.

When America became Suburban (Minneapolis: University of Minnesota Press, 2006).

Beer, David, "Thoughtful Territories: Imagining the Thinking Power of Things and Spaces," *City* 11, 2 (2007), pp. 229–238.

Becker, Anne, and Markus-Michael Müller, "The Securitization of Urban Space and the 'Rescue' of Downtown Mexico City Vision and Practice," *Latin American Perspectives* 40, 2 (2013), pp. 77–94.

Belcher, Oliver, Lauren Martin, Anna Secor, Stephanie Simon, and Tommy Wilson, "Everywhere and Nowhere: The Exception and the Topological Challenge to Geography," *Antipode* 40, 4 (2008), pp. 499–503.

Bell, David, and Mark Jayne (eds.), *City of Quarters: Urban Villages in the Contemporary City* (Burlington, VT: Ashgate, 2004).

Benevolo, Leonardo, *The Origins of Modern Town Planning* (Cambridge, MA: The MIT Press, 1967).

Benjamin, Walter [edited by Michael Jennings], *The Writer of Modern Life: Essays on Charles Baudelaire* (Cambridge, MA: Harvard University Press, 2006).

Ben-Joseph, Eran, "Double Standards, Single Goal: Private Communities and Design Innovation," *Journal of Urban Design* 9, 2 (2004), pp. 131–151.

Benton, Laura, *A Search for Sovereignty: Law and Geography in European Empires, 1400–1900* (Cambridge: Cambridge University Press, 2010).

Berger, Alan, *Drosscape: Wasting Land in Urban America* (New York: Princeton Architectural Press, 2006).

Berger, Stefan, "The Study of Enclaves – Some Introductory Remarks," *Geopolitics* 15, 2 (2010), pp. 312–328.

Berman, Marshall, *All That is Solid Melts into Air: The Experience of Modernity* (New York: Penguin, 1998).

Berney, Rachel, "Pedagogical Urbanism: Creating Citizen Space in Bogotá Colombia," *Planning Theory* 10, 16 (2011), pp. 16–34.

"Public Space versus Tableau: The Right-to-the-City Paradox in Neoliberal Bogotá, Columbia," in Tony Samara, Shenjing He, and Guo Chen (eds.), *Locating the Right to the City in the Global South* (New York: Routledge, 2013), pp. 152–170.

Berry-Chikhaoui, Isabelle, "Major Urban Projects and the People Affected: The Case of Casablanca's Avenue Royale," *Built Environment* 36, 2 (2010), pp. 216–229.

Bethke, Maria, and Dominik Bender, *The Living Conditions of Refugees in Italy* (Frankfurt am Main: Förderverein PRO ASYL e.V., 28 February 2011).

Bey, Hakim, *T. A. Z. The Temporary Autonomous Zone, Ontological Anarchy, Poetic Terrorism* (Brooklyn, NY: Autonomedia, 1991).

Bhatia, Neerag, "Introduction: Floating Frontiers," in Neeraj Bhatia and Mary Casper (eds.), *The Petropolis of Tomorrow* (New York: Actar, 2013), pp. 12–19.

Biehl, João, "Vita: Life in a Zone of Social Abandonment," *Social Text* 19, 3 (2001), pp. 131–149.

"*Vita: Life in a Zone of Social Abandonment* (Berkeley: University of California Press, 2005).

Bishop, Peter, and Lesley Williams, *The Temporary City* (New York: Routledge, 2012).

Bishop, Ryan, and John Phillips. "The Urban Problematic," *Theory, Culture & Society* 30, 7–8 (2013), pp. 221–241.

Bishop, Ryan, John Phillips, and Wei Wei Yeo, "Perpetuating Cities: Excepting Globalization and the Southeast Asia Supplement," in Ryan Bishop, John Phillips, and Wei Wei Yeo (eds.), *Postcolonial Urbanism: Southeast Asian Cities and Global Processes* (New York: Routledge, 2003), pp. 1–36.

(eds.), *Postcolonial Urbanism: Southeast Asian Cities and Global Processes* (New York: Routledge, 2003).

Blackwell, Adrian "Shenzhen – Topology of a Neoliberal City," in Rodolphe El-Khoury and Edward Robbins (eds.), *Shaping the City: Studies in History, Theory and Urban Design* (New York: Routledge, 2013), pp. 278–311.

Blokland, Talja, and Mike Savage (eds.), *Networked Urbanism: Social Capital in the City* (Aldershot, UK: Ashgate, 2008).

Blomley, Nicholas, "Making Private Property: Enclosure, Common Right and the Work of Hedges," *Rural History* 18, 1 (2007), pp. 1–21.

"Enclosure, Common Right and the Property of the Poor," *Social and Legal Studies* 17, 3 (2008), pp. 311–331.

"Making Space for Law," in Kevin Cox, Murray Low and Jennifer Robinson (eds.), *The Sage Handbook of Political Geography* (London: Sage, 2008), pp. 155–168.

Blumenfield, Hans, *The Modern Metropolis: Its Origins, Growth, Characteristics, and Planning: Selected Essays* [edited by Paul Spreiregen] (Cambridge, MA: The MIT Press, 1967).

Boano, Camillo, and Ricardo Martén, "Agamben's Urbanism of Exception: Jerusalem's Border Mechanics and Biopolitical Strongholds," *Cities* 34, 1 (2013), pp. 6–17.

Boddy, Trevor, "Underground and Overhead: Building the Analogous City," in Michael Sorkin (ed.), *Variations on a Theme Park* (New York: Noonday Press, 1992), pp. 123–153.

Body-Gendrot, Sophie, Jacques Carré, and Romain Garbaye, "Introduction," in Sophie Body-Gendrot, Jacques Carré, Romain Garbaye (eds.), *A City of One's Own: Blurring the Boundaries between Private and Public* (Aldershot, UK: Ashgate, 2008), pp. 1–10.

Boland, Philip, "Sexing Up the City in the International Beauty Contest: The Performative Nature of Spatial Planning and the Fictive Spectacle of Place Branding," *Town Planning Review* 84, 2 (2013), pp. 251–274.

Bollens, Scott, *City and Soul in Divided Societies* (New York and London: Routledge, 2012).

Booth, Philip, "Partnerships and Networks: The Governance of Urban Regeneration in Britain," *Journal of Housing and the Built Environment* 20, 3 (2005), pp. 257–269.

Borges, Marcelo, and Susana Torres, "Company Towns: Concepts, Historiography, and Approaches," in Marcelo Borges and Susana Torres (eds.), *Company Towns: Labor, Space, and Power Relations across Time and Continents* (New York: Palgrave Macmillan, 2012), pp. 1–40.

(eds.), *Company Towns: Labor, Space, and Power Relations across Time and Continents* (New York: Palgrave Macmillan, 2012).

Bottomley, Anne, and Nathan Moore, "From Walls to Membranes: Fortress Polis and the Governance of Urban Public Space in twenty-first Century Britain," *Law and Critique* 18, 2 (2007), pp. 171–206.

Bovaird, Tony, "Public–Private Partnerships: from Contested Concepts to Prevalent Practice," *International Review of Administrative Sciences* 70, 2 (2004), pp. 199–215.

Boyer, M. Christine, *Dreaming the Rational City: The Myth of American City Planning* (Cambridge, MA: The MIT Press, 1983).

"The City of Illusion: New York's Public Places," in Paul Knox (ed.), *The Restless Urban Landscape* (Englewood Cliffs, NJ: Prentice Hall, 1993), pp. 111–126.

CyberCities: Visual Perception in the Age of Electronic Communications (New York: Princeton Architectural Press, 1996).

The City of Collective Memory: Its Historical Imagery and Architectural Entertainments (Cambridge, MA: The MIT Press, 1998).

Brautigam, Deborah, and Tang Xiaoyang, "African Shenzhen: China's Special Economic Zones in Africa," *Journal of Modern African Studies* 49, 1 (2011), pp. 27–54.

Breitung, Werner, "Macau Residents as Border People: A Changing Border Regime from a Socio-cultural Perspective," *Journal of Current Chinese Affairs* 38, 1 (2009), pp. 101–127.

"Borders and the City: Intra-Urban Boundaries in Guangzhou (China)," *Quaestiones Geographicae* 30, 4 (2011), pp. 55–61.

"Enclave Urbanism in China: Attitudes towards Gated Communities in Guangzhou," *Urban Geography* 33, 2 (2012), pp. 278–294.

Brenner, Neil, "Globalisation as Reterritorialisation: The Re-scaling of Urban Governance in the European Union," *Urban Studies* 36, 3 (1999), pp. 431–451.

"Theses on Urbanization," *Public Culture* 25,1 (2013), pp. 85–114.

"Urban Theory without an Outside," in Neil Brenner (ed.), *Implosions/Explosions: Towards a Study of Planetary Urbanization* (Berlin: Jovis, 2013), pp. 14–35.

Brenner, Neil, and Christian Schmid, "Planetary Urbanization," in Matthew Gandy (ed.), *Urban Constellations* (Berlin: Jovis, 2011), pp. 10–13.

"The 'Urban Age' in Question," *International Journal of Urban and Regional Research* 38, 3 (2013), pp. 731–755.

"The 'Urban Age' in Question," in Neil Brenner (ed.), *Implosions/Explosions: Towards a Study of Planetary Urbanism* (Berlin: Jovis, 2014), pp. 310–337.

"Towards a New Epistemology of the Urban?" *City* 19, 2–3 (2015), pp. 151–182.

Briffault, Richard, "A Government for Our Time? Business Improvement Districts and Urban Governance," *Columbia Law Review* 99, 2 (1999), pp. 365–477.

Brittain-Catlin, William, *Offshore: The Dark Side of the Global Economy* (New York: Picador, 2005).

Bromley, Ray, "Street Vending and Public Policy: A Global Review," *International Journal of Sociology and Social Policy* 20, 1 (2000), pp. 1–29.

Broudehoux, Anne-Marie, "Spectacular Beijing: The Conspicuous Construction of an Olympic Metropolis," *Journal of Urban Affairs* 29, 4 (2007), pp. 383–399.

"Neoliberal Exceptionalism in Rio de Jainero's Olympic Port Redevelopment," in Michael Leary and John McCarthy (eds.), *The Routledge Companion to Urban Regeneration* (London: Routledge, 2013), pp. 558–568.

Brown, Wendy, *Walled States, Waning Sovereignty* (New York: Zone Books, 2010).

Brugmann, Jeb, *Welcome to the Urban Revolution: How Cities Are Changing the World* (St Lucia: University of Queensland Press, 2009).

Brunet-Jailly, Emmanuel, "Theorizing Borders: An Interdisciplinary Perspective," *Geopolitics* 10, 4 (2005), pp. 633–649.

Brunetta, Grazia, and Stefano Moroni, *Contractual Communities in the Self-Organising City* (Dordrecht, Netherlands: Springer, 2011).

Buck-Morss, Susan, *Dreamworld and Catastrophe: The Passing of Mass Utopia in East and West* (Cambridge, MA: The MIT Press, 2000).

Buğra, Ayşe, "The Immoral Economy of Housing in Turkey, *International Journal of Urban and Regional Research* 22, 2 (1998), pp. 282–302.

Buijs, Steef, Wendy Tan, and Devisari Tunas (eds.), *Megacities: Exploring a Sustainable Future* (Rotterdam: Naio10 Publishers, 2010).

Bull, Hedley, *The Anarchical Society: A Study of Order in World Politics [2nd Edition]* (London: Macmillan, 1995).

Bunnell, Tim, "Views from Above and Below: The Petronas Twin Towers and/in Contesting Visions of Development in Contemporary Malaysia," *Singapore Journal of Tropical Geography* 20, 1 (1999), pp. 1–23.

Bunnell, Tim, Daniel Goh, Chee-Kien Lai, and Choon-Piew Pow, "Introduction: Global Urban Frontiers? Asian Cities in Theory, Practice and Imagination," *Urban Studies* 49, 13 (2012), pp. 2785–2793.

Bunnell, Tim, and Anant Maringanti, "Practicing Urban and Regional Research beyond Metrocentricity," *International Journal of Urban and Regional Research* 34, 2 (2010), pp. 415–420.

Bunnell, Tim, and Michelle Ann Miller, "Jakarta in Post-Suharto Indonesia: Decentralisation, Neoliberalism and Global City Aspiration," *Space and Polity* 15, 1 (2011), pp. 35–48.

Burdett, Ricky, "Designing Urban Democracy: Mapping Scales of Urban Identity," *Public Culture* 25, 2 (2013), pp. 349–367.

"Accretion and Rupture in the Global City," in Pedro Gadanho (ed.), *Uneven Growth: Tactical Urbanisms for Expanding Megacities* (New York: Museum of Modern Art, 2014), pp. 32–39.

Burdett, Ricky, and Deyan Sudjic (eds.), *The Endless City: The Urban Age Project by the London School of Economics and Deutsche Bank's Alfred Herrhausen Society* (London: Phaidon, 2011).

Burdett, Ricky, and Philipp Rode, "Living in the Urban Age," in Ricky Burdett and Deyan Sudjic (eds.), *Living in the Endless City: The Urban Age Project by the London School of Economics and Deutsche Bank's Alfred Herrhausen Society* (London: Phaidon, 2011), pp. 8–43.

Burgess, Ernest, "The Growth of the City: An Introduction to a Research Project," in Robert Park, Ernest Burgess, and Roderick McKensie (eds.), *The City* (Chicago: University of Chicago Press, 1925 [Reprinted 1987]), pp. 1–14.

Burgess, Rod, and Marisa Carmona, "The Shift of Master Planning to Strategic Planning," in Marisa Carmona (ed.), *Planning through Projects: Moving from Master Planning to Strategic Planning. 30 Cities* (Amsterdam: Techne Press, 2009), pp. 12–42.

Butler, Tim, and Loretta Lees, "Super-Gentrification in Barnsbury, London," *Transactions of the British Institute of Geographers* 31, 4 (2006), pp. 467–487.

Button, Mark, "Private Security and the Policing of Quasi-Public Space," *International Journal of the Sociology of Law* 31, 3 (2003), pp. 227–237.

Byers, Jack, "The Privatization of Downtown Public Space: The Emerging Grade-separated City in North America," *Journal of Planning Education and Research* 17, 3 (1998), pp. 189–205.

Cairncross, Frances, *The Death of Distance: How the Communications Revolution is Changing our Lives* (Boston: Harvard Business School Press, 1997).

Caldeira, Teresa, "Building up Walls: The New Pattern of Spatial Segregation in São Paulo," *International Social Science Journal* 147 (1996), pp. 55–66.

"Fortified Enclaves: The New Urban Segregation," *Public Culture* 8, 2 (1996), pp. 303–328.

City of Walls: Crime, Segregation, and Citizenship in São Paulo (Berkeley: University of California Press, 2000).

Campbell, Scott, "Green Cities, Growing Cities, Just Cities? Urban Planning and the Contradictions of Sustainable Development," *Journal of the American Planning Association* 62, 3 (1996), pp. 296–312.

Cameron, Angus, and Ronen Palan, *The Imagined Economies of Globalization* (London: Sage, 2004).

Can, Ayşegül, "Neo-Liberal Urban Politics in the Historical Environment of İstanbul – The Issue of Gentrification," *Planning* 23, 2 (2013), pp. 95–104.

Canclini, Nestor Garcia, "Mexico City: Cultural Globalization in a Disintegrating City," *American Ethnologist* 22, 4 (1995), pp. 743–755.

Carlson, Linda, *Company Towns of the Pacific Northwest* (Seattle: University of Washington Press, 2003).

Carmody, Pádraig, "Cruciform Sovereignty, Matrix Governance and the Scramble for Africa's Oil: Insights from Chad and Sudan," *Political Geography* 28, 6 (2009), pp. 353–361.

Carmona, Matthew, "Contemporary Public Space: Critique and Classification, Part One: Critique," *Journal of Urban Design* 15, 1 (2010), pp. 123–148.

"Contemporary Public Space, Part Two: Classification," *Journal of Urban Design* 15, 2 (2010), pp. 157–173.

Carmona, Matthew, and Claudio De Magalhães, "Public Space Management – Present and Potential," *Journal of Environmental Planning and Management* 49, 1 (2006), pp. 75–99.

Carmona, Matthew, Claudio De Magalhães, and Leo Hammond, *Public Space: The Management Dimension* (London: Routledge, 2008).

Carmona, Matthew, Tim Heath, Taner Oc, and Steve Tiesdell, *Public Places Urban Spaces, The Dimensions of Urban Design* (Oxford: Architectural Press, 2003).

Carmona, Matthew, and Filipa Matos Wunderlich, *Capital Spaces: The Multiple Complex Public Spaces of a Global City* (New York: Routledge, 2012).

Cartier, Carolyn, "Megadevelopment in Malaysia: From Heritage Landscapes to 'Leisurescapes' in Melaka's Tourism Sector," *Singapore Journal of Tropical Geography*, 19, 2 (1998), pp. 151–176.

"The State, Property Development and the Symbolic Landscape in High-rise Hong Kong," *Landscape Research* 24 (1999), pp. 185–208.

"'Zone Fever', the Arable Land Debate, and Real Estate Speculation: China's Evolving Land Use Regime and its Geographical Contradictions," *Journal of Contemporary China* 10, 28 (2001), pp. 445–469.

"Transnational Urbanism in the Reform-era Chinese City: Landscapes from Shenzhen," *Urban Studies* 39, 9 (2002), pp. 1513–1532.

"Neoliberalism and the Neoauthoritarian City in China – Contexts and Research Directions: Commentary in Conversation with Jennifer Robinson's Urban Geography Plenary Lecture," *Urban Geography* 32, 8 (2011), pp. 1110–1121.

"Territorial Urbanization and the Party-State in China," *Territory, Politics, Governance* 3, 3 (2015), pp. 294–320.

Casper, Mary, "On Land, At Sea: Formalizing Public Edges in the Archipelago," in Neeraj Bhatia and Mary Casper (eds.), *The Petropolis of Tomorrow* (New York: Actar, 2013), pp. 106–199.

Castel, Robert, "The Roads to Disaffiliation: Insecure Work and Vulnerable Relationships," *International Journal of Urban and Regional Research* 24, 3 (2000), pp. 519–535.

Castells, Manuel, *The Rise of the Network Society, Volume 1* [2nd edition] (Cambridge, MA: Blackwell, 2000).

Centner, Ryan, "Microcitizenships: Fractious Forms of Urban Belonging after Argentine Neoliberalism," *International Journal of Urban and Regional Research*, 36, 2 (2012), pp. 336–362.

"Distinguishing the Right Kind of City: Contentious Urban Middle Classes in Argentina, Brazil, and Turkey," in Tony Samara, Shenjing He, and Guo Chen (eds.), *Locating Right to the City in the Global South* (New York: Routledge, 2013), pp. 247–263.

Chalana, Manish, "Of Mills and Malls: The Future of Urban Industrial Heritage in Neoliberal Mumbai," *Future Anterior* 9, 1 (2012), pp. a-15.

"Slumdogs vs. Millionaires: Balancing Urban Informality and Global Modernity in Mumbai, India," *Journal of Architectural Education* 63, 2 (2010), pp. 25–37.

Chalana, Manish, and Tyler Sprague, "Beyond Le Corbusier and the Modernist City: Reframing Chandigarh's 'World Heritage' Legacy," *Planning Perspectives* 28, 2 (2013), pp. 199–222.

Chalfin, Brenda, "Governing Offshore Oil: Mapping Maritime Political Space in Ghana and the Western Gulf of Guinea," *South Atlantic Quarterly* 114, 1 (2015), pp. 101–118.

Charlesworth, Esther, *Architects without Frontiers: War, Reconstruction and Design Responsibility* (Oxford and Burlington: Architectural Press Elsevier, 2006).

Charney, Igal, and Gillad Rosen, "Splintering Skylines in a Fractured City: High-rise Geographies in Jerusalem," *Environment and Planning D* 32, 6 (2014), pp. 1088–1101.

Chatterjee, Partha, *Politics of the Governed: Reflections on Popular Politics in Most of the World* (New York: Columbia University Press, 2004).

Lineages of Political Society: Studies in Postcolonial Democracy (New York: Columbia University Press, 2011).

Chatzidakis, Andreas, Pauline Maclaran, and Alan Bradshaw, "Heterotopian Space and the Utopics of Ethical and Green Consumption," *Journal of Marketing Management* 28, 3–4 (2012), pp. 494–515.

Chen, Jia Ching, "Greening Dispossession: Environmental Governance and Sociospatial Transformation in Yixing, China," in Tony Samara, Shenjing He, and Guo Chen (eds.), *Locating the Right to the City in the Global South* (New York: Routledge, 2013), pp. 81–104.

Chen, Xiangming, "The Evolution of Free Economic Zones and the Recent Development of Cross-national Growth Zones," *International Journal of Urban and Regional Research* 19, 4 (1995), pp. 593–621.

"The Evolution of Free Economic Zones and the Recent Development of Cross-national Growth Zones," *International Journal of Urban and Regional Research* 19, 5 (1995), pp. 593–621.

As Borders Blend: Transnational Spaces on the Pacific Rim (New York: Rowman & Littlefield, 2005).

Chen, Xiangming, and Tomas de'Medici, "Research Note – The 'Instant City' Coming of Age: Production of Spaces in China's Shenzhen Special Economic Zone," *Urban Geography* 31, 8 (2010), pp. 1141–1147.

Cheong, Kee-Cheok, and Kim-Leng Goh, "Hong Kong as Charter City Prototype – When Concept Meets Reality," *Cities* 35 (2013), pp. 100–103.

Cherry, Gordon, "Introduction: Aspects of Twentieth-century Planning," in Gordon Cherry (ed.), *Shaping an Urban World* (London: Mansell, 1980), pp. 1–21.

Chiodelli, Franceso, "Planning Illegality: The Roots of Unauthorized Housing in Arab East Jerusalem," *Cities* 29, 2 (2012), pp. 99–106.

"Re-shaping Jerusalem: The Transformation of Jerusalem's Metropolitan Area by the Israeli Barrier," *Cities* 31 (2013), pp. 417–424.

"The Next Jerusalem: Potential Futures of the Urban Fabric," *Jerusalem Quarterly* 53 (2014), pp. 50–60.

Choi, Narae, "Metro Manila through the Gentrification Lens: Disparities in Urban Planning and Displacement Risks," *Urban Studies* 53, 3 (2016), pp. 577–592.

Christiansen, Thomas, and Knut Erik Jørgensen, "Transnational Governance above and below the State: The Changing Nature of Borders in Europe," *Regional and Federal Studies* 10, 2 (2000), pp. 62–77.

Clarke, John, "Dissolving the Public Realm? The Logics and Limits of Neoliberalism," *Journal of Social Policy* 33, 1 (2004), pp. 27–48.

Clunan, Anne, and Harold Trinkunas, "Conceptualizing Ungoverned Spaces: Territorial Statehood, Contested Authority, and Softened Sovereignty," in Anne Clunan and Harold Trinkunas (eds.), *Ungoverned Spaces: Alternatives to State Authority in an Era of Softened Sovereignty* (Stanford: Stanford University Press, 2010), pp. 17–33.

Coaffee, Jon, *Terrorism, Risk and the City: The Making of a Contemporary Urban Landscape* (Burlington, VT: Ashgate, 2003).

"Urban Renaissance in the Age of Terrorism: Revanchism, Automated Social Control or the End of Reflection," *International Journal of Urban and Regional Research* 29, 2 (2005), pp. 447–454.

Cochrane, Allan, *Whatever Happened to Local Government* (Milton Keynes, England: Open University Press, 1993).

Coleman, Matthew, "Immigration Geopolitics beyond the Mexico-US Border," *Antipode* 38, 1 (2007), pp. 54–76.

Coleman, Roy, "Images from a Neoliberal City: The State, Surveillance and Social Control," *Critical Criminology* 12, 1 (2004), pp. 21–42.

Connell, Jon, "Beyond Manila: Walls, Malls, and Private Spaces," *Environment and Planning A* 31, 3 (1999), pp. 417–439.

Cook, Ian, and Kevin Ward, "Conferences, Informational Infrastructures and Mobile Policies: The Process of Getting Sweden 'BID Ready'," *European Urban and Regional Studies* 19, 2 (2012), pp. 137–152.

Cooke, Miriam, "Beirut Reborn: The Political Aesthetics of Auto-Destruction," *The Yale Journal of Criticism* 15, 2 (2002), pp. 393–424.

Coppola, Alessandro, and Alberto Vanolo, "Normalising Autonomous Spaces: Ongoing Transformations in Christiania, Copenhagen," *Urban Studies* 52, 6 (2015), pp. 1152–1168.

Coquery-Vidrovitch, Catherine, "Review Essays: Is L.A. a Model or a Mess?" *American Historical Review* 105, 5 (2000), pp. 1683–1691.

Correa, Felipe, "Forward: Alternative Post-Oil Cities," in Neeraj Bhatia and Mary Casper (eds.), *The Petropolis of Tomorrow* (New York: Actar, 2013), pp. 8–9.

Correa-Jones, Michael, "The Origins and Diffusion of Racial Restrictive Covenants," *Political Science Quarterly* 115, 4 (2000), pp. 541–568.

Coutard, Olivier, "Placing Splintering Urbanism: Introduction," *Geoforum* 39, 6 (2008), pp. 1815–1820.

Coy, Martin, "Gated Communities and Urban Fragmentation in Latin America: The Brazilian Experience," *GeoJournal* 66, 1–2 (2006), pp. 121–132.

Crang, Mike, and Stephen Graham, "SENTIENT CITIES Ambient Intelligence and the Politics of Urban Space," *Information, Communication & Society* 10, 6 (2007), pp. 789–817.

Crawford, Margaret, *Building the Workingman's Paradise: The Design of American Company Towns* (London and New York: Verso, 1995);

"Blurring the Boundaries: Public Space and Private Life," in John Chase, Margaret Crawford, and John Kaliska (eds.), *Everyday Urbanism* (New York: The Monacelli Press, 1999), pp. 22–35.

Crilley, Darrell, "Megastructures and Urban Change: Aesthetics, Ideology, and Design," in Paul Knox (ed.), *The Restless Urban Landscape* (Englewood Cliffs, NJ: Prentice-Hall, 1993), pp. 126–164.

Cross, Jamie, "Neoliberalism as Unexceptional: Economic Zones and the Everyday Precariousness of Working Life in South India," *Critique of Anthropology* 30, 4 (2010), pp. 355–373.

Dream Zones: Anticipating Capitalism and Development in India (London: Pluto, 2014).

Cross, John, *Informal Politics: Street Vendors and the State in Mexico City* (Stanford, CA: Stanford University Press, 1998).

"Pirates on the High Streets: The Street as a Site of Local Resistance of Globalization," in John Cross and Alfonso Morales (eds.), *Street Entrepreneurs: People, Place and Politics in Local and Global Perspectives* (New York: Routledge, 2007), pp. 125–144.

Cross, John, and Marina Karides, "Capitalism, Modernity, and the 'Appropriate' Use of Space," in John Cross and Alfonso Morales (eds.), *Street Entrepreneurs: People, Place and Politics in Local and Global Perspectives* (New York: Routledge, 2007), pp. 19–35.

Crossa, Veronica, "Resisting the Entrepreneurial City: Street Vendors' Struggle in Mexico City's Historic Center," *International Journal of Urban and Regional Research* 33, 1 (2009), pp. 43–63.

"Reading for Difference on the Street: De-homogenising Street Vending in Mexico City," *Urban Studies* 53, 2 (2016), pp. 287–301.

Cruz, Teddy, "Tijuana Case Study: Tactics of Invasion – Manufacturing Sites," *Architectural Design* 75, 5 (2005), pp. 32–37.

"Rethinking Urban Growth: It's about Inequality, Stupid," in Pedro Gadanho (ed.), *Uneven Growth: Tactical Urbanisms for Expanding Megacities* (New York: The Museum of Modern Art, 2014), pp. 48–55.

"Border Tours: Strategies of Surveillance, Tactics of Encroachment," in Michael Sorkin (ed.), *Indefensible Space: The Architecture of the National Insecurity State* (New York: Routledge, 2008), pp. 111–140.

Cuff, Dana, "Los Angeles: Urban Development in the Postsuburban Megacity," in André Sorensen and Junichiro Okata (eds.), *Megacities: Urban Form, Governance, and Sustainability* (Tokyo: Springer, 2011), pp. 273–287.

Cutler, A. Clair, *Private Power and Global Authority: Transnational Merchant Law and the Global Political Economy* (Cambridge: Cambridge University Press, 2003).

Cybriwsky, Roman, and Larry Ford, "City Profile Jakarta," *Cities* 18, 3 (2001), pp. 199–210.

Daher, Rami Farouk, "Amman: Disguised Genealogy and Recent Urban Restructuring and Neoliberal Threats," in Yasser Elsheshtawy, (ed.), *The Evolving Arab City: Tradition, Modernity and Urban Development* (London: Routledge, 2008), pp. 37–68.

Datta, Anoya, "India's Ecocity? Environment, Urbanisation, and Mobility in the Making of Lavasa," *Environment and Planning C* 30, 10 (2012), pp. 982–996.

"Encounters with Law and Critical Urban Studies: Reflections on Amin's Telescopic Urbanism," *City* 17, 4 (2013), pp. 517–522.

Davidson, Kathryn, and Brendan Gleeson, "The Sustainability of an Entrepreneurial City?" *International Planning Studies* 19, 2 (2014), pp. 173–191.

Davidson, Mark, and Kevin Ward, "'Picking up the Pieces': Austerity Urbanism, California and Fiscal Crisis," *Cambridge Journal Regions, Economy and Society* 7, 1 (2014), pp. 81–97.

Davidson, Mar, and Kurt Iveson, "Beyond City Limits: A Conceptual and Political Defense of 'the City' as an Anchoring Concept for Critical Urban Theory," *City* 19, 5 (2015), pp. 646–664.

Davies, Stephan, "Laissez-faire Urban Planning," in David Beito, Peter Gordon, and Alexander Tabarrok (eds.), *The Voluntary City: Choice, Community and Civil Society* (Ann Arbor: University of Michigan Press, 2002), pp. 18–46.

Davis, Mike, *City of Quartz: Excavating the Future of Los Angeles* (New York: Vintage, 1992).

"Planet of Slums," *New Left Review* 26 (2004), pp. 5–34.

"Fear and Money in Dubai," *New Left Review* 41 (2006), pp. 47–68.

Planet of Slums (New York: Verso, 2006).

Davis, Mike, and Daniel Bertrand Monk, "Introduction," in Mike Davis and Daniel Bertrand Monk (eds.), *Evil Paradises: Dreamworlds of Neoliberalism* (New York: The New Press, 2007), pp. ix–xvi.

Davis, Sasha, "The US Military Base Network and Contemporary Colonialism: Power Projection, Resistance and the Quest for Operational Unilateralism," *Political Geography* 30, 4 (2011), pp. 215–224.

Dear, Michael, "Postmodernism and Planning," *Environment and Planning D* 4, 3 (1986), pp. 367–384.

(ed.), *From Chicago to LA: Making Sense of Urban Theory* (Thousand Oaks, CA: Sage, 2001).

"Los Angeles and the Chicago School: Invitation to a Debate," *City & Community* 1, 1 (2002), pp. 5–32.

"Cities without Centers and Edges," in Roger Sherman and Dana Cuff (eds.), *Fast-Forward Urbanism: Rethinking Architecture's Engagement with the City* (New York: Princeton Architectural Press, 2011), pp. 226–242.

"The Urban Question after Modernity," in Heiko Schmid, Wolf-Dietrich Sahr, and John Urry (eds.), *Cities and Fascination: Beyond the Surplus of Meaning* (Burlington, VT: Ashgate, 2011), pp. 17–32.

Dear, Michael, and Steven Flusty, "Postmodern Urbanism," *Annals of the Association of American Geographers* 88, 1 (1998), pp. 50–72.

"Engaging Postmodern Urbanism," *Urban Geography* 20, 5 (1999), pp. 393–416.

Deboulet, Agnès, "Urban Highways as an Embodiment of Mega and Elite Projects: A New Realm of Conflicts and Claims in Three Middle Eastern Capital Cities," *Built Environment* 36, 2 (2010), pp. 146–161.

Deboulet, Agnès, and Mona Fawaz, "Contesting the Legitimacy of Urban Restructuring and Highways in Beirut's Irregular Settlements," in Diane Davis and Nora Libertun de Duren (eds.), *Cities and Sovereignty: Nationalist Conflicts in the Urban Realm* (Bloomington: Indiana University Press, 2010), pp. 117–151.

De Cauter, Lieven, "Towards a Phenomenology of Civil War: Hobbes Meets Benjamin in Beirut," *International Journal of Urban and Regional Research* 35, 2 (2011), pp. 221–230.

Degen, Monica, "Fighting for the Global Catwalk: Formalizing Public Life in Castlefield (Manchester) and Diluting Public Life in el Raval (Barcelona)," *International Journal of Urban and Regional Research* 27, 4 (2003), pp. 867–880.

Dehaene, Michiel, and Lieven De Cauter, "The Space of Play: Toward a General Theory of Heterotopia," in Michiel Dehaene and Lieven De Cauter (eds.), *Heterotopia and the City: Public Space in a Postcivil Society* (New York: Routledge, 2008), pp. 86–102.

Deleuze, Gilles, "Postscript on the Societies of Control," *October* 59 (1992), pp. 3–7.

Deleuze, Gilles, and Félix Guattari, *A Thousand Plateaus: Capitalism and Schizophrenia* (Minneapolis: University of Minnesota Press, 1987).

Deneç, Evren Aysev, "The Reproduction of the Historical Center of Istanbul in the 2000s: A Critical Account on Two Projects in Fener-a Balat," *METU JFA* 31, 2 (2014), pp. 163–188.

Desfor, Gene, and John Jørgensen, "Flexible Urban Governance: The Case of Copenhagen's Recent Waterfront Development," *European Planning Studies* 12, 4 (2004), pp. 479–496.

De Magalhães, Claudio, and Matthew Carmona, "Innovations in the Management of Public Space, Reshaping and Refocusing Governance," *Planning Theory and Practice* 17, 3 (2006), pp. 289–303.

Dembski, Sebastian, "Structure and Imagination of Changing Cities: Manchester, Liverpool and the Spatial In-between," *Urban Studies* 52, 9 (2015), pp. 1647–1664.

Denis, Eric, "Cairo as Neoliberal Capital? From Walled City to Gated Communities," in Diane Singerman and Paul Amar (eds.), *Cairo Cosmopolitan: Politics, Culture and Urban Space in the New Middle East* (Cairo: American University in Cairo Press, 2006), pp. 47–72.

DePalma, Anthony, David Slade, and Craig Whitaker, *Reclaiming the Waterfront – A Planning Guide for Waterfront Municipalities* (Hoboken, NJ: Fund for a Better Waterfront, 1996).

Dewey, Onesimo Flores, and Dianne Davis, "Planning, Politics, and Urban Mega-Projects in Developmental Context: Lessons from Mexico City's Airport Controversy," *Journal of Urban Affairs* 35, 5 (2013), pp. 531–551.

De Wit, Joop, and Erhard Berner, "Progressive Patronage? Municipalities, NGOs, CBOs and the Limits to Slum Dwellers' Empowerment," *Development and Change* 40, 5 (2009), pp. 927–947.

Diaz Orueta, Fernando, and Susan Fainstein, "The New Mega-Projects: Genesis and Impacts," *International Journal of Urban and Regional Research* 32, 4 (2008), pp. 759–767.

Dick, Howard, and Peter Rimmer, "Beyond the Third World City: The New Urban Geography of Southeast Asia," *Urban Studies* 35, 12 (1998), pp. 2303–2321.

Didier, Sophie, Marianne Morange, and Elisabeth Peyroux, "The Spreading of the City Improvement District Model in Johannesburg and Cape Town: Urban Regeneration and the Neoliberal Agenda in South Africa," *International Journal of Urban and Regional Research* 36, 5 (2012), pp. 915–935.

"City Improvement Districts and 'Territorialized Neoliberalism' in South African Cities (Johannesburg, Cape Town)," in Jenny Künkel and Margit Mayer (eds.), *Neoliberal Urbanism and its Contestations: Crossing Theoretical Boundaries* (New York: Palgrave, 2012), pp. 119–136.

"The Adaptative Nature of Neoliberalism at the Local Scale: Fifteen Years of City Improvement Districts in Cape Town and Johannesburg," *Antipode* 45, 1 (2013), pp. 121–139.

Diken, Bülent, "From Refugee Camps to Gated Communities: Biopolitics and the End of the City," *Citizenship Studies* 8, 1 (2004), pp. 83–106.

Diken, Bülent, and Carsten Bagge Laustsen, "Sea, Sun, Sex, and the Discontents of Pleasure," *Tourist Studies* 4, 2 (2004), pp. 99–114.

The Culture of Exception: Sociology Facing the Camp (New York: Routledge, 2005).

DiGaetano, Alan, and Elizabeth Strom, "Comparative Urban Governance: An Integrated Approach," *Urban Affairs Review* 38, 3 (2003), pp. 356–395.

Di Marco, and Anna Tozzi, "The Reshaping of Cairo's City of the Dead: Rural Identity versus Urban Arena in the Cairene Cultural Narrative and Public Discourse," *Anthropology of the Middle East* 6, 2(2011), pp. 38–50.

Dinçer, İclal, "The Impact of Neoliberal Policies on Historic Urban Space: Areas of Urban Renewal in Istanbul," *International Planning Studies* 16, 1 (2011), pp. 43–60.

Dinius, Oliver, and Angela Vergara (eds.), *Company Towns in the Americas: Landscape, Power, and Working-Class Communities* (Athens: University of Georgia Press, 2011).

Dirlik, Arif, "Architecture of Global Modernity, Colonialism and Places," in Sang Lee and Ruth Baumeister (eds.), *The Domestic and the Foreign in Architecture* (Rotterdam: 010 Publishers, 2007), pp. 37–46.

Dodds, Klaus, and Stephen Royle, "Introduction: Rethinking Islands," *Journal of Historical Geography* 29, 4 (2003), pp. 487–498.

Doevendans, Kees, and Anne Schram, "Creation/Accumulation City," *Theory, Culture & Society* 22, 2 (2005), pp. 29–43.

Domosh, Mona, "The Symbolism of the Skyscraper: Case Studies of New York's First Tall Buildings," *Journal of Urban History* 14, 3 (1998), pp. 320–345.

Donovan, Michael, "Informal Cities and the Contestation of Public Space: The Case of Bogota's Street Vendors, 1988–2003," *Urban Studies* 45, 1 (2008), pp. 29–51.

Dorio, Emma, "Decentralisation, Power and Networked Governance in Metro Manila," *Space and Polity* 16, 1 (2012), pp. 7–27.

Dorman, W. J., "Exclusion and Informality: The Praetorian Politics of Land Management in Cairo, Egypt," *International Journal of Urban and Regional Research* 37, 5 (2013), pp. 1584–1610.

Doron, Gil, "The Dead Zone and the Architecture of Transgression," *City* 42, 2 (2000), pp. 247–263.

"'...Those Marvelous Empty Zones on the Edge of our Cities': Heterotopia and the 'Dead Zone'," in Michiel Dehaene and Liven de Cauter (eds.), *Heterotopia and the City: Public Space in a Postcivil Society* (New York: Routledge, 2008), pp. 203–214.

Doucet, Isabelle, "[Centrality] and/or Cent][rality: A Matter of Placing the Boundaries," in Giovanni Maciocco (ed.), *Urban Landscape Perspectives* (Berlin and Heidelberg: Springer Verlag, 2008), pp. 93–121.

Douglass, Mike, "Globalization on the Edge: Fleeing the Public Sphere in the (Peri-) urban Transition in Southeast Asia," in Tôn Nữ Quỳnh Trân, Fanny Quertamp, Claude de Miras, Nguyễn Quang Vinh, Lê Văn Năm, Trương Hoàng Trương (eds.), *Trends of Urbanization and Suburbanization in Southeast Asia* (Ho Chi Minh City: General Publishing House, 2012), pp. 101–118.

Douglass, Mike, and Amrita Danière, "Urbanization and Civic Space in Asia," in Amrita Danière and Mike Douglass (eds.), *The Politics of Civic Space in Asia: Building Urban Communities* (London and New York: Routledge, 2009), pp. 1–18.

Douglass, Mike, and Liling Huang, "Globalizing the City in Southeast Asia: Utopia on the Urban Edge – the Case of Phu My Hung, Saigon," in Ronan Paddison, Peter Marcotullio, and Mike Douglass (eds.), *Connected Cities: Histories, Hinterlands, Hierarchies and Networks and Beyond. Volume III* (Thousand Oaks, CA: Sage, 2010), pp. 287–319.

Douglass, Mike, Bart Wissink, and Ronald Van Kempen, "Enclave Urbanism in China: Questions and Interpretations," *Urban Geography* 33, 2 (2012), pp. 167–182.

Dowling, Robyn, Rowland Atkinson, and Pauline McGuirk, "Privatism, Privatisation and Social Distinction in Master-planned Residential Estates," *Urban Policy and Research* 28, 4 (2010), pp. 391–410.

Doxiadis, Constantinos, and John Papaioanou, *Ecumenopolis: The Inevitable City of the Future* (New York: Norton, 1974).

Drakakis-Smith, David, *Third World Cities* [2nd Edition] (New York: Routledge, 2000).

Drummond, Lisa, "Street Scenes: Practices of Public and Private Space in Urban Vietnam," *Urban Studies* 37, 12 (2000), pp. 2377–2391.

Dumper, Michael, *Jerusalem Unbound: Geography, History and the Future of the Holy City* (New York: Columbia University Press, 2014).

Dupont, Veronique, "The Dream of Delhi as a Global City," *International Journal of Urban and Regional Research* 35, 3 (2011), pp. 533–554.

Durham, Scott, *Phantom Communities: The Simulacrum and the Limits of Postmodernism* (Stanford, CA: Stanford University Press, 1998), pp. 1–10.

Durrell, Lawrence, *Reflections on a Maritime Venus* (Mount Jackson, VA: Axios Press, 1953).

Easterling, Keller, "Siting Protocols," in Peter Lang and Tam Miller (eds.), *Suburban Discipline* (New York: Princeton Architectural Press, 1997), pp. 20–31.

    Enduring Innocence: Global Architecture and Its Political Masquerades (Cambridge, MA: The MIT Press, 2005).

    "The Corporate City is the Zone," in Christina de Baan, Joachim Declerk, and Veronique Patteeuw (eds.), *Visionary Power: Creating the Contemporary City* (Rotterdam: NAi Publishers, 2007), pp. 75–85.

    "Extrastatecraft," in Kanu Agrawal, *et al.* (eds.), *Perspecta 39: Re-Urbanism Transforming Capitals* (Cambridge, MA: The MIT Press, 2007), pp. 4–16.

    "Zone," in Ilka & Andreas Ruby (eds.), *Urban Transformation* (Berlin: Ruby Press, 2008), pp. 30–45.

    "Shadow States," in Jack Shelf and Shumi Bose (eds.), *Fulcrum: Real Estates: Life without Debt* (Germany: Bedford Press, 2014), pp. 27–33.

    Extrastatecraft: The Power of Infrastructure Space (New York: Verso, 2014).

Eder, Mine, and Özlem Öz, "Neoliberalization of Istanbul's Nightlife: Beer or Champagne?" *International Journal of Urban and Regional Research* 39, 2 (2015), pp. 284–304.

Edkins, Jenny, "Sovereign Power, Zones of Indistinction, and the Camp," *Alternatives* 25, 1 (2000), pp. 3–25.

Edmonds, Richard Louis, "Macau: Past, Present and Future," *Asian Affairs* 24, 1 (1993), pp. 3–15.

Efrat, Elisha, *Geography of Occupation* (Jerusalem: Carmel Publications, 2002).

Eick, Volker, "The Co-production of Purified Space: Hybrid Policing in German Business Improvement Districts," *European Urban and Regional Studies* 19, 2 (2012), pp. 121–136.

Ek, Richard, "Giorgio Agamben and the Spatialities of the Camp," *Geografiska Annaler B* 88, 4 (2006), pp. 363–386 (esp. pp. 372, 374).

Elden, Stuart, "Contingent Sovereignty, Territorial Integrity and the Sanctity of Borders," *SAIS Review* 26, 1 (2006), pp. 11–24.

    "Spaces of Humanitarian Exception," *Geografiska Annaler B* 88, 4 (2006), pp. 477–485.

    Terror and Territory: The Spatial Extent of Sovereignty (Minneapolis: University of Minnesota Press, 2009).

    "Thinking Territory Historically," *Geopolitics* 15, 4 (2010), pp. 757–761.

    "Secure the Volume: Vertical Geopolitics and the Depth of Power," *Political Geography* 34 (2013), pp. 35–51.

Ellin, Nan, *Postmodern Urbanism* [Revised Edition] (New York: Princeton Architectural Press, 1999).

    "Fear and City Building," *The Hedgehog Review* V, 3 (2003), pp. 43–61.

Ellison, Nick, and Roger Burrows, "New Spaces of (dis)engagement? Social Politics, Urban Technologies and the Rezoning of the City," *Housing Studies* 22, 3 (2007), pp. 295–312.

Elsheshtawy, Yasser, "The Middle East City: Moving beyond the Narrative of Loss," in
    Yasser Elsheshtawy (ed.), *Planning Middle Eastern Cities: An Urban Kaleidoscope
    in a Globalizing World* (London: Routledge, 2004), pp. 1–21.
"Redrawing Boundaries, Dubai an Emerging Global City," in Yasser Elsheshtawy
    (ed.), *Planning Middle Eastern Cities: An Urban Kaleidoscope* (New York: Rout-
    ledge, 2004), pp. 169–199.
Dubai: Behind an Urban Spectacle (New York: Routledge, 2010).
"Urban Dualities in the Arab World: From a Narrative of Loss to Neoliberal Urban-
    ism," in Michael Larice and Elizabeth MacDonald (eds.), *Urban Design Reader*
    (London: Routledge, 2013), pp. 475–496.
Elyachar, Julia, "Mappings of Power: The State, NGOs, and International Organizations
    in the Informal Economy of Cairo," *Comparative Studies in Society and History* 45,
    3 (2003), pp. 571–605.
Markets of Dispossession: NGOs, Economic Development and the State in Cairo
    (Durham, NC: Duke University Press, 2005).
Engel, Ulf, and Andreas Mehler, "Under Construction: Governance in Africa's New Vio-
    lent Social Spaces," in Ulf Engel and Gorm Rye Olsen (eds.), *The African Exception*
    (Burlington, VT: Ashgate, 2005), pp. 87–102.
Enlil, Zeynep Merey, "The Neoliberal Agenda and the Changing Urban Form of Istan-
    bul," *International Planning Studies* 16, 1 (2011), pp. 5–25.
Erkip, Feyzan, "Global Transformations versus Local Dynamics in Istanbul: Planning
    in a Fragmented Metropolis," *Cities* 17, 5 (2000), pp. 371–377.
Erman, Tahire, "The Politics of Squatter (*Gecekondu*) Studies in Turkey: The Changing
    Representations of Rural Migrants in the Academic Discourse," *Urban Studies* 38,
    7 (2001), pp. 983–1002.
Esin, Engin, and Kim Rygiel, "Of Other Global Cities: Frontiers, Zones, Camps," in
    Barbara Drieskens, Franck Mermier, and Heiko Wimmen (eds.), *Cities of the South:
    Citizenship and Exclusion in the 21st Century* (Beirut/London: Saqi Books, 2007),
    pp. 169–176.
Essex, Stephen, and Brian Chalkley "Mega-sporting Events in Urban and Regional
    Policy: A History of the Winter Olympics," *Planning Perspectives* 19, 2 (2004),
    pp. 201–232.
Evans, Graeme, "Branding the City of Culture: The Death of City Planning?" in Javier
    Monclús and Manuel Guardia (eds.), *Culture, Urbanism and Planning* (Aldershot:
    Ashgate, 2006), pp. 197–214.
Evers, Clifton, and Kirsten Seale, "Informal Urban Street Markets: International Per-
    spectives," in Clifton Evers and Kirsten Seale (eds.), *Informal Urban Street Markets:
    International Perspectives* (New York: Routledge, 2015), pp. 1–16.
Fahmi, Wael, and Keith Sutton, "Greater Cairo's Housing Crisis: Contested Spaces
    from Inner City Areas to New Communities," *Cities* 25, 5 (2008), pp. 277–
    297.
Fainstein, Susan, "Mega-Projects in New York, London and Amsterdam." *International
    Journal of Urban and Regional Research* 32, 4 (2008), pp. 768–785.
Falah, Ghazi-Walid, "Dynamics and Patterns of the Shrinking of Arab Lands in Pales-
    tine," *Political Geography* 22, 2 (2003), pp. 179–209.
Fall, Juliet, *Drawing the Line: Nature, Hybridity and Politics in Transboundary Spaces*
    (Burlington, VT: Ashgate Press, 2005).

Faludi, Andreas, "A Planning Doctrine for Jerusalem?" *International Planning Studies* 2, 1 (1997), pp. 83–102.

Fawaz, Mona, "An Unusual Clique of City-Makers: Social Networks in the Production of a Neighborhood in Beirut (1950–75)," *International Journal of Urban and Regional Research* 32, 3 (2008), pp. 565–585.

"Hezbollah as Urban Planner? Questions to and from Planning Theory," *Planning Theory* 8, 4 (2009), pp. 323–334.

"Neoliberal Urbanity and the Right to the City: A View from Beirut's Periphery," *Development & Change* 40, 5 (2009), pp. 827–852.

"The Politics of Property in Planning: Hezbollah's Reconstruction of Haret Hreik (Beirut, Lebanon) as Case Study," *International Journal of Urban and Regional Research* 38, 3 (2014), pp. 922–934.

Fenske, Gail, *The Skyscraper and the City: The Woolworth Building and the Making of Modern New York* (Chicago: University of Chicago Press, 2008).

Ferguson, James, *Expectations of Modernity: Myths and Meanings of Urban Life on the Zambian Copperbelt* (Berkeley: University of California Press, 1999).

"Seeing Like an Oil Company: Space, Security, and Global Capital in Neoliberal Africa," *American Anthropologist* 107, 3 (2005), pp. 377–382.

Global Shadows: Africa in the Neoliberal World Order (Durham: Duke University Press, 2006).

Fernandes, Edésio, "Constructing the 'Right to the City' in Brazil," *Social and Legal Studies* 16, 2 (2007), pp. 201–219.

Ferng, Jennifer, "Under Siege: Piracy, Borders, and Military Architecture" in Alexandra Brown and Andrew Leach (eds.), *Proceedings of the Society of Architectural Historians, Australia and New Zealand: 30, Open* [Volume 2] (Gold Coast, Queensland: SAHANZ, 2013), pp. 663–673.

Fink, Alexander, "The Hanseatic League and the Concept of Functional Overlapping Competing Jurisdictions," *Kyklos* 65, 2 (May 2012), pp. 194–217.

Firman, Tommy, "Urban Development in Bandung Metropolitan Region: A Transformation to a Desa-kota Region," *Third World Planning Review* 18, 1(1996), pp. 1–22.

"The Restructuring of Jakarta Metropolitan Area: A 'Global City' in Asia," *Cities* 15, 4 (1998), pp. 229–243.

"New Town Development in Jakarta Metropolitan Region: A Perspective of Spatial Segregation," *Habitat International* 28, 3 (2004), pp. 349–368.

"Demographic and Spatial Patterns of Indonesia's Recent Urbanization," *Population, Space and Place* 10, 6 (2004), pp. 421–434.

"The Continuity and Change in Mega-urbanization in Indonesia: A Survey of Jakarta–Bandung Region (JBR) Development," *Habitat International* 33, 4 (2009), pp. 327–339.

Fishman, Robert, *Urban Utopias in the Twentieth Century* [Revised Edition] (Cambridge, MA: The MIT Press, 1982).

"On Big Beaver Road: Detroit and the Diversity of American Metropolitan Landscapes," *Places* 19, 1 (2007), pp. 42–47.

Flint, John, "Cultures, Ghettos and Camps: Sites of Exception and Antagonism in the City," *Housing Studies* 24, 4 (2009), pp. 417–431.

Florentin, Daniel, "The 'Perforated City': Leipzig's Model of Urban Shrinkage Management," *Berkeley Planning Journal* 23, 1 (2010), pp. 83–101.

Flusty, Steven, "The Banality of Interdiction: Surveillance, Control and the Displacement of Diversity," *International Journal of Urban and Regional Research* 25, 3 (2001), pp. 658–664.

Flyvbjerg, Bent, "Machiavellian Megaprojects," *Antipode* 37, 1 (2005), pp. 18–22.

Flyvbjerg, Bent, Nils Bruzelius, and Werner Rothengatter, *Megaprojects and Risk: An Anatomy of Ambition* (Cambridge, UK: Cambridge University Press, 2003).

Foglesong, Richard, *Planning the Capitalist City: The Colonial Era to the 1920s* (Princeton: Princeton University Press, 2014).

Ford, Larry, *Cities and Buildings: Skyscrapers, Skid Rows and Suburbs* (Baltimore, MD: Johns Hopkins University Press, 1994).

"World Cities and Global Change: Observations on Monumentality in Urban Design," *Eurasian Geography and Economics* 49 (2008), pp. 237–262.

Forsberg, Tuomas, "Beyond Sovereignty, Within Territoriality: Mapping the Space of Late-Modern (Geo)Politics," *Cooperation and Conflict* 31, 4 (1996), pp. 355–386.

Foster, George, "South Seas Cruise a Case Study of a Short-lived Society," *Annals of Tourism Research* 13, 2 (1986), pp. 215–238.

Foucault, Michel, *Discipline and Punish: The Birth of the Prison* [Translated by Alan Sheridan] (New York: Vintage, 1979).

"The Subject and the Power," in Hubert Dreyfus and Paul Rabinow (eds.), *Michel Foucault: Beyond Structuralism and Hermeneutics* (Brighton: Harvester, 1982), pp. 208–226.

"Of Other Spaces?" *Diacritics* 16, 1 (1986), pp. 22–27.

"Space, Knowledge, and Power (interview with Paul Rabinow)," in Michael Hays (ed.), *Architecture Theory Since 1968* (Cambridge, MA: The MIT Press, 1998), pp. 428–439.

Franke, Anselm, Eyal Weizman, and Ines Geisler (Ines Weizman), "Islands: The Geography of Extraterritoriality," *ARCHIS* 6 (2003), pp. 18–54.

Franke, Anselm, and Eyal Weizman, *Territories: Islands, Camps and Other States of Utopia* (Berlin and Cologne: Kunst Werke and Walter Koenig Press, 2003).

Fraser, Nancy, "Rethinking the Public Sphere: A Contribution to the Critique of Actually Existing Democracy," in Craig Calhoun (ed.) *Habermas and the Public Sphere* (Cambridge, MA: The MIT Press, 1991), pp. 109–142.

Fregonese, Sara, "The Urbicide of Beirut? Geopolitics and the Built Environment in the Lebanese Civil War," *Political Geography* 28, 5 (2009), pp. 309–318.

"Between a Refuge and a Battleground: Beirut's Discrepant Cosmopolitanisms," *Geographical Review* 102, 3 (2012), pp. 316–336.

"Beyond the 'Weak State': Hybrid Sovereignties in Beirut," *Environment and Planning D* 30, 4 (2012), pp. 655–674.

Fricke, Adrienne, "Forever Nearing the Finish Line: Heritage Policy and the Problem of Memory in Postwar Beirut," *International Journal of Cultural Property* 12 (2005), pp. 163–181.

Friedrichs, Jörg, "The Meaning of New Medievalism," *European Journal of International Relations* 7, 4 (2001), pp. 475–501.

Frisby, David, *Cityscapes of Modernity: Critical Explorations* (Malden, MA: Polity Press, 2001).

Frey, Hildebrand, *Designing the City: Towards a More Sustainable Form* (New York: Spon, 1999).

Friedman, Patri, and Brad Taylor, "Seasteading: Competitive Governments on the Ocean," *Kyklos* 65, 2 (2012), pp. 218–235.

Fuentes, Gabriel, "The Real New Urbanism: Engaging Developing World Cities," *The Journal of Spatial Syntax* 4, 2 (2013), pp. 167–178.

Fyfe, Nicholas, "Making Space for 'Neo-communitarianism'? The Third Sector, State and Civil Society in the UK," *Antipode* 37, 3 (2005), pp. 536–557.

Fyfe, Nicholas, and Christine Milligan, "Space, Citizenship, and Voluntarism: Critical Reflections on the Voluntary Welfare Sector in Glasgow," *Environment and Planning A* 35, 11 (2003), pp. 2069–2086.

Fuller, Mia, *Moderns Abroad: Architecture, Cites, and Italian Imperialism* (New York: Routledge, 2007).

Gadanho, Pedro, "Mirroring Uneven Growth: A Speculation on Tomorrow's Cities Today," in Pedro Gadanho (ed.), *Uneven Growth: Tactical Urbanisms for Expanding Megacities* (New York: Museum of Modern Art, 2014), pp. 14–25.

Gaffikin, Frank, and David Perry, "The Contemporary Urban Condition: Understanding the Globalizing City as Informal, Contested, and Anchored," *Urban Affairs Review* 48, 5 (2012), pp. 701–730.

Gaffney, Chris, "Mega-events and Socio-spatial Dynamics in Rio de Janeiro, 1919–2016," *Journal of Latin American Geography* 9, 1 (2010), pp. 7–29.

Galey, John, "Industrialist in the Wilderness: Henry Ford's Amazon Venture," *Journal of Inter-American Studies and World Affairs* 21, 2 (1979), pp. 261–289.

Galloway, Anne, "Intimations of Everyday Life: Ubiquitous Computing and the City," *Cultural Studies*, 18, 2–3 (2004), pp. 384–408.

Gandelsonas, Mario, "Slow Infrastructure," in Dana Cuff and Roger Sherman (eds.), *Fast-Forward Urbanism: Rethinking Architecture's Engagement with the City* (New York: Princeton Architectural Press, 2011), pp. 122–131.

Gandin, Greg, *Fordlândia: The Rise and Fall of Henry Ford's Forgotten Jungle City* (New York: Metropolitan Books, 2009).

Gandolfo, Daniella, *City at Its Limits: Taboo, Transgression, and Urban Renewal in Lima* (Chicago: University of Chicago Press, 2009).

Gandy, Matthew, *Concrete and Clay: Reworking Nature in New York City* (Cambridge, MA: The MIT Press, 2003).

"Learning from Lagos," *New Left Review* 33 (2005), pp. 37–53.

"Cyborg Urbanization: Complexity and Monstrosity in the Contemporary City," *International Journal of Urban and Regional Research* 29, 1 (2005), pp. 26–49.

"Planning, Anti-planning and the Infrastructure Crisis Facing Metropolitan Lagos," *Urban Geography* 43, 2 (2006), pp. 371–396.

"Urban Flux," *Architectural Design* 79, 5 (2009), pp. 12–17.

"When Does the City End?" in Neil Brenner (ed.), *Implosions/Explosions: Towards a Study of Planetary Urbanization* (Berlin: Jovis, 2014), pp. 86–89.

Gans, Deborah, and Matthew Jelacic, "The Refugee Camp: Ecological Disaster of Today, Metropolis of Tomorrow," *Architectural Design* 74, 2 (2004), pp. 82–86

Glassner, Martin Ira, *Political Geography* (New York: John Wiley, 1993).

Garner, John, *The Model Company Town Urban Design through Private Enterprise in Nineteenth-Century New England* (Amherst: University of Massachusetts Press, 1984).

 The Company Town: Architecture and Society in the Early Industrial Age (Oxford: Oxford University Press, 1992).

Garreau, Joel, *Edge City: Life on the New Frontier* (New York: Doubleday, 1991).

Garrido, Marco, "Civil and Uncivil Society: Symbolic Boundaries and Civic Exclusion in Metro Manila," *Philippine Studies* 56, 4 (2008), pp. 443–466.

 "The Sense of Place behind Segregating Practices: An Ethnographic Approach to the Symbolic Partitioning of Metro Manila," *Social Forces* 91, 4 (2013), pp. 1343–1362.

 "The Ideology of the Dual City: The Modernist Ethic in the Corporate Development of Makati City, Metro Manila," *International Journal of Urban and Regional Research* 37, 1 (2013), pp. 165–185.

Garza, Gustavo, "Global Economy: Metropolitan Dynamics and Urban Policies in Mexico," *Cities* 16, 3 (1999), pp. 149–170.

Gazit, Nir, "Social Agency, Spatial Practices and Power: The Micro-Foundations of Fragmented Sovereignty in the Occupied Territories," *International Journal of Politics, Culture and Society* 22, 1 (2009), pp. 83–103.

 "Boundaries in Interaction: The Cultural Fabrication of Social Boundaries in West-Jerusalem," *City & Community* 9, 4 (2010), pp. 390–413.

Gazit, Nir, and Robert Latham, "Spatial Alternatives and Counter-Sovereignties in Israel/Palestine," *International Political Sociology* 8, 1 (2014), pp. 63–81.

Gellert, Paul, and Barbara Lynch, "Mega-projects as Displacements," *International Social Science Journal* 55, 175 (2003), pp. 15–25.

Geniş, Serife, "Producing Elite Localities: The Rise of Gated Communities in Istanbul," *Urban Studies*, 44, 4 (2007), pp. 771–798.

Gerlach, Julia, "Three Areas: Manshiet Nasser, City of the Dead, Boulaq al-Dakrour," in Regina Kipper and Marion Fischer (eds.), *Cairo's Informal Areas: Between Urban Challenges and Hidden Potentials. Facts. Voices. Visions* (Cairo: German Technical Cooperation [GTZ], 2009), pp. 49–52.

Ghannam, Farha, "The Visual Re-Making of Urban Space: Relocation and the Use of Public Housing in 'Modern' Cairo," *Visual Anthropology* 10, 2–4 (1998), pp. 264–280.

 Remaking the Modern: Space, Relocation, and the Politics of Identity in a Global Cairo (Berkeley: University of California Press, 2002).

 "Two Dreams in a Global City: Class and Space in Urban Egypt," in Andreas Huyssen (ed.), *Other Cities, Other Worlds: Urban Imaginaries in a Globalizing Age* (Durham: Duke University Press, 2008), pp. 267–287.

 "Mobility, Liminality, and Embodiment in Urban Egypt," *American Ethnologist* 38, 4 (2011), pp. 790–800.

Ghosn, Rania, "The Expansion of the Extractive Territory," in Neeraj Bhatia and Mary Casper (eds.), *The Petropolis of Tomorrow* (New York: Actar, 2013), pp. 228–237.

Glaeser, Edward, *Triumph of the City* (New York: Penguin, 2011).

Glaeser, Edward, Stuart Rosenthal, and William Strange, "Urban Economics and Entrepreneurship," *Journal of Urban Economics* 67, 1 (2010), pp. 1–14.

Gleeson, Brendan, "Critical Commentary. The Urban Age: Paradox & Prospect," *Urban Studies* 49, 5 (2012), pp. 931–943.

Gilbert, Alan (ed.), *The Mega-City in Latin America* (Tokyo, Paris, and New York: The United Nations University Press, 1996).

"Housing in Third World Cities: The Critical Issues," *Geography* 85, 2 (2000), pp. 145–155.

"The Return of the Slum: Does Language Matter?" *International Journal of Urban and Regional Research* 31 (2007), pp. 697–713.

"Extreme Thinking about Slums and Slum Dwellers: A Critique," *SAIS Review* 29, 1 (2009), pp. 35–48.

Gilbert, Alan, and Joseph Gugler (eds.), *Cities, Poverty and Development* (Oxford: Oxford University Press, 1981).

Gill, Stephen, "Globalisation, Market Civilisation, and Disciplinary Neoliberalism," *Millennium* 24 (1995), pp. 399–423.

Gillham, Oliver, *The Limitless City: A Primer on the Urban Sprawl Debate* (Washington, DC: Island Press, 2002).

Gillis, John, *Islands of the Mind: How the Human Imagination Created the Atlantic World* (New York: Palgrave Macmillan, 2004).

Gindroz, Ray, "City Life and New Urbanism," *Fordham Urban Law Journal* 29, 4 (2001), pp. 1419–1437.

Giorgi, Gabriel, and Karen Pinkus, "Zones of Exception: Biopolitical Territories in the Neoliberal Era," *Diacritics* 36, 2 (2006), pp. 99–108.

Giroir, Guillaume, "The Purple Jade Villas (Beijing): A Golden Ghetto in Red China," in Georg Glasze, Chris Webster, and Klaus Frantz (eds.), *Private Cities: Global and Local Perspectives* (London: Routledge, 2005), pp. 142–152.

Glasze, Georg, Klaus Frantz, and Chris Webster, "The Global Spread of Gated Communities," *Environment and Planning B* 29, 3 (2002), pp. 315–320.

Glasze, Georg, Chris Webster, and Klaus Frantz, "Introduction: Global and Local Perspectives on the Rise of Private Neighbourhoods," in Georg Glasze, Chris Webster, and Klaus Frantz (eds.), *Private Cities: Global and Local Perspectives* (New York: Routledge, 2010), pp. 1–9.

Glover, Will, "The Troubled Passage from 'Village Communities' to Planned New Town Developments in Mid-Twentieth-Century South Asia," *Urban History* 39, 1 (2012), pp. 108–127.

Goldberger, Paul, "The Rise of the Private City," in Julia Vitullo-Martin (ed.), *Breaking Away: The Future of Cities* (New York: Century Fund Press, 1996), pp. 135–147.

Goldblum, Charles, and Tai-Chee Wong, "Growth, Crisis and Spatial Change: A Study of Haphazard Urbanisation in Jakarta, Indonesia," *Land Use Policy* 17, 1 (2000), pp. 29–37.

Goh, Daniel, and Tim Bunnell, "Recentring Southeast Asian Cities," *International Journal of Urban and Regional Research* 37, 3 (2013), pp. 825–833.

Goheen, Peter, "Public Space and the Geography of the Modern City," *Progress in Human Geography* 24, 4 (1998), pp. 479–496.

Gold, Peter, *Europe or Africa? A Contemporary Study of the Spanish North African Enclaves of Ceuta and Melilla* (Liverpool: Liverpool University Press, 2000).

Goldman, Michael, "Speculative Urbanism and the Making of the Next World City," *International Journal of Urban and Regional Research* 35, 3 (2011), pp. 555–581.

"Speculating on the Next World City," in Ananya Roy and Aiwha Ong (eds.), *Worlding Cities: Asian Experiments and the Art of Being Global* (Malden, MA: Wiley-Blackwell, 2011), pp. 229–258.

"Speculative Urbanism and the Making of the Next World City," *International Journal of Urban and Regional Research* 35, 3 (2011), pp. 555–581.

Goldstein, Donna, *Laughter Out of Place: Race, Class, Violence and Sexuality in a Rio Shantytown* (Berkeley: University of California Press, 2003).

González, Sara, "Bilbao and Barcelona 'in Motion': How Urban Regeneration 'Models' Travel and Mutate in the Global Flows of Policy Tourism," *Urban Studies* 48, 7 (2011), pp. 1397–1418.

Gordon, Ian, "The Resurgent City: What, Where, How, and for When?" *Planning Theory and Practice* 5, 3 (2004), pp. 371–379.

Gotham, Kevin Fox, "From 9/11 to 8/29: Post-Disaster Recovery and Rebuilding in New York and New Orleans," *Social Forces* 87, 2 (2008), pp. 1039–1062.

"Creating Liquidity Out of Spatial Fixity: The Secondary Circuit of Capital and the Subprime Mortgage Crisis," *International Journal of Urban and Regional Research* 33, 2 (2009), pp. 355–371.

"Mechanisms of Mutation: Policy Mobilities and the Gulf Opportunity (GO) Zone," *Urban Geography* 35, 8 (2014), pp. 1171–1195.

"Re-anchoring Capital in Disaster Devastated Spaces: Financialisation and the Gulf Opportunity (GO) Zone Programme," *Urban Studies* (2014) 53, 7 (2016), pp. 1362–1383.

Gotham, Kevin Fox, and Miriam Greenberg, "Post-Disaster Recovery and Rebuilding in New York and New Orleans," *Social Forces* 87, 2 (2008), pp. 1039–1062.

Crisis Cities: Disaster and Redevelopment in New York and New Orleans (New York: Oxford University Press, 2014).

Gottmann, Jean, *Megalopolis: The Urbanized Northeastern Seaboard of the United States* (Cambridge, MA: The MIT Press, 1964).

"Why the Skyscraper?" *Geographical Review* 56, 2 (1966), pp. 190–212.

Graham, Stephen, "The End of Geography or the Explosion of Place? Conceptualising Space, Place, and Information Technology," *Progress in Human Geography* 22, 2 (1998), pp. 165–185.

"Constructing Premium Network Spaces: Reflections on Infrastructure Networks and Contemporary Urban Development," *International Journal of Urban and Regional Research* 24, 1 (2000), pp. 183–200.

"The Spectre of Splintering Metropolis," *Cities* 18, 6 (2001), pp. 365–368.

"Flow City: Networked Mobilities and the Contemporary Metropolis," *Journal of Urban Technology* 9, 1 (2002), pp. 1–20.

"Urban Network Architecture and the Structuring of Future Cities," in Henning Thomsen (ed.), *Future Cities – The Copenhagen Lectures* (Copenhagen: Fonden Realdania, 2002), pp. 110–122.

(ed.), *Cities, War, and Terrorism: Towards an Urban Geopolitics* (Malden, MA: Blackwell, 2004).

"Switching Cities Off," *City* 9, 2 (2005), pp. 169–194.

"Spectres of Terror," in Philipp Misselwtiz and Tim Rieniets (eds.), *City of Collision: Jerusalem and the Principles of Conflict Urbanism* (Basel, Switzerland: Birkhauser, 2006), pp. 156–162.

"Cities and the 'War on Terror'," in Michael Sorkin (ed.), *Indefensible Space: The Architecture of the National Insecurity State* (New York: Routledge, 2007), pp. 1–28.

"Cities as Battlespace: The New Military Urbanism," *City* 13, 4 (2009), pp. 383–402.

Cities under Siege: The New Military Urbanism (New York and London: Verso, 2010).

"Interview with Stephen Graham," in Ignatio Farias and Thomas Bender (eds.), *Urban Assemblages: How Actor-Network Theory Changes Urban Studies* (London: Routledge, 2010), pp. 197–206.

"Luxified Skies," *City* 19, 5 (2015), pp. 618–645.

Graham, Stephen, and Alessandro Aurigi, "Virtual Cities, Social Polarization, and the Crisis in Urban Public Space," *The Journal of Urban Technology* 4, 1 (1997), pp. 19–52.

Graham, Stephen, and Simon Marvin, *Splintering Urbanism: Reworked Infrastructures, Technological Mobilities and the Urban Condition* (London: Routledge, 2001).

Graham, Stephen, Renu Desai, and Colin McFarlane, "Water Wars in Mumbai," *Public Culture* 25, 1 (2013), pp. 115–141.

Graham, Stephen, and Lucy Hewitt, "Getting Off the Ground: On the Politics of Urban Verticality," *Progress in Human Geography* 37, 1 (2013), pp. 72–92.

Graham, Stephen, and Sobia Ahmad Kaker, "Living the Security City: Karachi's Archipelago of Enclaves," *Harvard Design Magazine* 37 (2014), pp. 12–16.

Grant, Bruce, "The Edifice Complex: Architecture and the Political Life of Surplus in the New Baku," *Public Culture* 26, 3 (2014), pp. 501–528.

Gratton, Peter, *The State of Sovereignty: Lessons from the Political Fictions of Modernity* (Albany: State University of New York Press, 2012).

Gray, Neil, and Libby Porter, "By Any Means Necessary: Urban Regeneration and the 'State of Exception' in Glasgow's Commonwealth Games," *Antipode* 47, 2 (2015), pp. 380–400.

Green, Hardy, *The Company Town: The Industrial Edens and Satanic Mills That Shaped the American Economy* (New York: Basic Books, 2010).

Greenwood, Dan, and Peter Newman, "Markets, Large Projects and Sustainable Development: Traditional and New Planning in the Thames Gateway," *Urban Studies* 47, 1 (2010), pp. 105–119.

Gregory, Derek, *The Colonial Present* (Oxford: Blackwell, 2004).

"The Black Flag: Guantánamo Bay and the Space of Exception," *Geografiska Annaler* 88 B, 4 (2006), pp. 405–427.

"Vanishing Points: Law, Violence, and Exception in the Global War Prison," in Derek Gregory and Alan Pred (eds.), *Violent Geographies: Fear, Terror, and Political Violence* (New York: Routledge, 2007), pp. 205–236.

Grubbauer, Monika, "Architecture, Economic Imaginaries and Urban Politics: The Office Tower as Socially Classifying Device," *International Journal of Urban and Regional Research* 38, 1 (2014), pp. 336–359.

Guano, Emanuela, "Spectacles of Modernity: Transnational Imagination and Local Hegemonies in Neoliberal Buenos Aires," *Cultural Anthropology* 17, 2 (2002), pp. 181–209.

"The Denial of Citizenship: 'Barbaric' Buenos Aries and the Middle-class Imaginary," *City & Society* 16, 1 (2004), pp. 69–97.

Gugler, Josef (ed.), *World Cities beyond the West: Globalization, Development, Inequality* (New York: Cambridge University Press, 2004).

Mauro Guillén, "Modernism without Modernity: The Rise of Modernist Architecture in Mexico, Brazil, and Argentina, 1890–1940," *Latin American Research Review* 39, 2 (2004), pp. 6–34.

Gülöksüz, Elvan, "Negotiation of Property Rights in Urban Land in İstanbul," *International Journal of Urban and Regional Research* 26, 3 (2002), pp. 462–476.

Gunay, Zeynep, and Vedia Dokmeci, "Culture-led Regeneration of Istanbul Waterfront: Golden Horn Cultural Valley Project," *Cities* 29, 4 (2012), pp. 213–222.

Gunay, Zeynep, T. Kerem Koramaz, and A. Sule Ozuekren, "From Squatter Upgrading to Large-scale Renewal Programmes: Housing Renewal in Turkey," in Richard Turkington and Christopher Watson (eds.), *Renewing Older Housing: A European Perspective* (Bristol: Policy Press, 2014), pp. 215–244.

Gundogdu, Ibrahim, and Jamie Gough, "Class Cleansing in Istanbul's World Class Project," in Libby Porter and Kate Shaw (eds.), *Whose Urban Renaissance? An International Comparison of Urban Regeneration* (New York: Routledge, 2009), pp. 16–24.

Gunewardena, Nandini, and Mark Schuller (eds.), *Capitalizing on Catastrophe: Neoliberal Strategies in Disaster Reconstruction* (Lanham, MD: Alta Mira, 2008).

Guzey, Ozlem, "Neoliberal Urbanism Restructuring the City of Ankara: Gated Communities as a New Life Style in a Suburban Settlement," *Cities* 36, 1 (2014), pp. 93–106.

Habermas, Jürgen, *The Philosophical Discourse of Modernity* [Translated by Frederick Lawrence] (Cambridge, MA: The MIT Press, 1987).
  The Structural Transformation of the Public Sphere: An Inquiry into a Category of Bourgeois Society (Cambridge, MA: The MIT Press, 1989).

Haila, Ann, "Real Estate in Global Cities: Singapore and Hong Kong as Property States," *Urban Studies* 37,12 (2000), pp. 2241–2256.

Hailey, Charlie, *Camps: A Guide to 21st Century Space* (Cambridge, MA: The MIT Press, 2009).

Hajer, Maarten, "The Generic City," *Theory, Culture & Society* 16, 4 (1999), pp. 137–144.
  "Policy without Polity? Policy Analysis and the Institutional Void," *Policy Sciences* 36, 2 (2003), pp. 175–195.

Hajer, Maarten, and Arnold Reijndorp, *In Search of New Public Domain: Analysis and Strategy* (Rotterdam: NAi Publishers, 2001).

Halegoua, Germaine, "The Policy and Export of Ubiquitous Place: Investigating South Korean U-Cities," in Marcus Foth, Laura Forlano, Christine Satchell, and Martin Gibbs (eds.), *From Social Butterfly to Engaged Citizen: Urban Informatics, Social Media, Ubiquitous Computing, and Mobile Technology to Support Citizen Engagement* (Cambridge, MA: The MIT Press, 2011), pp. 315–334.

Halfacree, Keith, "Rethinking 'Rurality'," in Anthony Champion and Graeme Hugo (eds.), *New Forms of Urbanization: Beyond the Urban-Rural Dichotomy* (Aldershot, UK: Ashgate, 2004), pp. 285–304.

Hall, Tim, and Phil Hubbard, "The Entrepreneurial City: New Urban Politics, New Urban Geography?" *Progress in Human Geography* 20, 2 (1996), pp. 153–174.

(eds.), *The Entrepreneurial City: Geographies of Politics, Regime, and Representation* (London: John Wiley, 1998).

Hall, Peter, "Global City-Regions in the Twenty-first Century," in Alan Scott (ed.), *Global City-Regions: Trends, Theory, Policy* (Oxford: Oxford University Press, 2001), pp. 59–77.

Cities of Tomorrow: An Intellectual History of Urban Planning and Design in the Twentieth Century [Third Edition] (Malden, MA: Blackwell, 2002).

Hall, Peter, and Kathy Pain, "From Metropolis to Polyopolis," in Peter Hall and Kathy Pain, (eds.), *The Polycentric Metropolis: Learning from Mega-City Regions in Europe* (New York: Earthscan, 2006), pp. 3–18.

Hall, Stephen, and Andrew Jonas, "Urban Fiscal Austerity, Infrastructure Provision and the Struggle for Regional Transit in 'Motor City'," *Cambridge Journal of Regions, Economy and Society* 7, 1 (2014), pp. 189–206.

Halpern, Orit, Jesse LeCavalier, Nerea Calvillo, and Wolfgang Pietsch, "Test-Bed Urbanism," *Public Culture* 25, 2(2013), pp. 272–306.

Hananel, Ravit, "Planning Discourse versus Land Discourse: The 2009–12 Reforms in Land-Use Planning and Land Policy in Israel," *International Journal of Urban and Regional Research* 37, 5 (2013), pp. 1611–1637.

Handel, Ariel, "Gated/Gating Community: The Settlement Complex in the West Bank," *Transactions of the Institute of British Geographers* 39, 4 (2014), pp. 504–517.

Hannigan, John, *Fantasy City: Pleasure and Profit in the Postmodern Metropolis* (London: Routledge, 1998).

Hansen, Thomas Blom, and Finn Stepputat, "Sovereignty Revisited," *Annual Reviews of Anthropology* 35 (2006), pp. 295–315.

Harb, Mona el-Kak, "Transforming the Site of Dereliction into the Urban Culture of Modernity: Beirut's Southern Suburb and Elisar Project," in Peter Rowe and Hashim Sarkis (eds.), *Projecting Beirut: Episodes in the Construction and Reconstruction of a Modern City* (Munich: Prestel, 1998), pp. 173–182.

"Post-War Beirut: Resources, Negotiations, and Contestations in the Elissar Project," *Arab World Geographer* 3, 4 (2000), pp. 272–288.

"Postwar Beirut: Resources, Negotiations, and Contestations in the Elyssar Project," in Seteney Shami (ed.), *Capital Cities: Ethnographies of Urban Governance in the Middle East* (Ottawa: University of Toronto Press, 2001), pp. 111–133.

"Faith-Based Organizations as Effective Development Partners? Hezbollah and Postwar Reconstruction in Lebanon," in Gerald Clarke and Michael Jennings (eds.), *Development, Civil Society and Faith-Based Organizations* (New York: Palgrave Macmillan, 2008), pp. 214–239.

Harders, Cilja, "The Informal Social Pact: The State and the Urban Poor in Cairo," in Eberhard Kienle (ed.), *Politics from Above, Politics from Below: The Middle East in the Age of Economic Reform* (London: Saqi, 2003), pp. 91–213.

Harker, Christopher, "New Geographies of Palestine/Palestinians," *The Arab World Geographer* 13, 3–4 (2010), pp. 199–216.

"The Only Way is Up? Ordinary Topologies in Ramallah," *International Journal of Urban and Regional Research* 38, 1(2014), pp. 318–335.

Harms, Erik, *Saigon's Edge: On the Margins of Ho Chi Minh City* (Minneapolis: University of Minnesota Press, 2011).

"Beauty as Control in the New Saigon: Eviction, New Urban Zones, and Atomized Dissent in a Southeast Asian City," *American Ethnologist* 39, 4 (2012), pp. 735–750.

"Eviction Time in the New Saigon: Temporalities of Displacement in the Rubble of Development," *Cultural Anthropology* 28, 2 (2013), pp. 344–368.

"Knowing into Oblivion: Clearing Wastelands and Imagining Emptiness in Vietnamese New Urban Zones," *Singapore Journal of Tropical Geography* 35 (2014), pp. 312–327.

Harris, Andrew, "From London to Mumbai and Back Again: Gentrification and Public Policy in Comparative Perspective," *Urban Studies* 45, 12 (2008), pp. 2407–2428.

"Vertical Urbanism: Flyovers and Skywalks in Mumbai," in Matthew Gandy (ed.), *Urban Constellations* (Berlin: Jovis, 2011), pp. 118–123.

"The Metonymic Urbanism of Twenty-First-Century Mumbai," *Urban Studies* 49, 13 (2012), pp. 2955–2973.

"Concrete Geographies: Assembling Global Mumbai through Transport Infrastructure," *City* 17, 3 (2013), pp. 343–360.

Harvey, David, *The Condition of Postmodernity: An Enquiry into the Origins of Cultural Change* (Malden, MA: Basil Blackwell, 1989).

"From Managerialism to Entrepreneurialism: The Transformation in Urban Governance in Late Capitalism," *Geografiska Annaler Series B, Human Geography* 71, 1 (1989), pp. 3–17.

Spaces of Hope (Berkeley: University of California Press, 2000).

"The Right to the City," *International Journal of Urban and Regional Research* 27, 4 (2003), pp. 939–941.

"The 'New' Imperialism: Accumulation by Dispossession," *Socialist Register* 40 (2004), pp. 63–87.

"From Globalization to the New Imperialism," in Richard Appelbaum and William Robinson (eds.), *Critical Globalization Studies* (New York: Routledge, 2005), pp. 91–100.

Spaces of Global Capitalism: Towards a Theory of Uneven Geographical Development (London and New York: Verso, 2006).

"The Right to the City," *New Left Review* 53 (2008), pp. 23–40.

Cosmopolitanism and the Geographies of Freedom (New York: Columbia University Press, 2009).

Social Justice and the City [Revised Edition] (Athens: University of Georgia Press, 2009).

Hasson, Shlomo, "Local Politics and Split Citizenship in Jerusalem," *International Journal of Urban and Regional Research* 20, 1 (1996), pp. 116–133.

Haughton, Graham, "Trojan Horse or White Elephant? The Contested Biography of the Life and Times of the Leeds Development Corporation," *Town Planning Review* 70 (1999), pp. 173–190.

Haughton, Graham, and Phil Allmendinger, "The Soft Spaces of Local Economic Development," *Local Economy* 23, 2 (1998), pp. 138–148.

"Spatial Planning and the New Localism," *Planning Practice and Research* 28, 1 (2013), pp. 1–5.

Haughton, Graham, Phil Allmendinger, David Counsell, and Geoff Vigar, *New Spatial Planning: Territorial Management with Soft Spaces and Fuzzy Boundaries* (New York and London: Routledge, 2010).

Haughton, Graham, Phil Allmendinger, and Stijn Oosterlynck, "Spaces of Neoliberal Experimentation: Soft Spaces, Postpolitics, and Neoliberal Governmentality," *Environment and Planning A* 45, 1 (2013), pp. 217–234.

Hauka, Codi, "Spaces of Exception and Suspended Logic: Redefining Agamben's Biopolitical Paradigm on Sovereignty, Law and Space," *Hemispheres* 36 (2013), pp. 67–80.

Hayes, Graeme, and John Horne, "Sustainable Development: Shock and Awe? London 2012 and Civil Society," *Sociology* 45, 5 (2011), pp. 749–764.

Hayek, Ghenwa, *Beirut, Imagining the City: Space and Place in Lebanese Literature* (London: I. B. Taurus, 2015).

Hayward, David, "The Privatized City: Urban Infrastructure, Urbanism and Service Provision in the Era of Privatization," *Urban Policy and Research* 15, 1 (1997), pp. 55–56.

He, Shenjing, "Evolving Enclave Urbanism in China and its Socio-spatial Implications: The Case of Guangzhou," *Social & Cultural Geography* 14, 3 (2013), pp. 243–275.

Healey, Patsy, "Introduction: The Transnational Flow of Knowledge and Expertise in the Planning Field," in Patsy Healey and Robert Upton (eds.), *Crossing Borders: International Exchange and Planning Practices* (London: Routledge, 2010), pp. 1–26.

Making Better Places: The Planning Project in the Twenty-first Century (New York: Palgrave Macmillan, 2010).

"The Universal and the Contingent: Some Reflections on the Transnational Flow of Planning Ideas and Practices," *Planning Theory* 11, 2 (2012), pp. 188–207.

"Circuits of Knowledge and Techniques: The Transnational Flow of Planning Ideas and Practices," *International Journal of Urban and Regional Research* 37, 5 (2013), pp. 1510–1526.

Healey, Patsey, Stuart Cameron, Simin Davoudi, Stephen Graham, and Ali Madani-Pour, "Challenges for Urban Management," in Patsy Healey, Stuart Cameron, Simin Davoudi, Stephen Graham, and Ali Madani-Pour (eds.), *Managing Cities: The New Urban Context* (Chichester, UK: Wiley, 1995), pp. 273–290.

Heben, Andrew, *Tent City Urbanism: From Self-Organized Camps to Tiny Villages* (Eugene, OR: The Village Collaborative, 2014).

Hefetz, Amir, and Mildred Warner, "Beyond the Market versus Planning Dichotomy: Understanding Privatisation and its Reverse in U.S. Cities," *Local Government Studies* 33, 4 (2007), pp. 555–572.

Held, David, and Anthony McGrew, "Globalization and the Liberal Democratic State," *Government and Opposition* 28, 2 (1993), pp. 261–278.

Heller-Roazen, Daniel, *The Enemy of All: Piracy and the Law of Nations* (Cambridge, MA: The MIT Press, 2009).

Henders, Susan, "So What If It's Not a Gamble? Post-Westphalian Politics in Macau," *Pacific Affairs* 74, 3 (2001), pp. 342–360.

Hentshel, Christine, "City Ghosts: The Haunted Struggles for Downtown Durban and Berlin Neukölln," in Tony Samara, Shenjing He, and Guo Chen (eds.), *Locating the Right to the City in the Global South* (New York: Routledge, 2013), pp. 195–218.

Herbert, Claire, and Martin J. Murray, "Building New Cities from Scratch: Privatized Urbanism and the Spatial Restructuring of Johannesburg after *Apartheid*," *International Journal of Urban and Regional Research* 39, 3 (2015), pp. 471–494.

Herwitz, Daniel, "Modernism at the Margins," in Hilton Judin and Ivan Vladislavić (eds.), *Blank___: Architecture, Apartheid and After* (Rotterdam: NAi, 1999), pp. 405–421.

Herzog, Lawrence, *Return to the Center: Culture, Public Space, and City Building in the Global Era* (Austin: University of Texas Press, 2006).

Hettne, Björn, *Development Theory and the Three Worlds* (Harlow: Longman, 1995).

Hill, David, "Jane Jacobs' Ideas on Big, Diverse Cities: A Review and Commentary," *Journal of the American Planning Association* 54, 3 (1988), pp. 302–314.

Hinchliffe, Steve, and Sarah Whatmore, "Living Cities: Towards a Politics of Conviviality," *Science as Culture* 15, 2 (2006), pp. 123–138.

Hing, Lo Shiu, "Casino Politics, Organized Crime and the Postcolonial State in Macau," *Journal of Contemporary China* 14, 43 (2005), pp. 207–224.

Hirt, Sonia, "Premodern, Modern, and Postmodern? Placing New Urbanism in a Historical Perspective," *Journal of Planning History* 8, 3 (2009), pp. 248–273.

, *Iron Curtains: Gates, Suburbs and Privatization of Space in the Post-Socialist City* (New York: John Wiley & Sons, 2012).

Hodkinson, Stuart, "The New Urban Enclosures," *City* 16, 5 (2012), pp. 500–518.

Hodson, Mike, and Simon Marvin, "Urbanism in the Anthropocene: Ecological Urbanism or Premium Ecological Enclaves?" *City* 14, 3 (2010), pp. 298–313.

Hogan, Trevor, and Julian Potter, "Big City Blues," *Thesis Eleven* 121, 1 (2014), pp. 3–8.

Hogan, Trevor, and Christopher Houston, "Corporate Cities – Urban Gateways or Gated Communities against the City? The Case of Lippo, Jakarta," in Tim Bunnell, Lisa Drummond and K. C. Ho (eds.), *Critical Reflections on Cities in Southeast Asia* (Singapore: Times Academic, 2002), pp. 243–264.

Hogan, Trevor, Tim Bunnell, Choon-Piew Pow, Eka Permanasari, and Sirat Morshidi, "Asian Urbanisms and the Privatization of Cities," *Cities* 29, 1 (2012), pp. 59–63.

Holcombe, Randall, "Planning and the Invisible Hand: Allies or Adversaries?" *Planning Theory* 12, 2 (2012), pp. 199–210.

Holden, Adam, and Kurt Iveson, "Designs on the Urban: New Labour's Urban Renaissance and the Spaces of Citizenship," *City* 7, 1 (2003), pp. 57–72.

Holston, James, *The Modernist City: An Anthropological Critique of Brasília* (Chicago: University of Chicago Press, 1989).

"Spaces of Insurgent Citizenship," in Leonie Sandercock (ed.), *Making the Invisible Visible: A Multicultural Planning History* (Berkeley and Los Angeles: University of California, 1998), pp. 37–56.

"Spaces of Insurgent Citizenship," in James Holston and Arjun Appudurai (eds.), *Cities and Citizenship* (Durham, NC: Duke University Press, 1999), pp. 155–173.

Insurgent Citizenship: Disjunctions of Democracy and Modernity in Brazil (Princeton, NJ: Princeton University Press, 2007).

"Insurgent Citizenship in an Era of Global Urban Peripheries," *City & Society* 21, 2 (2009), pp. 245–267.

Holston, James, and Arjun Appadurai, "Introduction: Cities and Citizenship," in James Holston and Arjun Appudurai (eds.), *Cities and Citizenship* (Durham: Duke University Press, 1999), pp. 1–18.

Home, Robert, *Of Planting and Planning: The Making of British Colonial Cities* [Second Edition] (New York: Routledge, 2013).

Hommels, Anique, "Studying Obduracy in the City: Toward a Productive Fusion between Technology Studies and Urban Studies," *Science, Technology, & Human Values* 30, 3 (2005), pp. 323–351.

Unbuilding Cities: Obduracy in Urban Sociotechnical Change (Cambridge, MA: The MIT Press, 2005).

Hönke, Jana, "New Political Topographies. Mining Companies and Indirect Discharge in Southern Katanga (DRC)," *Politique africaine* N° 120, 4 (2011), pp. 105–127.

Transnational Companies and Security Governance: Hybrid Practices in a Postcolonial World (New York: Routledge, 2013).

Horovitz, Jacques, and Anne–Valérie Ohlsson, "Dubai Internet City: Serving Business," *Asian Journal of Management Cases* 2, 2 (2005), pp. 163–209.

Hosagrahar, Jyoti, *Indigenous Modernities: Negotiating Architecture and Urbanism* (London: Routledge, 2005).

Hourani, Najib, "Transnational Pathways and Politico-Economic Power: Globalisation and the Lebanese Civil War," *Geopolitics* 15, 2 (2010), pp. 290–311.

"From National Utopia to Elite Enclave: The Selling of the Beirut Souqs," in Gary McDonogh and Marina Peterson (eds.), *Global Downtowns* (Philadelphia: University of Pennsylvania Press, 2012), pp. 136–159.

"Urbanism and Neoliberal Order: The Development and Redevelopment of Amman," *Journal of Urban Affairs* 36, 2 (2014), pp. 634–649.

"Capitalists in Conflict: The Lebanese Civil War Reconsidered," *Middle East Critique* 24, 2 (2015), pp. 137–160.

Hourani, Najib, and Ahmed Kanna, "Arab Cities in the Neoliberal Moment," *Journal of Urban Affairs* 36, s2 (2014), pp. 600–604.

Hoyt, Lorlene, "Importing Ideas: The Transnational Transfer of Urban Revitalization Strategy," *International Journal of Public Administration* 29, 1–3 (2006), pp. 221–243.

Huang, Youqin, "Collectivism, Political Control, and Gating in Chinese Cities," *Urban Geography* 27, 6 (2006), pp. 507–535.

Hou, Jeffrey, "(Not) your Everyday Public Space," in Jeffrey Hou, (ed.), *Insurgent Public Space: Guerrilla Urbanism and the Remaking of Contemporary Cities* (New York: Routledge, 2010), pp. 1–18.

"Vertical Urbanism, Horizontal Urbanity: Notes from East Asian Cities," in Vinayak Bharne (ed.), *The Emerging Asian City: Concomitant Urbanites and Urbanisms* (New York: Routledge: 2013), pp. 234–243.

Hsing, You Tien, *The Great Urban Transformation: Politics of Land and Property in China* (Oxford: Oxford University Press, 2010).

Hsu, Cathy H. C., and Zheng Gu, "Ride on the Gaming Boom: How Can Hong Kong, Macau and Zhuhai Join Hands to Develop Tourism in the Region?" *Asia Pacific Journal of Tourism Research* 15, 1 (2010), pp. 57–77.

Hu, Xiuhong, and David Kaplan, "The Emergence of Affluence in Beijing: Residential Social Stratification in China's Capital City," *Urban Geography* 22, 1 (2001), pp. 54–77.

Huang, Philip C. C., "Chongqing Equitable Development Driven by a 'Third Hand'?" *Modern China* 37, 6 (2011), pp. 569–622.

Huchzermeyer, Marie, *Cities with 'Slums': From Informal Settlement Eradication to a Right to the City in Africa* (Cape Town: University of Cape Town Press, 2011).

Hudson, Alan, "Placing Trust, Trusting Place: on the Social Construction of Offshore Financial Centres," *Political Geography* 17, 8 (1998), pp. 913–937.

   "Beyond the Borders: Globalisation, Sovereignty and Extra-territoriality," *Geopolitics* 3, 1 (1998), pp. 89–105.

   "Offshores Onshore: New Regulatory Spaces and Real Historical Places in the Landscape of Global Money," in Ron Martin (ed.), *Money and the Space Economy* (London: Wiley, 1999), pp. 139–195.

   "Offshoreness, Globalization and Sovereignty: A Postmodern Geo-Political Economy?" *Transactions of the Institute of British Geographers* 25, 3 (2000), pp. 269–283.

Hughes, Thomas, "The Evolution of Large Technological Systems," in Wiebe Bijker, Thomas Hughes, and Trevor Pinch (eds.) *The Social Construction of Technological Systems: New Directions in the Sociology and History of Technology* (Cambridge, MA: The MIT Press, 1987), pp. 51–82.

Humphreys, Stephen, "Legalizing Lawlessness: On Giorgio Agamben's *State of Exception*," *The European Journal of International Law* 17, 3 (2006), pp. 677–687.

Hunt, Stacey, "Citizenship's Place: The State's Creation of Public Space and Street Vendors' Culture of Informality in Bogota, Columbia," *Environment and Planning* D 27, 2 (2009), pp. 331–351.

Hutcheon, Linda, "The Politics of Postmodernism: Parody and History," *Cultural Critique* 5 (1986–1987), pp. 179–207.

Hvidt, Martin, "Public–Private Ties and their Contribution to Development: The Case of Dubai," *Middle Eastern Studies* 43, 4 (2007), pp. 557–577.

Hyndman, John, *Managing Displacement: Refugees and the Politics of Humanitarianism* (Minneapolis: University of Minnesota Press, 2000).

Ibelings, Hans, *Super-Modernism: Architecture in the Age of Globalization* (Rotterdam: NAi Publishers, 2002).

Innes, Judith, Sarah Connick, and David Booher, "Informality as a Planning Strategy," *Journal of the American Planning Association* 73, 2 (2007), pp. 195–210.

Iossifova, Deljana, "Searching for Common Ground: Urban Borderlands in a World of Borders and Boundaries," *Cities* 34 (2013), pp. 1–5.

   "Borderland Urbanism: Seeing between Enclaves," *Urban Geography* 36, 1 (2015), pp. 90–108.

Ip, Wing Tong, "Casino Capitalism and Social Polarization in Macao," *Asian Education and Development Studies* 1, 3 (2012), pp. 276–293.

Irving, Allan, "The Modern/postmodern Divide in Urban Planning," *University of Toronto Quarterly* 62, 4 (1993), pp. 474–488.

Isin, Engin, and Kim Rygiel, "Abject Spaces: Frontiers, Zones, Camps," in Elizabeth Dauphinee, and Cristina Masters (eds.), *The Logics of Biopower and the War on*

Terror: Living, Dying, Surviving (London: Palgrave Macmillan, 2007), pp. 178–203.

Jabareen, Yosef Rafeq, "The Politics of State Planning in Achieving Geopolitical Ends: The Case of the Recent Master Plan for Jerusalem," *International Development Planning Review* 32, 1 (2010), pp. 27–43.

Jackson, Mark, and Veronica della Dora, "'Dreams so big only the Sea can hold Them': Man-made Islands as Anxious Spaces, Cultural Icons, and Travelling Visions," *Environment and Planning A* 41, 9 (2009), pp. 2086–2104.

Jacobs, Jane M., "A Geography of Big Things," *Cultural Geographies* 13, 1 (2006), pp. 1–27.

Jacobs, Jane, *The Death and Life of America's Great Cities* (New York: Vintage, 1961).

Jaglin, Sylvy, "The Differentiation of Technical Services in Cape Town: Echoing Splintering Urbanism?" *Geoforum* 39, 6 (2008), pp. 1897–1906.

Jaguaribe, Beatriz, "Modernist Ruins: National Narratives and Architectural Forms," *Public Culture* 11, 1 (1999), pp. 295–312.

Jameson, Frederic, *Archaeologies of the Future: The Desire Called Utopia and Other Science Fictions* (London: Verso, 2005).

Jasanoff, Sheila, "Future Imperfect: Science, Technology, and the Imaginations of Modernity," in Jasanoff, Sheila, and Sang-Hyun Kim (eds.), *Dreamscapes of Modernity: Sociotechnical Imaginaries and the Fabrication of Power* (Chicago: University of Chicago Press, 2015), pp. 1–33.

Jeffrey, Alex, Colin McFarlane, and Alex Vasudevan, "Rethinking Enclosure: Space, Subjectivity and the Commons," *Antipode* 44, 4 (2012), pp. 1247–1267.

Jessop, Bob, "From Keynesian Welfare State to Schumpeterian Workfare State," in Roger Burrows and Brian Loader (eds.), *Towards a Post-Fordist Welfare State*, (London: Routledge, 1994), 13–38.

"The Entrepreneurial City: Re-Imaging Localities, Redesigning Economic Governance, or Restructuring Capital?" in Nick Jewson and Susanne MacGregor (eds.), *Transforming Cities: Contested Governance and New Spatial Divisions* (London and New York: Routledge, 1997), pp. 28–41.

"The Narrative of Enterprise and the Enterprise of Narrative: Place Marketing and the Entrepreneurial City," in Tim Hall and Phil Hubbard (eds.), *The Entrepreneurial City: Geographies of Politics, Regime, and Representation* (New York: John Wiley & Sons, 1998), pp. 77–99.

"Liberalism, Neoliberalism and Urban Governance: A State-Theoretical Perspective," *Antipode* 34, 2 (2002), pp. 452–472.

Johnson, Cedric (ed.), *The Neoliberal Deluge: Hurricane Katrina, Late Capitalism, and the Remaking of New Orleans* (Minneapolis: University of Minnesota Press, 2011).

Jones, Gavin, "Southeast Asian Urbanization and the Growth of Mega Urban Regions," *Journal of Population Research* 19, 2 (2002), pp. 119–136.

Jones, Gavin, and Pravin Visaria (eds.), *Urbanization in Large Developing Countries: China, Indonesia, Brazil, and India* (Oxford: Oxford University Press, 1997).

Judd, Dennis, Dick Simpson, and Janet Abu-Lughod (eds.), *The City Revisited: Urban Theory from Chicago, Los Angeles, and New York* (Minneapolis: University of Minnesota Press, 2011).

Jun-Woo, Kim, and Young-Jin Ahn, "Songdo Free Economic Zone in South Korea: A Mega-Project Reflecting Globalization?" *Journal of the Korean Geographical Society* 46, 5 (2011), pp. 662–672.

Kabbani, Oussama, "Public Space as Infrastructure: The Case of the Postwar Reconstruction of Beirut," in Peter Rowe and Hashim Sarkis (eds.), *Projecting Beirut: Episodes in the Construction and Reconstruction of a Modern City* (Munich: Prestel, 1998), pp. 68–82.

Kaika, Maria, "Architecture and Crisis: Re-inventing the Icon, Re-imag(in)ing London and Re-branding the City," *Transactions of the Institute of British Geographers* [New Series] 35, 4 (2010), pp. 453–474.

Kaker, Sobia Ahmad, "Enclaves, Insecurity and Violence in Karachi," *South Asian History and Culture* 5, 1 (2014), pp. 93–107.

Kaminker, Sarah, "For Arabs Only: Building Restrictions in East Jerusalem," *Journal of Palestine Studies* 26 (1997), pp. 5–16.

Kanna, Ahmed, "The 'State Philosophical' in the 'Land without Philosophy': Shopping Malls, Interior Cities, and the Image of Utopia in Dubai," *Traditional Dwellings and Settlements Review* 16, 2 (2005), pp. 59–73.

"Flexible Citizenship in Dubai: Neoliberal Subjectivity in the Emerging 'City-Corporation,'" *Cultural Anthropology* 25, 1 (2010), pp. 100–129.

Dubai: The City as Corporation (Minneapolis: University of Minnesota Press, 2011).

Karaman, Ozan, "Urban Pulse – (Re)Making Space for Globalization in Istanbul," *Urban Geography* 29, 6 (2008), pp. 518–525.

"Urban Renewal in Istanbul: Reconfigured Spaces, Robotic Lives," *International Journal of Urban and Regional Research* 37, 2 (2013), pp. 715–733.

"Urban Neoliberalism with Islamic Characteristics," *Urban Studies* 50, 16 (2013), pp. 3412–3427.

"Resisting Urban Renewal in Istanbul," *Urban Geography* 35, 2 (2014), pp. 290–310.

Karaman, Ozan, and Tolga Islam, "On the Dual Nature of Intra-urban Borders: The Case of a Romani Neighborhood in Istanbul," *Cities* 29, 4 (2012), pp. 234–243.

Karpat, Kemal, *The Gecekondu, Rural Migration, and Urbanization* (Cambridge, UK: Cambridge University Press, 1976).

Kassab, Suzanne, "On Two Conceptions of Globalization: The Debate around the Reconstruction of Beirut," in Ayçe Oncu and Petra Weylande (eds.), *Space, Culture and Power: New identities in Globalizing Cities* (London: Zed Books, 1997), pp. 42–55.

Kayden, Jerold, *Privately Owned Public Space: The New York City Experience* (New York: Wiley, 2000).

Keil, Roger, and Douglas Young, "In Between Canada: The Emergence of the New Urban Middle," in Douglas Young, Patricia Burke Wood, and Roger Keil (eds.), *In-Between Infrastructure: Urban Connectivity in a Time of Vulnerability* (Toronto: Praxis(e) Press, 2013), pp. 1–18.

Keith, Kent, "Floating Cities: A New Challenge for Transnational Law," *Marine Policy* 1, 3 (1977), pp. 190–204.

Kelbaugh, Douglas, *Repairing the American Metropolis* (Seattle: University of Washington Press, 2002).

Kern, Leslie, "Selling the 'Scary City': Gendering Freedom, Fear and Condominium Development in the Neoliberal City," *Social & Cultural Geography* 11, 3 (2010), pp. 209–230.

Kesseiba, Karim, "Cairo's Gated Communities: Dream Houses or Unified Houses," *Procedia: Social and Behavioral Sciences* 170 (2012), pp. 728–738.

Keyder, Çaglar, "Liberalization from Above and the Future of the Informal Sector: Land, Shelter, and Informality in the Periphery," in Faruk Tabak and Michaeline Crichlow (eds.), *Informalization: Process and Structure* (Baltimore: The Johns Hopkins University Press, 2000), pp. 119–132.

"Globalization and Social Exclusion in Istanbul," *International Journal of Urban and Regional Research*, 29, 1 (2005), pp. 124–134.

Khamaisi, Rassem, "Resisting Creeping Urbanization and Gentrification in the Old City of Jerusalem and its Surroundings," *Contemporary Arab Affairs* 3 (2010), pp. 53–70.

Kilian, Ted, "Public and Private, Power and Space," in Andrew Light and Jonathan Smith (eds.), *Philosophy and Geography II: The Production of Public Space* (Lanham, MD: Rowman & Littlefield, 1998), pp. 115–134.

Kim, C.-G., "Place Promotion and Symbolic Characterization of New Songdo City, South Korea," *Cities*, 27, 1 (2010), pp. 13–19.

Kim, Jung In, "Making Cities Global: The New City Development of Songdo, Yujiapu and Lingang," *Planning Perspectives* 29, 3 (2014), pp. 329–356.

King, Anthony, *Colonial Urban Development: Culture, Social Power and Environment* (London and Boston: Routledge & Kegan Paul, 1976).

Urbanism, Colonialism, and the World-Economy: Cultural and Spatial Foundations of the World Urban System (London and Boston: Routledge Kegan & Paul, 1990).

"The Times and Spaces of Modernity (or who needs Postmodernism?)," in Mike Featherstone, Scott Lash, and Roland Robertson (eds.), *Global Modernities* (Thousand Oaks, CA: Sage, 1995), pp. 108–123.

"Worlds in the City: Manhattan Transfer and the Ascendance of Spectacular Space," *Planning Perspectives* 11, 2 (1996), pp. 97–114.

King, Russell, "The Geographical Fascination of Islands," in Douglas Lockhart, David Drakakis-Smith, and John Schembri (eds.), *The Development Process in Small Island States* (London: Routledge, 1993), 13–37.

Kingsbury, Benedict, "Sovereignty and Inequality," *European Journal of International Law* 9, 4 (1998), pp. 599–625.

Kipper, Regina, "Cairo: A Broader View," in Regina Kipper and Marion Fischer (eds.), *Cairo's Informal Areas: Between Urban Challenges and Hidden Potentials. Facts. Voices. Visions* (Cairo: German Technical Cooperation [GTZ], 2009), pp. 13–17.

Kirby, Andrew, "The Production of Private Space and its Implications for Urban Social Relations," *Political Geography* 27, 1 (2008), pp. 74–95.

Kirkpatrick, L. Owen, *Sovereignty and the Fragmented City: The Many Citizenships of Detroit, Michigan* (Detroit, MI: Wayne State University Press, 2016).

"Graduated Sovereignty and the Fragmented City: Mapping the Political Geography of Citizenship in Detroit," In Cherstin Lyon (ed.), *Place, (Dis)Place, and Citizenship* (Detroit: Wayne State University Press, forthcoming).

Kirkpatrick, L. Owen, and Michael Peter Smith, "The Infrastructural Limits to Growth: Rethinking the Urban Growth Machine in Times of Fiscal Crisis," *International Journal of Urban and Regional Research* 35, 3 (2011), pp. 477–503.

Kirshner, Joshua, and Marcus Power, "Mining and Extractive Urbanism: Postdevelopment in a Mozambican Boomtown," *Geoforum* 61 (2015), pp. 67–78.

Kleibert, Jana Marie, and Lisa Kippers, "Living the Good Life? The Rise of Urban Mixed-Use Enclaves in Metro Manila," *Urban Geography* 37, 3 (2016), pp. 373–395.

Klein, Naomi, *No Logo: Taking Action against the Brand Bullies* (London: Flamingo, 2000).

Kligmann, Anna, *Brandscapes: Architecture and the Experience Economy* (Cambridge, MA: The MIT Press, 2007).

Kobrin, Stephen, "Back to the Future: Neomedievalism and the Postmodern Digital World Economy," *Journal of International Affairs* 51, 2 (1998), pp. 361–386.

Koch, Natalie, "The Monumental and the Miniature: Imagining 'Modernity' in Astana," *Social & Cultural Geography* 11, 8 (2010), pp. 769–787.

Koenigsberger, Otto, "Book Review: *The City in Newly Developing Countries*," *Urban Studies* 8, 1 (1971), pp. 75–76.

    "Foreword," in Alan Turner (ed.) *Cities of the Poor: Settlement Planning in Developing Countries* (London: Croom Helm, 1980), pp. 11–15.

Kohn, Margaret, "Privatization and Protest: Occupy Wall Street, Occupy Toronto, and the Occupation of Public Space in a Democracy," *Perspectives on Politics* 11, 1 (2013), pp. 99–110.

    Brave New Neighbourhoods: The Privatisation of Public Space (London: Routledge, 2004).

Kolossov, Vladimir, "Border Studies: Changing Perspectives and Theoretical Approaches," *Geopolitics* 10, 4 (2005), pp. 606–632.

Kolson, Kenneth, *Big Plans: The Allure and Folly of Urban Design* (Baltimore: The Johns Hopkins University Press, 2001).

Kooijman, Dion, "Company Towns: Between Economic Dominance and Mass Media: A Review of Rassenga 70 (1998)," *Space and Culture* 3, 4–5 (2000), pp. 244–245.

Koolhaas, Rem, *Delirious New York: A Retroactive Manifesto for Manhattan* (New York: Monacelli Press, 1978).

    "The Past is too Small to Inhabit," *New Perspectives Quarterly* 30, 4 (2013), 13–18.

    "Whatever Happened to Urbanism?" in Rem Koolhaas and Bruce Mau (eds.), *S, M, L, XL* (New York: Monacelli Press, 1995), pp. 958–971.

    "Imagining Nothingness," in Rem Koolhaas and Bruce Mau (eds.), *S, M, L, XL* (New York: Monacelli Press, 1995), pp. 198–203.

    "Fragments of a Lecture on Lagos," in Okwui Enwezor, *et al.* (eds.), *Under Siege: Four African Cities: Freetown, Johannesburg, Kinshasa, Lagos* (Ostfildern-Ruit [Germany]: Hatje Cantz, 2002), pp. 173–183.

Koolhaas, Rem, and Bruce Mau [edited by Jennifer Singler], *S, M, L, XL* (Rotterdam and New York: 010 Publishers/The Monacelli Press, 1995).

Koonings, Kees, and Dirk Druijt, "The Rise of Megacities and the Urbanization of Informality, Exclusion, and Violence," in Kees Koonings and Dirk Druijt (eds.), *Megacities: The Politics of Urban Exclusion and Violence in the Global South* (London: Zed Press, 2009), pp. 8–26.

Kooy, Michelle, and Karen Bakker, "Splintered Networks: The Colonial and Contemporary Waters of Jakarta," *Geoforum* 39, 6 (2008), pp. 1843–1858.

Kotek, Joël, "Divided Cities in the European Cultural Context," *Progress in Planning* 52, 3 (1999), pp. 227–237.

Krasner, Stephen, *Sovereignty: Organized Hypocrisy* (Princeton, NJ: Princeton University Press, 1999).

    "Abiding Sovereignty," *International Political Science Review* 22, 3 (2001), pp. 229–251.

"Sharing Sovereignty: New Institutions for Collapsed and Failing States," *International Security* 29, 1 (2004), pp. 85–120.

Krasner, Stephen (ed.), *Problematic Sovereignty: Contested Rules and Political Possibilities* (New York: Columbia University Press, 2001).

Krause, Monika, "The Ruralization of the World," *Public Culture* 25,2 [70] (2013), pp. 233–248.

Krijnen, Marieke, *Facilitating Real Estate Development in Beirut: A Peculiar Case of Neoliberal Public Policy* (Unpublished Master's Thesis, American University of Beirut, 2010).

Krijnen, Marieke, and Mona Fawaz, "Exception as the Rule: High-End Developments in Neoliberal Beirut," *Built Environment* 36, 2 (2010), pp. 245–259.

Kudva, Neema, "The Everyday and the Episodic: The Spatial and Political Impacts of Urban Informality," *Environment and Planning A* 41, 7 (2009), pp. 1614–1628.

Kunzmann, Klaus, "The Future of the City Region in Europe," in Koos Bosma and Helma Hellinga (eds.), *Mastering the City: North European City Planning 1900–2000* (Rotterdam: NAi Publishers, 1997), pp. 16–29.

Kuppinger, Petra, "Exclusive Greenery: New Gated Communities in Cairo," *City & Society* 16, 2 (2004), pp. 35–61.

Kusno, Abidin, *Behind the Postcolonial: Architecture, Urban Space and Political Cultures in Indonesia* (New York: Routledge, 2000).

Kuyucu, Tuna, and Özlem Ünsal, "'Urban Transformation' as State-led Property Transfer: An Analysis of Two Cases of Urban Renewal in Istanbul," *Urban Studies* 47, 7 (2010), pp. 1479–1499.

Kwan, Fanny Vong Chuk, "Gambling Attitudes and Gambling Behavior of Residents of Macao: The Monte Carlo of the Orient," *Journal of Travel Research* 42, 3 (2004), pp. 271–278.

Lake, Robert, and Kathe Newman, "Differential Citizenship in the Shadow State," *GeoJournal* 58, 2–3 (2002), pp. 109–120.

Lang, Jon, *Urban Design: A Typology of Procedures and Products* (Amsterdam: Elsevier/Architecture Press, 2005).

Larkin, Craig, "Remaking Beirut: Contesting Memory, Space, and the Urban Imaginary of Lebanese Youth," *City & Community* 9, 4 (2010), pp. 414–442.

"Beyond the War? The Lebanese Postmemory Experience," *International Journal of Middle East Studies* 42, 4 (2010), pp. 615–635.

"Speaking in the Silence: Youthful Negotiations of Beirut's Postwar Spaces and Memories," in Wendy Pullan and Britt Bailie (eds.), *Locating Urban Conflicts: Ethnicity, Nationalism and the Everyday* (New York: Palgrave Macmillan, 2013), pp. 93–114.

Larson, Scott, "Whose City is it Anyway? Jane Jacobs vs. Robert Moses and Contemporary Redevelopment Politics in New York City," *Berkeley Planning Journal* 22, 1 (2009), pp. 33–41.

Latour, Bruno, *Science in Action* (Cambridge, MA: Harvard University Press, 1987).

Law, Lisa, "Defying Disappearance: Cosmopolitan Public Spaces in Hong Kong," *Urban Studies* 39, 9 (2002), pp. 1625–1645.

Leaf, Michael, "Land Rights for Residential Development in Jakarta, Indonesia: The Colonial Roots of Contemporary Urban Dualism," *International Journal of Urban and Regional Research* 17, 4 (1993), pp. 477–499.

"The Suburbanisation of Jakarta: A Concurrence of Economics and Ideology," *Third World Planning Review* 16, 4 (1994), pp. 341–356.

Lefebvre, Henri, *Writings on Cities* [edited and translated by Eleonore Kotman and Elizabeth Lebas] (Oxford: Blackwell, 1996).

The Urban Revolution (Minneapolis: University of Minnesota Press, 2003).

Lee, Sang Ho, Tan Yigitcanlar, Jung-Hoon Han, and Youg-Taek Leem, "Ubiquitous Urban Infrastructure: Infrastructure Planning and Development in Korea," *Innovation: Management, Policy & Practice* 10, 2–3 (2008), pp. 282–292.

Leenders, Reinhoud, "No Body Having Too Much to Answer For: Laissez-faire, Networks, and Postwar Reconstruction in Lebanon," in Steven Heydeman (ed.), *Networks of Privilege in the Middle East: The Politics of Economic Reform Revisited* (New York: Palgrave MacMillan, 2004), pp. 169–200.

Leggett, Gary, "Playgrounds: Radical Failure in the Amazon." *Architectural Design* 81, 3 (2011), pp. 68–75.

Leidenberger, Georg, "Review Essay: The Search for a Useable Past: Modernist Urban Planning in a Postmodern Age," *Journal of Urban History* 32, 3 (2006), pp. 451–465.

Lemanski, Charlotte, "Global Cities in the South: Deepening Social and Spatial Polarisation in Cape Town," *Cities* 24, 6 (2007), pp. 448–461.

Lemke, Thomas, "Foucault, Governmentality, and Critique," *Rethinking Marxism* 14, 3 (2000), pp. 49–64.

Lees, Loretta, "Super-Gentrification: The Case of Brooklyn Heights, New York City," *Urban Studies* 40, 12 (2003), pp. 2487–2509.

"The Geography of Gentrification: Thinking through Comparative Urbanism," *Progress in Human Geography* 36, 2 (2012), pp. 155–171.

Lees, Loretta, Tom Slater, and Elvin Wyly, *Gentrification* (New York: Routledge, 2013).

Le Goix, Renaud, "Gated Communities: Sprawl and Social Segregation in Southern California," *Housing Studies* 20, 2 (2005), pp. 323–343 (esp. 336–337).

"Gated Communities as Predators of Public Resources: The Outcomes of Fading Boundaries between Private Management and Public Authorities in Southern California," in Georg Glasze, Chris Webster, and Franz Klaus (eds.), *Private Cities: Global and Local Perspectives* (New York: Routledge, 2006), pp. 76–91.

Leisch, Harald, "Gated Communities in Indonesia," *Cities* 19, 5 (2002), pp. 341–350.

Lewis, Jim, "Phenomenon: The Exigent City," *The New York Times Magazine*, June 8, 2008. Available at www.nytimes.com/2008/06/08/magazine/08wwln-urbanism-t.html.

Levien, Michael, "Special Economic Zones and Accumulation by Dispossession in India," *Journal of Agrarian Change* 11, 4 (2011), pp. 454–483.

Li, Tania Murray, *The Will to Improve: Governmentality, Development and the Practice of Politics* (Durham: Duke University Press, 2007).

"To Make Live or Let Die?: Rural Dispossession and the Protection of Surplus Populations," *Antipode* 41, S1 (2009), pp. 66–93.

Lillie, Nathan, "Bringing the Offshore Ashore: Transnational Production, Industrial Relations and the Reconfiguration of Sovereignty," *International Studies Quarterly* 54, 3 (2010), pp. 683–704.

Lippert, Randy, "'Clean and Safe' Passage: Business Improvement Districts, Urban Security Modes, and Knowledge Brokers," *European Urban and Regional Studies* 19, 2 (2012), pp. 167–180.

Liu, Xiaozi, Gerhard K. Heilig, Junmiao Chen, and Mikko Heino, "Interactions between Economic Growth and Environmental Quality in Shenzhen, China's First Special Economic Zone," *Ecological Economics* 62, 3 (2007), pp. 559–570.

Lloyd, M. G., John McCarthy, Stanley McGreal, and Jim Berry, "Business Improvement Districts, Planning and Urban Regeneration," *International Planning Studies* 8, 4 (2003), pp. 295–321.

Lo, Sonny, "Casino Capitalism and Its Legitimacy Impact on the Politico-Administrative State in Macau," *Journal of Current Chinese Affairs* 38, 1 (2009), pp. 19–47.

Lo, Sonny, and Herbert Yee, "Legitimacy-Building in the Macau Special Administrative Region: Colonial Legacies and Reform Strategies," *Asian Journal of Political Science* 13, 1 (2005), pp. 51–79.

Loh, Carolyn, "The Everyday Emergency: Planning and Democracy under Austerity Regimes," *Urban Affairs Review* 52, 5 (2016), 832–863.

Loshitzky, Yosefa, "Fortress Europe. Introduction," *Third Text* 20, 6 (2006), pp. 629–634.

Loukaitou-Sideris, Anastasia, "Privatisation of Public Open Space: The Los Angeles Experience," *Town Planning Review* 64, 2 (1993), pp. 139–168.

"Cracks in the City: Addressing the Constraints and Potentials of Urban Design," *Journal of Urban Design* 1, 1 (1996), pp. 91–103.

Loukaitou-Sideris, Anastasia, and Tridib Banerjee, *Urban Design Downtown: Poetics and Politics of Form* (Berkeley: University of California Press, 1998).

Lovering, John, "The Relationship between Urban Regeneration and Neoliberalism: Two Presumptuous Theories and a Research Agenda," *International Planning Studies* 12, 4 (2007), pp. 343–366.

Lovering, John, and Hade Türkmen, "Bulldozer Neoliberalism in Istanbul: The State-led Construction of Property Markets, and the Displacement of the Urban Poor," *Urban Geography* 16, 1 (2011), pp. 73–96.

Low, Setha, "The Edge and the Center: Gated Communities and Urban Fear," in Setha Low and D. Lawrence Zuniga (eds.), *The Anthropology of Space and Place* (Cambridge, MA: Blackwell, 2003), pp. 387–407.

"How Private Interests Take over Public Space: Zoning, Taxes, and Incorporation of Gated Communities," in Setha Low and Neil Smith (eds.), *The Politics of Public Space* (New York: Routledge, 2006), pp. 81–103.

"The Erosion of Public Space and the Public Realm: Paranoia, Surveillance and Privatization in New York City," *City & Society* 18, 1 (2006), pp. 43–49.

Lowenthal, David, "Islands, Lovers, and Others," *The Geographical Review* 97 (2007), pp. 202–229.

Lütticken, Sven, "Parklife," *New Left Review* 10 [NS] (2001), pp. 111–118.

Luo, Xiaolong, and Jianfa Shen, "The Making of New Regionalism in the Cross-Boundary Metropolis of Hong Kong–Shenzhen, China," *Habitat International* 36, 1 (2012), pp. 126–135.

Luymes, Don, "The Fortification of Suburbia: Investigating the Rise of Enclave Communities," *Landscape and Urban Planning* 39, 2–3 (1997), pp. 187–203.

MacBurnie, Ian, "The Periphery and the American Dream," *Journal of Architectural Education* 48, 3 (1995), pp. 134–143.

Mack, Jennifer, "Urban Design from Below: Immigration and the Spatial Practice of Urbanism," *Public Culture* 26, 1 (2014), pp. 153–185.

MacLeod, Gordon, "From Urban Entrepreneurialism to a "Revanchist City"? On the Spatial Injustices of Glasgow's Renaissance," *Antipode* 34, 3 (2002), pp. 602–624.

Madanipour, Ali, *Public and Private Spaces of the City* (London: Routledge, 2003).

Mahmud, Tayyab, "Slums, Slumdogs, and Resistance," *Journal of Gender, Social Policy, & the Law* 18, 3 (2010), pp. 685–710.

Majdalani, Roula, "The Governance Paradigm and Urban Development: Breaking New Ground?" in Seteney Shami (ed.), *Capital Cities: Ethnographies of Urban Governance in the Middle East* (Ottawa: University of Toronto Press, 2001), pp. 135–140.

Makdisi, Saree, "Laying Claim to Beirut: Urban Narrative and Spatial Identity in the Age of *Solidère*," *Critical Inquiry* 23, 3 (1997), pp. 660–705.

Malkki, Lisa, "News from Nowhere: Mass Displacement and Globalized 'Problems of Organization'," *Ethnography* 3, 3 (2002), pp. 351–360.

Malo, Manasse, and P. J. M. Nas, "Queen City of the East and Symbol of the Nation: The Administration and Management of Jakarta," in Jürgen Rüland (ed.), *The Dynamics of Metropolitan Management in Southeast Asia* (Singapore: Institute of Southeast Asian Studies, 1996), pp. 99–132.

Manzanas, Ana, and Jesús Benito Sanchez, "Unbound Cities, Concentric Circles: Karen Tai Yamashita's Tropic of Orange," *Cities, Borders and Spaces in Intercultural American Literature and Film* (New York: Routledge, 2011), pp. 49–64 [Chapter 3].

Mannathukkaren, Nissim, "The 'Poverty' of Political Society: Partha Chatterjee and the People's Plan Campaign in Kerala, India," *Third World Quarterly* 31, 2 (2010), pp. 295–314.

Marcuse, Peter, "'Dual City': A Muddy Metaphor for a Quartered City," *International Journal of Urban and Regional Research* 13, 4 (1989), pp. 697–708.

"What's So New about Divided Cities?" *International Journal of Urban and Regional Research* 17, 3 (1993), pp. 355–365.

"Not Chaos but Walls: Postmodernism and the Partitioned City," in Sophie Watson and Katherine Gibson (eds.), *Postmodern Cities and Spaces* (Oxford: Blackwell, 1994), pp. 243–253.

"Space and Race in the Post-Fordist City: The Outcast Ghetto and Advanced Homelessness in the United States Today," in Enzo Mingione (ed.), *Urban Poverty and the Underclass* (Oxford: Blackwell, 1996), pp. 176–217.

"The Enclave, the Citadel, and the Ghetto: What has Changed in the Post-Fordist U.S. City," *Urban Affairs Review* 33, 2 (1997), pp. 228–264.

"The Ghetto of Exclusion and the Fortified Enclave: New Patterns in the United States," *American Behavioral Scientist* 41, 3 (1997), pp. 311–326.

"Space in the Globalizing City," in Neil Brenner and Roger Keil (eds.), *The Global Cities Reader* (New York: Routledge, 2006), pp. 26–269.

"From Critical Urban Theory to the Right to the City," *City* 13, 2–3 (2009), pp. 185–196.

Marquardt, Nadine, and Henning Füller, "Spillover of the Private City: BIDs as a Pivot of Social Control in Downtown Los Angeles," *European Urban and Regional Studies* 19, 2 (2012), pp. 153–166.

Marrero-Guillamón, Isaac, "Olympic State of Exception," in Hilary Powell and Isaac Marrero-Guillamón (eds.), *The Art of Dissent: Adventures in London's Olympic State* (London: Marshgate Press, 2012), pp. 20–29.

Martin, Diana, "From Spaces of Exception to 'Campscapes': Palestinian Refugee Camps and Informal Settlements in Beirut," *Political Geography* 44 (2015), pp. 9–18.

Martin, Lauren, and Matthew Mitchelson, "Geographies of Detention and Imprisonment: Interrogating Spatial Practices of Confinement, Discipline, Law, and State Power," *Geography Compass* 3, 1 (2009), pp. 459–477.

Marvin, Simon, and Steven Graham, *Splintering Urbanism: Networked Infrastructures, Technological Mobilities and the Urban Condition* (New York: Routledge, 2001).

Masri, Ghada, "Reconstructing Phoenicia: Tourist Landscapes and National Identity in the Heart of the Lebanese Capital," in Robert Maitland and Brent Ritchie (eds.), *City Tourism: National Capital Perspectives* (Cambridge, MA: CAB International, 2009), pp. 225–238.

Maurer, Bill, "Islands in the Net: Rewiring Technological and Financial Circuits in the 'Offshore' Caribbean," *Society for Comparative Study of Society and History* 43, 3 (2001), pp. 467–501.

"Re-regulating Offshore Finance," *Geography Compass* 2, 1 (2008), pp. 155–175.

May, Todd, *Gilles Deleuze: An Introduction* (Cambridge, UK: Cambridge University Press, 2005).

Mayer, Margit, "First World Urban Activism: Beyond Austerity Urbanism and Creative City Politics," *City* 17, 1 (2013), pp. 5–19.

Mbembe, Achille, "At the Edge of the World: Boundaries, Territoriality, and Sovereignty in Africa" [Trans. Steven Rendall] *Public Culture* 12, 1 (2000), pp. 259–284.

McCalla, Robert, "The Geographical Spread of Free Zones Associated with Ports," *Geoforum* 21, 1 (1990), pp. 121–134.

McCann, Eugene, "Collaborative Visioning or Urban Planning as Therapy? The Politics of Public–Private Policy Making," *The Professional Geographer* 53, 2 (2001), pp. 207–218.

"Urban Policy Mobilities and Global Circuits of Knowledge: Toward a Research Agenda," *Annals of the Association of American Geographers* 101, 1 (2011), pp. 107–130.

McCann, Eugene, and Kevin Ward, "Introduction: Urban Assemblages, Territories, and Relations, Practices, and Powers," in Eugene McCann and Kevin Ward (eds.), *Mobile Urbanism: Cities and Policymaking in the Global Age* (Minneapolis: University of Minnesota Press, 2011), pp. xiii–xxxv.

McConnell, Fiona, "The Fallacy and the Promise of the Territorial Trap: Sovereign Articulations of Geopolitical Anomalies," *Geopolitics* 15, 4 (2010), pp. 762–768.

McEwan, Cheryl, "Material Geographies and Postcolonialism," *Singapore Journal of Tropical Geography* 24, 3 (2003), pp. 340–355.

McFarlane, Colin, "The Comparative City: Knowledge, Learning, Urbanism," *International Journal of Urban and Regional Research* 34, 4(2010), pp. 725–742.

"Infrastructure, Interruption, and Inequality: Urban Life in the Global South," in Stephen Graham (ed.), *Disrupted Cities: When Infrastructure Fails* (New York: Routledge, 2010), pp. 131–144.

McGee, T. G., "The Emergence of Desakota Regions in Asia: Expanding a Hypothesis," in Norton Ginsburg, Bruce Koppel, and T. G. McGee (eds.), *The Extended Metropolis: Settlement Transition in Asia* (Honolulu: University of Hawaii Press, 1991), pp. 3–25.

McGee, T. G., and Ira Robinson (eds.), *Mega-Urban Regions of Southeast Asia* (Vancouver: University of British Columbia Press, 1995).

McGuirk, Pauline, "Neoliberalist Planning? Re-thinking and Re-casting Sydney's Metropolitan Planning," *Geographical Research* 43, 1 (2005), pp. 59–70.

McGuirk, Pauline, and Andrew MacLaran, "Changing Approaches to Urban Planning in an 'Entrepreneurial City': The Case of Dublin," *European Planning Studies* 9, 4 (2001), pp. 437–457.

McGuirk, Pauline, and Robyn Dowling, "Master-Planned Residential Developments: Beyond Iconic Spaces of Neoliberalism?" *Asia Pacific Viewpoint* 50, 2 (2009), pp. 120–134.

McGuirk, Pauline, and Robyn Dowling, "Neoliberal Privatization? Remapping the Public and Private in Sydney's Master-Planned Residential Estates," *Political Geography* 28, 3 (2009), pp. 174–185.

McKenzie, Evan, *Privatopia: Homeowner Associations and the Rise of Residential Private Government* (New Haven: Yale University Press, 1994).

Metzger, Jonathan, and Peter Schmitt, "When Soft Spaces Harden: The EU Strategy for the Baltic Sea Region," *Environment and Planning A* 44, 2 (2012), pp. 263–280.

Meagher, Sharon, "The Darker Underside of Scott's Third Wave," *City* 17, 3 (2013), pp. 395–398.

Mehrotra, Rahul, "One Space, Two Worlds," *Harvard Design Magazine* (Winter/Spring, 1997), pp. 40–41.

"Constructing Historic Significance: Looking at Bombay's Historic Fort Area," *Future Anterior* 1, 2 (2004), pp. 25–32.

"The Static and the Kinetic," in Ricky Burdett and Deyan Sudjic (eds.), *Living in the Endless City: The Urban Age Project by the London School of Economics and Deutsche Bank's Alfred Herrhausen Society* (London: Phaidon, 2011), pp. 108–115.

Melosi, Martin, *The Sanitary City: Environmental Services in Urban America from Colonial Times to the Present* (Baltimore: The Johns Hopkins University Press, 2000).

Meneses-Reyes, Rodrigo, "Out of Place, Still in Motion: Shaping (Im)Mobility Through Urban Regulation," *Social & Legal Studies* 22 (2013), pp. 335–356 (quotations from p. 335).

Meneses-Reyes, Rodrigo, and José A. Caballero-Juárez, "The Right to Work on the Street: Public Space and Constitutional Rights," *Planning Theory* 13, 4 (2014), pp. 370–386.

Mendieta, Eduardo, "Invisible Cities: A Phenomenology of Globalization from Below," *City* 5, 1 (2001), pp. 7–26.

"The Axle of Evil: SUVing through the Slums of Globalizing Neoliberalism," *City* 9, 2 (2005), pp. 195–204.

Merrifield, Andrew, "Public Space: Integration and Exclusion in Urban Life," *City* 5, 6 (1996), pp. 57–72.

"The Urban Question under Planetary Urbanization," *International Journal of Urban and Regional Research* 37, 3 (2013), pp. 909–922.

Merry, Sally, "Spatial Governmentality and the New Urban Social Order: Controlling Gender Violence through Law," *American Anthropologist* 103, 1 (2001), pp. 16–29.

Miao, Pu, "Deserted Streets in a Jammed Town: The Gated Community in Chinese Cities and Its Solution," *Journal of Urban Design* 8, 1 (2003), pp. 45–66.

Michel, Boris, "Going Global, Veiling the Poor Global City Imaginaries in Metro Manila," *Philippine Studies* 58, 3 (2010), pp. 383–406.

Miéville, China, "Floating Utopias," in Mike Davis and Daniel Bertrand Monk (eds.), *Evil Paradises: Dreamworlds of Neoliberalism* (New York: New Press, 2008), pp. 251–261.

Miles, Malcolm, and Tim Hall (eds.), *Urban Futures: Critical Commentaries on Shaping the City* (New York: Routledge, 2003).

Milgram, B. Lynne, "Reconfiguring Space, Mobilizing Livelihood: Street Vending, Legality, and Work in the Philippines," *Journal of Developing Societies* 27, 3&4 (2011), pp. 261–293.

Minton, Anna, *What Kind of World Are We Building? The Privatisation of Public Space* (London: RICS, 2006).

Ground Control: Fear and Happiness in the 21st Century City (London: Penguin, 2009).

Minca, Claudio, "Agamben's Geographies of Modernity," *Political Geography* 26 (2007), pp. 78–97.

Miraftab, Faranak, "Insurgent Planning: Situating Radical Planning in the Global South," *Planning Theory* 8, 1 (2009), pp. 32–50.

Miraftab, Faranak, and Shana Wills, "Insurgency and the Spaces of Active Citizenship: The Story of the Western Cape Anti-Eviction Campaign in South Africa," *Journal of Planning Education and Research* 25, 2 (2000), pp. 200–217.

Mirzoeff, Nicholas, "The Empire of Camps," *Situation Analysis* 1 (2002), pp. 20–25.

Mitchell, Don, "The End of Public Space? People's Park, Definitions of the Public, and Democracy," *Annals of the Association of American Geographers* 85 (1995), pp. 108–133.

"The Annihilation of Space by Law: The Roots and Implications of Anti-Homeless Laws in the United States," *Antipode* 29, 3 (1997), pp. 303–335.

The Right to the City: Social Justice and the Fight for Public Space (New York: Guilford, 2003).

Mitchell, Katharyne, "The Culture of Urban Space," *Urban Geography* 21, 5 (2000), pp. 443–449.

"Transnationalism, Neo-Liberalism, and the Rise of the Shadow State," *Economy and Society* 30, 2 (2001), pp. 165–189.

Mitchell, Jerry, "Business Improvement Districts and the Management of Innovation," *American Review of Public Administration* 31, 2 (2001), pp. 201–217.

"Business Improvement Districts and the 'New' Revitalization of Downtown," *Economic Development Quarterly* 15, 2 (2001), pp. 115–123.

Mitchell, Timothy, *Rule of Experts: Egypt, Techno-Politics, Modernity* (Berkeley: University of California Press, 2002).

"Dreamland," in Mike Davis and Daniel Monk (eds.), *Evil Paradises: Dreamlands of Neoliberalism* (New York: Verso, 2007), pp. 1–33.

Mitchell, William, *The City of Bits: Space, Place and the Infobahn* (Cambridge, MA: The MIT Press, 1995).

Mitchell-Weaver, Clyde, and Brenda Manning, "Public–Private Partnerships in Third World Development: A Conceptual Overview," *Studies in Comparative International Development* 26, 4 (1991–1992), pp. 45–67.

Moeller, Kim Christian, "Police Crack Down on Christiania in Copenhagen," *Crime, Law, and Social Change* 32, 4 (2009), pp. 337–345.

Mol, Annemarie, *The Body Multiple: Ontology in Medical Practice* (Durham, NC: Duke University Press, 2002).

Monstadt, Jochen, "Conceptualizing the Political Ecology of Urban Infrastructures: Insights from Technology and Urban Studies," *Environment and Planning A* 41, 8 (2009), pp. 1924–1942.

Morales, Alfonso, "Conclusion: Law, Deviance, and Defining Vendors and Vending," in John Cross and Alfonso Morales (eds.), *Street Entrepreneurs: People, Place and Politics in Local and Global Perspectives* (New York: Routledge, 2007), pp. 262–269.

Morton, Stephen, *States of Emergency: Colonialism, Literature, and the Law* (Liverpool: Liverpool University Press, 2013).

Morshed, Md. Manjur, and Yasushi Asami, "The Role of NGOs in Public and Private Land Development: The Case of Dhaka City," *Geoforum* 60 (2015), pp. 4–13.

Moroni, Stefano, and David Emanuel Andersson, "Introduction: Private Enterprise and the Future of Urban Planning," in David Emanuel Andersson and Stefano Moroni (eds.), *Cities and Private Planning: Property Rights, Entrepreneurship and Transaction Costs* (Northampton, MA: Edgar Elgar, 2014), pp. 1–16.

Moss, Timothy, "Socio-Technical Change and the Politics of Urban Infrastructure: Managing Energy in Berlin between Dictatorship and Democracy," *Urban Studies* 51, 7 (2014), pp. 1432–1448.

Moulier-Boutang, Yann, *Cognitive Capitalism* (Cambridge, UK: Polity Press, 2011).

Mountz, Alison, "The Enforcement Archipelago: Detention, Haunting, and Asylum on Islands," *Political Geography* 30, 3 (2011), pp. 118–128.

"Political Geography I: Reconfiguring Geographies of Sovereignty," *Progress in Human Geography* 37, 6 (2013), pp. 829–841.

Mozingo, Louise, *Pastoral Capitalism: A History of Suburban Corporate Landscapes* (Cambridge, MA: The MIT Press, 2011).

Meuser, Philipp, "Astana, Almaty, and Aktau: Architectural Experiments in the Steppes of Kazakhstan," in Alfrun Kliems and Marina Dmitrieva (eds.), *The Post-Socialist City: Continuity and Change in Urban Space and Imagery* (Berlin: Jovis, 2010), pp. 230–247.

Munck, Ronaldo, "Neoliberalism, Necessitarianism and Alternatives in Latin America: There is no Alternative (Tina)?" *Third World Quarterly* 24, 3 (2003), pp. 495–511.

Murray, Martin J., *Taming the Disorderly City: The Spatial Landscape of Johannesburg after Apartheid* (Ithaca: Cornell University Press, 2008).

"The City in Fragments: Kaleidoscopic Johannesburg after Apartheid," in Gyan Prakash and Kevin Kruse (eds.), *The Spaces of the Modern City* (Princeton: Princeton University Press, 2008), pp. 144–178.

"Fire and Ice: Unnatural Disasters and the Disposable Urban Poor in Post-Apartheid Johannesburg," *International Journal of Urban and Regional Research* 33, 1 (2009), pp. 165–192.

City of Extremes: The Spatial Politics of Johannesburg (Durham, NC: Duke University Press, 2011).

"Afterword: Re-engaging with Transnational Urbanism," in Tony Samara, Shenjing He, and Guo Chen (eds.), *Locating the Right to the City in the Global South* (New York: Routledge, 2013), pp. 285–310.

"City of Layers: The Making and Shaping of Affluent Johannesburg after Apartheid," in Marie Huchzermeyer and Christoph Haferburg (eds.), *Urban Governance in Post-Apartheid Cities* (Stuttgart: Schweizerbart, 2014), pp. 179–196.

"'City Doubles': Re-Urbanism in Africa," in Faranak Miraftab, David Wilson, and Ken Salo (eds.), *Cities and Inequalities in a Global and Neoliberal World* (New York: Routledge, 2015), pp. 92–109.

"Waterfall City (Johannesburg): Privatized Urbanism *in Extremis*," *Environment & Planning A* 47, 3 (2015), pp. 503–520.

Nagel, Caroline, "Ethnic Conflict and Urban Redevelopment in Down Town Beirut," *Growth and Change* 31, 2 (2000), pp. 211–234.

"Reconstruction Space, Re-creating Memory: Sectarian Politics and Urban Development in Postwar Beirut," *Political Geography* 21, 5 (2002), pp. 717–725.

Nairn, Tom, "Sovereignty after the Election," *New Left Review* 1/224 (1997), pp. 3–18.

Naphade, Milind, Guruduth Banavar, Colin Harrison, Jurij Paraszczak, and Robert Morris, "Smarter Cities and their Innovation Challenges," *Computer* 44, 6 (2011), pp. 32–39.

Nasr, Joe, and Eric Verdeil, "The Reconstruction of Beirut," in Salma Jayyusi, Renata Holod, Attilio Petruccioli, and André Raymond (eds.), *The City in the Islamic World*. Volume 2 (Leiden and Boston: Brill, 2008), pp. 1116–1141.

Nasrallah, Rami, "The Jerusalem Separation Wall: Facts and Political Implications" in Robert Brooks (ed.), *The Wall Fragmenting the Palestinian Fabric in Jerusalem* (Jerusalem: The International Peace and Cooperation Center, 2007), pp. 13–26.

Natrasony, Shawn, and Don Alexander, "The Rise of Modernism and the Decline of Place: The Case of Surrey City Centre, Canada," *Planning Perspectives* 20, 4 (2005), pp. 413–433.

Nedoroscik, Jeffrey, *The City of the Dead: A History of Cairo's Cemetery Communities* (Westport, CT: Greenwood Press, 1997).

Needham, Andrew, and Allen Dieterich-Ward, "Beyond the Metropolis: Metropolitan Growth and Regional Transformation in Postwar America," *Journal of Urban History* 35, 7 (2009), pp. 943–969.

Neilson, Brett, "Zones: Beyond the Logic of Exception?" *Concentric: Literary and Cultural Studies* 40, 2 (2014), pp. 11–28.

Németh, Jeremy, "Defining a Public: The Management of Privately Owned Public Space," *Urban Studies* 46, 11 (2009), pp. 2463–2490.

Németh, Jeremy, and Stephan Schmidt, "Toward a Methodology for Measuring the Security of Publicly Accessible Spaces," *Journal of the American Planning Association* 73, 3 (2007), pp. 283–297.

Németh, Jeremy, and Justin Hollander, "Security Zones and New York City's Shrinking Public Space," *International Journal of Urban and Regional Research* 34, 1 (2010), pp. 20–34.

Neumann, Dietrich "The Unbuilt City of Modernity," in Thorsten Scheer, Josef-Paul Kleihues, Paul Kahlfeldt, (eds.), *City of Architecture/Architecture of the City/Berlin 1900–2000* (Berlin: Nicolaische Verlagsbuchhandlung, 2000), pp. 161–173.

Newman, David, "Geopolitics Renaissant: Territory, Sovereignty, and the World Political Map," *Geopolitics* 3, 1 (1998), pp. 1–16.

"The Lines that Continue to Separate Us: Borders in a Borderless World," *Progress in Human Geography* 30, 2 (2006), pp. 1–19.

"The Resilience of Territorial Conflict in an Era of Globalization," in Miles Kahler and Barbara Walter (eds.), *Globalization, Territoriality and Conflict* (Cambridge: Cambridge University Press, 2006), pp. 85–110.

"Territory, Compartments and Borders: Avoiding the Trap of the Territorial Trap," *Geopolitics* 15, 4 (2010), pp. 773–778 (esp. p. 773).

Newman, David, and Anssi Paasi, "Fences and Neighbours in the Post-Modern World: Boundary Narratives in Political Geography," *Progress in Human Geography* 22, 2 (1998) pp. 186–207.

Ng, Mee Kam, "Sustainable Urban Development Issues in Chinese Transitional Cities: Hong Kong and Shenzhen," *International Planning Studies* 7, 1 (2002), pp. 7–36.

"Shenzhen," *Cities* 20, 6 (2003), pp. 429–441.

Ng, Mee Kam, and Wing-Shing Tang, "Land-Use Planning in 'One Country, Two Systems': Hong Kong, Guangzhou and Shenzhen," *International Planning Studies* 4, 1 (1999), pp. 7–27.

Noble, Aleen, and Elisha Efrat, "The Geography of the Intifada," *Geographical Review* 80, 3 (1990), pp. 288–307.

Noland, Peter, "Imperial Archipelagos: China, Western Colonialism and the Law of the Sea," *New Left Review* 80 (2013), pp. 77–95.

Nordstrom, Caroline, "Shadows and Sovereigns," *Theory, Culture & Society* 17, 4 (2000), pp. 35–54.

Norton, Augustus Richard, *Hezbollah: A Short History* (Princeton, NJ: Princeton University Press, 2007).

Nye, David, *American Technological Sublime* (Cambridge, MA: The MIT Press, 1994).

Nyers, Peter, "Emergency or Emerging Identities? Refugees and Transformations in World Order," *Millennium* 28, 1 (1999), pp. 1–26.

Nyíri, Pál, "Enclaves of Improvement: Sovereignty and Developmentalism in the Special Zones of the China-Lao Borderlands," *Comparative Studies in Society and History* 54, 3 (2012), pp 533–562.

"Guest Editorial: The Renaissance of Concessions," *Political Geography* 31 (2012), pp. 195–196.

Nyman, Elizabeth, "Island Exceptionalism and International Maritime Conflicts," *The Professional Geographer* 65, 2 (2013), pp. 221–229.

O'Brien, Richard, *Global Financial Integration: The End of Geography* (London: Pinter Publishers, 1992).

Oc, Taner, and Steve Tiesdell (eds.), *Safer City Centres: Reviving the Public Realm* (London: Paul Chapman, 1997).

O'Connor, Carol, "Sorting Out the Suburbs: Patterns of Land Use, Class, and Culture," *American Quarterly* 37, 3 (1985), pp. 382–394.

O'Donnell, Mary Anne, "Becoming Hong Kong, Razing Baoan, Preserving Xin'An: An Ethnographic Account of Urbanization in the Shenzhen Special Economic Zone," *Cultural Studies* 15, 3–4 (2001), pp. 419–443.

O'Dowd, Liam, "From a 'Borderless World' to a 'World of Borders': 'Bringing History Back In'," *Environment and Planning D* 28, 6 (2010), pp. 1031–1050.

"From a 'Borderless World' to a 'World of Borders': 'Bringing History Back In'," *Environment and Planning D* 28, 6 (2010), pp. 1031–1050.

Ohmae, Kenichi, "The Rise of the Region State," *Foreign Affairs* 72, 2 (Spring 1993), pp. 78–87.

    The End of the Nation State: The Rise of Regional Economies (New York: The Free Press, 1995).

    The Borderless World: Power and Strategy in the Interlinked Economy [Revised Edition] (New York: Harper Business, 1999).

Öktem, Binnur, "The Role of Global City Discourses in the Development and Transformation of the Buyukdere–Maslak Axis into the International Business District of Istanbul," *International Planning Studies* 16, 1 (2011), pp. 27–42.

Oldenburg, Ray, *The Great Good Place: Cafes, Coffee Shops, Bookstores, Bars, Hair Salons and the Other Hangouts at the Heart of a Community* [2nd edition] (New York: Marlowe, 1999).

Öncü, Ayşe, "The Politics of Urban Land Market in Turkey: 1950–1980," *International Journal of Urban and Regional Research* 12, 1 (1988), pp. 38–64.

    "The Myth of the 'Ideal Home' Travels across Cultural Borders to Istanbul," in Ayse Öncü and Petra Weyland (eds.), *Space Culture and Power: New Identities and Globalizing Cities* (London: Zed Books, 1997), pp. 56–72.

    "The Politics of Istanbul's Ottoman Heritage in the Era of Globalism: Refractions through the Prism of a Theme Park," in Barbara Drieskens, Franck Mermier, and Heiko Wimmen (eds.), *Cities of the South: Citizenship and Exclusion in the 21st Century* (Beirut/London: Saqi Books, 2007), pp. 233–264.

O'Neill, Kevin, and Benjamin Fogarty-Valenzuela, "Verticality," *Journal of the Royal Anthropological Institute [N.S.]* 19, 2 (2013), pp. 378–389.

Ong, Aihwa, *Flexible Citizenship: The Cultural Logic of Transnationality* (Durham, NC: Duke University Press, 1999).

    "Graduated Sovereignty in Southeast Asia," *Theory, Culture, & Society* 17, 4 (2000), pp. 55–75.

    "The Chinese Axis: Zoning Technologies and Variegated Sovereignty," *Journal of East Asian Studies* 4 (2004), pp. 69–96.

    Neoliberalism as Exception: Mutations in Citizenship and Sovereignty (Durham, NC: Duke University Press, 2006).

    "Hyperbuilding: Spectacle, Speculation, and Hyperspace of Sovereignty," in Ananya Roy and Aihwa Ong (eds.), *Worlding Cities: Asian Experiments and the Art of Being Global* (Malden, MA: Wiley-Blackwell, 2011), pp. 205–226.

Ong, Aiwha, and Stephen Collier (eds.), *Global Assemblages: Technology, Politics, and the Ethics of Anthropological Problems* (Malden, MA: Blackwell, 2004).

Ophir, Adi, Michal Givoni, and Sari Hanafi, "Introduction," in Adi Ophir, Michal Givoni, and Sari Hanafi (eds.), *The Power of Inclusive Exclusion: Anatomy of Israeli Rule in the Occupied Palestinian Territories* (Cambridge, MA: The MIT Press; New York: Zone Books, 2009), pp. 15–30.

Opitz, Sven, and Ute Tellmann, "Global Territories: Zones of Economic and Legal Dis/connectivity," *Distinktion: Scandinavian Journal of Social Theory* 13, 3 (2012), pp. 261–282.

Orenstein, Dara, "Foreign Trade Zones and the Cultural Logic of Frictionless Production," *Radical History Review* 109 (2011), pp. 36–61.

Ortega, Arnisson Andre C., "Desakota and Beyond: Neoliberal Production of Suburban Space in Manila's Fringe," *Urban Geography* 33, 8 (2012), pp. 1118–1143.

Osborne, Stephen, *Public–Private Partnerships: Theory and Practice in International Perspective* (New York: Routledge, 2002).

Osinulu, Adedamola, "The Road to Redemption: Performing Pentecostal Citizenship in Lagos," in Mamadou Diouf and Rosalind Fredericks (eds.), *The Arts of Citizenship in African Cities: Infrastructures and Spaces of Belonging* (New York: Palgrave Macmillan, 2014), pp. 115–136.

Ó Tuathail, Gearoid, and Timothy Luke, "Present at the (Dis)integration: Deterritorialization and Reterritorialization in the New Wor(l)d Order," *Annals of the Association of American Geographers* 84, 3 (1994), pp. 381–398.

Ouis, Pernilla, "'Greening the Emirates': The Modern Construction of Nature in the United Arab Emirates," *Cultural Geographies* 9, 3 (2002), pp. 334–347.

"Engineering the Emirates: The Evolution of a New Environment," in Stanley Brunn (ed.), *Engineering Earth: The Impacts of Mega-engineering Projects* (Amsterdam: Springer Netherlands, 2011), pp. 1409–1423.

"'And an Island Never Cries': Cultural and Societal Perspectives on the Mega Development of Islands in the United Arab Emirates," in Viorel Badescu and Richard Cathcart (eds.), *Macro-engineering Seawater in Unique Environments* (Berlin Heidelberg: Springer, 2011), pp. 59–75.

Owais, Abdalla, "Transformations between East Jerusalem and its Neighborhoods," in Omar Yousef, Abdalla Owais, Rasseem Khamaisi, and Rami Nasrallah (eds.), *Jerusalem and its Hinterland* (Jerusalem: International Peace and Cooperation Center, 2008), pp. 53–65.

Özkan, Suha, and Philip Jodidio, *A Vision in Architecture: Projects for the Istanbul Zorlu Center* (New York: Rizzoli International Publications, 2012).

Pacione, Michael, "Mumbai," *Cities* 23, 3 (2006), pp. 229–238.

Paddison, Ronan, and Joanne Sharp, "Questioning the End of Public Space: Reclaiming Control of Local Banal Spaces," *Scottish Geographical Journal* 123, 2 (2007), pp. 87–106.

Painter, Joe, "Prosaic Geographies of Stateness," *Political Geography* 25, 7 (2006), pp. 752–774.

Palen, Ronan, "Trying to Have Your Cake and Eat It: How and Why the State System Has Created Offshore," *International Studies Quarterly* 42, 4 (1998), pp. 625–644.

"The Emergence of an Offshore Economy," *Futures* 30, 1 (1998), pp. 63–67.

"Offshore and the Structural Enablement of Sovereignty," in Mark Hampton and Jason Abbott (eds.), *Offshore Finance Centres and Tax Havens: The Rise of Global Capital* (London: Macmillan, 1999).

"Tax Havens and the Commercialization of State Sovereignty," *International Organization* 56, 1 (2002), pp. 151–176.

The Offshore World: Sovereign Markets, Virtual Places, and Nomad Millionaires (Ithaca, New York: Cornell University Press, 2003).

Palermo, Pier Carlo, and Davide Ponzini, *Bottom of Form Place-making and Urban Development: New Challenges for Contemporary Planning and Design* (New York: Routledge, 2015).

Paling, William, "Planning a Future for Phnom Penh: Mega Projects, Aid Dependence and Disjointed Governance," *Urban Studies* 49, 13 (2012), pp. 2889–2912.

Pallister-Wilkins, Polly, "The Separation Wall: A Symbol of Power and a Site of Resistance?" *Antipode* 43, 5 (2011), pp. 1851–1882.

Papadopoulos, Nicolas, and Shavin Malhotra, "Export Processing Zones in Development and International Marketing: An Integrative Review and Research Agenda," *Journal of Macromarketing* 27, 2 (2007), pp. 148–161.

Park, Bae Gyoon, "Spatially Selective Liberalization and Graduated Sovereignty: Politics of Neoliberalism and 'Special Economic Zones' in South Korea," *Political Geography* 24, 7 (2005), pp. 850–873.

Parker, Christopher, "Tunnel-bypasses and Minarets of Capitalism: Amman as Neoliberal Assemblage," *Political Geography* 28, 2 (2009), pp. 110–120.

Parker, Geoffrey, *Sovereign City: The City-State through History* (Chicago: University of Chicago Press, 2005).

Parker, Simon, *Urban Theory and the Urban Experience: Encountering the City* [2nd Edition] (New York: Routledge, 2015).

Parnell, Susan, and Sophie Oldfield (eds.), *The Routledge Handbook for Cities of the Global South* (New York: Routledge, 2014).

Parnell, Susan, and Edgar Pieterse, "The 'Right to the City': Institutional Imperatives of a Developmental State," *International Journal of Urban and Regional Research* 34, 1 (2010), pp. 146–162.

Parnell, Susan, and Jennifer Robinson, "(Re)theorizing Cities from the Global South: Looking Beyond Neoliberalism," *Urban Geography* 33, 4 (2012), pp. 593–617.

Parnreiter, Christof, "Commentary: Toward the Making of a Transnational Urban Policy?" *Journal of Planning Education and Research* 31, 4 (2011), pp. 416–422.

Passi, Anssi, "Boundaries as Social Processes: Territoriality in the World of Flows," *Geopolitics* 3, 1 (1998), pp. 69–88.

"The Changing Discourses on Political Boundaries Mapping the Backgrounds, Contexts and Contents," in Henk van Houtum, Olivier Kramsch, and Wolfgang Zierhofer (eds.), *B/ordering Space* (Burlington, VT: Ashgate, 2005), pp. 17–32.

"Generations and the Development of Border Studies," *Geopolitics* 10, 4 (2005), pp. 663–671.

Pawson, Eric, "Gottmann, J. 1961: Megalopolis. The Urbanized Northeastern Seaboard of the United States. New York: The Twentieth-Century Fund," *Progress in Human Geography* 32, 3 (2008), pp. 441–444.

Peck, Jamie, "Liberating the City: Between New York and New Orleans," *Urban Geography* 27, 8 (2006), pp. 681–713.

"Austerity Urbanism: American Cities under Extreme Economy," *City* 16, 6 (2012), pp. 626–655.

"Pushing Austerity: State Failure, Municipal Bankruptcy and the Crises of Fiscal Federalism in the USA," *Cambridge Journal of Regions, Economy and Society* 7, 1 (2014), pp. 17–44.

"Framing Detroit," in Michael Peter Smith and L. Owen Kirkpatrick (eds.), *Reinventing Detroit: The Politics of Possibility* (New Brunswick, NJ: Transaction, 2015), pp. 145–165.

Peck, Jamie, and Adam Tickell, "Neoliberalizing Space," *Antipode* 34, 3 (2002), pp. 380–404.

Peck, Jamie, Nik Theodore, and Neil Brenner, "Neoliberal Urbanism Redux?" *International Journal of Urban and Regional Research* 37, 3 (2013), pp. 1091–1099.

Percival, Tom, and Paul Waley, "Articulating Intra-Asian Urbanism: The Production of Satellite Cities in Phnom Penh," *Urban Studies* 49, 13 (2012), pp. 2873–2888.

Peresthu, Andrea, "Questioning the JABOTABEK Growth Centre Strategies," in Marisa Carmona, Devisari Tunas, and Marinda Schoonraad (eds.), *Globalization, Urban Form and Governance: Globalization and the Return of the Big Plans* [Volume 7] (Delft: Delft University Press, 2003), pp. 57–75.

Perlman, Janice, *Favela: Four Decades of Living on the Edge in Rio de Janeiro* (Oxford and New York: Oxford University Press, 2010).

Peron, Françoise, "The Contemporary Lure of the Island," *Tijdschrift voor Economische en Sociale Geografie* 95, 3 (2004), pp. 326–339.

Peteet, Julie, *Landscape of Hope and Despair: Palestinian Refugee Camps* (Philadelphia: University of Pennsylvania Press, 2009).

Peterson, J. E., "Life after Oil: Economic Alternatives for the Arab Gulf States," *Mediterranean Quarterly* 20, 3 (2009), pp. 1–18.

Petti, Alessandro, "Dubai Offshore Urbanism," in Michiel Dehaene and Lieven De Cauter (eds.), *Heterotopia and the City: Public Space in a Postcivil Society* (New York: Routledge, 2008), pp. 287–296.

Peyroux, Elisabeth, "City Improvement Districts in Johannesburg: An Examination of the Local Variations of the BID Model," in *Business Improvement Districts: Ein Neues Governance-Modell aus Perspektive von Praxis und Stadtforschung*, Robert Pütz (ed.), Geographische Handelsforschung 14 (Passau, Germany: L. I. S. Verlag, 2008), pp. 139–162.

"Legitimating Business Improvement Districts in Johannesburg: A Discursive Perspective on Urban Regeneration and Policy Transfer," *European Urban and Regional Studies* 19, 2 (2012), pp. 181–194.

Peyroux, Elisabeth, Robert Pütz, and Georg Glasze, "Business Improvement Districts (BIDs): The Internationalization and Contextualization of a 'Travelling Concept'," *European Urban and Regional Studies* 19, 2 (2012), pp. 111–120.

Phelps, Nicholas, Tim Bunnell, and Michelle Ann Miller, "Post-disaster Economic Development in Aceh: Neoliberalization and other Economic-Geographical Imaginaries," *Geoforum* 42, 2 (2011), pp. 418–426.

Pieterse, Edgar, *City Futures: Confronting the Crisis of Urban Development* (Cape Town: UCT Press, 2008).

Piffero, Elena, "Beyond Rules and Regulations: The Growth of Informal Cairo," in Regina Kipper and Marion Fischer (eds.), *Cairo's Informal Areas: Between Urban Challenges and Hidden Potentials. Facts. Voices. Visions* (Cairo: German Technical Cooperation [GTZ], 2009), pp. 20–27.

Pinder, David, *Visions of the City: Utopianism, Power and Politics in Twentieth-Century Urbanism* (New York: Routledge, 2013).

Pinos, Jaume Castan, "Assessing the Significance of Borders and Territoriality in a Globalized Europe," *Regions & Cohesion* 3, 2 (2013), pp. 47–68.

Pírez, Pedro, "Buenos Aires: Fragmentation and Privatization of the Metropolitan City," *Environment & Urbanization* 14, 1 (2002), pp. 145–158.

Pizarro, Rafael, Liang Wei, and Tridip Banerjee, "Agencies of Globalization and Third World Urban Form: A Review," *Journal of Planning Literature* 18, 2 (2003), pp. 111–130.

Pope, Albert, "From Form to Space," in Roger Sherman and Dana Cuff (eds.), *Fast-Forward Urbanism: Rethinking Architecture's Engagement with the City* (New York: Princeton Architectural Press, 2011), pp. 143–175.

"The Unified Project," *Architectural Design* 82, 5 (2012), 80–87.

"The Island Organism: Hilberseimer in Rockford," in Neeraj Bhatia and Mary Casper (eds.), *The Petropolis of Tomorrow* (New York: Actar, 2013), pp. 92–105.

Popescu, Gabriel, *Bordering and Ordering the Twenty-first Century: Understanding Borders* (Plymouth: Rowland & Littlefield, 2012).

Potuoğlu-Cook, Ökyü, "Beyond the Glitter: Belly Dance and Neoliberal Gentrification in Istanbul," *Cultural Anthropology* 21, 4 (2006), pp. 633–60.

Pow, Choon-Piew, "Urban Entrepreneurialism, Global Business Elites and Urban Mega-development: A Case Study of Suntec City," *Asian Journal of Social Science* 30, 1 (2002), pp. 53–72.

"Securing the 'Civilized' Enclaves: Gated Communities and the Moral Geographies of Exclusion in (Post-)Socialist Shanghai," *Urban Studies* 44, 8 (2007), pp. 1539–1558.

"Constructing a New Private Order: Gated Communities and the Privatization of Urban Life in Post-Reform Shanghai," *Social & Cultural Geography*, 8, 6 (2007), pp. 813–833.

"Living it Up: Super-rich Enclave and Transnational Elite Urbanism in Singapore," *Geoforum* 42, 3 (2011), pp. 382–393.

Pow, Choon-Piew, and Lily Kong, "Marketing the Chinese Dream Home: Gated Communities and Representations of the Good Life in (Post-) Socialist Shanghai," *Urban Geography* 28, 2 (2007), pp. 129–159.

Prakash, Gyan, "Introduction," in Gyan Prakash and Kevin Kruse (eds.), *The Spaces of the Modern City: Imaginaries, Politics and Everyday Life* (Princeton, NJ: Princeton University Press, 2008), pp. 1–18.

"Mumbai: The Modern City in Ruins," in Andreas Huyssen (ed.), *Other Cities, Other Worlds: Urban Imaginaries in a Globalizing Age* (Durham: Duke University Press, 2008), pp. 181–204.

"Introduction: Imagining the Modern City, Darkly," in Gyan Prakash (ed.), *Noir Urbanism: Dystopic Images of the Modern City* (Princeton, NJ: Princeton University Press, 2010), pp. 1–14.

Pryzbylski, Maya, "Re-Rigging Transborder Logics across the Bounded Site," in Neeraj Bhatia and Mary Casper (eds.), *The Petropolis of Tomorrow* (New York: Actar, 2013), pp. 258–271 (esp. 260).

Pullan, Wendy, "Frontier Urbanism: The Periphery at the Centre of Contested Cities," *The Journal of Architecture* 16, 1 (2011), pp. 15–35.

Pullan, Wendy, Philipp Misselwitz, Rami Nasrallah, and Haim Yacobi, "Jerusalem's Road 1: An Inner City Frontier? *City* 11, 2 (2007), pp. 176–198.

Pugalis, Lee, and David McGuinness, "From a Framework to a Toolkit: Urban Regeneration in an Age of Austerity," *Journal of Urban Regeneration and Renewal* 6, 4 (2013), pp. 339–353.

Pugalis, Lee, and Joyce Liddle, "Austerity Era Regeneration: Conceptual Issues and Practical Challenges, Part 1," *Journal of Urban Regeneration and Renewal* 6, 4 (2013), pp. 333–338.

Purcell, Mark, "Excavating Lefebvre: The Right to the City and its Urban Politics of the Inhabitant," *GeoJournal* 58, 2 (2002), pp. 99–108.

"Citizenship and the Right to the Global City: Reimagining the Capitalist World Order," *International Journal of Urban and Regional Research* 27, 3 (2003), pp. 564–590.

"Resisting Neoliberalization: Communicative Planning or Counter-hegemonic Movements?" *Planning Theory* 8, 2 (2009), pp. 140–65.

Quilty, Jim, and Lysandra Ohrstrom, "The Second Time as Farce: Stories of Another Lebanese Reconstruction," *MERIP* 37, 2 (2007), pp. 31–41.

Raco, Mike, "Remaking Place and Securitizing Space: Urban Regeneration and the Strategies, Tactics and Practices of Policing in the UK," *Urban Studies* 40, 9 (2003), pp. 1869–1887.

"The Privatisation of Urban Development and the London Olympics 2012," *City* 16, 4 (2012), pp. 452–460.

Rael, Ronald, "Border Wall as Architecture," *Environment and Planning D* 29, 3 (2011), pp. 409–420.

Rajagopalan, Shruti, and Alexander Tabarrok, "Lessons from Gurgaon, India's Private City," in David Emanuel Andersson and Stefano Moroni (eds.), *Cities and Private Planning: Property Rights, Entrepreneurship and Transaction Costs* (Northhampton, MA: Edward Elgar, 2014), pp. 199–213.

Rai, Pallavi Tak, "Townships for Sustainable Cities," *Procedia: Social and Behavioral Sciences* 37 (2012), pp. 417–442.

Rao, Vyjayanthi, "Proximate Distances: The Phenomenology of Density in Mumbai," *Built Environment* 33, 2 (2007), pp. 227–248 (quotation from p. 245).

Ramirez-Lovering, Diego (ed.), *Opportunistic Urbanism* (Melbourne, Australia: RMIT Publishing, 2008).

Reed, Stephen, "Amsterdam: Beyond Inside and Out," in Stephen Read, Jürgen Rosemann, and Job van Eldijk (eds.), *Future City* (London and New York: Spon Press, 2006), pp. 194–211.

Reeve, Alan, "The Private Realm of the Managed Town Centre," *Urban Design International* 1, 1 (1996), pp. 61–80.

Reid-Henry, Simon, "Exceptional Sovereignty? Guantanamo Bay and the Re-Colonial Present," *Antipode* 39, 4 (2007), pp. 627–648.

"The Territorial Trap Fifteen Years On," *Geopolitics* 15, 4 (2010), pp. 752–756.

Relph, Edward, *The Modern Urban Landscape* (London: Croon Helm, 1986).

Reno, Russell, "Non-Euclidean Zoning: The Use of the Floating Zone," *Maryland Law Review* 23, 2 (1963), pp. 105–120.

Rizzo, Agatino, "Rapid Urban Development and National Master Planning in Arab Gulf Countries: Qatar as a Case Study," *Cities* 39 (2014), pp. 50–57.

Robbins, Steven, "At the Limits of Spatial Governmentality: A Message from the Tip of Africa," *Third World Quarterly* 23, 4 (2002), pp. 665–689.

Roberts, John Michael, "Public Spaces of Dissent," *Sociology Compass* 2, 2 (2008), pp. 654–674.

Robertson, Roland, "Glocalization: Time-Space and Homogeneity-Heterogeneity," in Mike Featherstone, Scott Lash, and Roland Robertson (eds.), *Global Modernities* (London: Sage, 1995), pp. 25–44.

Robinson, Jennifer, "Global and World Cities: A View from off the Map," *International Journal of Urban and Regional Research* 26, 3 (2002), pp. 531–554.

"Urban Geography: World Cities, or a World of Cities," *Progress in Human Geography* 29, 6 (2005) pp. 757–765.

Ordinary Cities: Between Modernity and Development (New York: Routledge, 2003).

"The Spaces of Circulating Knowledge: City Strategies and Global Urban Governmentality," in Eugene McCann and Kevin Ward (eds.), *Mobile Urbanism: Cities and Policymaking in the Global Age* (Minneapolis: University of Minnesota Press, 2011), pp. 15–40.

"2010 Urban Geography Plenary Lecture – The Travels of Urban Neoliberalism: Taking Stock of the Internationalization of Urban Theory," *Urban Geography* 32, 8 (2011), pp. 1087–1109.

"Cities in a World of Cities: The Comparative Gesture," *International Journal of Urban and Regional Research* 35, 1 (2011), pp. 1–23.

"The Urban Now: Theorising Cities beyond the New," *European Journal of Cultural Studies* 16, 6 (2013), pp. 659–677.

Rodgers, Dennis, "'Disembedding' the City: Crime, Insecurity and Spatial Organization in Managua, Nicaragua," *Environment & Urbanization* 16, 2 (2004), pp. 113–124.

"'Nueva Managua': The Disembedded City," in Mike Davis and Daniel Monk (eds.), *Evil Paradises: Dreamworlds of Neoliberalism* (New York: New Press, 2007), pp. 127–139.

"Haussmannization in the Tropics: Abject Urbanism and Infrastructural Violence in Nicaragua," *Ethnography* 13, 4 (2012), pp. 413–438.

Roitman, Janet. "Garrison-Entrepôt," *Cahiers d'études Africaines* 38, 150 (1998), pp. 297–329.

"Modes of Governing: The Garrison-Entrepôt," in Aihwa Ong and Stephen Collier (eds.), *Global Anthropology: Technology, Politics, and Ethics as Anthropological Problems* (Malden, MA: Blackwell, 2005), pp. 417–436.

Fiscal Disobedience: An Anthropology of Economic Regulation in Central Africa (Princeton, NJ: Princeton University Press, 2005).

"New Sovereigns? Regulatory Authority in the Chad Basin," in Thomas Callaghy, Ronald Kassimir, and Robert Latham (eds.), *Intervention and Transnationalism in Africa. Global-Local Networks of Power* (Cambridge, UK: Cambridge University Press, 2010), pp. 240–263.

Rose, Gillian, Monica Degen, and Begum Basdas, "More on 'Big Things': Building Events and Feelings," *Transactions of the Institute of British Geographers [New Series]* 35, 3 (2010), pp. 334–349.

Rose, Nikolas, and Peter Miller, "Political Power Beyond the State: Problematics of Government," *British Journal of Sociology* 43, 2 (1992), pp. 173–205.

Rowe, Colin, and Fred Koetter, *Collage City* (Cambridge, MA: The MIT Press, 1979).

Roy, Ananya, "Urban Informality: Toward an Epistemology of Planning," *Journal of the American Planning Association* 71, 2 (2005), pp. 147–158.

"Praxis in the Time of Empire," *Planning Theory* 5, 1 (2006), pp. 7–29.

"Why India Cannot Plan its Cities: Informality, Insurgence and the Idiom of Urbanization," *Planning Theory* 8, 1 (2009), pp. 76–87.

"Civic Governmentality: The Politics of Inclusion in Beirut and Mumbai," *Antipode* 41, 1 (2009), pp. 159–179.

"The 21st-Century Metropolis: New Geographies of Theory," *Regional Studies* 43, 6 (2009), pp. 819–830.

"Civic Governmentality: The Politics of inclusion in Beirut and Mumbai," *Antipode* 41, 1 (2009), pp. 159–179.

"Urbanisms, Worlding Practices and the Theory of Planning," *Planning Theory* 10, 1 (2011), pp. 6–15.

"Slumdog Cities: Rethinking Subaltern Urbanism," *International Journal of Urban and Regional Research* 35, 2 (2011), pp. 223–238.

"Postcolonial Urbanism: Speed, Hysteria, Mass Dreams," in Ananya Roy and Aihwa Ong (eds.), *Worlding Cities: Asian Experiments and the Art of Being Global* (Oxford: Blackwell, 2011), pp. 307–335.

"Whose Afraid of Postcolonial Theory?" *International Journal of Urban and Regional Research* [40, 1 (2016), pp. 200–209.

Roy, Ananya, and Aihwa Ong (eds.), *Worlding Cities: Asian Experiments and the Art of Being Global* (Malden, MA: Wiley-Blackwell, 2011).

Ruby, Ilka, and Andreas Ruby, "Forward," in Ilka and Andreas Ruby (eds.), *Urban Transformations* (Berlin: Ruby Press, 2008), pp. 10–13.

Ruggeri, Laura, "'Palm Springs': Imagineering California in Hong Kong," in Mike Davis and Daniel Monk (eds.), *Evil Paradises: Dreamlands of Neoliberalism* (New York: Verso, 2007), pp. 102–113.

Ruggie, John, "Review: Continuity and Transformation in World Politics: Towards a Synthesis," *World Politics* 35, 2 (1983), pp. 261–285.

"Territoriality and Beyond: Problematizing Modernity in International Relations," *International Organization* 47, 1 (1993), pp. 139–174.

Sakizlioglu, Nur Bahar, and Justus Uitermark, "The Symbolic Politics of Gentrification: The Restructuring of Stigmatized Neighborhoods in Amsterdam and Istanbul," *Environment and Planning A* 46, 6 (2014), pp. 1369–1385.

Samara, Tony Roshan, "Policing Development: Urban Renewal as Neoliberal Security Strategy," *Urban Studies* 47, 1 (2010), pp. 197–214.

Samara, Tony, Roshan, Shenjing He, and Guo Chen, "Introduction: Locating the City in the Global South," in Tony Samara, Shenjing He, and Guo Chen (eds.), *Locating the Right to the City in the Global South* (New York: Routledge, 2013), pp. 1–20.

Sánchez, Fernanda, and Anne-Marie Broudehoux, "Mega-Events and Urban Regeneration in Rio de Janeiro: Planning in a State of Emergency," *International Journal of Urban Sustainable Development* 5, 2 (2013), pp. 132–155.

Sandercock, Leonie, *Towards Cosmopolis* (Chichester: John Wiley, 1998).

[Images by Peter Lyssiotis], *Cosmopolis II: Mongrel Cities of the 21st Century* (London: Continuum, 2003).

Sanyal, Romola, "Squatting in Camps: Building and Insurgency in Spaces of Refuge," *Urban Studies* 48, 5 (2011), pp. 877–890.

"Urbanizing Refuge: Interrogating Spaces of Displacement," *International Journal of Urban and Regional Research* 38, 2 (2014), pp. 558–572.

Sarkis, Hashim, and Peter Rowe, "The Age of Physical Reconstruction," in Peter Rowe and Hashim Sarkis (eds.), *Projecting Beirut: Episodes in the Construction and Reconstruction of a Modern City* (Munich: Prestel, 1998), pp. 275–284.

Sassen, Saskia, *Cities in World Economy* (Thousand Oaks, CA: Pine Forge Press, 1994).

"The Informal Economy: Between New Developments and Old Regulations," *The Yale Law Journal* 103, 8 (1994), pp. 2289–2304.

Losing Control? Sovereignty in an Age of Globalization (New York: Columbia University Press, 1996).

"New Frontiers Facing Urban Sociology at the Millennium," *British Journal of Sociology* 51, 1 (2000), pp. 143–159.

The Global City: New York, London, Tokyo [second edition] (Princeton, NJ: Princeton University Press, 2001).

(ed.), *Global Networks, Linked Cities* (London: Routledge, 2002).

"Introduction: Locating Cities on Global Networks," in Saskia Sassen (ed.), *Global Networks, Linked Cities* (New York: Routledge, 2002), pp. 1–36.

"Reading the City in a Global Digital Age: Between Topographical Representation and Spatialized Power Projects," in Stephen Read, Jürgen Rosemann, and Job van Eldijk (eds.), *Future City* (London and New York: Spon Press, 2006), pp. 145–155.

"Toward a Multiplication of Specialized Assemblages of Territory, Authority, and Rights," *Parallax* 13, 1 (2007), pp. 87–94.

Territory•Authority•Rights: From Medieval to Global Assemblages [Updated Edition] (Princeton: Princeton University Press, 2008).

"Neither Global nor National: Novel Assemblages of Territory, Authority, and Rights," *Ethics & Global Politics* 1, 1–2 (2008), pp. 61–79.

"The Economies of Cities," in Ricky Burdett and Deyan Sudjic (eds.), *Living in the Endless City: The Urban Age Project by the London School of Economics and Deutsche Bank's Alfred Herrhausen Society* (London: Phaidon, 2011), pp. 56–65.

Expulsions: Brutality and Complexity in the World Economy (Cambridge, MA: Harvard University Press, 2014).

Sather, Clifford, *The Bajau Laut: Adaptation, History, and Fate in a Maritime Fishing Society of Southeastern Sabah* (Oxford: Oxford University Press, 1997).

Saunders, Doug, *Arrival City: How the Largest Migration in History is Reshaping Our World* (New York: Pantheon Books, 2011).

Sawalha, Aseel, "'Healing the Wounds of the War': Placing the War-Displaced in Post-war Beirut," in Jane Schneider and Ida Susser (eds.), *Wounded Cities: Destruction and Reconstruction in a Globalized World* (Oxford: Berg, 2003), pp. 271–290.

Reconstructing Beirut: Memory and Space in a Postwar Arab City (Austin: University of Texas Press, 2010).

Sawyer, Suzana, "Commentary: The Corporation, Oil, and the Financialization of Risk," *American Ethnologist* 39, 4 (2012), pp. 710–715.

Schatz, Edward, "What Capital Cities Say About State and Nation Building," *Nationalism and Ethnic Politics* 9, 4 (2004), pp. 111–140.

Scherr, Richard, "The Synthetic City: Excursions into the Real-Not Real," *Places* 18, 2 (2005), pp. 6–15.

Scheper-Hughes, Nancy, *Death without Weeping: The Violence of Everyday Life in Brazil* (Berkeley: University of California Press, 1992).

Schindler, Seth, "Governing the Twenty-First Century Metropolis and Transforming Territory," *Territory, Politics, Governance* 3, 1 (2015), pp. 7–26.

Schinkel, Willem, and Marguerite van den Berg, "City of Exception: The Dutch *Revanchist* City and the Urban *Homo Sacer*," *Antipode* 43, 5 (2011), pp. 1911–1938.

Schlichtman, John Joe, and Jason Patch, "Gentrifier? Who, Me? Interrogating the Gentrifier in the Mirror," *International Journal of Urban and Regional Research* 38, 4 (2014), pp. 1491–1508.

Schmid, Christian, "Networks, Borders, Differences: Towards a Theory of the Urban," in Neil Brenner (ed.), *Implosions/Explosions: Towards a Study of Planetary Urbanization* (Berlin: Jovis, 2013), pp. 67–80.

"Patterns and Pathways of Global Urbanization: Towards Comparative Analysis," in Neil Brenner (ed.), *Implosions/Explosions: Towards a Study of Planetary Urbanization* (Berlin: Jovis, 2013), pp. 203–217.

Schmid, Heiko, "Economy of Fascination: Dubai and Las Vegas as Examples of Themed Urban Landscapes [Ökonomie der Faszination: Dubai und Las Vegas als Beispiele thematisch inszenierter Stadtlandschaften]," *Erdkunde* 60, 4 (2006), pp. 346–361.

Schmidt, Stephan, and Jeremy Németh, "Space, Place and the City: Emerging Research on Public Space Design and Planning," *Journal of Urban Design* 15, 4 (2010), pp. 453–457.

Schmidt, Stephan, Jeremy Németh, and Erik Botsford, "The Evolution of Privately Owned Public Spaces in New York City," *Urban Design International* 16, 4 (2011), pp. 270–284.

Schneider, Jane, and Ida Susser, "Wounded Cities: Destruction and Reconstruction in a Globalized World," in Jane Schneider and Ida Susser (eds.), *Wounded Cities: Destruction and Reconstruction in a Globalized World* (Oxford, UK: Berg, 2003), pp. 1–25.

Schrijver, Lara, "The Archipelago City: Piercing Together Collectivities," *OASE* 71 [*Journal for Architecture, Urban Formation & Collective Spaces*] (2006), pp. 18–36.

Schulenburg, Alexander Hugo, "'Island of the Blessed': Eden, Arcadia, and the Picturesque in the Textualizing of St Helena," *Journal of Historical Geography* 29, 4 (2003), pp. 535–553.

Schuyler, David, "The New Urbanism and the Modern Metropolis," *Urban History* 24, 3 (1997), pp. 344–358.

Scobey, David, *Empire City: The Making and Meaning of the New York City Landscape* (Philadelphia: Temple University Press, 2002).

Scott, Allen, "Creative Cities: Conceptual Issues and Policy Questions," *Journal of Urban Affairs* 28, 1 (2006), pp. 1–17.

   "Capitalism and Urbanization in a New Key? The Cognitive-Cultural Dimension," *Social Forces* 85, 4 (2007), pp. 1465–1482.

   "Cultural Economy and the Creative Field of the City," *Geografiska Annaler: Series B, Human Geography* 92, 2 (2010), pp. 115–130.

   "Emerging Cities of the Third Wave," *City* 15, 3/4 (2011), pp. 289–381.

   "Retrospect," *City* 17, 3 (2013), pp. 384–386.

   "Beyond the Creative City: Cognitive–Cultural Capitalism and the New Urbanism," *Regional Studies* 48, 4 (2014), pp. 565–578.

Scott, Allen, and Michael Storper, "Regions, Globalization, and Development," *Regional Studies* 37, 6&7 (2003), pp. 579–593.

   "The Nature of Cities: The Scope and Limits of Urban Theory," *International Journal of Urban and Regional Research* 39, 1 (2015), pp. 1–15.

Scott, James, *Seeing Like a State: How Certain Schemes to Improve the Human Condition Have Failed* (New Haven: Yale University Press, 1998).

Scully, Eileen, "Taking the Low Road to Sino-American Relations: Open Door Expansionists and the Two China Markets," *Journal of American History* 82, 1 (1995), pp. 62–83.

   Bargaining with the State from Afar: American Citizenship in Treaty Port China (New York: Columbia University Press, 2001).

Secchi, Bernardo, "Rethinking and Redesigning the Urban Landscape," *Places* 19, 1 (2007), pp. 6–11.

Seabrook, Jeremy, *In the Cities of the South: Some Scenes from a Developing World* (London: Verso, 1996).

Seidman, Steven, "The Politics of Cosmopolitan Beirut from the Stranger to the Other," *Theory, Culture & Society* 29, 2 (2012), pp. 3–36.

Séjourné, Marion, "The History of Informal Settlements," in Regina Kipper and Marion Fischer (eds.), *Cairo's Informal Areas: Between Urban Challenges and Hidden Potentials. Facts. Voices. Visions* (Cairo: German Technical Cooperation [GTZ], 2009), pp. 17–20.

Sellars, Simon, "Hakim Bey: Repopulating the Temporary Autonomous Zone," *Journal for the Study of Radicalism* 4, 2 (2010), pp. 83–108 (quotation from p. 84).

Semiaticky, Matt, "Message in a Metro: Building Urban Rail Infrastructure and Image in Delhi, India," *International Journal of Urban and Regional Research* 30, 2 (2006), pp. 277–292.

Sennett, Richard, "Boundaries and Borders," in Ricky Burdett and Deyan Sudjic (eds.), *Living in the Endless City: The Urban Age Project by the London School of Economics and Deutsche Bank's Alfred Herrhausen Society* (London: Phaidon, 2011), pp. 324–341.

Seshadri, Triyakshana, "An Analysis of the Feasibility of Private Land Assembly for Special Economic Zones in India," *Urban Studies* 49, 10 (2012), pp. 2285–2300.

Shaftoe, Henry, *Convivial Public Spaces: Creating Effective Public Places* (London: Earthscan, 2008).

Shapira, Harel, "The Border: Infrastructure of the Global," *Public Culture* 25, 2 (2013), pp. 249–260.

Sharma, R. N., "Mega Transformation of Mumbai: Deepening Enclave Urbanism," *Sociological Bulletin* 59, 1 (2010), pp. 69–91.

Sharman, Jason, "Offshore and the New Political Economy," *Review of International Political Economy* 17, 1 (2010), pp. 1–19.

Shatkin, Gavin, "Planning to Forget: Informal Settlements as 'Forgotten Places' in Globalising Metro Manila," *Urban Studies* 41, 12 (2004), pp. 2469–2484.

"Colonial Capital, Modernist Capital, Global Capital: The Changing Political Symbolism of Urban Space in Metro Manila, the Philippines," *Pacific Affairs* 78, 4 (2006), pp. 577–600.

"Global Cities of the South: Emerging Perspectives on Growth and Inequality," *Cities* 24, 1 (2007), pp. 1–15.

"The City and the Bottom Line: Urban Megaprojects and the Privatization of Planning in Southeast Asia," *Environment and Planning A* 40, 2 (2008), pp. 383–401.

"Planning Privatopolis: Representation and Contestation in the Development of Urban Integrated Mega-Projects," in Ananya Roy and Aihwa Ong (eds.), *Worlding Cities: Asian Experiments and the Art of Being Global* (Malden, MA: Blackwell, 2011), pp. 77–97.

"Coping with Actually Existing Urbanisms: The Real Politics of Planning in the Global Era," *Planning Theory* 10, 1 (2011), pp. 79–87.

Shatkin, Gavin, and Sanjeev Vidyarthi, "Introduction: Contesting the Indian City: Global Visions and the Politics of the Local," in Gavin Shatkin (ed.), *Contesting the Indian City: Global Visions and the Politics of the Local* (Malden, MA: Wiley-Blackwell, 2014), pp. 1–38.

Shaw, Annapurna, "Planning and Local Economies in Navi Mumbai: Processes of Growth and Governance," *Urban Geography* 24, 1 (2003), pp. 2–15.

The Making of Navi Mumbai (Hyderabat: Orient Longman Private Limited, 2004).

Shenhav, Yehouda, and Yael Berda, "Juxtaposing the Israeli Occupation of the Palestinian Territories with Colonial Bureaucratic History," in Adi Ophir, Michal Givoni,
   and Sari Hanafi (eds.), *The Power of Inclusive Exclusion: Anatomy of Israeli Rule
   in the Occupied Palestinian Territories* (Cambridge, MA: The MIT Press; and New
   York: Zone Books, 2009), pp. 337–374.
Shepard, Cassim, "Montage Urbanism: Essence, Fragment, Increment," *Public Culture*
   25, 2 (2013), pp. 223–232.
Sheikh, Hassan Ismae'l, "An Urbanity of Exile: Palestinian Refugee Camps," *A10: New
   European Architecture* 27 (2009), pp. 60–62.
Shepard, Mark, (ed.), *Sentient City: Ubiquitous Computing, Architecture, and the Future
   of Urban Space* (Cambridge, MA: The MIT Press, 2011).
Shin, Dong-Hee, "Ubiquitous City: Urban Technologies, Urban Infrastructure and
   Urban Informatics," *Journal of Information Science*, 35, 5 (2009), pp. 515–526.
Shin, Hyun Bang, "Unequal Cities of Spectacle and Mega-Events in China," *City* 16, 6
   (2012), pp. 728–744.
Shlay, Anne, and Gillian Rosen, "Making Place: The Shifting Green Line and the Devel-
   opment of 'Greater' Metropolitan Jerusalem," *City & Community* 9, 4 (2010),
   pp. 358–389.
   Jerusalem: The Spatial Politics of a Divided Metropolis (London: Polity Press, 2015).
Short, John Rennie, "Globalization, Cities and the Summer Olympics," *City* 12, 3
   (2008), pp. 321–340.
Short, James, *The Social Fabric of the Metropolis: Contributions of the Chicago School
   of Urban Sociology* (Chicago: University of Chicago Press, 1971).
Short, Michael, *Planning for Tall Buildings* (London: Routledge, 2012).
Shwayri, Sofia, "A Model Korean Ubiquitous Eco-City? The Politics of Making
   Songdo," *Journal of Urban Technology* 20,1 (2013), pp. 39–55.
Shwayrik, Sofia, "From Regional Node Backwater and Back to Uncertainty: Beirut,
   1943–2006," in Yasser Elsheshtawy (ed.), *The Evolving Arab City: Tradition,
   Modernity and Urban Development* (London: Routledge, 2008), pp. 69–98.
Sidaway, James, *Imagined Regional Communities: Integration and Sovereignty in the
   Global South* (London: Routledge 2002).
   "Sovereign Excesses? Portraying Postcolonial Sovereigntyscapes," *Political Geogra-
   phy* 22, 2 (2003), pp. 157–178.
   "On the Nature of the Beast: Re-charting Political Geographies of the European
   Union," *Geografiska Annaler, Series B* 88, 1 (2006), pp. 1–14.
   "Spaces of Postdevelopment," *Progress in Human Geography* 31, 3 (2007), pp. 345–
   361.
   "Enclave Space: A New Metageography of Development?" *Area* 39, 3 (2007),
   pp. 331–339.
   "'One Island, One Team, One Mission': Geopolitics, Sovereignty, 'Race' and Rendi-
   tion," *Geopolitics* 15, 4 (2010), pp. 667–683.
Sieverts, Thomas, *Cities without Cities: An Interpretation of the Zwischenstadt* (Lon-
   don: Spon Press, 2003).
   "The In-Between City as an Image of Society: From the Impossible Order towards
   a Possible Disorder in the Urban Landscape," in Douglas Young, Patricia Burke
   Wood, and Roger Keil (eds.), *In-Between Infrastructure: Urban Connectivity in a
   Time of Vulnerability* (Toronto: Praxis(e) Press, 2013), pp. 19–27.

Silver, Christopher, *Planning the Megacity: Jakarta in the Twentieth Century* (New York: Routledge, 2008).

Silver, Hilary, "Divided Cities in the Middle East," *City & Community* 9, 4 (2010), pp. 34–357.

Simon, David, "Colonial Cities, Postcolonial Africa and the World Economy: A Reinterpretation," *International Journal of Urban and Regional Research* 13, 1 (1989), pp. 68–91.

"Situating Slums," *City* 15, 6 (2011), pp. 674–685.

Simone, Abdoumaliq, "Straddling the Divides: Remaking Associational Life in the Informal African City," *International Journal of Urban and Regional Research* 25, 1 (2001), pp. 102–117.

"Resource of Intersection: Remaking Social Collaboration in Urban Africa," *Canadian Journal of African Studies* 37, 2–3 (2003), pp. 513–538.

For the City Yet to Come: Urban Life in Four African Cities (Durham, NC: Duke University Press, 2004).

"People as Infrastructure: Intersecting Fragments in Johannesburg," *Public Culture* 16, 3 (2005), pp. 407–429.

"Pirate Towns: Reworking Social and Symbolic Infrastructures in Johannesburg and Douala," *Urban Studies* 43, 2 (2006), pp. 357–370.

City Life from Jakarta to Dakar: Movements at the Crossroads (New York: Routledge, 2010).

Simpson, Tim, "Macao, Capital of the 21st Century?" *Environment and Planning D* 26 (2008), pp. 1053–1079.

"Materialist Pedagogy: The Function of Themed Environments in Post-Socialist Consumption in Macau," *Tourist Studies* 9, 1 (2009), pp. 60–80.

"Scintillant Cities: Glass Architecture, Finance Capital, and the Fictions of Macau's Enclave Urbanism," *Theory, Culture & Society* 30, 7–8 (2013), pp. 343–371.

"Macau Metropolis and Mental Life: Interior Urbanism and the Chinese Imaginary," *International Journal of Urban and Regional Research* 38, 3 (2014), pp. 823–842.

Sims, David, *Egypt's Desert Dreams: Development or Disaster?* (New York and Oxford: Oxford University Press, 2015).

Sims, David, and Janet Abu-Lughod, "A History of Modern Cairo: Three Cities in One," in David Sims (ed.), *Understanding Cairo: The Logic of a City out of Control* (Cairo: American University in Cairo, 2010), pp. 45–90.

Singerman, Diane, "Cairo Cosmopolitan: Citizenship, Urban Space, Publics, and Inequality," in Barbara Drieskens, Franck Mermier, and Heiko Wimmen (eds.), *Cities of the South: Citizenship and Exclusion in the 21st Century* (London: Al-Saqi Books, 2007), pp. 82–111.

"The Contested City," in Dianne Singerman (ed.), *Cairo Contested: Governance, Urban Space, and Global Modernity* (Cairo: American University in Cairo Press, 2009), pp. 3–38.

Singerman, Diane, and Paul Amar, "Contesting Myths, Critiquing Cosmopolitanism, and Creating the Cairo School of Urban Studies," in Diane Singerman and Paul Amar (eds.), *Cairo Cosmopolitan: Politics, Culture and Urban Space in the New Middle East* (Cairo: American University in Cairo Press, 2006), pp. 1–43.

Slaughter, Anne-Marie, "Disaggregated Sovereignty: Towards the Public Accountability of Global Government Networks," *Government and Opposition* 39, 2 (2004),
pp. 159–190.

Smith, Neil, "Disastrous Accumulation," *South Atlantic Quarterly* 106, 4 (2007),
pp. 769–787.

Smith, Neil, and Setha Low, "Introduction: The Imperative of Public Space," in Setha
Low and Neil Smith (eds.), *The Politics of Public Space* (New York: Routledge,
2006), pp. 1–16.

Smith, Richard, "Dubai in Extremis," *Theory, Culture & Society* 31, 7–8 (2014),
pp. 291–296.

Smith, Vanessa, and Ron Edmond, "Introduction," in Vanessa Smith and Ron
Edmond (eds.), *Islands in History and Representation* (London: Routledge, 2003),
pp. 1–18.

Sopher, David, *The Sea Nomads: A Study of the Maritime Boat People of Southeast Asia*
(Singapore: National Museum Press, 1977).

Sorkin, Michel, "Container Riff," in *Some Assembly Required* (Minneapolis: University
of Minnesota Press, 2001), pp. 185–190.

Soja, Edward, "Inside Exopolis: Scenes from Orange County," in Michael Sorkin (ed.),
Variations on a Theme Park: The New American City and the End of Public Space
(New York: Hill and Wang, 1992), pp. 94–122.

"Los Angeles: 1965–1992: From Crisis-led Restructuring to Restructuring-Generated
Crisis," in Allen Scott and Edward Soja (eds.), *The City: Los Angeles and Urban
Theory at the End of the Twentieth Century* (Berkeley: University of California
Press, 1996), pp. 426–446.

ThirdSpace: Journeys to Los Angeles and Other Real-and-Imagined Places (Oxford:
Basil Blackwell, 1996).

Postmetropolis: Critical Studies of Cities and Regions (Malden, MA: Blackwell Publishers, 2000).

"Borders Unbound: Globalization, Regionalism, and the Postmetropolitan Transition," in Henk van Houtum, Olivier Kramsch, and Wolfgang Zierhofer (eds.),
B/ordering Space (Burlington, VT: Ashgate, 2005), pp. 33–46.

"Regional Urbanization and the Future of Megacities," in Steef Bujijs, Wendy Tan,
and Devisari Tunas (eds.), *Megacities: Exploring a Sustainable Future* (Rotterdam:
010 Publishers, 2010), pp. 56–75.

"Regional Urbanization and the End of the Metropolis Era," in Gary Bridge and
Sophie Watson (eds.), *New Companion to the City* (Chichester, UK: Wiley-
Blackwell, 2011), pp. 679–689.

"Regional Urbanization and Third Wave Cities," *City* 17, 5 (2013), pp. 688–
694.

"Regional Urbanization and the End of the Metropollis Era," in Neil Brenner (ed.),
Implosions/Explosions: Towards a Study of Planetary Urbanization (Berlin: Jovis,
2013), pp. 276–287.

My Los Angeles: From Urban Restructuring to Regional Urbanization (Berkeley: University of California Press, 2014), p. 185–186.

Soja, Edward, and Miguel Kanai, "The Urbanization of the World," in Ricky Burdett
and Deyan Sudjic (eds.), *The Endless City: The Urban Age Project by the London
School of Economics and the Deutsche Bank's Alfred Herrhausen Society* (London:
Phaidon, 2007), pp. 54–69.

Sorkin, Michael, "Introduction," in Michael Sorkin (ed.), *Variations on a Theme Park: The New American City and the End of Public Space* (New York: Hill and Wang, 1992), pp. xi–xv.

Spruyt, Hendrik, *The Sovereign State and Its Competitors* (Princeton: Princeton University Press, 1994).

Staeheli, Lynn, "Political Geography: Where's Citizenship?" *Progress in Human Geography* 35, 3 (2011), pp. 393–400.

Stanek, Łukasz, "Biopolitics of Scale: Architecture, Urbanism, the Welfare State and After," in Jakob Nilsson and Sven-Olov Wallenstein (eds.), *Foucault, Biopolitics, and Governmentality* (Stockholm: Södertörn Philosophical Studies, 2013), pp. 105–122.

Star, Susan Leigh, "The Ethnography of Infrastructure," *American Behavioral Scientist* 43, 3 (1999), pp. 377–393.

Stavrides, Stavros, "Contested Urban Rhythms: from the Industrial City to the Post-Industrial Urban Archipelago," *The Sociological Review* 61 [Issue Supplement S1] (2013), pp. 34–50.

"Occupied Squares and the Urban 'State of Exception': In, Against and Beyond the City of Enclaves," in Estela Schindel and Pamela Colombo (eds.), *Spaces and Memories of Violence: Landscapes of Erasure, Disappearance and Exception* (New York: Palgrave Macmillan, 2014), pp. 231–243.

Steinberg, Philip, *The Social Construction of the Ocean* (Cambridge, UK: Cambridge University Press, 2001).

"Insularity, Sovereignty and Statehood: The Representation of Islands on Portolan Charts and the Construction of the Territorial State," *Geographiska Annaler* 87, 4 (2005), pp. 253–265.

"Sovereignty, Territory, and the Mapping of Mobility: A View from the Outside," *Annals of the Association of American Geographers* 99, 3 (2009), pp. 467–495.

"The Deepwater Horizon, the Mavi Marmara, and the Dynamic Zonation of Ocean Space," *Geographical Journal* 177, 1 (2011), pp. 12–16.

"Liquid Urbanity: Re-engineering the City in a Post-Terrestrial World," in Stanley Brunn (ed.), *Engineering the Earth: The Impacts of Mega-Engineering Projects* (Berlin: Springer 2011), pp. 2113–2122.

Steinberg, Philip, Elizabeth Nyman, and Mauro Caraccioli, "Atlas Swam: Freedom, Capital, and Floating Sovereignties in the Seasteading Vision," *Antipode* 44, 4 (2012), pp. 1532–1550.

Steiner, Christian, "From Heritage to Hyperreality? Tourism Destination Development in the Middle East between Petra and the Palm," *Journal of Tourism and Cultural Change* 8, 4 (2010), pp. 240–253.

Stern, Michael, and William Marsh, "Editors' Introduction. The Decentered City: Edge Cities and the Expanding Metropolis," *Landscape and Urban Planning* 36, 4 (1997), pp. 243–246.

Stiles, Kendall, "International Support for NGOs in Bangladesh: Some Unintended Consequences," *World Development* 30, 5 (2002), pp. 835–846.

Stoker, Gerry, "Governance as Theory: Five Propositions," *International Social Science Journal* 50, 155 (1998), pp. 17–28.

Stoker, Gerald, "Public–Private Partnerships in Urban Governance," in Jon Pierre (ed.), *Partnerships in Urban Governance: European and American Experience* (Basingstoke: Macmillan, 1998), pp. 34–51.

Stoler, Ann Laura, "On Degrees of Imperial Sovereignty," *Public Culture* 18, 1 (2006), pp. 125–146.

"Imperial Debris: On Ruins and Ruination," *Cultural Anthropology* 23, 2 (2008), pp. 191–219.

Storper, Michael, "Governing the Large Metropolis," *Territory, Politics, Governance* 2, 2 (2014), pp. 115–134.

Strain, Garrett, "Neighborhood and Nation in Neoliberal Times: Urban Upheaval, Resistance, and National Identity in Buenos Aires," *intersections* 12, 1 (2012), pp. 14–91.

Strange, William, Walid Hejazi, and Jianmin Tang, "The Uncertain City: Competitive Instability, Skills, Innovation and the Strategy of Agglomeration," *Journal of Urban Economics* 59, 3 (2006), pp. 331–351.

Strong, Michael, and Robert Himber, "The Legal Autonomy of the Dubai International Financial Centre: A Scalable Strategy for Global Free–Market Reforms," *Economic Affairs* 29, 2 (2009), pp. 36–41.

Sudjic, Deyan, *The 100-Mile City* (San Diego: Harcourt Brace & Company, 1993).

The Edifice Complex: How the Rich and Powerful Shape the World (New York: Penguin, 2005).

Sum, N. L., "Theorizing the Development of East Asian Newly Industrializing Countries: A Regulationist Perspective," in Bob Jessop (ed.), *Regulation Theory and the Crisis of Capitalism* (Cheltenham: Edward Elgar, 2001), pp. 354–390.

Summerton, Jane, "Introductory Essay: The Systems Approach to Technological Change," in Jane Summerton (ed.), *Changing Large Technical Systems* (Boulder, CO: Westview Press, 1994), pp. 1–21.

Swanson, Kate, "Revanchist Urbanism Heads South: The Regulation of Indigenous Beggars and Street Vendors in Ecuador," *Antipode* 39, 4 (2007), pp. 708–728.

Swyngedouw, Erik, "Governance Innovation and the Citizen: The Janus Face of Governance-beyond-the-State," *Urban Studies* 42, 11 (2005), pp. 1991–2006.

"Exit 'Post' – The Making of 'Glocal' Urban Modernities," in Stephen Read, Jürgen Rosemann, and Job van Eldijk (eds.), *Future City* (London and New York: Spon Press, 2005), pp. 125–144.

"City or Polis? Profitable Politics … or the End of the Political," in Steef Buijs, Wendy Tan, and Devisari Tunis (eds.), *Megacities: Exploring a Sustainable Future* (Rotterdam: 010 Publishers, 2010), pp. 214–234.

Swyngedouw, Erik, Frank Moulaert, and Arantxa Rodriguez, "Neoliberal Urbanization in Europe: Large-Scale Urban Development Projects and the New Urban Policy," *Antipode* 34, 3 (2002), pp. 542–577.

Tabb, William, "The Wider Context of Austerity Urbanism," *City* 18, 2 (2014), pp. 87–100.

Tadiar, Neferti, "Manila's New Metropolitan Form," *differences: A Journal of Feminist Cultural Studies* 5, 3 (1993), pp. 154–178.

Tait, Malcom, and Ole Jensen, "Travelling Ideas, Power, and Place: The Cases of Urban Villages and Business Improvement Districts," *International Planning Studies* 12, 2 (2007), pp. 107–127.

Tajbakhsh, Kian, *The Promise of the City: Space, Identity, and Politics in Contemporary Social Thought* (Berkeley: University of California Press, 2001).

Tanulku, Basak, "Gated Communities: From 'Self-Sufficient Towns' to 'Active Urban Agents," *Geoforum* 43, 3 (2012), pp. 518–528.

Taşan-Kok, Tuna, "Entrepreneurial Governance: Challenges of Large-Scale Property-led Urban Regeneration Projects," *Tijdshrift voor Economishe en Sociale Geografie* 101, 2 (2010), pp. 126–149.

Taşan-Kok, Tuna, and Guy Baeten (eds.), *Contradictions of Neoliberal Planning: Cities, Policies, and Politics* (New York: Springer, 2012).

Tarbush, Nada, "Cairo 2050: Urban Dream or Modernist Delusion?" *Journal of International Afffairs* 65, 2 (2012), pp. 171–186.

Taylor, Laura, "No Boundaries: Exurbia and the Study of Contemporary Urban Dispersion," *GeoJournal* 76, 4 (2011), pp. 323–339.

Taylor, Nigel, "Anglo-American Town Planning Theory since 1945: Three Significant Developments but no Paradigm Shifts," *Planning Perspectives* 14, 4 (1999), pp. 327–345.

Tedong, Peter Aning, Jill Grant, and Wan Nor Azriyati Wan Abd Aziz, "The Social and Spatial Implications of Community Action to Enclose Space: Guarded Neighbourhoods in Selangor, Malaysia," *Cities* 41 (Part A) (2014), pp. 30–37.

Tekeli, Îlhan, "Bridging Histories," in Ricky Burdett and Deyan Sudjic (eds.), *Living in the Endless City: The Urban Age Project by the London School of Economics and Deutsche Bank's Alfrde Herrhausen Society* (London: Phaidon Press, 2011), pp. 210–217.

"Governing Enclosure: The Role of Governance in Producing Gated Communities and Guarded Neighborhoods in Malaysia," *International Journal of Urban and Regional Research* 39, 1 (2015), pp. 112–128.

Tewdwr-Jones, Mark, and Donald McNeill, "The Politics of City-Region Planning and Governance: Reconciling the National, Regional and Urban in the Competing Voices of Institutional Restructuring," *European Urban and Regional Studies* 7, 2 (2000), pp. 119–134.

Till, Karen, "Neotraditional Towns and Urban Villages: The Cultural Production of a Geography of 'Otherness'," *Environment and Planning D* 11, 6 (1993), pp. 709–732.

Thompson, Carolyn, "Master-Planned Estates: Privatization, Socio-Spatial Polarization and Community," *Geography Compass* 7, 1 (2013), pp. 85–93.

Thuillier, Guy, "Gated Communities in the Metropolitan Area of Buenos Aires, Argentina: A Challenge for Town Planning," *Housing Studies* 20, 2 (2005), pp. 255–271.

Tochterman, Brian, "Theorizing Neoliberal Urban Development: A Genealogy from Richard Florida to Jane Jacobs," *Radical History Review* 112 (2012), pp. 65–87.

Tokunaga, Masahiro, "Enterprise Restructuring in the Context of Urban Transition: Analysis of Company Towns in Russia," *The Journal of Comparative Economic Studies* 1 (2005), pp. 79–102.

Tolosa, Hamilton, "The Rio/São Paulo Extended Metropolitan Region: A Quest for Global Integration," *The Annals of Regional Science* 37, 2 (2003), pp. 479–500.

Tonkiss, Fran, "Austerity Urbanism and the Makeshift City," *City* 17, 3 (2013), pp. 312–324.

Trudeau, Dan, "Towards a Relational View of the Shadow State," *Political Geography* 27, 6 (2008), pp. 669–690.

"Junior Partner or Empowered Community? The Role of Nonprofit Social Service Providers amidst State Restructuring," *Urban Studies* 45, 13 (2008), pp. 2805–2827.

"Constructing Citizenship in the Shadow State," *Geoforum* 43, 3 (2012), pp. 442–452.

Trudeau, Dan, and Luisa Veronis, "Enacting State Restructuring: NGOs as Translation Mechanisms," *Environment and Planning D* 27, 6 (2006), pp. 117–134.

Toledo Silva, Ricardo, "The Connectivity of Infrastructure Networks and the Urban Space of São Paulo in the 1990s," *International Journal of Urban and Regional Research* 24, 1 (2000), pp. 139–164.

Ó Tualthail, Gearóid (Gerald Toal), "Borderless Worlds? Problematising Discourses of Deterritorialization," in Nurit Kliot and David Newman (eds.), *Geopolitics at the End of the Twentieth Century: The Changing World Political Map* (London: Frank Cass, 2000), pp. 139–154.

Tugal, Cihan, "The Greening of Istanbul," *New Left Review* 51 (2008), pp. 65–80.

Türkün, Asuman, "Urban Regeneration and Hegemonic Power Relationships," *International Planning Studies* 16, 1 (2011), pp. 61–72.

Türeli, Ipek, "Modeling Citizenship in Turkey's Miniature Park," *Traditional Dwellings and Settlements Review* 17, 2 (2006), pp. 55–69.

Turok, Ivan, and Nick Bailey, "The Theory of Polycentric Urban Regions and its Application to Central Scotland," *European Planning Studies* 12, 3 (2004), pp. 371–389.

Turner, Alan, "Urban Planning in the Developing World: Lessons from Experience," *Habitat International* 16, 2 (1992), pp. 113–126.

Turner, Brian, "The Erosion of Citizenship," *British Journal of Sociology* 52, 2 (2001), pp. 189–209.

UN-Habitat, *Slums of the World* (Nairobi: United Nations Human Settlements Programme, 2003).

UN-Habitat, *State of the World's Cities 2010/2011: Bridging the Urban Divide* (Nairobi: United Nations Human Settlements Programme, 2008).

Üngör, Uğur Ümit, "Creative Destruction: Shaping a High-Modernist City in Interwar Turkey," *Journal of Urban History* 39, 2 (2012), pp. 297–314.

Ünsal, Özlem, and Tuna Kuyucu, "Challenging the Neoliberal Urban Regime: Regeneration and Resistance in Başıbüyük and Tarlabaşı," in Deniz Göktürk, Levent Soysal, and Ipek Türeli (eds.), *Orienting Istanbul: Cultural Capital of Europe?* (New York: Routledge, 2010), pp. 51–70.

Urry, John, *Offshoring* (Malden, Massachusetts: Polity Press, 2014).

Uzun, C. Nil, "The Impact of Urban Renewal and Gentrification on Urban Fabric: Three Cases in Turkey," *Tijdschrift voor economische en sociale geografie* 94, 3 (2003), pp. 363–375.

Valverde, Mariana, "Laws of the Street," *City & Society* 21, 2 (2009), pp. 163–181.

"Seeing like a City: The Dialectic of Modern and Premodern Ways of Seeing in Urban Governance," *Law & Society Review* 45, 2 (2011), pp. 277–312.

Van Houtum, Henk, and Ton Van Naerssen, "Bordering, Ordering and Othering," *Tijdschrift voor economische en sociale geografie* [TESG] 93, 2 (2002), pp. 125–136.

Van Houtum, Henk, Olivier Kramsch, and Wolfgang Zierhofer, "Prologue: B/ordering Space," in Henk van Houtum, Olivier Kramsch, and Wolfgang Zierhofer (eds.), *B/ordering Space* (Burlington, VT: Ashgate, 2005), pp. 1–13.

Vanolo, Alberto, "Alternative Capitalism and Creative Economy: The Case of Christiania," *International Journal of Urban and Regional Research* 37, 5 (2013), pp. 1785–1798.

Varna, George, and Steve Tiesdall, "Assessing the Publicness of Public Space: The Star Model of Publicness," *Journal of Urban Design* 15, 4 (2010), pp. 575–598.

Vasudevan, Alex, Colin McFarlane, and Alex Jeffrey, "Spaces of Enclosure," *Geoforum* 39, 5 (2008), pp. 1641–1646.

Veltz, Pierre, "European Cities in the World Economy," in Arnaldo Bagnasco and Patrick Le Galès (eds.), *Cities in Contemporary Europe* (Cambridge, UK: Cambridge University Press, 2000), pp. 33–47.

Vidler, Anthony, *The Architectural Uncanny: Essays in the Modern Unhomely* (Cambridge, MA: The MIT Press, 1992).

Viganò, Paola, The Contemporary European Urban Project: Archipelago City, Diffuse City and Reverse City," in C. Greig Crysler, Stephen Cairns, and Hilde Heynen (eds.), *The SAGE Handbook of Architectural Theory* (London: Sage, 2012), pp. 657–670.

Vinokurow, Evgeny, *A Theory of Enclaves* (Lanham, MD: Lexington Books 2007).

Virilio, Paul, *Speed and Politics* [Translated by Marc Polizzotti] (Los Angeles: Semiotext[e], 1977).

  Bunker Archeology (New York: Princeton Architectural Press, 1994).

Vlcek, William, "Behind an Offshore Mask: Sovereignty Games in the Global Political Economy," *Third World Quarterly* 30, 8 (2009), pp. 1465–1481.

  "Taking *Other* People's Money: Development and the Political Economy of Asian Casinos," *The Pacific Review* 28, 3 (2015), pp. 323–345.

Von Schnitzler, Antina, "Citizenship Prepaid: Water, Calculability, and Techno-Politics in South Africa," *Journal of Southern African Studies* 34, 4 (2008), pp. 899–917.

Voronkova, Lilia, and Oleg Pachenkov, "OPEN/CLOSED: Pubic Spaces in Modern Cities," *Berkeley Planning Journal* 24, 1 (2011), pp. 197–207.

Wachsmuth, David, "City as Ideology: Reconciling the Explosion of the City Form with the Tenacity of the City Concept," *Environment and Planning D* 32, 1 (2014), pp. 75–90.

Wainwright, Oliver, "Is Beirut's Glitzy Downtown Redevelopment all that it Seems?" *Guardian [UK]*, January 22, 2015.

Walker, David, "Resisting the Neoliberalization of Space in Mexico City," in Tony Samara, Shenjing He, and Guo Chen (eds.), *Locating the Right to the City in the Global South* (New York: Routledge, 2013), pp. 171–194.

Walker, Richard, "Building a Better Theory of the Urban: A Response to 'Towards a New Epistemology of the Urban'?" *City* 19, 5 (2015), pp. 183–191.

Wall, Alex, "Programming the Urban Surface," in James Corner (ed.), *Recovering Landscape* (New York: Princeton Architectural Press, 1999), pp. 233–249.

Walzer, Michael, "Pleasures and the Cost of Urbanity," *Dissent* 33, 4 (1986), pp. 470–475.

Wang, Ya Ping, Yanglin Wang, and Jiansheng Wu, "Urbanization and Informal Development in China: Urban Villages in Shenzhen," *International Journal of Urban and Regional Research* 33, 4 (2009), pp. 957–973.

Wang, James, and Daniel Olivier, "Port-FEZ Bundles as Spaces of Global Articulation: The Case of Tianjin, China," *Environment and Planning A* 38, 8 (2006), pp. 1487–1503.

Ward, Kevin, "Entrepreneurial Urbanism, State Restructuring and Civilizing 'New' East Manchester," *Area* 35, 2 (2003), pp. 116–127.

"'Politics in Motion,' Urban Management and State Restructuring: The Trans-Local Expansion of Business Improvement Districts," *International Journal of Urban and Regional Research* 30, 1 (2006), pp. 54–75.

"Business Improvement Districts: Policy Origins, Mobile Policies, and Urban Liveability," *Geography Compass* 1, 3 (2007), pp. 657–672.

Ward, Stephen, "Transnational Planners in a Postcolonial World," in Patsy Healey and Robert Upton (eds.), *Crossing Borders: International Exchange and Planning Practices* (London: Routledge, 2010), pp. 46–72.

Wari, Shahd, "Jerusalem: One Planning System, Two Urban Realities," *City* 15, 3–4 (2011), pp. 457–472.

Warner, Sam Bass, *The Private City: Philadelphia in Three Periods of Its Growth* (Philadelphia: University of Pennsylvania Press, 1987).

Watson, Sophie, *City Publics* (London: Routledge, 2006).

Watson, Vanessa, "The Usefulness of Normative Planning Theories in the Context of Sub-Saharan Africa," *Planning Theory* 1, 1 (2002), pp. 27–52.

"African Urban Fantasies: Dreams or Nightmares?" *Environment and Urbanization* 26, 1 (2014), pp. 215–231.

Weaver, Adam, "Spaces of Containment and Revenue Capture: 'Super-Sized' Cruise Ships as Mobile Tourism Enclaves," *Tourism Geographies: An International Journal of Tourism Space, Place and Environment* 7, 2 (2005), pp. 165–184.

"The McDonaldization Thesis and Cruise Tourism," *Annals of Tourism Research* 32, 2 (2005), pp. 346–366.

Webb, Alex, "Oil Rocks," in Neeraj Bhatia and Mary Casper (eds.), *The Petropolis of Tomorrow* (New York: Actar, 2013), pp. 192–223.

Webb, Martin, "Meeting at the Edges: Spaces, Places and Grassroots Governance Activism in Delhi," *South Asia Multidisciplinary Academic Journal* 8 (2013), pp. 1–14.

Webber, Melvin, "The Urban Place and the Nonplace Urban Realm," in *Explorations into Urban Structure* (Philadelphia: University of Pennsylvania Press, 1964), pp. 79–153.

Weber, Rachel, "Extracting Value from the City: Neoliberalism and Urban Redevelopment," *Antipode* 34, 3 (2002), pp. 519–540.

Webster, Chris, Georg Glasze, and Frantz Klaus, "Guest Editorial: The Global Spread of Gated Communities," *Environment and Planning B* 29, 3 (2002), pp. 315–320.

Webster, Chris, Fulong Wu, and Tanjing Zhao, "China's Modern Gated Cities," in Georg Glasze, Chris Webster, and Klaus Frantz (eds.), *Private Cities: Local and Global Perspectives* (London and New York: Routledge, 2005), pp. 153–169.

Weinstein, Lisa, Neha Sami, and Gavin Shatkin, "Contested Developments: Enduring Legacies and Emergent Political Actors in Contemporary Urban India," in Gavin Shatkin (ed.), *Contesting the Indian City: Global Visions and the Politics of the Local* (Malden, MA: Wiley-Blackwell, 2014), pp. 38–64.

Weinstein, Lisa, *The Durable Slum: Dharavi and the Right to Stay Put in Globalizing Mumbai* (Minneapolis: University of Minnesota Press, 2014).

Weinstein, Richard, "The First American City," in Allen Scott and Edward Soja (eds.), *The City: Los Angeles and Urban Theory at the End of the Twentieth Century* (Berkeley and Los Angeles: University of California Press, 1996), pp. 22–46.

Weinstock, Michael, with Mehran Gharleghi, "Intelligent Cities and the Taxonomy of Cognitive Scales," *Architectural Design* 83, 4 (3013), pp. 56–65.

Weintraub, Jeff, "The Theory and Politics of the Public/Private Distinction," in Jeff Weintraub and Krishan Kumar (eds.), *Public and Private in Thought and Practice: Perspectives on a Grand Dichotomy* (Chicago: University of Chicago Press, 1997), pp. 1–40.

Weiss, Lindsay, "Exceptional Space: Concentration Camps and Labor Compounds in Late 19th-Century Southern Africa," in Adrian Myers and Gabriel Moshenka (eds.), *Archaeologies of Internment* (New York: Springer, 2010), pp. 21–32.

Weizman, Eyal, "The Politics of Verticality," in Malkit Shoshan (ed.), *Territoria: Illustrations of the Israeli-Palestinian Conflict* [First Edition, Volume 1] (Haifa: Association of Forty, 2002), pp. 43–68.

"Strategic Points, Flexible Lines, Tense Surfaces, Political Volumes: Ariel Sharon and the Geometry of Occupation," *The Philosophical Forum* 35, 2 (2004), pp. 221–244.

Hollow Land: Israel's Architecture of Occupation (London: Verso, 2007).

"Principles of Frontier Geography," in Philipp Misselwitz and Tim Rieniets (eds.), *City of Collision: Jerusalem and the Principles of Conflict Urbanism* (Basel: Birkhäuser Publisher for Architecture, 2006), pp. 84–92.

Weizman, Eyal, Rafi Segal, and David Tartakover (eds.), *A Civilian Occupation: The Politics of Israeli Architecture* (London: Verso, 2003).

Welker, Marina, "'Corporate Security Begins in the Community': Mining, the Corporate Social Responsibility Industry, and Environmental Advocacy in Indonesia," *Cultural Anthropology* 24, 1 (2009), pp. 142–179.

Wettenhall, Roger, "The Rhetoric and Reality of Public–Private Partnerships," *Public Organization Review* 3, 1 (2003), pp. 77–107.

Wilkinson, Paul, "Caribbean Cruise Tourism: Delusion? Illusion?," *Tourism Geographies: An International Journal of Tourism Space, Place and Environment* 1, 3 (1999), pp. 261–282.

Williams, Stewart, "The Temporary City," *Australian Planner* 50, 3 (2013), pp. 278–279.

Willis, Carol, *Form Follows Finance: Skyscrapers and Skylines in New York and Chicago* (New York: Princeton Architectural Press, 1995).

Wilson, David, "Spaces of Neoliberalism: Urban Restructuring in North America and Western Europe," *Annals of the Association of American Geographers* 94, 3 (2004), pp. 676–678.

Wilson, Elizabeth, "The Rhetoric of Urban Space," *New Left Review* 1, 209 (1995), pp. 146–160.

Winters, Jeffrey, *Power in Motion: Capital Mobility and the Indonesian State* (Ithaca, NY: Cornell University Press, 1996).

Wissink, Bart, "Enclave Urbanism in Mumbai: An Actor-Network-Theory Analysis of Urban (Dis) Connection," *Geoforum* 47 (2013), pp. 1–11.

Wong, Kai Wen, and Tim Bunnell, "'New Economy' Discourse and Spaces in Singapore: A Case Study of 'one-north'," *Environment and Planning A* 38, 1 (2006), pp. 69–83.

Wood, Andrew, "Managing the Lady Managers: The Shaping of Heterotopian Spaces in the 1893 Chicago Exposition's Woman's Building," *Southern Communication Journal* 69, 4 (2004), pp. 289–302.

Wood, Robert, "Caribbean Cruise Tourism: Globalization at Sea," *Annals of Tourism Research* 27, 2 (2000), 345–370.

Woodward, Rachel, "Military Landscapes: Agendas and Approaches for Future Research," *Progress in Human Geography* 38, 1 (2014), pp. 40–61.

Wu, Fulong, "Transplanting Cityscapes: The Use of Imagined Globalization in Housing Commodification in Beijing," *Area* 36, 3 (2004), pp. 227–234.

"Rediscovering the 'Gate' under Market Transition: From Work-Unit Compounds to Commodity Housing Enclaves," *Housing Studies* 20, 2 (2005), pp. 235–254.

Wu, Fulong, and Klaire Webber, "The Rise of Foreign Gated Communities in Beijing: Between Economic Globalization and Local Institutions," *Cities* 21, 3 (2004), pp. 203–213.

Xaveer de Geyter Architects, *After-Sprawl: Research for the Contemporary City* (Rotterdam: NAi Publishers, 2002).

Yacobi, Haim, "The NGOization of Space: Dilemmas of Social Change, Planning Policy, and the Israeli Public Sphere," *Environment and Planning D* 25, 4 (2007), pp. 745–758.

"God, Globalization, and Geopolitics: on West Jerusalem's Gated Communities," *Environment and Planning A* 44 (2012), pp. 2705–2720.

Ye, Lin, "State-led Metropolitan Governance in China: Making Integrated City Regions," *Cities* 41 (Part B) (2014), pp. 200–208.

Yeoh, Brenda, and Tou Chuang Chang, "Globalising Singapore: Debating Transnational Flows in the City," *Urban Studies* 38, 7 (2001), pp. 1025–1044.

Yessenova, Saulesh, "The Tengiz Oil Enclave: Labor, Business, and the State," *PoLAR: Political and Legal Anthropology Review* 35, 1 (2012), pp. 94–114.

Yeung, H. W., "Capital, State, and Place: Contesting the Borderless Word," *Transactions of the Association of British Geographers NS* 23, 3 (1998), pp. 291–309.

Yiftachel, Oren, "Planning and Social Control: Exploring the Dark Side," *Journal of Planning Literature* 12, 4 (1998), pp. 395–406.

Ethnocracy: Land and Identity in Israel/Palestine (Philadelphia: University of Pennsylvania Press, 2006).

"Critical Theory and 'Gray Space': Mobilization of the Colonized," *City* 13, 2 (2009), pp. 246–263.

Yiftachel, Oren, and Haim Yakobi, "Planning a Binational Capital: Should Jerusalem Remain United?" *Geoforum* 33, 1 (2002), pp. 137–145.

"Barriers, Walls, and Diacritics: The Shaping of 'Creeping Apartheid' in Israel/Palestine," in Michael Sorkin (ed.), *Against the Wall: Israel's Barrier to Peace* (New York: The New Press, 2005), pp. 138–157.

Yigitcanlar, Tan, and Melih Bulu, "Dubaization of Istanbul: Insights from the Knowledge-based Urban Development Journey of an Emerging Local Economy," *Environment and Planning A* 47, 1 (2015), pp. 89–107.

Yonucu, Deniz, "A Story of a Squatter Neighborhood: From the Place of the 'Dangerous Classes' to the 'Place of Danger'," *The Berkeley Journal of Sociology* 52 (2009), pp. 50–72.

Yu, Xiaojiang, "Growth and Degradation in the Orient's 'Las Vegas': Issues of Environment in Macau," *International Journal of Environmental Studies* 65, 5 (2008), pp. 667–683.

Yunianto, Tunggul, "On the Verge of Displacement: Listening to Kampong Dwellers in the Emotional Economy of Contemporary Jakarta," *Thesis Eleven* 121, 1 (2014), pp. 101–121.

Zacharias, John, and Yuanzhou Tang, "Restructuring and Repositioning Shenzhen, China's New Mega City," *Progress in Planning* 73, 4 (2010), pp. 209–249.

Zacher, Mark, "The Decaying Pillars of the Westphalian Temple: Implications for International Order and Governance," in James Rosenau and Ernest-Otto Czempiel, (eds.), *Governance without Government: Order and Change in World Politics* (Cambridge, UK: Cambridge University Press, 1992), pp. 58–101.

Zalik, Anna, "Zones of Exclusion: Offshore Extraction, the Contestation of Space and Physical Displacement in the Nigerian Delta and the Mexican Gulf," *Antipode* 41, 3 (2009), pp. 557–582.

Zayim, Ayca, "Differentiated Urban Citizenship and Housing Rights: Analysing the Social Impacts of Urban Redevelopment in Globalizing Istanbul," *International Planning Studies* 19, 3–4 (2014), pp. 268–291.

Zeiderman, Austin, Sobia Ahmad Kaker, Jonathan Silver, and Astrid Wood, "Uncertainty and Urban Life," *Public Culture* 27, 2 (2015), pp. 281–304.

Zérah, Marie-Hélène, "Splintering Urbanism in Mumbai: Contrasting Trends in a Multilayered Society," *Geoforum* 39, 6 (2008), pp. 1922–1932.

Zhang, Jun, "From Hong Kong's Capitalist Fundamentals to Singapore's Authoritarian Governance: The Policy Mobility of Neoliberalising Shenzhen, China," *Urban Studies* 49, 13 (2012), pp. 2853–2871.

Zukin, Sharon, *Landscapes of Power: From Detroit to Disney World* (Berkeley and Los Angeles: University of California Press, 1991).

"The City as a Landscape of Power: London and New York as Global Financial Capitals," in Lester Budd and Sam Whimster (eds.), *Global Finance and Urban Living: A Study of Metropolitan Change* (New York: Routledge, 1992), pp. 195–223.

Zureik, Elia, David Lyon, and Yassem Abu-Laban, *Surveillance and Control in Israel/Palestine: Population, Territory and Power* (London: Routledge, 2010).

Internet Sources

Abourahme, Nasser, "Contours of the Neoliberal City: Fragmentation, Frontier Geographies, and the New Circularity," *Occupied London*, No. 4 (2009) [n.p.]. Available at www.occupiedLondon.org/contours.

Borsdorf, Axel, and Rodrigo Hidalgo, "The Fragmented City: Changing Patterns in Latin American Cities," The Urban Reinventors Paper Series. *The Urban Reinventors Online Journal*, Issue 3/09, pp. 1–18. Available at www.urbanreinventors.net.

Easterling, Keller, "Enduring Innocence" (Presentation at the Symposium "Archipelago of Exceptions. Sovereignties of Extraterritoriality," Centre du Cultura Contemporània de Barcelona (CCCB), November 10, 2005. Available at www.publicspace.org/en/text-library/eng/b019-enduring-innocence.

"Zone: The Spatial Softwares of Extrastatecraft," *Places: Forum of Design for the Public Realm*, June 11, 2012]. Available at http://places.designobserver.com/feature/zone-the-spatial-softwares-of-extrastatecraft/34528/html.

Ghandour, Marwan, and Mona Fawaz, "Spatial Erasure: Reconstruction Projects in Beirut," *ArteEast Quarterly* (Spring, 2010). Available at www.arteeast.org.

Honsa, Jesse, "Istanbul's Fading Metabolism," *Failed Urbanism*, October 17, 2014. Available at www.failedarchitecture.com/istanbuls-fading-metabolism.

Judt, Tony, "What Is Living and What Is Dead in Social Democracy," *New York Review of Books*, December 17, 2009. Available at www.nybooks.com/articles/archives/2009/dec/17.

Katsikis, Nikos, "On the Geographical Organization of World Urbanization," *MONU #20: Geographical Urbanism*, April 2014. Available at www.terraurbis.com.

Morrow, Greg, "The Privatization of Cities," *Critical Planning* 13 (2006), n.p. (*Journal of the UCLA Department of Urban Planning*). Available at https://criticalplanning .squarespace.com/volume-13.

Pieterse, Edgar, "Cityness and African Urban Development" (Working Paper No. 42 [2010], *World Institute for Development Economics Research*), quotation from p. 2. Available at http://hdl.handle.net/10419/54110.

Rao, Anupama, and Paul Rabé, "Workshop Report: 'Public City, Private City', Institute for Public Knowledge, New York University, August 27–28, 2014. Available at www.rethinking.asia/report/public-city-private-city.

Srivastava, Rahul, and Matias Eshanove, "Why Mumbai's Slums Are Villages," *Airoots* (November 26, 2006). Available at www.airoots.org/why-mumbai%E2 %80%99s-slums-are-villages.

Weizman, Eyal, "Introduction to the Politics of Verticality," *Open Democracy* (2002). Available at www.opendemocracy.net/ecology-politicsverticality/article_801.jsp.

"On Extraterritoriality," Lecture at the Symposium "*Archipelago of Exception. Sovereignties of Extraterritoriality*" (November 10–11, 2005). Available at www .publicspace.org/en/text-library/eng/b011-on-extraterritoriality.

Periodicals

Adarkar, Neera, "Gendering the Culture of Building," *Economic & Political Weekly* 38 [Number 43], (October 25–31, 2003), pp. 4527–4534.

Anonymous, "Urban Dreamscapes: Starting from Scratch," *Economist*, September 7, 2013.

Elshadhed, Mohamend, "From Tahrir Square to Emaar Square: Caoro's Private Road to a Private City," The Guardian, April 7, 2014.

Freshton, Tom, "'You are now Leaving the European Union'," *Vanity Fair*, September 12, 2013.

Khanna, Parag, "Beyond City Limits," *Foreign Policy* (August 16, 2010), pp. 120–123 and 126–128.

Kohn, Margaret, "The Mauling of Public Space," *Dissent* (Spring, 2001), pp. 71–77.

Krier, Léon [interviewed by Nikos Salingaros], "The Future of Cities: The Absurdity of Modernism," *Planetizen* (November 5, 2001).

Lee, Mark, "Two Deserted Islands," *San Rocco Magazine* (2014), pp. 4–10.

Lemann, Nicholaus, "Get Out of Town," *The New Yorker* (June 27, 2011), pp. 76–80.

Ramachandraiah, C., "Maytas, Hyderabad Metro and the Politics of Real Estate," *Economic and Political Weekly* 44, 3 (January 17–23, 2009), pp. 36–40.

Sundaram, Ravi, "Uncanny Networks: Pirate, Urban and New Globalization," *Economic and Political Weekly* 34 (3 January 2004), pp. 6–41.

Pirate Modernity: Delhi' Media Urbanism (New York: Routledge, 2010).

White, Jon, "Floating Cities could redefine Human Existence," *New Scientist* 215, 2883 (September 22, 2012), pp. 26–27.

Working Papers

Athalye, Shubhangi, "Rebuilding Mumbai – Dreams and Reality," *Ethnographic Praxis in Industry Conference Proceedings* 1 (2012), pp. 350–353.

Bender, Thomas, "History, Theory & the Metropolis" (*CMS Working Paper Series*, No. 005–2206. Center for Metropolitan Studies: Technical University Berlin D-10587, 2006), [15 pp.].

Brenner, Neil, and Christian Schmid, "Combat, Caricature and Critique in the Study of Planetary Urbanization," Urban Theory Lab, Graduate School of Design, Harvard University (April 2015), pp. 1–11.

Christiaanse, Kees, Mark Michaeli, and Tim Rieniets, "Istanbul's Spatial Dynamics," *Urban Age* (Cities Programme, London School of Economics, 2009), pp. 1–2.

Friedman, Patri, and Brad Taylor, "Seasteading: Institutional Innovation on the Open Ocean" (Paper presented at the Australasian Public Choice Society Conference, December 9–10, 2010, Seasteading Institute, University of Canterbury, Christchurch, New Zealand),.

Glaeser, Edward, and Joshua Gottlieb, "The Wealth of Cities: Agglomeration Economies and Spatial Equilibrium in the United States," National Bureau Economic Research Working Paper, No. 14806 (March 2009).

Gunday, Zeynep, "Renewal Agenda in Istanbul: Urbanisation vs. Urbicide" (49th ISO-CARP Congress, 2013, Brisbane, Australia).

Hanafi, Sari, "Palestinian Refugee Camps in Lebanon as a Space of Exception," *REVUE Asylon(s) N°5* (2008), [n.p.].

Hönke, Jana, "Transnational Pockets of Territoriality: Governing the Security of Extraction in Katanga (DRC)" (Working Paper Series of the Graduate Centre Humanities and Social Sciences of the Research Academy Leipzig, Leipzig, 2009).

Khayat, Nadine, *Case Studies: The Elyssar Reconstruction Project; The Ministry of the Displaced; The Economic and Social Fund for Development, Lebanon 2007* (Beirut: Lebanese Center for Policy Studies (LCPS); and London: Tiri, 2007).

McCallam, Jamie, "Export Processing Zones: Comparative Data from China, Honduras, Nicaragua, and South Africa" [Working paper No. 21] (Geneva: International Labour Office, 2011).

Miller, Michelle Ann, and Tim Bunnell, "Post-Disaster Urban Renewal: Memories of Trauma and Transformation in an Indonesian City," *Asia Research Institute Working Papers Series*, No. 154 (National University of Singapore, 2011).

Murray, Martin J., "The Evolving Spatial Form of Cities in a Globalizing World Economy: Johannesburg and Sao Paulo" (Democracy and Governance Programme, Occasional Paper #5. Human Sciences Research Council, Cape Town, 2005).

Randall, Edward, "Reconstruction and Fragmentation in Beirut" (Conflict in Cities and the Contested State: Everyday Life and the Possibilities for Transformation in Belfast, Jerusalem and Other Divided Cities. *Divided Cities/Contested States*), Working Paper No. 29 (2014).

Segel, Arthur, "New Songdo City," *Harvard Business School Occasional Paper 9-206–019* (2006).

Zhu, Jieming, "Symmetric Development of Informal Settlements and Gated Communities: Capacity of the State: The Case of Jakarta, Indonesia," (Asia Research institute, National University of Singapore, Working Paper Series No. 135, February 2010).

Weizman, Eyal, Anselm Franke, and Thomas Keenan, *Archipelago of Exception – Sovereignties of Extraterritoriality* (Barcelona: Centro de Cultura Contemporánea (CCCB) (November, 2005).

World Bank Group, "Special Economic Zones: Performance, Implications and Lessons Learned for Zone Development," *Paper #45869* (Washington, DC: World Bank, 2008).

Newspaper Sources

Aaen, Christian, "North of Beijing, California Dreams Come True," *New York Times*, February 3, 2003.

Buncombe, Andrew, "Slumdogs who Seek Success," *The Independent [London]*, January 16, 2009.

Cambanis, Thanassis, "To Catch Cairo Overflow, 2 Megacities Rise in Sand," *New York Times*, August 24, 2010.

Elshahed, Mohamed, "From Tahrir Square to Emaar Square: Cairo's Private Road to a Private City," *The Guardian*, April 7, 2014.

French, Howard, "Chinese Success Story Chokes on its own Growth," *New York Times*, December 19, 2006.

Gamble, Jessa, "Has the Time Come for Floating Cities?" *The Guardian*, March 18, 2014.

Gorvett, Jon, "Mixed-Use Zorlu Center Raises Stakes in Istanbul," *New York Times*, July 14, 2011.

Gough, Neil, "The Overnight Metropolis," *New York Times*, December 24, 2015.

Limpin, Rogelio, "Cavite Ecozone Slams Manila Truck Ban," *Manila Times*, March 3, 2014.

Magnier, Mark, "Mumbai Billionaire's Home Boasts 27 Floors, Ocean and Slum Views," *The Los Angeles Times*, October 24, 2010.

Mouawad, Jad, "The Construction Site Called Saudi Arabia," *New York Times*, January 20, 2008.

O'Connell, Pamela Licalzi, "Korea's High-Tech Utopia, Where Everything Is Observed," *The New York Times*, October 5, 2005.

Ouroussoff, Nicholai, "In Arabian Desert, a Sustainable City Arises," *New York Times*, September 25, 2010.

Poveledo, Elisabetta, "Migrants' Lives in Ruin as Camp is Razed in Rome," *New York Times*, May 17, 2015.

Reich, Robert, "Succession of the Successful," *New York Times Magazine*, January 20, 1991 (p. 42).

Masters and Ph.D. Dissertations

Dorman, J. W., *The Politics of Neglect: The Egyptian State in Cairo, 1974–98* (Unpublished Ph.D. Thesis, School of Oriental and African Studies, University of London, 2007).

Hourani, Najib, Capitalists in Conflict: A Political Economy of the Life, Death, and Rebirth of Beirut (Unpublished Ph.D. dissertation, New York University, 2005).

Krijnen, Marieke, *Facilitating Real Estate Development in Beirut: A Peculiar Case of Neoliberal Public Policy* (Unpublished Master's Thesis, Center for Arab and Middle East Studies, American University of Beirut, 2010).

Makarem, Hadi, "Actually Existing Neoliberalism: The Reconstruction of Downtown Beirut in Post-Civil War Lebanon" (Unpublished Ph.D. dissertation, London School of Economics and Political Science, 2014).

Özkan, Derya, The Misuse Value of Space: Spatial Practices and the Production of Space in Istanbul (Unpublished Ph.D. Dissertation, University of Rochester, 2008).

Ramos, Viktor, *The Continuous Enclave: Strategies in Bypass Urbanism* (Unpublished Master's Thesis, School of Architecture, Rice University, 2009).

Weizman, Eyal, "Introduction to the Politics of Verticality," in Malkit Shoshan (ed.), *Territoria: Illustrations of the Israeli-Palestinian Conflict*, First Edition, Volume 1 (Haifa: Association of Forty, 2002), pp. 43–68.

Index